Corporations at Climate Crossroads

Corporations at Climate Crossroads

Multilevel Governance, Public Policy, and Global Climate Action

Lily Hsueh

The MIT Press
Cambridge, Massachusetts
London, England

The MIT Press
Massachusetts Institute of Technology
77 Massachusetts Avenue, Cambridge, MA 02139
mitpress.mit.edu

The open access edition of this book was made possible by generous funding and support from MIT Press Direct to Open.

The MIT Press would like to thank the anonymous peer reviewers who provided comments on drafts of this book. The generous work of academic experts is essential for establishing the authority and quality of our publications. We acknowledge with gratitude the contributions of these otherwise uncredited readers.

This book was set in Stone Serif and Stone Sans by Westchester Publishing Services. Printed and bound in the United States of America.

Library of Congress Cataloging-in-Publication Data

Names: Hsueh, Lily author
Title: Corporations at climate crossroads : multilevel governance, public policy, and global climate action / Lily Hsueh.
Description: Cambridge, Massachusetts : The MIT Press, [2025] | Includes bibliographical references and index.
Identifiers: LCCN 2024057104 (print) | LCCN 2024057105 (ebook) | ISBN 9780262553186 paperback | ISBN 9780262384469 pdf | ISBN 9780262384476 epub
Subjects: LCSH: Social responsibility of business | Climate change mitigation
Classification: LCC HD60 .H78 2025 (print) | LCC HD60 (ebook) | DDC 658.4/08—dc23/eng/20250320
LC record available at https://lccn.loc.gov/2024057104
LC ebook record available at https://lccn.loc.gov/2024057105

EU Authorised Representative: Easy Access System Europe, Mustamäe tee 50, 10621 Tallinn, Estonia | Email: gpsr.requests@easproject.com

To my beloved family
this is for you

Contents

List of Figures

List of Tables

Acknowledgments

As a problem-driven economist and policy scholar, my research resides at the nexus of economics, political economy, and management. My quest to understand the role of global businesses in climate economics, policy, and governance began a decade ago when I participated in the Oxford Workshop on Transnational Climate Governance and Domestic Politics at the Blavatnik School of Government. It was there among policy scholars and political scientists of environmental politics that I began to think about the ways in which multinational companies operate in a nested structure of governance, whereby firm-level incentives and constraints are as salient as regulatory and global-level drivers and the ways in which economics and politics are inseparable for understanding climate policy and governance. Global businesses have the market leverage and political and economic authority to help change the course of human history. But what drives corporate behavior on climate change? In this book, I make the case that the dynamic interactions of firm-level managerial and organizational drivers and regulatory and global governance are where the rubber meets the road in explaining the demand for and supply of proactive climate action by global businesses.

On the eve of the Paris Agreement, I presented the genesis of this book project at the Arizona State University (ASU) Global Institute of Sustainability and Innovation, at the invitation of Chris Boone, now the dean of the USC Sol Price School of Public Policy. The positive feedback from the interdisciplinary audience encouraged me to continue with this research. Several of this book's empirical chapters draw from and extend my published articles.

At ASU, at the School of Public Affairs and across campus I am grateful to Stu Bretschneider, Chingwen Cheng, Elizabeth Corley, Chandra Crudup,

Jonas Gamso, Brian Gerber, Chris Herbst, Yushim Kim, Joanna Lucio, Spiro Maroulis, Angel Molina, Karen Mossberger, Shannon Portillo, Daniel Schugurensky, Don Siegel, Akheil Singla, and Justin Stritch for their academic camaraderie. At the Center for Environmental Economics and Sustainability Policy, Josh Abbott, Kelly Bishop, Jeffrey Englin, Danae Hernandez-Cortez, Michael Hanemann, Kailin Kroetz, Nick Kumnioff, Bryan Leonard, Alvin Murphy, Valerie Mueller, Deborah Salon, and Glenn Sheriff gave me helpful feedback on early versions of this book's econometric analyses.

Fellowships and grants from the Arizona State University, Stanford University, and the American Association of University Women supported research and writing. My gratitude goes to ASU President Michael Crow for encouraging this ambitious research agenda and book project with the President's Strategic Initiative Grant, which gave me the freedom to hire research assistants, train graduate students, travel to conduct interviews, and share my research with colleagues afar. I am grateful to the following professional associations and academic institutions, which hosted conferences, presentations, talks, and workshops where I received critical and incisive feedback. These include the American Economic Association, Association of Environmental and Resource Economists, American Political Science Association, Association of Public Policy Analysis and Management, Environmental Politics and Governance, Federal Reserve Bank of San Francisco, Centre for Economic Policy Research, International Studies Association, and the National Bureau of Economic Research Summer Institute. I am also grateful to Stanford University, Texas A&M University, the University of Arizona, the University of California, Berkeley, the University of California, Davis, the University of California, Santa Cruz, the University of Maryland, University of Pennsylvania, University of Toronto, and the University of Washington.

At different stages of research and analysis, I received helpful insights and feedback from the following individuals: Liliana Andonova, David Anthoff, Max Auffhammer, Laura Bakkensen, Tim Bartley, Patrick Bayer, Jon Bendor, Daniel Berliner, Thomas Bernauer, Steven Bernstein, Kelly Bishop, Elin Boasson, Mark Buntaine, Bruce Cain, Ben Cashore, Xun Cao, Chris Costello, Cary Coglianese, Meri Davlasheridze, Kevin Dooley, Jeffrey Englin, Mary Evans, Robert Falkner, Chris Field, Neil Fligstein, Meredith Fowlie, Jessica Green, Jennifer Hadden, Emilie Hafner-Burton, Tom Hale, Michael Hanemann, Chris Herbst, Matt Hoffmann, Roselyn Hsueh, Joseph Huang, Nathan Hultman, Oscar Jorda, Charlie Kolstad, David Konisky, Jonathan Koppell, Matthew

Kotchen, Rachel Krause, Nick Kumnioff, David Layton, Bryan Leonard, Rob Letzer, Tze-Luen Lin, Tom Lyon, Doug MacMartin, Alfred Marcus, Dan Matisoff, Jonas Meckling, Qing Miao, Axel Michaelow, Katherina Michaelow, Valerie Mueller, Alvin Murphy, Kate O'Neill, Kimberly Nicholas, Aseem Prakash, Lucy Qiu, Varun Rai, Mar Reguant, Stefan Renckens, Jorge Rivera, Brigitte Roth Tran, Charlie Roger, Glenn Rudebusch, Deborah Salon, Jim Sanchirico, Philip Schleifer, Jay Shimshack, Yixian Sun, Sonia Seneviratne, Glenn Sheriff, Marty Smith, Craig Thomas, Wenling Tu, Rama Mohana Turaga, Hamish van der Ven, Andrew Waxman, Daniel Wilson, and Hongtao Yi.

I am grateful to Elizabeth Corley, Kirsten Foot, Matt Hoffmann, David Layton, Kate O'Neill, Aseem Prakash, Jim Sanchirico, Marty Smith, and Craig Thomas for their inspiration, support, and encouragement over the years. At the MIT Press, Emily Taber was the first to inquire if I had plans to write a book. I am grateful to her and the invaluable feedback of anonymous reviewers that led to my book contract and publication. Catherine Woods and Caroline Helms shepherded the editorial production process at the MIT Press.

My gratitude goes to David Archibeque at the ASU Carey School of Business and Alice Kalinowski at the Stanford Graduate School of Business for their patience and help in navigating public and proprietary databases. I received helpful research assistance from Jessica Bass, Pooja Chandramohan, Eugene Cho, Jacob Emnett, Elliott Harwood, Nihaal Konda, Elizabeth Kuttner, Sang Eun Lee, and Won No.

During the writing of this book, I benefited from a sabbatical at the Stanford Woods Institute for the Environment. There I presented my ideas, fine-tuned my framework, and received helpful feedback. I arrived at the university in 2022 at an exciting time, during the inaugural year of Stanford's new Doerr School of Sustainability. I am grateful to Steve Graham, the former dean of Stanford Earth, who connected me with Woods Institute director Chris Field and other faculty on campus. I am indebted to Chris Field for his hospitality and advice. The extraordinary Woods staff and researchers and fellow visiting scholars made it a joy to write in my sabbatical office.

With Woods as my base, I am grateful to Jon Bendor at the Stanford Graduate School of Business, who generously commented on multiple drafts of this book's framework chapter. Thank you, Jon, for our lively discussions about firm behavior in the face of uncertainty, at time *t* and *t*+1 and beyond. Special thanks to Charlie Kolstad, who invited me to give a talk at the Stanford

Environmental and Energy Policy Analysis Center, a cross-campus effort of the Percourt Institute for Energy and the Stanford Institute for Economic Policy Research, and to Larry Goulder at the Department of Economics, who attended my multiple talks across campus and paired every constructive feedback with words of encouragement. Thank you to Bruce Cain of Stanford Political Science and the Doerr School for our conversations about the ways in which subnational politics have spurred climate policy innovations in the United States and beyond. My gratitude goes to Arun Majumdar, the founding dean of the Stanford Doerr School of Sustainability, for introducing me to leaders in finance and technology.

At Stanford, I also benefited from conversations with Steve Callander and Neil Malhotra at the Graduate School of Business; Bill Barnett and Bard Harstad of GSB and the Doerr School; Hunt Allcott, Gretchen Daily, Noah Diffenbaugh, and Eric Lambin at the Doer School; Colleen Honigsberg at the Stanford Law School; and Roger Howe, Jim Sweeney, and Wilman Tsai at the Stanford Engineering School, among others. I attended and presented at conferences focused on organizations and the environment, political economy and sustainability, and corporate carbon disclosures cohosted by GSB and the Doerr School.

During my Bay Area sabbatical, I was also blessed by the hospitality of Elliott Campbell, Kate O'Neill, and Jim Sanchirico at UC Santa Cruz, UC Berkeley, and UC Davis, where I shared my book's findings at invited talks and received valuable feedback from faculty and students. I am thankful for Neil Fligstein's feedback on multiple book chapters and his encouragement to be bold and to take a stand.

This book's research and analysis would not have been completed without the on-the-ground knowledge and insights of numerous people working for companies, governments, and international organizations. I have learned tremendously from these insiders who shared openly with me. Special thanks go to Kelli Kreiser at the ASU Thunderbird School of Global Management for inviting me to the 2020 GreenBiz 20 conference, where I launched my field research. My gratitude goes to Thomas Catlaw, Jonas Gamos, Joseph Huang, Ana Maria Ibanez, and Rachel Kirvan for making the initial introductions that led to this book's interviews and qualitative data collection.

Thank you to my cul de sac neighbors Tina and Sead Bahor, Sheri and John Koponen, Indira and Kevin Jeffrey, and Sumana and Aravind Pinto. Your love and support sustained my family.

My gratitude goes to friends at Redemption Tempe, Peninsula Bible Church, and the Stanford Christian Faculty and Staff Fellowship who provided spiritual nourishment for the marathon that is writing a book. I am thankful for Mary Ellen Azada and Mark Labberton's encouragement and prayers over the years.

I thank my identical twin sister Rosie, a political scientist who has written two influential books; she has been a steadfast encourager, supporter, and advisor all in one. Thank you to dear friends Evelyn Baca, Lauren De Witt, Jen Hanson, Bonnie Hensen, Chasya Hiebert, Jenny Larson Huang, Anita Kishore, Britta Martens, Andrea Ng, Allison Phillips, and Veronica So for your friendship, encouragement, and support through the research and writing of this book. I am also grateful for my brother, Peter, sister-in-law Robin, sister-in-law Esther, and brother-in-law Andy for being part of my village.

Last but not least, I thank my husband Joseph, who is the ultimate partner and coparent. I dedicate this book to Joseph and our daughters, and to my parents Shay and Pauline for instilling in me a love for nature, economics, and politics, which Joseph and I have passed on to our daughters. As I write this book's acknowledgments, I am sitting next to Mirror Lake, at the foot of Yosemite's famed Half Dome. The breathtaking beauty of the scenery around me and the reflection of Half Dome in the lake remind me of the resilience of planet Earth.

I Introduction, Framework, Firm-Level Drivers

1 The Supply and Demand of Corporate Climate Action

In a 2023 annual letter to shareholders, Pat Gelsinger, Intel's former chief executive officer, explained that corporate responsibility and sustainability has been "deeply ingrained in Intel's DNA" because Intel's cofounder Gordon Moore "established [the company's] commitment to environmental sustainability during a time when companies were not thinking about it the way they are today."[1]

Intel Corporation has consistently ranked among the world's top 100 sustainable corporations according to Corporate Knights, a Toronto-based media and research company that has ranked companies annually based on corporate environmental, social, and governance performance since 2000. Intel is the only firm in the global semiconductor industry with this distinction; other semiconductor companies, notably ASML Holdings NV, Nvidia Corporation, Samsung Electronics, and the Taiwan Semiconductor Manufacturing Company, have also ranked among Corporate Knight's annual top 100 lists at least once from 2011 to 2020.[2]

Suzanne Fallender, former global director of corporate responsibility at Intel, shared that Intel's prior experience in green chemistry initiatives helped to establish the company as an "early mover [on climate action]."[3] Intel led an industry-wide voluntary reduction of chemicals with high global warming potential.[4] Moreover, the company started environmental, social, and governance (ESG) reporting in 2003, and for over two decades Intel has disclosed its carbon management and carbon emissions to CDP (formerly the Carbon Disclosure Project), the largest and oldest nonprofit that houses voluntary climate disclosures, ahead of many of its industry peers.

In 2014, during the national policy discussions in the United States over the US Environmental Protection Agency's promulgated Clean Power Plan and a year before the 2015 Paris Agreement, Intel articulated the company's "handprint" approach to climate action. Conceived by Stephen Harper, Intel's former global director of environmental, energy, and sustainability policy, the premise was that, in addition to the global semiconductor company's direct climate "footprint," Intel would use its technologies to help customers reduce their own climate and energy footprints, as an extension of the company's "handprint."[5] The idea is that customers—even a climate leader like Microsoft—cannot reduce their carbon footprints without Intel "because Intel's chips, notebooks, data centers, and Internet of Things, powered computing worldwide," said Fallender.[6]

By 2017, Intel had developed a fully integrated strategy for environmental, social, and governance performance, which mapped into the United Nations Sustainable Development Goals, with climate change as one of Intel's four pillars of corporate social responsibility, along with supply chain responsibility, diversity and inclusion, and social impact. Intel's vice president of investor relations and the chief financial officer regularly meet with the global firm's corporate responsibility team and sustainability managers across Intel's worldwide operations.

Intel's engagement with regulators and policymakers has extended beyond the traditional activities of its corporate government relations. For the company's voluntary use and procurement of renewable electricity sources, Intel has been recognized many times by the US Environmental Protection Agency's (EPA) Green Power Partnership as a national top 100 organization, alongside Microsoft and Apple, two other technology mainstays on the EPA list.[7] In Europe, Intel has contributed to the Green Deal for Europe by extending its handprint to "build European capacity to design and manufacture the most powerful and energy-efficient processors."[8]

By all accounts, Intel's sustainability leadership among its semiconductor peers and global businesses during the years leading up to and after the Paris Agreement was a period of mediocre revenue growth and tepid profits for this US-based multinational firm. Intel's carbon intensity fell during the first decade of the twenty first century, as shown in figure 1.1. From 2011 to 2020 (this book's study period), the carbon intensity has held steady, even while the global firm's total carbon emissions have grown as the company increased in size. As such, corporate financial prowess or market power alone is unlikely to explain this global chipmaker's sustainability credentials.

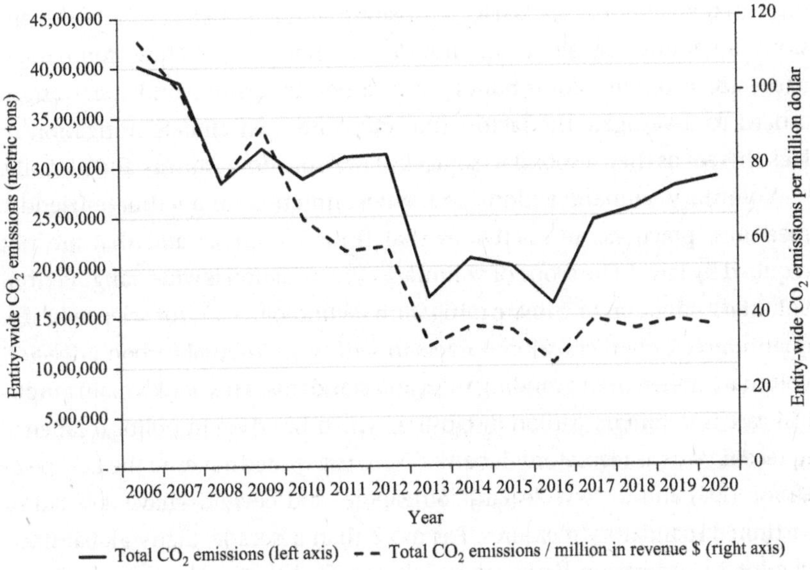

Figure 1.1
Intel Corporation's entity-wide carbon emissions and carbon emissions intensity (2005–2020).
Source: LSEG Data and Analytics.

Instead, Intel's climate change story is characterized by the role of executive and managerial leadership in sustainability, complementary capabilities in adjacent areas, such as green chemistry, firm-initiated corporate social responsibility, and strategic and proactive engagement with the regulatory process in the United States and Europe and with global governance. This book's multilevel governance framework on climate change theorizes and shows that Intel's and global businesses' participation and effort in corporate self-regulation on climate change and environmental performance are a consequence of the interaction and complementarities between corporate, regulatory, and global governance, including firm-level managerial and organizational capabilities and structures.

This book shines light on global businesses like Intel Corporation[9]—namely, the Fortune Global 500 companies and firms listed on the S&P 500 index—to ask whether, why, and how the world's largest corporations (as measured by sales revenue) have taken proactive or voluntary action on climate change during the years leading up to and after the Paris Agreement (2011–2020). Global businesses represent close to 70 percent of annual global industrial greenhouse gas (GHG) emissions, and a majority of carbon emissions are emitted by about one hundred corporations.[10] These companies' sheer size, economic contribution, and carbon footprint worldwide warrant a need to investigate the factors that motivate their climate mitigation or lack thereof as they respond to sources of pressure domestically and globally.

Voluntary climate actions are environmental and climate-friendly measures, practices, and activities that firms undertake and that are not required by law.[11] The scope of voluntary climate action is wide, ranging from voluntary adoption of climate mitigation technologies and/or science-based, quantitative carbon emissions targets to setting an internal carbon price and voluntary adherence to binding rules and standards. This book's main empirical case is voluntary carbon disclosure, which has risen in political salience in recent years as regulators globally—from the United States to the European Union (EU) and to New Zealand, Singapore, and beyond—have debated or instituted mandatory measures. For more than a decade, many global firms like Intel Corporation have voluntarily reported their carbon management and carbon emissions to CDP.

In the call to arms of nonstate actors such as multinational firms, there is a tendency to view these actors either as acting unilaterally and unconditionally or entrenched in insurmountable institutional and organizational barriers or political quagmires. This is a far cry from reality. *Corporations at Climate Crossroads* highlights the agency of global businesses, nation states, and international organizations and their interactions. Specifically, this book asks the following questions:

- Many global businesses talk a good game, but which firm, regulatory, and global governance factors (and their cross-level interactions) compel global businesses to participate in voluntary climate action?
- Do global businesses that participate in voluntary climate action emit less carbon emissions?
- How do the interactions of firm, regulatory, and global governance conditions vary across sectors and between the Global North and the Global South?

Specifically, *Corporations at Climate Crossroads* develops a multilevel governance framework on climate change and tests related propositions. In this political economic framework, corporations are key players in a nested structure of climate change governance with interactions between bottom-up and top-down incentives and institutions involving firm, regulatory, and global governance.[12]

The book shows that in order to navigate uncertainty in the face of climate change, senior- and executive-level managers often have discretion over internal firm or corporate policy or how that policy will be executed. Managers form governing coalitions inside the firm to delineate and mobilize support for voluntary climate action. They serve as what this book terms "regulation brokers": when regulatory pressure is high and the marginal cost of self-regulation is low, there is a hastening of efforts led by managers to signal the firms' ability to internalize externalities, earn regulatory goodwill, and avoid costly liabilities. Managers are also "norm brokers" in shaping, translating, and disseminating global best practices that could someday become market norms or laws.

Beyond that, firms' learning and norming (often led by managers) in global governance institutions largely mirror current and prospective requirements and pressures of domestic regulation and distributive conflicts among political and economic stakeholders in nation-states. Regulatory pressures and demands can shape how firms' learning and norming translate into corporate self-regulation on climate change with varying benefits and costs. Thus, global governance, while a harbinger of future regulation, seldom fully fills the regulatory void or governance gap that firm managers may be empowered to shape.

The book further shows that the more stringent existing or impending regulation is, the greater the effort firms will devote to, and the more likely firms will engage in, costly (as opposed to less costly) voluntary climate action. By contrast, in the absence of strong regulation, the weaker the self-regulation on climate change is, the more likely it is that firms will engage in greenwashing behavior.

Empirical testing of the multilevel governance framework on climate change reveals that despite evidence of, and increasing media attention on, corporate greenwashing, the past decade (2011–2020) has been characterized by partial success in galvanizing corporate climate action. The global firms that are the best managed and most stringently regulated and are active participants of global governance institutions are today's corporate climate leaders. In response to the global demand for corporate self-regulation in the climate change area, firms supply climate mitigation without the force of law because they are catalyzed by executive leadership and innovative management practices and compelled by public and private politics arising domestically and internationally.

This book's main conclusions are the following. First, while some global firms act on their own, the majority of global firms do not. Rather, on the whole, their proactive climate action is in response to regulatory pressures coming from domestic regulation of their country of origin or export country of largest sales. Despite the fact that global governance institutions are replete with opportunities for learning about global best practices, most firms' climate mitigation reinforces what they are already doing and reflects existing corporate management practices and regulations on the books or on the horizon, rather than first-mover climate leadership.

Second, in developed countries, where regulations are by and large more robust, corporate, domestic, and global governance are complements. The EU is an exemplar of how firm, regulatory, and global interactions and the blurring of the private and public governance spheres in Europe explicate the climate leadership of global firms based there. By contrast, developing country–based firms respond foremost to the stringency of laws and regulations of their country of origin or in their largest export markets rather than to nonmandatory global norms and best practices, despite the fact that developing countries have fewer resources and governance capacity than developed countries. Global South–based firms' corporate self-regulation on climate change does not on its own fill the vacuum left by weak domestic governance. That being said, the relative influence of cross-level governance dynamics could shift once new or emerging climate policy innovations, such as quantitative emissions targets, becomes an industry or business norm or standard.

Moreover, while some firms have engaged in "cheap talk," technology firms led the way on voluntary climate action and carbon emission efficiency from 2011 to 2020. Carbon-efficient corporations from greenhouse gas–intensive sectors, under regulatory pressure, have also used their proactive climate action to signal their climate leadership to regulators, investors, and consumers. By contrast, on the whole, global businesses in retail, health care, and financial services—these are low (direct) emitters of carbon to begin with—prioritized the promotion of their sustainability credentials without consistently delivering on actual environmental performance.

Finally, neither firms nor regulation nor global norms and pressures by themselves will be able to achieve the substantive climate action that is required for reducing global temperatures enough to avert a climate change crisis. Civil society stakeholders—from institutional investors to environmental watchdog groups to universities—are more important than ever to keep firms accountable for their pledges and acts of corporate social responsibility on the environment and beyond. To ensure that their climate action translates into real environmental performance, the program design of voluntary as well as mandatory climate mitigation and adaptation programs is key.

Empirically, *Corporations at Climate Crossroads* follows an original author-constructed census of Fortune Global 500 and S&P 500 firms' climate disclosure, mitigation, and performance over time (2011–2020), across scales of governance (firm, state, country, and global levels) and sectors, and between developed and developing countries. The multilevel governance framework on climate change's testable implications, in the form of propositions, are substantiated by large-*N* cross-sectional and panel data analyses—with attention to causal inference by exploiting a natural experiment and employing quasi-experimental methods. Illustrative company case studies provide narratives of exemplar climate leaders that underscore and elaborate on the key managerial, political economy, and governance variables that have been identified as major drivers of corporate climate action in this book's statistical analysis. A novel empirical contribution is the book's distinction between firms' greenwashing behavior and actual climate leadership by statistically distinguishing between firms' decision to engage in and their actual level of voluntary climate action (i.e., sustainability outputs) and carbon footprints (i.e., environmental performance). Moreover, the book's multimethod approach is an answer to the call for causal inference and mechanism studies of proenvironmental behavior by actors (firm managers) who are typically omitted from the climate governance story and their interactions across regulatory and global governance.

The rest of this chapter begins with an exposition of the assumptions that underlie the book's arguments and analysis, starting with a commonly held premise that climate change is a problem of the global commons, which defies easy governance. Next, the chapter expounds on the existing explanations in economics, political science, management, and related fields of the demand for and supply of corporate self-regulation on climate change. Examining and unraveling the interactive effects of the different levels of climate governance on firm-level climate action, the book's multilevel governance framework on climate change departs from the often dichotomous approach that either privileges agency over structure or vice versa and focuses on firm-, country-, or global-level explanations.[13] From there, chapter 1 introduces the book's empirical setting and cases. The final section provides a roadmap for the rest of the book.

1.1 Is Climate Change a Collective Action Problem?

The science is clear. There is evidence that from 2011 to 2020, the period of this book's focus, planet Earth experienced a temperature increase of 1.1°C compared to 1850–1990.[14] Data suggest that this warming was largely human-caused and could be irreversible (see figure 1.2). Throughout the book "climate change" is used interchangeably with "global warming" to refer to the larger phenomenon of human-caused climate change.[15]

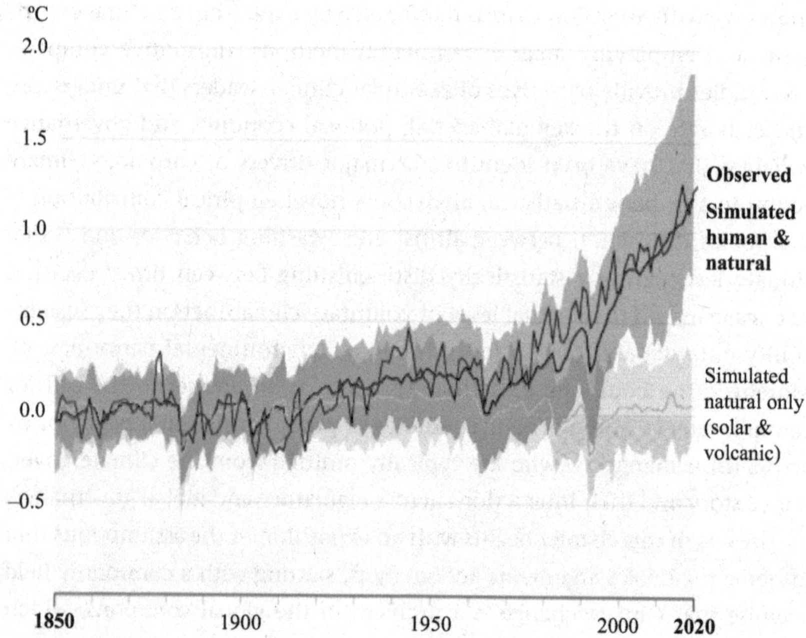

Figure 1.2
Changes in global surface temperature (annual average) as observed and simulated using human and natural and only natural factors (1850–2020).
Source: IPCC Sixth Assessment Reports Working Group 1 figure SMP.1(b), https://www.ipcc.ch/report/ar6/wg1/figures/summary-for-policymakers/.

While the scientific consensus on the existence of climate change is clear,[16] the physical and socioeconomic impacts of a changing climate are characterized by risks and uncertainties that are complex and not easily quantified.[17] The implication of this complexity is that there are no straightforward or easy solutions, and much of contemporary debate is about the *how* of climate policy and governance.

In the collective action paradigm, GHG emissions—unlike point source pollutants such as tailpipe emissions from the internal combustion engine of a conventional car—defy traditional regulatory approaches because they are transboundary in nature. The costs and benefits of limiting them are diffuse and, thus, not easily assigned to the offending polluter(s). This is to say, each actor (individual, firm, or country) has an incentive to free ride and let others shoulder the cost of the destruction and maintenance of the global commons.

Yet the public good (such as clean air and biodiversity) will not be provided if every actor behaves this way; unilateral cooperation is irrational given that no actors will be willing to suffer the costs associated with others' free riding. As such, both the "cause" (GHG emissions) and "effect" (congestion, overuse, or degradation of the global commons) of climate change present challenging problems for effective governance.

The long-sought-after solution to this collective action problem is cooperation among all nations to mitigate greenhouse gas emissions. The conventional wisdom is that nations will reduce emissions as long as they are guaranteed that others will do the same: once a foolproof international mechanism is set up to prevent nations from shirking their respective obligations to reduce their share of GHG emissions, coupled with a mechanism to incentivize as well as punish nations that fail to meet their goals, climate change would be slowed and eventually halted.[18] Up until the Paris Agreement, the United Nations Framework Convention on Climate Change (UNFCCC) followed this idealized global governance logic. A notable example is the 1997 Kyoto Protocol. Yet the Kyoto Protocol has largely been viewed by both scholars and the policy community as a policy and governance failure.[19]

This top-down, global governance logic is juxtaposed with the Coasean provision, which is a decentralized governance approach. In an influential 1960 article, the economist Ronald Coase posited that even in the presence of externalities or the impact on third parties of a transaction or activity not involving them,[20] an economy can always reach an efficient solution if property rights are well defined and transaction costs are sufficiently low.[21] The Coase theorem is predicated by the rationale that individuals (or firms) have an incentive to find a way to make mutually beneficial deals through decentralized bargaining that lead them to "internalize the externality."

Despite the stylized benefits, its applicability for solving real-world externality problems remains debated, whether on efficiency or equitable grounds. As it relates to climate change, Jean Tirole writes that "the strategy of voluntary commitments has several defects and is an inadequate response to the climate change challenge."[22] In aggregate, voluntary climate action, as part of the Paris Agreement's pledge and review process, is predicted to contribute (even) less to global carbon emissions reductions than the bargaining outcome of the Kyoto Protocol.[23]

Without assuming that the Coasean provision results in first-best, efficient outcomes (or equitable outcomes for that matter), this book acknowledges the fact that decentralized and private solutions on climate change have occurred frequently, before and after the Paris Agreement, and puts the emergence, diffusion, and impact of corporate self-regulation on climate change front and center as puzzles to examine. Specifically, to explain the rise and impact of corporate self-regulation on climate change, *Corporations at Climate Crossroads* argues that there is a need to understand what is going on at the firm level vis-à-vis interactions with higher levels of governance (regulation and global governance). Thus, the book shines light on firms and the senior- and executive-level managers inside them who are exercising their agency in their response to internal firm and external political economy opportunities and constraints.

1.2 Demand for and Supply of Corporate Climate Action

Extant economics, political science, and management literatures on the role of corporations in climate change shows that among the diverse set of twenty-first-century "global governors,"[24] which includes international organizations, intergovernmental organizations, professional associations, advocacy groups, and the like, are the multinational corporations. The global demand for corporate climate action is part of the global trend toward "governance with government" rather than "governance by government"—namely, the rise of nonregulatory and decentralized governance of environmental protection.[25] Firms (and managers within them) serve as agents or "global governors" in navigating the push and pull of regulatory regimes and global governance to supply climate action without the force of law.

While corporations often "back into governance roles and may even drag their feet,"[26] global businesses also gain authority because others perceive them as capable of achieving results. What, then, drives some companies to meet the demand for corporate self-regulation on climate change while other companies continue business as usual? In other words, why don't all firms take climate action or engage in climate action at the same level of effort? The following sections situate the book's multilevel governance framework on climate change (MGFCC) in the dominant research in economics, political science, and management that has primarily focused on either the firm, subnational, country, or global level. The MGFCC bridges the firm and domestic political economy and global governance and contends that the interactions between corporate governance and regulation, corporate and global governance, and regulation and global governance are the salient drivers of corporate climate action.

1.2.1 Firm-Level Explanations

Firm-level explanations about the rise and diffusion of corporate self-regulation in the environmental area have historically been the purview of economists and management scholars, respectively, albeit not exclusively, and have in recent years become an area of interest to political scientists. For these scholars, the "firm" is the primary unit of analysis. The preoccupation is to explain why profit-maximizing firms would participate in costly voluntary environmental programs, which are decentralized environmental policy tools to encourage proactive environmental behavior by firms, that have spawned a rich literature across public and environmental economics, public policy, and management.[27] Since the 1990s, empirical scholarship in this area has focused on the diffusion and performance of voluntary environmental programs sponsored by the government, the private sector, and NGOs or bilateral voluntary agreements negotiated between regulators and industry.[28]

This literature presupposes a broader set of attitudes, preferences, and calculations for considering prosocial or altruistic behavior by firms or individuals.[29] Buchanan was the first scholar to define the joint provision of a public and private good as an "impure public good": in the equilibrium, firms sometime produce a public good or an externality jointly with their main task of providing private goods or services for consumption.[30] Given incomplete contracts, in the absence of ex post bargaining frictions, a public good will be owned by the party that values it more, in relative terms, the benefits it generates by the related investments.[31] In this setup, scholars have explicitly linked the private provision of public goods to corporate social responsibility (CSR)—namely, the corporate provision of public goods or curtailment of public bads independent of legal benchmarks.[32] CSR has also been referred to in the literature as "industry self-regulation," and as "corporate environmentalism"[33] in the environmental area.

CSR arises in a political economy context characterized by imperfect and asymmetric information between firms and external stakeholders, including regulators. Firms engage in self-regulation as a way to deflect private or public politics and to improve stakeholder and regulatory relations today with the aim of getting preferential treatment tomorrow in the face of impending regulation.[34] The political economic framework presupposes a broader set of attitudes, preferences, and calculations for considering firms' prosocial or altruistic behavior.[35] The MGFCC adopts this political economic paradigm as a point of departure.

Both private politics (i.e., social activism by NGOs or civil society stakeholders) and public politics (actual or potential government interaction with firms via laws and regulation) have gained scholarly attention because of extensive empirical evidence that suggests political motivations are salient factors for explaining the diffusion of corporate self-regulation on the environment, including climate change.[36]

A key implication is that firms will act preemptively based on microlevel incentives: when the threat of activism or regulation is high and the marginal cost of self-regulation is relatively low, it is the rational calculus of firms to engage in self-regulation as a form of deterrence. For firms, the mere threat of negative publicity may be sufficient to integrate voluntary environmentalism as a part of corporate strategy; this is because the cost of deflecting negative publicity enters into firms' profit maximization on the cost side. At the equilibrium, ex ante agreements involving self-regulation are reached and coordinated at the firm and industry level by firms and industries.[37]

The incentive to join voluntary environmental programs could also be derived from the threat of public rather than private politics. Potential changes in regulation and related adjustment costs may lead firms to hedge against such an event and build a strategic buffer zone in the form of overcompliance. Self-regulation involves cultivating and maintaining regulatory goodwill in anticipation of future regulation.[38] As such, firms that engage in self-regulation are positioning themselves to influence the behavior of regulatory authorities in their favor.

While distinct from corporate political lobbying, corporate self-regulation may be part of firms' larger political strategy to preempt more stringent public regulations.[39] For example, corporations' participation in modest voluntary environmental programs could dissuade voters, activists, and government officials from seeking more draconian government regulations.[40] The magnitude of these effects is the strongest when all companies within an industry join the voluntary effort.[41] Similarly, if firms expect stochastic shocks to their environmental performance, overcompliance today may reduce the risk of future noncompliance.[42]

The firm-level studies discussed above seldom consider external factors beyond the domestic political economy or how internal firm organizational dynamics and managerial agency serve as mediators vis-à-vis domestic regulation and global governance. A rich literature on business and the environment examines the drivers of corporate participation in voluntary climate disclosures (notably, participation in CDP, which is an empirical case in this book) and evaluates the effects of climate disclosures on financial outcomes and firms' carbon emissions.[43] This body of research by and large underscores external factors, such as supply chain pressures, shareholder actions, and regulatory threats, including the threat of direct economic consequences, as drivers of corporate environmental behavior,[44] despite a recent call by management scholars for a focus on the complementary impacts (rather than separate influences) of mandatory and voluntary programs on organizations' environmental strategies and performance.[45] As this book theorizes and empirically demonstrates, the interactions across corporate, regulatory, and global governance levels are where the rubber meets the road in explaining global businesses' proactive climate action over the past decade.

1.2.2 Domestic- and Global-Level Perspectives

Domestic and global-level explanations for corporate self-regulation on climate change historically dominated political science—notably, the international political economy and private regulation and private authority literatures. This body of research has examined "country" or "international organization" as the primary unit of analysis and has typically explored the unconditional effects of domestic and international or transnational regulatory pressures, respectively. The central puzzle is to explain the groundswell of climate change activity that heterogeneous actors have created and provided through a complex network structure involving institutions at different levels of governance.[46]

The rise of private actors in transnational climate governance has upended the traditional view that the state is the central actor in both domestic governance and international regimes.[47] Scholars have identified bottom-up or mixed approaches to climate change governance as institutional innovations for "wedging the gap" between what countries are able to achieve and what is necessary to keep temperature rise below 2°C.[48] Nongovernmental or private actors—such as trade associations, professional bodies, technical organizations, and activist groups—have established private governance institutions to coordinate their activities.[49] The emphasis is on transnational "diffusion" processes, such as advocacy pressures and commodity chains, through which social and material pressures are transmitted.[50]

Notably, country- and global-level perspectives have primarily focused on analyses at the level of international agreements and strategic actions of nation-states to explain the political conflict over climate policy, with a preoccupation among both economists and political scientists with how to solve the large-scale free riding concerns in global climate negotiations and policymaking. Proposed solutions include technological breakthroughs, rulemaking or issue linkages at the international level, or climate coalitions or clubs made up of "essential" actors in developed countries and developing countries.[51]

Despite this, recent research departs from the conventional collective action theory to develop a "distributive politics meta-theocratical alternative"[52] and a "dynamic theory of climate politics"[53] based on the present and future revaluation of assets, both of which emphasize a distributive conflict lens. Through this lens, there is a contest between those who benefit from climate change, such as owners of assets that accelerate climate change (e.g., fossil fuel plants) and owners of assets vulnerable to climate change (e.g., coastal properties). This contest can be played out in the political arena between politicians over the livelihoods of their constituencies. Climate politics create new economic winners and losers, as a function of the power play and dynamics of political and economic stakeholders. The sharp divisions in material interests potentially reshape political alignments within and across countries.

Such recent development in the macropolitical literature parallels the attempt to "bring the state back in" in the study of private authority regimes in climate governance and environmental governance more generally.[54] Empirical research shows that certain domestic political and institutional contexts favor some actors' participation in transnational governance and their effectiveness more than that of others. Participation in transnational climate governance is greatest in countries with strong civil liberties, decentralized government, competent bureaucracies, and proenvironment policies.[55] This suggests a synergetic relationship between national policies and transnational private governance in the aggregated uptake of transnational climate initiatives across countries.

These studies capture important mechanisms of interplay between domestic political structures and the agency of nonstate actors in global governance. Public-private interactions create a "blurring" between public and private authority, with private authority serving as a complement (rather than a substitute) to public regulatory arrangements.[56] A cross-national study found that national policies and transnational initiatives are likely to reinforce each other in their influence of a country's participation in transnational climate initiatives.[57] Similar goals between state and nonstate actors increase the likelihood of success of hybrid regimes comprising public, commercial, and civil society actors that occupy a common issue.[58] In other words, state actors play a supporting role and increase the legitimacy of private actors.

Notwithstanding, little if any of the above-mentioned research examines how national policies and governance structures interact with microlevel dynamics and incentives at the firm level, despite findings of a multilevel comparison study—which models firms as nested within countries—indicating that firm-level factors account for a majority of the variance in their climate action.[59] As this book argues, given global businesses' strategic considerations, the ways in which domestic regulation and global governance shape corporate self-regulation in the climate change area vary by firms' corporate management and choices about their internal management structures and practices.

1.2.3 Gaps in the Firm-Level and Domestic- and Global-Level Explanations

The multilevel governance framework on climate change (MGFCC) brings together these disparate literatures into a framework to explain how micro- and macro-incentives and institutions have spurred multinational corporations, at every level of governance, to engage proactively in climate action. To elaborate on these interactions, the MGFCC articulates the corporate, regulatory, and global governance levels as part of a nested structure of climate change governance. Operational rules at the firm-level affect day-to-day decisions; in turn, collective-choice rules that form domestic regulatory regimes affect operational activities. Constitutional-choice rules serve as a covering set of rules shaping the collections of rules nested under it (see chapter 2 for details).[60] All three levels are intricately linked, and the causal mechanism is complex—the specificity of which is often context and issue specific.

First and foremost, the MGFCC opens the black box of the firm to delineate the role of managerial agency and uncover internal firm management and organization-level structures and incentives to shed light on global businesses as strategic actors and nodes of decision-making. Testable implications of the MGFCC link the proposed multilevel governance interactions (i.e., corporate × regulation, corporate × global, and regulation × global) to global firms' participation and effort in voluntary climate action and to their environmental performance or carbon footprints. These multilevel governance interactions are predicated on the fact that global businesses are "decision-making coalitions"[61] with a business imperative to reassure a diverse set of stakeholders—including shareholders, employees, customers, regulators, and investors in domestic and global markets—that they are well managed and well run.

1.3 Empirical Setting, Research Design, Methods, and Cases

This book's empirical setting is the five years leading up to and the aftermath of the 2015 Paris Agreement. The empirical evidence to substantiate *Corporations at Climate Crossroads*'s framework about multilevel governance interactions is large-*N* cross-sectional and panel data analyses (with attention to causal inference) from 2011 to 2020 about the ways in which global businesses (through managers) respond to regulatory pressure arising from domestic regulation and global governance and to heterogeneous effects in their corporate self-regulation on climate change. Global firms' participation and effort (i.e., intensity of participation) in voluntary carbon disclosure through CDP serve as the main dependent variables of interest. Other outcome variables investigated include global businesses' adoption of quantitative emissions targets and an internal carbon price. The firm is the unit of analysis in a majority of the book's empirical chapters.

In addition to the multilevel governance framework on climate change, this book makes several empirical contributions: First, large-*N* econometric analyses are based on an original author-constructed database—the Global Sustainable Business and Climate Action Database. This novel dataset is the first of its kind to track a census of the largest multinational companies worldwide by sales revenue—namely, the Fortune Global 500 and S&P 500 index firms—and follows their voluntary climate action and performance from 2011 to 2020.[62] Illustrative case studies illuminate and elaborate on quantitative results to further underscore the explanatory power of the book's multilevel governance framework on climate change.

Second, this book distinguishes "green" or climate change leadership from global businesses' greenwashing behavior by employing discrete-continuous econometric models to disentangle whether a firm participates and how much it participates in corporate self-regulation. Not all companies that make climate net-zero pledges in fact carry out their proactive commitments. Thus, a unique contribution of this book is the conceptual and empirical distinction and measurement of a firm's binary decision about participation in proactive climate action (or not) and the intensity or extent of that action. Relatedly, attention is paid to causal inference through the use of a natural experiment (described below) along with quasi-experimental methods. Individual empirical chapters contain information about empirical models and main analyses, whereas appendices contain additional supporting materials and robustness checks.

1.3.1 Voluntary Carbon Disclosure and CDP

Founded in 2000, CDP represents an ideal case for examining corporate self-regulation in the climate change area because it is the oldest and largest non-profit organization in the world that houses voluntary carbon disclosure by corporations.[63] Second, CDP holds the largest environmental database in the world, with approximately 15,000 companies reporting to it.[64] Moreover, recent mandatory climate disclosure rules introduced in the United Kingdom (UK), the EU, New Zealand, India, Singapore, Hong Kong, and the United States have all to varying degrees built on CDP's success as a global disclosure system for investors, companies, cities, states, and regions to manage their environmental impact. Moreover, CDP has partnered with subnational governments from Thailand to Italy and has participated in high-level political processes like the European Commission's Technical Expert Group on Sustainable Finance. In fact, CDP has been regarded as a "primary building block" of public rules.[65]

On January 13, 2025, several federal agencies at the behest of President Trump announced that they are withdrawing from this proposed rule. As such, I am deleting this sentence.

At the behest of more than 650 institutional investors with approximately $90 trillion in assets, CDP invites midsize to large global companies across sectors, domiciled in developed and emerging markets across industries, including all of the Global 500 and S&P 500 firms that make up this book's empirical analysis, to respond to an annual climate change questionnaire. Firms are requested to voluntarily disclose their entity-wide GHG emissions as well as their plans for measuring, reporting, and reducing scope 1, scope 2, and scope 3 GHG emissions, including the adoption of science-based, quantitative emissions targets and an internal price on carbon.[66]

In addition to tracking corporate strategies and emissions, CDP grades corporations on the substantive contents of their climate disclosures, publishing disclosure scores for companies that report to it on an annual basis. In this book's empirical analyses, CDP's disclosure scores, including letter grades, serve as a proxy for firms' varying levels of voluntary climate action, as defined in the rest of the book.[67]

1.3.2 Regulatory Stringency and the US Case

Empirically, to substantiate the role of domestic regulation in the multilevel governance framework on climate change, this book conceptualizes and measures regulatory pressure and stringency in four separate ways. First, the book adopts the standard practice in the international political economy literature to measure regulatory stringency across countries by their respective ratifications of international environmental agreements (IEAs), which are compiled and made publicly available by the International Environmental Agreements Database Project, maintained at Université Laval. While not a perfect representation of the strength of a country's regulatory regime, IEAs reflect what each country is willing to legally commit to with respect to the breadth and depth of environmental regulation at the domestic level. The book also employs alternative ways of assessing a country's range and ambitiousness of environmental and climate policymaking, such as the number of climate change–related laws that a country passed from 2011 to 2020 from the London School of Economics and Political Science's Climate Change Laws of the World database, and a composite index of environmental performance indicators (e.g., air quality, biodiversity and habitat, ecosystems, and climate change) or the Environmental Performance Index (EPI) from the Yale University Center for Environmental Law & Policy and Columbia University's Center for International Earth Science Information Network.

Furthermore, this book makes use of the US EPA's Clean Power Plan (CPP)—first introduced by the EPA in 2013 and officially announced by President Obama in 2015—as a plausible natural experiment or an exogenous shock of regulatory pressure. As the book's empirical analyses in chapters 5 and 7 demonstrate, coming off the tail of more than a decade of failed US legislative action, the CPP was a driver of US-based global businesses' participation and effort in voluntary carbon disclosure and was linked to firms' entity-wide carbon emissions and carbon emissions intensity.

The United States is the largest emitter of planet-warming GHG emissions in human history, second only to China. The top three GHG emitters (China, the United States, and India) together contribute 43 percent, while the bottom one hundred countries account for about 3 percent. However, the US per capita emission is the highest in the world. As such, there is a widely held view that without swift emissions reductions by the United States, it is less likely for the rest of the world to limit the rise of global average temperatures. Moreover, failure to pass climate legislation in the US takes away "diplomatic leverage to press other countries to take climate action of their own."[68]

For more than two decades leading up to the 2022 Inflation Reduction Act,[69] numerous climate change–related proposals in the US Congress either died in committee or failed a vote in the US Senate or in the House of Representatives, leading up to the 2015 Paris Agreement (figure 1.3), as detailed in chapter 5.[70] Since 2015, President Barack Obama joined, President Donald Trump exited, and President Joe Biden rejoined the Paris Agreement, when he took office in 2020. There was much uncertainty about climate and clean energy provisions in the Build Back Better Bill, the predecessor of the 2022 Inflation Reduction Act.

In the backdrop of the multidecade federal inaction on climate change, on the eve of the Paris Agreement, momentum was building in the United States under the auspices of President Obama's administration. The Obama

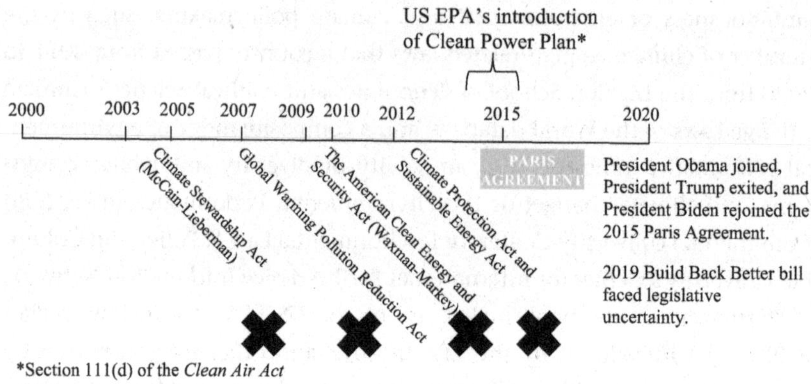

Figure 1.3
Timeline of failed climate change proposals in the US Congress (2000–2020).

administration pledged to take the lead, along with China, to cut carbon emissions, tackle climate change as a national policy priority, and innovate in alternative fuel technology, including solar and biofuels.

By year-end 2013, the US Environmental Protection Agency had introduced the Clean Power Plan, which set standards for new power plants, as an amendment to the 1990 Clean Air Act. Many companies at the time perceived that broader climate change regulation was forthcoming and attempted to get ahead of expected climate regulations by engaging in proactive climate action.[71]

1.3.3 Global Governance and the United Nations Global Compact

Throughout this book, the United Nations Global Compact is the main case of global governance. In 2000, more than a decade before the 2015 United Nations Framework of Climate Change Conference (UNFCCC) in Paris or Conference of the Parties (COP) 21 in December 2015, the supranational organization was founded to enhance "international dialogues" among businesses and governments about socially responsible policies and "universal sustainability principles" across all aspects of corporate sustainability—environment, social policy, sustainable development, governance, financial markets, and supply chains. The international and supranational organization is predicated on the belief that firms are the main driver of change, rather than governments.

According to UN Global Compact (UNGC) founder and Harvard professor John Ruggie, the UNGC is "meant to serve as a framework of reference and dialogue to stimulate best practices and to bring about convergence in corporate practices around universally shared values . . . [Furthermore,] . . . how does the [Global Compact] propose to induce corporate change? . . . The hope and expectation [are] that good practices will help to drive out bad ones through the power of dialogue, transparency, advocacy, and competition."[72]

This book's multilevel governance framework on climate change (MGFCC) contends that global governance institutions like the UNGC are viewed as a harbinger of domestic regulation and therefore a form of regulatory pressure to be reckoned with through active engagement. As a low-cost, nonbinding international voluntary program, the UN Global Compact serves as a lower-bound test for the validity of the MGFCC in explaining corporate behavior as an outcome of corporate, regulatory, and global governance interactions.

Notably, as the book's empirical analysis shows, the UN Global Compact has had success in influencing corporations when exogenous actors—in the private or public spheres—also place pressure on firms. Firms engage in global governance through the UNGC—led by senior- and executive-level managers working on climate change—when there is an increase in the stringency of existing and potential domestic regulations. As this book shows, this is true even for global businesses based outside the EU and Europe where intrafirm norms on climate and associated expectations about regulatory pressure are less pronounced.

1.3.4 Illustrative Company Cases

In *Corporations at Climate Crossroads*, illustrative company cases in the consumer-oriented and technology sectors and a descriptive analysis of the Oil and Gas Climate Initiative (OGCI) highlight how the various component parts or key independent variables and their interactions that make up this book's multilevel governance framework on climate change (MGFCC) have taken shape on the ground as salient drivers of corporate climate leaders' voluntary climate action. The qualitative case studies and large-*N* econometric analyses reinforce each other in providing evidence to support the book's multilevel governance theory about corporate climate action centered on firms.

The illustrative company cases highlight the main results of the book, which show that global firms that are the best managed and most stringently regulated and are active participants of global governance institutions are today's corporate climate leaders. Despite this, empirical results also show that neither firms themselves nor regulation or global norms and pressures alone will be able to achieve the substantive climate action that is required for reducing global temperatures enough to avert a climate change crisis. Civil society stakeholders—from institutional investors to environmental watchdog groups to universities—are more important than ever to keep firms accountable for their pledges and acts of corporate social responsibility on the environment and beyond.

1.4 Roadmap for the Rest of the Book

The first three chapters make up part I of the book, which establishes the basis for understanding the multilevel governance drivers of voluntary climate action by global businesses. This chapter (chapter 1) has articulated the empirical puzzles and situated the study at the nexus of related but scholastically disparate fields—namely, economics, political science, and management. Chapter 1 has also previewed the book's multilevel governance analysis, underscoring that proactive climate action by global businesses is a function of the synergic interaction between private governance and public governance at multiple levels—corporate managerial agency (firm level), regulatory pressures and public policy (domestic level), and global governance institutions (global level).

Chapter 2 presents the multilevel governance framework on climate change (MGFCC), which argues that corporations supply climate mitigation without the force of law in response to public and private politics (domestically and internationally), along with the discretion of managerial agency to navigate uncertainty. Testable implications, in the form of propositions, assert that global businesses are free agents (namely, agency of firm managers) and that their interaction with the stringency of existing and potential regulation and in the domestic and global governance spheres are key drivers of corporate self-regulation on climate change. These propositions about internal firm and external political economy catalysts of corporate climate action become subjects of empirical testing in rest of the book.

Chapter 3 "opens up the firm" to test the propositions in chapter 2 regarding corporate management—namely senior- and executive-level leadership dedicated to climate mitigation, which as this chapter argues, plays a key role in steering a corporation's self-regulation on climate change. Other firm-level organizational capabilities—namely, company-initiated corporate social responsibility practices (as opposed to socially responsible practices that have become industry or institutional norms) and complementary assets or capabilities in adjacent areas—are introduced to further underscore the firm-level managerial and organizational capabilities that lower firms' marginal cost of self-regulation. Spillover benefits and cost savings from these internal firm capabilities increase firms' effort in proactive climate action.

Chapter 3 also introduces the book's main empirical case, CDP, to which a majority of global firms have proactively disclosed their carbon management and emissions. Subsequent chapters also draw on CDP's climate disclosure data for empirical evidence.

Part II of the book provides empirical evidence to substantiate the propositions formed in chapter 2 that link cross-level governance interactions with voluntary climate action among the world's largest corporations by sales revenue, namely Fortune Global 500 and S&P 500 firms. After chapter 3 has established managerial agency and internal firm capabilities as important drivers of voluntary climate action, chapter 4 empirically links corporate management with domestic regulation and global governance to delineate cross-level governance interactions, as proposed in the MGFCC in chapter 2.

Chapter 5 presents the US case. The Clean Power Plan, which was introduced by the U.S. EPA during a period absent of federal climate legislation, had exerted regulatory pressure on GHG-intensive firms. This chapter makes use of the Clean Power Plan as a natural experiment to quantify the causal impact of the interaction between managerial agency and regulatory pressure, in shaping global firms' proactive climate action during the five years leading up to the Paris Agreement.

Chapter 6 provides quantitative and qualitive empirical evidence for the complementary interplay between domestic regulation and global governance in inducing global firms' adoption of global best practices, such as science-based, quantitative emissions targets and an internal price on carbon. An illustrative case study details the multiple institutional venues, such as the Global Compact Local Networks, in the UN Global Compact for fostering business-government dialogue and partnerships and for firms to learn about global best practices in carbon management.

Part III of *Corporations at Climate Crossroads* links voluntary climate action to firms' carbon footprints in chapter 7 and examines sectoral variation in chapter 8, along with illustrative company cases of exemplar corporate climate leaders based on interviews with sustainability leaders across consumer, technology, and GHG-intensive sectors. Chapters 7 employs a similar quasi-experimental approach as chapter 5 to link firms' voluntary adoption of carbon management practices with environmental performance by quantifying whether firms that disclose climate change information reduce entity-wide GHG emissions and GHG emissions intensity. This chapter exploits heterogeneity in the substantive contents of firms' climate disclosures—ranging from basic transparency to a higher level of climate mitigation, such as third-party GHG verification—to show that some firms use voluntary carbon disclosure to obfuscate and enable greenwashing when regulatory pressure is low.

Chapter 9 highlights variations between the Global North and Global South in the propensity of global firms based there to engage in industry self-regulation on climate change. A plethora of descriptive data analyses in chapters 8 and 9 underline the results of the large-*N* cross-sectional and panel data analyses of the previous empirical chapters and provide nuanced sectoral and regional distinctions. The empirically verified key takeaway is that once sectoral and regional heterogeneity are accounted for, corporations and managerial and executive leaders inside them (who are often omitted from the climate story) are key players in a nested structure of climate change governance with interactions between bottom-up and top-down incentives and institutions involving firm, regulatory, and global governance. Corporate environmentalism in the climate change area by multinational companies originating from the European Union, as highlighted in chapter 9, exhibits the complementarities between corporate, regulatory, and global governance as theorized in this book's multilevel governance framework on climate change.

Chapter 10 summarizes and highlights how the book's key findings set the stage for a proposed research agenda about the potential pitfalls and necessity of safeguards for corporate self-regulation on climate change. Ultimately, markets can fail, and so can governments. Companies and their technologies alone are unlikely avert the global climate change crisis, nor can governments' sheer will and iron fists. The polycentric governance structure with checks and balances of the multilevel governance framework on climate change is consistent with a proposal for a portfolio approach to climate change—notably, in an era of contentious politics and uncertainty about climate denialism or pragmatism.

The rise of stakeholder capitalism, and a growing emphasis on corporate social responsibility (CSR) and corporate political responsibility (CPR), coexist with incidences of corporate greenwashing. This final chapter features a Stanford University student movement, which is part of a global campaign to dissociate the university from the fossil fuel industry's influence on research. The student activists and administrators have found common ground in ensuring transparency in university research funding involving the fossil fuel industry. This chapter also spotlights the state of California's new mandatory corporate climate disclosure rules to show how the book's framework sheds light on how regulatory developments in California, Europe, and elsewhere, help to mainstream climate disclosures and other climate policy innovations and expedite industry norms and standards in the United States and beyond.

2 Theory of Multilevel Governance Drivers of Corporate Self-Regulation on Climate Change

This chapter presents a multilevel governance framework on climate change (MGFCC) to explain the various and interacting roles of corporate, regulatory, and global governance in driving and shaping voluntary climate action by global businesses. The MGFCC challenges the often-dichotomous approach in the economics, political science, and management literatures that either privileges agency over structure or vice versa and focuses either on micro- or macroexplanations (see chapter 1 for a review of the literature). Instead, the MGFCC posits that multinational corporations engage in climate mitigation without or beyond the force of law, in response to public and private politics emanating domestically and globally, and in concert with the discretion of managerial leadership inside the firm.

In order to navigate uncertainty in the face of climate change, senior management or executive-rank leaders (henceforth, managers) often have some discretion over either firm policy or how that policy will be executed. Looking inside the "black box" of firm decision-making is therefore warranted. This chapter presents a theoretical framework to explicate the interaction between managerial agency and regulatory stringency and managerial agency and global governance as drivers of corporate self-regulation on climate change. Extending existing research, the theoretical framework accounts for how multinational corporations, the book's subject and unit of analysis, engage in self-regulation on climate change—thus signaling their "green" leadership—but exert varying degrees of actual green behavior.[1]

Chapter 2 begins with an exposition of the nested structure of climate change governance to highlight the distinctions among corporate, regulatory, and global governance as an analytically useful way to contextualize the complementarities of business, regulation, and global governance. In subsequent sections in this chapter, propositions are formed about how corporate × regulation, corporate × global, regulation × global interactions impact the firms' decision about their participation and effort in voluntary climate action, which are then examined empirically in the rest of the book. Together, the component parts of the three governance-level interactions make up the MGFCC to explain corporate behavior on climate change, as summarized at the end of the chapter.

2.1 A Nested Structure of Climate Change Governance

Elinor Ostrom's (2007b) nested structure of institutions provides a starting point from which this book builds and extends, for explaining the ways in which corporate, regulatory, and global governance complement and interact in the MGFCC.

For Ostrom, and in this book, "institutions" refers to both organizations and the rules used to structure patterns of interaction within and across organizations. Diverse institutional arrangements—several of which are subjects of this book (italicized), include *markets*, hierarchies, *firms*, families, *voluntary associations*, *national governments*, and *international regimes*.

Ostrom distinguishes between operational rules, which affect day-to-day decisions, collective-choice rules, which in turn affect operational activities, and constitutional-choice rules, which serve as a covering set of rules shaping the collections of rules nested under them. All three levels are intricately linked, and the causal mechanism is complex—the specificity of which is often context- and issue-specific.

For concreteness, under the MGFCC, the United Nations Global Compact (UNGC) is an example of a constitutional-choice institution with a universalistic objective as shown in an inverted representation of Ostrom's (2007b) nested structure of institutions (figure 2.1). The UNGC is a nonbinding United Nations (UN) initiative based on voluntary CEO commitments to adopt global best practices and standards on environmental sustainability and socially responsible policies and to report their implementation. While the UNGC does not possess coercive powers, it has established itself as the global authority on corporate sustainability and relies on democratic decision-making and norms of inclusiveness to elicit the cooperation of and coordination among corporate members and nation-states in which the firms are domiciled.

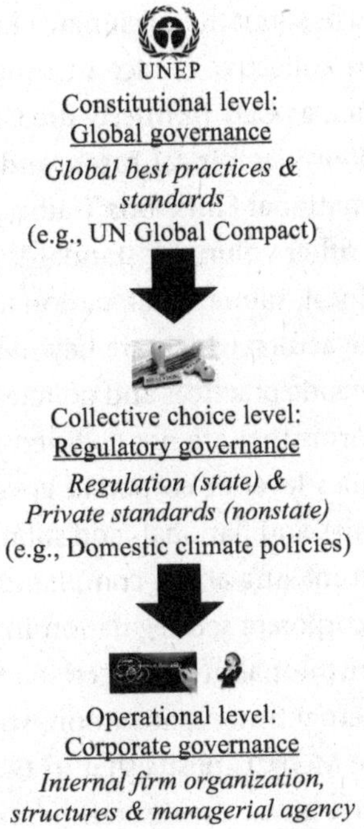

Figure 2.1
A nested structure of climate change governance.
Source: Author's adaptation of (an inverted) Ostrom's (2007b) nested structure of institutions.

The collective and operational rules that the UNGC promotes reflect the convention's purpose of harmonizing national regulations to contribute to the "mainstreaming of the [Sustainable Development Goals]." For example, the UNGC's local networks "advance corporate sustainability at the grassroots level by helping companies understand what responsibilities business mean within a national context."[2] Moreover, the UN Global Compact Academy is a "premier online learning platform" for companies to "fast-track your sustainability strategy and skills."[3] As the chapter theorizes, global governance institutions are viewed by firms as harbingers of future regulatory requirements at the country (or subnational) level and therefore as a form of regulatory pressure to be reckoned with through active engagement.

Below the constitutional choice institutions are the collective choice institutions, which comprise both formal and informal, state/public, and nonstate/private institutions. Regulations are formal and government-promulgated policies, such as national or subnational climate change policies. By contrast, private actor–sponsored collective choice institutions include third-party-sponsored programs, such as CDP (formerly the Carbon Disclosure Project), which is one of this book's empirical cases, and industry-sponsored programs such as the International Emissions Trading Association.

There are numerous other voluntary standards and programs on climate change initiated at the local, subnational, national, and transnational levels by public and/or private actors, which are beyond the scope of this book.[4] Informal institutions include practices and policies that are experimental in nature or established norms that are not codified or officially sanctioned.

At the operational rules level or corporate governance, individual firms are nested within countries and national- and subnational-level institutions. They engage in decision-making about compliance with government policies or participation in corporate self-regulation in the climate change area. Firms respond to constitutional and collective choice opportunities and constraints through internal firm organization, structures, and managerial agency. At this level, the MGFCC posits that in the face of and to navigate uncertainty, managers are given the discretion and authority to steer and execute corporate policy and respond to climate change.

Governance takes place at all three levels—constitutional, collective choice, and operational. The operational level is nested under the collective choice level, which is nested under the constitutional level. The constitutional level serves as a covering set of institutions, ultimately to set the agenda and "a call to companies to align strategies and operations with universal principles on human rights, labour, environment and anti-corruption, and take actions that advance societal goals."[5]

The rest of the chapter delineates elements of the MGFCC, first at the firm level to highlight managerial agency (section 2.3). Next, sections 2.4 and 2.5 explicate how corporate governance through managers interacts with the regulatory and global governance levels, synergistically or otherwise. Section 2.6 theorizes how domestic regulation delimits global governance's influence on firms as a driver of corporate self-regulation on climate change. Altogether, seven testable implications in the form of propositions delineate a causal mechanism about the internal and external drivers of voluntary climate action by global businesses (see figure 2.2 in section 2.7 for an illustration). These empirical predictions are the subjects of large-*N* cross-sectional and panel data analyses (with attention to causal inference) and illustrative case studies in the empirical chapters of the book.

2.2 Firms, Uncertainty, Bounded Rationality, and Norms

In a 1970 op-ed for the *New York Times*, Milton Friedman famously declared, "There is one and only one social responsibility of business—to use its resources and engage in activities designed to increase its profits so long as it stays within the rules of the game, which is to say, engages in open and free competition without deception or fraud."[6]

Fifty years later, Fama objects to the rise in stakeholder capitalism on similar grounds,[7] with an emphasis on the high contract costs of optimizing across stakeholders. He writes, "Unlike wealth, welfare has multiple dimensions (for example, E and S and G), and tastes for different dimensions vary across shareholders. . . How do we write and enforce a payment function in which managers are evaluated on wealth along with multiple dimensions of welfare, with the likelihood of randomness in outcomes on all dimensions? [This] puts us in a quagmire of satisfying the divergent tastes of shareholders, . . . a problem that implies high contract costs."[8,9]

In spite of Friedman and Fama's skepticism, corporate social responsibility and/or stakeholder capitalism are part of today's business realities.[10] This may be because what is considered "market equilibrium" is not easily defined: uncertainty abounds about the future of how technology can be improved, what customers really want, and which regulation and policy will prevail. This is the world in which global businesses across sectors and countries of domicile have operated in the past decade, amid mounting scientific evidence about the threat and impacts of global warming as well as the increased societal pressure to respond.

Several assumptions undergird the multilevel governance framework on climate change introduced in this chapter and book. First, this book assumes that in a world defined by the reality of climate change, a stable "long-run" equilibrium is not an easy target in a substantive sense. Rather, as Nelson and Winter (2002) write, "It is always in a transient phase, groping toward its temporary target." Second, decision-makers face informational constraints and cognitive limitations; in other words, they are boundedly rational.

These boundedly rational decision-makers are influenced by both rationality and norms.[11] Norms are behavioral rules and institutions and can be a single standard of behavior or a collection of practices that are not codified in law.[12] Norms could be backed by third-party sanctions, although even norms that carry punitive consequences are "soft" laws as opposed to "hard" laws because they are by definition not legally binding. Notwithstanding, norms are characterized by prescriptive qualities of "oughtness" and "appropriate" behavior,[13] and once internalized, could acquire a taken-for-granted quality. Following Fearon (1999, 27), norms take the generic form "Good people do (or do not do) X in situations A, B, C."[14] The implication is that norms are shared by people and at least partly sustained by their approval and disapproval. This is because what is appropriate is subject to the judgment of a community or society.

Furthermore, companies do not have complete contingency plans or perfect knowledge at time *t*. The capacity of the human mind and of the organizations that they make up is small compared with the size of the problems whose solution is required for objectively rational behavior.[15] Rather, decision-makers in firms, government, and other private and public organizations possess imperfect and/or limited information, foresight, and computational capability and face uncertainty.[16] Despite this, they have and continue to tackle problems of great complexity and difficulty, often reasonably well. The MGFCC articulates the way in which interactions between managerial agency at the firm level and regulatory pressures emanating from the domestic and international realms serve as the mechanism by which "wicked problems" like climate change—which are characterized by complexity and uncertainty—are contended with, often preemptively, by multinational corporations.

2.3 Managerial Agency: Policy Supporters and Champions Inside the Firm

In a world of informational and cognitive constraints and in the face of uncertainty, dedicated managers at the senior or executive level responsible for a firm's climate policy, management, and mitigation activities are "policy supporters" as opposed to "policy skeptics" or "policy neutrals."[17] They are agents of change inside the firm because they capture or win the attention of top management and actively engage with investors and help to either secure consensus on or compromise in proclimate policies and activities.[18] Given that firms do not have complete contingency plans at time *t*, companies give discretion to and rely on managers to navigate uncertainty, respond to internal firm opportunities and constraints, and interact with and respond to the demands of the external political economy.[19]

When climate change managers are in or near top management, they exercise more control over firm decision-making processes and thus can drive and direct priorities and resources toward corporate climate action in ways that champions in lower ranks are less likely to be able to do.[20] These senior- or executive-level managers perform three key tasks to build relational contracts inside the firm for tackling risks under uncertainty. First, they attract climate-neutral or climate-conscious employees in their designated role as sustainability officers. In contrast to a climate-neutral employee, a climate-conscious employee cares not only about monetary payoffs (or incentives) but also about her reputation and identity and the social impact of her actions.

Second, as agents of change, managers dedicated to climate mitigation seek to align the beliefs of employees with those of the firm to improve coordination and solve a range of agency problems. When managers successfully engage in sustainability efforts on behalf of the company, a climate-conscious employee's identity (her own belief about herself and her type) and reputation (others' beliefs about that person's type) are strengthened.[21] In this way, firms become what Henderson and Van den Steen (2015) refer to as "carriers of identity and reputation" since both firm membership and actions, particularly those of multinational corporations, are visible to the public.[22]

Third, managers form governing coalitions made up of leaders and employees across ranks inside the firm. Coalition-building is achieved through a continuous bargaining-learning process, whereby managers mobilize support for the firm's approach to sustainability practice.[23] As key players in a "meso level social order,"[24] managers possess the social skills and ability to empathize with others and thereby bring people together toward collective action of corporate self-regulation on climate change.[25] Managers help set the agenda and shape the narrative and framing for a given approach.[26]

Through these three tasks, climate change managers facilitate the necessary incentives and coordination for effective beyond-compliance climate action by firms: namely, the alignment of values, learning, creativity, and innovation. This is because a manager's bias toward a particular course of action can increase employees' (and the company's) effort and investments.[27]

And, as such, dedicated managers responsible for firms' response to climate change help to shape the narratives and counternarratives related to firms' sustainability practices.[28]

At times, these managers' efforts could result in increasing returns to scale in sustainability output (e.g., carbon management) or outcome (e.g., environmental performance). Two propositions link global firms' installation of managers dedicated to climate mitigation to companies' participation and effort (i.e., intensity of participation in climate-related self-regulation).

Proposition 1 (participation and manager): The likelihood of corporate participation in voluntary climate action increases when there is a manager responsible for carbon management and climate risks at the senior management or executive rank inside the firm.

Proposition 2 (intensity of participation and manager): A firm's level of voluntary climate action increases where there is a manager responsible for carbon management and climate risks at the senior management or executive rank inside the firm.

2.4 Corporate and Domestic Regulation (Corporate × Regulation)

Economics and political science literatures have agreed that public politics (actual or potential government interaction with firms via laws and regulation) are salient drivers of corporate self-regulation on climate change.[29] As explicated in chapter 1, a recent literature in political science focuses on distributive politics (i.e., relationship between politicians/legislation and their constituencies, which include corporations) as a limiting factor to solutions to environmental problems such as climate change.[30] Notably, powerful corporate actors that stand to lose from decarbonization transitions often stall or block policy progress. These firms have heavily engaged in political lobbying and other activities in order to veto a regulatory initiative or shape environmental policy in favor of least-cost instruments and designs.

Rather than a focus on firms' political strategies (including political lobbying), the MGFCC explicates firms' *internal* managerial capacity and how they interact with regulation to influence corporate self-regulation on climate change. Political lobbying and related activities typically occur as a separate function and are housed separately from functions responsible for a firm's climate policy, mitigation, and sustainability practices more generally.[31]

To elucidate the relationship between firms and public politics, the MGFCC adapts and extends the concept of "bargaining under the shadow of war" in international relations theory.[32] The general idea is that of bargaining when each party has an outside option. Firm A offers the government a deal (i.e., corporate self-regulation), with both parties anticipating that there will be regulation by the government if there is no deal.[33] Both firm A and the government would rather not have regulation because regulation is a costly endeavor for both parties, in terms of compliance costs for firms and implementation and enforcement costs for regulators. Moreover, in a world in which politicians seek reelection, regulation—notably, policies that impose a highly visible and concentrated cost—can be unpopular with the electorate.[34]

If firm A goes first in offering a deal (self-regulation), then firm A must offer the government something that is at least as good as the government's "outside offer," which is the expected utility of regulation, and can be interpreted as the threat of actual or impending regulation (e.g., forthcoming carbon standards or a carbon tax). The stronger the threat of regulation by the government, the more credible and higher quality is firm A's self-regulation.

A corollary is that the weaker the threat of regulation,[35] the weaker will be corporate self-regulation, and the more likely it is that firm A will engage in greenwashing behavior or false or misleading advertising of corporate social responsibility. This is because there is no incentive for firm A to offer something that is beyond what is as good as the government's outside offer.[36] Consequently, the likelihood of greenwashing behavior by firm A is increased compared to the case in which the threat of regulation (the government's outside offer) is strong.

Firm A's internal champion on climate change, namely, the dedicated manager responsible for the company's response to climate change (see previous section), serves as an intermediary to broker a deal between firm A and the government, facilitating firm A's choice of self-regulation over regulation by the government. The existence of these "policy supporters"—who are also "regulation" brokers—is critical because companies facing similar regulatory environments may not always respond in the same way.

In the face of both existing and impending regulation, when regulatory pressure is high and the marginal cost of self-regulation is low, there will be a hastening of efforts, led by managers, to signal to regulators and other external stakeholders firms' ability to internalize externalities and reduce their negative impacts on the environment. Managers readily respond to regulatory pressures in order to earn goodwill with both regulators and stakeholders and to avoid complex, inflexible, and costly regulatory processes and legal liabilities.

As long as firm A does not renege on its promise to self-regulate, the bargain between firm A and the government is secure.[37] That being said, a corporation can participate and signal that it has environmental sustainability policies without actually integrating these policies into business as usual. Rather, once a company has made the decision to participate in voluntary climate action, a firm's effort or intensity of participation helps to distinguish leaders from greenwashers.[38]

The creation and installation of a chief sustainability officer, for example, could merely be "symbolic management"[39] when promises or policies are not backed by corresponding actions. When there is a disconnect between the structures (participation) and the activities of an organization (intensity of participation), "decoupling" is a common result.[40] This policy-practice gap is a chief variety of greenwash.[41]

To decrease the incidence of greenwashing requires effectively aligning internal and intrafirm structures, processes, and incentives. Regulatory pressure is one expedient way to align structures, processes, and incentives within firms for environmental performance. In particular, there is a constructive interaction between regulation and management practices that help to mainstream a policy into business operations, which in turn influence corporate environmental performance.

When companies have made the necessary alignments in their business operations toward a low-carbon economy, such as by managing and integrating climate risks into day-to-day decision-making—further incentivized by regulatory pressure—the marginal cost of additional voluntary climate action is relatively low, because they already possess supporting management structures and practices that help to maximize the firm's profits.[42] With more intensive participation (i.e., more effort) in beyond-compliance or proactive climate action, these firms safeguard their brand reputation and may even capture new markets because they are signaling to "caring" consumers about their corporate social responsibility bona fides.[43]

Proposition 3 (participation and corporate × regulation): Firms with a dedicated manager responsible for carbon management and climate risks are more likely than firms without a dedicated manager to participate in voluntary climate action when they face strong pressure from existing or impending regulation.

Proposition 4 (intensity of participation and corporate × regulation): Firms that integrate climate risks into their business operations will engage in a higher level of voluntary climate action when they face strong pressure from existing or impending regulation.

2.5 Corporate and Global Governance (Corporate × Global)

In the MGFCC, firms, through managers, view global governance institutions as harbingers of future regulatory requirements at the domestic level and, as such, a form of regulatory pressure to be reckoned with through active engagement. They face stakeholder and regulatory pressure from a diverse array of global governance institutions that are often deliberately orchestrated, aimed at targeting one or multiple dimensions of climate change governance.[44] With backing from private industry, governments, or NGOs, global governance institutions make up a "coral reef" of diverse organizational forms in transnational climate governance, which include informal institutions, transgovernmental networks, intergovernmental organizations, and private transnational regulatory organizations.[45] This organization ecology accommodates local diversity and fosters learning and norming from a decentralized implementation experience.[46]

No global governance institution possesses the same coercive authority as domestic regulatory regimes. This is notably true for global governance institutions with high organizational flexibility and a low cost of entry, such as the UN Global Compact (UNGC), which is this book's empirical case for global governance. These primarily norm-based institutions recruit firms as members and are replete with opportunities for learning and norming, building brand reputation, and showcasing industry leadership. A study shows that membership in the UNGC increases firms' propensity to respond transparently to stakeholder allegations because of the reputational benefits that membership in the global governance institution confers, lowering firms' reputational cost of transparent response.[47]

Through firms' participation in global governance institutions, managers dedicated to climate mitigation join epistemic communities, in which—as knowledge-based experts—they learn about and help to define the problems that corporations face, identify policy solutions, and assess policy outcomes. In doing so, managers serve as "norm brokers": they represent their employers at climate forums, workshops, and meetings convened by global governance institutions to learn about, contest, and translate global best practices—many of which could someday become market norms and rules of law.

In particular, managers dedicated to climate mitigation are critical for norm emergence around corporate sustainability because they call attention to issues or even "create" issues through framing. By using language that names, interprets, and dramatizes them, managers—through forums and platforms that global governance institutions provide—shape broader public understandings and convince industry peers and competitors to adopt new ways of talking about and understanding issues and adopt specific policy instruments.

Given that no company has a complete plan of action or knowledge of what is an optimal plan for corporate insurance against climate change, managers help to determine which are "'pretty good' heuristics and which are mediocre" when comprehensive contingency planning is not possible.[48] Consequently, while global governance institutions—a majority of which lack monitoring or sanctioning mechanisms—may not directly induce corporate environmental performance, they could have conditioning effects on firms' participation and intensity of participation in corporate self-regulation on climate change through managerial agency.

Proposition 5 (participation and corporate × global): Firms with a dedicated manager responsible for carbon management and climate risks are more likely to participate in voluntary climate action when they participate in global governance institutions that seek to align business operations with universally accepted best practices about the environment.

Proposition 6 (intensity of participation and corporate × global): Firms that integrate climate risks into their business operations will engage in a higher level of voluntary climate action when they participate in global governance institutions that seek to align business operations with universally accepted best practices about the environment.

2.6 Regulation and Global Governance (Regulation × Global)

As introduced in the previous section, in addition to being harbingers of future regulatory requirements, global governance institutions are sites of norming and learning. When firms join global governance institutions, they face numerous opportunities for norming and learning about new worldviews, frameworks, and policy objectives as well as technical and esoteric aspects of policy tools and implementation designs and processes.[49] These lessons are an accumulation of technological, managerial, and organizational knowledge that foster the build-up of local technological capabilities.

The economics of innovation and technical change literatures identify this iterative process of adaptation and experimentation as learning by doing, learning by using, and learning by interacting.[50] Economists have linked such experiential and experimental learning to game theory. Contemporary game theory, informed by empirical data from lab experiments, views Nash equilibrium (i.e., pareto optimality at which no conflict-free moves can be taken because every deviation will make someone else worse off) to arise from a nonequilibrium adaptive process of learning, imitation, and evolution.[51]

In global governance institutions, learning can come from a plurality of sources such as epistemic communities, by trial and error, or as the result of a competition of beliefs and ideas, including divergent causal reasoning about policy problems.[52] The transfer of ideas and information via networks in international organizations, in the spread of norms, standard setting, and development of professional communities, promotes harmonization and policy coordination and can be rapid and frequent.[53]

That being said, in the face of complexity and uncertainty, firms rarely conduct a systematic search for emergent policy problems or the optimal solutions to solve them.[54] In circumstances where there is an overload of information or conflicting information or a "complex and changing nature of the world,"[55] corporate actors will fall back on existing knowledge and expectations, with all entailed and relevant financial consequences.[56] In other words, firms learn discriminatively inside global governance institutions. This is the case when corporate actors are confronted with evidence of a mismatch between policy objectives and the consequences of the planned course of action.[57]

The implication is that even while firms, through managers, view global governance institutions as potential signals of ensuing regulation on the horizon and thus have the incentive to learn, there is also a contrasting force at play. The multilevel governance framework on climate change (MGFCC) posits that, all else being equal, firms' learning is by and large mirrored by the current and prospective requirements and pressures of the domestic regulatory regime. Public politics emanating from firms' domicile country constrain and delimit the type and extent of learning and the translation of such learning into sustainability outputs or outcomes at the firm level.[58] Strong domestic regulation incentivizes firms' learning about relatively costly sustainability innovations and about how to define, implement, measure, and communicate their climate mitigation strategies because the domestic regulatory regime sets the performance baseline for firms.

In other words, when the stringency of domestic regulation is high, it follows that a firm's marginal cost of voluntary climate action will be low compared to a company facing weak domestic regulation and the same opportunities for learning in global governance institutions. Hence, the firm facing stricter domestic regulation has the incentive to engage in relatively costly climate action. Conversely, when domestic regulation is weak, the marginal cost of self-regulation will be high compared to a firm faced with stringent domestic regulation and the same opportunities for learning. This leads the firm facing less stringent regulation to engage in less costly climate action.

Consequently, while it is unlikely that corporate behavior will change as a result of participation in global governance institutions alone without formal rules of accountability, global governance institutions are likely to have success in influencing corporate behavior when regulators also place pressure on the firms.[59] In fact, the UN Global Compact views itself as a complement to (not a substitute for) legal regulation at the national or international levels.[60]

The outcome of the learning and norming that take place inside global governance institutions for corporate participants is global best practices that are in line with the scope and stringency of existing regulation or the credible threat of future regulation. All things considered, in their benefit-cost calculus a majority of firms have little incentive to adopt policy or innovations—as introduced by global governance institutions—that go beyond regulation on the books or on the horizon.

In this way, domestic regulation serves as an intermediary between knowledge production in global governance institutions and corporate climate action, leading to minor adjustments from preexisting expectations and requirements. This suggests that global governance is ultimately a complement to rather than a substitute for domestic rules.

Proposition 7 (participation and regulation × global): For firms originating from countries with (less) stringent regulations, their participation in global governance institutions leads them to engage in (less) costly voluntary climate action.

2.7 Multilevel Governance Framework on Climate Change: Explaining Corporate Self-Regulation on Climate Change

The multilevel governance framework on climate change (MGFCC) articulates a causal mechanism for global firms' decision-making about proactive climate action. The various component parts—manager, corporate × regulation, corporate × global, and regulation × global—as presented in sections 2.1 through 2.6 make up the MGFCC. The propositions (propositions 1 to 7) that accompany each component part are subjected to empirical tests in subsequent chapters. Manager, corporate × regulation, corporate × global, and regulation × global serve as key independent variables to be empirically verified as a "cause" or "driver" of participation and effort in corporate climate action, the dependent variables of interest. In other words, managerial agency and its interaction with domestic regulation and global governance as well as the interplay between domestic regulation and global governance are hypothesized to independently affect corporate behavior on climate change that surpasses current regulation.

One could conceive of other causal structures involving corporate, regulatory, and global governance and the actors operating in them. For instance, a concrete example describing the possibility of nonindependence of corporate governance and domestic regulation is the following, occurring at the industry level: the opposition of the fossil fuel industry in the United States to a carbon tax impacts the chance that any such legislation will pass. Their collective position affects the stringency of the regulatory environment, which could in turn shape the oil and gas firms' participation and effort in proactive climate action. There are still other (and more complex) causal structures; in particular, corporate leadership could affect self-regulation both directly and indirectly, via domestic or global governance, all or some of which could impact corporate decision-making on voluntary climate action.

The potentially complex directions of the causal arrows or endogeneity of managerial agency, domestic regulation, and global governance are addressed in the empirical chapters by exploiting a natural experiment (see chapters 5 and 7) to ensure the exogeneity or independence of regulatory pressure as a driver of corporate proactive behavior. Furthermore, a variety of econometric models and statistical techniques are employed to account for how previous year's corporate actions impact contemporaneous decisions about participation and effort, how contemporaneous policy or market shocks in the economy affect all firms, or how industry-specific factors and actions could impact corporate climate action. Appendices 3 to 7 describe the book's methodologies in detail.

In the MGFCC, corporate self-regulation on climate change is predicated on the interactions between regulatory pressure emanating from domestic regulation and global governance (external to the firm) and managerial capacity (internal to the firm), respectively. The MGFCC posits and the empirical analyses show that firms' ambitions typically reflect the policy ambition of their governments. In other words, global firms' voluntary climate action and public politics are complements, not substitutes.

As, as shown in figure 2.2, whether firms are "green" or "gray" (i.e., greenwashing) firms are unknown ex-ante because both types of firms have the incentive to respond to public politics (regulation or regulatory pressure), market forces, and private politics (stakeholder activism) in their sustainability outputs (namely, participation and intensity of participation in voluntary climate action, respectively). Environmental performance or sustainability outcome is secured (and green firms are revealed) if and when, along with a high level of effort, firms are faced with external accountability, namely monitoring, enforcement, and sanctioning for nonadherence.

2.7.1 Managerial Agency

With respect to managerial capacity, firms install senior- and executive-level managers responsible for climate mitigation on their behalf. These managers attract climate-neutral or climate-conscious employees, align beliefs of employees and the firm, and create informal and formal governing coalitions made up of leaders and employees inside the company. Through the alignment of values, creativity, and innovation, managers appropriate the necessary incentives and secure the coordination needed for corporate self-regulation on climate change.

2.7.2 Corporate × Regulation

In the face of actual regulation or regulation pressure, managers serve as "regulation brokers." When regulatory pressure is high and the marginal cost of self-regulation is low, there will be a hastening of efforts, led by managers, to signal firms' ability to internalize externalities, earn regulatory goodwill, and avoid legal liabilities. The higher the regulatory stringency and more credible the regulatory threat, the more effort managers devote to voluntary climate action.

2.7.3 Corporate × Global

Another source of public politics is regulatory pressure emanating internationally from global governance institutions. Global governance, which firms view as a harbinger of future regulatory requirements, is a form of regulatory pressure (albeit a weak source compared to binding rules of law) to be reckoned with through active engagement. These primarily norm-based institutions are replete with opportunities for learning and norming, building brand reputation, and showcasing industry leadership.

Through a firm's participation in global governance institutions, managers dedicated to climate mitigation join epistemic communities, in which, as knowledge-based experts, they learn about and help to define the environmental problems that corporations face, identify policy solutions, and assess the policy outcomes. In doing so, managers serve as "norm brokers": they represent their employers, as well as help formulate and translate the global best practices—which are likely to someday become market norms and rules of law—that they learn about and that are disseminated at public forums that global governance institutions convene.

2.7.4 Regulation × Global

Global governance institutions seldom fill a regulatory void or governance gap. Rather, national and subnational government pressures and demands originating from outside the global governance institutions trigger, influence, and shape members' learning and norming. Consequently, firms' learning and norming (led by managers) in global governance institutions are bounded by and thus mirror pressures and requirements of domestic regulation and distributive conflicts among political and economic stakeholders

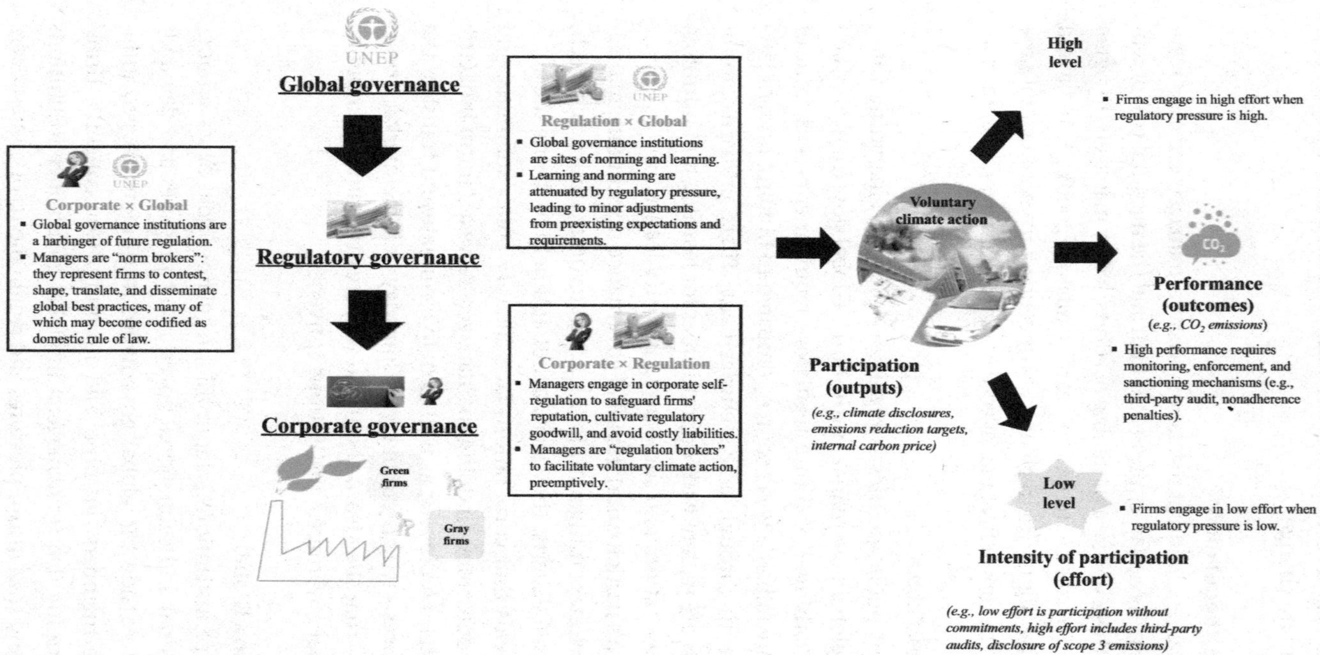

Figure 2.2

Multilevel governance interactions and voluntary climate action: a causal mechanism.

Notes: Assumptions undergirding this causal mechanism: (1) Under uncertainty, firms do not have complete contingency plans in their response to climate change at time *t*. (2) Firms account for political economic costs and benefits in their profit maximization. Alternative explanations enter into this book's large-*N* empirical analyses in the form of control variables: for example, stakeholder activism, markets (prices), sectors, states, countries, firm size, and time trends.

in nation-states. The more stringent existing or impending regulation is, the more likely corporate participants of global governance institutions are to engage in costly (as opposed to less costly) climate action.

2.7.5 Intensity of Participation and Environmental Performance

How much effort companies exert on their voluntary climate action is an outcome of the interaction of regulatory stringency or credibility of regulatory pressure and their existing managerial capacity. Taking a cue from regulatory pressure, dedicated managers responsible for climate mitigation facilitate and implement a firm's self-regulation by integrating climate risks into the firm's business operations and in turn engage in higher levels of self-regulation.

The stronger the threat of regulation, the more credible and higher quality is a firm's self-regulation. In contrast, the weaker the threat of regulation, the weaker self-regulation will be, and the more likely it is that firms will engage in greenwashing behavior.

Notwithstanding, to what extent firms' effort in self-regulation translates into environmental performance depends on the stringency of program obligations and standards, monitoring, enforcement, and sanctioning mechanisms. Accountability is paramount to ensure firms' fulfillment of their pledges about corporate social responsibility on climate change.

3 Opening Up the Firm: Internal Management and Organizational Drivers

This chapter "opens up the firm" to take a look inside its internal management and organizational structures.[1] In doing so, chapter 3 substantiates and extends chapter 2's theorizing about corporate management drivers of global firms' voluntary climate action. In the multilevel governance framework on climate change (MGFCC), while firms are nested within domestic regulatory and global governance, national (and subnational) policy drivers are necessary but not sufficient conditions for corporate climate action. In fact, on the eve of the 2015 Paris Agreement, close to two-thirds of the Fortune Global 500 firms' proactive climate action was attributable to the firm rather than to the domestic political economy drivers.[2] The fraction of the variance among firms that could be explained by country-level heterogeneity was 30 to 35 percent, leaving the rest to be explained by firm-level characteristics, as shown in table 3.1. This is to say, while external political economy drivers are important—notably, cross-level corporate × regulation, corporate × global, and regulation × global drivers that are examined in subsequent chapters of the book—this chapter underscores that supportive management and organizational structures and internal firm dynamics are catalysts for corporate self-regulation on climate change.

In the previous chapter, the MGFCC explicated the management factors *internal* to the corporation (i.e., executive and managerial leadership) that are the determinants of a global firm's participation and effort in beyond-compliance climate action, as propositions 1 and 2 articulate. This chapter proposes additional organizational factors and dynamics—namely, a firm's complementary assets—which are the basic building blocks by which firms profit from successful commercializing of an innovation,[3] and company-initiated corporate social responsibility (CSR) practices (as opposed to socially

Table 3.1
Variance decomposition: Ratio of between-country variance to total variance

Model	Country-level share of total variance	Standard error
Participation in voluntary climate action	0.35	(0.110)
Participation in voluntary carbon disclosure	0.32	(0.113)

Note: The results are based on a multilevel mixed-effects model that separately identifies the relative weight of internal firm and external political economy drivers of corporate self-regulation on climate change.

responsible practices that have become industry or institutional norms). These firm-level managerial and organizational capabilities lower firms' marginal cost of self-regulation on climate change. Spillover benefits and cost savings from these internal firm capabilities can facilitate and galvanize firms' effort in voluntary climate action. These are less-emphasized internal determinants in the extant business management literature, which by and large focuses on external factors, such as supply chain pressures, shareholder actions, and external political economy threats (including the threat of regulation and direct economic consequences) as drivers of firms' proactive action on climate change.

To test the validity of propositions 1 and 2 and these other germane internal firm organizational characteristics, this chapter focuses on the Global 500 firms' participation in CDP (formerly the Carbon Disclosure Project) on the eve of the 2015 Paris Agreement. Subsequent chapters also draw on CDP's annual climate change questionnaire for empirical evidence.[4] CDP, founded in 2000, is an ideal case study for examining firms' participation and effort in corporate self-regulation because it is the oldest and largest nonprofit organization in the world that tracks voluntary carbon disclosure by corporations.[5] This international nonprofit organization—made up of more than 650 institutional investor signatories with approximately $90 trillion in assets—invites all Global 500 companies across industries to disclose their entity-wide plans for measuring, reporting, and reducing greenhouse gas (GHG) emissions, including the adoption of science-based, quantitative emissions targets.

In this chapter's empirical analysis, like the rest of the book, a distinction is made between a firm's decision to disclose (i.e., participation) and the linked but subsequent decision of how much information to disclose about corporate carbon management and entity-wide carbon emissions (i.e., intensity of participation or effort) to CDP. This modeling approach explicitly accounts for the fact that firms may engage in self-regulation—thus signaling their "green" leadership—only to exert varying degrees of actual green behavior, some of which may be no more than greenwashing.[6]

Results show that, all else being equal, the main drivers of participation and effort in voluntary carbon disclosure among the Global 500 firms is the existence of senior- and executive-level managers responsible for carbon management and climate risks (which substantiate propositions 1 and 2) and the adoption of environment, social, and governance (ESG) principles by global businesses. Notwithstanding, global firms endowed with environmental research and development (R&D) investments disclose information about their climate management strategies and carbon emissions at higher levels than firms that do not possess existing capabilities to capitalize on climate innovations.

3.1 Internal Firm Management and Organizational Drivers

In a world that is characterized by uncertainty about the future of how technology can be improved, what customers really want, and which regulations and policies will prevail, firms do not have a complete contingency plan for their response to the threat and impacts of climate change. A firm's senior- or executive-level manager, such as a chief sustainability officer, can help a firm's executive team align its vision of "strategic sustainability initiatives"[7] with its business strategy and allocate the necessary resources and responsibilities toward these efforts. Other firm-level organizational capabilities—namely, complementary assets and company-initiated CSR practices—further lower firms' marginal cost of self-regulation on climate change. Spillover benefits and cost savings from these existing internal firm capabilities increase firms' participation and effort in voluntary climate action.

3.1.1 Managerial Agency

As established in chapter 2, companies give discretion to and rely on senior- and executive-level managers to navigate uncertainty, respond to internal firm opportunities and constraints, and interact with and respond to the demands of the external political economy. In this setting, managers who are "policy supporters" are agents of change inside the firm: they capture the attention of top management, actively engage with investors, and help to either secure consensus on or compromise in proclimate policies and activities. To build relational contracts for tackling risks under uncertainty, managers attract employees who care not only about monetary payoffs but also about their own reputation and identity and the social impact of their actions. Moreover, managers align beliefs of employees with that of the firm, in part, by forming governing coalitions comprising leaders and employees across ranks inside the firm.

Through these tasks, climate change managers facilitate the necessary incentives and coordination for effective voluntary climate action by firms: namely, the alignment of values, learning, creativity, and innovation. These managers have the capacity to create new issues, interests, and strategies as well as new modes of action. In doing so, they promote both participation and effort in voluntary climate action as central to business objectives. At times, these managers efforts result in increasing returns to scale in output (e.g., carbon management) or outcome (e.g., environmental performance), as propositions 1 and 2 in chapter 2 posit and as shown again here.[8]

Proposition 1 (participation and manager): The likelihood of corporate participation in voluntary climate action increases when there is a manager responsible for carbon management and climate risks at the senior management or executive rank inside the firm.

Proposition 2 (intensity of participation and manager): A firm's level of voluntary climate action increases where there is a manager responsible for carbon management and climate risks at the senior management or executive rank inside the firm.

3.1.2 Other Organizational Capabilities: Complementary Assets

Complementary assets are part of the basic building blocks by which firms profit from the successful commercialization of an innovation. The innovating firm needs to establish a "prior position in these complementary assets," in order to maximize economic returns from an innovation.[9] Complementary assets are often specialized and make up parts of a system, depending on the innovation in question.[10]

For example, preexisting firm resources and capabilities enable a firm to gain a cost advantage from implementing best practices in environmental management. Firms improve their economic and environmental performance through green innovation by increasing operational efficiency, lowering costs, and meeting the demands of environmentally sensitive customers.[11] In turn, green innovation capacity helps firms not only to obtain competitive advantage, but to maintain it. Studies have found that the adoption of ISO 14001 standards—an environmental management process innovation first developed in 1996—increased the likelihood that manufacturing facilities engaged in more advanced voluntary environmental practices, such as the adoption of green supply chain management.[12]

Whether firms possess complementary assets or not is going to impact a firm's decision about participation and effort in voluntary climate action. This is because given the heterogeneity of firms, due to complementary assets or lack thereof, firms will experience different compliance costs under the same regulation. As such, the cost-benefit analysis will yield an "ideal" level of corporate self-regulation on climate change as a function of corporate R&D, which could include green innovation, among other demand and supply factors.[13] The existence of green innovation expands firms' capacity to engage in climate mitigation and at higher levels, beyond what is required by law. Through green innovation, firms build a routinized framework to report their carbon information, as well as establish capability to reduce their carbon footprints.

3.1.3 Other Organizational Capabilities: Explicit Corporate Social Responsibility Initiatives and Practices

Firms that engage in "explicit" corporate social responsibility (CSR) initiatives and practices articulate and communicate widely their responsibility policies, programs, and practices to stakeholders and the public as a reflection of company discretion and initiative.[14] By contrast, "implicit" CSR is not a voluntary and deliberate corporate decision but, rather, a reflection of a global firm's institutional environment.[15] In other words, the majority of issues that count as corporate responsibilities toward society are not part of the multinational corporation's explicit policies but are *implicitly* codified and "embedded" in the norms, standards, and legal framework, notably in Europe.[16] Even with a rise in explicit CSR worldwide, European companies have less discretion in the area of environmental protection because of their distinctive national business system, which is different from that of the United States or other countries. This is to say, what is considered "proactive" in the United States and elsewhere may already be required—and even if not codified in law, there may be strong norms—in the European Union (EU).[17]

For global businesses, explicit CSR may take various forms. Firms have brand reputations to protect, and they work proactively to ensure that they are out in front of emerging issues by detailing how they are upholding their vision and values and then integrating that vision and those values into strategies and operating practices.[18] As such, many sustainability-inclined firms publicly declare "sustainability" as core to their business in their mission statement and/or create dedicated websites and platforms that contain detailed information about the company's sustainable practices, investments, or special projects related to environmental sustainability.

Moreover, firms may embed ESG principles into their businesses to screen investments for environmental stewardship, equitable and fair business relationships, and accurate and transparent accounting methods and voting procedures.[19] According to the United Nation's (UN), "[the] environmental, social and corporate governance (ESG) issue can affect the performance of investment portfolios."[20] As an indication of the importance of ESG, there is a proliferation of third-party data providers that rate companies on their ESG performance or activities and consulting firms that assist companies from start-ups to global businesses in not only improving but communicating their ratings to stakeholders.[21]

Participation and effort in voluntary climate action should be the domain of firms that previously have engaged in explicit CSR practices for several reasons. First, for these firms, the marginal cost of participation is low since they are already engaged in CSR activities related to environmental protection more generally, which they have explicitly publicized to consumers, investors, and other stakeholders. Second, for firms that participate in proactive climate action, engaging in higher levels of climate mitigation activity enables them to safeguard their brand reputations and to corner new markets; by doing so, they are further signaling their corporate social responsibility to consumers. Finally, it is in these firms' benefit-cost calculus to execute to a greater extent what they have already adhered to publicly to prevent negative stock market impacts, reduce risk, and preserve firm value under uncertain times.[22]

3.2 Model and Data

To test propositions 1 and 2, this chapter's empirical analysis examines the Global 500 firms' participation and intensity of participation in CDP or voluntary carbon disclosure in 2015, as a function of the firms' corporate managerial leadership on climate change. Measures for firms' complementary assets and explicit corporate social responsibility practices are also included to fully account for explanatory power of firm-level managerial and organizational capabilities.

Unlike the extant empirical literature that models carbon disclosure as either a binary or continuous variable, this chapter distinguishes between a firm's decision to disclose, which is a binary, "yes or no" decision, and the linked but subsequent decision of how much climate change information to disclose in a double-hurdle model.[23] This modeling approach explicitly accounts for the fact that private actors may engage in self-regulation—thus signaling their green leadership—only to exert varying degrees of actual green behavior, some of which may be no better than greenwashing behavior or false or misleading advertising of corporate social responsibility.[24] The double-hurdle model is the first of several discrete-continuous econometric models (see also chapters 4, 5, and 7) that are employed in this book to disentangle *whether* a firm participates (i.e., first hurdle decision) and *how much* it participates in corporate self-regulation (i.e., second hurdle decision).

The global firms examined in this chapter are from diverse sectors. As figure 3.1 shows, the firms operate in consumer discretionary (13 percent), consumer staples (9 percent), energy (9 percent), financials (25 percent), health care (10 percent), industrials (10 percent), information technology and telecommunications (15 percent), materials (5 percent), and utilities (4 percent). Close to 30 percent of the Global 500 firms are in the greenhouse gas–intensive sectors—namely the energy, industrial, materials, and utility sectors.

Forty-three percent of the Global 500 companies originate from the United States, as shown in figure 3.2. Most other firms have headquarters in Japan (7 percent), the UK (7 percent), France (5 percent), Canada (4 percent), Hong Kong (3 percent), Germany (3 percent), Switzerland (3 percent), India (3 percent), China (2 percent), Australia (2 percent), Brazil (2 percent), Netherlands (2 percent), Spain (2 percent), and Sweden (2 percent). Altogether,

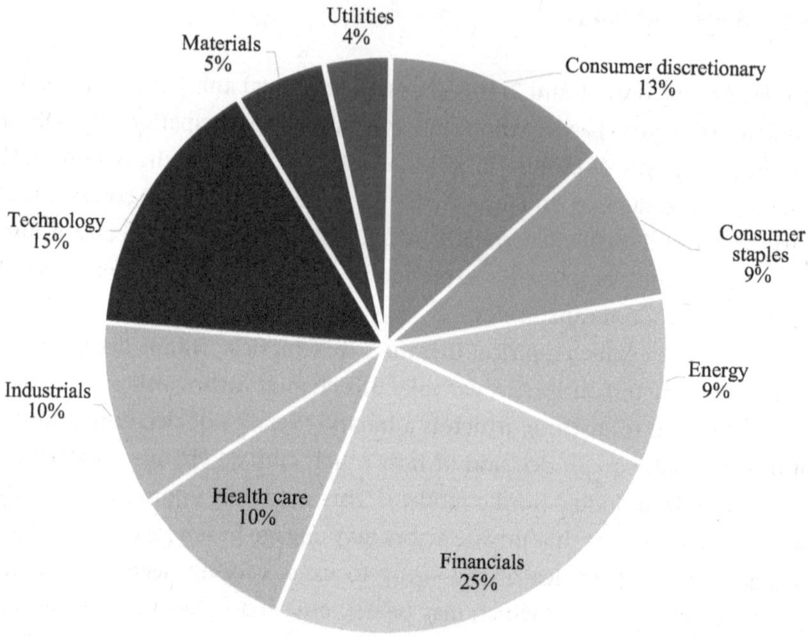

Figure 3.1
Fortune Global 500 firms by industry sector (2015).
Note: Technology comprises the information technology and telecommunications sectors. Industrial sectors are defined by the Global Industry Classification Standard.
Data source: "Fortune Global 500," 2015, https://fortune.com/ranking/global500/2015/.

companies originating from the EU make up close to a quarter share of the Global 500 firms based on market capitalization.

There are two dependent variables: one for measuring the binary choice of participation in voluntary disclosure (*participation*) and the other for measuring effort or the intensity of participation. The intensity of participation is operationalized as a firm's level of voluntary carbon disclosure as represented by its *carbon disclosure score*, which is based on its responses to CDP's 2015 climate change questionnaire.[25] A carbon disclosure score above 80 (out of 100) means that a company not only voluntarily participates in carbon disclosure but does so publicly and verifies carbon disclosures with third-party audits.

These dependent, or outcome, variables, respectively, make up the two stages, or hurdles, of decision-making in the double-hurdle model. Appendix 3 provides the technical details for the creation of these variables as

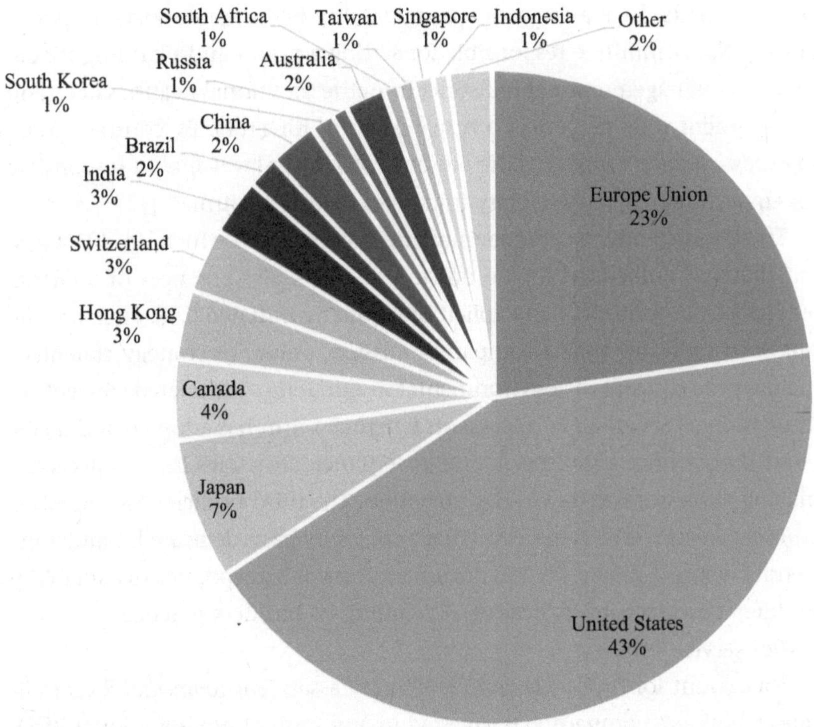

Figure 3.2
Fortune Global 500 firms by country (2015).
Note: Global firms based in the EU are domiciled in Belgium, Czech Republic, Denmark, Finland, France, Germany, Italy, Luxembourg, Netherlands, Poland, Spain, and Sweden. The other category comprises Colombia, Israel, Malaysia, Mexico, Norway, Peru, and Thailand.
Data source: "Fortune Global 500," 2015, https://fortune.com/ranking/global500/2015/.

well as a justification for the appropriateness of the modeling approach in fitting the underlying data,[26] which as shown in figure A3.1 is characterized by a concentration of zeros (i.e., nonparticipation) and a bias toward high levels of carbon disclosure among firms reporting to CDP.

With respect to key independent variables, the empirical analysis includes measures for managerial agency at varying levels inside the firm. *Policy supporter—upper management* represents the presence of a senior management-level officer (e.g., vice president or head of sustainability) or an executive-level officer (e.g., chief sustainability officer) responsible for environmental sustainability initiatives, including climate mitigation.[27] This indicator variable also represents the existence of a sustainability or corporate social responsibility (CSR) committee responsible for setting a vision and planning for climate risk management that is distinct from the traditional health, safety, and environment roles as part of a firm's board of directors. By contrast, *policy supporter—analyst* represents the presence of a lower-level analyst responsible for environmental sustainability initiatives within the firm.[28]

Three independent variables measure the extent to which, in 2015, sustainability is embedded in the mission and business practices of a Global 500 firm as indicators of an explicit or company-initiated CSR. First, *mission statement* indicates that a company's mission, value, or strategy statement includes the concept of "environmental sustainability" or related concepts in its wording.[29] Second, *ESG* represents whether a firm has adopted and incorporated environmental, social, and governance principles into its decision-making processes and day-to-day operation. The third explicit CSR variable is *dedicated website*, which indicates that a company has a dedicated, standalone website where it publicizes and documents how it incorporates sustainability in different aspects of its business, including its business practice, products, and/or service delivery.

To account for firm-level complementary assets, *environmental R&D* indicates whether a company has invested in any form of environmental R&D, such as investments in technologies that increase energy efficiency or investments in management process improvements that incorporate principles of environmental sustainability. As an alternative measure, *ISO 14001 certification* indicates whether a company is certified with the ISO 14001 environmental management system.

Other variables in the model control for additional plausible drivers of corporate self-regulation as identified in existing empirical studies. Financial economics-based research on ESG and CSR has shown that firms' social responsibility activities are strongly related to market, leadership, and ownership characteristics.[30] Scholars of voluntary environmental programs have long identified that larger firms are more likely to participate in voluntary environmental programs;[31] this is because larger facilities have a greater capacity to bear the fixed cost of participating in voluntary programs, seeking certification, and providing environmental training to personnel. Moreover, external pressures from regulators, competitors, and the public may also be greater; consequently, large firms have more incentive than small firms to join voluntary programs, including voluntary carbon disclosure, to mitigate the potential negative impacts of a tarnished image.[32] *Revenues*, *assets*, and *employees* serve as control variables for firm size.

The empirical analysis also includes a variable (*government-owned*) that indicates whether a global firm is at least 50 percent government-owned. A study of environmental management system (EMS) adoption in the United States found that government-owned facilities have fewer capabilities and accrue higher EMS adoption costs; this suggests that firms that are owned partially or wholly by the government may not participate as readily or exert as much effort in voluntary carbon disclosure.[33]

Moreover, the empirical analysis includes an indicator variable, *GHG-intensive (broad)*, for whether or not a firm operates in a greenhouse gas–intensive sector—namely, energy, materials, utilities, or industrials. The effect of sectoral heterogeneity has been mixed. Voluntary program participation rates have been higher in industries with greater consumer contact.[34] Recent studies have shown that firms and organizations that operate in sectors that emit substantial amounts of greenhouse gases are more likely to engage in voluntary climate mitigation and related activities, including carbon disclosure, because they do so to preempt regulatory scrutiny and/or to capture relatively cheaply the marginal benefits of action in terms of technical efficiencies or reputational gains.[35] Sector effects could also be important because of competitive pressures for proactive climate action among firms operating in the same sector.

The double-hurdle regressions also include country indicator variables and robust standard errors with sector-level cluster correction, the latter of which are standard for reliable statistical inference. The country indicator variables control for exogenous factors that affect, in some unobserved way, global firms originated in a given country. These exogenous factors could include country-specific political, regulatory, and institutional factors (e.g., high levels of commitment to climate mitigation and protection of shareholder rights) that motivate proactive climate action by firms based there.

Appendix 2 (table A2.1) provides information about how these firm-level management and organizational variables as well as control variables are constructed and coded and where they come from. A statistical test to confirm variable independence and summary statistics of the dependent and independent variables are reported in appendix 3. There is also a discussion in appendix 3 about how the cross-sectional nature of the data is dealt with to improve the data's representiveness and to thwart threats of endogeneity.

3.3 Results and Discussion

Table 3.2 presents the results based on the double-hurdle model. For ease of interpretation, the results are reported in the form of average and conditional marginal effects (AMEs and CAMEs) or differences in the predicted probability of participation and intensity of participation, respectively, associated with the presence of a policy supporter, an explicit CSR practice, and complementary assets while holding all other variables at their mean value. Tier 1 results report the first-hurdle decision of participation, and tier 2 results report the second-hurdle decision about intensity of participation, conditional on the participation decision being positive.

Appendix 3 contains technical explanations as to how the AME and CAME are computed as well as results of additional analyses that serve as a robustness check of this chapter's main models with alternative measures of the key explanatory variables. Moreover, chapter 9 reports results based on a split sample of EU firms to underscore distinctive national business systems across countries and regions.

3.3.1 Managerial Agency—Policy Supporters

The econometric results, as shown in table 3.2, provide strong support for propositions 1 and 2 on the role of policy supporters in upper management for all Global 500 firms. With respect to proposition 1, which postulates a positive relationship between policy supporters or managers at the senior- or executive-level and the probability of participation, policy supporters in upper management are estimated to be correlated with participation at the 1 percent significance level for all Global 500 firms. A global firm that houses a policy supporter in upper management is nearly 12 percent more likely to engage in voluntary carbon disclosure than firms without a vice president or chief sustainability officer dedicated to corporate environmental sustainability (see "AME" column). This result indicates that the existence of policy supporters in the decision-making ranks of a multinational corporation elevates environmental protection, including proactive climate action such as voluntary carbon disclosure, as a priority within the firm.[36]

The results in the second-hurdle decision show that the existence of upper management as policy supporters is both a correlate of participation in voluntary carbon disclosure (first-hurdle decision) as well as a correlate of a corporation's level of voluntary carbon disclosure, confirming proposition 2,

Table 3.2

Internal firm determinants of participation and effort in voluntary carbon disclosure, double-hurdle model (Fortune Global 500 firms)

Tier 1 (Participation in voluntary disclosure)	Coefficient	Robust standard errors[a]	AME
Policy supporter—upper management	0.576***	0.105	0.116
Mission statement	0.109	0.322	0.022
ESG principles[c]	0.664***	0.180	0.134
Dedicated website	–0.001	0.392	0.000
Environmental R&D	–0.085	0.254	–0.017
Revenues (log)	0.294***	0.069	0.059
Government-owned	–0.113	0.367	–0.023
GHG-intensive (broad)	–0.126	0.349	–0.025
Constant	2.430***	0.815	
Tier 2[b] (Level of voluntary carbon disclosure)	**Coefficient**	**Robust standard errors[a]**	**CAME[d]**
Policy supporter—upper management	6.328***	1.578	6.328
Mission statement	2.888**	1.449	2.887
ESG principles[c]	5.215***	1.273	5.214
Dedicated website	2.487	2.494	2.487
Environmental R&D	3.779***	1.067	3.779
Revenues (log)	1.571***	0.552	1.571
Government-owned	–0.478	5.560	–0.478
GHG-intensive (broad)	–2.128*	1.250	–2.128
Constant	72.486***	5.437	
Lnsigma			
Constant	2.492***	0.067	
Chi-square	19.894		
N	500		

Note: Abbreviation: AME, average marginal effect. **p*<0.1, ***p*<0.05, ****p*<0.01 (two-tailed tests).

[a] Robust standard errors with sector-level cluster correction.

[b] Country indicator variables are included to control for exogenous factors such as country-specific political and institutional factors (e.g., high levels of general commitment to climate mitigation and shareholder rights protection) that motivate a national trend of proactive climate action by firms that are based there.

[c] Environmental, social, and governance (ESG) principles.

[d] AME conditional on $y>0$ (CAME).

which links sustainability leadership with a firm's intensity of participation (second-hurdle decision). This is likely because senior-level champions in the firm are better positioned with the authority to convince "policy skeptics" and "policy neutrals" of the long-term financial benefits of investments in carbon management, including third-party audit and verification protocols. *Policy supporter—upper management* is associated with approximately a six-point increase in carbon disclosure scores according to the conditional average marginal effects.

3.3.2 Explicit CSR Practices

There are three measures for explicit corporate social responsibility (CSR) practices—namely, mission statement, ESG, and dedicated website. In table 3.2, only ESG has a positive and statistically significant association with a Global 500 firm's participation in voluntary carbon disclosure. A firm's prior adoption of ESG principles is associated with a 13 percent higher likelihood of participation in CDP for all Global 500 firms (see "AME" column).

The results in table 3.2 also show that explicit CSR practices are positively associated with a firm's intensity of participation in CDP. When it comes to corporate decision-making about the level of carbon disclosure, Global 500 companies that earn higher scores on their level of carbon disclosure by three to five points (on a scale of 100) are associated with the incorporation of ESG principles in day-to-day operations and the existence of a sustainability-oriented mission or vision statement according to the conditional average marginal effect. Explicit CSR practices in the form of an articulated vision and mission statement for environmental sustainability correspond to two additional points in a firm's level of carbon disclosure, conditional on participation in voluntary carbon disclosure.

For the Global 500 firms on the whole, these explicit "signals" of corporate social responsibility suggest that the marginal cost of going the extra mile in voluntary disclosure is relatively low when a firm is already engaged in proactive actions related to sustainability. In fact, higher levels of carbon disclosure may help safeguard brand reputations because a firm is further signaling to consumers that it is a socially responsible corporation.

3.3.3 Complementary Assets

The results for the Global 500 firms provide evidence to show that while participation in voluntary carbon disclosure (first-hurdle decision) is not associated with firms' endowment of complementary assets, the level of carbon disclosure (second-hurdle decision) is a function of the presence of complementary assets, namely, firms' investments in environmental R&D once a firm has made the decision to participate in CDP. In fact, global firms that have invested in environmental R&D on average participated in voluntary carbon disclosure at a higher level (approximately two to four points higher) than firms without environmental R&D investments.

The bottom-line is that all corporate CDP participants—regardless of country of origin—that are endowed with complementary assets are associated with higher levels of carbon disclosure. Therefore, global firms' intensity of participation is a function of a cost-benefit calculation rather than an outcome of mere participation; this is because the cost of participation, while not nothing, is relatively low.[37] Firms with complementary assets possess a lower marginal cost of disclosing information about their carbon management and climate mitigation, including carbon emissions, since they have already invested in energy-efficient technologies and other related innovations, all of which make reducing and tracking carbon emissions relatively more cost effective.

Among the control variables, an increase in firm size—namely, a 1 percent increase in corporate revenues—is associated with an increase in the likelihood of voluntary carbon disclosure by 5–7 percent, and is associated with two additional points in the carbon disclosure score, conditional on participation. Moreover, while a greenhouse gas–intensive firm is no less likely than a non-greenhouse-gas–intensive firm to have participated in the CDP on the eve of the Paris Agreement, a firm that operates in a greenhouse gas–intensive sector is associated with about a two- to three-point penalty in its carbon disclosure score, conditional on participation. As chapter 7 explicates in more detail, empirical evidence from a prior study shows that firms will pull back on corporate environmental disclosure when there is no good news to share.[38]

3.4 Conclusion

One private voluntary climate initiative that has emerged over the past two decades as a prominent institutional arrangement for firms around the globe to signal and demonstrate their proactive climate leadership is CDP (formerly the Carbon Disclosure Project). This chapter provides large-*N* empirical evidence from a cross-sectional econometric analysis to show that management and organizational factors and dynamics internal to firms are important correlates of decision-making by a global business about their related but distinct and subsequent decisions about participation and effort or intensity of participation in voluntary carbon disclosure. In doing so, proposition 1 and proposition 2, which link firms' managerial agency to their participation and effort in voluntary climate action, respectively, are substantiated, in the case of voluntary carbon disclosure. Moreover, this chapter identifies other firm-level organizational capabilities, namely company-initiated corporate social responsibility (CSR) practices (as opposed to socially responsible practices that have become industry or institutional norms) and complementary assets as drivers of corporate self-regulation on climate change. This chapter characterizes the "leaders among leaders" of global firms that choose not only to disclose their climate change information but to go the extra mile in disclosing their carbon management strategies and carbon emissions.

Once firm size, greenhouse gas intensity, and external factors (e.g., country-specific political and institutional characteristics) are considered, the firm-level antecedents of participation are not always the same as the drivers of the intensity of participation in voluntary carbon disclosure. On the whole, for Fortune Global 500 firms, participation is the domain of "policy supporters"—namely senior or executive leadership dedicated to environmental sustainability and corporate practices of firm-initiated corporate social responsibility or explicit CSR practices. By contrast, once firms have chosen to participate, their decisions about their level of disclosure depend on their possession of complementary assets—that is, their prior endowments of organizational or technological capabilities and/or financial capital. These complementary assets give firms the experience and competencies they need to gain cost advantages for implementing global best practices on carbon management or mitigating negative climate impacts.

Despite "opening up of the firm," this chapter's analysis is limited by the fact that the empirical analysis merely captures a snapshot of global businesses at one point in time—namely the year 2015. This static frame cannot adequately establish causality or measure the momentum and dynamics of the spread of explicit CSR. To do so, one needs to examine temporal changes in a longitudinal study, which is beyond the scope of this chapter. That being said, 2015 is a significant point in time, on the eve of the Paris Agreement. Subsequent chapters examine dynamic interactions over time between existing institutions and structures—namely, regulatory and global governance—and corporate managerial agency in global firms' responses to climate change, in the context of changing public policies and global norms during 2011–2020.

An important question that is worth asking—and of relevance throughout the rest of this book—is whether and/or under what conditions the results of a study on the largest firms by revenue generalize to a broader population of firms, notably smaller and privately held enterprises. Without the benefit of data on other firms, the conjecture is that this chapter explains participation and effort in voluntary carbon disclosure (and voluntary climate action) in the private sector more generally. In fact, these empirical results are likely to be lower-bound estimates in an analysis that includes firms of various sizes and scope. If multinational corporations—which by virtue of their size and scope of production invite more public scrutiny than privately held firms—require the leadership of sustainability champions at the senior management and executive levels, it is highly probable that firms facing fewer stakeholder pressures would also require internal champions to capture the attention of corporate leaders, align employees' preferences with that of the firm, and build governing coalitions. This same logic should apply regarding the extent of the adoption of sustainability values and principles in influencing the proactive carbon disclosure of firms of various sizes and scopes of business.

Finally, a couple of implications follow from this chapter, which subsequent chapters address. First, this chapter's findings suggest that there needs to be more scholarly attention to firms' management structures and explicit demonstrations of corporate value and commitments toward sustainability. It may be that climate mitigation and adaptation at the global scale require more than big sticks; they also require leadership and creativity. With the right leadership and vision, corporations will be less likely to drag their feet.[39] Insights from illustrative company cases demonstrate qualitatively the decisive actions of individual leaders in the context of supportive internal firm managerial and organizational resources. Nonetheless, questions remain about the link between the scope of participation in voluntary climate action, including voluntary carbon disclosure, and effectiveness. Prior research suggests that there is one-way causation from carbon emissions to disclosures but little or no evidence of reverse causality.[40] This question of sustainability outcomes versus outputs is taken up in chapter 7, where the question of whether firms that disclose climate change information emit less carbon emissions is examined in a panel data analysis of US firms in the S&P 500 index.

II Corporate Climate Action and Cross-Level Governance Interactions

4 Global Firms' Interactions with Domestic Regulation and Global Governance

Whereas chapter 3 established that internal firm capabilities—notably, managerial agency and supportive organizational structures—are key drivers of global firms' voluntary climate action, chapter 4 links corporate management with domestic regulation and global governance to delineate cross-level governance interactions, as proposed in the multilevel governance framework on climate change (MGFCC) in chapter 2.[1] This chapter provides empirical evidence to substantiate propositions 3–6 (see sections 2.4 and 2.5 of chapter 2), which together contend that corporate, regulatory, and global governance positively reinforce each other as drivers of corporate self-regulation on climate change.

This chapter extends the cross-sectional analysis in the previous chapter to a cross-country and cross-sector panel data analysis following the 683 global firms that were listed at least once as a Fortune Global 500 company from 2010–2015. The results lend validity to the hypothesized corporate×regulation and corporate×global interactions in chapter 2, underscoring the fact that firms do not act in a vacuum. They are individual agents with distinct management structures and practices *and* they interact with and are constrained by regulatory and global governance institutions.

As in the rest of the book, this chapter distinguishes between firms' decision to participate and their decision about the intensity of their participation in voluntary climate action, which earlier studies have not considered sufficiently, if at all.[2] In doing so, this chapter's empirical analysis underscores that to fully understand in an unbiased way the drivers of "deeper" participation, it is important to account for the nonrandom and strategic decision by firms to engage in self-regulation in the first place, the factors of which are not fully observed.

4.1 Corporate Management vis-à-vis Domestic Regulation and Global Governance

As laid out in chapter 2, the book's MGFCC adapts the concept of "bargaining under the shadow of war" in international relations theory to explicate the deal-making that happens between firms and the government, when the government's "outside offer" is the threat of actual or impending regulation. The stronger the threat of regulation by the government, the more credible and higher quality is a firm's self-regulation. By contrast, if the threat of regulation is weak, corporate self-regulation will be weaker, and it will be more likely that a firm will engage in greenwashing behavior.

Aside from government, another source of public politics is regulatory pressure emanating internationally from global governance institutions. Global governance, which firms view as a harbinger of future regulatory requirements, is a form of regulatory pressure (albeit a weak source compared to the binding rules of law) to be reckoned with through active engagement.

In summary, firms engage in corporate self-regulation on climate change as a way to deflect domestic and global sources of public politics and to gain improved stakeholder and regulatory relations today with the aim of getting preferential treatment tomorrow (e.g., neutral or positive rather than negative publicity by consumer or activist groups and/or less enforcement by regulators) in the face of future or potentially forthcoming regulation.[3] A key implication is that firms will act preemptively based on micro-level incentives: when the threat of regulation is high and the marginal cost of self-regulation is relatively low, it is the rational calculus of firms to engage in self-regulation as a form of deterrence.

4.1.1 Corporate × Regulation Interactions

Where does corporate managerial agency enter in this cross-level governance interaction? With respect to corporate × regulation interactions, dedicated managers responsible for a company's response to climate change serve as an intermediary to broker a deal between the firm and the government and thus facilitate the firm's choice of self-regulation over government regulation. Specifically, in the face of actual regulation or regulatory pressure, managers serve as "regulation brokers."

When regulatory pressure is high and the marginal cost of self-regulation is low, there will be a hastening of efforts led by managers to signal firms' ability to internalize externalities, earn regulatory goodwill, and avoid legal liabilities. The higher is regulatory stringency and more credible is the regulatory threat, the more effort managers devote to voluntary climate action. These regulation brokers serve a critical role given that companies facing similar regulatory environments may not always respond in the same way.

The following testable implications (in the form of propositions) are from chapter 2, about corporate × regulation interactions as drivers of global firms' participation and effort in voluntary climate action. In this and several other chapters, this climate action should be understood to be voluntary carbon disclosure, which serves as this book's main empirical case of voluntary climate action by global businesses.

Proposition 3 (participation and corporate × regulation): Firms with a dedicated manager responsible for carbon management and climate risks are more likely than firms without a dedicated manager to participate in voluntary climate action when they face strong regulatory pressure from existing or impending regulation.

Proposition 4 (intensity of participation and corporate × regulation): Firms that integrate climate risks into their business operations will engage in a higher level of voluntary climate action when they face strong regulatory pressure from existing or impending regulation.

4.1.2 Corporate × Global Interactions

While global governance institutions do not have the same coercive authority as domestic regulatory regimes, they are viewed by private actors to be a harbinger of future regulatory requirements and thus a form of regulatory pressure to be reckoned with. In Green's (2013) analysis of privately initiated carbon standards within the regime complex for climate change, the author found that more than 75 percent of standards created by private actors recognize rules created under the Kyoto Protocol, which is an offshoot of the United Nations Framework Convention on Climate Change (UNFCCC). This finding suggests an unintended consequence of private authority—that it can serve as a venue for the embedding of public rules perpetuated or normalized by international institutions.

One such international institution is the United Nations Global Compact (UNGC), which is a flexible and low-cost voluntary regulatory program that seeks to align business operations and strategies with universally accepted principles drawn from declarations and conventions adopted by the United Nations in the areas of human rights, labor, environment, and the fight against corruption.[4] An interesting question, which this chapter's empirical analysis addresses, is whether participation in norm-based programs like the UNGC will condition firm-level management structures and practices by means of social mechanisms—such as norms and learning—to induce participation and intensity of participation in private governance regimes.[5]

As chapter 2 explicates, with respect to corporate×global interactions, through a firm's participation in global governance institutions, managers dedicated to climate mitigation join epistemic communities. As knowledge-based experts, they learn about and help to define the environmental problems that corporations face, identify policy solutions, and assess the policy outcomes. In doing so, managers serve as "norm brokers": they represent their employers, as well as translate, on behalf of global governance institutions, the global best practices that are likely to someday become market norms and rules of law.

Propositions 5 and 6 from chapter 2 refer to corporate×global interactions as drivers of global firms' participation and effort in corporate self-regulation on climate change.

Proposition 5 (participation and corporate×global): Firms with a dedicated manager responsible for carbon management and climate risks are more likely to participate in voluntary climate action when they participate in global governance institutions that seek to align business operations with universally accepted best practices about the environment.

Proposition 6 (intensity of participation and corporate×global): Firms that integrate climate risks into their business operations will engage in a higher level of voluntary climate action when they participate in global governance institutions that seek to align business operations with universally accepted best practices about the environment.

4.2 Model and Data

To test these propositions about the interplay between corporate management and domestic regulation, and corporate management and global governance, this chapter's empirical analysis extend the cross-sectional analysis in chapter 3 to a panel data analysis of the Fortune Global 500 companies' participation and extent (intensity) of participation in voluntary carbon disclosure in the CDP during 2011–2015. As in chapter 3, the first dependent variable of interest is the binary choice of participation in voluntary carbon disclosure (*participation*). The second dependent variable is a continuous variable and a measure of the intensity of participation or the level of voluntary carbon disclosure (*carbon disclosure score*). The two dependent variables represent discrete-continuous choices that firms make: the binary choice of participation in voluntary disclosure and the decision about effort or level of disclosure.

Unlike the previous chapter, instead of a focus on firm-level managerial and organizational characteristics as independent variables on the right-hand side of the equation, the subject of chapter 4's panel data analysis is the cross-level corporate, regulation, and global governance interactions. The following discussion introduces new firm- and country-level independent and interaction variables that were not in chapter 3's cross-sectional analysis. Technical information about sources and the construction and coding of the variables are in appendix 2.

4.2.1 Firm-Level Variables

The panel data analysis's firm-level variables are *manager* and *target*, both of which come from company responses to CDP's annual climate change questionnaire between 2011 and 2015.[6] These two internal firm managerial agency variables are the key independent variables, along with *regulatory stringency* and *UNGC member*, that make up this chapter's four propositions.

In a given year, *manager* represents either the presence of a senior- or executive-level manager responsible for climate change, environmental sustainability, or environmental policy or the existence of a committee responsible for setting vision and planning for climate risk management as part of a company's board of directors.[7]

Target indicates whether a firm has adopted a quantitative emissions target in a given year; it is a proxy for whether a firm has integrated climate risks into its modus operandi. Each year, companies are given the opportunity to report to CDP any changes made to their management structures.

Another firm-level variable, and a key independent variable, is *UNGC member*: it is an indicator variable about whether a company is a member of the United Nations Global Compact in a given year during the study period, 2011–2015. *UNGC member* is interacted with *manager* and *target* to assess whether there is evidence to support proposition 3 and proposition 4, respectively.

As in the previous chapter and all the empirical analyses in this book, a company's annual *revenues* are a measure of firm size. As an alternative measure, a company's *assets* are included as a robustness check.

Furthermore, the empirical analysis includes controls for variation in market- and sector-level characteristics. *GHG-intensive* indicates that a firm is part of the materials and utilities sectors, as defined by the Global Industry Classification Standard. According to CDP's 2016 Climate Change Report, companies in materials and utilities emit the largest amount of aggregated scope 1 and scope 2 emissions compared to other sectors. This analysis also controls for other sectors, excluding the materials and utilities sectors that are already covered by *GHG-intensive*. These sector-specific indicator variables account for cross-sector variation—such as variation in consumer orientation or energy intensity in production—that may influence a corporation's decision to engage in voluntary climate action but does not change systematically over time within a sector.

Natural gas price, which represents an annual average of monthly natural gas prices, allows for an alternative explanation of corporate voluntary carbon disclosure. Since burning natural gas, a factor of production, produces nearly half as much carbon dioxide per unit of energy as coal,[8] the downward trend in natural gas prices in during the study period could instead be a driver of voluntary climate action rather than internal firm management and organizational structures and practices or pressures coming from domestic regulatory or global governance institutions.

4.2.2 Country-Level Variables

There is no measure of the de jure stringency of countries' environmental policies or regulatory institutions with sufficiently broad and long coverage. That being said, this chapter's analysis adopts a standard proxy used in the international political economy literature to represent *regulatory stringency*:[9] countries' environmental treaty commitments—namely, a count of a country's ratifications of international environmental agreements (IEAs) in a given year. Environmental treaty commitments by countries are "efforts to regulate human interactions with the environment that involve legally binding commitments . . . among governments . . . that have environmental protection as a primary objective."[10] In other words, IEAs are a proxy for regulatory stringency at the country level because a country's ratifications of environmental treaties reflect what each country is willing to legally commit to with respect to the breadth and depth of regulation at the domestic level.

An alternative measure of the strength a country's regulatory regime on the environment is also considered: The Environmental Performance Index (EPI) measures a country's range and ambitiousness of environmental policymaking. The EPI provides "a gauge at a national scale of how close countries are to established environmental policy targets. . . . [Relative] rankings indicate which countries are best at addressing the environmental challenges that every nation faces."[11] In this sense, the EPI captures the rigor of a country's regulatory institutions dedicated to environment protection.[12]

Other country-level variables serve as controls to contextualize the political economies in which the Global 500 firms domicile. These variables are based on Andonova et al.'s (2017) findings that participation in transnational climate governance is greatest in countries with strong civil liberties, a decentralized government, competent bureaucracies, and proenvironment policies. Country-level controls include civil liberties—namely, freedom of expression and belief, associational and organizational rights, rule of law, and personal autonomy and individual rights—GDP per capita, presence of a federalist system of government, EU membership, and country-level counts of company certifications to the ISO 14001 environmental management standard.[13] As a robustness check, the variable for "civil liberties" is replaced with a variable for "political rights," which is a measure of a country's electoral process, political pluralism and participation, and functioning of government.

Liberal and decentralized institutions have enabled networks of cities, voluntary markets for carbon offsets, and regional initiatives, notably in the United States, Canada, and Europe.[14] That being said, European Union (EU) countries have by and large led national climate policymaking worldwide. A vast majority of EU countries have proportional electoral systems (i.e., electoral systems in which coalitions of parties share political power). Studies have shown that proportional electoral systems are associated with more stringent climate policies—in particular, policies that impose direct costs on consumers, such as carbon taxes—than those with majoritarian electoral systems (i.e., where the party with the majority governs).[15] Moreover, EU citizens' preferences for sustainability in corporate practices are well articulated.[16] By contrast, advanced economies such as the United States, Canada, and Australia have substantial civil liberties and a degree of decentralization but limited national commitment to climate mitigation or adaptation compared to the EU.

In contrast to chapter 3's firm-level measure, certification counts at the country-level for firms' adoption of the ISO 14001 environmental management standard are a measure of broader business interest in transnational private governance and investments in corporate social sustainability, which is related to supply chain–based demand from firms in proenvironmental jurisdictions.[17]

A country-level international nongovernmental organization (INGO) or stakeholder activism variable is not included in the analysis because a premise of this chapter is that institutional investors are viewed as stakeholders,[18] and they have empowered CDP to serve on their behalf to target and invite the Fortune Global 500 companies to proactively disclose climate change information. By this token, stakeholder politics, which have been found in the literature to be a driver of transnational climate governance,[19] is held constant in the empirical analysis.

4.2.3 Cross-Level Interaction Terms

To test the four proposed propositions about the cross-level governance interaction effects, four separate interaction terms have been created. First, *manager×regulatory stringency* and *target×regulatory stringency* are associated with the first two propositions about corporate management and domestic regulation (propositions 3 and 4). *Manager×UNGC member* and *target×UNGC member* assess the latter two propositions about corporate management and global governance (propositions 5 and 6). Together, these interaction terms evaluate this chapter's main argument, which is that the interaction of a firm's agency and the multilevel structures in which it operates condition a firm's choices about whether and to what extent it will engage in beyond-compliance climate action.

4.2.4 Estimation Model

Even though the CDP invites *all* of the Global 500 firms to participate in its annual climate change questionnaire, not all global business invitees respond to CDP's information request. The mechanism by which firms decide whether to disclose or not disclose to CDP is unobserved and unknown to the researcher (i.e., an omitted variable). As such, this chapter's panel data analysis employs the Heckman selection model, which accounts for the fact that firms' decisions about participation and intensity of participation in voluntary carbon disclosure are nonrandom and likely to be deliberate and strategic. Appendix 4 contains technical details about the Heckman selection model, including how the model treats *carbon disclosure score*, which is not observed for nonparticipants, and how the chapter's empirical analysis is robust to alternative measures and to the endogenous binary-variable model, which is an alternative model that is also employed in chapter 5, where the attention is turned to the US case.

4.3 Results and Discussion

The results based on the Heckman selection model are reported for the Global 500 companies in table 4.1. Model 1 results are based on the Heckman selection model with the full set of firm- and country-level variables along with corporate×regulation interactions.[20] Model 2 replicates model 1 but with corporate×global interactions.[21] The corporate×regulation and corporate×global interactions represent the four propositions on corporate and domestic regulation and corporate and global governance, respectively. Results for both firms' participation and intensity of participation (level of carbon disclosure) are reported side by side in table 4.3. Appendix 4 contains the results of a base or reference model without the cross-level interactions (table A4.2), as well as alternative analyses that serve as robustness checks, with alternative measures of the main explanatory variables and an alternative modeling approach. See tables A4.3–A4.9 in appendix 4 for the results.

4.3.1 Corporate Management and Domestic Regulation

As shown in table 4.1, there is strong evidence among the Global 500 companies for proposition 3 and proposition 4. Regardless of a company's country of origin, the strength of regulatory institutions matters, and the effects of the domestic regulatory context are conditioned by whether there is a dedicated manager responsible for climate change inside firms and whether firms have integrated climate risks into their business operations. In other words, the stringency of (national-level) regulations is a driver of participation in voluntary carbon disclosure through firm-level management levers (i.e., via *manager* or *target*). Firms with a climate change manager are 10 percent more likely to participate in voluntary carbon disclosure than firms without

Table 4.1

Multilevel determinants of participation and effort in voluntary carbon disclosure, Heckman selection model (Fortune Global 500 firms)

	Model 1		Model 2	
	Corporate × regulation		Corporate × global	
	Participation in voluntary carbon disclosure b/se[a]	Level of voluntary carbon disclosure b/se[a]	Participation in voluntary carbon disclosure b/se[a]	Level of voluntary carbon disclosure b/se[a]
Firm, market, and sector variables				
Manager[b]			1.529*** (0.12)	
Target[b]				13.118*** (1.76)
UNGC member	0.836*** (0.17)	3.122*** (1.10)		
Revenues[c] (log)	0.198*** (0.06)	1.358*** (0.51)	0.251*** (0.06)	1.515*** (0.51)
Natural gas price (log)	0.003 (0.08)	−10.270*** (0.75)	0.000 (0.09)	−10.324*** (0.75)
GHG-intensive	−0.406* (0.22)	4.668** (1.90)	−0.392* (0.22)	4.962*** (1.89)
Country-level variables				
Regulatory stringency (log)	−0.011 (0.08)	−2.330 (1.63)	0.171** (0.08)	−0.422 (1.69)

Civil liberties	–0.153** (0.07)	–8.153*** (1.60)	–0.149** (0.07)	–7.958*** (1.59)
GDP per capita (log)	0.206** (0.08)	–3.173** (1.44)	0.148* (0.08)	–3.379** (1.44)
Federalism	0.025 (0.21)	–0.527 (1.55)	–0.064 (0.20)	–0.874 (1.57)
ISO 14001 (log)	–0.001 (0.06)	–0.167 (0.66)	–0.007 (0.06)	–0.215 (0.67)
EU member	0.130 (0.26)	–0.698 (1.61)	0.173 (0.25)	–0.190 (1.64)
Cross-level interactions				
Manager × regulatory stringency	0.329*** (0.03)			
Target × regulatory stringency		2.811*** (0.32)		
Manager × UNGC member			0.587*** (0.19)	
Target × UNGC member				1.925* (1.10)
Constant	-4.055*** (1.14)	123.893*** (16.60)	–4.634*** (1.09)	116.638*** (16.76)
Athrho Constant	–0.153** (0.07)		–0.193** (0.08)	
Lnsigma Constant	2.672*** (0.04)		2.677*** (0.04)	

(*continued*)

Table 4.1 (*continued*)

	Model 1		Model 2	
	Corporate × regulation		Corporate × global	
	Participation in voluntary carbon disclosure b/se[a]	Level of voluntary carbon disclosure b/se[a]	Participation in voluntary carbon disclosure b/se[a]	Level of voluntary carbon disclosure b/se[a]
N	2,588		2,588	
Sector fixed effects	Yes		Yes	
Year fixed effects	Yes		Yes	

Note: $^{*}p<0.1$, $^{**}p<0.05$, $^{***}p<0.01$. Year indicator variables for 2011 and the technology sector, which includes information technology and telecommunications, serve as the base, respectively.

[a] Robust standard errors with firm-level cluster correction.

[b] *Manager* and *target* are lagged by one year to allow for the possibility of reverse causation. Moreover, the installation of a climate change manager and the adoption of a quantitative emissions target may be jointly determined with the decision about participation in voluntary carbon disclosure or the level of disclosure. Companies that commit to voluntary carbon disclosure are more likely to devote resources to meet the program's goals, including integrating climate risks and/or hiring a dedicated manager. There could also be unobserved factors that influence participation in the CDP that are also likely to influence current management choices.

[c] These contemporaneous time-varying variables are lagged by one year in the analysis to mitigate the possibility of reverse causation in the sense that larger, more deep-pocketed firms may be financially better positioned to cope with the costs of meeting CDP's requirements (including but not limited to disclosure requirements) and therefore more likely to self-select into the CDP.

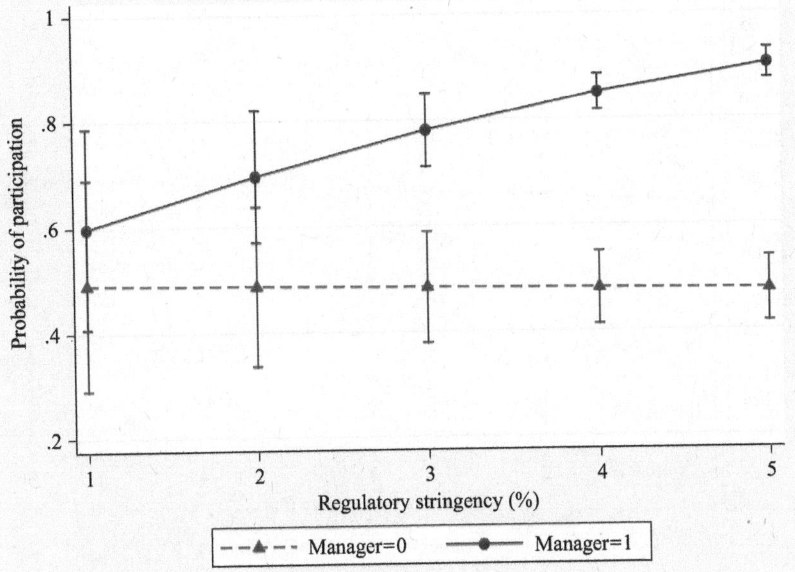

Figure 4.1
Manager × regulatory stringency: predicted probability of voluntary carbon disclosure (Fortune Global 500 firms).
Note: The error bars represent 95 percent confidence intervals.
Source: Lily Hsueh, "Corporations at a Crossroads: How Multilevel Governance Interactions Shape Participation and Efforts in Private Governance Regimes," *Governance* 32, no. 4 (2019): 731, https://doi.org/10.1111/gove.12406.

a manager responsible for carbon management and climate risks. Conditional on participation, a firm that has adopted a quantitative emissions target discloses their carbon management activities and plans at a higher level (by three more points in the carbon disclosure score according to estimated model results).[22]

Figure 4.1 and figure 4.2 plot the predicted probability of participation and intensity of participation for firms with and without a manager or a target, respectively, for a given (percent) change in regulatory stringency. The error bands in these and all following figures represent 95 percent confidence intervals. Companies' propensity for and their intensity of participation are greater with than without climate change managerial capacity at all levels of regulatory stringency (although confidence bands are wider when domestic regulation is relatively weak).

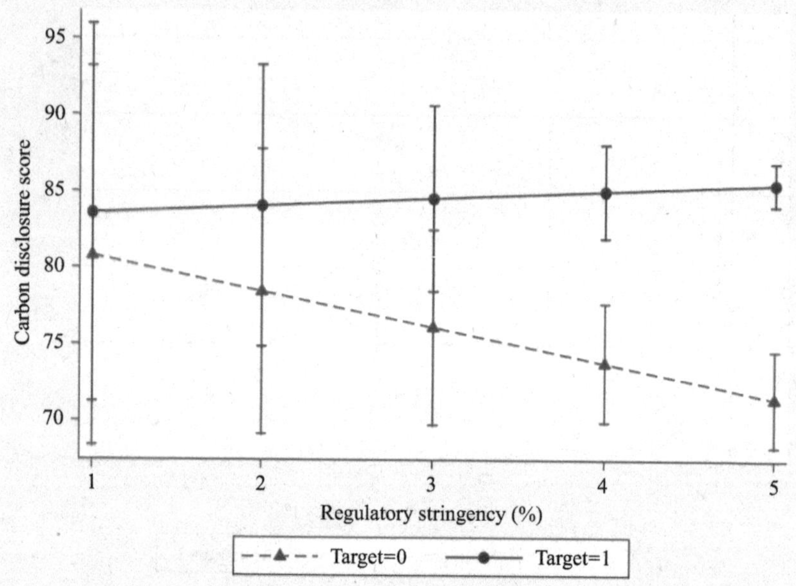

Figure 4.2
Target × regulatory stringency: predicted probability of voluntary carbon disclosure (Fortune Global 500 firms).
Note: The error bars represent 95 percent confidence intervals.
Source: Lily Hsueh, "Corporations at a Crossroads: How Multilevel Governance Interactions Shape Participation and Efforts in Private Governance Regimes," *Governance* 32, no. 4 (2019): 732, https://doi.org/10.1111/gove.12406.

As regulatory stringency increases, firms possessing a manager or a target are more likely to participate in voluntary carbon disclosure or disclose at higher levels, respectively. Responses of firms without similar carbon management capabilities or capacities are considerably less sensitive to increases in regulatory stringency. In fact, the average marginal effect could be in the reverse (although with large error bars) with respect to the level of carbon disclosure for participants without a target. This suggests that without facilitating corporate management structures and practices, strong regulatory institutions alone do not lead to greater participation or higher intensity of participation in voluntary carbon disclosure.

4.3.2 Corporate Management and Global Governance

Propositions 5 and 6, which posit that firms with carbon management structures and practices are more likely to participate in voluntary carbon disclosure and disclose at higher levels if they have adopted global governance principles that seek to align business operations with universally accepted best practices, are by and large substantiated by the empirical results. Global firms that have installed climate change managers or adopted quantitative emissions targets, respectively, *and* embedded public rules spawned by global governance regimes by joining the United Nations Global Compact (UNGC), are more likely to participate in voluntary carbon disclosure and disclose at higher levels (at the 10 percent significance level), according to the results in table 4.1.

Figure 4.3 shows the probability of participation for different combinations of *manager* and *UNGC member*, respectively, as predicted by model 2 (see table 4.1). Firms that have installed a manager are more likely to participate in voluntary carbon disclosure than firms without a climate change manager, regardless of whether or not they possess membership in the UNGC. That being said, firms that install a manager responsible for climate mitigation and join the UNGC have a near-perfect chance (0.9 out of 1) of participating in voluntary carbon disclosure.

Despite this, the slope of the dashed line (representing *manager*=0) is steeper than the slope of the solid line (*manager*=1), which indicates that the average marginal effect of *UNGC member* on participation is higher than that of *manager*. In other words, moving from not being a member to becoming a member of the UNGC has a larger marginal impact on a firm's probability of participation when a firm has not installed a manager. The UN Global Compact, by construction, has built-in institutional mechanisms for learning and normalization of global practices on climate mitigation, such as carbon disclosure, as further explored in chapter 6. On its own, *UNGC member* is positively associated with participation, and this association is strengthened when firms also install a manager responsible for climate mitigation.

Turning to figure 4.4, the results are qualitatively similar to those in figure 4.3 for the predicted level of voluntary carbon disclosure for different combinations of *target* and *UNGC member* in model 2 (see table 4.1). When a participating company possesses both *target* and *UNGC member*, its carbon disclosure score is predicted to be close to 90 points (out of 100), which is about 20 points higher than if a firm has neither adopted a quantitative emissions target nor joined the UNGC.

Together, these results suggest that managers dedicated to carbon management and climate risks are as much agents of regulation as they are agents of the market. In response to regulatory pressure, they will align

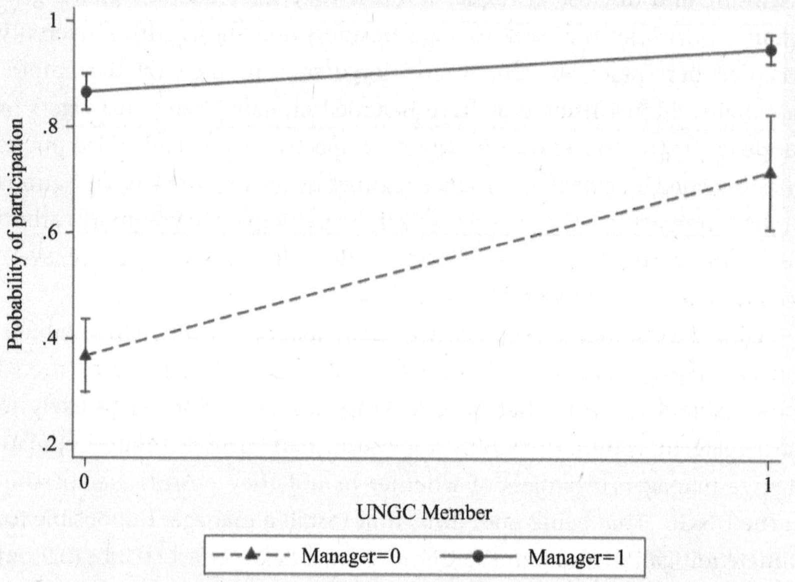

Figure 4.3
Manager × UNGC member: predicted probability of voluntary carbon disclosure (Fortune Global 500 firms).
Note: The error bars represent 95 percent confidence intervals.
Source: Lily Hsueh, "Corporations at a Crossroads: How Multilevel Governance Interactions Shape Participation and Efforts in Private Governance Regimes," *Governance* 32, no. 4 (2019): 732, https://doi.org/10.1111/gove.12406.

and steer their companies toward policies and practices—including engaging in voluntary climate action, such as participation in the CDP—that are in congruence with rules on the books, as well as rules in the making, espoused by domestic regulatory and global governance institutions. By the same token, conditional on participation, firms that have implemented quantitative emissions targets on GHG emissions will engage in higher levels of voluntary carbon disclosure when they originate from countries with strong regulatory institutions and have adopted universal principles of sustainability espoused by the UN Global Compact.

Of note, the results of the control variables on the whole mirror findings in the literature: by and large, open societies characterized by political freedoms allow for a vibrant associational life and the strengthening of social capital,

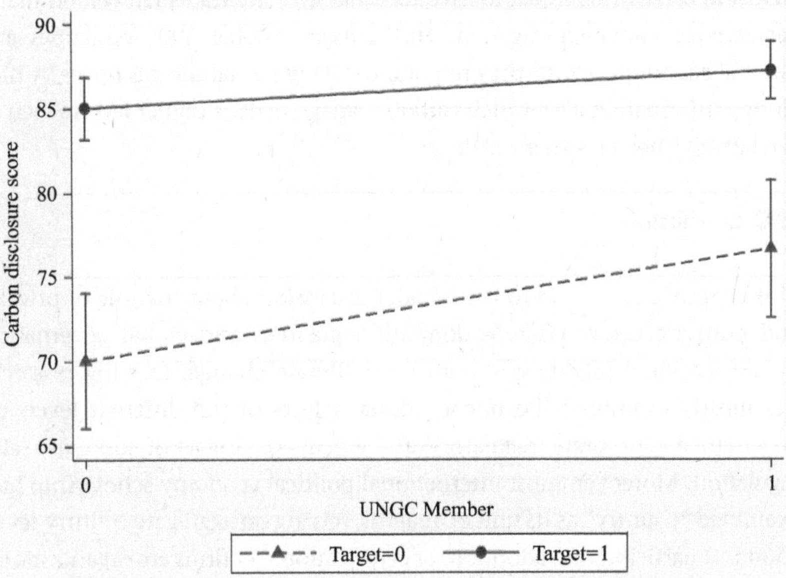

Figure 4.4
Target × UNGC member: predicted probability of voluntary carbon disclosure (Fortune Global 500 firms).
Note: The error bars represent 95 percent confidence intervals.
Source: Lily Hsueh, "Corporations at a Crossroads: How Multilevel Governance Interactions Shape Participation and Efforts in Private Governance Regimes," *Governance* 32, no. 4 (October 2019): 733, https://doi.org/10.1111/gove.12406.

which in turn create capacity for taking collective action in the management of natural resources and protection of the environment.[23] Large firms, firms originating from countries with relatively high civil liberties, firms that participate in global governance institutions, and those with dedicated corporate management structures are more likely to engage in voluntary climate action through CDP. These firms also participate more intensively, with a few exceptions.

While companies operating in GHG-intensive sectors are less likely to participate in voluntary carbon disclosure, the carbon-intensive firms that do disclose to CDP, go the extra mile in their level of disclosure (by 5–6 points in the carbon disclosure score). They do so by certifying with a third-party verification system or reporting their GHG emissions. In doing so, these

GHG-intensive firms signal to investors that they are leaders in carbon management or climate mitigation. Furthermore, Global 500 companies are rational economic actors: they respond to changing natural gas prices by disclosing information about their carbon management at higher levels when it is relatively cheap for them to do so.

4.4 Conclusion

This chapter contributes to the broader discussion about the role of private and nonstate actors vis-à-vis domestic regulation and global governance in transnational private governance on climate change. Existing research has mostly examined the unconditional effects of the different levels of governance—corporate, regulatory, and global—as drivers of corporate self-regulation. Moreover, most international political economy scholarship has examined "country" as its unit of analysis, relying on aggregate country-level counts of participation, adoption, or certification. Yet firms are organizations with distinct management structures and practices.

This chapter provides empirical evidence for the book's claim that the interactions between a firm's agency in corporate management and the multilevel governance structures in which it resides and operates condition a firm's decisions about whether and to what extent it will engage in voluntary climate action. Senior- or executive-level managers dedicated to carbon management and climate risks serve as firm-level channels through which domestic regulations are implemented and global rules and best practices are disseminated and diffused. These managers have agency, and their actions on behalf of their firms are constrained by national and global governance institutions. Propositions 3–6 about corporate × regulation and corporate × global interactions are by and large substantiated by the panel data analysis of the Fortune Global 500 firms' participation in the CDP and their level of voluntary carbon disclosure over the period 2011–2015.

This chapter leaves open the question of whether there are differences between developed versus developing countries with respect to how global businesses based there engage with domestic regulation and interact with global governance institutions. Chapter 9 returns to this question,[24] with an emphasis on variations in domestic regulatory governance regimes in the Global North and the Global South, respectively. In particular, as chapter 9 highlights, the intrafirm norms on climate and associated expectations about regulatory pressure—notably, in the energy sector—are distinct for European firms compared to US firms and for the rest of the Fortune Global 500. Nevertheless, as this chapter demonstrates, firms' participation in the UN Global Compact—when combined with managerial agency—promotes "norming" in *all* global businesses, including those domiciled in the United States or outside Europe.

5 The US Case: Regulatory Pressure and the Clean Power Plan

Chapter 5 builds on the previous chapter's empirical establishment that there is a variation in the willingness of global firms to participate and engage in voluntary climate action at different levels of effort. This is due in large part to firm heterogeneity with respect to firm management factors, external political economy dynamics (regulatory and global governance), and their interactions. Businesses will act preemptively in anticipation of a more stringent regulatory environment, and they are more likely to do so, and at higher levels, when there are favorable management structures and practices that give agency to corporate management.

In this chapter, the US case is featured to underscore this book's argument that the interaction between managerial agency and regulatory stringency is a driver of corporate self-regulation on climate change. In this regard, this chapter makes use of the US Environmental Protection Agency's (EPA) introduction of the Clean Power Plan (CPP) as an exogenous policy shock and natural experiment,[1] which in 2011–2015 exerted regulatory pressures on greenhouse gas–intensive firms, to examine the role that regulatory pressure played in shaping global firms' participation and effort in voluntary carbon disclosure during the five years leading up to the Paris Agreement.[2] Many businesses talk a good game, but under what conditions are they compelled to participate in carbon disclosure, and at higher levels?

To isolate the causal impact of regulatory pressure on global firms' participation and intensity of participation in voluntary carbon disclosure, and the interaction between regulatory pressure and corporate management, this chapter employs a quasi-experimental research design. Moreover, as in the previous chapters, chapter 5 distinguishes between the Fortune Global 500 firms' participation and effort in voluntary carbon disclosure. Specifically, this chapter is an empirical analysis of the Global 500 firms' participation in the CDP (formerly the Carbon Disclosure Project) and their level of carbon disclosure over the period 2011–2015, which is carried out in the endogenous binary-variable (EBV) model. The EBV model allows for correlation between the unobservables—that is, phenomena or variables that are not easily observed, measured, or quantified—that affect a firm's participation in voluntary carbon disclosure and the unobservables that affect the level of carbon disclosure, such as any learning-by-doing effects on the extent of carbon disclosure from firms' prior-year participation.

5.1 Failed Climate Change Proposals and the Clean Power Plan

The conventional wisdom is that climate change is a global commons problem.[3] Under the United Nations Framework Convention on Climate Change, nations agree on reductions in greenhouse gas (GHG) emissions. Governments introduce the necessary policies and incentives for emissions reductions in their jurisdiction. Companies, cities, and citizens then take measures to reduce their carbon footprints—namely, the total GHG emissions caused directly or indirectly by a firm. This stylized framework does not align with the reality of climate change policymaking in the United States. The United States did not ratify the 1997 Kyoto Protocol, which committed industrial countries and economies in transition to adopt binding emissions reduction targets and to report periodically on their climate mitigation.[4] Moreover, in the first two decades of the new millennium, the US Congress was not able to reach agreement on environmental protection, energy, and other legislation central to climate change due to legislative gridlock. In the absence of legislative options, the federal government mainly focused on climate research and voluntary reduction, leaving climate change policies up to the states.[5] Thousands of US firms participated in voluntary programs sponsored by various levels of government and/or the private sector; they proactively increased energy efficiency, invested in renewable energy sources, and disclosed information about carbon management, among other activities that went beyond the law.[6]

For three presidential administrations from 1993 to 2009 under Bill Clinton and George W. Bush, the US federal government did not pass major laws related to the environment, energy, or climate change. Even though Presidents George H. W. Bush and Bill Clinton were involved in the initial Kyoto Protocol negotiations, it had become clear that the US Senate was

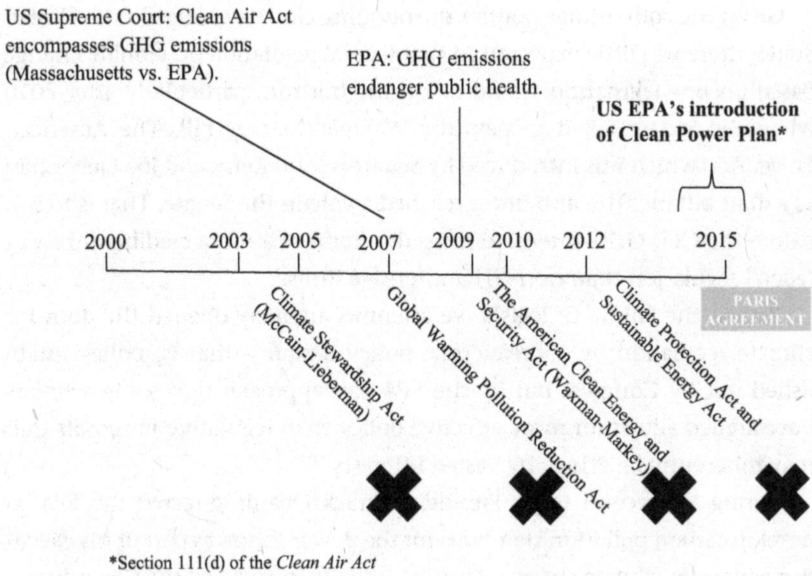

Figure 5.1
Timeline of the Clean Power Plan and other (failed) climate change proposals in the US Congress (2000–2015).

against it.[7] The focus on research and voluntary reductions rather than outright growth in carbon emissions continued during President George W. Bush's administration because of the disagreement among senior federal officials in the executive and legislative branches about the urgency of climate change.[8]

As figure 5.1 shows, over the last two decades all legislative proposals related to climate change have failed to pass in the US Congress.[9] The first proposals for federal legislation on climate change were introduced well over a decade ago. The McCain-Lieberman Climate Stewardship Act failed a Senate vote twice, in 2003 and 2005, and died in 2007 in committee before reaching the full Senate for a vote. The Global Warming Pollution Reduction Act of 2007, introduced by Senators Bernie Sanders and Barbara Boxer, died in committee, as did two additional bills proposed in early 2013—the Climate Protection Act and the Sustainable Energy Act. The House of Representatives approved the American Clean Energy and Security Act of 2009, commonly referred to as the Waxman-Markey bill, but it was never brought to the Senate floor for discussion or a vote.[10]

Given the contentious politics surrounding climate change in the United States, there was little expectation that federal regulation on climate change based on *new* legislation would be on the horizon, particularly after 2010 when the Senate failed to pass the Waxman-Markey bill. The American Power Act, which was introduced by Senators John Kerry and Joe Lieberman as a draft bill in 2010, also never reached a vote in the Senate. That is to say, before the CPP, GHG-intensive firms did not face a more credible threat of federal regulation than non-GHG-intensive firms.

Rather, the failure of legislative attempts arguably opened the door for climate regulation by "bureaucratic policy design"—that is, policy established not by Congress but by the EPA—an approach that some scholars have argued allows for more effective policy than legislative proposals that may inherently be driven by vested interests.[11]

During his second term, President Barack Obama directed the EPA to develop carbon pollution standards for the power sector, as part of his executive action on climate change. The EPA initially introduced the Clean Power Plan (CPP) in June 2014 as a set of regulations under Section 111(d) of the Clean Air Act. The EPA issued its final CPP in August 2015, establishing standards on carbon dioxide emission performance rates for new coal and natural gas–fired power plants.

Multiple events leading up to the CPP helped to boost its credibility with firms. The first was the US Supreme Court's decision in *Massachusetts vs. EPA* in 2007 that the Clean Air Act's protection includes GHG emissions.[12] Second, the EPA's own science-based determination showed that these current and projected concentrations of GHG emissions endangered public health and welfare.[13] In light of President Obama's executive order, the EPA's subsequent issuance of rules for regulating GHG emissions from fossil fuel electricity-generating units served as a harbinger of future regulation beyond the power sector for US firms, notably GHG-intensive firms in the materials, energy, and industrial sectors.

Furthermore, the CPP is a performance-based standard specific to each power plant; this means that it is likely to have higher costs of compliance than an alternative policy (e.g., carbon tax or cap-and-trade regulation) for a given level of aggregate abatement.[14] Consequently, firms viewed the CPP as a credible regulatory threat with consequential adjustment costs, which likely led utilities and other firms in the GHG-intensive sectors to respond to impending regulation, even before the CPP was enshrined in law.[15]

Despite opposition to President Obama's climate change policy, including lawsuits that reached the Supreme Court, the private sector in 2014 and 2015 saw that federal regulation on carbon emissions was imminent.[16] At the time, the Paris Agreement was gaining momentum, and the United States and China were increasingly engaged in galvanizing global climate action.[17]

As such, the CPP was arguably viewed as a credible regulatory threat with consequential adjustment costs for corporations.[18] By engaging in rational proactive climate action *today*, corporations—particularly those based in the United States—hedged against forthcoming regulation to improve regulatory relations and signal climate leadership with the aim of obtaining preferential treatment *tomorrow* if and when the CPP were to become law.

5.2 Model and Data

5.2.1 DD and DDD Frameworks

Before introducing the endogenous binary-variable (EBV) model, the logic of the quasi-experimental research design in the form of difference-in-differences (DD) and difference-in-difference-in-differences (DDD) frameworks is presented. Figure 5.2 plots the 2011–2015 time series of the average carbon disclosure score for Global 500 firms based in the United States (treatment group) next to the time series of the average carbon disclosure score for companies that are headquartered outside the United States (control group). The vertical dotted line represents the introduction of the CPP in 2014. From 2011 to 2013, US firms' average level of voluntary carbon disclosure was approximately equal to that of firms based outside the United States. The two carbon disclosure score series diverged sharply in 2014, which coincided with the introduction of the CPP.

This divergence in parallel trends in the posttreatment period (i.e., the post-CPP period) is confirmed with a formal parallel trends test, where an indicator variable representing US firms is interacted with year indicators as regressors in an ordinary least squares (OLS) regression of the carbon disclosure score. Table A5.1 in appendix 5 shows that the coefficients associated with the 2012 and 2013 year indicators are statistically insignificant, which means that the outcome trends between the treatment and the control group

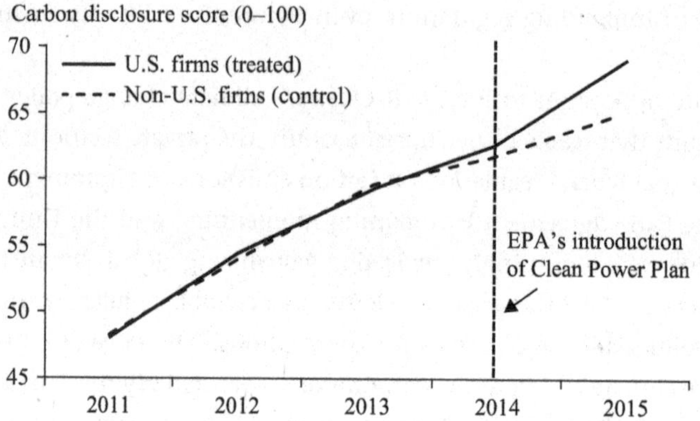

Figure 5.2
Level of voluntary carbon disclosure, 2011–2015 (US versus non-US firms).
Source: Lily Hsueh, "Voluntary Climate Action and Credible Regulatory Threat: Evidence from the Carbon Disclosure Project," *Journal of Regulatory Economics* 56 (2019): 195. https://doi.org/10.1007/s11149-019-09390-z.

are the same. This suggests that the "difference in differences" is not significantly different between US and non-US companies in the pretreatment, or pre-CPP, period.

A more precise model can be obtained by exploiting further variation that exists between the treatment and control firms. As hypothesized in propositions 3 and 4 in chapter 2, a firm's affirmative response to impending regulation in their participation and effort in voluntary carbon disclosure could be predicated by having favorable corporate management factors. Table A5.2 in appendix 5 shows the variation in the level of voluntary carbon disclosure for firms with and without a dedicated manager responsible for carbon management and climate risks in the pre- and post-CPP periods. A simple difference-in-means test indicates that firms with a manager had a significantly higher carbon disclosure score than those without a manager in both periods; this suggests that variation in management factors matter, both directly on its own and indirectly through its interaction with regulatory pressure.

Figure 5.3 shows that there was a positive gap in the level of voluntary carbon disclosure for firms with and without a manager responsible for climate mitigation from 2011 to 2013; that being said, both trends were on balance fairly stable pre-CPP. By contrast, the divergence in trends became apparent

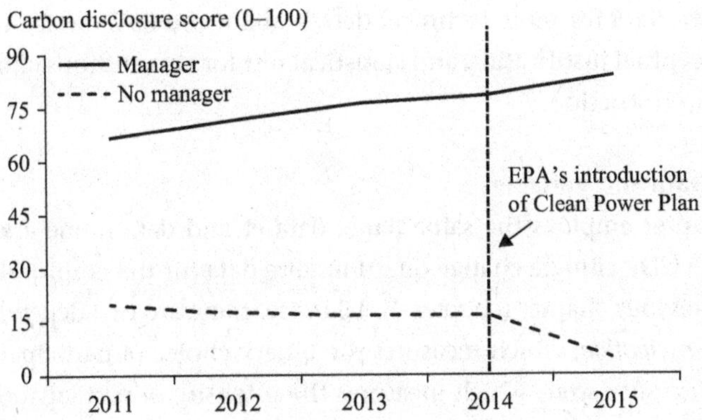

Figure 5.3
Level of voluntary carbon disclosure, 2011–2015 (manager versus no manager).
Source: Lily Hsueh, "Voluntary Climate Action and Credible Regulatory Threat: Evidence from the Carbon Disclosure Project," *Journal of Regulatory Economics* 56 (2019): 196. https://doi.org/10.1007/s11149-019-09390-z.

in the post-CPP period. Nevertheless, whether this divergence is exclusively a function of regulatory pressure via the CPP is unclear because it appears that companies without a manager may also have altered their behavior post-CPP; that is to say, the precise causal mechanisms by which companies with or without a climate change manager responded to regulatory pressure could be confounded. To alleviate this concern, alternative specifications in which *manager* is fixed at 2011, 2012, or 2013 levels are included as robustness checks in appendix 5 (see table A5.7).

5.2.2 Estimation Model

Both the DD and DDD estimators are nested within an EBV model.[19] The EBV model is a linear potential-outcome model that allows for a specific correlation structure between the unobservables that affect a firm's decision to participate in voluntary carbon disclosure, represented by the binary variable *participation*, and the unobservables that affect the potential outcome, that is, the level of carbon disclosure or carbon disclosure score. Typically, one such unobservable is regulatory pressure, which is explicitly modeled in this chapter as *Clean Power Plan (CPP)*, an indicator variable. In essence, the average marginal effect and the other parameters of a linear regression model are augmented with the endogenous binary participation variable.

See appendix 5 for more technical details about the EBV model, including the conceptual justification and statistical test for this author's choice of an exclusion restriction.

5.2.3 Data and Variables

This chapter employs the same panel dataset and data frame and utilizes the same CDP climate change questionnaire data for the empirical analysis as the previous chapter (chapter 4). Likewise, there are two dependent variables: *participation*, which measures the binary choice of participation, and *carbon disclosure score*, which measures the intensity of participation or the level of carbon disclosure.[20] In this chapter, the latter covariate is the outcome variable in the OLS (model 1) and endogenous binary-variable (EBV) models (models 2 and 3), whereas the former is the endogenous binary participation variable in the EBV models (models 2 and 3). The OLS model serves as a reference model, whereas the EBV models are the main models of interest.

A unique feature of this chapter's empirical analysis is that *carbon disclosure score* is coded 0 for companies that did not participate in CDP's annual climate change questionnaire in 2011–2015. Unlike the Heckman selection model in chapter 4, this coding scheme assumes that aside from CDP no other institutions have built a more comprehensive international database of self-reported climate change information and have developed a reputation for impartiality.[21] Nonetheless, this coding scheme is robust to the Heckman selection model, in which nonparticipation is coded as missing values. Altogether, 232 companies did not disclose to the CDP at some point from 2011 to 2015, making 903 company×year observations, or close to 30 percent of the sample. By contrast, 532 companies in 2011–2015 have a *carbon disclosure score* greater than 0, making 2,348 company×year observations (which is equivalent to 72 percent of the sample).

In what follows below, explanatory variables that have not already been laid out in a previous chapter are explicated here—namely, the variables that make up the interaction terms for the DD and DDD estimators. Toward this regard, an indicator variable, *Clean Power Plan (CPP)*, was constructed to represent that the EPA introduced the CPP in June 2014 and published its final standards on carbon emissions for new coal- and natural gas–fired power plants in August 2015. Moreover, *USA* is a indicator variable that signifies whether a firm is based in the United States. *USA×CPP* is an interaction term between *USA* and *Clean Power Plan (CPP)*, which designates US firms in the years following the EPA's introduction of the CPP. These three variables make up the DD estimator. By contrast, pair interaction terms between *USA*, *Clean Power Plan (CPP)*, and *manager*, as well as the three variables interacting together in the form of *USA* × *CPP* × *manager*, make up the separate regressors of the DDD estimator.

Details about the construction of and data source for the control variables, such as *revenues*, *natural gas price*, and *target* are given in appendix 2. In this chapter's analysis, standard econometric controls such as sector and year fixed effects, are included to account for sector heterogeneity and to control for exogenous macroeconomic, political, and institutional factors that affect, in some unobserved way, all US multinational firms in a given year. For example, two other EPA regulatory initiatives during this period impacted the use and production of coal-fired power (not directly related to the Clean Power Plan): the EPA's mercury rule and cross-state air pollution rule that limit emissions of mercury, fine particulate matter, and nitrogen oxide and sulfur dioxide, which contribute to ozone pollution. Both of these rules were expensive for firms (in some sectors more than others) to comply with and negatively affected the viability of coal-fired power and factories.

Table 5.1 reports summary statistics for the covariates pre- and post-CPP periods. Panel A presents descriptive statistics for US-based companies (treatment), and panel B reports descriptive statistics for the non-US firms (control). On average, 70 to 75 percent of Global 500 companies have participated in voluntary carbon disclosure at least once from 2011 to 2015. US firms participated at higher rates than non-US companies in the pre-CPP period, and that gap widened in the post-CPP period; the gap between the two groups' levels of voluntary carbon disclosure also increased during the post-CPP period.

5.3 Results and Discussion

Table 5.2 presents the chapter's estimation results. On balance, these results are robust to a trimmed matching sample that established balance on observables for the treatment and control firms and alternative specifications (e.g., sector-specific regressions and a Heckman selection model), all of which can be found in appendix 5.

In table 5.2, model 1 is the DD estimator in the OLS model, whereas model 2 and model 3 are the nested DD and DDD estimators in the EBV

Table 5.1
Summary statistics for treatment and control groups, before and after the Clean Power Plan

	Pre-CPP (2011–2013)		Post-CPP (2014–2015)	
Variable	Mean	Standard deviation	Mean	Standard deviation
		A. Treatment group—US-based companies		
Participation in CDP (% share)	73.25	44.30	76.01	42.75
Carbon disclosure score (0–100)	53.83	37.01	65.83	39.69
Revenues (millions)	$31,314.31	$50,409.89	$34,180.55	$50,107.94
Assets (millions)	$93,423.17	$266,454.00	$104,216.90	$282,618.50
Manager (% share)	71.33	45.25	79.62	40.33
Target (% share)	53.36	49.92	63.06	48.32
Natural gas price (Dow Jones)	2.51	0.89	1.65	0.47
Natural gas price (S&P GSCI)	81.09	28.81	53.33	15.30
N	729		471	
		B. Control group—Non-US companies		
Participation in the CDP (% share)	71.37	45.22	70.77	45.51
Carbon disclosure score (0–100)	53.90	37.54	63.47	42.72
Revenues (millions)	$33,197.01	$46,496.79	$33,138.29	$46,108.47
Assets (millions)	$180,874.90	$415,481.40	$185,062.90	$396,438.70
Manager (% share)	63.72	48.10	73.53	44.15
Target (% share)	55.90	49.67	65.50	47.57
Natural gas price (Dow Jones)	2.51	0.89	1.65	0.47
Natural gas price (S&P GSCI)	81.26	28.86	53.43	15.29
N	1,254		797	

Table 5.2

Quasi-experimental approach to participation and effort in voluntary carbon disclosure, difference-in-differences and difference-in-difference-in-differences estimations in OLS and nested in EBV models

	Model 1	Model 2		Model 3	
	DD Level of voluntary carbon disclosure b/se[a]	DD Participation in voluntary carbon disclosure b/se[a]	Level of voluntary carbon disclosure b/se[a]	DDD Participation in voluntary carbon disclosure b/se[a]	Level of voluntary carbon disclosure b/se[a]
USA	2.718 (1.98)	0.121 (0.11)	–0.098 (1.05)	0.057 (0.17)	–0.932 (1.64)
Clean Power Plan (CPP)	N/A	N/A	N/A	N/A	N/A
USA×CPP	1.73 (1.51)	0.058 (0.07)	–0.024 (0.90)	0.456*** (0.17)	1.805 (1.73)
Manager				2.037*** (0.14)	5.135*** (1.72)
USA×manager				–0.291 (0.22)	0.449 (1.95)
CPP×manager				0.518*** (0.12)	9.103*** (1.10)
USA×CPP×manager				–0.384* (0.22)	–2.743 (2.06)
Revenues (log)	5.420*** (0.94)	0.425*** (0.05)	1.968*** (0.36)	0.304*** (0.05)	1.343*** (0.35)
Natural gas price (log)	–7.054*** (1.16)	–0.002 (0.04)	–12.411*** (0.68)	0.784*** (0.08)	–5.973*** (0.79)

(continued)

Table 5.2 *(continued)*

	Model 1	Model 2		Model 3	
	DD Level of voluntary carbon disclosure b/se[a]	DD Participation in voluntary carbon disclosure b/se[a]	Level of voluntary carbon disclosure b/se[a]	DDD Participation in voluntary carbon disclosure b/se[a]	Level of voluntary carbon disclosure b/se[a]
Target	48.483*** (2.25)		15.272*** (1.48)		13.847*** (1.46)
Participation last year			62.683*** (1.82)		61.748*** (2.06)
Constant	–17.922*** (9.15)	–3.349*** (0.49)	–6.037* (3.64)	–4.143*** (0.55)	–10.349*** (3.60)
Athrho Constant		0.281*** (0.03)		0.185*** (0.03)	
Lnsigma Constant		2.641*** (0.03)		2.614*** (0.03)	
Year fixed effects	Yes	Yes	Yes	Yes	Yes
Sector fixed effects	Yes	Yes	Yes	Yes	Yes
R^2	0.49				
F-stat	84.893***				
Chi-square			10,239.141***		20,202.868***
N	3,209		3,209		3,209

Note: *$p<0.1$, ***$p<0.01$. Model 1 is a difference-in-differences estimation in the OLS model; model 2 is a difference-in-differences estimation nested in the EBV model; and model 3 is a difference-in-difference-in-differences estimation nested in the EBV model. *Clean Power Plan (CPP)* is excluded from the model because it is collinear with the year fixed effects; N/A, or not applicable, denotes this fact.

[a] Robust standard errors with firm-level cluster correction.

model, respectively. According to the DD estimator in the EBV model (model 2), which accounts for firms' participation in the CDP but does not account for variation in firm management, participation in the CDP is primarily a function of firm size. By contrast, once we account for the role of a dedicated manager responsible for carbon management and climate risks as part of a DDD specification in the EBV model (model 3), the results show US firms were more likely to participate in the CDP after the EPA's introduction of the CPP. Specifically, post-CPP, US companies were nearly 10 percent more likely to take part in voluntary carbon disclosure than non-US firms.[22]

While it was not (yet) codified in law, the EPA's introduction of the CPP was generally viewed by US firms as a credible harbinger of impending regulation given the reasons described in section 5.1, including the fact that the CPP was part of the Clean Air Act, which is a legally binding legislation with broad jurisdiction that encompassed GHG emissions. Thus, engaging in industry self-regulation through the CDP was one way for US firms to proactively signal their climate mitigation readiness in the face of a regulatory threat.

The positive effect of the CPP for US companies is attenuated by the presence of a manager responsible for carbon management and climate risks (at the 10 percent significance level), as shown by the estimated coefficient on the triple interaction term, $USA \times CPP \times manager$; this represents the treatment effect in the DDD estimator of the EBV model. One possible interpretation is that managers play multiple roles: in addition to serving as policy supporters, they also serve as internal firm monitors, making sure that any form of industry self-regulation, of which voluntary carbon disclosure is a case, is viewed as a positive signal of climate change readiness rather than greenwashing behavior in the post-CPP world.

That being said, when comparing US firms with and without a manager, those with an executive officer responsible for climate risks post-CPP were close to 55 percent more likely to participate in the CDP than firms without a manager. For corporations with existing managerial capacity, the marginal cost of voluntary carbon disclosure was relatively low since they were more likely to be equipped for climate mitigation than their counterparts without a dedicated manager in the post-CPP period.

With respect to the intensity of participation in voluntary carbon disclosure, the estimated coefficients on $USA \times CPP$ in all three models are not statistically significant, indicating that regulatory pressure (in the form of the

CPP)—with or without the presence of a manager—did not induce US firms to increase their level of voluntary carbon disclosure.

Nevertheless, the fact that *CPP×manager* in model 2 and model 3 is positive and statistically significant on its own without a *USA* interaction term suggests that, on balance, non-US companies also responded to changes in the regulatory environment originating in the United States. In fact, model 3 suggests that after the introduction of the CPP, firms with a dedicated climate change manager were 65 percent more likely to participate in voluntary carbon disclosure than firms without climate change managers, regardless of country of origin. Moreover, among firms making carbon disclosures, the Clean Power Plan (CPP) was associated with about 14 additional points (out of 100) in the carbon disclosure score among firms with a dedicated climate change manager compared to firms without a manager responsible for carbon management and climate risks.[23]

Since nearly if not all Global 500 corporations sell to US markets, changes in the regulatory environment in the United States arguably affect all of these firms in some way, although differently. A little over a quarter of non-US Global 500 firms generate their largest or second-largest sales in the United States.[24] That being said, it is impossible to separately identify the effects of the CPP on non-US firms from common trends that are not part of the CPP. For example, the Obama administration's executive actions on climate change also articulated a vision for increased global leadership, in addition to directing the EPA to promulgate regulation as part of the Clean Air Act. Multinational companies and shareholders worldwide recognized and anticipated that the United States was to play a significant role at the 2015 Paris Agreement, which it did.

Confirming prior results in the literature, the control variables on balance produced expected results. Across all three models, large firms were more likely than smaller firms to participate in voluntary carbon disclosure or to disclose at higher levels. Companies that have established quantitative emissions targets disclosed at higher levels (14–50 points) than their counterparts without the concrete tool for climate mitigation. Moreover, by and large, firms responded to economic incentives in their level of carbon disclosure: when natural gas prices fell, it became less costly for firms to invest in voluntary carbon disclosure, so they disclosed at higher levels (see models 2 and 3). That being said, model 3 results show that firms chose to participate in the CDP even when natural gas prices were increasing (and thus it was relatively more expensive to reduce emissions); this may be because firms participated in the CDP to communicate and promote their climate leadership irrespective of substantive contents, which is relatively inexpensive compared to the cost of engaging in substantive climate mitigation.[25] Chapter 7 links global firms' disclosure about substantive climate mitigation to their actual environmental performance.

Finally, participation in the previous year in the CDP accounted for a substantial extent of firms' disclosure scores; this is a feature of the endogenous binary-variable model, which allows for correlation between participation and intensity of participation in voluntary carbon disclosure. Prior participation represents a form of learning effects: firms may not participate fully in the CDP during the first year that they join, but once they participate they accumulate knowledge both about how the disclosure framework works and about best practices. With this information, they could modify their behavior, which allows them to increase their scores in subsequent years.

5.4 Conclusion

In many countries outside the United States, center-right and center-left political parties have largely accepted the consensus on climate science and the need to mitigate carbon emissions sooner rather than later. By contrast, during 2011–2020 the United States lagged behind the EU and the rest of the world in national-level climate change legislation and policies, including laws and policies that promote low carbon transition in areas of energy, transport, land use, and climate resilience. This chapter has focused on the US case and examined the role that the US Environmental Protection Agency's introduction of the Clean Power Plan (CPP)—which increased the likelihood of climate change regulation in the United States in 2011–2015—played in motivating Global 500 firms' participation and intensity of participation in voluntary carbon disclosure.

This chapter's quasi-experiments and discrete-continuous models show that when there was credible regulatory pressure, combined with internal firm managerial capabilities and competencies, such as senior- and executive-level managers dedicated to climate mitigation, US firms acted preemptively in their participation and effort in climate disclosures. When corporate management was not considered, however, empirical results show that there was not a statistically significant relationship between regulatory pressure—that is, the CPP—and firms' participation and the intensity of participation in voluntary carbon disclosure.

On balance, as this chapter's evidence shows, managers dedicated to addressing climate change impacts played dual roles. On one hand, managers represented managerial capacity and capability for climate mitigation. On the other hand, managers served as internal firm monitors to ensure that industry self-regulation would be viewed by the markets, including shareholders, as a positive signal of climate change readiness rather than greenwashing behavior in a world of increasing regulatory scrutiny and stakeholder activism.

Regardless of country of origin, in the post-CPP period global firms with a dedicated manager responsible for carbon risk management compared to firms without such a manager, notably those operating in GHG-intensive sectors, were also associated with increases in their carbon disclosure scores. Given President Obama's executive action, which formed the basis for the CPP, and the Obama administration's articulation of global leadership on the eve of the Paris Agreement, multinational firms and shareholders worldwide anticipated the United States' significant role at the 2005 UN climate change conference in Paris.

6 An Interplay of Domestic and Global Governance: Global Firms' Learning and Norming in the UN Global Compact

A throughline of the previous two chapters—chapter 4 and chapter 5—is the interaction between corporate management with domestic regulation and global governance, respectively, in shaping firms' decision-making about corporate self-regulation on climate change. This chapter, in turn, examines the complementary interplay of domestic regulation and global governance in steering voluntary climate action by firms. The focus of this chapter is empirical evidence to support proposition 7 of the multilevel governance framework on climate change (MGFCC) about regulation × global drivers of corporate proactive behavior on climate change, which is covered in chapter 2.

The main thrust of this proposition is that, all else being equal, global firms' participation in global governance institutions are attenuated by pressures and requirements of domestic regulation and distributive conflicts among political and economic stakeholders in nation-states. The more stringent existing or impending regulation is, the more likely corporate participants of global governance are to engage in costly (as opposed to less costly) climate action. Given that learning by firms could be costly and thus not an automatic process,[1] the learning that takes place inside global governance institutions is rarely Schumpeterian in nature.[2] That is, a fundamental change in purpose or strategies for achieving learning is unlikely unless political economy conditions at the domestic level change.

This chapter presents both case-based qualitative and quantitative evidence for substantiating proposition 7. An illustrative case study details the multiple institutional venues for learning and norming in the United Nations Global Compact (UNGC). Large-*N* panel data analyses evaluate firms' adoption of costly carbon management tools, namely, quantitative emissions targets and an internal carbon price, as a function of regulatory stringency and global

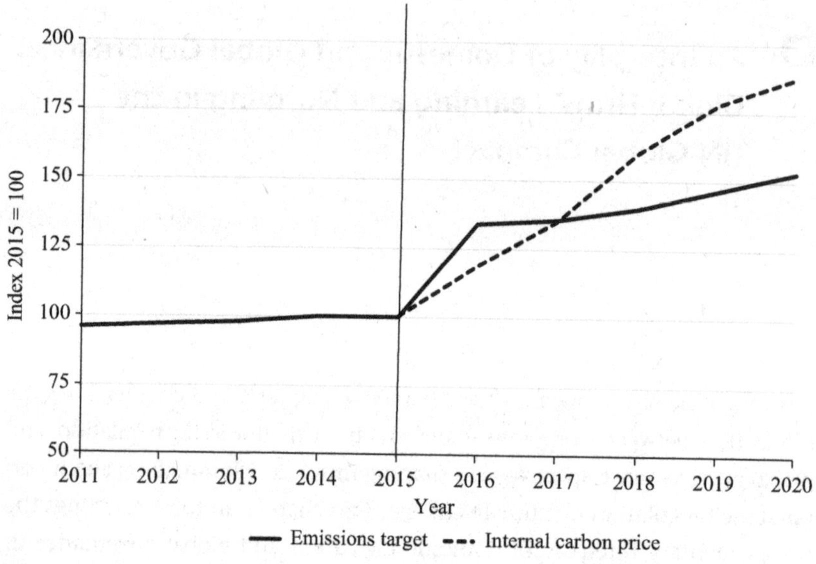

Figure 6.1
The rise of global firms' adoption of quantitative emissions targets and an internal carbon price (2011–2020).
Note: Index 2015 = 100 means that 2015 is the base year.
Data source: Author's calculations based on data from CDP and individual company websites and annual reports.

governance membership. Like in the other chapters, global firms are regarded as strategic actors and thus are the unit of analysis in the case study about institutional venues with the UNGC that promote learning and norming as well as the multicountry and multisector panel data analysis of the uptake of costly voluntary climate action by global firms.

Figure 6.1 illustrates the rise in firms' adoption of quantitative emissions targets and an internal price on carbon after 2015. From 2011 to 2015, the emissions target adoption rate grew by four basis points, whereas it jumped fifty-three basis points from 2015 to 2020. In 2011, about half of the Fortune Global 500 firms had set a quantitative emissions target. By 2020, more than 80 percent of firms regardless of sector had adopted targets. Adopting quantitative targets for reducing carbon emissions had become ubiquitous for global businesses by 2020.

With respect to setting a benchmark price, in 2015, 20 percent of firms had established an internal price on carbon. In 2020, nearly 40 percent of the Fortune Global 500 companies had placed a monetary value on carbon operational efficiencies. This chapter's empirical analysis quantifies the extent to which this is due to the influence of domestic regulation and global governance interactions, controlling for secular trends and alternative explanations.

6.1 Domestic Regulation and Global Governance Interactions

When firms join global governance institutions (such as the UN Global Compact in this book), they face numerous opportunities for learning and norming about new worldviews, frameworks, and policy objectives as well as technical and esoteric aspects of policy tools and implementation designs and processes. Lessons about and involving paradigm shifts tend to be less frequent, and typically, are an outcome of a "focusing event"—that is, a sudden event that is harmful or reveals a potentially greater future harm and becomes known to policymakers and the public simultaneously.[3] This reflexive type of learning and norming is infrequent because fundamental changes associated with underlying shifts in worldviews are costly to firms, all else being equal.[4]

Given this, firms engage primarily in lessons about the viability of policy instruments or implementation designs inside global governance institutions.[5] These lessons are an accumulation of technological, managerial, and organizational knowledge that foster the buildup of local technological capabilities.[6] The economics of innovation and technical change literature identifies this iterative process of adaptation and experimentation as learning-by-doing, learning-by-using, or learning-by-interacting.[7]

As presented in chapter 2 (section 2.6), learning can come from a plurality of sources, such as epistemic communities, by trial and error, or as the result of a competition of beliefs and ideas, including divergent causal reasoning about policy problems.[8] The "soft" transfer of ideas and information via networks in international organizations, in the spread of norms, standard setting, and development of professional communities, promotes harmonization and policy coordination and can be rapid and frequent.[9]

This iterative and incremental process of learning is a result of firms' benefit-cost calculus as they confront and engage with new knowledge, norms, and best practices that emanate from knowledge systems inside global governance institutions. As corporate members learn about the broader scope, technicalities, and implementation design of a new policy tool or practice, there are feedback loops between existing expectations and structures that individual firms face and the outcomes of the learning processes.

This bounded learning implies that firms rarely, if ever, conduct a systematic search for emergent policy problems or the optimal solutions to solve them.

In circumstances where there is an overload of information or conflicting or ever-changing information,[10] policy actors will fall back on what they know or what is expected of them.[11] To find a way forward, firms learn by adapting existing heuristics to problems. This is the case even when policy actors are confronted with evidence of a mismatch between policy objectives and the consequences of the planned course of action.[12] In this vein, firms learn discriminatively because, all else being equal, their learning is bounded by and reflects current or prospective requirements and pressures of the domestic regulatory regime.

When the stringency of domestic regulation is high, it follows that a firm's marginal cost of proactive climate action will be relatively low compared to a company facing low domestic regulation and the same opportunities for learning, leading to a "high level of climate action" that goes beyond existing legal requirements. Strong domestic regulation incentivizes firms' learning about relatively expensive sustainability innovations and how to define, implement, measure, and communicate their climate mitigation strategies because the domestic regulatory regime sets a high baseline and framework that firms use to acquire and assimilate new knowledge in global governance institutions.

The following is proposition 7 from chapter 2, which refers to regulation × global interactions as drivers of global firms' participation and effort in increasingly costly forms of corporate self-regulation on climate change.

Proposition 7 (participation and regulation × global): For firms originating from countries with (less) stringent regulations, their participation in global governance institutions leads them to engage in (less) costly voluntary climate action.

6.2 Illustrative Case Study: Institutional Venues for Learning and Norming in the UN Global Compact

The UNGC serves as the empirical setting to examine the interplay between domestic regulation and global governance in steering corporate self-regulation on climate change. Founded in 2000 by the UN Environmental Programme, the UN Global Compact's primary role is a "learning forum," as articulated by the largest voluntary corporate sustainability initiative's founding director, John Ruggie.[13] The international voluntary initiative seeks to enhance "international dialogues" by businesses and governments about socially responsible policies and "universal sustainability principles" across all aspects of corporate sustainability—environment, social policy, sustainable development, governance, financial markets, and supply chains—with firms as the main driver of change (or action), rather than governments.[14]

There are at least two main institutional venues by which corporate members of the UN Global Compact collect, process, and disseminate knowledge and thus learn: the Global Compact Local Networks and the UN Global Compact Academy (henceforth, the Local Networks and the Academy, respectively). The Local Networks is a business-led, multistakeholder platform for businesses to engage with "stakeholders from Government, the UN, civil society and communities to map a shared approach . . . to drive outreach, learning, policy dialogue, collective action and partnerships . . . [and] guide them as they put their sustainability commitments into action."[15] A common theme across these activities is the Local Networks' emphasis on aligning businesses with national challenges and priorities ("Companies must understand their responsibility to comply with all relevant legislation [at the national level]"[16]) and fostering business-government synergies while upholding internationally recognized minimum standards and principles.

By contrast, the Academy does not assume locality; it is a digital learning platform for firms to learn about global best practices and "actionable skills to help companies move further faster in implementing the Ten Principles of the UN Global Compact and the Sustainable Development Goals."[17] Since participation is not localized, the Academy enables inclusivity: companies around the globe, domiciled in developed and developing countries alike, learn about global norms and best practices. Despite this, inherently, the activities of the Academy as well as that of the Local Networks show that participating firms' learning and norming by and large mirror and are demarcated by current and prospective ambitions of the domestic regulatory regimes of these firms' countries of origin or largest export markets.

6.2.1 Global Compact Local Networks

The Local Networks help companies understand what "responsible business" means in a corporation's country of origin, with the aim of "[facilitating] outreach, learning, policy dialogue, collective action and partnerships."[18] The activities of the Local Networks emphasize the synergic relationship between the UNGC and a "national context" and take place primarily at the country level.

Corporate members of the UNGC are by default members of their country of origin's Local Network; that being said, Local Networks support both local firms and subsidiaries of multinational corporations for a nominal fee.[19] There are over 9,000 business participants and over 3,000 nonbusiness participants in the UNGC's more than 80 Local Networks worldwide.[20] In 2018 alone, Local Networks organized 205 initiatives across multiple countries to facilitate public-private policy dialogues; more than 6,000 companies attended these forums.

Several Local Network programs illustrate the interplay between the UNGC and national governments in shaping corporate member's learning about global best practices on climate change. Launched in 2007, the UN Global Compact Network USA regularly organizes events that bring together Network members and subnational (state) and federal government officials. In 2020, the US participants of the Young SDG Innovators Programme gathered in Phoenix, Arizona, at the Arizona State University's Thunderbird School of Global Management for a series of training and networking workshops aimed at helping that year's Young Innovators to develop scalable projects for their respective companies to implement companywide.[21]

As part of the workshop agenda, there was an informal "lunch and learn" event with Marie Royce, who was at the time the assistant secretary of the US State Department's Bureau of Education and Cultural Affairs (ECA).[22] The main topic of conversation was public-private partnerships, with a focus on how companies could better communicate and engage with the ECA on a myriad of issues, from international trade to climate change. Before engaging in an open forum, the deputy assistant secretary for ECA made a presentation about the bureau's existing outreach programs to corporations and outlined concrete ways that the bureau could collaborate with the Young SDG Innovators and Network USA's corporate members on enhancing climate communication.

In addition to dialogues with government officials, Network USA organizes roundtable panels and workshops—in-person events and webinars—that bring together, for example, corporate financial and social responsibility officers and US state and federal government treasurers and other officials, to share their views, learn from one another, and preview and discuss proposed policies in the regulatory horizon.[23] In 2021, Network USA and the United Nations Principles for Responsibility Investment cohosted a series of webinars on recent developments and an overview of the landscape on corporate climate disclosures, including the US Securities and Exchange Commission's request to companies for information and comments about its planned proposal for mandatory disclosures. Several webinars were devoted to technical details such as materiality, scenario analysis, corporate social responsibility (CSR) reports and assurance, physical and transition risks, the role of auditors, and critical price assumptions.[24]

Outside the United States, Local Networks have also collaborated directly with national governments to create and strengthen a national incentive-based strategy around sustainability and CSR. One notable example is the UN Global Compact Network Tunisia's launch of a multistakeholder study of CSR, as part of new legislation that was introduced in Tunisia's Parliament in 2015. On behalf of its sixty-six corporate members, Network Tunisia actively engaged with the Tunisian government. According to an UNGC annual report, Network Tunisia was a "vocal advocate in the country, calling for the establishment of a national strategy around sustainability and corporate social responsibility with particular incentives for business to adopt responsible and principled practices."[25]

Tunisia's CSR legislation, which was subsequently adopted by the Parliament in 2018, established and institutionalized a committee responsible for monitoring, tracking, and evaluating CSR programs on an annual basis. The information disclosure inventory, which is to be submitted to Tunisia's three presidencies of the Republic, the Government, and the National Assembly, does not go beyond a repository of corporate sustainability activities, however.

6.2.2 UN Global Compact Academy

In 2018, the UNGC launched the UN Global Compact Academy to provide "learning opportunities" and "learning sessions,"[26] regardless of whether Local Networks exist in global businesses' country of origin or export markets. The Academy distributes information, builds capacity, and trains and assists companies in the adoption and implementation of global best practices on climate mitigation. The Academy aims to be "both accessible and solutions oriented" and "offers both learning and practical tools" and "a principles-based approach that puts respect for human rights at the center of business action."[27]

The Academy is effectively a virtual epistemic community, in which corporate members learn about and help to define the environmental problems that corporations face, identify policy solutions, and assess the policy outcomes. All UNGC members have access to virtual sessions, e-learning courses, influencer series (i.e., seminars and lectures by UN leaders and "companies shaping the sustainability agenda"), as well as an online community of "like-minded firms" working toward social responsibility.[28] Furthermore, the Academy provides participating UN Global Compact members with certificates of completion and a tracker for their progress through the Academy Learning Platform.

The Academy offers a series of webinars tailored to promoting climate action. Featured sessions include "Raising Ambition—How to Set Science-Based Targets Aligning with 1.5 Degrees Celsius Pathways," "The Ambition Loop," and "Setting a Price on Carbon." The stated objective undergirding these learning opportunities is that climate action will help members identify new business opportunities and prepare them for the transition to a low-carbon economy. These sessions emphasize the spread of new scientific knowledge, indigenous learning, and capacity building, and collaboration with governments.

"The Ambition Loop" teaches the concept of "positive feedback loops" in which "private sector leadership and Government policies reinforce each other . . . [to] fast-track zero-carbon economic growth."[29] In another webinar, "Setting a Price on Carbon," the Academy aims to demonstrate "why carbon pricing makes good business sense" and to show how a company can use an internal price on carbon as a tool to mitigate climate-related financial risks by integrating carbon pricing into a firm's long-term investment decisions. These knowledge-based courses and workshops instruct companies in how to work with and comply with existing regulation in their domiciles and export markets as well as how to go beyond what is currently on the books to align with global best practices in anticipation of potential regulations in the horizon. Fundamentally, the emphasis is existing and potential domestic regulations as baselines.

6.3 Model and Data

The above-described illustrative case study explicates the two key institutional venues for learning and norming in the UNGC, which are the learning mechanisms by which corporate members of the UNGC interact with the global governance institution. The following large-*N* panel data analysis provides an empirical test for proposition 7. Proposition 7 contends that global firms' propensity to engage in costly voluntary climate action is a function of the interaction between the stringency of domestic regulation in firms' country of origin and firms' membership in global governance institutions.

This chapter employs a two-stage binomial logistic analysis of a panel of the Fortune Global 500 firms' adoption of quantitative emissions targets during 2011–2020 and internal carbon prices or both during 2015–2020. In the first stage, a reduced-form binomial logistic regression predicts firms' participation in the UNGC. The rationale for the first stage is to account for the possibility of selection bias. Firms that join the UN Global Compact could be the companies that already have active CSR programs in the climate change area and/or originate from countries that are more deeply embedded in international nongovernmental or intergovernmental organization networks. The predicted covariates on firms' participation in the UNGC then enters into the second stage of the binomial logistical regressions on firms' likelihood to adopt these costly carbon management tools as a function of the interactions between firms' participation in the UNGC and domestic regulatory stringency.

6.3.1 Dependent Variables

Chapter 6 employs three dependent variables of interest to represent increasingly more costly adoption of climate mitigation tools by Global 500 firms: *target, carbon price,* and *target and price. Target* indicates whether a firm has adopted a quantitative emissions target; it is a proxy for whether a firm has proactively integrated climate risks into a firm's modus operandi in a given year.

Carbon price concerns whether a company uses an internal price on carbon. A firm's internal price on carbon places a monetary value (typically on a per ton basis) on greenhouse gas (GHG) emissions.[30]

Target and price represents a firms' adoption of both an emissions *target* and an internal *carbon price*. All three variables are time-variant variables, which means that the year(s) preceding adoption is (are) coded as 0. Data for *price* and *target and price* are available for 2015–2020, as detailed in appendix 2, when CDP included a question in its annual climate change questionnaire asking firms about an internal carbon price.

Firms' adoptions of an emissions target and/or internal price on carbon represent increasingly stringent forms of corporate self-regulation because these carbon management tools do not possess immediate financial payoffs. Instead, they enable medium- to long-run risk mitigation and business operations planning for firms' shift to low-carbon alternatives. Moreover, emissions targets and internal carbon prices prepare firms for future government policies that restrict carbon emissions and thus could take multiple fiscal periods for firms to fully appropriate these investments. As shown in figure 6.1, emissions targets are more commonplace and thus relatively less costly to implement, while an internal carbon price is an emerging global best practice.

6.3.2 Firm, Market, and Sector Variables

As this book posits, corporate managerial leadership generates, persuades, accumulates, and disseminates knowledge to influence aggregate decision-making about environmental management inside the firm.[31] First introduced in chapter 4, *manager* is a time-variant indicator variable concerning whether a company has a senior- or executive-level manager responsible for climate change, environmental sustainability, or environmental policy in a given year. *Manager* also represents whether a firm has a committee responsible for setting vision and planning for climate risk management as part of its board of directors. Appendix 1 describes this book's treatment of missing data due to nonresponse for *manager* in the CDP climate change questionnaire.

Also introduced in chapter 4, *UNGC member* is an indicator variable for a firm's annual membership in the UN Global Compact. This time-variant variable allows for the fact that longer-term members of the UNGC have learned more or accumulated more knowledge than new members. Additionally, while members are by default a member of their country of origin's Local Network, the longer they have been a member of the UNGC, the more likely they are to be active participants of Local Networks.

UNGC member enters into this chapter's first-stage (reduced form) regression to predict global firms' membership in the UN Global Compact. The predicted $\widehat{\textit{UNGC member}}$ then enters the second-stage regression as an independent variable in the form of a cross-level interaction term (namely, $\widehat{\textit{UNGC member}} \times \textit{regulatory stringency}$).

Following the empirical analyses in the previous chapters, this chapter's empirical analysis includes *revenues*, *natural gas price*, and *GHG-intensive*. *GHG broad*, which includes not only materials and utilities but also energy and industrial, serves as an alternative (broader) measure of carbon intensity.

Moreover, industry sector fixed effects (with the information technology and telecommunications sector serving as the base), excluding the materials and utilities sectors already covered by *GHG-intensive*, are also part of this chapter's logistic panel regressions. These sector-specific indicator variables account for cross-sector variation—such as variation in consumer orientation or energy intensity in production—which may influence a corporation's decision to engage in voluntary climate action but does not change systematically over time within a sector.

6.3.3 Country-Level Variables

Following chapter 4, *regulatory stringency* represents (in log form) a country's international environmental treaty ratifications in a given year. The premise is that a country's ratification of environmental treaties reflects what each country is willing to commit to with respect to the breadth and depth of domestic regulation.

An alternative measure of regulatory stringency is a climate change–specific variable, *climate change laws*, which is the log form of the cumulative or year-to-date numbers of climate change–related laws (i.e., legislation and executive actions) that a country has passed from 2011 to 2020. This variable represents the extent of a country's ambition in climate change policymaking.

Another explanatory variable at the country level is *civil liberties*, similar to chapter 4's empirical analysis. Other country-level controls include gross domestic products (GDP) per capita (log), federalism, EU membership, and country-level counts of ISO 14001 certifications (log). The rationales for inclusion of these controls are explained in chapter 4.

Table A6.1 in appendix 6 reports summary statistics for firm, market, sector, and country variables, including alternative measures used in robustness checks for UNGC members and nonmembers.

6.3.4 Cross-Level Interaction Terms

To test proposition 7, *regulatory stringency* × $\widehat{\textit{UNGC member}}$ is an interaction term that represents regulation × global drivers of corporate proactive behavior on climate change. *Regulatory stringency* × $\widehat{\textit{UNGC member}}$ appraises this chapter's main argument, which is that the interaction between the domestic regulation of firms' country of origin and firms' participation in global private governance institutions predicate firms' decision-making about whether to engage in increasingly costlier climate mitigation.

6.4 Results and Discussion

Results for the first-stage UNGC participation regressions are reported in appendix 6 (see table A6.2). Second-stage binomial logistic regression results with sector and year fixed effects are reported for the Fortune Global 500 firms in tables 6.1, 6.2, and 6.3 for *target, carbon price,* and *target and price,* respectively. In all three tables, model 1 is the base or reference model, which comprises firm, market, sector, and country covariates without the cross-level *regulatory stringency* × $\widehat{\textit{UNGC member}}$ interaction. A second specification (model 2) is a replication of the base model with an inclusion of the regulation × global interaction.[32] Estimated coefficients are reported as odds ratios to facilitate interpretation.[33] All three tables report robust standard errors with firm-level cluster correction.

Appendix 6 contains a series of robustness checks, including alternative specifications of key independent variables, such as a measure of regulatory stringency that is based on a global business's largest export market (see tables A6.2 to A6.10). By and large, this chapter's empirical results representing increasingly costlier voluntary climate action are robust to alternative specifications.

6.4.1 Domestic Regulation and Global Governance

As shown tables 6.1–6.3, there is evidence to support proposition 7 (see model 2), which states that the likelihood of voluntary adoption of costly climate actions increases when corporate members of global governance institutions originate from countries with strong regulatory institutions. For a 1 percent increase in the stringency of domestic regulation, the odds of engaging in proactive adoption of an emissions target are 1.29 times larger for firms that have joined the UN Global Compact than for firms that are not members of the UNGC, all else being equal. The odds are a little higher (1.35–1.37 times) for firms' adoption of relatively more costly climate actions—namely, an internal carbon price or both an emissions target and a carbon price, when regulatory stringency increases by 1 percent.

These results suggest that there is a productive interplay between domestic regulation and global governance in inducing corporate self-regulation on climate change. The more credible is the threat of regulation or the higher in stringency is domestic regulation, the more likely it is that firms'

Table 6.1
Adoption of a quantitative emissions target, stage 2 logistics panel data models (Fortune Global 500 firms)

	Model 1	Model 2
	Base b/se[a]	Regulation × global b/se[a]
Firm, market, sector variables		
Manager	4.744*** (0.727)	4.819*** (0.736)
UNGC member	3.857*** (1.999)	
Revenues (log)	1.425*** (0.124)	1.432*** (0.125)
Natural gas price (log)	0.780 (0.132)	0.784 (0.132)
GHG-intensive	0.783 (0.252)	0.793 (0.255)
Country-level variables		
Regulatory stringency (log)	1.389** (0.179)	1.371** (0.177)
Civil liberties	0.843* (0.074)	0.846* (0.075)
GDP per capita (log)	1.253* (0.145)	1.183 (0.135)
Federal	0.795 (0.169)	0.797 (0.171)
ISO 14001 (country-level) (log)	0.935 (0.081)	0.933 (0.080)
EU member	0.586* (0.183)	0.584* (0.187)
Post–Paris Agreement (2016–onward)	2.010* (0.784)	2.035* (0.790)
Cross-level interactions		
Regulatory stringency × UNGC member		1.291** (0.139)
Constant	0.005*** (0.008)	0.006*** (0.011)
Chi-square	524.949	520.40
N	6,091	6,091
Sector fixed effects	Yes	Yes
Year fixed effects	Yes	Yes

Note: $^{*}p<0.1$, $^{**}p<0.05$, $^{***}p<0.01$.

[a] Robust standard errors with firm-level cluster correction.

Table 6.2
Adoption of an internal carbon price, stage 2 logistics panel data models (Fortune Global 500 firms)

	Model 1	Model 2
	Base b/se[a]	Regulation × global b/se[a]
Firm, market, and sector variables		
Manager	2.792*** (0.556)	2.778*** (0.559)
UNGC member	4.255** (2.582)	
Revenues (log)	1.222** (0.105)	1.220** (0.105)
Natural gas price (log)	0.900 (0.082)	0.899 (0.083)
GHG-intensive	6.485*** (2.164)	6.502*** (2.172)
Country-level variables		
Regulatory stringency (log)	1.413* (0.276)	1.326 (0.259)
Civil liberties	0.660*** (0.078)	0.665*** (0.078)
GDP per capita (log)	0.801 (0.118)	0.798 (0.118)
Federal	0.745 (0.176)	0.783 (0.197)
ISO 14001 (country-level) (log)	0.839* (0.080)	0.848* (0.081)
EU member	0.802 (0.240)	0.759 (0.240)
Cross-level interactions		
Regulatory stringency × UNGC member		1.351** (0.174)
Constant	0.286 (0.569)	0.356 (0.683)
Chi-square	218.70	220.30
N	3,631	3,631
Sector fixed effects	Yes	Yes
Year fixed effects	Yes	Yes

Note: *$p<0.1$, **$p<0.05$, ***$p<0.01$.

[a] Robust standard errors with firm-level cluster correction.

Table 6.3

Adoption of both a quantitative emissions target and an internal carbon price, stage 2 logistics panel data models (Fortune Global 500 firms)

	Model 1	Model 2
	Base b/se[a]	Regulation × global b/se[a]
Firm, market, and sector variables		
Manager	2.839*** (0.564)	2.844*** (0.571)
UNGC Member	4.686*** (1.378)	
Revenues (log)	1.198** (0.103)	1.199** (0.104)
Natural gas price (log)	0.939 (0.093)	0.940 (0.093)
GHG-intensive	5.305*** (1.736)	5.337*** (1.749)
Country-level variables		
Regulatory stringency (log)	1.388 (0.282)	1.300 (0.261)
Civil liberties	0.687*** (0.080)	0.692*** (0.081)
GDP per capita (log)	0.790* (0.110)	0.783* (0.109)
Federal	0.758 (0.175)	0.792 (0.196)
ISO 14001 (country-level) (log)	0.874 (0.082)	0.884 (0.083)
EU member	0.856 (0.246)	0.819 (0.249)
Cross-level interactions		
Regulatory stringency × UNGC member		1.367** (0.169)
Constant	0.239 (0.467)	0.313 (0.586)
Chi-square	217.312	218.951
N	3,634	3,634
Sector fixed effects	Yes	Yes
Year fixed effects	Yes	Yes

Note: $*p<0.1$, $**p<0.05$, $***p<0.01$.

[a] Robust standard errors with firm-level cluster correction.

engagement through learning and norming in the UN Global Compact will lead to costly investments in climate mitigation.

As reported in all three tables, results for the firm, market, sector, and political economy controls indicate that large firms, firms that participate in the UNGC, firms with dedicated corporate management structures, firms that originate from countries with relatively strong regulatory institutions, and firms that are based in countries with relatively high civil liberties are more likely to engage in voluntary climate action. These results mirror findings in the prior literature and in the rest of the book.

6.5 Conclusion

A new school of political economists contends that the diffusion of knowledge about climate change in international organizations is akin to the "catalytic" forces and institutions that lead to "increasing returns" in global climate cooperation, which go beyond any existing institutional solution to free riding.[34] In this vein, the building and strengthening of coalitions—through global governance institutions such as the UN Global Compact—can help secure the necessary investments for more effective climate policies. Proposition 7, as articulated in chapter 2 and tested for validity in this chapter, builds on this premise. Specifically, this chapter examines how participation in the UN Global Compact interacts with the stringency of domestic regulation in global businesses' country of origin to drive firms' adoption of costly carbon management tools—namely, science-based, quantitative emissions targets and an internal carbon price.

An illustrative case study details the multiple institutional venues in the UN Global Compact for firms to learn about global best practices in carbon management. The UNGC encourages members to actively engage in the Global Compact Local Networks, which take place at the country level with the main objective of aligning businesses with national challenges and priorities. By contrast, the UN Global Compact Academy is a digital learning platform for firms, domiciled anywhere in the globe, to learn about global best practices and norms.

Substantiated by a panel data analysis of the Fortune Global 500 firms' adoption of costly carbon management tools (namely, emissions targets, an internal carbon price, or both) and their participation in the UNGC over the period 2011–2020, this chapter demonstrates that there is a limit to the assertive display of self-regulation by global firms: firms will readily adopt widely accepted and relatively less costly carbon management practices, such as quantitative emissions targets, but may pause on their adoption of an internal price on carbon, which is an emerging practice that is costlier for firms. There is, on balance, less marginal gain from engaging in more costly forms of self-regulation. This is because domestic regulation influence and shape global firms' learning about and eventual adoption of global best practices. Unlike emissions targets, internal carbon prices have not yet proliferated as a regulatory imperative or corporate norm in 2011–2020.

This chapter highlights the role of nation-states as well as the agency of global firms and international organizations. In doing so, this chapter heeds the call for grappling with the unique epistemological and methodological challenges of "drill[ing] research down to domestic levels while considering global context . . . and to better address interests and ideas at the international, state and subnational levels."[35] Firms are the ones who join global governance institutions that are replete with opportunities and institutional venues for learning, such as the UNGC's Local Networks and the Academy. They help to legitimate new ideas, consolidate and strengthen networks, and provide the logistics by which companies can convert carbon management concepts into concrete best practices. Importantly, these learning mechanisms emphasize collaborations with national and subnational governments, as well as advocacy for the adoption of emerging policies and global best practices. More often than not, the learning that takes place is limited to learning about the viability of policy instruments or implementation designs, with the cost of this learning being weighed against the domestic regulatory baselines. There is less of an incentive for firms to go beyond the rules on the books or anticipated regulation.

Based on this chapter's empirical results, the UNGC appears to have accomplished its objectives about learning and norming, at least in the climate change area, which is to "promote corporate sustainability and encourage innovative solutions and partnership." As this chapter shows, the resultant proactive climate actions by these firms are the consequence of the interplay between their participation in the UNGC, which focuses on the dissemination and transmission of global best practices, and domestic regulatory stringency. A separate inquiry is whether or not firms' voluntary climate action translates into actual and quantifiable environmental performance, which is the subject of chapter 7.

III Carbon Footprints, Sectoral and Regional Variations, and Conclusion

7 Linking Global Firms' Corporate Climate Action and Carbon Footprints

Part I and part II of the book have examined the internal firm and external political economy drivers of corporate self-regulation on climate change. As explicated in chapter 2's multilevel governance framework on climate change, inside firms, senior- and executive-level managers dedicated to climate mitigation attract climate-neutral or -conscious employees, align employees' beliefs with those of the firm through incentives and coordination, and form governing coalitions comprising internal stakeholders across ranks for proactive climate action. In the face of public politics (i.e., actual or potential government interaction with firms via laws and regulation), managers with the support of internal stakeholders across ranks will readily heed regulatory pressure by engaging in beyond-compliance climate action (which includes strategic decisions about which activities to engage in) in an attempt to earn goodwill with regulators and to avoid complex, inflexible, and costly regulatory processes and legal liabilities. Managers' active engagement with global governance strengthens global firms' climate mitigation. Part II ends with chapter 6, which provides evidence for this book's argument that global firms' proactive climate action is a response to the stringency of domestic regulation on the books and on the horizon, as firms, often through managers, interact with and help to shape global best practices inside global governance institutions.

The empirical focus thus far has been on firms' sustainability outputs, such as the voluntary carbon disclosure or the adoption of quantitative emissions targets, rather than on environmental outcomes or performance as the dependent variable of interest. Part III begins with chapter 7, which details an investigation of whether global businesses' sustainability outputs—namely, voluntary carbon disclosure, translate to a reduction in a company's actual carbon emissions. The premise is that voluntary carbon disclosure can augment environmental regulation by inducing a firm to reduce its carbon footprint above and beyond what is legally mandated. The question is, Do global firms that proactively disclose information about their climate mitigation activities (i.e., participate in a voluntary disclosure program) necessarily emit less carbon emissions?

Answering this question is not straightforward, because determining the independent and actual effect of firms' climate disclosures on their carbon emissions is fundamentally difficult when the researcher cannot randomly assign firms with different levels of climate mitigation activity to participate (or not) in voluntary carbon disclosure. Earlier research,[1] in the first decade of the US Department of Energy's Voluntary Greenhouse Gas Registry, found that participating in the registry had no significant effect on the companies' carbon emissions intensity (CO_2 per unit of generation) but that many of the companies, by being selective in what they reported, reported emissions reductions. Another study,[2] which focused on the power sector's participation in CDP's (formerly the Carbon Disclosure Project) annual climate change questionnaires, found either no impact or an increase in carbon intensity.[3]

Unlike the prior studies that have examined firms' choice between two alternatives (namely, to disclose or not to disclose), this chapter exploits heterogeneity in firms' effort or intensity of participation in voluntary carbon disclosure through CDP—proxied by firms' disclosures about the extent or level of their climate mitigation activities (i.e., firms' substantive contents of climate disclosures)—to show that some firms use voluntary carbon disclosure to obfuscate and enable greenwashing when regulatory pressure is low. Firms' substantive contents of disclosure about their (commitments to) climate mitigation range from basic transparency about their carbon management to higher levels of climate mitigation, such as third-party verification of their reported greenhouse gas (GHG) emissions or reporting about emissions that extends beyond direct operations. Similar to chapter 5, this chapter makes use of the United States Environmental Protection Agency's (EPA) introduction of the Clean Power Plan as an exogenous policy shock to identify the causal impact of firms' voluntary carbon disclosure on their entity-wide GHG emissions and GHG emissions intensity.

7.1 Voluntary Carbon Disclosure and Carbon Emissions

Aside from the empirical studies mentioned above, little research links voluntary carbon disclosure by firms to carbon emissions.[4] Furthermore, fewer still are studies that examine how firms' disclosures about the extent or level of their climate mitigation activities impact their carbon emissions. That being said, numerous studies link corporate environmentalism, including firms' environmental disclosures to their business valuation.[5] In particular, two studies found empirical evidence that regulatory pressure—via the Kyoto Protocol in one of the studies—explains the link between firms' disclosures, whether firm-initiated or third-party initiated, and market outcomes.[6]

Closer to this chapter's focus on estimating the carbon emissions impact of firms' effort or intensity of participation in voluntary carbon disclosure is a recent study, although firm value is again the outcome variable of interest. Specifically, the authors investigate the stock market response to firms' disclosures about their environmental activities.[7] The authors' findings suggest that the relevance of the content of information disclosure matters if it is to have the hypothesized impact on the dependent or outcome variable. What matters most for significant stock returns is content that contains relatively high "newness of information" and expected net financial benefit.

In this chapter, the type of information disclosures that will most likely be correlated with reduced carbon emissions are voluntary disclosures about corporate actions that represent global best practices and concrete actions to advance climate mitigation, such as firms' implementation of entity-wide emission reduction plans and strategies, disclosures of third-party-verified GHG emissions from firms' direct operations, and transparency about indirect emissions, including emissions from their supply chains, business travel, employees' commutes, and the way customers use their products. These disclosures constitute information about higher levels of proactive climate mitigation activity by firms. By contrast, disclosures about lower levels of climate mitigation activity represent basic carbon transparency and initial assessments of the environment impacts of business activities without concrete actions to address potential harms and risks associated with climate change.

Ultimately, the antithesis of greenwashing or false or misleading advertising of corporate social responsibility by global firms is when corporations' disclosures of climate mitigation activities are backed up with corresponding actions related to implementation—for example, when third-party audits of actual carbon emissions ensure that quantitative emissions targets and other carbon management tools and practices are carried out. This elimination of the gap between policy and practice (i.e., sustainability outputs) leads to reductions in carbon emissions (i.e., sustainability outcomes) and an increase in environmental performance and regulatory compliance more generally.[8]

7.2 Managers, Regulatory Pressure, and Corporate Self-Regulation on Climate Change

As explicated in chapter 2, corporate management's proclivity to engage in public politic and to build a strategic "buffer zone" in the form of overcompliance suggests that firms that proactively disclose their climate mitigation activities are likely to have systematically different carbon emissions profiles than nonparticipants, aside from their participation in voluntary carbon disclosure.[9] One rationale, which this book argues, based on insights from environmental economics, political economy, and the management, strategy, and organizational behavior literature, is that managers dedicated to climate mitigation facilitate the strategic alignment between prosocial employees, suppliers, customers, and the firm and build loyalty, trust, and cooperation within the organization toward proenvironment policies and activities that aim to reduce a firm's carbon footprint.[10]

A firm's decision to participate in CDP (voluntary carbon disclosure) and their substantive level of participation are functions of the interaction between regulatory pressure (which is in the form of the EPA's Clean Power Plan) and corporate management through dedicated managers responsible for carbon management and climate risks. This does not preclude the fact that firms could (also) use private regulation as a political strategy to preempt more stringent public regulations.[11] In fact, it is through managers dedicated to climate mitigation inside the firm (as distinct from lobbyists, who operate in a different unit/division inside the company) that firms engage in preemptive behavior.

As depicted in this book's multilevel governance framework on climate change, in the face of uncertainty, senior- and executive-level managers perform several key tasks to build relational contracts to tackle business risks posed by global climate change. They attract climate-conscious employees, align beliefs of employees and the firm, and form governing coalitions with internal stakeholders across ranks and investors.[12] These managerial functions ultimately allow for and facilitate the necessary incentives and coordination for effective corporate social responsibility. If regulatory pressure is high and the marginal cost of self-regulation is low, managers will hasten efforts to signal firms' ability to internalize externalities, earn good will, and avoid legal and financial liabilities.

7.3 Model and Data

In an ideal research setting, the researcher would randomly assign firms to participate (or not) in voluntary carbon disclosures with different levels of effort. While random assignment is not feasible, this chapter, like chapter 5, exploits the EPA's introduction of the Clean Power Plan (CPP) (which was part of President Barack Obama's signature climate change policy) as a natural experiment for the identification of the causal impact of voluntary carbon disclosure on carbon emissions. During 2011–2016, before the start of Donald Trump's first presidency, the CPP, which placed limits on carbon emissions from US power plants, exerted regulatory pressure on US-based GHG-intensive firms in the power sector and beyond.[13] This chapter employs the same quasi-experimental framework and empirical models as chapter 5—namely, the difference-in-difference-in-differences (DDD) estimator, nested in an endogenous binary-variable (EBV) model. The unit of analysis is firm×year.

Unlike chapter 5, this chapter utilizes data on the decade-long CDP participation status of 581 companies listed in the S&P 500 index during 2011–2020. In CDP's annual climate change questionnaire, a company's disclosure of direct and indirect GHG emissions are reported at the entity level, so as to prevent firms from reporting only on outcomes of successful projects or initiatives.[14]

To isolate the effect of S&P 500 firms' participation in voluntary carbon disclosure on their entity-wide carbon emissions, 2011–2020 data have been collected from a number of sources for fitting the stage 1 (participation) and stage 2 (CO_2 emissions) of the empirical models. There are two dependent variables: the binary choice of participation and entity-wide carbon emissions. The latter covariate is the outcome variable, whereas the former is the endogenous binary participation variable in the EBV models.

7.3.1 Dependent Variables

Following the previous chapters, *participation* is operationalized as 1 for participation in the CDP in a given year for a firm or 0 otherwise. A firm can decide to participate in CDP in one year but not the next year.[15] In the second stage of the EBV model, entity-wide scope 1 and scope 2 emissions data (at the annual level) are aggregated for each firm to represent entity-wide *CO_2 emissions, CO_2 emissions per dollar, CO_2 emissions per full-time employees*, respectively. The natural log transformation is then taken of the carbon emissions and carbon emissions intensity variables to reduce fluctuations and facilitate the interpretation of the results in percent changes.

Figure 7.1 shows the participation rates in CDP by GHG-intensive and non-GHG-intensive sectors from 2011 to 2016. In the past decade non-GHG-intensive firms in the S&P 500 index participated at higher rates than GHG-intensive firms. The heterogeneity in sectoral participation in voluntary carbon disclosure, at least in the years leading up to the introduction of the Clean Power Plan, was not surprising given earlier studies showing that voluntary program participation rates are higher in industries with greater consumer contact due to a firm's preemptive response to consumer group activism.

That being said, other studies have shown that firms operating in sectors that emit substantial amounts of GHG emissions are more likely to engage in climate disclosure and mitigation activities to preempt regulation or private politics;[16] this is in line with a recent study that shows that both environmental groups and clean energy interests are concentrated where the politics are most opportune or the carbon footprints are greatest.[17] Together, these studies suggest that participation levels could be different but that trends in the participation rates of consumer-oriented and carbon-intensive sectors would more or less track each other and continue on a parallel and increasing path. This is due to competitive pressures for voluntary carbon disclosure in both sectors, as shown by the dotted lines, which are linear predictions based on 2011–2013 trends (see figure 7.1).

Instead, with the introduction of the CPP (as shown in figure 7.2) non-GHG-intensive firms increased their participation as expected, while participation rates for firms in the GHG-intensive sectors went in the opposite direction. This may appear nonintuitive, but a prior study found empirical

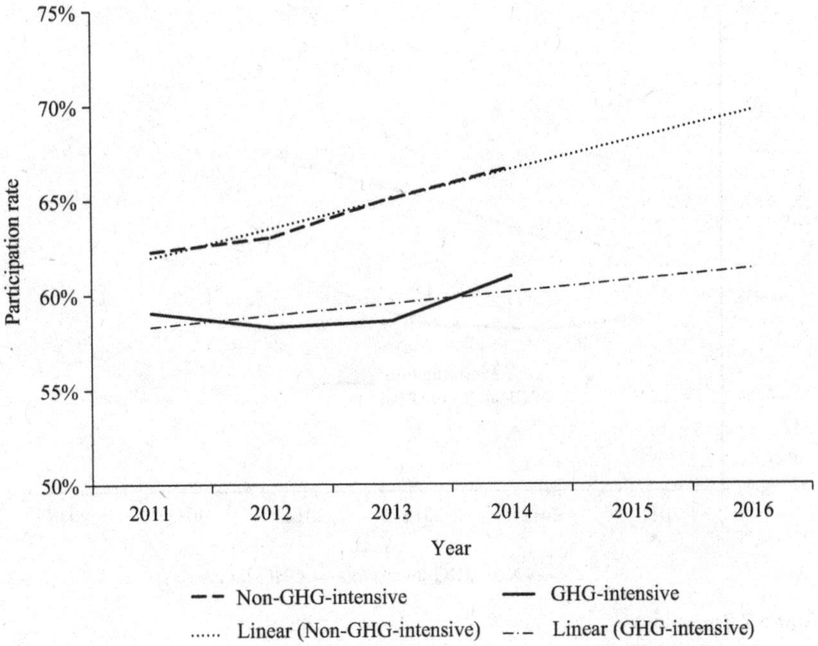

Figure 7.1
Participation in the CDP: GHG-intensive versus non-GHG-intensive sectors (2011–2016).
Note: Dotted lines are linear predictions. GHG-intensive sectors are energy, industrials, materials, and utilities.
Data source: CDP.

evidence to show that firms will pull back on corporate environmental disclosure when there is no good news to share.[18]

Another study found that unilateral domestic climate change policy imposes significant economic costs on energy-intensive sectors, leading to a decrease in production and increase in net imports, which reduces overall competitiveness relative to less-intensive industries.[19] Together, these studies suggest that it is no wonder that when faced with regulatory pressures, GHG-intensive firms shied away from voluntary carbon disclosure.

After 2016, when the Clean Power Plan was taken off the US national climate policy agenda, GHG-intensive sectors no longer faced the same kind of regulatory pressure. As figure 7.3 shows, participation trends in voluntary carbon disclosure fluctuated for all S&P 500 firms regardless of carbon

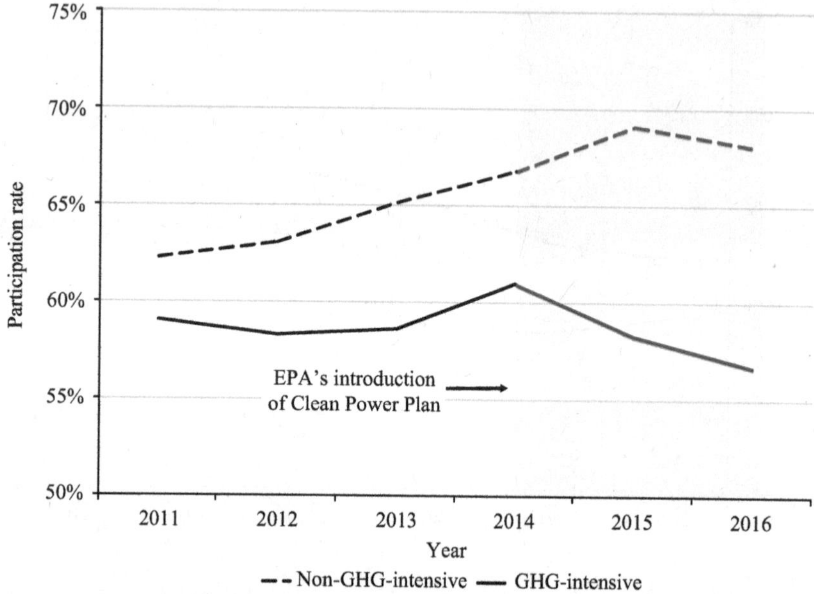

Figure 7.2
The Clean Power Plan and participation in the CDP: GHG-intensive versus non-GHG-intensive sectors (2011–2016).
Note: Results from a parallel trends test show that post-CPP participation trends are statistically different for GHG-intensive firms relative to non-GHG-intensive firms. GHG-intensive sectors are energy, industrials, materials, and utilities.
Data source: CDP.

intensity. After the CPP, and during the Paris Agreement regime (2015–2020), trends in participation rates for GHG-intensive and non-GHG-intensive firms tracked each with differences only in the levels, similar to the pre-CPP era (2011–2013).

7.3.2 Independent Variables

This chapter uses CDP's assignment of letter grades to firms as measures of their intensity of participation in voluntary carbon disclosure. CDP assigns letter grades ranging from A to D based on individual firms' substantive level of (self-disclosed) climate action, as shown in figure 7.4; however, CDP's grading does not assess actual environmental performance. This means that a firm can be on CDP's A-list regardless of whether it has reduced greenhouse gas emissions, as long as the firm has achieved the requirements of sustainability outputs, such as quantitative emissions targets and environmental

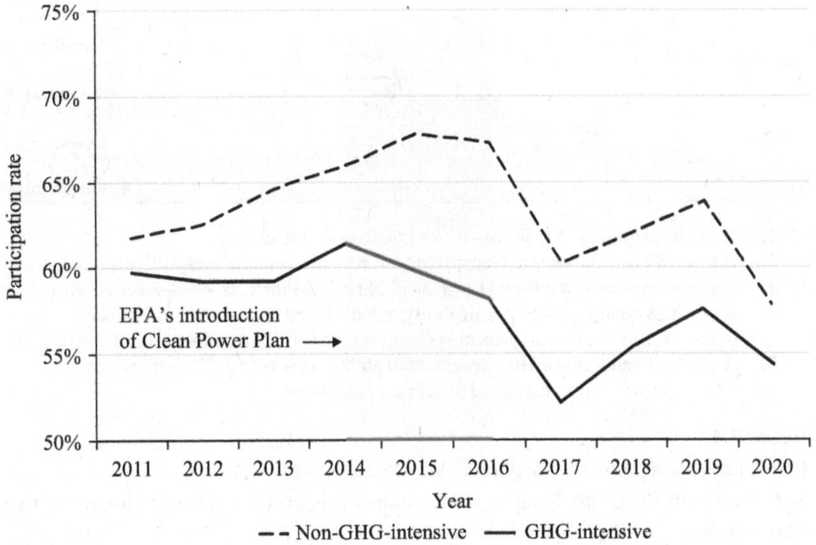

Figure 7.3
Participation in the CDP: GHG-intensive versus non-GHG-intensive sectors (2011–2020).
Note: GHG-intensive sectors are energy, industrials, materials, and utilities.
Data source: CDP.

management systems.[20] This chapter's empirical analysis investigates whether and to what extent there is a causal link between sustainability outputs and outcomes (i.e., does carbon disclosure at different substantive levels lead to reductions in carbon footprints).

In CDP's scoring system, points are allocated for each question on the CDP climate change questionnaire, and at the end of scoring, the number of points that a firm has been awarded is divided by the maximum number that could have been awarded at the transparency, awareness, management, and leadership levels. The fraction is then converted to a percentage by multiplying by 100 and rounded to the nearest whole number (see appendix 1 for more information).

From here, a minimum score of 75 is required in order to be assessed at the next level. This means that each performance grade represents an additive effect; that is, a higher grade implies that the lower grade and associated substantive level of climate action have been achieved.[21]

For this chapter's analysis, the A to D letter grades are translated into indicator variables to represent the intensity of participation in the second stage

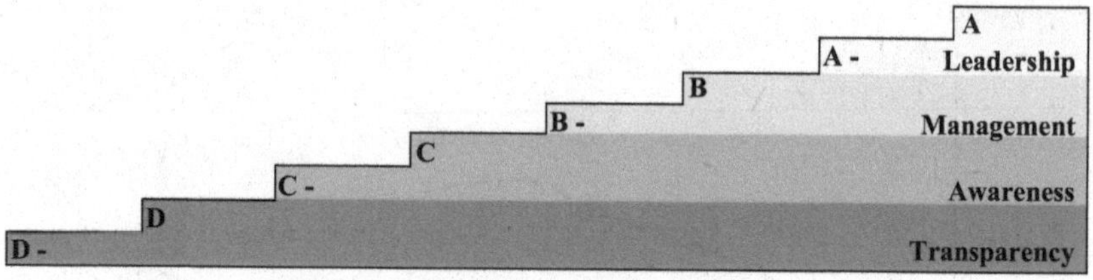

1. **Non-participation:** No disclosures or insufficient disclosures.
2. **D grade (Transparency):** Transparency in survey responses irrespective of contents
3. **C grade (Awareness):** Initial assessment of business impacts ←→ ecosystems
4. **B grade (Management):** Sustainability outputs based on results of assessments (e.g., environmental management systems, science-based quantitative emissions targets)
5. **A grade (Leadership):** High-level sustainability outputs (e.g., 3rd party audits, internal carbon price, disclosure of scope 3 emissions)

Figure 7.4
CDP's grading scheme for corporate climate disclosure.
Note: Based on firms' disclosures, CDP grades firms on their level of climate mitigation activity.
Source: CDP.

of the endogenous binary-variable (EBV) model. *CDP—transparency* indicates whether a company has received a letter grade in the range of D to D–; this designation means that the firm has responded to a majority of CDP's climate change questionnaire irrespective of the contents of the disclosure.[22] Firms at this level of climate mitigation activity are considered low- or basic-level participants in voluntary carbon disclosure.

CDP—awareness measures whether a firm has moved beyond mere disclosure of climate change information or carbon transparency to a demonstration of an awareness about climate change issues; in this case, firms are awarded a letter grade in the range of C to C–. In order to receive a C-range grade, companies' evaluations must include the impacts of business activities on the environment, and how these activities affect people and ecosystems, as well as impacts that the environment may have on business activities. Importantly, a C grade does not mean that a company has taken any actions to address environmental issues beyond initial screenings or assessments.[23] In this chapter, *CDP—awareness* is equivalent to a medium-low level of substantive climate action.

To receive a score in the B range, as indicated by *CDP—management*, a firm needs to demonstrate that management action has been taken to address issues that have been raised in its assessments of the company's impacts on the environment and the environment's impacts on business operations. At this medium-high level of climate mitigation activity, firms have adopted and implemented an environmental management system and established quantitative emissions targets.

Firms that have been designated at this level of climate mitigation activity have made efforts to "mitigate risk, advance environmental accounting in at-risk sites, make risk assessments more robust and comprehensive, implement an environmental policy and integrate environmental issues into business strategy."[24] These climate mitigation activities are associated with how CDP and its partner organizations, such as Ceres and the World Wide Fund for Nature, define what is considered to be effective corporate environmental management.

The final and highest level of substantive climate action is the A-list status, as measured by *CDP—leadership*. To be designated a climate change A-list firm, companies must have disclosed climate actions that "represent best practice as formulated by partner organizations with CDP to advance environmental stewardship."[25] According to CDP, "best practice" includes third-party verification of at least 70 percent of total scope 1 and scope 2 emissions with no significant exclusions.

These A-list carbon disclosers are required to publicly disclose their actual gross scope 1 and scope 2 emissions to CDP, along with disclosures about the way in which their emissions reduction strategies encompass company-wide goals.[26] Firms that voluntarily disclose scope 3 emissions are allotted additional points in CDP's scoring. As mentioned earlier, CDP does not benchmark or grade firms based on their *actual* environmental performance. In other words, firms in the *CDP—leadership* level of disclosure are designated "climate leaders" by CDP regardless of whether they have reduced carbon emissions.[27]

In this chapter's analysis, participants have been grouped into four distinct categories: D range, C range, B range, and A range. There are no distinctions made between D- and D, C- and C, and so on, because of the concern about low statistical power given the small number of observations and, thus, miniscule degrees of freedom available for analysis.[28]

7.3.3 DDD Variables

The DDD variables in both the participation and outcome stages of the endogenous binary-variable (EBV) model include the following: Like in previous chapters, *GHG-intensive* is an indicator variable that signifies whether a firm is part of the materials and utilities sectors, as defined by the Global Industry Classification Standard. According to CDP, companies in materials and utilities emit the largest amount of aggregated scope 1 and scope 2 emissions compared to other sectors. Importantly, the power sector (classified under utilities), which is the direct target of the Clean Power Plan, is considered part of the *GHG-intensive* designation.

Clean Power Plan (CPP), which is also an indicator variable, is coded as 1, or turned on, in the years 2014, 2015, and 2016 and turned off, or coded as 0, thereafter. In June 2014, the Environmental Protection Agency (EPA) introduced a draft version of the CPP and sought public comments. In August 2015, the EPA published its final standards on carbon emissions for new coal- and natural gas–fired power plants. In November 2016, Donald Trump was elected US president for the first time, and he was sworn in as president in January 2017. He had campaigned on repealing the regulation, and under his first administration, the Clean Power Plan was replaced with the Affordable Clean Energy Rule, which was a much weaker measure and was projected to increase greenhouse gas emissions.[29]

Manager is a time-varying variable drawn from the CDP climate change questionnaire from 2011 to 2020 and from corporate websites and published reports, such as a company's annual reports or corporate social responsibility reports, for firms that did not report to CDP during the study period. Like in previous chapters, *manager* represents, in a given year, whether a company has a senior- or executive-level manager responsible for climate change–related policies and activities as well as whether it has a committee responsible for climate risk management as part of its board of directors. In this chapter's robustness checks, *manager* is fixed in separate years (2011–2015) to test the sensitivity of the main analysis to the exogeneity assumption about firms' decision to install managers dedicated to climate mitigation (see appendix 7).

Moreover, interactions between *GHG-intensive* and *CPP*, and *GHG-intensive* and *manager*, as well as the three variables interacting together in the form of *CPP* × *GHG-intensive* × *manager*, make up the separate regressors of the DDD estimator.

As shown in figure 7.5, the S&P 500 firms' participation in CDP varies by whether firms have installed a senior- and executive-level manager responsible for carbon management and climate risks and whether firms operate in sectors that were targets of regulatory pressure from 2011 to 2016. Those with

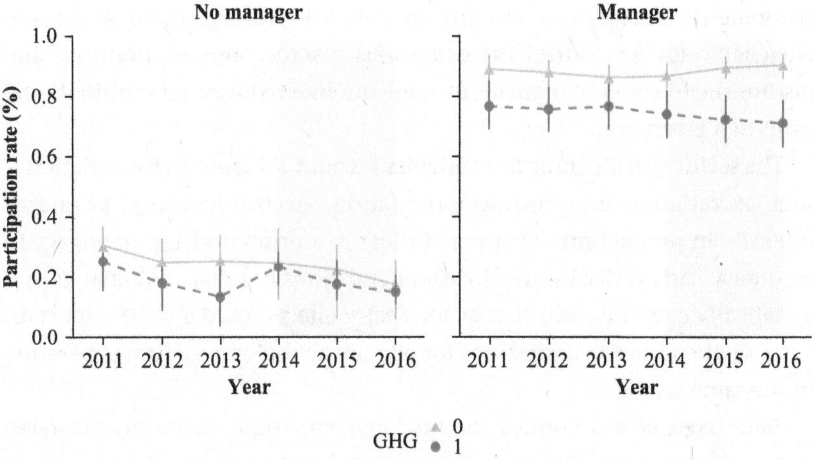

Figure 7.5
Participation in the CDP: manager versus no manager (2011–2016).
Note: GHG-intensive firms are denoted by the dashed line. Non-GHG-intensive firms are denoted by the solid line. The error bars represent 95 percent confidence intervals. GHG-intensive sectors are energy, industrials, materials, and utilities.
Data sources: CDP and individual company websites and annual reports.

managers, regardless of belonging in GHG-intensive or non-GHG-intensive sectors, participated at high rates in voluntary carbon disclosure compared to those without managers before and during the CPP period. The differences (*manager* versus *no manager*) are statistically significant. This suggests that variation in corporate management matters, directly on its own and indirectly through its interaction with regulatory pressure.

That being said, participation by firms in GHG-intensive sectors decreased while participation by non-GHG-intensive sectors tended to increase post-CPP. This is a harbinger for strategic action by participants in these sectors; non-GHG-intensive sectors were more likely to participate (and at higher levels), but irrespective of their carbon footprints.

7.3.4 Other Controls

This chapter's main analysis includes similar control variables for firm size and market conditions, namely *revenues* and *natural gas price*, respectively, as in the previous chapters. Also, both the first- and second-stage regressions include sector, state, and year fixed effects, which are standard econometric strategies to account for state-level variation and sector heterogeneity and to control for exogenous macroeconomic, political, and institutional factors that affect, in some unobserved way, all multinational firms in a given year.

The sector-specific indicator variables account for cross-sector variation—such as variation in consumer orientation, electric fuel mix, or energy intensity in production—that may influence a firm's decision to engage in voluntary carbon disclosure or carbon emissions but does not change systematically over time within a sector. Sector effects could also be important because of competitive pressures for climate action among firms operating in the same sector.

State fixed effects control for time-invariant state characteristics relating to the regulatory climate, environmental preferences, and corporation-friendly policies of US states in which the S&P 500 firms are headquartered. Year fixed effects control for exogenous factors, such as high levels of general commitment to climate mitigation and protection of shareholder rights that motivate a secular trend of proactive climate action by all firms. These and related secular trends have become more salient in the years following the 2015 Paris Agreement. In one of this chapter's sensitivity analyses, an indicator variable (*Paris Agreement*) is turned on in 2015 and thereafter to demarcate a regime shift in international climate governance.

7.4 Results and Discussion

7.4.1 Participation in CDP

Table 7.1 presents the main results for the first stage, or participation stage, of the endogenous binary-variable (EBV) model. Model 1 is the main model, which contains the DDD estimator on a full sample of the S&P 500 firms. Model 2 represents a split sample of the S&P 500 firms in the broad GHG-intensive sectors (i.e., energy, industrials, materials, and utilities), whereas model 3 is a split sample comprising firms in non-GHG-intensive or consumer-oriented sectors (i.e., consumer discretionary, consumer staples, financial services, and health care).

A full set of results, which include estimated coefficients for control variables, for the stage 1 regressions is given in appendix 7 (table A7.2). Appendix 7 also contains results of alternative analyses that serve as robustness checks for sensitivity to changes in alternative measures, modeling assumptions, and error structures.[30]

Table 7.1
Participation in voluntary carbon disclosure, stage 1 difference-in-difference-in-differences estimation nested in EBV models (S&P 500 index firms)

	Model 1	Model 2	Model 3
Voluntary carbon disclosure	All S&P 500 b/se[c]	GHG-intensive (broad)[a] b/se[c]	Consumer-oriented[b] b/se[c]
GHG-intensive	–0.698* (0.41)		
Clean Power Plan (CPP)[d]	N/A	N/A	N/A
Manager	1.190*** (0.16)	1.391*** (0.24)	1.049*** (0.24)
CPP × GHG-intensive	–0.645 (0.45)		
CPP × manager	0.282 (0.25)	0.273 (0.43)	0.633* (0.34)
GHG-intensive × manager	0.059 (0.33)		
CPP × GHG-intensive × manager	0.341 (0.50)	N/A	N/A

Note: $*p<0.1$, $***p<0.01$. All models include controls and sector, year, and state fixed effects (not shown). A full set of results are presented in appendix 7. *Clean Power Plan (CPP)* is excluded from the model because it is collinear with the year fixed effects; N/A, or not applicable, denotes this fact.

[a] Energy, industrials, materials, and utilities sectors.

[b] Consumer discretionary, consumer staples, financial services, and health care sectors.

[c] Robust standard errors with firm-level cluster correction.

With respect to participation in voluntary carbon disclosure, GHG-intensive firms are less likely to participate in CDP (at the 10 percent confidence level). That being said, on balance, companies that have installed senior- or executive-level managers dedicated to climate mitigation are more likely to disclose to CDP than companies without managerial capacity, irrespective of sector. For consumer-oriented sectors, after the introduction of the Clean Power Plan and before the proposed rule's fate was in jeopardy after President Trump's election, companies with managers were more likely to participate in CDP, despite the fact that the CPP's performance standards only targeted the power sector. This result and the higher CDP participation rate of consumer-oriented firms relative to GHG-intensive firms during 2014–2016 (see figure 7.1) suggest that these firms could have strategically engaged in voluntary carbon disclosure to appeal to consumers and institutional stakeholders, notably in the lead-up to the Paris Agreement.

7.4.2 Entity-Wide Carbon Emissions

Table 7.2 contains the main results on key independent variables—namely, the different levels of substantive climate mitigation activities for stage 2 EBV regressions. A full set of results, including estimated coefficients for control variables, is given in appendix 7 (table A7.2). There are several key takeaways. At first glance, it appears that, conditional on participation, global businesses that report to CDP, regardless of the contents of their information disclosure or D-grade disclosures, are associated with reductions in entity-wide GHG emissions.

By contrast, firms that receive a B grade (i.e., *CDP–management*) are associated with *increases* in CO_2 emissions, as shown in the "Model 1" column (all S&P 500) in table 7.2. Beyond completing CDP's annual climate change questionnaire, these firms disclosed that they undertook assessments of their business impacts on the environment and integrated climate risk management

Table 7.2
Entity-wide carbon emissions, stage 2 difference-in-difference-in-differences estimation nested in EBV models (S&P 500 index firms)

	Model 1	Model 2	Model 3
Model 1	All S&P 500 b/se[c]	GHG-intensive[a] b/se[c]	Consumer-oriented[b] b/se[c]
CDP—transparency	–0.203**	–0.665***	–0.071
	(0.10)	(0.20)	(0.13)
CDP—awareness	0.012	–0.241	0.081
	(0.11)	(0.21)	(0.13)
CDP—management	0.229**	–0.096	0.350**
	(0.12)	(0.22)	(0.14)
CDP—leadership	0.181	–0.219	0.537***
	(0.15)	(0.28)	(0.18)

Note: $^{**}p<0.05$, $^{***}p<0.01$. All models include controls and sector, year, and state fixed effects (not shown). A full set of results is shown in appendix 7.
[a] Energy, industrials, materials, and utilities sectors.
[b] Consumer discretionary, consumer staples, financial services, and health care sectors.
[c] Robust standard errors with firm-level cluster correction.

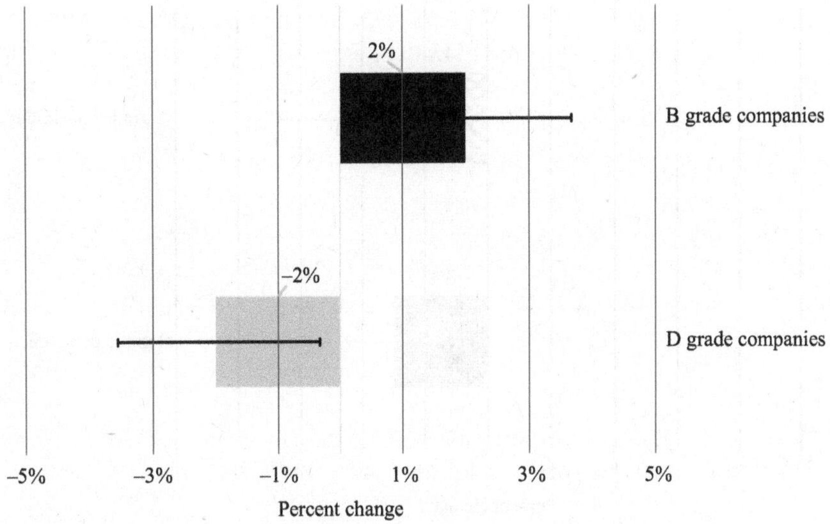

Figure 7.6
S&P 500 index firms' change in entity-wide emissions (2011–2020).
Note: Data show estimated percent changes based on the author's analysis of corporate disclosures on emissions. The error bars represent 95 percent confidence intervals.
Data sources: CDP and LSEG Data and Analytics.

into their business strategy (e.g., setting a quantitative emissions target).[31] Firms that earned a B grade for their carbon management did not have to adhere to stringent protocols, such as third-party audits, or report scope 3 emissions.

Despite receiving a B grade in their reported substantive level of climate mitigation activity, these firms' total carbon emissions increased nearly 2 percent, as shown in figure 7.6. This estimated magnitude of emissions increase, taken alongside a 2 percent estimated emissions reductions of firms that report at a basic level of disclosure, suggest that, on balance, voluntary carbon disclosure had negligible if not perverse, or opposite of the expected, impact on firms' carbon footprints for the S&P 500 companies overall.

Analysis of split samples of S&P 500 data shows that there is sectoral heterogeneity. Table 7.1 model 3 results indicate that firms' high levels of sustainability outputs in the financial, health care, and other consumer-oriented sectors, on average, not only did not lead to reduced entity-wide carbon emissions but were associated with *increases* in GHG emissions.[32] Entity-wide

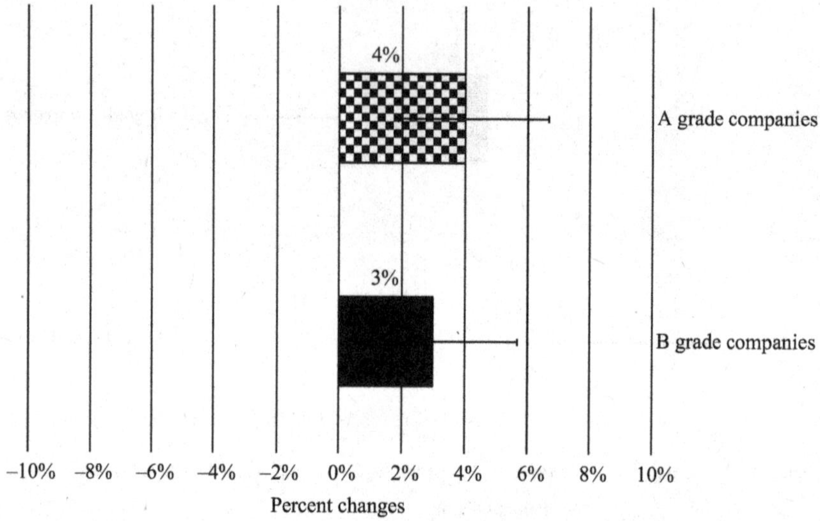

Figure 7.7
Consumer-oriented firms' change in entity-wide emissions (2011–2020).
Note: Data show estimated percent changes based on the author's analysis of corporate disclosures on emissions. The error bars represent 95 percent confidence intervals.
Data sources: CDP and LSEG Data and Analytics.

carbon emissions are estimated to have increased for consumer-oriented firms by 3 to 4 percent for firms that earned a B grade or an A grade from CDP (see figure 7.7).

B-grade firms have voluntarily committed to improving their environmental performance at the level of *CDP—management*, whereas A grade or *CDP—leadership*-level firms are considered the most elite or A-list companies that are leading on environmental transparency and action.[33] The latter companies have set an internal carbon price, subjected their scope 1 and scope 2 emissions to third-party audits, or voluntarily reported their scope 3 emissions.

For both *CDP—management* and *CDP—leadership*, the 95 percent confidence bands are wide, although the lower bounds are above zero and there is an increase in entity-wide carbon emissions of nearly 5 and 7 percent, respectively, for the upper bounds. These perverse outcomes suggest evidence of "cheap talk"[34] with respect to their substantive contents of voluntary carbon disclosure or greenwashing behavior by global firms that did not experience the same level of regulatory pressure as GHG-intensive firms.

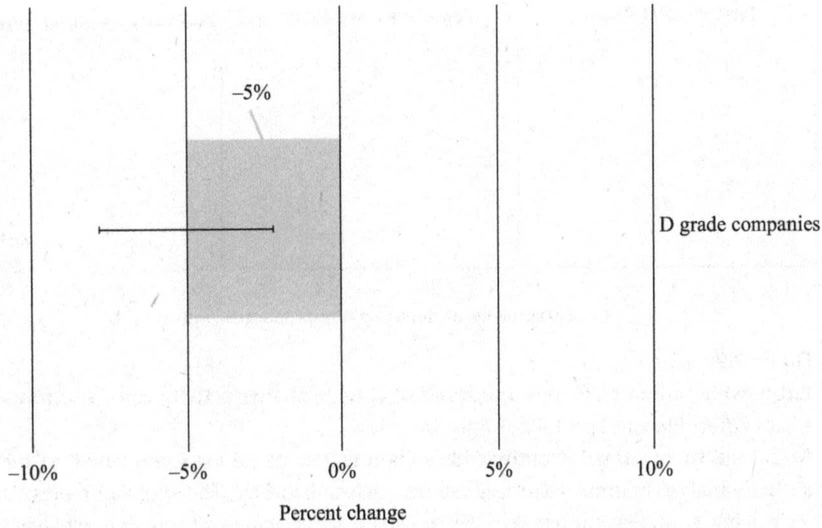

Figure 7.8
GHG-intensive firms' change in entity-wide emissions (2011–2020).
Note: Data show estimated percent changes based on the author's analysis of corporate disclosures on emissions. The error bar represents the 95 percent confidence interval.
Data sources: CDP and LSEG Data and Analytics.

By contrast, reporting firms in the GHG-intensive sectors, which faced more pressure from expected climate regulations, were associated with declines in overall carbon emissions. In fact, merely answering CDP's climate change questionnaire questions (basic transparency), irrespective of substantive contents or the designation of a D (lowest) grade by CDP, is associated with a statistically significant reduction in total carbon emissions at the 5 percent level (see model 2 results).

The discrepancies between firms in the GHG-intensive and consumer-oriented sectors are shown visually in figure 7.7 and figure 7.8, respectively. As shown in figure 7.8, the change in entity-wide carbon emissions for carbon-intensive companies, such as utilities, is predicted to be negative (–5 percent) for the lowest, or *CDP—transparency*, level of participation in the CDP; the confidence band is sizable, in the range of –1.8 percent to –7.5 percent. These firms earned a D grade from CDP.

Figure 7.9 shows three panels representing model-fitted entity-wide CO_2 emissions with respect to levels of firms' climate mitigation activity for three regimes: pre–Clean Power Plan (CPP) (2011–2013), post-CPP (2014–2016),

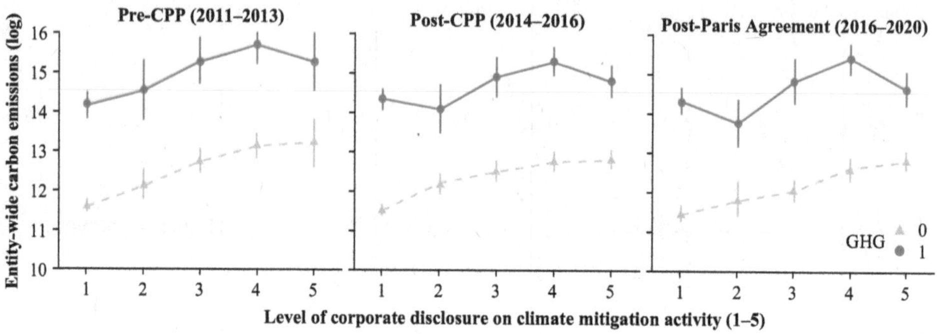

Figure 7.9

Entity-wide carbon emissions and levels of climate change activity (pre– and post–Clean Power Plan and post–Paris Agreement).

Note: Data show estimated entity-wide carbon emissions (in log form) based on the author's analysis of firms' voluntary carbon disclosure to CDP. The error bars represent 95 percent confidence intervals. CDP assigns a letter grade to firms that achieve a certain level of corporate disclosure on climate mitigation activity. The levels are represented by the numbers 1 through 5 on the x-axis: 1, non-participation: no disclosures or insufficient disclosures; 2, D grade (transparency): transparency in survey responses irrespective of contents; 3, C grade (awareness): formal assessment of business impacts on ecosystems and vice versa; 4, B grade (management): adoption of sustainability outputs based on results of formal assessments (e.g., environmental management systems, quantitative emissions targets); 5, A grade (leadership): adoption of more advanced sustainability outputs such as internal carbon price, third-party audits, and reporting of scope 3 emissions. GHG-intensive sectors are energy, industrials, materials, and utilities.
Data sources: CDP and LSEG Data and Analytics.

and post–Paris Agreement (2016–2020). Voluntary carbon disclosure (levels 2–5, or grades D, C, B, and A) appears to map into higher levels of CO_2 emissions than nonparticipation (level 1); this was certainly true before the CPP.

That being said, after the CPP, moving from nonparticipation in CDP to participation at the lowest level, or basic carbon transparency, was associated with a lower entity-wide carbon emission compared to the pre-CPP era for the GHG-intensive sectors, although the confidence bar is relatively large (see middle panel in figure 7.9). The third regime, or post–Paris Agreement era, does not look qualitatively different from the post-CPP regime with respect to S&P 500 firms' carbon footprints, for both carbon- and non-carbon-intensive sectors. After 2016, the writing was (increasingly) on the wall for what the future will look like for GHG-intensive companies with mounting scientific evidence about global warming and regulatory and stakeholder pressure toward decarbonization. There is evidence that A-list firms (*CDP—leadership* level), while high polluters, are associated with a sharper decline in entity-wide emissions than those that are focused on sustainability outputs (*CDP—management* level) without third-party audits.

There are a couple of explanations for the predicted heterogeneity between GHG-intensive and consumer-oriented firms. First, there were likely to be low-hanging fruits with respect to emission reductions for dirty firms relative to less dirty firms (particularly since scope 3 emissions are not part of this chapter's analysis). Second, GHG-intensive firms faced more regulatory pressure from expected climate regulations than non-GHG-intensive firms after the Clean Power Plan and in the post–Paris Agreement regime. These firms' participation in the CDP or any display of corporate social responsibility was likely to have been scrutinized by stakeholders, including institutional investors. As such, participation in voluntary carbon disclosure—even at the lowest level of climate mitigation activity—was associated with reduced entity-wide carbon emissions. There is evidence that (relatively more) carbon-efficient GHG-intensive firms have used their proactive transparency to signal corporate climate leadership.[35]

On the other hand, results suggest that consumer-oriented firms likely engaged in strategic behavior by appealing to key stakeholders in order to communicate their proactive corporate social responsibility irrespective of their actual carbon footprints. Conditional on participation, firms that have reportedly committed to the integration of carbon risk management in their business operations, among other relatively advanced climate mitigation activities, did not reduce their entity-wide carbon emissions.

7.4.3 Carbon Emissions Intensity

S&P 500 firms that proactively disclosed their emissions to CDP, on average, reduced their carbon emissions per capita of full-time employees; this is one measure of entity-wide CO_2 emissions intensity. Table 7.3 reports the regression results of the second-stage DDD in endogenous binary-variable (EBV) models for two separate measures of carbon emissions intensity for all S&P 500 firms.

This means that as a company increases in size, it is estimated to reduce its carbon footprint on a per-employee basis. In fact, emissions per full-time employee for S&P 500 firms filing carbon disclosures fell by an average of 16 percent from 2011 to 2020, as shown in figure 7.10.

Table 7.3
Carbon emissions intensity, stage 2 difference-in-difference-in-differences estimation nested in EBV models (S&P 500 index firms)

Carbon emissions intensity (log)	CO_2 emissions per dollar b/se[a]	CO_2 emissions per full-time employee b/se[a]
CDP—transparency	–0.190* (0.10)	–0.360*** (0.12)
CDP—awareness	0.02 (0.11)	–0.168 (0.13)
CDP—management	0.243** (0.12)	0.076 (0.14)
CDP—leadership	0.199 (0.15)	0.064 (0.19)

Note: *$p<0.1$, **$p<0.05$, ***$p<0.01$. All models include controls and sector, year, and state fixed effects (not shown). A full set of results are given in appendix 7.
[a] Robust standard errors with firm-level cluster correction.

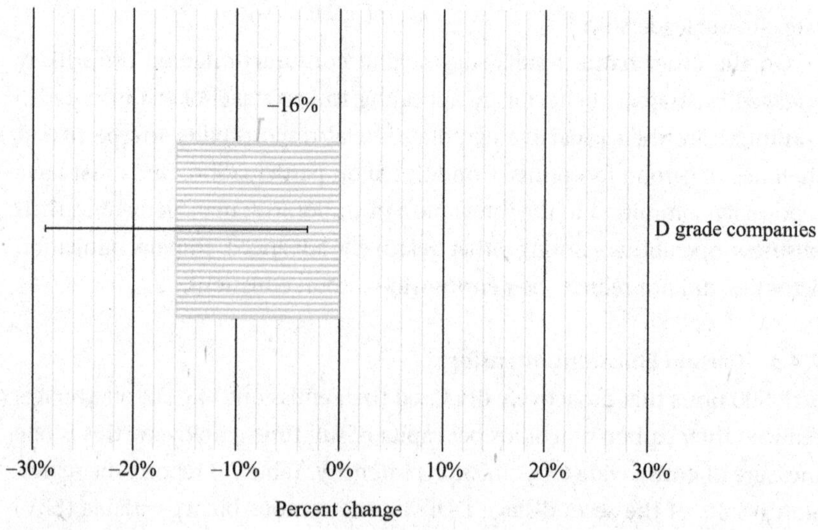

Figure 7.10
S&P 500 index firms' change in carbon emissions per full-time employee (2011–2020). *Note*: Data show estimated percent changes based on the author's analysis of corporate disclosures on emissions. Error bars show the 95 percent confidence intervals. *Data sources*: CDP and LSEG Data and Analytics.

Table 7.4
Carbon emissions intensity, stage 2 difference-in-difference-in-differences estimation nested in EBV models (GHG-intensive firms)

Carbon emissions intensity (log)	CO_2 emissions per dollar (b/se[a])	CO_2 emissions per full-time employee (b/se[a])
CDP—transparency	−0.669***	−0.982***
	(0.20)	(0.24)
CDP—awareness	−0.26	−0.645***
	(0.21)	(0.25)
CDP—management	−0.117	−0.537*
	(0.23)	(0.27)
CDP—leadership	−0.238	−0.595*
	(0.28)	(0.31)

Note: $^*p<0.1$, $^{***}p<0.01$. All models include controls and sector, year, and state fixed effects (not shown). A full set of results is shown in appendix 7.
[a] Robust standard errors with firm-level cluster correction.

This does not, however, necessarily translate to a reduction in a company's overall carbon emissions. Much of the decline involved large emissions-intensive companies, such as utilities, that were trying to get ahead of expected climate regulations.

7.4.4 Control Variables

Quasi-experimental and discrete-continuous modeling results on the control variables (see table A7.2) provide additional insights about the strategic behavior by GHG-intensive and non-GHG-intensive sectors. Across all three models, large firms were more likely to participate in voluntary carbon disclosure or to emit more carbon emissions than smaller firms, as expected. Furthermore, having a senior executive responsible for climate change's impact on business operations increased the probability of participation in the CDP, notably in GHG-intensive sectors (model 2), and this propensity remains positive in the face of regulatory pressure (although the magnitude wanes and is not statistically significant).

In the split sample of firms in the consumer-oriented sectors (model 3), the interaction term between *CPP* and *manager* is positive and statistically significant at the 10 percent level despite the fact that the CPP's performance standards targeted the power sector. As mentioned above, firms with climate-related managerial capacity that regularly interacted with consumers may have engaged in voluntary carbon disclosure strategically to appeal to them and other stakeholders, such as institutional investors, especially in the lead-up to and immediately after the 2015 Paris Agreement. This result also reveals a potential weakness of the Clean Power Plan measure (an indicator variable), which is that it is not able to fully distinguish the impact of the CPP from that of other concurrent events in the political economy, such as President Barack Obama's broader action plan to address the threat of climate change.[36]

Finally, it is worth pointing out that the DDD interaction term, *CPP×GHG-intensive×manager*, is not statistically significant in both the participation and outcome stages of model 1, although with the expected signs. This is in line with the fact that climate change managers play dual roles.[37] On one hand, these managers represent firm capacity and capability for climate mitigation, and it is their functional role to demonstrate that on behalf of their companies. On the other hand, these managers serve as an internal firm monitor to ensure that industry self-regulation is viewed by markets, including shareholders, as a positive signal of climate change readiness rather than greenwashing in the post-CPP world.

7.5 Conclusion

Do businesses that proactively disclose information about their carbon management and climate mitigation strategies emit less carbon emissions? Voluntary carbon disclosure is a crucial case of voluntary climate action that has become increasingly salient and policy-relevant as lawmakers in the United States (including California), United Kingdom (UK), European Union (EU), New Zealand, and Asian hubs such as Singapore and Hong Kong have either mandated or are in the process of mandating climate disclosures by publicly traded companies and, in some cases, by private firms. Unlike prior literature, this chapter exploits the interaction between regulatory pressure and the agency of corporate management to identify how heterogeneity in firms' disclosure about their substantive level of climate mitigation impacts their entity-wide carbon emissions and carbon emissions intensity. In doing so, this chapter distinguishes corporate climate leadership from greenwashing—namely, false or misleading advertising of corporate social responsibility.

The empirical setting of this chapter is the S&P 500 firms' participation and effort or intensity of participation in CDP, the oldest and largest non-profit organization in the world that houses voluntary carbon disclosure by corporations. The chapter uses CDP's grading of firms' information disclosure based on established criteria of transparency (D grade), awareness (C grade), management (B grade), and leadership (A grade) as proxies of firms' varying levels of "green" behavior in climate mitigation.

Empirical results based on quasi-experimental estimation embedded in discrete-continuous models show that companies that have proactively disclosed their emissions to CDP on average reduced their entity-wide carbon emissions intensity by one measure: carbon emissions per capita of full-time employees. This means that as a company increases in size, it is estimated to reduce its carbon footprint on a per-employee basis. This does not, however, necessarily translate to a reduction in a company's overall carbon emissions.[38] Much of the decline involved large emissions-intensive companies, such as utilities,[39] that were trying to get ahead of expected climate regulations.

The results identify a potential source of greenwashing by the S&P 500 firms. From 2011 to 2020, carbon disclosure by companies that received a B grade from CDP increased their entity-wide carbon emissions on average. Notably, those in the financial, health care, and other consumer-oriented sectors that did not experience the same level of regulatory pressure as GHG-intensive firms led the increase. More than a quarter of the S&P 500 firms that completed CDP's annual climate change questionnaire undertook assessments of their business impacts on the environment and integrated climate risk management into their business strategy. Yet entity-wide emissions still increased.

Even companies that made CDP's coveted A-list of climate leaders were not necessarily be free of greenwashing. A company earns an A grade when it has met criteria of disclosure, awareness, management, and leadership, including adopting global best practices, such as a quantitative emissions target, regardless of whether these practices translate into improved environmental performance.

Because CDP grades companies based on sustainability outputs rather than environmental performance, an A-list company could be carbon neutral when it counts only the facilities it owns and not the factories that make its products.[40] Moreover, a firm that has earned an A could commit to removing all emitted carbon but maintain partnerships with oil and gas companies to "generate new exploration opportunities."[41]

Retail and apparel giants Walmart, Target, and Nike—all in the B to A range in recent years—offer an example of the challenge. They regularly disclose their carbon management plans and emissions to CDP. However, they are also part of the industry-led Sustainable Apparel Coalition, which has controversially portrayed petroleum-based synthetics as the most sustainable choice above natural fibers in the Higgs Index,[42] a supply chain measurement tool that some clothing companies use to show a social and environmental footprint to consumers.[43] Walmart has been sued by the Federal Trade Commission over products described as bamboo and "eco-friendly and sustainable" that were made from rayon, a semisynthetic fiber made using toxic chemicals.[44]

By contrast, for firms that operate in GHG-intensive sectors (i.e., materials, utilities, energy, and industrials), participation at the basic level of disclosure (i.e., completion of CDP's climate change questionnaire, which does not require substantive climate mitigation) was associated with reductions in entity-wide carbon emissions and carbon emissions intensity. These relatively dirty firms had faced higher regulatory pressure, particularly after 2013 when the EPA introduced the Clean Power Plan. These firms' participation in CDP (and other forms of corporate social responsibility) were heavily scrutinized by diverse stakeholders, including institutional investors.[45] Moreover, it was likely that even small operational alterations to individual plants increased efficiencies; when aggregated to the entity-level, these efficiency savings represented relatively large emissions reductions. On the other hand, non-GHG-intensive firms, with a lower carbon footprint to begin with, were less scrutinized during 2011–2020 and likely engaged in strategic behavior by appealing to key stakeholders in order to communicate their green image and reputation irrespective of their actual carbon footprints.

The sources of greenwashing identified in this chapter are consistent with earlier studies that show that voluntary programs, including information disclosure programs, could be leveraged as a policy tool to encourage carbon transparency.[46] Without stringent obligations that are coupled with monitoring and penalties for nonadherence, firms will shirk their obligations, or their (non)action may have negligible effects on their environmental performance.[47] Proactive corporate climate actions taken by high-profile companies—notably, large retailers such as Walmart and Unilever as well as by technology companies such as Microsoft and Amazon in recent years—may not necessarily translate to reductions in entity-wide carbon emissions unless these same companies are willing to commit to more stringent forms of accountability and adherence, such as explicit commitments to reducing carbon emissions, with material penalties for nonadherence to stringent obligations.[48]

Making carbon disclosure mandatory—which is what California, the UK, the EU, and New Zealand have done in establishing a regulatory framework and announcing a timeline for implementation—is one way of inducing environmental performance by firms. Even so, ultimately, to ensure long-term decarbonization, there needs to be built-in incentives designed in these carbon disclosure programs to harmonize across disparate global markets and to encourage firms not only to report their climate risks and carbon emissions but also to benchmark their emission targets based on historical emissions, undergo independent audits, and report concrete changes.[49] Otherwise, firms become "greenhoused organizations": while disciplined in developing new management structures around sustainability and transforming organizational processes around data (see chapter 3), they engage in deflection, which prevents data collection from effecting more substantive impacts.[50]

In light of this chapter's findings, financial markets and institutions globally could be at the forefront of advocating for ranking systems like the one developed by CDP but refining what it means to be a "climate leader." This way, rewarding or penalizing of firms will be based on tangible environmental performance rather than mirages of corporate social responsibility in the "market for virtues."[51] Awarding climate performers-leaders means that capital will reach sustainable projects and ensure that the financial system itself addresses all relevant risks and builds resilience.

8 Consumer-Facing and Carbon-Intensive Sectors: A Race to the Top or Bottom?

Policy and governance scholars have posited that how firms engage with environmental politics varies across and within sectors and institutional contexts and over the course of the policy cycle.[1] Prior literature on firms' participation in voluntary environmental programs finds that the effect of sector heterogeneity or cross-sector variation has been mixed. There is some evidence that participation rates are higher in industries with greater consumer contact regardless of issue area (from toxics to climate change).[2] Studies focused on climate change have shown that firms operating in sectors that emit substantial amounts of greenhouse gas (GHG) emissions are more likely to engage in climate mitigation.[3] Sector-specific effects could also be important because of competitive pressures for seeking market dominance or first-mover advantage in technological disruptions among firms operating in the same sector.[4]

While the empirical results presented in the previous chapters (with the exception of chapter 7) were based on large-*N* panel data analyses that accounted for sector heterogeneity through standard econometric techniques (e.g., sector fixed effects), results predicted the "average" behavior of global firms across sectors.[5] By contrast, this chapter investigates how global businesses across sectors have responded to internal firm management and organizational structures, domestic regulation, and global governance in their voluntary climate action from 2011 to 2020. Which sectors are engaging in corporate self-regulation on climate change, and what are the main drivers of sectoral differences in corporate environmental behavior and performance?

To answer these questions, empirical results from the previous chapters about global businesses' participation and effort in voluntary carbon disclosure and adoption of global best practices (sustainability outputs) and carbon emissions (sustainability outcomes) are analyzed, with a focus on explaining the differences across consumer-oriented, technology, and greenhouse gas-intensive sectors.[6] Moreover, this chapter presents illustrative company cases in the consumer-oriented and technology sectors and a descriptive analysis of the Oil and Gas Climate Initiative (OGCI) to reinforce the results of this book's large-*N* statistical analyses, concerning how the various component parts—manager, corporate × regulation, corporate × global, and regulation × global—that make up the book's multilevel governance framework on climate change (MGFCC) have taken shape on the ground as salient drivers of corporate climate leaders' voluntary climate action (see chapter 2 for an exposition of the MGFCC).[7] As detailed later in this chapter, the OGCI was founded in 2014 by the chief executive officers of twelve of the largest energy companies that are responsible for more than 30 percent of global oil and gas production. The OGCI's stated mission is to reduce unabated carbon emissions through carbon capture, utilization and storage, and methane emissions reduction, among other initiatives.

8.1 Which Sectors Are Taking More Proactive Climate Action and Why?

In 2011, about half of the largest firms in the world (by revenue) installed a senior- or executive-level manager responsible for the firm's carbon management and climate risks, as shown in table 8.1. By the end of the decade, the share of multinational corporations with vice presidents or chief sustainability officers presiding over a firm's climate mitigation increased to 85 percent. Needless to say, chief sustainability officers and similar roles have become ubiquitous among Fortune Global 500 firms. In 2020, nearly 90 percent of firms in GHG-intensive sectors—namely, energy, industrials, materials, and utilities—which faced the most regulatory pressure and activist scrutiny, delegated senior management and executive-level leaders with direct responsibility for climate mitigation or climate change policy in their organizations. The managerial shift of climate-related duties to upper management by and large happened during the post–Paris Agreement period, or from 2016 to 2020, for global businesses.

At the start of the decade, firms across sectors with climate managerial capacity readily invested in carbon-management tools—such as quantitative emissions targets—with significantly higher propensity than firms without managers, and the proliferation of these sustainability outputs increased over

Table 8.1
Climate change managerial agency: Existence of senior- or executive-level managers, across sectors

Year or period	Global 500 (%)	Consumer-oriented[a] (%)	Technology[b] (%)	GHG-intensive (broad)[c] (%)
2011	54	52	55	57
2014	74	72	74	77
2017	82	80	83	85
2020	85	82	88	89
Before Paris Agreement (2011–2015)	68	65	69	71
After Paris Agreement (2016–2020)	83	81	84	86

[a] Consumer discretionary, consumer staples, financial services, and health care sectors.
[b] Information technology and telecommunications sectors.
[c] Energy, industrials, materials, and utilities sectors.
Data sources: CDP and corporate websites and annual reports.

time. By 2020, a higher share (over 90 percent) of global businesses in the technology, financials, health care, other consumer-oriented sectors had set targets for reducing their entity-wide carbon emissions or carbon emissions intensity than those operating in GHG-intensive sectors, despite emitting less than 10 percent of the combined entity-wide carbon emissions of the energy, industrials, materials, and utilities sectors.

8.1.2 Multilevel Governance Interactions and Voluntary Climate Action

When multilevel governance interactions are accounted for, firms' likelihood of adopting quantitative emissions targets rose both at the beginning and at the end of the 2011–2020 decade (see table 8.2). In both 2011 and 2020, the firms that had installed a senior- or executive-level manager originated from a country (or exported to a country) with high regulatory stringency and joined global governance institutions focused on corporate sustainability (namely, the United Nations Global Compact) were 10 percent more likely to have set emissions targets than firms that possess managerial capabilities alone. This result holds across consumer-oriented, technology, and GHG-intensive sectors.

Table 8.2

Quantitative emissions targets and multilevel governance interactions, across sectors

	Global 500 (%)	Consumer-oriented[b] (%)	Technology[c] (%)	GHG-intensive (broad)[d] (%)
Corporate adoption rates for quantitative emissions targets, 2011				
No manager	31	30	41	29
Manager	69	72	80	61
Regulation	61	62	70	54
Global	72	78	80	60
Manager × regulation	70	75	79	59
Manager × global	78	81	89	68
Regulation × global	81	84	87	75
Manager × regulation × global[a]	81	85	85	70
Corporate adoption rates for quantitative emissions targets, 2014				
No manager	14	13	23	12
Manager	68	70	77	61
Regulation	62	63	70	57
Global	74	81	78	63
Manager × regulation	71	75	76	64
Manager × global	81	84	89	72
Regulation × global	83	85	88	79
Manager × regulation × global	85	86	88	80
Corporate adoption rates for quantitative emissions targets, 2017				
No manager	24	19	29	29
Manager	84	87	90	78

Regulation	79	81	86	73
Global	90	97	88	83
Manager × regulation	86	90	89	78
Manager × global	94	100	93	87
Regulation × global	95	99	94	88
Manager × regulation × global	96	100	94	90
Corporate adoption rates for quantitative emissions targets, 2020				
No manager	41	37	42	52
Manager	90	93	92	86
Regulation	88	88	91	85
Global	95	99	98	89
Manager × regulation	92	95	94	87
Manager × global	97	100	97	91
Regulation × global	98	100	100	94
Manager × regulation × global	99	100	100	96

[a] Manager × regulation × global for a given year represents a firm that installed a dedicated senior- or executive-level manager responsible for climate mitigation, originating from a country that scored equal to or above the mean in regulatory stringency of all Global 500 firms, and is a member of the UN Global Compact.

[b] Consumer discretionary, consumer staples, financial services, and health care sectors.

[c] Information technology and telecommunications sectors.

[d] Energy, industrials, materials, and utilities sectors.

Data sources: CDP and corporate websites and annual reports.

In 2011, 85 percent of consumer-oriented and technology firms that possessed climate managerial capabilities, stringently regulated, and participated in global governance had established an emissions target. Only half of firms without these cross-level (manager × regulation × global) governance characteristics had set an emissions target (not shown in the table). By 2020, all Global 500 firms that operated in the consumer discretionary, consumer staples, health care, and information technology and telecommunication sectors had set and publicly declared quantitative targets for reducing GHG emissions. This is compared with an adoption rate of about 75 percent for consumer-oriented and technology firms that either did not delegate climate change responsibility to senior- or executive-level managers, face regulatory stringency, or engage in global governance. Over the decade, target-setting has become pervasive across sectors, and is a universal imperative for consumer-facing multinational companies that have hired senior- or executive-level managers responsible for climate change and joined the UN Global Compact. These latter consumer-facing firms, by and large, are domiciled in countries with relatively stringent regulation.

Notably, the 2015 Paris Agreement marked a significant regime shift across consumer-oriented, technology, and GHG-intensive sectors. This is to say, what was once an "opportunistic expansion strategy" in voluntary climate action morphed into a "strategic imperative"[8] in the five years following the Paris Agreement across most if not all sectors. In the months leading up to the 2015 Paris Agreement, more than two thousand companies across sectors—from Baosteel Group Corporation to ExxonMobil Corporation to Taiwan Semiconductor Manufacturing Company Limited to Walmart, Inc.—pledged to reduce carbon emissions, increase energy use efficiencies, and invest in renewable energy sources. By 2023, more than 15,500 companies of all sizes had pledged to engage in climate action, such as setting a climate action commitment, participating in cooperative initiatives, adopting climate action plans, and undertaking specific mitigation, adaptation, or finance actions.[9]

As table 8.2 shows, corporate adoption rates for emissions targets in 2014, a year before the Paris Agreement, mirrored those of 2011 in all but one measure. GHG-intensive firms in materials, industrials, energy, and utilities sectors that installed a dedicated climate change manager, faced regulatory pressure, and participated in global governance engaged in voluntary climate action at a higher rate, increasing from 70 to 80 percent from 2011 to 2014, compared to a rise from 85 to 88 percent for the technology sector.

The GHG-intensive sector's shift toward a climate future started before the Paris Agreement, driven by sectoral developments and regional- and country-level developments: Germany's green industry initiatives, which began in 2000 with Germany's Renewable Energy Sources Act, and the EU's Emissions Trading System, which was launched in 2005. In the United States, President Barack Obama's executive actions on climate change and the Environmental Protection Agency's intended implementation of the Clean Power Plan (while falling short of Europe's precautionary principal-driven climate policy and governance) also showed how the interplay of corporate, regulatory, and global governance spurred corporate self-regulation on climate change.[10]

The 2015 Paris Agreement represented a major global climate change regime shift away from the one set in motion with the 1997 Kyoto Protocol, which was primarily a top-down rather than a bottom-up regime.[11] Public attitudes and sentiment in the United States and beyond experienced a shift as well. Figure 8.1 shows the rise in volume of media coverage in the United States before and after the twenty-first session of the Conference of the Parties (COP 21), or the Paris Agreement.[12] The public's attention increasingly focused on climate change, with spikes in media attention linked to the annual global United Nations Climate Change Conference events aimed at bolstering international cooperation. As table 8.1 indicates, global firms' voluntary climate action as a whole and across sectors correlated with this shift in global climate change regime.

Figure 8.2 shows the rise of and peak in media attention on "climate change" whenever an annual Conference of the Parties (COP) was underway, starting in 2011 at COP 17, or the seventeenth session of the Conference of the Parties to the United Nations Framework Convention on Climate Change (UNFCCC), which was held in Durban, South Africa. US news stories discussing "climate change" were by far the greatest for COP 21, followed by the twenty-sixth session of the Conference of the Parties to the UNFCCC, or COP 26, in Glasgow, UK.

Strikingly, while global businesses' adoption of carbon management tools increased substantially in 2016–2020 (post–Paris Agreement) compared to 2011–2015 (pre–Paris Agreement), their voluntary carbon disclosure declined. This retrenchment in voluntary carbon disclosure was sharper for GHG-intensive firms, which faced more regulatory pressure than consumer-oriented and technology companies.

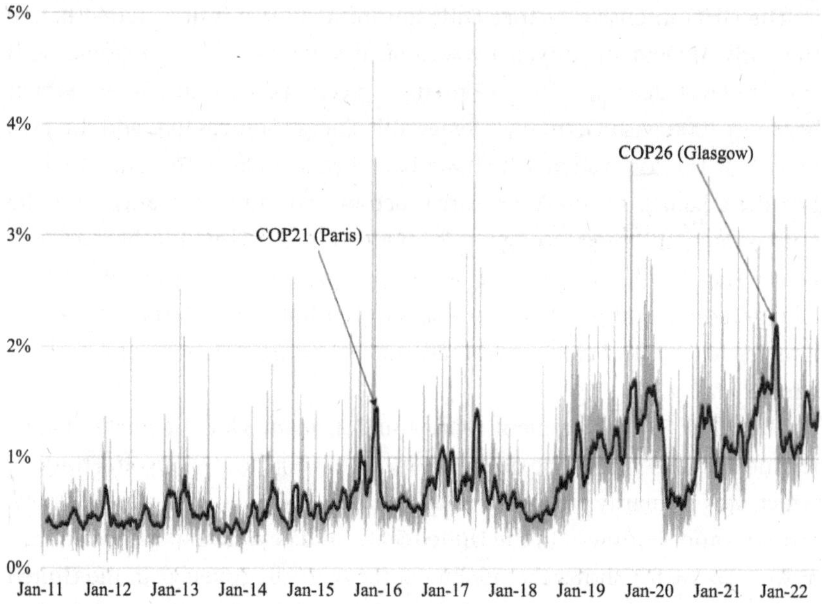

Figure 8.1
Monthly average percentage of US media stories that mentioned "climate change" (2011–2022).
Note: The gray lines represent the daily values, whereas the blue line is a monthly smoothed average. Certain events, like COP 21 and COP 26, as well as President Trump's announced withdrawal from the Paris Agreement (July 2017), represent significant spikes in coverage.
Source: Media Sound; this figure is published as figure 1 in a commentary by David G. Victor and Parker Bolstad for the Brookings Institution, February 10, 2023, https://www.brookings.edu/articles/good-news-about-global-warming-the-publics-paying-attention.

This phenomenon is unsurprising because, according to the extant literature, it is better not to disclose if and when there is no "good news" to share. In anticipation of tightening of domestic climate policymaking across the globe, firms pulled back voluntary carbon disclosure to reassess and bolster their internal carbon management (as evidenced by the increase in the adoption of quantitative emissions targets, for example). While overall, global firms' participation in the CDP (formerly the Carbon Disclosure Project) fell, for the firms that did proactively disclose their carbon management plans and emissions, their intensity of participation increased, as large-*N* econometric results from the previous chapters reveal.

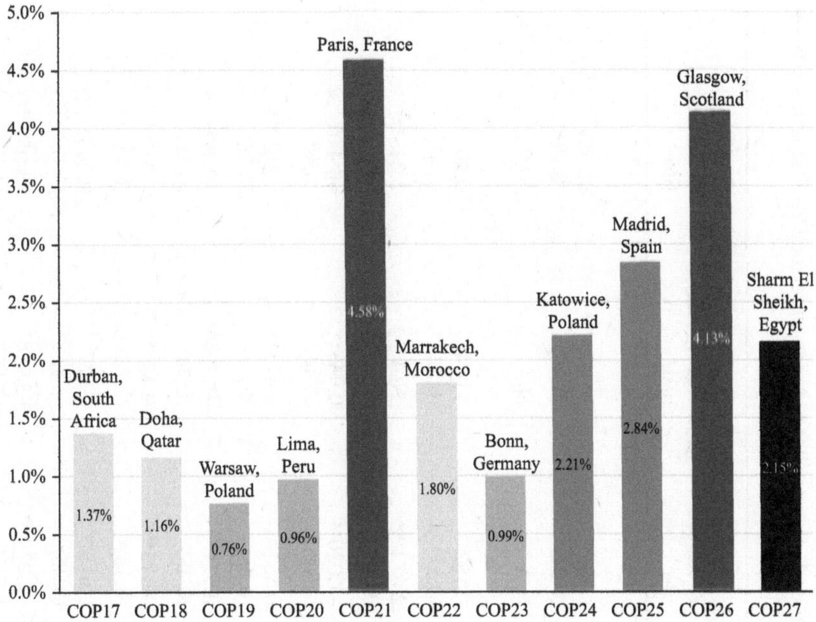

Figure 8.2
Peak percentage of all US news stories discussing "climate change" for each COP.
Note: The peak percentage represents maximum daily coverage for each Conference of the Parties (COP) to the United Nations Framework Convention on Climate Change. The bars are color-coded in a gradient such that the darker bars correspond to higher values and the lighter bars correspond to lower values. COP 27 appears in the darkest color to indicate that it is the most recent COP as of July 2023.
Source: Media Sound; this figure is published as figure 2 in a commentary by David G. Victor and Parker Bolstad for the Brookings Institution, https://www.brookings.edu/articles/good-news-about-global-warming-the-publics-paying-attention.

8.1.3 Participation and Intensity of Participation in Voluntary Carbon Disclosure

Tables 8.3 and 8.4 report the results of sector-specific endogenous binary-variable (EBV) regressions based on the quasi-experiments presented in chapter 5.[13]

Consumer-oriented sectors make up the first few columns of table 8.3—namely, consumer discretionary, consumer staples, financials, and health care. Results for the technology sector follow. Table 8.4 reports results for energy, industrials, materials, and utilities, or GHG-intensive sectors.

Table 8.3

Quasi-experimental approach to participation and effort in voluntary carbon disclosure, difference-in-difference-in-differences estimations in EBV models (consumer-oriented and technology sectors)

	Consumer discretionary b/se[a]	Consumer staples b/se[a]	Financials b/se[a]	Health care b/se[a]	Technology b/se[a]
Participation in voluntary carbon disclosure[b]					
USA	–0.093 (0.42)	0.125 (0.42)	0.442 (0.31)	–1.177*** (0.44)	0.739 (0.49)
Clean Power Plan (CPP)	N/A	N/A	N/A	N/A	N/A
USA × CPP	0.593 (0.52)	N/A	0.182 (0.31)	1.011* (0.52)	0.601 (0.41)
Manager	1.511*** (0.42)	N/A	2.572*** (0.39)	N/A	2.245*** (0.41)
USA × manager	–0.110 (0.61)	N/A	–1.030** (0.51)	0.943** (0.44)	–0.446 (0.57)
CPP × manager	0.299 (0.39)	3.040*** (0.59)	0.551 (0.36)	1.871*** (0.62)	0.681*** (0.23)
USA × CPP × Manager	–0.230 (0.78)	0.078 (0.66)	0.171 (0.45)	–1.796** (0.74)	–0.908 (0.55)
Revenues (log)	0.553*** (0.18)	0.657*** (0.21)	0.345*** (0.13)	0.457** (0.21)	0.232** (0.11)
Natural gas price (log)	0.097 (0.31)	–0.335 (0.33)	0.615** (0.26)	0.577* (0.33)	0.263* (0.15)
Constant	–5.681*** (1.64)	–5.353** (2.11)	–4.299*** (1.31)	–3.988* (2.15)	–3.059*** (1.09)

Level of voluntary carbon disclosure[b]					
USA	–0.237 (4.29)	–2.909 (2.82)	–4.436 (2.98)	–5.536 (4.01)	3.930 (4.88)
CPP	3.846 (3.29)	–5.026 (4.15)	–1.896 (2.55)	1.735 (5.75)	–0.839 (2.61)
USA × CPP	N/A	N/A	N/A	N/A	N/A
Manager	–0.753 (6.27)	N/A	5.311 (3.57)	N/A	11.523* (6.02)
USA × manager	–2.818 (5.56)	N/A	8.290** (3.85)	5.445 (4.20)	–6.002 (5.25)
CPP × manager	5.470 (4.28)	11.273*** (4.23)	9.679*** (2.05)	12.930** (6.25)	9.352*** (2.56)
USA × CPP × manager	0.669 (6.64)	–2.201 (2.46)	–6.659 (4.49)	–3.767 (7.35)	–4.193 (5.21)
Revenues (log)	3.394*** (1.05)	1.927 (1.33)	0.866 (0.92)	0.483 (1.31)	1.929** (0.78)
Natural gas price (log)	–3.893* (2.24)	–10.144*** (2.11)	–5.119*** (1.66)	–3.651 (3.25)	–8.220*** (1.61)
Target	18.077*** (5.47)	12.866*** (4.39)	15.350*** (3.44)	20.458*** (5.38)	16.042*** (3.41)
Participation last year	59.467*** (5.65)	64.947*** (4.99)	57.980*** (4.03)	52.091*** (7.85)	56.115*** (7.45)
Constant	–32.143*** (10.00)	–7.853 (11.68)	–3.147 (8.40)	1.992 (11.81)	–15.209* (7.79)

(continued)

Table 8.3 (*continued*)

	Consumer discretionary b/se[a]	Consumer staples b/se[a]	Financials b/se[a]	Health care b/se[a]	Technology b/se[a]
Athrho	0.195**	0.214	0.282***	0.358**	0.146*
Constant	(0.10)	(0.13)	(0.05)	(0.17)	(0.08)
Lnsigma	2.619***	2.418***	2.634***	2.597***	2.561***
Constant	(0.10)	(0.07)	(0.09)	(0.11)	(0.07)
Year fixed effects	Yes	Yes	Yes	Yes	Yes
Chi-square	4,070.193***	2,480.427***	5,253.527***	1,511.878***	4,818.727***
N	392	276	725	257	473

Note: *$p<0.1$, **$p<0.05$, ***$p<0.01$. *Clean Power Plan (CPP)* is excluded from the model because it is collinear with the year fixed effects; N/A or "not applicable" denotes this fact.

[a] Robust standard errors with firm-level cluster correction.

[b] Variables are dropped to ensure variance matrix is symmetric, denoted by N/A.

Table 8.4
Quasi-experimental approach to participation and effort in voluntary carbon disclosure, difference-in-difference-in-differences estimations in EBV models (GHG-intensive sectors)

	Energy b/se[a]	Industrials b/se[a]	Materials b/se[a]	Utilities b/se[a]
Participation in voluntary carbon disclosure[b]				
USA	−0.390 (0.31)	−0.331 (0.54)	6.426*** (0.33)	−0.094 (0.43)
Clean Power Plan (CPP)	N/A	N/A	N/A	N/A
USA × CPP	N/A	0.767 (0.49)	−0.643** (0.31)	N/A
Manager	N/A	2.080*** (0.48)	N/A	N/A
USA × manager	N/A	−0.093 (0.72)	N/A	N/A
CPP × manager	2.575*** (0.45)	0.250 (0.31)	2.894*** (0.55)	2.128*** (0.47)
USA × CPP × manager	−0.229 (0.38)	−0.829 (0.51)	N/A	−0.170 (0.57)
Revenues (log)	0.058 (0.10)	0.302 (0.20)	0.205 (0.15)	0.414** (0.19)
Natural gas price (log)	0.815*** (0.26)	0.545 (0.40)	0.035 (0.28)	0.433*** (0.16)
Constant	−1.099 (0.99)	−3.537* (2.06)	−1.554 (1.42)	−3.988** (1.94)
Level of voluntary carbon disclosure[b]				
USA	4.207* (2.46)	−5.661 (6.92)	4.297 (3.98)	−3.160 (3.24)
Clean Power Plan (CPP)	−4.820 (4.70)	−1.311 (4.83)	−7.537** (3.59)	5.778*** (2.06)
USA × CPP	N/A	N/A	N/A	N/A
Manager	N/A	−1.886 (5.03)	N/A	N/A
USA × manager	N/A	7.655 (8.29)	N/A	N/A
CPP × manager	18.570*** (3.53)	11.752*** (4.48)	13.244*** (3.43)	7.847*** (2.26)
USA × CPP × manager	−7.446** (3.44)	−4.435 (6.62)	0.000 (0.00)	−2.582 (3.87)
Revenues (log)	0.817 (0.96)	2.053 (1.80)	2.133** (1.05)	0.898 (1.16)

(*continued*)

Table 8.4 (*continued*)

	Energy b/se[a]	Industrials b/se[a]	Materials b/se[a]	Utilities b/se[a]
Natural gas price (log)	−7.121**	−7.886***	−10.513***	−0.639
	(3.05)	(2.47)	(2.62)	(1.40)
Target	12.542***	15.049**	6.631**	4.014
	(3.21)	(6.61)	(2.90)	(2.75)
Participation last year	60.673***	62.486***	69.504***	84.747***
	(5.43)	(6.43)	(4.61)	(2.83)
Constant	−4.028	−13.859	−6.545	−14.871
	(10.27)	(17.84)	(10.27)	(12.50)
Athrho	0.231	0.180*	0.331*	0.003
Constant	(0.16)	(0.10)	(0.20)	(0.06)
Lnsigma	2.629***	2.739***	2.508***	2.243***
Constant	(0.08)	(0.09)	(0.10)	(0.10)
Year fixed effects	Yes	Yes	Yes	Yes
Chi-square	847.131***	1,947.857***	2,692.558***	5,981.223***
N	311	316	282	177

Note: *$p<0.1$, **$p<0.05$, ***$p<0.01$. *Clean Power Plan (CPP)* is excluded from the model because it is collinear with the year fixed effects; N/A or "not applicable" denotes this fact.

[a] Robust standard errors with firm-level cluster correction.

[b] Variables are dropped to ensure that variance matrix is symmetric, denoted by N/A.

Chapter 5 presented a rationale (and statistical test) for how the US Environmental Protection Agency's introduction of the Clean Power Plan (CPP), as part of the Clean Air Act, served as a natural experiment or an exogenous shock whereby US firms moved from a less stringent environment to an expectation of a more stringent regulatory environment. Following more than a decade of failed legislative action, the CPP was viewed by global firms as a credible regulatory threat with consequential adjustment costs, leading firms in the GHG-intensive sector to hedge against impending regulation in the mid-2010s, even before the CPP became enshrined in law (which it never did).

Regression results in tables 8.3 and 8.4 show that there is sector heterogeneity with respect to the effects of regulatory pressure (by the way of the CPP) on US firms. What is consistent across sectors, with the exception of the consumer discretionary sector is the positive and statistically significant response to regulatory pressure by companies that have installed a dedicated manager responsible for climate mitigation with respect to their intensity of participation in voluntary carbon disclosure. Once a global firm had committed to reporting to the CDP, the presence of senior- or executive-level managers combined with regulatory pressure was associated with higher, as opposed to lower, levels of climate disclosure. Of note, both US and non-US firms with dedicated managers operating in GHG-intensive sectors were about 20 to 50 percent more likely to participate in voluntary carbon disclosure and disclosed at higher levels (8–18 points) in the post-CPP period than firms without managerial leadership capacity to address climate risks in these sectors.

In the following sections, illustrative company cases illuminate the ways in which corporate, regulatory, and global governance and their interactions (with managers leading the way) have propelled voluntary climate action in the consumer-oriented, technology, and oil and gas sectors, in spite of sector-specific challenges. Semistructured interviews with senior- and executive-level managers dedicated to carbon management and climate risks at global businesses are supplemented by primary and secondary data sources, such as annual corporate sustainability and corporate social responsibility reports and company websites.

8.2 Retail, Apparel, and Assertive Climate Action: Therein Lies the Challenge

Global retail and apparel brands, such as Walmart, Tesco, Target, Abercrombie & Fitch, H&M, and Nike, regularly disclosed their carbon management plans and emissions to CDP in the last decade (2011–2020). All have received a grade of B to A- from CDP. However, these global firms are members of the industry-led Sustainable Apparel Coalition, which has controversially portrayed petroleum-based synthetics as the most sustainable choice, above natural fibers in the Higgs Index,[14] a supply chain measurement tool that some clothing companies use to demonstrate their social and environmental footprint to consumers.[15]

The US Federal Trade Commission (FTC) sued Walmart, along with Kohl's, over products described as bamboo and "eco-friendly and sustainable"[16] that were made from rayon, a semisynthetic fiber made using toxic chemicals.[17] The FTC argued that these firms allegedly engaged in greenwashing in violation of the Federal Trade Commission Act and the Textile Products Identification Act, which regulate deceptive trade practices and prohibit misbranding and false advertising, respectively, in the United States.[18]

Despite the fact that there is much media attention on corporate greenwashing in the consumer-oriented sector—which has faced less regulatory pressure than carbon-intensive sectors—two illustrative company cases (Moody's Corporation and Adidas AG) instantiate how multilevel governance interactions or the interplay of firm, regulatory, and global governance have propelled corporate climate action that goes beyond the legal requirements in the consumer-oriented sector.

Impressive sustainability outputs notwithstanding, Moody's and Adidas, along with the vast majority of consumer-oriented firms, do not have direct control over the carbon emissions of their supply chains (i.e., scope 3 emissions or indirect emissions), including, for example, the manufacturing and transport of the merchandises that they sell (see table 8.5). Scope 3 emissions make up over 90 percent of these firms' carbon footprints. Scope 1 emissions are the direct emissions from a firm's chimneys and tailpipes. Scope 2 emissions are associated with the power that a company consumes.

8.2.1 Moody's: A Climate Financial Solutions Provider

Founded in 1909, Moody's Corporation, often referred to as Moody's, is the holding company for Moody's Investors (MIS), a United States-based credit rating agency, and Moody's Analytics (MA), an American provider of financial analysis software and services. While Moody's has not been considered a "first mover" among global firms like Unilever (which has been the subject of numerous case studies as a corporate exemplar), the global financial services company actively participates in the UN Global Compact as a leader in climate finance, due in no small part to influential managers who convinced upper management that climate action has become a business imperative.

Managerial and Organizational Capabilities Policy supporters among senior managers and at the executive level have advocated for the integration of climate change risk assessment and ESG more broadly, as an integral part of Moody's products and business solutions. Under the leadership of Mark Kaye, Moody's former chief financial officer (CFO), Moody's has viewed its primary role as an "impartial arbiter reporting a new reality"

Table 8.5
Share of scope 1, 2, and 3 emissions in company cases, across sectors

Company	Scope 1 emissions (%)	Scope 2 emissions (%)	Scope 3 emissions (%)
Consumer-oriented sector			
Moody' Corporation	0.1	0.5	99.5
Adidas AG	6.0	5.8	93.7
Technology sector			
Microsoft Corporation	0.7	33.4	65.9
Intel Corporation	8.2	22.7	69.1
GHG-intensive sector			
Oil and Gas Climate Initiative[a]			
Saudi Aramco	N/A	N/A	N/A
BP PLC	11.2	1.0	87.8
Chevron Corporation	N/A	N/A	N/A
China National Petroleum Corporation	N/A	N/A	N/A
Eni SPA	18.0	0.4	81.7
Equinor (formerly Statoil and StatoilHydro)	4.0	0.9	95.1
ExxonMobil Corporation	N/A	N/A	N/A
Occidental Petroleum Corporation	7.4	2.1	90.6
Petróleo Brasileiro SA	9.7	0.1	90.3
Repsol SA	17.1	0.4	82.5
Shell PLC	4.0	0.6	95.3
TotalEnergies (formerly Total SE)	9.1	0.7	90.2

Note: N/A denotes the lack of available data for these companies.

[a] Oil and Gas Climate Initiative (OGCI) members are Saudi Aramco, BP, Chevron, China National Petroleum Corporation, Eni, Equinor (formerly Statoil and Statoil-Hydro), ExxonMobil, Occidental, Petrobras, Repsol, Shell, and TotalEnergies. OGCI has pledged to reduce the group's collective average methane intensity of upstream gas and operations to below 0.25 percent by 2025.

Data source: "Actor Tracking," Global Climate Action, https://climateaction.unfccc.int/Actors.

through its climate risk scores, sustainable bond and loan reviews, and environmental, social, and governance (ESG) specialty indices, and as a provider of climate risk assessment tools and solutions to help its clients navigate a "new world." This new world is one in which the financial returns on fossil fuel technologies and reserves are increasingly unfavorable; there are existing or emerging mission regulations as well as rapidly shifting stakeholder expectations. Moody's acquisitions of big data analytics and related strategic businesses have allowed the company to harvest and quantify diverse sources of climate risks because "stakeholders have become even more important, amplified by social media, in a nonlinear way."[19]

Leadership champions notwithstanding, according to Johannes Wassenberg, former head of operations, ESG, and managing director in Moody's London office, climate change is not the first time Moody has pivoted in response to and in the direction of global trends. The experience and expertise—i.e., complementary assets (see chapter 3 for an explication)—gained from the Enron accounting scandal facilitated Moody's climate readiness. "When the Enron case happened, corporate governance [became] an important focus. Moody hired corporate governance specialists and accounting specialists. A major challenge then though was the governance data to relate and correlate with financial performance. COP21/Paris sharpened focus/picked up speed in ESG business—initially in environmental and climate change but now equal focus on social and governance sides," commented Wassenberg.[20]

Notably, Moody's leaders viewed ESG as an "opportunistic expansion strategy," which by 2019 morphed into a "strategic imperative," with the acquisitions of Vigeo Eiris and Four-Twenty-Seven.[21] Both were ESG start-ups, based in Paris and the San Francisco Bay Area, respectively, that offered specialized research and decision-making tools employing big data analytics in ESG risk assessment. By 2020, there was a recognition that all products and business lines need ESG-enabled capabilities, with some being more climate-focused and others being more social-focused: "That year, it became a strategic topic in board discussions, and [even] more clearly in 2021, into a recognition that all of our products (analytics, risk management, and solutions) need to be ESG-enabled. We need to have probability of defaults that include climate dimensions, climate scenarios, [and] expressed in financial tools. So that we can provide tools to central banks, banks, and asset managers [everywhere] to [better] manage capital."[22]

Corporate × Regulation In 2012, MIS downgraded Alpha Natural Resources, Inc., an American mining company, across a suite of Moody's ratings on debt securities, including the probability of a default rating. According to Moody's, the downgrade reflected the company's exposure to Central Appalachian coal, citing "increasing costs due to difficult geology and regulatory pressures . . . weak domestic demand for steam coal [because of] ongoing coal to gas substitution . . . and environmental regulations that disadvantage coal," among other market factors, such as a deterioration of prices that could impact output and cost.[23] Moody's business action on Alpha Natural Resources, Inc. represented the beginning of a shift and an indication of changes to come at Moody's with respect to the company's integration of climate risks in its rating system as a systemic investment risk to not only extractive companies but other businesses and governments more generally.

Corporate × Global Moody's focus on product development and global leadership has safeguarded the company and its private and public sector clients from the risks of regulatory burden that are associated with climate change. The Paris Agreement "highlighted the momentum and sharpened the focus" that "it not only made business sense, it is a business necessity,"[24] according to Wassenberg. In 2015 and 2016, Moody's "sharpened its focus" on climate financing, notably in the company's ESG analytics and benchmarking business, in parallel to and as part of this global firm's response to the Paris Agreement. Influential senior managers inside Moody's, including head of ESG rating Brian Cahill and head of MIS assessment Myriam Durrand, led the way "to convince upper management [that] these are trends we should focus on . . . whether it's ESG or other trends, it takes people to build their case, that this should be reflected in asset classes, not just in one rating or one sector but across different sectors."[25]

Under Moody's former CFO Mark Kaye's leadership, the company joined the UN Global Compact in 2019 for the first time. Kaye regarded the global governance institution as an "impartial institution" and "neutral movement" where Moody's is recognized as "a subject matter expert." Moody's was a founding member of the Global Compact's CFO Taskforce, which ran from 2019 to 2021. In the company's participation in supranational initiatives like the UNGC, Moody's has emphasized its advisory role to CFOs and chief risk officers. According to Wassenberg, Moody's role is to help its clients quantify ESG opportunities and risks in the "transition of the internalization of external costs [of climate change]."[26] The MIS's vice chairperson currently serves as a member of the TCFD Taskforce, along with leaders from S&P Global Ratings, Deloitte, PwC, and other global financial services firms.

8.2.2 Adidas: A Green Company and "Own the Game" with Sustainable Materials

Germany-based Adidas AG is a leading sportswear firm globally, with 2,500 retail stores in 160 countries. With a global workforce of about 62,000 employees, Adidas designs, distributes, and markets athletic and sports lifestyle products worldwide under the Adidas brand.[27] In 2017 and again in 2020, Adidas was ranked among the world's top 100 companies for "clean capitalism" and corporate sustainability by Corporate Knights, a Toronto-based media and research company that consults with and advises firms, governments, and other organizations on clean energy transition.[28] Aside from the company's recent participation in global initiatives, Adidas has actively positioned itself for more than two decades as a leader among its industry peers,[29] through Green Company, a companywide "explicit" corporate social responsibility (CSR) initiative (see chapter 3 for an explication of explicit CSR).

Until 2020, Green Company published an annual sustainability report distinct from Adidas's annual financial report. In 2010, Green Company tracked the environmental impact of 67 in-house locations out of 300 offices, manufacturing sites, and distribution centers worldwide. Some of them are owned by Adidas, and some are leased or rented. A decade later, more than 120 in-house locations are part of Green Company's tracking and reporting scope.

Managerial and Organizational Capabilities At its origin, Green Company and its predecessor (Green Teams) were sponsored by the Adidas chief executive office and existed organizationally under Global Operations, with regular reports to the Adidas Sustainability Sponsor Board, which ensures cross-functional alignment (namely, global brands, global operations, digital, sales, and other functions) and monitoring of the company's sustainability strategy (from water- to climate change–related topics). According to a Green Company director, Adidas's vision is for the deployment of interdisciplinary teams made up of sustainability-minded managers, operators, and analysts, from junior to senior positions, that are embedded across every level of the company.[30] Currently, with Green Company's expanded scope, Workforce

& Governance continues to report to the Sustainability Sponsor Board but is organizationally part of Global Human Resources, People, and Culture.

Established in the early to mid-2000s, Adidas's Green Company tracked, measured, and reported the company's internal environmental impact across Adidas's corporate offices, distribution centers, and showrooms longer than most of its industry peers. Based at the global apparel and footwear company's headquarters in Germany, Green Company—and its current expanded scope, which includes all aspect of workplace governance—served as Adidas's vehicle for driving its corporate headquarters' climate change strategy and other sustainability initiatives across its global operations, beyond what is required by the EU or other jurisdictions.[31]

"We [at Green Company] pushed the envelope on local [country-level] practices and went beyond regulatory compliance, because [we have been] driven by headquarters' values and objectives and global sustainability trends. The main message is that: we started this [over] 15 years ago . . . in Green Company, we are a pioneer, while a lot of companies are [just] now coming to this strategy" according to a senior director at Green Company.[32]

In its first decade or so (2005–2015), Green Company's focus was energy efficiency and paper and water recycling at Adidas's sites. By 2015, Adidas developed the "second phase of our Green Company programme": the emphasis became standardization, tracking, and reporting on a long list of environmental outputs, outcomes, and quantitative emissions targets, such as the certifications of corporate environmental, energy, occupational health and safety management standards, total generated waste, total printing paper consumption, total water consumption, and scope 1 and scope 2 carbon emissions, among other metrics.[33] In 2015, the United Nations recognized Adidas as a leader in "Measure, Reduce, Contribute" and reporting on its action and invited Adidas to join the Climate Neutral Now initiative.[34]

Aside from tracking and reporting internal energy use and carbon footprint information, Green Company encouraged environmental sustainability at local sites and showrooms worldwide by providing employee incentives. Green Company created Green Teams, with a goal of erecting a Green Team at every location with more than fifty employees. Each Green Team is made up of a team manager and team captain, along with Green Team members, all of whom are employee-volunteers. Incentivized by an allocated budget or "green funds," Green Team members serve as local champions of environmental sustainability and organize and participate in two to three green projects a year, such as Earth Hour, Earth Day, World Cleanup Day, and Adidas×Parley Run for the Oceans.[35] "It's a positive message, to engage people . . . they are mostly millennials, they love it."[36] By 2020, Adidas' green funds had subsidized projects to replace the use of fossil fuels with renewable energy and monitor ongoing performance in real time.

Corporate×Regulation From 2010 to 2020, Adidas's scope 1 and scope 2 emissions intensity (total CO_2 emissions/millions in revenue dollars) fell 12 percent in annualized percent change, ranking the company consistently among the top five firms in its peer industry group of global textiles and apparel businesses.[37] That being said, in light of the growing scrutiny over scope 3 emissions in Germany, Adidas's domicile country, and the EU, Adidas is increasingly pressured to track and report scope 3 emissions. Starting in 2025, Adidas and other stock exchange–listed companies with more than 500 employees in the EU will have to submit detailed reports of their carbon emissions. Scope 3, or emissions outside Adidas's direct operations, made up 97.9 percent of Adidas's total carbon footprint in 2022.[38]

A senior director at Green Company emphasized that Adidas is once again aspiring to and getting ahead of future regulatory targets. As an example, preemptively, Adidas' Green Company reporting is no longer separate from Adidas' reporting on products and brands but, rather, has been integrated in its annual financial reporting starting in 2021. This integration of sustainability and profits coincided with Adidas' launch of its "Own the Game" strategy focused on brand creditability, unique consumer experience, and sustainable materials procured from the company's vast supply chain. Adidas's slogan is "For the places we play . . . without a beautiful planet, there is no beautiful game."[39]

Corporate×Global Unlike Moody's, Adidas is not a member of the UN Global Compact. However, the apparel and footwear company is a signatory of the Fashion Industry Charter for Climate Action (FCCA), which is a UN-sponsored industry initiative that was launched at the twenty-fourth session of the Conference of Parties (COP 24) to the United Nations Framework Convention on Climate Change in Katowice, Poland, in December 2018. As an active participant of FCCA, Adidas has set ambitious science-based, quantitative targets to reduce absolute scope 1, 2, and 3 emissions by 30 percent by 2030 and achieve net-zero carbon emissions by 2050. In addition to the FCCA, Adidas is a founding member of or participant in twenty global governance collaborations and accords on human rights, sustainable textiles, responsible sourcing, and other issue areas. In the climate change area, Adidas is a signatory of Race to Zero, Science Based Targets Initiative (SBTi), and Climate Ambition Alliance.

Regulation × Global With sites located globally, from Western Europe to emerging markets to North America Latin America, and Asia, Green Company has aligned sustainability initiatives across its own sites in order to ensure "credible and seamless data collection" on key environmental and energy metrics, while also adapting to local infrastructures and regulations.[40]

According to a Green Company director, "My recommendation is that a site [develops] a 5-year plan, you try to do as much as you can, even if there is no local regulation to support it. [We connect and work] with the General Manager of the country or regional office. First, we explain our [Adidas's] sustainability commitment. We are a German company [in the European system], we want to do this. Second, we check the local regulations and the market. It's super easy in Tokyo but not in Istanbul or Colombia. We try to standardize as much as we can even though we allow sites to adapt to local regulations and look for other options/other solutions."[41]

Green Company came up with a "creative solution in Adidas' Chinese sites" where plastic use is prevalent: Adidas has partnered with Starbucks to give employees a discount on purchases at Starbucks if they bring their own cups to the Seattle-based coffeeshop. In Colombia, where the government's recycling program and waste-tracking systems were nascent,[42] Adidas's headquarters in Germany supported the additional cost of private recycling services to ensure that recycling was properly collected and processed at Adidas sites in Colombia, because "we are checking. We do audits. We check the [local] regulations, and if we can't do this, we ask what are the options."[43]

8.3 Technology Firms Lead on Proactive Climate Action

On the eve of the Paris Agreement, global firms operating in the technology sector were two times more likely than other multinational corporations to engage in proactive climate action.[44] Among the notable technology companies worldwide that engaged in voluntary climate action—including

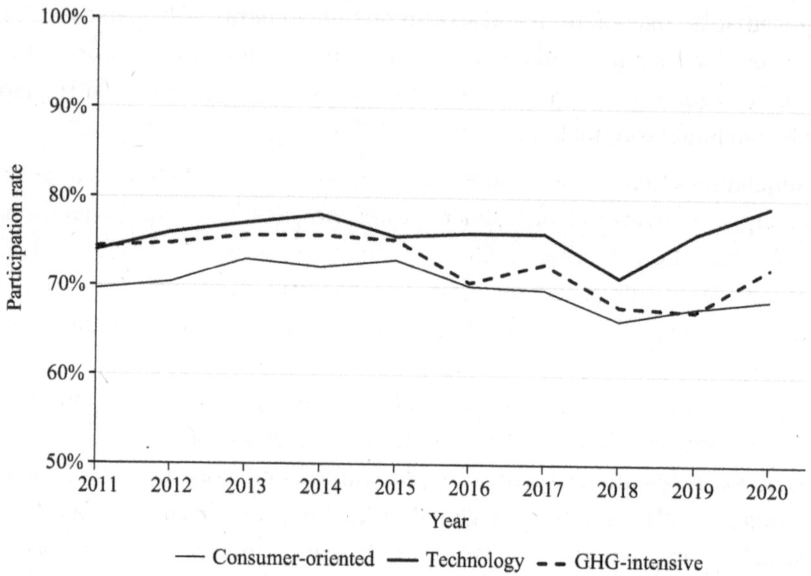

Figure 8.3
Participation in voluntary carbon disclosure, by sector.
Data sources: Author's calculations based on data from CDP and individual company websites and annual reports.

annually reporting to CDP—were Apple, Inc., Google LLC, Hitachi, Ltd., LG Innotek Co., Ltd., Microsoft Corporation, Ericsson, and Telefonica, SA.

These and other technology firms' higher likelihood of adopting a quantitative emissions target and participating in voluntary carbon disclosure continued post–Paris Agreement. By 2020, close to 80 percent of technology multinationals were regular respondents to CDP's annual climate change questionnaire. Nearly 90 percent of them have set ambitious emissions reduction plans to halve emissions or achieve net-zero carbon emissions by 2050. The rest of the Global 500 firms in the consumer-oriented and GHG-intensive sectors are not far behind, but the technology sector has led in voluntary carbon disclosure and emissions target–setting, as shown in figure 8.3 and figure 8.4, respectively.

There are several reasons why technology companies have been in a better position than other firms to play a proactive role in climate action in the last decade (2011–2020). First, technology firms, as a sector, tend to be wealthier, not only in terms of asset holdings but also in profitability, and

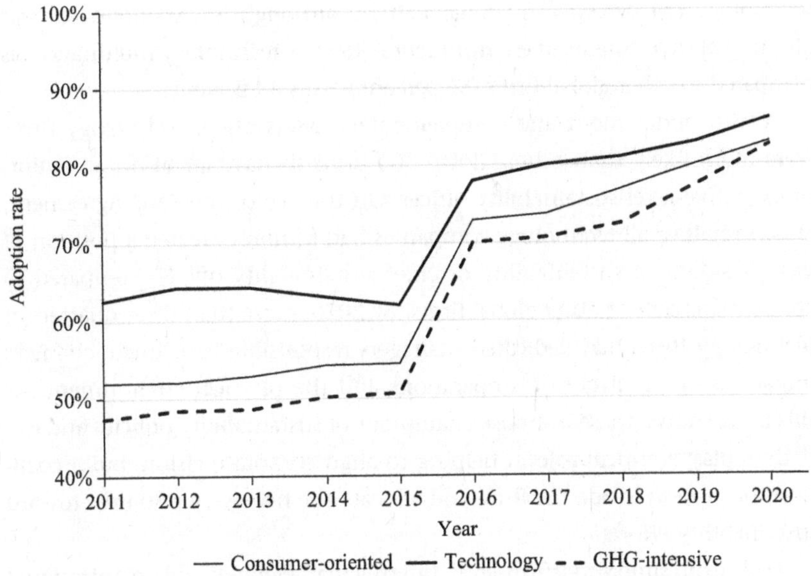

Figure 8.4
Adoption of quantitative emissions target, by sector.
Data source: Author's calculations based on data from CDP and individual company websites and annual reports.

employ a larger number of workers than other companies. Large and well-resourced firms are more able to afford the costly investments necessary for deploying renewable energy and related technologies and for undertaking carbon accounting and emissions management. Wealthy companies that employ a large number of workers have two to four times higher odds of beyond-compliance climate action than firms with smaller asset holdings and employee base.[45]

Second, more often than not, when a company demonstrates a commitment to sustainability through complementary capabilities and competencies, such as investments in environmental research and development (R&D) or certification with the ISO 14001 environmental management standard, the odds are higher that the company also engages in voluntary carbon disclosure and other proactive climate commitments, as chapter 3's analysis shows. For example, by the time of COP 21, a larger share of global firms in the technology sector (75 percent) were certified with the ISO 14001 environmental management standard than Global 500 companies excluding technology (54 percent). A similar pattern, although less pronounced, was also true of investments in environmental R&D by technology multinationals compared to other global firms (56 percent versus 48 percent).

Wealth endowment and complementary assets aside, technology firms were more likely than other Global 500 firms to have an in-house senior- or executive-level sustainability officer. On the eve of the Paris Agreement, close to half of all technology companies had formally created a position of vice president of sustainability or chief sustainability officer, compared to about 40 percent of other global firms. By 2020, more than three quarters of technology firms had dedicated managers responsible for climate change's impact on internal business operations and the physical environment. As this book shows, these in-house champions of sustainability policies and initiatives play a critical role in helping to align corporate vision, build coalitions of support inside the firm, and allocate the necessary resources toward sustainability efforts.

Aside from supportive firm-level, internal management and organizational capabilities, global businesses in the technology sector are by and large (85 percent) based in developed countries with relatively more stringent regulations and robust climate policies. Many are also active participants in global governance. Notably, all technology firms that are ranked in the top ten for how well a firm addresses risk and concerns related to environmental, social, and governance (ESG) issues in day-to-day operations are also members of the UN Global Compact and have in recent years received an A or A- grade from CDP for setting a quantitative emissions target and for committing to decarbonization by 2050.[46] The top ten technology firms ranked by ESG performance are Microsoft, SAP SE, Nokia, Infosys, Ltd., Hitachi, Ltd., Cisco Systems, Inc., Intel Corporation, Deutsche Telekom AG, Wipro, and Telecom Italia SPA.

A majority of these firms are also members of the UN-backed international cooperative initiatives on climate change, such as Race to Zero,[47] the Climate Ambition Alliance,[48] and the Business Ambition for 1.5°C.[49] These technology companies and others, such as Apple, Autodesk, Inc., BT Group PLC, and Salesforce, Inc., have also joined forces with Aviva PLC, Inter IKEA Holding BV, Starbucks Corporation, Walmart, Marks and Spencer Group PLC, and Johnson & Johnson, as part of RE100, which is a business-led, cross-sector global corporate renewable energy initiative founded in 2003 with the stated goal of securing 100 percent of their electricity from renewable sources.

While not free of accusations of corporate greenwashing, firms in the technology sector stand out for their deployment of technology to reduce both their own and their customers' carbon emissions, as two illustrative cases—Microsoft and Intel—depict. Multilevel governance interactions also explain corporate self-regulation on climate change in the technology sector with emphases on the sector's unique firm-level managerial and organizational capabilities and competitive pressures within the sector that characterized a "race to the top" as opposed to a "race to the bottom."

With that said, similar to other consumer-oriented companies, a majority of technology firms are by no means carbon-intensive in their operations. Over 75 percent of technology firms' total emissions are from their supply chain and product use or scope 3 emissions, for those that track and report scope 3 emissions. There are currently no uniform metrics or a requirement by the CDP, let alone an industry norm in the technology or other sectors, for reporting non-operations-related emissions.

8.3.1 Microsoft: A Holistic Approach to Climate Action

Among the world's largest companies by revenue, Microsoft consistently ranked in the top five in 2011–2020 and was first in 2020 for ESG performance among its peers in software and information technology services. On the eve of the Paris Agreement, ahead of global firms of its size by market capitalization, Microsoft achieved a commitment that it set just three years earlier to becoming carbon neutral for its operations across 100 countries and inclusive of the firm's data centers, software development labs, offices, and air travel.

Managerial and Organizational Capabilities Toward these efforts, Microsoft was among the first multinational company to set an internal carbon price, under the leadership of Robert Bernard, Microsoft's first chief environmental strategist from 2007 to 2018. The company credits its internal fee on carbon emissions as a key tool for the company to reduce emissions at scale and generate funding for its carbon removal efforts. According to the company, "[its] initial carbon fee focused on scope 1, scope 2, and business air travel. The proceeds from the fee provided funding for [its] carbon-neutral commitment at the time. In 2020 [the company] began charging [its] internal business groups for all scope 3 emissions and, in parallel, worked with [its] suppliers to help them understand their carbon contributions and how to reduce them."[50]

Microsoft's strategic use of its internal carbon fee could be one way for technology firms to avoid greenwashing. That being said, because CDP grades companies based on sustainability outputs rather than outcomes, an A-list company could be "carbon neutral" when it counts only the facilities it owns and not the factories that make its products.[51] Even a climate leader like Microsoft, which has consistently earned an A since 2013, could commit to removing all emitted carbon but maintain partnerships with oil and gas companies to "generate new exploration opportunities,"[52] using a similar backbone cloud computing technology it built for tracking building emissions and sustainability performance.

Corporate × Regulation In 2015, Microsoft and Apple were the only two private sector entities that earned the US Environmental Protection Agency (EPA) Green Power Partner of the Year award, which recognizes leadership in green power use and overall strategy and impact on the green power market. The EPA defines green power as electricity produced from solar, wind, geothermal, biogas, eligible biomass, and low-impact small hydroelectric sources. To qualify as green power, the renewable electricity must also go above and beyond what is otherwise required by mandate or requirement.[53]

Microsoft was also a 2016 recipient of the EPA's Climate Leadership Award for Organizational Leadership. In 2020, Microsoft earned recognition again for its "sustained excellence in green power use" from the EPA. In fact, the company has consistently topped the EPA's national top 100 list as number one or among the top three green power users in the United States, often alongside other technology global firms, such as Google, Apple, and Intel. Microsoft actively engages domestic regulatory institutions outside of political lobbying and goes beyond-compliance in specific areas, such as renewable energy use and procurement, that the well-endowed company has identified as key for decarbonization.

Corporate × Global As an early joiner of RE100, by 2020, Microsoft was in a position to fulfill 100 percent of its entity-wide electricity consumption from renewable sources across its global operations, up from 70 percent in 2014 and seven years ahead of the company's initial target date.[54] Microsoft has also made progress well ahead of its medium- and long-term goals with respect to the company's targets of reducing operational (scope 1 and scope) CO_2 emissions by 75 percent (2013 baseline). Microsoft also announced commitments to halve its emissions by 2023 and achieve net-zero carbon emissions by 2050.

Moreover, Microsoft announced its plan to offset by 2050 all the carbon releases from the environment that the company has emitted since its founding in 1975. For Microsoft, carbon dioxide removal, or CDR, includes everything from nature-based solutions—like using soils and trees to absorb CO_2—to more technical, engineered solutions like deploying direct air capture machines that remove CO_2 from the air. To meet this ambitious goal, Microsoft has a taken a "holistic," cross-sector, and collaborative approach. First, the company established a $1 billion climate innovation fund to accelerate the global development of carbon reduction and removal technologies. According to Lucas Joppa, Microsoft's chief environmental officer from 2018 to 2022, "If we are going to properly stabilize our climate systems, it's going to require a true accounting of our carbon emissions and removal."[55]

Second, toward this effort, Microsoft has begun to report and improve on the corporation's buildings' emissions performance. It has also developed a cloud-based, artificial intelligence–driven software tool to help companies measure and manage building emissions.[56] Moreover, along with a dozen multinational corporations spanning the retail, banking, automobile, and health care sectors, Microsoft formed a coalition—Transform to Net-Zero (TONZ)—to share guidance and best practices with other companies that have also pledged to meet net-zero targets by 2050.[57]

Microsoft's leadership in forming TONZ followed the company's earlier efforts in helping to establish an industry consortium in which the company partnered with industry competitors and peers, including Apple, Google, Dell Technologies, SAP, and Accenture, to set industry standards and influence national and global climate policy. These partnerships yielded the Information Technology Industry Council's Digital Energy and Sustainability Solutions Campaign and the Global e-Sustainability Initiative, a collaborative effort between leading technology companies and the United Nations Environmental Programme and International Telecommunication Union.

8.3.2 Intel: A "Handprint" for the World

From 2011 and 2020, Intel was ranked among the world's top 100 sustainable corporations eight out of ten years by Corporate Knights, a Toronto-based media and research company that has ranked companies annually based on corporate environmental, social, and governance (ESG) performance since 2000.[58] Intel is the only firm in the semiconductor industry with this distinction. ASML Holdings NV, a Netherlands-based company, trails behind Intel with six top 100 awards, whereas South Korea's Samsung Electronics has been ranked in the Corporate Knights top 100 five times in the past decade. The Taiwan Semiconductor Company has also joined the top 100 during 2011–2020.

Managerial and Organizational Capabilities In a 2023 letter, Intel's then chief executive officer Pat Gelsinger identified executive leadership as key to "why corporate responsibility and sustainability remain deeply engrained in Intel's DNA." According to Gelsinger, Intel's cofounder Gordon Moore, who passed away in March 2023, "established [Intel's] commitment to environmental sustainability during a time when companies were not thinking about it the way they are today."[59]

Corporate responsibility related to climate change evolved over time at Intel. The initial emphasis was a "business focus [toward] risk management [and] cost efficiencies . . . from a purely engineering mindset."[60] Like a majority of the Global 500 firms, sustainability was part of the company's environmental health and safety division. "We started with energy conservation in which we set aside capital budget and privileged [returns on investment]."[61] Since 2001, Intel regularly made the US Environmental Protection Agency's quarterly National Top 100 green power list, along with Microsoft and Apple, two other notable mainstays on that list.[62]

In this engineering framework, "Intel is an early mover [on climate action] . . . [its] supply chain initiatives started in the 2000s"[63] with Intel's green chemistry initiatives, which led to a voluntary reduction of chemicals with high global warming potential throughout the global semiconductor industry.[64] Moreover, "Intel had a voluntary report in 1994 before it became popular to have [corporate responsibility] reports and before the creation of the [Global Reporting Initiative] in 1997. [The company] started ESG reporting in 2003," explained Suzanne Fallender, a former global director of corporate responsibility at Intel.[65]

That being said, there was a sense that "Intel was losing its edge to other tech companies in making bolder statements after the Paris Agreement," despite Intel's industry leadership in alternative green chemistry and water use, restoration, and conservation,[66] which are complementary capabilities in adjacent areas. Facing competitive pressures among its peers, Intel engaged in external benchmarking, which started with an external scan of what other firms were doing in the technology sector and beyond. Over time, there was a realization that across the board—investors, customers, employees, and pool talents all needed to be engaged.[67] Starting in 2017, investor relations and the finance team became involved in corporate responsibility reporting. Intel's vice president of investor relations and the chief financial officer met with the corporate responsibility team on a regularly basis.

By the end of the decade (2020), Intel's corporate responsibility office moved from the manufacturing division to human resources, similar to how Adidas had merged Green Company with workplace governance. Intel's leadership began to asked the question "Are you building the right teams, the right environment, the right culture, so that you can bring your purpose to life?"[68] The idea was that corporate responsibility at Intel—encompassing environmental, social, and governance—should be part of the culture and talent pool, according to Fallender.

Corporate × Regulation In 2014, during the national policy discussions in the United States over the US Environmental Protection Agency's promulgated Clean Power Plan and a year before the Paris Agreement, Intel released its new climate change policy statement, which articulated the company's "handprint" approach to climate action. Stephen Harper, Intel's former global director of environmental, energy, and sustainability policy from 1998 to 2022, created the "handprints" versus "footprints" metaphor. The premise was that, in addition to the global semiconductor company's direct climate footprint, Intel established the goal of using its technologies to help customers reduce their climate and energy footprints, as an extension of the company's handprint.[69] "The idea is that customers—even a climate leader like Microsoft—cannot reduce their carbon footprints without Intel" because Intel's chips, notebooks, data centers, and Internet of Things, powered computing worldwide, according to Fallender.[70]

Intel's handprint approach, to use its technology to enable customers downstream to act on climate change, dovetailed well with the global firm's pioneering Copy EXACTLY! model for its semiconductor fabrication plants. With Copy EXACTLY!, Intel and its suppliers in effect have complied with regulations in the United States, its country of domicile, or those in Ireland/Europe and Israel, where Intel operates manufacturing plants.[71]

In this vein, Intel also supports market-based solutions when possible, such as trading across a larger market (linking the EU's Emissions Trading

System with other compatible schemes) as well as gaining credit for prior voluntary industry effort to reduce climate-harming emissions. Moreover, it has contributed to the "Green Deal for Europe," by extending its handprint to strengthen the EU's capability for decarbonization of the economy and digitization of resource-intensive sectors.

Corporate × Global By 2017, Intel had developed a fully integrated strategy for environmental, social, and governance performance. Climate change is one Intel's four pillars of corporate social responsibility, along with supply chain responsibility, diversity and inclusion, and social impact. Together, these four pillars are codified as part of Intel's 2030 RISE Framework, which was announced in 2020 and maps into the UN Sustainable Development Goals. This is in line with Intel's involvement as a signatory of the "We Are Still In" declaration as part of an effort by a coalition of American communities, businesses, and nonfederal institutions in support of an ambitious new US climate target and to mobilize whole-of-society climate action.

Since 2019, Intel's corporate responsibility office meets monthly for a global "face to face" with team members and sustainability experts across Intel's worldwide operations. Trends in current and emerging regulatory issues as well as global governance are frequently on the agenda for discussion. For example, Intel states that "[it prefers] state actions that are coordinated on a regional or multi-state basis, increasing the size of policy markets, reducing the patchwork effect of localized action and decreasing cost impacts."

8.4 Are GHG-Intensive Sectors Laggards on Climate Action?

This book's multilevel governance framework on climate change (MGFCC) is also salient for explicating the drivers of global firms' proactive climate action in the GHG-intensive sector. Without the interplay of corporate, regulatory, and global governance drivers, a race to the bottom would likely have characterized the materials, utilities, energy, and industrials sectors during the 2011–2020 decade. Rather than showcasing how the various component parts of the MGFCC played out in illustrative company case studies, this section provides a descriptive analysis on the GHG-intensive sector as a whole and presents climate action and corporate, regulatory, and global governance data on the world's largest publicly traded and investor-owned oil and gas firms,[72] which have joined the Oil and Gas Climate Initiative (OGCI). As is the case for the rest of the global businesses, corporate climate leaders in the GHG-intensive sector are global firms that are the best managed, regulated stringently, and actively engaged in global governance.

Similar to the consumer-oriented and technology sectors, the pre- and post–Paris Agreement periods were distinct regimes for climate action by multinational corporations operating in carbon-intensive sectors, but even more so. COP 26 in Glasgow, Scotland, and indicting Intergovernmental Panel on Climate Change publications on the seriousness of a warming climate, the rise in climate activism, and regulatory discussions in Europe, Canada, and elsewhere signaled that formal regulation was likely to be on the horizon.

In a chief executive officer–led initiative, comprising twelve of the largest energy companies and more than 30 percent of global oil and gas production, the Oil and Gas Climate Initiative (OGCI) "[seeks] action . . . to accelerate and participate in the energy transition." Founded in 2014, OGCI has partners across the industry and in other sectors focused on reducing unabated carbon emissions through carbon capture, utilization and storage; methane emissions reduction; and tracking transport emissions. Since its founding, OGCI has faced scrutiny and accusations of greenwashing because environmentalists criticized the "the 'big oil' business model as fundamentally incompatible with avoiding dangerous climate change."[73]

As figure 8.5 shows, GHG-intensive firms readily adopted quantitative emissions targets after 2015. By contrast, these GHG-intensive firms, notably in the industrial and energy sectors, pulled back their disclosures to CDP for several years, more so than the rest of the Global 500 firms (see table 8.6). The oil and gas sector accounted for around 15 percent of total energy-related emissions globally, the equivalent of 5.1 billion tons of greenhouse gas emissions.

In 2011, half of the members of OGCI had set a quantitative emissions target. By 2020, only two of these twelve oil and gas producers had not set an emissions target, and only one company had not established an internal carbon price. From 2011 to 2020, the OGCI members together reduced entity-wide carbon emissions by nearly 20 percent, compared to a 13 percent reduction for the GHG-intensive sector as a whole and a 3 percent increase in total emissions for the rest of the Global 500 firms in the consumer-oriented and technology sectors.[74]

Among the OGCI members there are several noteworthy climate leaders, as ranked by Corporate Knights. Six of the twelve OCGI members—Equinor ASA (Norway), Eni SPA (Italy), Petrobras (Brazil), TotalEnergies (France), Repsol SA

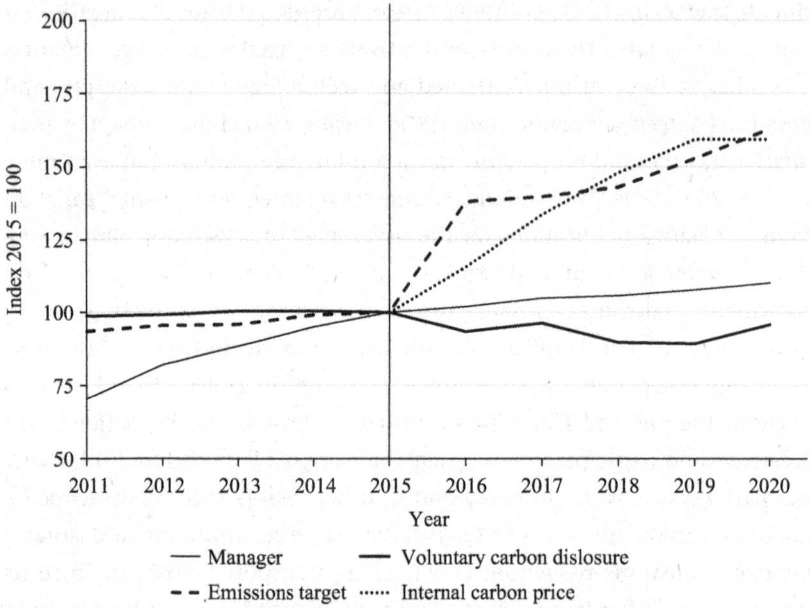

Figure 8.5
Trends in global firms' sustainability outputs in the GHG-intensive sector.
Note: Index 2015 = 100 means that 2015 is the base year.
Data sources: Author's calculations based on data from CDP and individual company websites and annual reports.

(Spain), and Shell LLC (UK)—were ranked among Corporate Knights' Global 100 list of the top 100 firms for "clean capitalism" and corporate sustainability at least once from 2011 to 2020.[75] Equinor (formerly Statoil) was ranked among the top 100 most sustainable corporations seven times throughout the 2011–2020 decade. Notably, Corporate Knights ranked the Norway-based firm first in 2011 and among the top five most sustainable firms four times from 2011 to 2015. The OCGI members that had not received commendation (e.g., ExxonMobil, BP PLC, China National Petroleum Corporation) on average received lower ESG performance scores than the OCGI members that did. That being said, none of the OCGI members domiciled in the EU (or Europe) has made the *Financial Times'* lists of Europe's climate leaders, which require that firms achieve reduction in their scope 1 and 2 greenhouse gas emissions intensity over a five-year period.[76]

By 2019, OGCI stepped up their engagement in the United Nations Climate Action Summits, leading critics to say they were attempting to influence

Table 8.6

Corporate climate action (sustainability outputs), GHG-intensive sectors versus other Fortune Global 500 firms

	Rest of Global 500[a]	GHG-intensive (broad)[b]	Materials and utilities	Energy and industrials	Oil and Gas Climate Initiative[c]
Before Paris Agreement (2011–15)					
Manager (%)	66	71	71	70	87
Voluntary carbon disclosure (%)	73	75	73	77	100
Emissions target (%)	55	49	53	45	45
Environmental, social, governance (ESG) score[d] (0–100)	59	62	66	59	76
ESG environment	60	64	69	61	75
ESG social	61	61	64	59	79
ESG governance	59	62	65	60	70
ESG controversies	75	78	78	78	51
N	1,320	1,150	470	680	55
After Paris Agreement (2016–20)					
Manager (%)	81	86	87	85	100
Voluntary carbon disclosure (%)	70	70	74	68	80
Emissions target (%)	78	75	79	72	71
Internal carbon price[4] (%)	25	44	59	33	91
Emissions target and internal carbon price[e] (%)	24	39	57	27	62
Environmental, social, governance (ESG) score (0–100)	69	67	69	66	78
ESG Environment	67	68	71	66	77

(continued)

Table 8.6 (*continued*)

	Rest of Global 500[a]	GHG-intensive (broad)[b]	Materials and utilities	Energy and industrials	Oil and Gas Climate Initiative[c]
ESG Social	73	69	70	68	83
ESG Governance	65	64	65	64	70
ESG Controversies	72	75	77	75	41
N	1517	1,146	470	680	55

[a] Consumer discretionary, consumer staples, financial services, health care, information technology, and telecommunication sectors.

[b] Energy, industrials, materials, and utilities sectors.

[c] The Oil and Gas Climate Initiative (OGCI) members are Saudi Aramco, BP, Chevron, China National Petroleum Corporation, Eni, Equinor, ExxonMobil, Occidental, Petrobras, Repsol, Shell, and TotalEnergies.

[d] The ESG score measures a company's relative environmental, social, and governance performance, commitment, and effectiveness based on company-reported data, which include information covering ten themes—resource use, emissions, environmental product innovation, workforce, human rights, community, product responsibility, management, shareholders, and corporate social responsibility strategy. Scores in the 50 to 75 range indicate "good relative ESG performance" and above-average degree of transparency in a firm's public reporting of environmental, social, and governance data. Scores above 75 indicate "excellent relative ESG performance and high degree of transparency in reporting material ESG data publicly." "LSEG ESG Score," LSEG Data and Analytics, accessed April 13, 2024, https://www.lseg.com/en/data-analytics/sustainable-finance/esg-scores.

[e] Data for global firms' adoption of an internal carbon price and an emissions target and an internal carbon price, respectively, are only available for 2016–2020.

Data sources: CDP, LSEG Data and Analytics, and corporate websites and annual reports.

negotiations in favor of fossil fuel companies. The OGCI hosted an "invitation-only forum" featuring a "closed high-level discussion" with stakeholders on the day of the 2020 Climate Action Summit, which was hosted by UN Secretary General António Guterres in New York City.[77] Critics accused the OGCI of "[attempting] to influence negotiations in favour of fossil fuel companies."[78]

As shown above in table 8.2, in the GHG-intensive sector, firms' adoption rates for quantitative emissions targets increased when there was higher regulatory stringency, upper management responsibility for climate mitigation, and corporate participation in global governance. The positive link between corporate, regulatory, and global governance interactions and sustainability outputs mirrored a similar phenomenon in the consumer-oriented and technology sectors. In fact, corporate, regulatory, and global governance interactions became even more significant drivers of global firms' emissions target–setting by the end of the decade. In 2020, nearly all carbon-intensive firms in the Global 500 had published GHG reduction targets that cover emissions from their oil and gas production and from the power those operations consume, or scope 1 and scope 2 emissions targets.[79]

Is the presence of multilevel governance interactions associated with higher environmental performance with respect to entity-wide carbon emissions for global firms? As reported in section 8.1, S&P 500 index firms that proactively disclosed their emissions to CDP, on average, reduced their carbon emissions per capita of full-time employees (see chapter 7 for full analysis). For US firms, much of the decline involved large GHG–intensive companies, such as utilities, that were trying to get ahead of expected climate regulations. While this did not necessarily translate to a reduction in a company's overall carbon emissions in the United States, for GHG-intensive firms worldwide, the presence of a dedicated manager on climate change along with regulatory stringency or membership in the UN Global Compact were associated with reduced entity-wide carbon emissions compared to when either corporate, regulatory, or global governance was not present.

As table 8.7 shows, firms that have an upper-management champion, are facing regulatory pressure, and have (sustained) participation in global governance, on average, have lower overall carbon emissions. This was notable (with statistical significance) in the materials and utilities sectors and for the members of the OGCI, as well as for the energy and industrials sectors in the post–Paris Agreement period (2016–2020). From 2011 to 2020, a nearly 20 percent reduction in entity-wide carbon emissions was recorded for the

Table 8.7
Entity-wide carbon emissions (metric tons) and multilevel governance interactions, across sectors

	Rest of Global 500[a]	GHG-intensive (broad)[b]	Materials & utilities	Energy & industrials	Oil and Gas Climate Initiative[c]
Before Paris Agreement (2011–2015)					
No manager	914,071	26,800,000	42,600,000	12,500,000	41,000,000
Manager	1,257,950	21,600,000	30,700,000**	14,500,000	55,100,000
Regulation	1,114,066	21,100,000**	31,500,000	13,800,000	51,300,000
Global	1,140,050	25,200,000	34,400,000	15,600,000	43,900,000**
Manager × regulation	1,162,518**	20,800,000	30,400,000	14,200,000	53,300,000
Manager × global	1,059,636	23,800,000	31,500,000	15,500,000	44,500,000**
Regulation × global	991,404**	22,300,000	26,600,000**	17,000,000	38,400,000**
Manager × regulation × global[d]	964,802**	20,500,000	23,400,000**	16,800,000	39,900,000**
After Paris Agreement (2016–20)					
No manager	850,564***	26,300,000*	36,200,000*	19,300,000	N/A
Manager	1,297,528***	21,400,000*	27,100,000*	17,000,000	53,193,438
Regulation	1,091,947***	18,200,000***	26,300,000	13,200,000***	46,214,290***
Global	1,190,694	22,300,000	27,200,000	17,900,000	39,902,720***
Manager × regulation	1,139,168**	17,900,000***	25,800,000*	12,800,000***	46,214,290***
Manager × global	1,133,496*	20,800,000	27,300,000	14,600,000*	3,990,2720***

Regulation × global	1,050,745*	17,100,000**	20,900,000**	13,200,000*	35,483,264***
Manager × regulation × global	1,062,557*	17,400,000**	20,900,000**	13,600,000*	35,483,264***

Note: *$p<0.1$, **$p<0.05$, ***$p<0.01$. Entity-wide carbon emissions refer to a firms' scope 1 and scope 2 emissions, as is the case throughout this book.

[a] Consumer discretionary, consumer staples, financial services, health care, information technology, and telecommunication sectors.

[b] Energy, industrials, materials, and utilities sectors.

[c] The Oil and Gas Climate Initiative (OGCI) members are Saudi Aramco, BP, Chevron, China National Petroleum Corporation, Eni, Equinor, ExxonMobil, Occidental, Petrobras, Repsol, Shell, and TotalEnergies.

[d] Manager × regulation × global for a given year represents a firm that installed a dedicated senior- or executive-level manager responsible for climate mitigation, originated from a country that scored above the mean in regulatory stringency of all Global 500 firms, and is a member of the UN Global Compact.

Data sources: LSEG Data and Analytics, and corporate websites and annual reports.

ten out of twelve OGCI members for which entity-wide carbon emissions are available.

8.5 Conclusion

In this chapter, sectoral analyses and illustrative company cases reveal that from 2011 to 2020, global firms operating in sectors with greater consumer contact readily undertook climate action pledges and widely communicated about them irrespective of their actual environmental performance. For consumer-oriented sectors (e.g., retail and apparel), global firms' carbon footprints are not in their operations but, rather, are in the supply chains. The challenge was that the "cheap talk" was accompanied by inadvertent greenwashing that was widely reported in the news media. That being said, two company archetypes—Moody's and Adidas—illustrate how visionary leaders, managerial and organizational capabilities, and proactive interaction with regulatory and global governance distinguish leaders from laggards in the consumer-oriented sectors.

In the technology sector, Microsoft and Intel are two standouts for the ways their leadership employed complementary capabilities and actively engaged with regulatory global governance (distinct from political lobbying) to emerge as sustainability leaders in their industries. The oil and gas sector lagged behind the rest of the Global 500 in their adoption of quantitative emissions targets and internal carbon price. But GHG-intensive firms that exercised managerial agency, faced relatively stringent regulation, and actively engaged in global governance were more successful, including several companies that were part of the Oil and Gas Climate Initiative.

Across the consumer-oriented, technology, and carbon-intensive sectors, the focus in the first half of the decade was on carbon management rather than emissions reduction. In the post–Paris Agreement period, global firms' proactive climate action accelerated. Notably, companies in the technology sector competed with one another to deploy big data and artificial intelligence to reduce their own carbon footprints and those of their customers. That being said, there has been increased attention on the dire impacts of climate change, pressures from institutional investors and climate activists, and the realization from firms that climate change is unavoidable and that climate regulation of some form is inevitable. Consequently, there is evidence of a shifting tide in the GHG-intensive sector. Despite bad publicity, for global firms in the power sector that faced regulatory pressure in the United States, as well as oil and gas and other energy companies based in the EU—where there are more stringent climate policies and industry-level initiatives—when regulatory pressure was combined with internal firm-level managerial and organizational capabilities and engagement with global governance, both sustainability outputs and environmental performance were improved during 2011–2020.

9 Developed and Developing Countries: What Drives Differences in Corporate Climate Action?

Chapter 9 examines how global firms based in developed versus developing countries differ in their proactive climate action.[1] In the developing countries, corporate, regulatory, and global governance are complements rather than substitutes. This means that in developed countries, these three governance levels positively reinforce each other as effective drivers of corporate self-regulation on climate change. The European Union (EU) is an exemplar of how firm, regulatory, and global interactions and the blurring of the private and public governance spheres in Europe characterize the climate leadership of global firms based there.

By contrast, developing country–based global firms are motivated by corporate managerial agency and the stringency of domestic regulation and their interactions. In other words, in developing countries global firms' voluntary climate action is an outcome of internal firm managerial and organizational structures and practices that are influenced by domestic laws and statutes. This is because in the medium- to long-run time horizon, it is economically and politically advantageous for firms in the Global South to act, at times preemptively, in anticipation of local rules and policies that could carry sanctions for noncompliance in their country of domicile or in their largest export markets.

This chapter begins with a descriptive analysis of the landscape of voluntary climate action by global firms in developed and developing countries. The rest of chapter 9 presents econometric models and results that distinguish a global firm's decision to participate and the intensity of their participation in voluntary carbon disclosure—first introduced in chapters 3 and 4—with separate analyses conducted for developed and developing countries. Section 9.2 illuminates internal firm managerial and organizational drivers and regulatory and global governance interactions to underscore corporate climate leadership in the EU and Europe. The next section (section 9.3) focuses on global firms based in developing countries and their proclivity to respond to regulatory pressure as opposed to nonmandatory global best practices. In low- and middle-income economies, domestic regulation (and not global firms' overcompliance) set the baseline for the proactive climate action of firms based there. Section 9.4 concludes the chapter.

9.1 Corporate Self-Regulation on Climate Change in the Global North and Global South

From 2011 to 2020, 84 percent of Fortune Global 500 firms were based in the Global North or in developed countries. The remaining 16 percent originated in the Global South or developing and emerging countries. During the same period, global firms domiciled in the United States and EU made up 36 and 21 percent, respectively, of the Global 500 and together represent more than 50 percent of the largest firms by revenue in the world.

By contrast, no individual country in the Global South was home base to more than 4 to 5 percent of the Global 500. India-based firms represented close to a fifth of global firms domiciled in developing countries, followed by Brazil (16 percent) and China (10 percent) (see figure 9.1).

As table 9.1 shows, during the 2011–2020 decade, multinational firms domiciled in the EU and the United Kingdom (UK) engaged in corporate self-regulation on climate change—namely, voluntary carbon disclosure and the adoption of quantitative emissions targets and an internal price on carbon—at higher rates than their peers in other developed countries (i.e., Global North excluding the EU and UK).[2]

Like their European peers, large numbers of global firms based in Canada and Australia participated in voluntary climate action in the periods before and after the 2015 Paris Agreement, as panel A in table 9.2 shows. Notably, in the post–Paris Agreement period, a majority if not all Global 500 firms from the two countries hired a senior- or executive-level manager to lead climate mitigation efforts and disclosed their carbon management and carbon emissions data to CDP (formerly the Carbon Disclosure Project).

Moreover, in the post–Paris Agreement period more than three-quarters of global firms based in Canada and Australia had adopted a quantitative emissions target for reducing carbon emissions. In 2016–2020, more than 50 percent of these firms adopted an internal carbon price, which was on

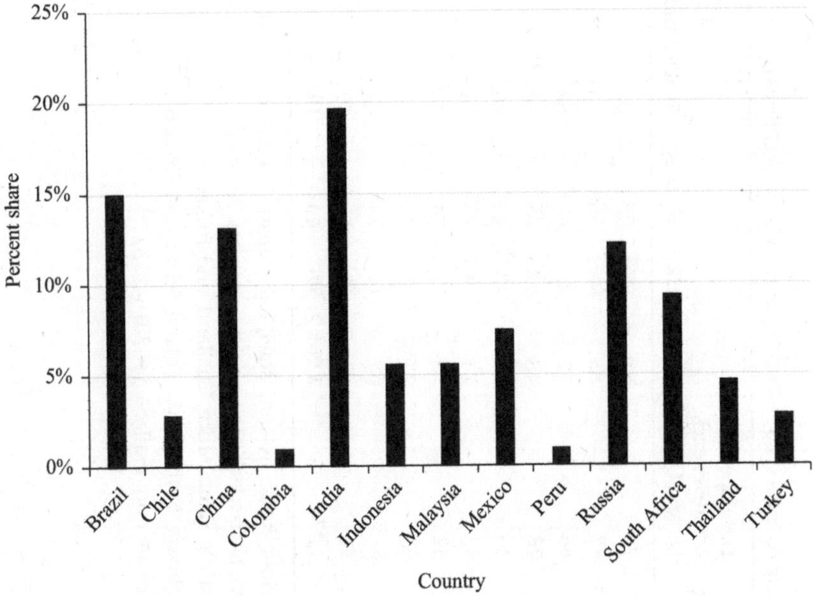

Figure 9.1
Percent share of Fortune Global 500 firms in the Global South, by country (2011–2020). *Data source*: Author's calculations based on data on the Fortune Global 500 from https://fortune.com/ranking/global500/.

par with or slightly above the adoption rates of multinational firms based in the EU or UK.

While Japanese firms and Korean firms invested in global best practices on climate change at lower rates than European, British, Canadian, or Australian firms during the first half of the 2011–2020 decade, in the post–Paris Agreement period they readily engaged in voluntary climate action and nearly caught up to corporate climate leaders in Europe, the UK, Canada, and Australia.

By contrast, a smaller share of global firms domiciled in developing countries engaged in corporate self-regulation on climate change (see panel B in table 9.2). From 2011 to 2020, about half of these firms installed a dedicated senior- or executive-level manager responsible for carbon management and climate risks inside the firm (compared to nearly 80 percent in the developed countries). Forty-five percent of developing country–based firms reported their carbon management or carbon emissions data to the CDP during the

Table 9.1

Corporate climate action (sustainability outputs), developed versus developing countries, 2011–2020 (Fortune Global 500 firms)

	Developed countries[a]	Developing countries[b]	Developed countries excl. EU and UK	EU[c]	UK	Norway	Switzerland
Manager (%)	79	53	76	88	97	78	65
Voluntary carbon disclosure (%)	77	45	73	85	92	100	73
Emissions target (%)	70	39	66	82	82	63	68
Internal carbon price[d] (%)	33	20	28	48	47	45	60
Emissions target and internal carbon price[e] (%)	31	19	26	48	43	45	60
Environmental, social, governance (ESG) score	65	58	63	74	74	73	73
ESG environment	66	55	62	78	75	74	76
ESG social	67	61	63	77	77	72	74
ESG governance	63	57	62	65	70	74	69
ESG controversies	73	84	74	73	60	66	69
N	5,729	1,040	4,274	1,065	390	40	196

[a] Australia, Belgium, Canada, Czech Republic, Denmark, Finland, Germany, Hong Kong, Ireland, Israel, Italy, Japan, Luxembourg, Netherlands, Norway, Poland, Singapore, South Africa, South Korea, Spain, Sweden, Switzerland, Taiwan, United States, and UK.

[b] Brazil, Chile, China, Colombia, India, Indonesia, Malaysia, Mexico, Peru, Russia, South Africa, Thailand, and Turkey.

[c] Belgium, Czech Republic, Denmark, Finland, France, Germany, Italy, Luxembourg, Netherlands, Poland, Spain, and Sweden.

[d] Data for internal carbon price and emissions target and internal carbon price are only available for 2016–2020.

[e] ESG score measures a company's relative environmental, social, and governance performance, commitment, and effectiveness, based on company-reported data, which include information covering ten themes (namely, resource use, emissions, environmental product innovation, workforce, human rights, community, product responsibility, management, shareholders, and corporate social responsibility strategy). Scores in the 50 to 75 range indicate "good relative ESG performance" and above average degree of transparency in a firm's public reporting of environmental, social, and governance data. Scores above 75 indicate "excellent relative ESG performance and high degree of transparency in reporting material ESG data publicly." "LSEG ESG Score," LSEG Data and Analytics, accessed April 13, 2024, https://www.lseg.com/en/data-analytics/sustainable-finance/esg-scores.

Data sources: CDP, LSEG Data and Analytics, and corporate websites and annual reports.

Table 9.2

Corporate climate action (sustainability outputs), developed versus developing countries, before and after the Paris Agreement (Fortune Global 500 firms)

Panel A
Developed countries

	Developed countries[a]	Developed countries excl. EU and UK	EU[c]	UK	Canada	US	Australia	Japan	South Korea	Taiwan
Before Paris Agreement (2011–2015)										
Manager (%)	72	67	83	95	81	73	92	59	54	49
Voluntary carbon disclosure (%)	78	74	89	98	93	76	98	79	69	38
Emissions target (%)	58	54	71	72	61	57	67	61	71	20
Environmental, social, governance (ESG) score[d] (0–100)	62	58	71	71	64	57	75	60	67	45
ESG environment	63	59	77	74	66	56	73	68	66	42
ESG social	62	58	73	74	65	59	75	50	66	40
ESG governance	61	60	63	66	65	58	78	66	68	55
ESG controversies	74	74	77	62	78	68	70	82	81	90
N	2,868	2,138	535	195	160	1,233	60	270	70	45
After Paris Agreement (2016–2020)										
Manager (%)	87	84	93	100	99	88	100	83	90	43
Voluntary carbon disclosure (%)	75	73	80	85	83	74	90	89	76	73
Emissions target (%)	81	77	92	93	84	77	85	86	97	76
Internal carbon price[e] (%)	33	28	48	47	62	21	50	35	39	31
Emissions target and internal carbon price[e] (%)	31	26	48	43	53	19	50	35	39	31

Environmental, social, governance (ESG) score[d] (0–100)	69	67	76	78	69	67	79	66	69	61
ESG environment	69	66	79	77	73	64	70	71	67	62
ESG social	72	69	81	81	72	70	84	62	72	64
ESG governance	66	65	67	74	62	65	80	64	62	53
ESG controversies	72	73	68	58	79	69	53	79	76	96
N	2,861	2,136	530	195	160	1,235	60	270	70	45

Panel B
Developing countries

	Developing countries[b]	Developing countries excl. China	China	Brazil	India	Russia
Before Paris Agreement (2011–2015)						
Manager (%)	44	48	17	63	65	12
Voluntary carbon disclosure (%)	48	47	54	70	41	28
Emissions target (%)	23	26	3	44	24	8
Environmental, social, governance (ESG) score[d] (0–100)	54	55	42	60	56	43
ESG environment	53	54	44	61	55	44
ESG social	54	58	35	66	60	39
ESG governance	55	55	59	54	52	49
ESG controversies	88	87	92	91	74	86
N	520	450	70	80	105	65
After Paris Agreement (2016–2020)						
Manager (%)	62	63	50	76	76	37

(continued)

Table 9.2 *(continued)*

Panel B
Developing countries

	Developing countries[b]	Developing countries excl. China	China	Brazil	India	Russia
Voluntary carbon disclosure (%)	43	44	40	70	34	32
Emissions target (%)	56	56	50	84	54	35
Internal carbon price[e] (%)	20	22	1	39	14	14
Emissions target and internal carbon price[e] (%)	19	21	1	39	14	11
Environmental, social, governance (ESG) score[d] (0–100)	63	63	58	67	61	57
ESG environment	58	58	58	62	55	52
ESG social	68	70	55	73	72	61
ESG governance	58	57	63	62	49	55
ESG controversies	81	79	91	72	60	81
N	520	450	70	80	105	65

[a] Australia, Belgium, Canada, Czech Republic, Denmark, Finland, Germany, Hong Kong, Ireland, Israel, Italy, Japan, Luxembourg, Netherlands, Norway, Poland, Singapore, South Africa, South Korea, Spain, Sweden, Switzerland, Taiwan, United States, and UK.

[b] Brazil, Chile, China, Colombia, India, Indonesia, Malaysia, Mexico, Peru, Russia, South Africa, Thailand, and Turkey.

[c] Belgium, Czech Republic, Denmark, Finland, France, Germany, Italy, Luxembourg, Netherlands, Poland, Spain, and Sweden.

[d] ESG score measures a company's relative environmental, social, and governance performance, commitment, and effectiveness, based on company-reported data, which include information covering ten themes (namely, resource use, emissions, environmental product innovation, workforce, human rights, community, product responsibility, management, shareholders, and corporate social responsibility strategy). Scores in the 50 to 75 range indicate "good relative ESG performance" and above average degree of transparency in a firm's public reporting of environmental, social, and governance data. Scores above 75 indicate "excellent relative ESG performance and high degree of transparency in reporting material ESG data publicly." "LSEG ESG Score," LSEG Data and Analytics, accessed April 13, 2024, https://www.lseg.com/en/data-analytics/sustainable-finance/esg-scores.

[e] Data for internal carbon price and emissions target and internal carbon price are only available for 2016–2020.

Data sources: CDP, LSEG Data and Analytics, and corporate websites and annual reports.

same time period. Close to 40 percent had set a quantitative emissions target. Furthermore, these firms' environmental, social, and governance (ESG) performances were 5 to 10 points lower than those of their peers domiciled in the developed countries.

That being said, the post–Paris Agreement period witnessed an increase in proactive climate action among developing country–based firms, notably Chinese firms. China and the United States played a major role in the twenty-first session of the Conference of the Parties (COP 21) to the United Nations Framework Convention on Climate Change despite the US exit from the Paris Agreement by President Donald Trump in 2017.[3] In 2016–2020, Brazilian firms exhibited a corporate sustainability profile closer to that of Japan than to those of other developing country–based firms. Global firms based in India stood out as intermediate cases of corporate environmentalism on climate change, performing in between developed country- and developing country-based firms. In India, the top 1,000 publicly listed companies by market capitalization are required to make ESG disclosures under the country's 2023 Business Responsibility and Sustainability Reporting framework, and at the writing of this book, Indian financial institutions must disclose climate risk disclosures starting in 2025.[4]

9.2 European Firms Lead on Proactive Climate Action

Starting in 2021, the *Financial Times*, in collaboration with the research company Statista, has compiled an annual list of Europe's climate leaders. Comprising 300 to 500 firms, the annual listing showcases firms domiciled in the EU as well as in the UK, Norway, and Switzerland that have achieved the greatest reduction in their greenhouse gas (GHG) emissions intensity over a five-year period.[5] From the inaugural 2021 list until 2023, the UK was home to the largest number of leading firms (90–120), ahead of Germany (30–52), France (40–45), and Switzerland (30–35). Of note, several firms on the Europe's Climate Leaders list have increased their revenues faster than their rate of energy usage, which means that carbon emissions have increased in absolute terms even as their emissions intensity has fallen.

Table 9.3 features twenty-eight Global 500 firms on the 2022 Europe's Climate Leaders list that have also been ranked among Corporate Knight's Global 100 list of the world's most sustainable corporations at least once from 2011 to 2020. The French company L'Oreal, Germany's Siemens AG,

Table 9.3

Europe's corporate climate leaders, 2020

Global 500 firm	Country	Sector	Reduction of core emissions intensity YoY, 2015–2020[a] (%)	Number of times on Corporate Knights' Global 100 ranking[b]	Manager[c]	CDP score[d]	Emissions target[c]	Internal carbon price[c]	UN Global Compact member	ESG score[e]
Kering	France	Consumer discretionary	30	5	✓	A–	✓	✓	✓	81
Ericsson	Sweden	Technology	29	8	✓	B	✓		✓	85
Lloyds Banking Group	UK	Financials	22	1	✓	B	✓		✓	84
AstraZeneca	UK	Health care	20	6	✓	A	✓	✓	✓	95
Adidas	Germany	Consumer discretionary	17	2	✓	B	✓	✓		92
DNB ASA	Norway	Financials	17	4	✓	A	✓	✓	✓	70
Iberdrola SA	Spain	Utilities	16	6	✓	A–	✓	✓	✓	86
GlaxoSmith-Kline	UK	Health care	16	5	✓	B	✓		✓	94
AXA Group	France	Financials	15	1	✓	C	✓		✓	81
Accenture	Ireland	Technology	15	6	✓	A	✓		✓	79
Siemens AG	Germany	Industrials	15	9	✓	A–	✓	✓	✓	90
H&M Group	Sweden	Consumer discretionary	14	9	✓	A	✓	✓	✓	71
Unilever PLC	UK	Consumer staples	14	8	✓	A	✓	✓	✓	90

L'Oréal	France	Consumer staples	14	9	✓	A	✓		✓	79
Vodafone Group	UK	Technology	13	2	✓	A	✓	✓	✓	84
Centrica	UK	Utilities	13	7	✓	A	✓	✓	✓	65
ABB	Switzer-land	Industrials	12	3	✓	A–	✓	✓	✓	94
Atlas Copco	Sweden	Industrials	9	5	✓	A–	✓		✓	84
LVMH	France	Consumer discretionary	9	1	✓	B	✓	✓	✓	70
SAP AG	Germany	Technology	9	4	✓	A	✓	✓	✓	93
Allianz SE	Germany	Financials	9	2	✓	A–	✓	✓	✓	94
Daimler AG	Germany	Consumer discretionary	9	6	✓	A–	✓	✓	✓	94
SANOFI	France	Health care	7	5	✓	A-	✓	✓	✓	89
Nestlé	Switzer-land	Consumer staples	6	4	✓	A–	✓		✓	91
Novartis	Switzer-land	Health care	6	5	✓	A–		✓	✓	86
Henkel AG	Germany	Consumer staples	6	6	✓	B	✓	✓	✓	82
Renault	France	Consumer discretionary	5	5	✓	A–	✓	✓	✓	82

(*continued*)

Table 9.3 *(continued)*

Global 500 firm	Country	Sector	Reduction of core emissions intensity YoY, 2015–2020[a] (%)	Number of times on Corporate Knights' Global 100 ranking[b]	Manager[c]	CDP score[d]	Emissions target[c]	Internal carbon price[c]	UN Global Compact member	ESG score[e]
Inditex	Spain	Consumer discretionary	5	3	✓	A–	✓	✓	✓	84
BT Group	UK	Technology	5	6	✓	A	✓	✓	✓	73

[a] YoY, year over year. Compound annual reduction rate (CARR) is based on the sum of scope 1 and 2 emissions and is adjusted by revenue growth from 2015 to 2020.

[b] The number of times a firm landed on Corporate Knight's Global 100 or the top 100 firms for "clean capitalism" from 2011 to 2020.

[c] Indicates whether a firm installed a senior- or executive-level manager dedicated to climate mitigation, adopted a quantitative emissions target, or set an internal carbon price.

[d] CDP (formerly the Carbon Disclosure Project) assesses how well firms report on and reduce their environmental impact with a letter grade (A–D).

[e] ESG score measures a company's relative environmental, social, and governance performance, commitment, and effectiveness, based on company-reported data, which include information covering ten themes (namely, resource use, emissions, environmental product innovation, workforce, human rights, community, product responsibility, management, shareholders, and corporate social responsibility strategy). Scores in the 50 to 75 range indicate "good relative ESG performance" and above average degree of transparency in a firm's public reporting of environmental, social, and governance data. Scores above 75 indicate "excellent relative ESG performance and high degree of transparency in reporting material ESG data publicly." "LSEG ESG Score," LSEG Data and Analytics, accessed April 13, 2024, https://www.lseg.com/en/data-analytics/sustainable-finance/esg-scores.

Data sources: CDP, LSEG Data and Analytics, and corporate websites and annual reports.

and Sweden's H&M Group have all landed on Corporate Knight's Global 100 list nine out of the ten years during 2011–2020. Across consumer-oriented, technology, and GHG-intensive sectors these firms have achieved on average close to a 15 percent reduction in their GHG emissions intensity from 2015 to 2020, as reported by the *Financial Times*. At the top of this list of select firms,[6] Kering, a French apparel and luxury goods company, reduced its emissions intensity by 30 percent. Following right behind is Ericsson, a Swedish telecommunications firm that reported 29 percent reductions in tons of emissions of CO_2-equivalent per 1 million euros in revenue.

All but one of these firms are signatories to the United Nations Global Compact; many of them are also participants in the Race to Zero, Fashion Industry Charter for Climate Action, RE100, Science-Based Targets Initiatives, or Climate Ambition Alliance, among other international cooperative initiatives on climate change. All of the firms in table 9.3 have designated responsibility for the firm's carbon management and climate risks to senior- or executive-level leadership. With respect to sustainability outputs, all of them have disclosed to CDP and implemented a quantitative emissions target. Furthermore, all but one GHG-intensive firm have set an internal price on carbon. More than one-third of these firms were recipients of CDP's Europe Awards, first held in 2017, to recognize A-list high-ranking corporate disclosers.[7]

The corporate sustainability dominance of these "select of the select" was also borne out in their environmental, social, and governance (ESG) performance. Their overall ESG scores were above those of their EU peers and the rest of the Global 500 firms (see tables 9.1 and 9.2).

These and other Global 500 firms featured on the 2021 *Financial Times* list and the 2022 and 2023 lists of Europe's climate leaders are archetypes of this book's multilevel governance framework on climate change, along with the multinational corporations featured in previous chapter's illustrative company cases. As table 9.3 indicates, and the rest of this section explicates in more detail, EU firms are well endowed with internal firm managerial and organizational capabilities, have faced relatively more stringent regulation and robust climate policies, and have participated at higher rates in global governance than global businesses of similar size and scope based in other countries and regions.

The EU's lead on corporate climate action does not come as a surprise, because of the "Brussels effect"—the term coined by legal scholar Anu Bradford to describe the EU's actual and perceived power to promulgate regulations that shape the global business environment.[8] In the environmental area, the EU has influenced global environmental standards through its regulation on hazardous substances and electronic waste, the protection of animal welfare, energy policy for buildings, renewables, and the mitigation of climate change through an emissions trading system.[9] This Europeanization of many aspects of global commerce extends to corporate self-regulation on climate change.

Scholars have argued that, for decades, the blurring of the private and public governance spheres in Europe[10]—to a greater extent than in any other part of the world—is responsible for the EU's distinctive national business system. In particular, the interactions of public and private actors in the climate disclosure policy domain across firm, country, and global governance levels has led to both ratcheting up of regulations in the EU and the competition among firms across sectors for a place on the *Financial Times*'s list of Europe's climate leaders.

9.2.1 Managerial and Organizational Capabilities

Chapter 3 of this book underscores that supportive internal firm management together with organizational structures and incentives are catalysts for corporate self-regulation on climate change. This chapter demonstrates that the combination of internal firm management and organizational drivers of participation and effort in voluntary carbon disclosure look different in European firms than in non-European firms. This is because of the EU's distinctive national business systems framework in conjunction with global supply chain imperatives. Even with an increase in explicit corporate social responsibility (CSR) worldwide—that is, a firm's publicly communicated policies, programs, and practices to external stakeholders as a reflection of company discretion and initiative—European companies have exercised less discretion in the area of corporate environmentalism. This is because corporate responsibilities toward society have *implicitly* been codified in the norms, standards, and legal framework of the EU.[11]

In 2015, the year of the Paris Agreement, EU-based firms were on average better resourced than the rest of the Global 500 firms with respect to the existence of policy supporters, complementary assets, or specific forms of explicit CSR practices, such as the adoption of ESG principles (see table A8.1 in appendix 8). As theorized in chapter 2, policy supporters are dedicated managers at the senior or executive level responsible for a firm's carbon management and climate risks; they are agents of change inside the firm because they capture or win the attention of top management and actively engage with investors and help to either secure consensus on or compromise in proclimate policies and activities. Complementary assets are the basic building blocks by which firms profit from successful commercializing of an innovation. See chapters 2 and 3 for detailed explication on and empirical testing of the role of internal firm managerial agency and organizational structures as drivers of voluntary climate action.

Despite the European firms' higher proclivity for supportive firm-level managerial capabilities and organizational structures compared to all Global 500 firms, the only correlate of participation in the European firms' voluntary carbon disclosure is firm size, according to the double-hurdle model results in table 9.4.[12] As noted in chapter 3, the double-hurdle model is a discrete-continuous econometrics model that accounts for the fact that firms may engage in self-regulation—thus signaling their green leadership—only to exert varying degrees of actual green behavior.

Given the EU's distinctive national business systems framework, as described above, the role of policy supporters in upper management inside European companies is likely to be less of a driver than that of the rest of the Global 500 firms because European CSR initiatives have been largely driven by programs and initiatives of external industry associations or of an "enabling state."[13] As shown in table 9.4, unlike the Global 500 firms as a whole, EU-based firms' decision to participate in voluntary carbon disclosure is not a function of upper management responsibility or a firm's proactive adherence to ESG principles on their own, respectively.[14] As the case of the EU's Non-Financial Reporting Directive illustrates (see next section), there is a blurring of the private and public spheres in the climate disclosure policy domain in Europe.

That being said, conditional on participation in voluntary carbon disclosure, European companies that disclosed to CDP at higher levels were the ones that had articulated a corporate vision for environmental sustainability, adopted ESG principles, and invested in complementary capabilities in the form of environmental research and development (R&D), similar to all Global 500 firms (see table 9.4). In fact, both *mission statement* and *ESG* are associated with conditional marginal effects (CAMEs) of three to five additional points in carbon disclosure score. Like their Global 500 peers, EU firms determined their effort or intensity of participation in voluntary carbon

Table 9.4

Internal firm determinants of participation and effort in voluntary carbon disclosure, double-hurdle model (EU-based Fortune Global 500 firms)

Tier 1 (Participation in voluntary carbon disclosure)	Coefficient	Robust standard errors[a]	AME
Policy supporter—upper management	0.402	0.389	0.133
Mission statement	0.111	0.673	0.005
ESG principles[b]	0.118	0.233	0.198
Dedicated website	0.037	0.543	0.004
Environmental R&D	0.091	0.328	–0.021
Revenues (log)	0.360***	0.063	0.060
Government-owned	N/A		
GHG-intensive (broad)	0.681	0.441	–0.053
Constant	–2.052***	0.546	
Tier 2 (Level of voluntary carbon disclosure)	**Coefficient**	**Robust standard errors[a]**	**CAME[c]**
Policy supporter—upper management	1.581	1.593	6.328
Mission statement	4.049*	2.087	2.887
ESG principles[b]	2.537*	1.37	5.214
Dedicated website	–0.834	1.625	2.487
Environmental R&D	1.879**	0.814	3.779
Revenues (log)	1.300**	0.544	1.571
Government-owned	N/A		
GHG-intensive (broad)	–3.392**	1.682	–2.128
Constant	80.840***	5.720	
Lnsigma			
Constant	1.677***	0.186	
Chi-square	153.757		
N	114		

Note: Abbreviations: AME, average marginal effect; *$p<0.1$, **$p<0.05$, ***$p<0.01$ (two-tailed tests). N/A or "not applicable" denotes the fact that *government-owned* has been dropped from the model due to multicollinearity.

[a] Robust standard errors with sector-level cluster correction.

[b] Environmental, social, and governance (ESG) principles.

[c] AME conditional on $y>0$ (CAME).

disclosure via a cost-benefit analysis based on an assessment of existing technologies and capabilities inside the firm.

The significance of explicit CSR in explaining the intensity of participation (tier 2 decision) but not participation (tier 1 decision) in voluntary carbon disclosure by EU-based firms may in part be explained by the fact that there is contemporary evidence of the spread of US-style, explicit CSR in Europe and elsewhere,[15] which some scholars have called "Americanization" of management practices.[16] Furthermore, while European firms have less discretion about whether or not to participate in carbon disclosure because of the EU's institutional framework, there is still room for discretion on the margins—based on individual company's benefit-cost analysis—regarding how much effort a firm chooses to devote to voluntary carbon disclosure. Adidas, which is featured in chapter 8 as an illustrative company case, is an exemplar of an EU-based company that has engaged in explicit CSR initiatives (notably, Adidas' Green Company) that not only embodied the ethos but also went beyond the legal requirements of the EU.

As a robustness check of table 9.4's results, *policy supporter—chief sustainability officer*, a measure of managerial agency at the highest level, is associated with a greater likelihood of participation in CDP for EU firms (see table A8.2). This could be because while on average corporate management in European firms did not exercise the same kind of discretion that other global firms have regarding CSR activities, the chief executive officer responsible for environmental sustainability and climate mitigation exercised discretion in ways that senior managers below the chief executive did not. In fact, a 2012 study showed that for Scandinavia-based publicly traded corporations, companies with a CSR top management position were three times more likely to be included in the Dow Jones Sustainability World Index than firms that did not install an executive leader overseeing corporate sustainability.[17]

9.2.2 Corporate × Regulation

Ahead of the rest of world, the European Commission was the first governing institution to establish guidance for firms and to set standards on an EU-wide classification for what constitutes sustainable or "green" economic activities. In 2014, the European Parliament passed the Non-Financial Reporting Directive (NFRD) mandating disclosure of environmental information for "public interest entities" (i.e., firms, banks, and insurers) with more than 500 employees. The NFRD dovetailed with the EU's 2016 plan of ten specific actions ("Action Plan: Financing Sustainable Growth") to move toward mandatory climate risk disclosure, as part of a new set of regulations to finance sustainable growth and support the transition to a low-carbon economy.[18]

Number nine of the ten-point action plan called for "strengthening sustainability disclosure accounting rule making,"[19] which made way for the establishment of standards and labels for financial products such as green bonds or green investment funds. The EU's Sustainable Finance Disclosure Regulation, which was a byproduct of the Action Plan,[20] requires firms to report how sustainability risks are integrated into investment decision-making. A related set of rules, the EU's Corporate Sustainability Reporting Directive, introduced detailed sustainability reporting requirements for EU companies and non-EU companies meeting certain thresholds for net turnover in the EU and firms with securities listed on a regulated EU market.

In these EU regulatory developments, CDP positioned itself as the data platform of choice for EU firms, relying on the fact that firms were already disclosing their climate-related information voluntarily to their platform. Since the early 2010s, CDP has been an increasingly regular voice in European public affairs, with engagement in more than twenty EU legislative proposals or policies. In fact, the European Commission's Guidelines on Non-Financial Reporting explicitly referenced CDP first among voluntary platforms as a means for firms to comply with the NFRD.[21]

In the EU, private and public interactions in the climate disclosure policy domain are sustained and complementary in a mutually reinforcing manner. Recent research has shown the complementarity between public and private governance—as evidenced by CDP's notable role in the EU's climate disclosure policymaking—is influenced by the degree to which a nonstate or private organization has access to the policymaking process, leverage of authority, and ability to strategically adapt and evolve to shifting priorities in politics and the economy.[22]

By contrast, several years behind the EU, the US Securities and Exchange Commission (SEC) proposed a similar set of corporate climate disclosure rules for publicly traded companies in 2022 but has faced, from the start, political opposition from Republican lawmakers.[23] Moreover, Republican state attorneys general in the United States, emboldened by a Supreme Court ruling that limited the Environmental Protection Agency's (EPA) ability to regulate greenhouse gas emissions, have threated multiple lawsuits, claiming that SEC regulators do not have the authority to promulgate corporate climate disclosure rules.[24]

Time will tell whether the normalization role that CDP played in climate disclosure in the EU could have positive spillover effects in the United States for corporate acceptance of mandatory disclosure rules. Like the European Commission, the SEC has emphasized that the "proposed disclosures are similar to those that many companies already provide based on broadly accepted disclosure frameworks . . . [and that] . . . the CDP questionnaire . . . exhibits full alignment" with the proposed rules.[25] While CDP has not played a similar role in the United States as it did in the EU, Elizabeth Small, general counsel and head of policy at CDP America, stated, "CDP has prepared the world for this. Now our theory of change has become the norm . . . CDP is delighted that climate disclosure has taken the mainstream stage [in the United States] and looks forward to dialogue in the months ahead."[26]

9.2.3 Corporate × Global

During 2011–2020, about a third of the Global 500 firms participated in global governance as members of the UN Global Compact (UNGC), which is a UN-led voluntary initiative based on chief executive officer commitment worldwide to adopt sustainable and socially responsible policies and to report on their implementation. As table 9.5 shows, EU firms stood out in their high rate of participation in the UNGC before and after the Paris Agreement (77–80 percent). By contrast, while making up the largest share of the Global 500, US firms were the least likely among developed country–based firms to join the UNGC, with 14 percent for the 2011–2020 decade.

Launched in 2004, the Global Compact Network Spain is the largest local (country) network of signatories to the UNGC, with more than 2,200 members from large- to small- and medium-sized enterprises, the public sector, educational entities, and nongovernmental organizations. All Spanish firms in the Global 500 have been UNGC members since at least 2012.

With more than 2020 members, Europe's second-largest local network is Global Compact Network France, which was established in 2005. Europe's third-largest local network is Germany's Global Compact Network, comprising more than 1,000 members from business, civil society, and government. Many of these active participants in global governance through the UNGC, rank among Europe's corporate Climate Leaders (see table 9.3).

Table 9.5
Participation rates in the UN Global Compact, developed versus developing countries (Fortune Global 500 firms)

	Year joined	2011–2020 (%)	Before Paris Agreement (%)	After Paris Agreement (%)
Developed countries[a]	2008	34	31	38
EU[b]	2005	77	75	80
UK	2007	51	46	55
Canada	2005	66	64	69
United States	2012	14	10	17
Australia	2010	53	47	58
Japan	2010	39	34	43
South Korea	2010	56	49	64
Developed countries excluding (excl.) EU	2009	25	21	28
Developed countries excl. EU and UK	2010	22	19	26
Developing countries[c]	2007	37	35	39
Brazil	2007	58	54	61
India	2003	48	48	48
China	2006	21	21	21
Russia	2011	18	15	22
Developing countries excl. China	2008	39	37	42

[a] Australia, Belgium, Canada, Czech Republic, Denmark, Finland, Germany, Hong Kong, Ireland, Israel, Italy, Japan, Luxembourg, Netherlands, Norway, Poland, Singapore, South Africa, South Korea, Spain, Sweden, Switzerland, Taiwan, United States, and UK.

[b] Belgium, Czech Republic, Denmark, Finland, France, Germany, Italy, Luxembourg, Netherlands, Poland, Spain, and Sweden.

[c] Brazil, Chile, China, Colombia, India, Indonesia, Malaysia, Mexico, Peru, Russia, South Africa, Thailand, and Turkey.

Data source: UN Global Compact, https://unglobalcompact.org/what-is-gc/participants.

After the Paris Agreement, nearly all EU-based corporate members of the UNGC had designated a senior- or executive-level manager responsible for climate mitigation and established a quantitative emissions target (see table 9.6). Half of these firms also set an internal carbon price. UNGC members based in other developed countries also adopted sustainability best practices at high rates, albeit at lower rates than the EU firms. While developing country–based firms were less likely than developed country–based firms to engage in corporate self-regulation on climate change overall, their corporate climate action increased substantially after the Paris Agreement, notably China. Non-UNGC members, regardless of country or region, were 20 to 50 percent less likely than UNGC members to adopt global best practices of sustainability before and after the Paris Agreement (data not shown).

9.3 Regulation Matters More for Corporate Climate Action in Developing Countries than in Developed Countries

Table 9.7 shows the adoption rates for quantitative emissions target–setting by global firms headquartered in developed versus developing countries, with respect to whether a firm has installed a dedicated senior- or executive-level manager responsible for climate mitigation, originates in a country with relatively stringent regulations, and is a member of the UN Global Compact. The combination of managerial agency, regulatory stringency, and participation in global governance is correlated with the highest adoption rates of quantitative emissions targets whether firms were domiciled in the Global North or the Global South and before or after the Paris Agreement.

However, the impacts of the cross-level governance interactions (relative to corporate, regulatory or global governance on their own) were more pronounced for firms in developing countries than those in developed countries, notably in the first half of the 2011–2020 decade. Moreover, developing country–based firms with senior- or executive-level managers responded more readily to domestic regulatory stringency than to nonmandatory global norms and best practices compared to their peers in the Global North during the same period.

While these divergent cross-level governance dynamics are true for new or emerging climate policy innovations, once a carbon management tool becomes the industry or business norm or standard, the relative influence

Table 9.6
Corporate climate action (sustainability outputs) for UNGC members, before and after the Paris Agreement (Fortune Global 500 firms)

	Developed countries[a]	Developed countries excl. EU+UK	Developing countries[b]	Developing countries excl. China	EU[c]	UK	China
Before Paris Agreement (2011–2015)							
Manager (%)	88	83	65	67	90	100	40
Voluntary carbon disclosure (%)	97	95	64	63	97	100	80
Emissions target (%)	80	81	39	43	83	67	0
Environmental, social, governance (ESG) score[d] (0–100)	74	73	66	68	75	78	49
ESG environment	79	75	65	67	83	79	47
ESG social	75	72	68	71	77	82	38
ESG governance	69	72	66	65	66	71	74
ESG controversies	70	67	85	85	76	52	89
N	892	403	181	166	399	90	15
After Paris Agreement (2016–2020)							
Manager (%)	97	95	82	81	98	100	100
Voluntary carbon disclosure (%)	91	92	59	58	88	94	73
Emissions target (%)	96	94	77	75	97	97	100
Internal carbon price[e] (%)	47	44	35	37	51	52	7
Emissions target and internal carbon price[e] (%)	47	44	33	36	51	50	7
Environmental, social, and governance (ESG) score[d] (0–100)	77	76	69	70	78	81	61
ESG environment	79	77	67	68	83	79	59

ESG social	81	79	75	77	83	84	54
ESG governance	70	71	64	63	69	77	76
ESG controversies	64	65	75	74	66	54	88
N	1,077	545	203	188	424	108	15

[a] Australia, Belgium, Canada, Czech Republic, Denmark, Finland, Germany, Hong Kong, Ireland, Israel, Italy, Japan, Luxembourg, Netherlands, Norway, Poland, Singapore, South Africa, South Korea, Spain, Sweden, Switzerland, Taiwan, United States, and UK.

[b] Brazil, Chile, China, Colombia, India, Indonesia, Malaysia, Mexico, Peru, Russia, South Africa, Thailand, and Turkey.

[c] Belgium, Czech Republic, Denmark, Finland, France, Germany, Italy, Luxembourg, Netherlands, Poland, Spain, and Sweden.

[d] ESG score measures a company's relative environmental, social, and governance performance, commitment, and effectiveness, based on company-reported data, which include information covering ten themes (namely, resource use, emissions, environmental product innovation, workforce, human rights, community, product responsibility, management, shareholders, and corporate social responsibility strategy). Scores in the 50 to 75 range indicate "good relative ESG performance" and above average degree of transparency in a firm's public reporting of environmental, social, and governance data. Scores above 75 indicate "excellent relative ESG performance and high degree of transparency in reporting material ESG data publicly." "LSEG ESG Score," LSEG Data and Analytics, accessed April 13, 2024, https://www.lseg.com/en/data-analytics/sustainable-finance/esg-scores.

[e] Data for internal carbon price and emissions target and internal carbon price are only available for 2016–2020.

Data sources: CDP, UN Global Compact, LSEG Data and Analytics, and corporate websites and annual reports.

of regulatory versus global governance alongside firm-level managerial and organizational capabilities could shift. In the latter half of the decade, or the post–Paris Agreement period, developing country–based global firms with managers and membership in the UN Global Compact were just as likely or more likely to adopt quantitative emissions targets as firms that had managers and faced regulatory pressure. In other words, when a sustainability practice is new, Global South firms proactively adopted it when they faced strong regulatory pressure. Once a sustainability practice became mainstreamed, however, the presence of senior- or executive-level managers responsible for climate mitigation is associated with firms' setting of an emissions target, whether firms faced regulatory pressure or participated in global governance.

These descriptive statistics align with the fact that, as shown in figures 9.3 and 9.4 (see below), by the end of the decade, more than a majority of developing country–based firms (notably Brazil and India) had installed dedicated upper management leaders responsible for carbon management and climate risks. Furthermore, by 2020 previously novel corporate management tools such as quantitative emissions targets had become a business norm for global firms in both developed and developing countries with high adoption rates (86 percent and 67 percent, respectively).

9.3.1 Managerial and Organizational Capabilities

As senior- and executive-level management over climate change have become ubiquitous in developed countries (notably in Europe), developing country–based firms have trended in the same direction. As shown in table 9.8, the proportion of developing country–based global firms that have installed senior- or executive-level managers dedicated to climate mitigation doubled from 2011 to 2020, from just over one-third in 2011 to 70 percent at the end of the decade. Notably, global firms in Brazil and India have nearly caught up to their peers in the Global North. China and Russia experienced, on average, the largest increases in the proportion of firms that have conferred the responsibility for carbon management and climate risks to upper management.

This upward trend emphasizing climate managerial capacity and capabilities was especially striking among Chinese firms. At the beginning of the 2011–2020 decade less than 10 percent of multinational companies based in China regarded corporate sustainability, including climate mitigation, as a business imperative that involved leadership and decision-making at the

Table 9.7
Corporate adoption rates for quantitative emissions targets and multilevel governance interactions, developed versus developing countries

	Developed countries (%)[a]	Developing countries (%)[b]
Before Paris Agreement (2011–2015)		
No manager	28	5
Manager	71	46
Regulation	62	42
Global	81	39
Manager × regulation	72	68
Manager × global	83	57
Regulation × global	81	44
Manager × regulation × global[c]	83	56
After Paris Agreement (2016–2020)		
No manager	32	28
Manager	88	73
Regulation	83	68
Global	96	77
Manager × regulation	89	79
Manager × global	98	82
Regulation × global	96	76
Manager × regulation × global[c]	98	81

Note: All adoption rates are distinct at the 1 percent statistical significance level.

[a] Australia, Belgium, Canada, Czech Republic, Denmark, Finland, Germany, Hong Kong, Ireland, Israel, Italy, Japan, Luxembourg, Netherlands, Norway, Poland, Singapore, South Africa, South Korea, Spain, Sweden, Switzerland, Taiwan, United States, and UK.

[b] Brazil, Chile, China, Colombia, India, Indonesia, Malaysia, Mexico, Peru, Russia, South Africa, Thailand, and Turkey.

[c] Manager × regulation × global for a given year represents a firm that installed a dedicated senior- or executive-level manager responsible for climate mitigation, originating from a country that scores equal to or above the 75th percentile in regulatory stringency of Global 500 firms based in developing countries, and is a member of the UN Global Compact. The regulatory stringency threshold is lower than that for the rest of this book's analyses on the full sample (i.e., all Global 500 firms) because no developing country scored equal to or above the mean in regulatory stringency for the full sample.

Data sources: CDP, LSEG Data and Analytics, and corporate websites and annual reports.

senior or executive level. By 2020, a majority of Chinese firms had installed a climate change senior- or executive-level manager.

These internal firm management trends coincided with the initiation of dedicated programs by private sector consulting firms as well as nonprofit organizations, such as the US-based Conference Board, which seeks to provide a "peer network" and training to "deepen knowledge, sharpen skills, and share experiences and actionable solutions for the management of China-specific sustainability issues."[27] External experts in integrating sustainability and energy efficiency into business strategy and circular economy concepts and new sustainable business models—a majority of them from the US and Europe—regularly consulted corporate executives in charge of sustainability, corporate responsibility, community engagement, or other activities closely related to sustainability for mainland China as well as other developing countries.

Russian firms followed a similar trajectory as firms in China (both starting at a low baseline) with respect to their appointment of senior- or executive-level managers responsible for climate mitigation from 2011 to 2020, with China leading with higher proportion of firms with corporate climate leadership roles until the end of the decade (see figure 9.2). By contrast, corporate management trends in Brazil and India tracked each other and generally mirrored those of the developed countries, as shown in figure 9.3. By the middle of the decade, European and British firms had achieved a (near) universal practice of delegating senior and executive leadership with responsibility over carbon management and climate mitigation (not shown).

9.3.2 Corporate × Regulation

Few scholars have focused on explaining corporate self-regulation as an outcome of the interaction between corporate management and regulatory governance cross-nationally and comparatively over time in a quantitative study, as this chapter and book do. That being said, there is research on examining the role of regulatory pressure on specific cases of voluntary environmental programs in developing countries. An empirical study focused on Chinese manufacturers showed that there were moderating effects of institutional pressures, including government regulation, on emergent green supply chain practices and performance.[28] An analysis of Mexico's flagship voluntary regulatory initiative, the Clean Industry Program, found that the voluntary program attracted participants under pressure from regulators but did not result

Table 9.8
Climate change managerial agency: Existence of senior- or executive-level managers, developed versus developing countries

	Developed countries[a] (%)	Developed countries excl. EU + UK (%)	Developing countries[b] (%)	Developing countries excl. China (%)	EU[c] (%)	UK (%)	China (%)	Brazil (%)	India (%)	Russia (%)
2011	58	52	34	38	70	87	7	50	52	8
2014	78	74	50	54	90	97	21	69	67	15
2017	86	83	61	62	93	100	50	75	76	31
2020	89	86	68	70	93	100	57	81	76	62
Before Paris Agreement (2011–2015)	72	67	45	49	83	95	17	63	65	12
After Paris Agreement (2016–2020)	87	84	62	64	93	100	50	76	76	37

[a] Australia, Belgium, Canada, Czech Republic, Denmark, Finland, Germany, Hong Kong, Ireland, Israel, Italy, Japan, Luxembourg, Netherlands, Norway, Poland, Singapore, South Africa, South Korea, Spain, Sweden, Switzerland, Taiwan, United States, and UK.
[b] Brazil, Chile, China, Colombia, India, Indonesia, Malaysia, Mexico, Peru, Russia, South Africa, Thailand, and Turkey.
[c] Belgium, Czech Republic, Denmark, Finland, France, Germany, Italy, Luxembourg, Netherlands, Poland, Spain, and Sweden.
Data sources: CDP and corporate websites and annual reports.

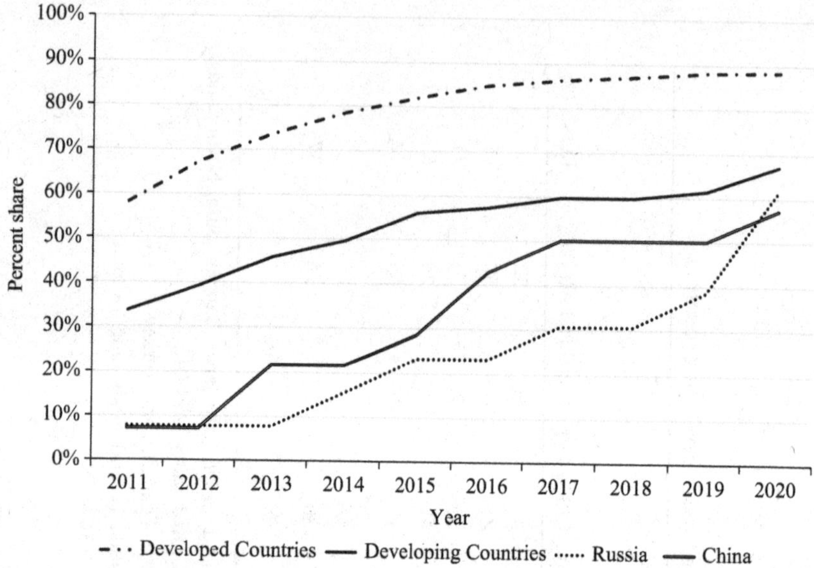

Figure 9.2

Percent share of senior- or executive-level managers on climate mitigation, 2011–2020 (developed versus developing countries, China, and Russia).

Data sources: CDP and corporate websites and annual reports.

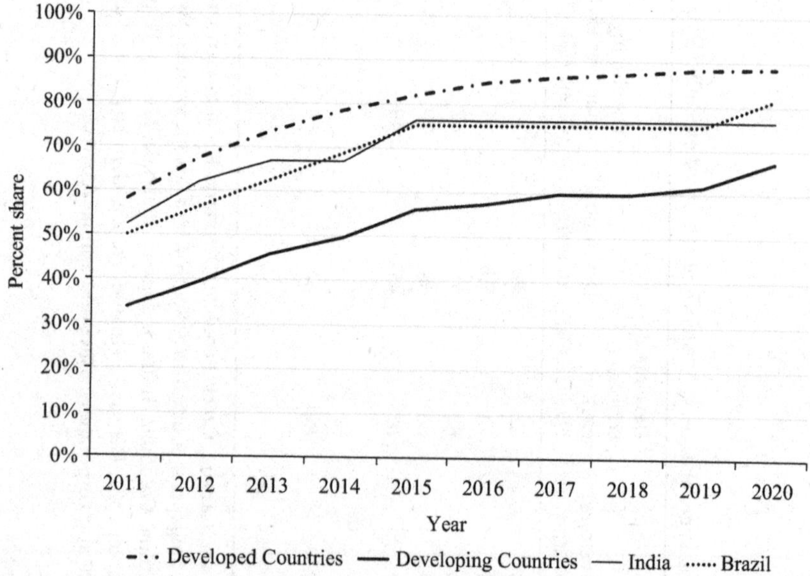

Figure 9.3

Percent share of senior- or executive-level managers on climate mitigation, 2011–2020 (developed versus developing countries, Brazil, and India).

Data sources: CDP and corporate websites and annual reports.

in a large, lasting impact on their environmental performance.[29] Moreover, one of the first studies on the Costa Rican Certification for Sustainable Tourism program identified that participation was related to government monitoring, along with other isomorphic institutional pressures and firm-level factors, such as trade association membership.[30]

These and other studies that are focused on the developing country context have demonstrated that industry and other privately driven self-regulation in the Global South functions in the shadow of, and in conjunction with, public regulation.[31] The expectation is that the corporate × regulation interactions that make up the propositions 3 and 4—as delineated in chapter 2—of this book's multilevel governance framework on climate change are just as (or more) salient drivers of participation and intensity of participation in the Global South as in the Global North.

Empirical evidence for this conjecture is reported in table 9.9, which displays results based on a split sample analysis of the Global South firms' participation in the CDP (first dependent variable) and their level of voluntary carbon disclosure (second dependent variable). This analysis based on the Heckman selection model complements chapter 4's panel data analysis for the Global 500 firms at-large, which established a statistically significant relationship between firm and domestic regulatory governance (corporate × regulation) and firm and global governance (corporate × global) interactions.

While on average global firms based in developed countries are more likely to participate in voluntary carbon disclosure (78 percent) than firms based in developing countries (47 percent), the average marginal effects (AMEs) associated with the interaction terms for managerial agency and regulatory stringency are more pronounced for firms based in developing countries than in developed countries (see model 1 results in panels A and B of table 9.9).[32] Given the existence of a senior- or executive-level manager dedicated to climate mitigation, a 1 percent increase in regulatory stringency is associated with a 16 percent increase in the probability of participation in voluntary carbon disclosure by a firm based in the Global South, compared to 6 percent for a firm based in the Global North.[33]

Moreover, conditional on participation, developing country firms that have adopted climate management tools—namely, quantitative emissions targets—are more responsive to regulatory pressures in their extent of voluntary carbon disclosure (i.e., level of carbon disclosure) than firms that are based in developed countries. These results are robust to whether or not

Table 9.9
Multilevel determinants of participation and effort in voluntary carbon disclosure, Heckman selection model, developed versus developing countries

	Model 1		Model 2	
	Corporate × regulation		Corporate × global	
	Participation in voluntary carbon disclosure b/se[a]	Level of voluntary carbon disclosure b/e[a]	Participation in voluntary carbon disclosure b/se[a]	Level of voluntary carbon disclosure b/e[a]
Panel A Developed countries				
Cross-level interactions				
Manager × regulatory stringency	0.331*** (0.03)			
Target × regulatory stringency		2.760*** (0.34)		
Manager × UNGC member			0.984*** (0.25)	
Target × UNGC member				1.749 (1.13)
Panel B Developing countries				
Cross-level interactions				
Manager × regulatory stringency	0.420*** (0.05)			

Target × regulatory stringency	3.277*** (0.82)		
Manager × UNGC member		0.002 (0.39)	
Target × UNGC member			–3.914 (2.98)

Note: ***$p < 0.01$. Models 1 and 2 in panels A and B include firm- and country-level controls and sector and year fixed effects (data not shown). A full set of results is given in appendix 8. See chapter 4 and appendix 4 for information about the dependent and independent variables and the Heckman selection model as well as information about how endogeneity concerns (e.g., reverse causation) are dealt with in the analysis.

[a] Robust standard errors with firm-level cluster correction.

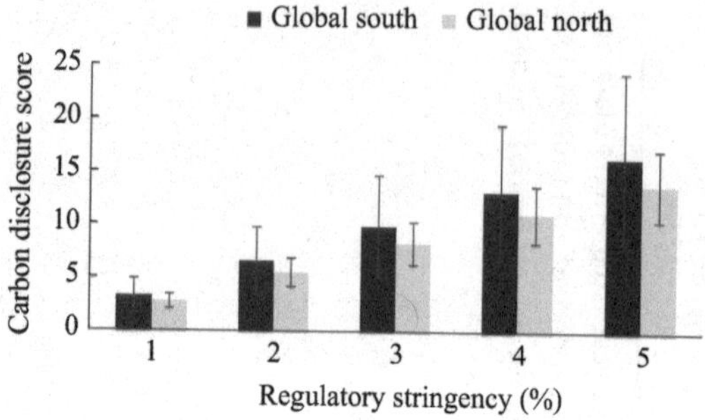

Figure 9.4
Global North versus Global South: average marginal effects of regulatory stringency, given quantitative emissions targets and conditional on participation.
Note: The 95 percent confidence intervals are shown by the error bars. A paired sample *t* test of the two series' estimated AMEs, assuming unequal variance, indicate that they are significantly different.
Source: Lily Hsueh, "Corporations at a Crossroads: How Multilevel Governance Interactions Shape Participation and Efforts in Private Governance Regimes," *Governance* 32, no. 4 (2019): 737, https://doi.org/10.1111/gove.12406.

global firms are based in China, Russia, or India, the three largest economies in the developing countries.

Figure 9.4 plots the estimated average marginal effects (AMEs) of regulatory stringency on a global firm's carbon disclosure score for increasing stringency of domestic regulation, given the adoption of quantitative emissions targets by firms (i.e., target = 1) and conditional on participation in the CDP. Notably, regulatory stringency's AMEs on the intensity of participation is higher for Global South firms than for Global North firms, although there is more noise in the Global South estimates, as shown by the wider error bars. A difference of means test assuming unequal variances confirms that the Global South and Global North AMEs are statistically different. These results suggest that the impact of managerial agency in the face of stringent regulation is more pronounced in the Global South than in the Global North.

9.3.3 Corporate × Global

To complement propositions 5 and 6, first established in chapter 2, about the role of corporate × global interactions in explaining corporate self-regulation on climate change, this chapter's conjecture is that corporate × global interactions are salient drivers of participation and intensity of participation in the Global North but not in the Global South. Developing country–based firms are likely to respond to domestic regulatory pressures before responding to the demands of global governance institutions.

The likely precedence of state-based and enforced regulatory policies over global norms from the perspective of Global South firms' corporate management is because, first, it is economically and politically less costly to adhere to domestic regulations that carry sanctions for noncompliance than to refrain from adopting voluntary global norms. Along the same vein, these firms may inhibit the expansion of global governance and mobilize to defeat transnational rules pertaining to labor, environment, health, and safety because they profit from cross-national regulatory differences.[34] Global firms do so either by incorporating in tax and investment havens or by gravitating to sourcing destinations with less stringent enforcement of labor and environmental laws.[35]

Second, private regulations do not simply add new rules for previously ungoverned phenomena. In fact, firms generally resist rules that would limit their autonomy. If firms do not already live with similar rules domestically—which is more likely in the Global North than in the Global South—they may not have the incentives to voluntarily embed more stringent global norms or best practices in their modus operandi. An example of this is the fact that imbalances between developed and developing countries have persisted with respect to voluntary nonparty contributions to climate action by firms and other nonstate actors, since nonparty voluntary contributions were first compiled in 2014 at the annual United Nations Climate Summit.[36]

These two rationales imply that firms "on the ground" in the Global South will more likely respond to domestic regulatory stringency than to global norms in their participation and intensity of participation in voluntary carbon disclosure. In fact, prior research has shown that Global South firms are often "inhibitors" rather than "providers" of global governance.[37]

As panel A of model 2 in table 9.9 shows, global firms based in developed countries that have adopted global best practices are more likely to disclose such information to investors through CDP (in the participation stage of the model) when facilitated by dedicated managers, mirroring the results for the Global 500 firms as a whole (see model 2 in table 4.1). By contrast, there is no statistical significance on either the *manager × UNGC member* or *target × UNGC member* interaction term in the split sample for developing countries (see panel B, model 2). These results lend large-*N* evidence to the above-mentioned conjecture that developing country–based firms may be less motivated than developed country–based firms to embed global best practices on carbon management that are more stringent than required by domestic regulation of their domicile country or their largest export markets.

9.4 Conclusion

In developed countries, corporate, domestic, and global governance are complements. The EU's lead in corporate climate actions is likely not to be diminished, as corporate, regulatory, and global governance interact and lead to a race to the top in corporate climate leadership. In response to regulatory pressure, dedicated senior- and executive-level managers have aligned and steered their firms toward policies and practices, including proactive climate action, that are in congruence with rules on the books, as well as with rules in the making espoused by domestic regulatory institutions and global institutions that emphasize learning and diffusion of best practices. Moreover, in the climate disclosure context, complementarity and normalization, notably in Europe, have led private and public governance to reinforce one another in positive feedback effects, which have expanded both the role for corporate self-regulation as well as the scope for and stringency of rules and government. In this way, developed country–based firms are as much agents of domestic regulatory governance and global governance institutions as they are agents of the market, given facilitating corporate management structures and practices.

In the developing countries context, global firms are especially motivated by corporate management, regulatory stringency, and their interactions. Developing country–based firms respond to domestic regulatory stringency rather than to nonmandatory global norms and best practices because it is economically and politically advantageous for firms in the Global South to act, at times preemptively, in anticipation of local rules and policies that could carry sanctions for noncompliance in their country of domicile or in their largest export markets. Consequently, corporate self-regulation on climate change by developing country-based firms does not on its own fill the vacuum left by weak domestic governance.

That being said, global firms may strategically respond to, exacerbate, or reconcile the wedge between domestic and global governance institutions, and do so with the global economy and markets in mind and on their side.

This has become more likely with the managerial shift of climate-related duties to upper management during the post–Paris Agreement period. Senior and executive leadership can and will exercise agency as a strategy to signal to international markets their ability to play by the norms and rules of the global economy.

Examples include several China-based global businesses (such as SHEIN, the largest fast fashion retailer, and JinkoSolar, a behemoth that produces one in ten solar modules installed globally) that are members of the UN Global Compact and have adopted quantitative emissions targets and have either moved their headquarters and/or set up factories outside China to distance themselves from their home country.[38] These companies are eager to shed "the shoddy reputation that American buyers continue to associate with goods made in China . . . and to escape from the risk of a crackdown by the Chinese authorities."[39]

10 All-Hands-on-Deck: What Happens When Markets and Governments Fail?

The science is clear. Many of the changes in the climate are unprecedented in thousands, if not hundreds of thousands of years, according to the Intergovernmental Panel on Climate Change Sixth Assessment Reports.[1] More than that, data indicate that human activity is responsible for the increase in global temperatures since at least the 1950s. Fossil fuels produce 90 percent of carbon emissions (see figure 10.1). At the time of writing of *Corporations at Climate Crossroads*, 2023 was the hottest year on record: 1.19 degrees Celsius (°C) above the twentieth-century average baseline, as shown in figure 10.2. The 2015 Paris Agreement's stated long-term objective of maintaining global temperature rise "well below" 2°C with a global target of 1.5°C was conceived to avoid the worst impacts of global warming and to minimize the risks and costs of reaching even higher warming levels.

The United States, EU, and China have contributed the most to cumulative carbon emissions worldwide (see figure 10.3). In the United States, industrial emissions make up 30 percent of greenhouse gas (GHG) emissions,[2] which is representative of the average share of industrial emissions to overall carbon emissions in industrialized countries.

Industrial emissions primarily come from burning fossil fuels for energy, as well as GHG emissions from certain chemical reactions necessary to produce goods from raw materials. Global businesses represent close to 70 percent of annual global industrial carbon emissions, and a majority of the emissions are emitted by about 100 corporations.

At the inaugural 2015 Business & Climate Summit, which took place ahead of the twenty-first session of the Conferences of Parties (COP 21) to the United Nations Framework Convention on Climate Change, there was a call for global firms to lead the shift toward a "low-carbon economy,"

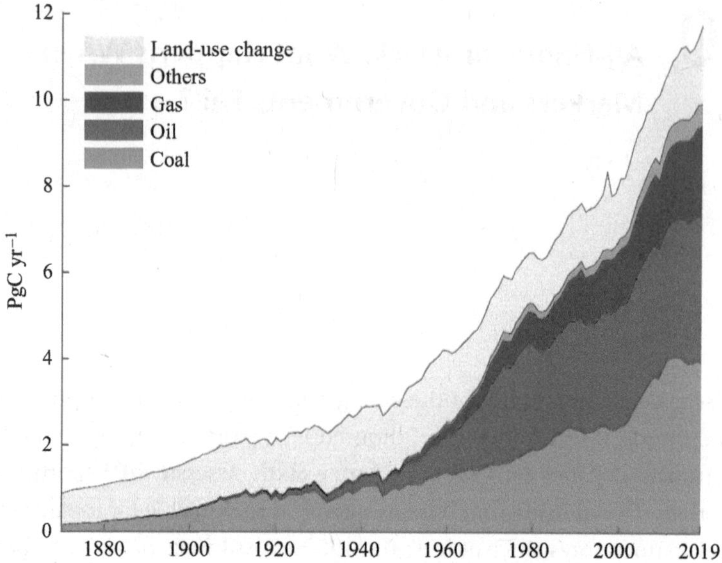

Figure 10.1
Share of global CO_2 emissions due to fossil fuel burning since 1870.
Note: The data in the figure represent historical trends of anthropogenic CO_2 emissions for the period 1870 to 2019, with "others" representing flaring, emissions from carbonates during cement manufacturing. The x-axis shows years, and the y-axis shows annual carbon exchange flux represented numerically in PgC yr-1 units, in which 1 PgC is equal to 1 billion metric tons of carbon.
Data source: IPCC Sixth Assessment Reports Working Group 6, figure 5.5(a), https://www.ipcc.ch/report/ar6/wg1/figures/chapter-5/.

highlighting the fundamental role of business in shaping the low-carbon transition. Fast-forward to less than a decade later and many of the world's largest public and private companies are now required to track and report nearly all of their GHG emissions if they do business in the EU, UK, New Zealand, India, Singapore, and in states such as California and cities like Hong Kong—including emissions from their supply chains, business travel, employee commutes, and the way customers use their products. That means oil and gas companies like Chevron Corporation and BP PLC will likely have to account for emissions from vehicles that use their gasoline, and Apple, Inc., will have to account for materials that go into producing iPhones.[3]

A majority of these firms—the largest companies in the world by sales revenues—have been preparing for mandatory disclosure rules for more than

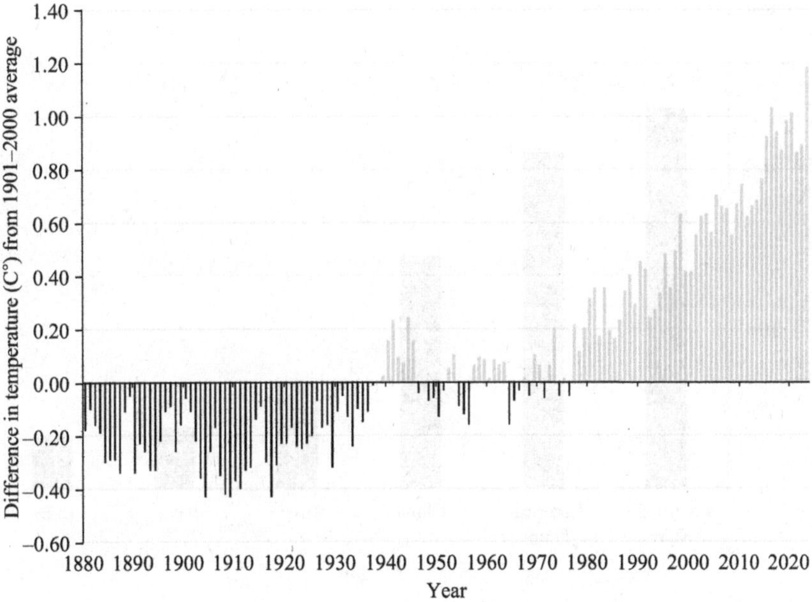

Figure 10.2
Yearly surface temperature from 1880 to 2023 compared to the twentieth-century (1901–2000) average.
Note: Black bars indicate cooler-than-average years; gray bars show warmer-than-average years. The y-axis is the difference from 1901–2000 average temperature (°C).
Data source: National Centers for Environmental Information, https://www.ncei.noaa.gov/access/monitoring/climate-at-a-glance/global/time-series.

a decade. In 2020, close to two-thirds of the firms listed in the S&P 500 index voluntarily reported to CDP (formerly the Carbon Disclosure Project), and an even greater share of the Fortune Global 500 (henceforth, Global 500) did so.[4]

As this book's main empirical case, CDP is a nonprofit organization that surveys companies on behalf of institutional investors about their carbon management and plans to reduce carbon emissions. As the oldest and largest nonprofit that houses voluntary carbon disclosure by corporations, CDP has played a significant role in the development of mandatory transparency and disclosure policies across levels of government. Recent mandatory climate disclosure rules introduced in the UK, EU, New Zealand, Singapore, Hong Kong, and the United States have all to varying degrees built on CDP's success as a global disclosure system for investors, companies, cities, states, and

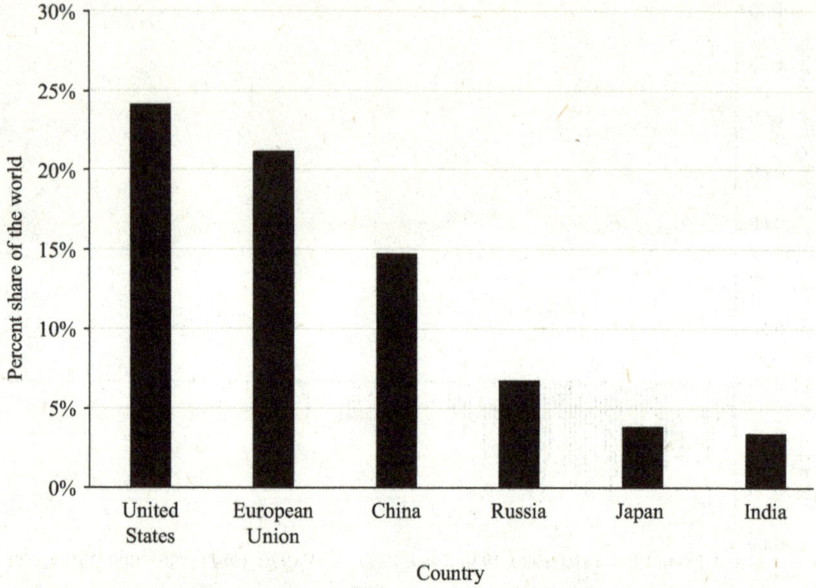

Figure 10.3
Share of world cumulative CO_2 emissions by country (1751–2022).
Note: Cumulative CO_2 emissions are based on emissions produced domestically from fossil fuel combustion and cement and do not correct for emissions embedded in international trade (e.g., consumption-based).
Data source: OurWorldInData.org, https://ourworldindata.org/co2-emissions.

regions to manage their environmental impact. CDP has also partnered with subnational governments in Thailand and Italy.

The rest of the chapter presents the thesis of this book's multiple governance framework of climate change and summarizes the book's major findings, before arguing that because markets and governments can fail and are unlikely, on their own, to resolve climate risks, an all-hands-on-deck approach is necessary for corporate accountability in the age of climate change. The polycentric governance structure with checks and balances of the multilevel governance framework on climate change is consistent with a proposal for a portfolio approach to climate change, notably in an era characterized by growing climate risks, political headwinds in many countries, and increasing challenges to international cooperation. A portfolio and all-hands-on-deck approach will also address the challenge of measuring, tracking, and ultimately, limiting global firms' indirect or non-operations-related emissions, or scope 3 emissions. Between 75 and 90 percent of global firms' total emissions are from their scope 3 emissions. There is currently no industry norm or uniform metric for reporting non-operations-related emissions.

10.1 Multilevel Governance Framework on Climate Change: Theory and Empirics

A lion's share of the global businesses that disclosed to CDP are also members of the United Nations Global Compact (UNGC). Established by the United Nations (UN) in 2000—which was the same year as CDP's founding—the UNGC seeks to bring together businesses and governments for "international dialogues" about socially responsible policies and "universal sustainability principles" across all aspects of corporate sustainability—environment, social policy, sustainable development, governance, financial markets, and supply chains.[5] Close to 90 percent of the UNGC members among the Global 500 proactively reported to CDP from 2011 to 2020.

At the firm level, these are the same global businesses that have installed senior- and executive-level managers dedicated to corporate climate policy and climate mitigation. In 2011, already nearly three-quarters of the Global 500 firms that reported to CDP designated upper management with the authority over carbon management and climate mitigation. By 2020, all global firm disclosers had invested in managerial capacity at the highest levels of corporate governance. By contrast, nearly all multinational firms (97 percent) that did not invest in climate change managerial leadership opted out of climate disclosure.

Corporate climate disclosure is but one case of corporate self-regulation on climate change. There has been no shortage of corporations taking climate action. In 2015, 2000 companies from 145 countries representing $37 trillion in revenues pledged proactive climate action. By 2022, the number of global businesses rose sixfold to nearly thirteen thousand companies. The scope of voluntary climate action is wide, ranging from voluntary adoption of climate mitigation technologies or science-based carbon emissions targets to setting an internal carbon price as well as voluntary adherence to binding rules and standards.

Pledges of and transparency about net-zero targets among the world's largest firms have in recent years proliferated and have become a corporate norm, especially in the wake of the 2018 Intergovernmental Panel on

Climate Change Special Report on 1.5°C. That being said, there is a general consensus among governmental and nongovernmental watchdogs that there are credibility gaps, which could undermine progress.

In light of this, this book sets out to answer the following questions: Many global businesses talk a good game, but which firm, country, and global governance factors (and their cross-level interactions) compel global businesses to participate in voluntary climate action? Do global businesses that participate in voluntary climate action emit less carbon emissions? How do favorable governance conditions vary across sectors and between developed and developing countries?

To answer these questions, *Corporations at Climate Crossroads* develops and tests propositions of a multilevel governance framework on climate change. In this political economic framework, corporations are key players in a nested structure of climate change governance with interactions between bottom-up and top-down incentives and institutions involving firm, regulatory, and global governance, as shown in figure 10.4. Whether a firm participates and how much it participates in corporate self-regulation depend on the interaction of managerial, economic, and political pressures that emanate from inside or outside the firm and across corporate, regulatory, and global governance levels.

10.1.2 A Theory about Corporate Self-Regulation on Climate Change

As chapter 2 delineates, this book's multilevel governance framework on climate change (MGFCC) bridges micro (firm) and macro (political economy and global governance) perspectives in economics, management, and political science to argue that corporate self-regulation on climate change is the result of the agency of senior- or executive-level managers and their interactions with domestic regulation and global governance. The MGFCC articulates a causal mechanism for global firms' decision-making about proactive climate action (see figure 2.2 for an illustration of this causal mechanism).

Corporate leaders face incomplete contingency planning, informational constraints, and cognitive limitations (i.e., decision-makers are boundedly rational). In order to navigate uncertainty in the face of climate change, senior- and executive-level managers often have discretion over internal firm or corporate policy or how that policy will be executed. They

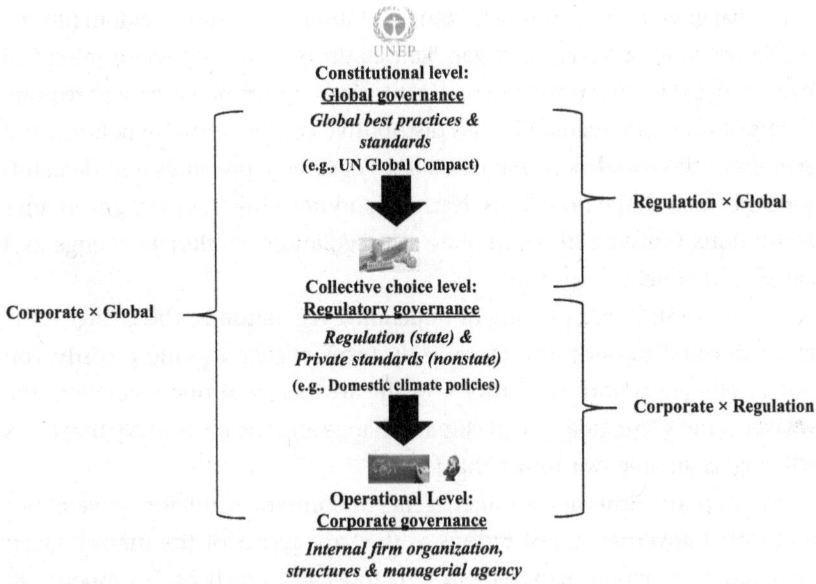

Figure 10.4
Multilevel governance framework on climate change: A nested structure of climate change governance with interactions between bottom-up and top-down incentives and institutions involving firm, regulatory, and global governance.

attract climate-neutral or climate-conscious employees and align the beliefs of employees and the firm through learning, creativity, and innovation. In doing so, managers form governing coalitions inside the firm to delineate and mobilize support as well as the necessary incentives and coordination for climate action that goes beyond the law. Company-initiated corporate social responsibility practices (as opposed to socially responsible practices that have become the industry or institutional norm), and the existence of complementary assets, are also necessary firm-level drivers of a corporation's participation and effort in proactive climate action.

Managers serve as "regulation brokers": when regulatory pressure is high and the marginal cost of self-regulation is low, there is a hastening of efforts led by managers to signal firms' ability to internalize externalities, earn regulatory goodwill, and avoid costly liabilities. Managers are also "norm brokers" in shaping, translating, and disseminating global best practices that could someday become market norms or rules of law.

Global governance, while a harbinger of future regulation, seldom fills the regulatory void or governance gap. Rather, firms' learning and norming (led by managers) in global governance institutions mirror pressures and requirements of domestic regulation and distributive conflicts among political and economic stakeholders in nation-states. Regulatory pressures and demands influence and shape how firms' learning and norming in global governance institutions translate into corporate self-regulation on climate change as a calculus of benefits and costs.

The more stringent existing or impending regulation is, the greater is the effort devoted to—and the more likely firms engage in—more costly voluntary climate action. By contrast, in the absence of strong regulation, the weaker is the self-regulation on climate change and the more likely that firms will engage in greenwashing behavior.

In summary, firms are as much agents of domestic regulatory governance and global governance institutions as they are agents of the market, given facilitating corporate management structures and practices. In response to regulatory pressure, dedicated senior- and executive-level managers will align and steer their firms toward policies and practices, including proactive climate action, that are in congruence with rules on the books, as well as with rules-in-the-making espoused by domestic regulatory institutions and global institutions that emphasize learning and diffusion of best practices.

10.1.3 Research Design and Methods

As delineated, the MGFCC articulates a causal mechanism for global firms' decision-making about corporate self-regulation on climate change. Chapter 2 presents testable implications in the form of seven propositions that accompany each component part, which are then subjected to empirical tests in subsequent chapters. Manager, corporate × regulation, corporate × global, and regulation × global serve as key independent variables to be empirically verified as a cause or driver of participation and effort in voluntary climate action, the dependent variables of interest.

Chapter 3 "opens up the firm" to empirically test propositions about corporate management as a key driver of voluntary climate action. Chapter 4 empirically links corporate management with regulation and global governance to delineate how cross-level governance interactions shape firms' decision-making in a panel data analysis of Fortune Global 500's participation in the CDP and their level of voluntary carbon disclosure. Chapter 5 presents the US case and makes use of the Environmental Protection Agency's (EPA) introduction of the Clean Power Plan as a natural experiment, which exerted regulatory pressure on greenhouse gas (GHG)–intensive firms domiciled in the United States, to quantify the extent to which the existence of senior and executive leadership responsible for carbon management and climate risks mediated the impact of regulatory pressure as a driver of global firms' participation and effort in voluntary climate action.

Chapter 6 provides empirical evidence for the complementary interplay between domestic regulation and global governance in inducing global firms' adoption of global best practices, such as science-based, quantitative emissions targets and an internal price on carbon. Chapters 7 employs a similar quasi-experimental approach as chapter 5 to link firms' voluntary adoption of carbon management practices with environmental performance by quantifying whether firms that disclose climate change information reduce entity-wide GHG emissions and GHG emissions intensity. Chapters 8 and 9 examine whether corporate self-regulation on climate change varies across sectors and in developed and developing countries.

Empirical evidence to substantiate the propositions are based on large-*N* cross-sectional and panel data analyses, which follow global firms' participation and effort in voluntary climate action, notably in voluntary carbon disclosure, from 2011–2020. This author-constructed census of Global 500 and S&P 500 firms' climate mitigation and performance from 2011 to 2020 and across scales of governance (firm, state, country, and global levels) and sectors, and in developed and developing countries, is the first of its kind to track a census of global companies and follows their voluntary climate action and performance over time.

A novel contribution is the book's empirical distinction between firms' decisions to engage in—and their actual level of—climate action as theorized in the multilevel governance framework on climate change. Throughout this book, discrete-continuous econometric models are employed to disentangle *whether* a firm participates and *how much* it participates in corporate self-regulation.

Of note, the complex directions of the causal arrows or endogeneity of managerial agency, domestic regulation, and global governance are addressed in the empirical chapters by exploiting a natural experiment (see chapters 5 and 7), which was arguably and statistically shown to be an exogenous policy shock. Furthermore, a variety of econometric models and statistical techniques are employed to account for how the previous year's corporate actions impact contemporaneous decisions about participation and effort, how contemporaneous policy or market shocks in the economy affect all firms, or how industry-specific factors and actions could impact corporate climate action.

10.2 How Do Favorable Governance Conditions Vary across Sectors and between Developed versus Developing Countries?

The general thesis of this book's multilevel governance framework on climate change (MGFCC) holds across time, sectors, and regions (i.e., developed and developing countries). That is, in any given year, sector, or region, corporate climate leaders are firms that actively manage the impacts of climate change, face actual or forthcoming regulatory pressures domestically, and engage in global governance. These multinational companies have proactively disclosed their carbon management and emissions, set a quantitative emissions target, or adopted a carbon price, among other acts of voluntary climate action.

Across consumer-oriented, technology, and carbon-intensive sectors, the pre- and post–Paris Agreement periods were distinct regimes for climate action by multinational corporations. COP 26 in Glasgow, Scotland, and indicting Intergovernmental Panel on Climate Change publications on the seriousness of a warming climate, the rise in climate activism, and regulatory discussions in Europe, Canada, and elsewhere signaled that a new era of more domestic regulation was on the horizon.

Table 10.1 shows that the proportion of global firms that have adopted a quantitative emissions target rises as the criteria of climate change managerial capacity, stringent regulation, and UN Global Compact membership are added, both before and after the Paris Agreement. From left to right, each column represents all Global 500 firms, GHG-intensive and non-GHG-intensive sectors, and developed and developing countries.

A similar story has emerged for global firms that set an internal price on carbon emissions, as shown in table 10.2. Businesses use internal carbon pricing to evaluate the impact of mandatory carbon prices on their operations and as a tool to identify potential climate risks. Again, firms that readily adopt an internal price on carbon are those that are well managed and stringently regulated and are active participants of global governance.

Table 10.1

Corporate adoption rates for quantitative emissions targets and multilevel governance interactions, before and after the Paris Agreement

	All Global 500 (%)	Non-GHG-intensive[b] (%)	GHG-intensive[c] (%)	Developed countries (%)	Developing countries (%)
Before Paris Agreement (2011–2015)					
No manager	22	23	18	28	5
Manager	68	72	61	71	46
Regulation	61	64	55	62	42
Global	73	80	63	81	39
Manager × regulation	71	75	64	72	68
Manager × global	80	84	72	83	57
Regulation × global	79	83	73	81	44
Manager × regulation × global[a]	82	85	76	83	56
After Paris Agreement (2016–2020)					
No manager	30	29	33	32	28
Manager	87	89	81	88	73
Regulation	82	85	78	83	68
Global	93	96	86	96	77
Manager × regulation	89	92	83	89	79
Manager × global	95	99	90	98	82
Regulation × global	94	97	90	96	76
Manager × regulation × global[a]	96	98	92	98	81

[a] Manager × regulation × global for a given year represents a firm that installed a dedicated senior- or executive-level manager responsible for climate change, originates from a country that scores equal to or above the 75th percentile in regulatory stringency of Global 500 firms based in developing countries, and is a member of the UN Global Compact. The regulatory stringency threshold is lower than that of the rest of this book's analyses on the full sample (i.e., all Global 500 firms) because no developing country scored equal to or above the mean in regulatory stringency for the full sample.

[b] Consumer discretionary, consumer staples, financial services, health care, information technology, and telecommunications sectors.

[c] Energy, industrials, materials, and utilities sectors.

Data sources: CDP, International Environmental Agreements (IEA) Database Project, UN Global Compact, and corporate websites and annual reports.

Table 10.2

Corporate adoption rates for internal carbon prices and multilevel governance interactions, after the Paris Agreement

	All Global 500 (%)	Non-GHG-intensive[b] (%)	GHG-intensive[c] (%)	Developed countries (%)	Developing countries (%)
No manager	8	7	12	10	5
Manager	36	29	49	37	29
Regulation	35	27	49	35	32
Global	45	39	57	48	35
Manager × regulation	38	30	53	37	40
Manager × global	48	41	62	49	44
Regulation × global	47	39	64	48	39
Manager × regulation × global[a]	49	41	66	50	46

Note: This table is based on data from 2016–2020 because consistent data on the Global 500 firms' adoption of an internal carbon price were only available from CDP after 2015.

[a] Manager × regulation × global for a given year represents a firm that installed a dedicated senior- or executive-level manager responsible for climate change, originates from a country that scores equal to or above the 75th percentile in regulatory stringency of Global 500 firms based in developing countries, and is a member of the UN Global Compact. The regulatory stringency threshold is lower than that for the rest of this book's analyses on the full sample (i.e., all Global 500 firms) because no developing country scored equal to or above the mean in regulatory stringency for the full sample.

[b] Consumer discretionary, consumer staples, financial services, health care, information technology, and telecommunications sectors.

[c] Energy, industrials, materials, and utilities sectors.

Data sources: CDP, International Environmental Agreements (IEA) Database Project, UN Global Compact, and corporate websites and annual reports.

The MGFCC's general principals about the complementarity of corporate, regulatory, and global governance notwithstanding, there are noteworthy differences across sectors and in developed versus developing countries, as summarized here.

10.2.1 Technology Firms Lead on Proactive Climate Action

As delineated in chapter 8, between 2011 and 2020, sectoral analyses and company case studies show that global firms operating in sectors with greater consumer contact readily committed to climate action pledges and widely communicated about them irrespective of their actual environmental performance (i.e., reduced carbon emissions or reduced carbon emissions intensity). For consumer-oriented sectors (notably retail and apparel), global firms' carbon footprints are not in their operations but rather in the supply chains. The challenge was that the "cheap talk" was accompanied by inadvertent greenwashing or false or misleading advertising of corporate social responsibility, which was widely reported in the news media.

By contrast, on the eve of the Paris Agreement, global firms operating in the technology sector were two times more likely than other multinational corporations to engage in proactive climate action.[6] Consumer staples, consumer discretionary, and information technology companies were more likely to engage in proactive climate action than firms operating in health care, energy, industrials, materials, and utilities sectors.

Technology firms, as a sector, tended to be wealthier, not only in terms of asset holdings but also profitability, and employed a larger number of workers than other companies. Moreover, technology firms also demonstrate a commitment to sustainability through complementary capabilities and competencies, such as investments in environmental research and development (R&D). For example, by the time of COP 21, a larger share of global firms in the technology sector (75 percent) were certified with the ISO 14001 environmental management standard than the rest of the Global 500 firms (54 percent). A similar pattern, although less pronounced, was also true of investments in environmental R&D by technology multinationals compared to other global firms (56 percent versus 48 percent).

Wealth endowment and complementary capabilities aside, technology firms were more likely than other Global 500 firms to have an in-house senior- or executive-level sustainability officer. On the eve of the Paris Agreement, close to half of all technology companies had formally created a position of vice president of sustainability or chief sustainability officer, compared to about 40 percent of other global firms. By 2020, more than three-quarters of technology firms had installed senior- to executive-level managers responsible for climate change's impact on internal business operations and the physical environment. As this book shows, these in-house champions of sustainability policies and initiatives play a critical role in helping to align corporate vision, build political coalitions inside the firm, and allocate the necessary resources toward sustainability efforts.

Aside from supportive firm-level internal management and organizational capabilities, global businesses in the technology sector are by and large (85 percent) based in developed countries with relatively more stringent regulations and robust climate policies. Many are also active participants in global governance. Notably, all technology firms that are ranked in the top ten for how well a firm addresses risk and concerns related to environmental, social, and governance (ESG) issues in day-to-day operations are also members of the UN Global Compact and have in recent years received an A or A- grade from the CDP for setting a quantitative emissions target and for committing to decarbonization by 2050.[7] The top ten technology firms ranked by ESG performance are Microsoft Corporation, SAP SE, Nokia Corporation, Infosys, Limited, Hitachi, Ltd., Cisco Systems, Inc., Intel Corporation, Deutsche Telekom AG, Wipro, and Telecom Italia SPA.

A majority of these firms are also members of the UN-backed Climate Ambition Alliance: Race to Zero,[8] Climate Ambition Alliance,[9] and the Business Ambition for 1.5°C,[10] among other international cooperative initiatives. These technology companies and others, such as Apple, Autodesk, Inc., BT Group PLC, and Salesforce, Inc., have also joined forces with Aviva PLC, Inter IKEA Holding BV (IKEA), Starbucks Corporation, Walmart, Marks and Spencer Group PLC, and Johnson & Johnson, among others, as part of RE100, which is a business-led, cross-sector global corporate renewable energy initiative founded in 2003 with the stated goal of securing 100 percent of their electricity from renewable sources.

While not immune to accusations of corporate greenwashing,[11] firms in the technology sector stand out for their deployment of technology to reduce both their own and their customers' carbon emissions, as two illustrative company cases—Microsoft and Intel—in chapter 8 depict. Multilevel governance interactions also explain corporate self-regulation on climate change in the technology sector with emphases on the sector's unique firm-level managerial and organizational capabilities and competitive pressures within the sector that characterized a "race to the top" as opposed to a "race to the bottom."

10.2.2 Without Multilevel Governance Drivers, GHG-Intensive Sectors Are Laggards on Climate Action

By contrast, during the 2011–2020 decade, GHG-intensive sectors (namely, energy, industrial, materials, and utilities) were less likely than non-GHG-intensive sectors to engage in corporate self-regulation on climate change. That being said, a subset of the GHG-intensive sector comprises corporate climate leaders that are best managed, regulated stringently, and engage in global governance, mirroring this book's thesis and empirical finding for global businesses as a whole. Without the interplay of corporate, regulatory, and global governance drivers, a "race to the bottom" would have characterized the materials, utilities, energy, and industrial sectors during the 2011–2020 decade. As noted in section 10.2, when US-based GHG-intensive firms faced regulatory pressure from the Clean Power Plan during 2011–2015, participants of voluntary carbon disclosure on average reduced their operational emissions.

After the Paris Agreement, global firms in GHG-intensive sectors stepped up their climate action, compared to before the Paris Agreement, regardless of subsectors' and firms' domicile country or region—that is, whether firms are based in the United States (less regulation), EU (more regulation), or the rest of the world. On the eve of the Paris Agreement, the world's largest publicly traded and investor-owned oil and gas firms joined the Oil and Gas Climate Initiative (OGCI), which was founded in 2014 by the CEOs of the twelve largest energy companies that are responsible for more than 30 percent of global oil and gas production.[12] In 2011, half of the OGCI members had set a quantitative emissions target. By 2020, all but two of these twelve oil and gas producers had set an emissions target, and only one company had not established an internal carbon price. Between 2011 and 2020, the OGCI members together reduced entity-wide carbon emissions by nearly 20 percent,[13] compared to a 13 percent reduction for the GHG-intensive sector as a whole and an increase of 3 percent total emissions in the consumer-oriented and technology sectors.

Six of the twelve OCGI members—Equinor ASA, Eni SPA, Petrobras, TotalEnergies, Repsol SA, and Shell LLC—have been ranked among Corporate

Knights' Global 100 of the top 100 firms for "clean capitalism" and corporate sustainability at least once from 2011 to 2020.[14] Since 2005, the Toronto-based Corporate Knights has published its Global 100 list of the world's 100 most sustainable public companies with more than $1 billion in revenue. Equinor (formerly Statoil) was ranked among the top 100 most sustainable corporations seven times throughout the 2011–2020 decade. Notably, Corporate Knights ranked the Norway-based firm first in 2011 and among the top five most sustainable firms four times from 2011 to 2015. The OCGI members that had not received commendation (i.e., ExxonMobil, BP, China National Petroleum Corporation) on average received lower ESG performance scores than their OCGI peers that did. Of note, none of the OCGI members domiciled in the EU (or Europe) have made the *Financial Times* lists of Europe's climate leaders, which require that firms have achieved reduction in their scope 1 and 2 greenhouse gas (GHG) emissions intensity over a five-year period.[15]

By 2019, OGCI stepped up their engagement in the United Nations Climate Action Summits, leading to criticism of an apparent attempt to influence negotiations in favor of fossil fuel companies. The OGCI hosted an "invitation-only forum" on the "sidelines" of the September Climate Action Summit hosted by UN Secretary General António Guterres in New York City. Oil and gas executives held a "closed, high-level discussion" with key stakeholders.[16] Critics accused the OGCI of "[attempting] to influence negotiations in favour of fossil fuel companies."[17]

10.2.3 European Firms Lead on Proactive Climate Action

As chapter 9 details, in developed countries, corporate, regulatory, and global governance are complements. This means that in developed countries, these three governance levels positively reinforce each other as drivers of corporate self-regulation on climate change. The EU is an exemplar of how firm, regulatory, and global interactions and the active engagement between the private and public governance spheres in Europe explain the climate leadership of global firms based there.

During the 2011–2020 decade, multinational firms domiciled in the EU and the United Kingdom (UK) engaged in corporate self-regulation on climate change—namely, voluntary carbon disclosure, quantitative emissions targets, and an internal price on carbon—at higher rates than their peers in other developed countries (i.e., Global North excluding the EU and UK). Sustainability outputs notwithstanding, from 2011 to 2020, three hundred to five hundred EU and European firms achieved 30 to 50 percent reduction in their greenhouse gas (GHG) emissions intensity, according to the *Financial Times* annual list of Europe's climate leaders.

A triangulation of Corporate Knights' Global 100 list of sustainable companies and the *Financial Times* list of sustainable companies with the Global 500 reveals the global firm archetypes of this book's multilevel governance framework on climate change. As chapter 9 explicates, EU firms are well-resourced, with internal firm managerial and organizational capabilities, have faced relatively more stringent (forthcoming) regulation and climate policies, and have participated at higher rates in global governance than global businesses of similar size and scope based in other countries and regions.

For decades, the blurring of the private and public governance spheres in Europe—to a greater extent than in any other part of the world—has been responsible for the EU's distinctive national business system.[18] Corporate responsibilities toward society have implicitly been codified in the norms, standards, and legal framework of the EU rather than necessarily manifested as explicit policies of individual corporations, as is the case in the United States and other parts of the world.[19] For example, the interactions of public and private actors in the climate disclosure policy domain have led to both ratcheting up of regulations in the EU and competition among firms across sectors for a place as Europe's climate leaders.

Ahead of the rest of world, the European Commission was the first governing institution to establish guidance for firms and to set standards on an EU-wide classification for what constitutes sustainable or "green" economic activities. In 2014, the European Parliament passed the Non-Financial Reporting Directive (NFRD), mandating disclosure of environmental information for "public interest entities" (i.e., firms, banks, and insurers) with more than five hundred employees. The NFRD dovetailed with the EU's 2016 plan to move toward mandatory climate risk disclosure as part of a new set of regulations to finance sustainable growth and support the transition to a low-carbon economy.[20]

In these EU regulatory developments, CDP positioned itself as the data platform of choice for EU firms and was a regular voice in European public affairs, with engagement in more than twenty EU legislative proposals or policies.[21] Several years behind the EU, the US Securities and Exchange Commission (SEC) proposed a similar set of corporate climate disclosure rules for publicly traded companies in 2022 but has faced political opposition from Republican lawmakers since the start. Time will tell whether the normalization role that CDP played in climate disclosure in the EU could have positive spillover effects in the United States for corporate acceptance of mandatory disclosure rules.

10.2.4 Developing Country–Based Firms Need Corporate Leaders and Regulation

In the developing country context, managerial *and* regulatory stringency, or corporate × regulation, interactions are more pronounced than in developed countries, as chapter 9's empirical analysis shows. Given the existence of a senior- or executive-level manager dedicate to climate mitigation, a 1 percent increase in regulatory stringency is associated with a 16 percent increase in the probability of participation in voluntary carbon disclosure by a firm based in the Global South, compared to 6 percent for a firm based in the Global North.[22] In the first half of the 2011–2020 decade, the impact of corporate × regulation interactions on the adoption of corporate sustainability outputs was more pronounced in developing countries than in developed countries. Moreover, developing country–based firms with senior- or executive-level managers responded more readily to domestic regulatory stringency than to nonmandatory global norms and best practices.

That being said, once a corporate climate management tool becomes the industry or business norm or standard, the relative importance of regulatory versus global governance could shift. In the latter half of the 2011–2020 decade, or the post–Paris Agreement period, developing country–based global firms with managers and membership in the UN Global Compact were just as or more likely to adopt quantitative emissions targets than firms with managers and facing domestic regulatory pressure. By the end of the decade more than half of developing country–based firms had installed dedicated leaders responsible for climate mitigation. For example, the upward trend emphasizing climate managerial capacity and capabilities was pervasive among Chinese firms, which coincided with the proliferation of dedicated programs by private and public sector consultancies seeking actionable carbon management solutions in these countries. By 2020, corporate management tools such as emissions targets had become a business and industry norm for global firms in both developed and developing countries, with high adoption rates (86 percent and 67 percent, respectively).

With respect to corporate×global interactions, Global South firms are often "inhibitors" rather than "providers" of global governance. These firms may inhibit the expansion of global governance and mobilize to defeat transnational rules pertaining to labor, environment, health, and safety because they profit from cross-national regulatory differences. Global firms do so either by incorporating in tax and investment havens or by gravitating to sourcing destinations with less stringent enforcement of labor and environmental laws.

In addition, if firms do not already live with similar rules domestically—which is more likely in the Global North than in the Global South—they have fewer incentives to embed more stringent global norms or best practices in their modus operandi. An example of this is the fact that imbalances between developed and developing countries have persisted with respect to voluntary "non-party" (i.e., non-country-level) contributions to climate actions.

Even so, global firms may still strategically respond to, exacerbate, or reconcile the wedge between domestic and global governance institutions, and do so with the global economy and markets in mind and on their side. In the post–Paris Agreement period, senior and executive leadership have exercised agency as a strategy to signal to international markets their ability to play by the norms and rules of the global economy. Examples include several China-based global businesses (such as SHEIN, the largest fast fashion retailer, and JinkoSolar Co., Ltd., a behemoth that produces one in ten solar modules installed globally) that are members of the UN Global Compact and have adopted quantitative emissions targets.[23] Both have either moved their headquarters or set up factories outside China to distance themselves from the Chinese government.[24]

10.3 Sustainability Outputs versus Environmental Performance: Do Global Businesses that Participate in Voluntary Action Emit Less Carbon?

The recent emergence of climate disclosure mandates globally suggests that policymakers and investors around the world perceive climate disclosure as driving actions that protect the environment. The big question is, Do global businesses that participate in climate disclosure actually reduce emissions?

Chapters 5 and 7 in this book focus on the US case and exploit the EPA's introduction of the Clean Power Plan as a natural experiment, which during 2011–2015 exerted regulatory pressures on GHG-intensive firms domiciled in the United States. Firms' heterogeneous participation in the CDP and their level of voluntary carbon disclosure show that some firms use voluntary carbon disclosure to obfuscate and enable greenwashing when regulatory pressure is low.

As chapter 7 of this book shows, voluntary carbon disclosure systems like that of CDP, which focus on reporting corporate sustainability outputs (e.g., science-based emissions targets) tend not to be as effective as those that focus on outcomes (e.g., a company's actual carbon emissions). For example, a company could earn an A or B grade from the CDP and still increase its entity-wide carbon emissions. Notably, companies in the financial, health care, and other consumer-oriented sectors that did not experience the same level of regulatory pressure as GHG-intensive firms led the increase during 2011–2020.

About a quarter of the S&P 500 companies that completed CDP's annual climate change survey undertook assessments of their business impacts on the environment and integrated climate risk management into their business strategy. Yet entity-wide emissions still increased. This is because a firm earns an A grade—including those on the CDP's coveted A-list—when it has met the criteria of disclosure, awareness, management, and leadership, including adopting global best practices regardless of whether those practices translate into improved environmental performance.[25]

An A-list company could be carbon neutral when it counts only the facilities it owns and not the factories that make its products.[26] Moreover, a company that has earned an A grade could commit to removing all emitted carbon but maintain partnerships with oil and gas companies to "generate new exploration opportunities."[27]

Retail and apparel giants Walmart, Inc., Target Corporation, and Nike, Inc.—all in the B to A—range in recent years—offer an example of the challenge. They regularly disclose their carbon management plans and emissions to CDP. That being said, they are also part of the industry-led Sustainable Apparel Coalition,[28] which has controversially portrayed petroleum-based synthetics as the most sustainable choice above natural fibers in the Higgs Index,[29] a supply chain measurement tool that some clothing companies use to demonstrate their social and environmental footprint to consumers.[30] The Federal Trade Commission has sued Walmart over products described as bamboo and "eco-friendly and sustainable" that were, in fact, made from rayon, a semi-synthetic fiber made using toxic chemicals.[31]

A hopeful prospect, however, is when large emissions-intensive firms, such as utilities in the United States, tried to get ahead of expected climate regulations by reducing their entity-wide carbon emissions intensity by at least one measure: carbon emissions per capita of full-time employees. This means that as a company increases in size, it is estimated to reduce its carbon footprint on a per-employee basis. However, this does not necessarily translate to a reduction in a company's overall carbon emissions.

In contrast, a recent study of the UK's 2013 disclosure mandate for UK-incorporated listed firms found that companies reduced their operational emissions by about 8 percent relative to a control group, with no significant changes to their profitability.[32] When firms uniformly report their emissions, they can gain important knowledge about inefficiencies in their operations and supply chains that were not evident before.[33]

10.4 A Call for All-Hands-on-Deck: What Happens When Markets and Governments Fail?

Markets can fail and so can governments. Sometimes they fail simultaneously because of regulatory capture—that is, when government and public policy are dominated by private industry that government is tasked to regulate. Research has shown that while close links between firms and politicians are associated with a higher rate of firm survival and growth in employment and revenues, political connections have also undermined productivity or innovation.[34] The reality of political lobbying in climate policy and governance (i.e., the organized attempts by corporations to interfere with the regulatory process and arguably an extension of corporate greenwashing) is well documented. Several books have been devoted to uncovering the impact of regulatory capture on the policymaking process, policies, and technology and the product winners and losers in the age of global climate change.[35]

A case in point is the multitrillion-dollar fossil fuel industry's decades-long interference in the US regulatory process to block climate action and obstruct public opinion. Multinational oil and gas giant ExxonMobil, for example, allegedly has known about the dangers of climate change since the 1970s, before climate change became a public issue, and spent millions to promote misinformation.[36] Nevertheless, what political interference looked like when climate denialism was at its height was different in 2015 on the eve of the Paris Agreement compared to now (in 2024), when Big Oil—the world's largest publicly traded and investor-owned oil and gas firms—continues to invest in new oil and gas exploration and development but has committed to net-zero emissions goals for their operations.[37] The chief executive officer–led Oil and Gas Climate Initiative (OGCI), which is made up of the twelve largest oil and gas producers in the world, has advocated for controversial climate solutions, such as carbon capture, utilization, and storage, that do not currently have broad support due to the technology's documented limitations.[38] That being said, new research on public perceptions of direct air capture has found conditional support for direct air capture deployment when there is community involvement in planning and implementation and community benefits such as local infrastructure and workforce development. When decision-making authority is shifted from the energy industry and involves citizen engagement and empowerment, the political economy and governance of decarbonization have the potential to be transformed.[39]

Business and management scholars have called on firms to be just as transparent about their corporate political responsibility as about their corporate social responsibility (CSR).[40] Metrics that better reflect actual corporate environmental behavior are in line with institutional investors' preferred approach of risk management and engagement, rather than divestment, to address climate-related risks.[41] The idea is that rating systems demand information from firms about their lobbying activities—notably as they relate to their public policy positions on the environment and climate change—and include evaluations of corporate political activity in their assessments of corporate environmental responsibility. When global firms' controversies, including negative information about their lobbying activities (proxied by global news media reports) are factored into environmental, social, and governance (ESG) metrics, their adjusted ESG scores were lower than their (unadjusted) ESG scores by 4 to 10 percentage points from 2011 to 2020, as shown in figure 10.5.

The rationale is that when firms are also graded on their public policy positions, they are forced to take meaningful steps to improve their environmental performance, especially when third-party watchdogs, nongovernmental organizations, and independent regulatory agencies alike publicize information about corporate political activity. This form of "climate shaming" utilizes corporate reputational sensitivities and the willingness of stakeholders

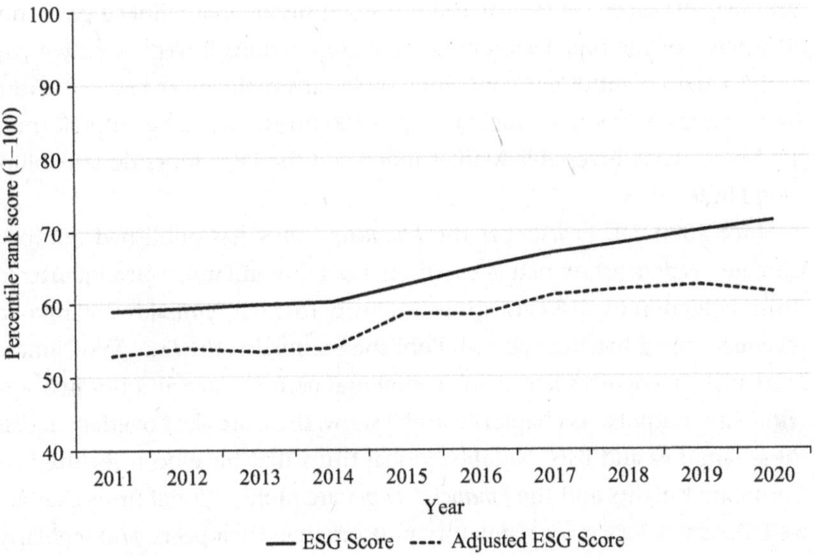

Figure 10.5
Average ESG score versus adjusted ESG score, 2011–2020 (Fortune Global 500 firms).
Note: The adjusted ESG score discounts the ESG score based on negative media stories. It does this by incorporating the impact of significant, material ESG controversies in the overall adjusted ESG score. The ESG controversy score is calculated based on twenty-three ESG controversy topics, from anticompetition to human rights to environmental to accounting and employee health to safety controversies, among others. During the year, if a scandal occurs, the firm involved is penalized, and this affects their overall adjusted ESG score and grading. The impact of the event may still be seen the following year if there are new developments related to the negative event—for example, lawsuits, ongoing legislation disputes, or fines. The adjusted ESG score accounts for the market capitalization bias from which firms with a large market capitalization (typically exceeding $10 billion) suffer, as they are likely to attract more media attention than firms with a smaller market capitalization. When companies are not involved in ESG controversies, the adjusted ESG score is equal to the ESG score.
Data source: LSEG Data and Analytics.

to hold firms accountable for their climate actions or inactions—that is, firms' greenwashing behavior in the climate change area.[42]

Third-party groups that have ranked and graded firms on some if not all aspects of the firms' ESG record and transparency include the Corporate Knights, whose data the author uses to underscore and triangulate findings from this book's empirical findings. Firms on the Corporate Knights' Global 100 list perform better on overall ESG metrics than do their peers. For example, 79 percent of Global 100 firms had sustainability-linked pay; only 30 percent of the broader multinational corporations linked executive pay to the achievement of environmental or social sustainability targets.[43] From 2005 to 2023, Corporate Knights' Global 100 firms financially outperformed the MSCI ACWI Investable Market Index and the Dow Jones Sustainability World Index.[44]

Since 2020, UK newspaper the *Financial Times* has published Europe's Climate Leaders list, which is based on a ranking of Europe-headquartered firms' reduction in GHG emissions intensity (namely, emissions relative to revenue) over a five-year period. Published annually, the Europe's Climate Leaders list recognizes firms' environmental performance and not just sustainability outputs. As chapters 8 and 9 show, there are clear overlaps across these rankings and lists. Notably, global firms that have been featured by Corporate Knights and the *Financial Times* are multinational firms that are well managed, face more regulatory pressure than their peers, and regularly participate in global governance; they provide further evidence to underscore this book's multilevel governance framework on climate change.

10.4.1 Civil Society Actors' Cross-Sector- and Cross-Governance-Level Climate Activism

Institutional investors and other civil society groups keep corporations accountable with respect to not only their CSR but also their corporate political responsibility. It can be especially effective when these groups engage in problem definition by shaping the understanding of the nature of a policy problem, adopt time-tested strategies from similar or adjacent realms that target firms and their partners across sectors and levels of government or governance, and bring their concerns to a decision setting at local, national, or global forums that offer the best prospect of reaching one's policy goals.[45] In fact, civil society actors' problem definition, strategies, and selection of venues for raising their concerns and requests align with those of this book's cross-level interactions of the multilevel governance framework on climate change. Societal leaders could engage with the powers that be at the local level of decision-making and engage with, or appeal to, the national or global level for legitimacy. A call to action by climate scientists argues for a similar all-hands-on-deck approach in locking in or reducing GHG emissions through five roles: as consumers, investors, role models, participants in organizations, and citizens.[46]

An example of this multilevel governance approach targeting corporations and their investment or research partners is the fossil fuel dissociation movement led by the Coalition for a True School of Sustainability at Stanford University (henceforth, the Coalition). In the words of one of the organizers of the student-led movement, the Coalition is part of a "global movement that works to dissociate the fossil fuel industry's influence on higher education," particularly as it relates to climate-related research.[47] The founding of the Coalition coincided with the launch of Stanford University's Doerr School of Sustainability, named after billionaire venture capitalist and philanthropist John Doerr who donated $1.1 billion to the new multidisciplinary school focused on climate change and sustainability.[48]

Made up of students, faculty, and staff, the Coalition urges Stanford's Doerr School of Sustainability to stop accepting funding from fossil fuel companies. Between 2011 and 2023, fossil fuel companies such as ExxonMobil, Shell, TotalEnergies, BP, Chevron, and Eni (all members of the Oil and Gas Climate Initiative) contributed to nearly 20 percent of the total sponsored research funding ($68 million out of $380 million) to departments housed in the Doerr School.[49]

The Coalition's campaign strategies are taken from "the playbook of what's happening" at other universities that are a step ahead with respect to fossil fuel dissociation as well as in an adjacent realm—the dissociation by public health schools in the United States and Canada from research money associated with the tobacco industry.[50] In 2017, Philip Morris International (PMI) announced its support for the establishment of the Foundation for a Smoke-Free World, with the stated mission of reducing illness and death from smoking and supporting research on harm reduction and smoking cessation, intervention, monitoring of industry action, and preparing tobacco farmers for a future of reduced demand.

A coalition of international and US organizations, including universities, banded together for a common cause. Along with the World Health Organization and other US and international organizations that support smoking prevention and tobacco control effects, seventeen schools of public health pledged not to work with the Foundation for a Smoke-Free World, which was to be solely funded by PMI.[51] The unified opposition by these diverse organizations across sectors and issue areas is based on their agreement that there is a "fundamental conflict of interest between the tobacco industry and public health."[52] In 2023, the once-PMI-backed foundation severed ties with the company and the tobacco industry.

Coalition student leaders have been quick to point out that Stanford University was not the first to launch a fossil fuel dissociation movement in higher education. Students from more than one hundred US colleges and universities have helped to bring about either partial or full commitment by their institutions to divest from fossil fuel companies.[53] These higher-education institutions include community colleges and state university systems, including the University of California, University of Illinois, and University of Maine, and private elite and liberal arts colleges, such as Columbia University, Harvard University, Princeton University, Dartmouth University, Oberlin College, and Williams College. To date (March 2024), over 250 education institutions worldwide, from the United States, Australia, Canada, the UK, and Europe to Israel and South Africa have made some form of fossil fuel divestment commitments.[54]

The Coalition's problem definition—that is, the narrative about the nature of a policy problem at hand—has been part and parcel of their campaign strategies. Following the template of existing activism in higher education against the tobacco and fossil fuel industries, the Coalition's core demand for greater transparency and disclosure echoed the mission and vision of Campus Climate Network (formerly Fossil Free Research), the organization and global movement that has supported students and faculty working to expose and dismantle the fossil fuel industry's influence on higher education. According to Campus Climate Network, when there is transparency, the "integrity of academia and the policy it informs" is protected, and "a more transparent, accessible, and democratic higher education system can unleash its full potential in contributing toward a rapid and socially just global energy transition."[55]

The Campus Climate Network and the Stanford Coalition's framing of fossil fuel dissociation around disclosure and transparency dovetailed with contemporary debates about misinformation and fake news in the digital age, as well as with frequent media attention about Big Oil's "Delaying, Diverting, and Deception."[56] There is also a continuity between what university student activists are trying to accomplish with removing oil and gas companies' influence on higher education and what younger youth climate activists have increasingly demanded with respect to structural, systemic change away from what they perceive as "a system that puts profits over people and planet," for the sake of their collective futures.[57] Students and their faculty supporters at the university believe that there is a synergistic relationship between academia and society: scholars need to inform the public, share their evidence-based research, and speak for science. June Choi, a Coalition organizer said, "We are in it because the future can be different and we are making it different."[58]

Toward these ends, in addition to traditional protests and demonstrations, members of the Coalition do not shy away from participating in university-led open forums and conversations related to research funded by fossil fuel companies. In fact, Coalition student activists joined forces with students in favor of maintaining an open dialogue with fossil fuel firms. The first of several jointly published recommendations called for the Stanford Doerr School of Sustainability to commit to an open and transparent process for industry-funded research. The students urged the Doerr School to "review, identify and eliminate benefits to industry donors that present a direct conflict of interest."[59] Other recommendations centered around fossil fuel companies' disclosure of "credible transition plans" and the establishment of a third-party enforcement board to ensure that dissociation and future reassociation processes are fair and transparent. The recommendations were accompanied by petitions to partner with global nonprofits, such as Climate Action 100,[60] InfluenceMaps,[61] and Science-Based Targets, Initiatives[62] for guidance on global best practices, performance metrics, and corporate accountability.

For the Coalition, transparency and disclosure are also about educating the public about the fact that science is not a value-free space and that "it improves [research's] impact to remove conflicts of interest."[63] A major concern is that when oil and gas firms join industrial affiliate programs at the university, they will not only have access to an early copy of new research but have a seat on research advisory boards.[64] According to a Coalition student organizer, "[The] oil and gas industry are saying we are just responding to market demand but they are actually shaping that future of that demand" through their influence on the trajectory of research.[65]

The Coalition's emphasis on transparency and disclosure turned out to be an olive branch; it was both an invitation and a low-hanging fruit for immediate action by the Doerr School. In February 2024, inaugural Dean Arun Majumdar echoed a similar value of disclosure and transparency in his announcement of the creation of an independent Industrial Affiliates Review Committee (IARC) to review and ensure that all industrial affiliate programs within the school follow university guidelines. The Doerr School emphasized that the IARC works independently of the university-wide Committee on Funding for Energy Research and Education,[66] established a year prior to evaluate research funding by fossil fuel companies across the university. Dean Arun Majumdar said, "Our affiliate programs provide unique opportunities for our faculty and students, and the IARC's work will not only ensure essential transparency but also foster potential avenues to improve and strengthen these programs."[67] In addition to the IARC, the Doerr School has also made financial and programmatic information about the school's industrial affiliate programs available on the school's website.[68]

At the writing of this book, it remains to be seen whether the Coalition's demands for fossil fuel dissociation—and recommendations on how to do it—will come to full fruition. With that said, the Coalition's early successes suggest that this stakeholder group engaged with local decision-makers while also appealing to activism at the national and global level for problem definition and legitimacy. They also brought their concerns and demands to key decision settings and found common ground with diverse groups, with a goal of identifying the best prospect of reaching its policy goal.

10.4.2 Subnational Actors and the Regulatory Process

Regulatory pressures and drivers for corporate self-regulation on climate change can come from different levels and sources. This book has focused on existing or forthcoming regulation at the national level and on global governance as a harbinger of future regulation. In the United States or countries with federalist systems, other potential sources are subnational, state- or provincial-level, and city- or local-level regulatory jurisdiction and oversight.[69] Local, state, and national governments play complementary roles in creating incentives for corporate investments in green jobs, green housing, clean energy, electric vehicle charging infrastructure, and mass transportation at affordable prices for a new decarbonized economy.

In the United States, California has a history of being a test bed for future federal policies.[70] In October 2023, California Governor Gavin Newsom signed two new rules into law. Under the new Climate Corporate Data Accountability Act, firms with annual revenues of $1 billion or more operating in California will be required to report both their direct and indirect greenhouse gas emissions starting in 2026 and 2027. The California Chamber of Commerce opposed the regulation, arguing that it would increase firms' costs; however, more than a dozen major corporations endorsed the rule, including Microsoft, Apple, Salesforce, and Patagonia, all of which report—and have for over a decade—to CDP (formerly the Carbon Disclosure Project). The second law, the Climate-Related Financial Risk Act, requires firms generating $500 million or more to report their financial risks related to climate change and their plans for risk mitigation. Both rules are huge leaps from current federal and state reporting requirements, which mandate reporting of only certain emissions from firms' direct operations.[71]

While the US government is considering broader emissions reporting requirements, California's new rules go further than either the Securities and Exchange Commission's (SEC) proposed corporate climate disclosure rules or President Joe Biden's proposed disclosure rules for federal contractors.[72] Table 10.3 shows how California climate disclosure rules compare to proposals by the SEC and the Biden Administration.

The most controversial part of California's disclosure rules involves scope 3 emissions for all reporting companies, unlike the proposed federal mandates. Scope 3 are emissions from a company's suppliers and its consumers' use of its products, and they are difficult to track accurately.

California's new emissions reporting law directs the California Air Resources Board, which will develop the regulations and administer them, to allow some leeway in scope 3 reporting as long as the reports are made with a reasonable basis and disclosed in good faith. At this point, the disclosure laws do not require firms to cut these emissions, only to report them. However, tracking scope 3 emissions highlights where companies could pressure suppliers to make changes. While carbon accounting experts consider this to be critical for successful decarbonization (since between 75 and 90 percent of global firms' total emissions are scope 3 emissions), investment banks and other financial market participants are concerned about double-counting and misallocation of responsibility.[73] Without credible pressures coming from public or private politics and emanating from global governance for the standardization of scope 3 emissions accounting, reporting and reducing nonoperational emissions and greening the supply chains more generally will less likely be a focus of (proactive) corporate climate action.[74]

Given their rigor and comprehensiveness, California's new rules represent a significant step toward mainstreaming corporate climate disclosures and potentially meaningful corporate climate actions. These rules will also have global ramifications because while California is not the first place to mandate

Table 10.3
Comparison of California and proposed US federal climate disclosure rules

	SEC proposal	Biden proposal	California emissions reporting law	California risk disclosure law
Title	Enhanced and Standardization of Climate-Related Disclosures for Investors	Federal Supplier Climate Risks and Resilience Rule	Corporate Data Accountability Act (SB 253)	Climate-Related Financial Risk (SB 261)
Target	Public firms doing business in the United States	Federal contractors	Public and private firms doing business in California that generate ≥ $1 billion in revenue	Public and private firms doing business in California that generate ≥ $500 million in revenue
Emissions disclosed[a]	Scope 1 and 2; scope 3 only if "material" or if registrant had set a target or goal including scope 3 emissions	Scope 1 and 2; scope 3 only for major contractors in receipt of ≥ $50 million from US federal government	Scope 1, 2, and 3	N/A
Climate-related financial risk disclosure[b]	Yes	Yes, for major contractors in receipt of ≥$50 million from US federal government	N/A	Yes
Third-party verification	Yes, for large accelerated filers, and only for scope 1 and 2 emissions	Yes, for major contractors only	Yes, with digital platform for public access	No

[a] Scope 1 emissions are the direct emissions coming out of a firm's chimneys and tailpipes. Scope 2 emissions are associated with the power a company consumes. Scope 3 includes emissions in a company's supply chain and through the use of its products.

[b] The SEC, Biden Administration, and California proposed climate-related financial risk disclosures followed the recommendations of the Task Force on Climate-Related Financial Disclosures (TCFD), which was a financial disclosures framework created by the Financial Stability Board (FSB), an international body that monitors and makes recommendations about the global financial system. FSB disbanded TCFD in October 2023 upon TCFD's fulfillment of its work. TCFD monitoring responsibilities was transferred to the International Sustainability Standards Board.

climate disclosures, it is the fifth-largest economy in the world. Subsidiaries of firms that did not have to report their emissions before will now be subject to disclosure requirements. California is in effect exercising its immense market leverage to establish climate disclosures as standard practice in the United States and beyond.

Most of the firms covered by California's climate disclosure rules are multinational corporations, which are the subject of this book. They include technology companies such as Apple, Google LLC, and Microsoft; giant retailers like Walmart and Costco Wholesale Corporation; and oil and gas companies such as ExxonMobil and Chevron. Global firms domiciled outside the United States, including developing country–based firms such as India's Infosys, China's AoGrand Group, Inc., and Brazil's Vale SA, are also subject to these disclosure laws when they do business in California.

Many of these firms also face reporting requirements elsewhere, including in the EU, the UK, New Zealand, India, Singapore, and cities like Hong Kong. Moreover, some of the same firms, notably banks and asset managers that operate or sell products in Europe,[75] have already started to comply with the EU's Sustainable Finance Disclosure Regulation.[76] Those regulations require firms to report how sustainability risks are integrated into investment decision-making.

10.5 Conclusion

While the science is clear about the dire consequences of global warming beyond 1.5°C, the politics and economics of climate change will likely continue to exhibit an ebb and flow of interference on climate policy and governance, either by climate deniers or private industry actors that bear the cost of decarbonization in the short to medium run. A case in point is the US federal government retrenchment during President Donald Trump's first administration (2016–2020), in the form of regulatory rollbacks regarding tailpipe emissions, fuel economy standards, and drilling and extraction, among others. The US Environmental Protection Agency's (EPA) promulgated Clean Power Plant, which is featured in this book as a natural experiment during an era of numerous failed climate legislative proposals in Congress (see chapter 5), never went into effect and was subject to multiple lawsuits.

Two years later (in 2022), the Inflation Reduction Act (IRA) was a landmark US federal law that purported to address multiple objectives—reduce the federal government budget deficit, lower prescription drug prices, and invest in domestic energy production and promote clean energy. Simultaneously praised and criticized for doing too much or too little,[77] the IRA is the largest piece of US federal legislation to address climate change. It is projected to invest nearly $800 billion to $1.2 trillion in provisions related to energy security and climate change.

In response to the Supreme Court case *West Virginia v. EPA*, which limited the EPA's authority to carry out the Clean Power Plan, the IRA amended the Clean Air Act (of which the Clean Power Plan is a part) to explicitly designate carbon dioxide, hydrofluorocarbons, methane, nitrous oxide, perfluorocarbons, and sulfur hexafluoride as air pollutants. In doing so, the EPA has been given formal congressional authorization to regulate carbon dioxide and other greenhouse gases, as well as to promote renewable energy.[78]

Fast forward to 2024 (at the writing of this book), and the era of climate denialism looks different than even a couple of years ago. Critics worry that the top-line messaging of some firms and trade associations, which outwardly supports climate-related policies like carbon pricing or emissions trading, is in fact different from their modus operandi. The twenty-eighth session of the Conference of Parties (COP 28) to the United Nations Framework Convention on Climate Change that took place in Dubai, in December 2023, was nicknamed the "Oil and Gas COP" because it was headed by Sultan Al Jaber, the chief executive of the Abu Dhabi National Oil Company and the United Arab Emirates' special envoy for climate change since 2020. Nongovernmental stakeholders and climate campaigners had low expectations and were concerned about the record number of fossil fuel lobbyists granted access to COP 28.[79]

Despite the perceived risk of greenwashing, the UN summit represented the top-down and bottom-up interactions posited by this book's multilevel governance framework on climate change. COP 28 resulted in new commitments by both countries and companies. It served a harbinger of what is to come with respect to regulatory development across rich and poor countries and of technological trajectories. On the second day of COP 28, the US EPA announced a rule to cut methane (CH_4) emissions from the oil and gas sector by 80 percent over fifteen years, less than a month behind an EU law that set tight methane leakage standards.[80] That news came with a $1 billion commitment to help smaller countries address the same problem.[81]

The EPA's methane rule and developing-country assistance dovetailed the strengthening of the Global Methane Pledge with several new countries joining the collective pledge, which was launched in COP 26 in Glasgow, to cut methane emissions 30 percent by 2030. Moreover, around fifty global oil and gas firms—including ExxonMobil, Shell, Saudi Aramco, and other members of the chief executive–led Oil and Gas Climate Initiative—committed to eliminate their own CH_4 emissions through carbon storage and removal technologies. There are concerns as to whether climate technological solutions could detract from the need to cut both methane and carbon emissions from fossil fuel use, and possibly invite moral hazard or riskier behavior as an unintended and undesired consequence.[82]

Regardless of the ebb and flow of the politics of climate change, and whether or not they are favorable toward decarbonization, the activities of external stakeholders are more important than ever. They are imperative to keep corporate management, regulatory regimes, and global governance institutions independent and accountable, as well as to facilitate the multilevel governance synergies that this book has argued and demonstrated. External stakeholders can also help to ensure that climate policies and programs are designed with accountability as a central feature and move beyond sustainability outputs to include substantive outcomes. Research has shown that, with careful policy design, alternative regulatory approaches using the fiscal system, such as a revenue-neutral carbon tax, a cap-and-trade program, or a clean energy standard, can achieve cost effective emissions reductions and avoid placing undesirable burdens on vulnerable industries or populations.[83] Environmental performance depends on the credibility and rigor of existing or forthcoming regulation as well as policy and program design features that not only incentivize participation (e.g., pledges) but also emphasize the stringency of obligations and deliverables, institutionalize monitoring and enforcement mechanisms that address the (material) consequences of nonadherence, and prevent firms from shirking their pledges and net-zero commitments.

This book's main conclusions are the following. First, while some global firms act on their own, the majority of global firms do not. Rather, on the whole, their proactive climate action is in response to regulatory pressures coming from domestic regulation of their country of origin or export country of largest sales. Despite the fact that global governance institutions are replete with opportunities for learning about global best practices, the majority of firms' climate mitigation reinforces what they are already doing and reflects existing corporate management practices and regulations on the books or on the horizon. Corporate climate leadership requires the alignment of corporate, regulatory, and global governance with senior and executive leaders inside the firm serving as regulation brokers and norm brokers, as argued and shown in this book.

Second, in developed countries, where regulations are by and large more robust, corporate, regulatory, and global governance enjoy complementarities. The European Union (EU) is an exemplar of how firm, regulatory, and global interactions and the blurring of the private and public governance spheres in Europe explicate the climate leadership of global firms based there. By contrast, developing country–based firms find it economically and politically advantageous to act, at times preemptively, in anticipation of local rules and policies that could carry sanctions for noncompliance in their country of domicile or in their largest export markets. Notwithstanding, global firms originating from countries with fewer political rights have joined global governance institutions in order to signal to international markets their willingness to play by the best practices and norms of the global economy. Finally, while some global firms, notably in the consumer-oriented sectors, have engaged in "cheap talk," technology firms led the way on voluntary climate action and carbon emission efficiency from 2011 to 2020. Carbon-efficient greenhouse gas–intensive corporations, under regulatory pressure, have used their proactive climate action to signal their climate leadership to regulators, investors, and consumers.

Finally, neither firms themselves nor regulation or global norms and pressures alone will be able to achieve the substantive climate action that is necessary for reducing global temperatures to avert a climate change crisis. The most effective incentives for industry-led climate mitigation and adaptation come from stable domestic regulation, including impending regulation that is viewed as credible and stable, and legislative flexibility for the private sector to exceed minimum (federal) standards when it is cost-effective for them to do so. When all is said and done, as this book argues and shows, global businesses that are the best managed and most stringently regulated and are active participants of global governance institutions are today's corporate climate leaders. In the face of climate change's complexity and uncertainty, corporate leaders possess the managerial agency to build governing coalitions and coordinate and align incentives within firms and with investors to ensure that multinational firms' interactions with regulatory and global governance lead to sustainable climate futures. To ensure that this becomes reality, civil society stakeholders—from institutional investors to environmental watchdog groups to universities—are more important than ever to keep firms accountable for their pledges and acts of corporate social responsibility on the environment and beyond.

Appendix 1

Explanation of Climate Disclosure and Greenhouse Gas Emissions Data

This book's author-constructed database—the Global Sustainable Business and Climate Action Database—is the first of its kind to track a census of firms that were listed as a Fortune Global 500 company or in the S&P 500 index at least once from 2011 to 2015.[1] The Global Sustainable Business Database comprises data on global firms' voluntary carbon disclosure to CDP (formerly the Carbon Disclosure Project), adoption of quantitative emissions targets, and setting of internal carbon prices. The database also contains other pledges of climate action, environmental, social, and governance (ESG) performance; environmental performance (namely, carbon emissions and carbon emissions intensity); participation in global governance; and information about the political, economic, and institutional characteristics of firms' country of origin and their largest export markets.

This unique database is drawn from diverse public and private proprietary sources, comprising pre- and post–2015 Paris Agreement data across scales of governance (firm, market, country, and global levels) for global firms that operate in diverse sectors and originate from thirty-eight countries, during 2011–2020, which is this book's study period. Appendix 2 includes a description of this book's variables, construction, operationalization, and sources.

This rest of this appendix contains information about the CDP survey data, including scoring and grading of firms' self-reported voluntary climate action as well as information about the methods by which the author collected data on firms that did not voluntarily report to CDP. The CDP survey data were verified by triangulation with primary and secondary sources. Appendix 1 also contains information about this book's sources of global firms' carbon emissions, carbon emissions intensity, and ESG performance.

Climate Disclosure Data from CDP

This book's Global Sustainable Business Database's carbon management and climate mitigation practices, strategies, and activities come primarily from CDP's annual climate change questionnaire from 2011 to 2020. Specifically, firm-level data on installation of senior- or executive-level managers dedicated to climate mitigation, adoption of quantitative emissions targets, an internal price on carbon, carbon disclosure scores, and letter grades, for this book's empirical analysis are drawn from the CDP annual climate change questionnaires.

As explicated in chapter 1, CDP is a private initiative founded in 2000 to encourage voluntary disclosure of greenhouse gas (GHG) emissions, water usage, and voluntary strategies for managing climate change, water, and deforestation risks by large and mid-size companies on an annual basis. Any organization wishing to publicly report their GHG emissions, climate change strategies, water stewardship approach, and deforestation risk management can do so through CDP.[2] CDP houses the largest repository of climate disclosure data in the world.

Every year, CDP invites executives of all Global 500 corporations and firms listed in the S&P 500 index to complete a survey to describe the risks and opportunities that climate change poses to their businesses, outline their corporate strategies for managing these risks and opportunities, and report their GHG emissions. The CDP climate change questionnaire is structured around the four thematic areas (namely, governance, strategy, risk management, and metrics and targets) of the Task Force for Climate-Related Financial Disclosure's recommendations.[3] A global firm's disclosures of direct and indirect GHG emissions must be reported at the "entity level"; this helps to prevent firms from reporting only on the outcomes of successful projects.[4]

Participation in CDP's annual climate change questionnaire is not free, although the costs are low relative to the global firms' revenues and market capitalization. CDP has a three-tier fee structure, which is based on increasing levels of program benefits: (1) essential, (2) foundation and (3) enhanced. For firms originating from United Kingdom, Europe, Japan, North America, Southeast Asia, South Korea, Australia, New Zealand, Hong Kong, and Taiwan, fees start at the foundation level. These firms also pay higher rates for participation at the foundation and enhanced fee levels than firms domiciled in China, Brazil, Latin America (excluding Brazil), and India. Firms that join CDP at the "essential" tier are awarded the lowest level of program benefits, whereas firms that pay the "enhanced" level enjoy additional benefits that include recognition at CDP-hosted events, promotion materials (e.g., CDP Supporter badge for external communication), complimentary sustainability screening of firms' suppliers, and access to the carbon disclosure data of up to one hundred industry peers and competitors.[5]

CDP's Carbon Disclosure Scores (before 2016)

CDP's rating methodology is based on scrutiny of the thoroughness or "level of detail and comprehensiveness of the content responses, as well as the company's awareness of climate change issues, management methods, and progress toward action on climate change" as reported in the firm's response to CDP's annual climate change questionnaire. This rating also considers a company's choice of measurement and verification of carbon emissions, such as a firm's selection of boundaries, adjustments, carbon accounting principles, and the verification status of the reported data.[6] CDP's scoring and grading (see below) do not measure actual environmental performance.

Before 2016, CDP graded firms on the level of detail and comprehensiveness of information disclosure by assigning scores (with a maximum score of 100; see below for more details). In this book's chapters 3–5, the disclosure scores serve as a proxy for global firms' intensity of participation or level of voluntary carbon disclosure.

In scoring a firm's comprehensiveness in climate disclosure, CDP gives more weight to company responses in some categories of the 2011–2015 climate change questionnaire than to others. The weights are based on the importance of a question to climate mitigation (as determined by CDP, along with stakeholder inputs from external partners to CDP) and the amount of data requested.[7]

For example, the three responses that correspond to the "highest points" attainable are those that relate to a firm's climate risks and opportunities (27 points) and information on a firm's GHG emissions—namely, boundary for GHG inventory, global scope 1 and 2 emissions, exclusions, and sources of uncertainty in data gathering, handling, and calculations (25 points). By contrast, the responses that correspond to the "lowest points" attainable are those about a corporation's climate change communications (3 points) and scope 1 and 2 emissions breakdowns (4 points). Information about corporate governance and adoption of emissions targets are allocated a maximum score of 5 and 15 points, respectively.

At the end of scoring, the number of points a company has been awarded (the numerator) is divided by the maximum number that could have been awarded (the denominator). The fraction is then converted to a percentage by multiplying by 100 and is rounded to the nearest whole number.[8]

(points awarded / points attainable) × 100 = disclosure score

All disclosure scores are public by default, but firms can request privacy or confidentiality of some or all of their responses to CDP, including performance scores (and carbon emissions). From 2011 to 2015, less than 5 percent of the Global 500 firms that disclosed to CDP requested privacy.[9] See appendices 3–5 for how the analyses in chapters 3–5, respectively, treat private versus public disclosures. The bottom line is that this book's empirical results are robust to whether or not these cases are included in the analyses.

CDP's Carbon Disclosure Letter Grades (after 2015)

CDP discontinued its publication of disclosure scores after 2015. Since 2016, CDP has published letter grades ranging from A to D based on individual firms' substantive level of (self-disclosed) climate action. A firm can be on CDP's A-list regardless of whether it has reduced GHG emissions, as long as the firm has achieved the requirements of sustainability outputs, such as quantitative emissions targets and environmental management systems. Chapter 7 uses CDP's assignment of letter grades to global firms as a measure of their effort or intensity of participation in voluntary carbon disclosure.

In CDP's scoring system, points are allocated for each question on the CDP climate change questionnaire, and at the end of scoring, the number of points that a firm has been awarded is divided by the maximum number that could been awarded at the transparency, awareness, management, and leadership levels, respectively. The fraction is then converted to a percentage by multiplying by 100 and is rounded to the nearest whole number.

From here, a minimum score of 75 is required in order to be assessed at the next level. If the minimum score threshold is not achieved, the company will not be scored at the next level.[10] This means that each performance grade represents an additive effect; that is, a higher grade implies that the lower grade and associated substantive level of climate action have been achieved. See chapter 7 for details on how letter grades are translated into indicator variables to represent the intensity of participation in the chapter's econometric analysis. They are listed in appendix 2 as variables in this book's Global Sustainable Business Database.

Treatment of Missing Climate Disclosure Data

The CDP's corporate climate disclosure data are incomplete because the survey data contain only firms that voluntarily responded to the CDP climate change questionnaire. There are two types of missing data for the variables (*manager* and *target*), drawn from the CDP climate change questionnaire: (1) companies that responded to CDP about their management structure and practices during some years but not others and (2) companies that did not participate in CDP during 2011–2020. In the author's treatment of both incidences of missing data, rather than impute missing data statistically, secondary information was gathered from corporate websites and published reports, such as a company's standard annual reports or their corporate social responsibility reporting during 2011–2020 to code missing data.

For *manager* and *target*, coding was straightforward: *manager* is coded 1 (0 otherwise) if there was a senior- or executive-level manager responsible for climate change, environmental sustainability, or environmental policy or if there was a board of directors committee devoted to addressing these issues in a given year from 2011 to 2020. *Target* is coded 1 (0 otherwise) when a company has adopted an emissions target in a given year of the study period.

Direct and Indirect Greenhouse Gas Emissions Data from LSEG

This book's data on global firms' entity-wide operational, or scope 1 and scope 2, GHG emissions data come from LSEG Data and Analytics (formerly Refinitiv ESG database and the Thomson Reuters ASSET4 database). Scope 1 emissions are the direct emissions from a firm's chimneys and tailpipes. Scope 2 emissions are associated with the power a company consumes and business travel. Given that there is currently no industry-wide consensus on how to measure emissions in a company's supply chain and through the use of its products (i.e., scope 3 emissions) and that few companies consistently report their scope 3 emissions, this book's analyses on firms' environmental performance encompass only scope 1 and scope 2 emissions. Following the Greenhouse Gas Protocol's emissions classifications by type, entity-wide operational emissions = direct (scope 1) + indirect (scope 2).

Of note, LSEG's scope 1 and scope 2 emissions data are highly correlated with data from other major sustainability data sources, such as Bloomberg, MSCI, Sustainalytics, CDP, and Trucost.[11] The data gathering and reporting practices of LSEG and its industry peers follow the Greenhouse Gas Protocol,[12] which comprises global standardized frameworks to measure and manage GHG emissions from private and public sector operations, value chains, and mitigation actions. The underlying sources of data come from corporate annual reports, sustainability reports, and stock exchange filings.

Environmental, Social, and Governance Data from LSEG

LSEG Data and Analytics is also the source of this book's environmental, social, and governance (ESG) performance data. Using company-reported data, LSEG assigns an ESG score to firms based on the environmental, social, and corporate governance pillars covering ten main themes (i.e., resource use, emissions, environmental product innovation, workforce, human rights, community, product responsibility, management, shareholders, and corporate social responsibility strategy). LSEG also gives firms an ESG controversy score, whereby according to LSEG, firms' actions are verified against commitments to "magnify the impact of significant controversies on the overall ESG scoring."[13]

The overall ESG score; subcategory scores for resource use, emissions, environmental product innovation, and so on; and other related metrics (e.g., ESG controversy) are each ranked between 0 and 100 and interpreted as percentile rank scores. Scores in the 50 to 75 range indicate good relative ESG performance and above average degree of transparency in making ESG data public. Chapters 8 and 9 contain additional information about and data descriptives for firms' ESG performance.

Appendix 2

Description of Global Sustainable Business and Climate Action Database: Variables, Construction, and Operationalization

Appendix 2 provides a description of the variables and their construction and operationalization in the author-constructed Global Sustainable Business and Climate Action Database. This novel dataset is the first of its kind to track a census of global firms across sectors and based in over thirty countries and follows their voluntary climate action and performance over time. Tables A2.1, A2.2, and A2.3 contain information about firm-level variables, market- and sector-level variables, and country-level variables, respectively. The last column of each table lists the chapters where the variables appear in this book's empirical analyses. The ways in which these variables enter into the empirical analyses are described in the chapters; technical details about the data and models are in the appendices.

Decisions about the inclusion of variables in this book's empirical analyses were made by the author based on a balance of unique contribution, parsimony, and internal and external validity, including whether a variable has been previously used in the extant economic, business management, public policy, and political science literatures.

The firm-, market-, sector-, and country-level data that make up the Global Sustainable Business and Climate Action Database come from public, private, and proprietary sources and are available for 2011 to 2020 unless otherwise noted.

Table A2.1
Firm-level variables

Variable	Description, construction, and operation	Source(s)	Chapter(s)
Assets (log)	Natural log of corporate annual, fiscal year-end assets in millions of dollars	Fidelity, Bloomberg, LSEG Data and Analytics	3–9
Carbon disclosure score	This index score ranges from 0 to 100 (100 is the maximum score). Before it was discontinued in 2016, CDP (formerly the Carbon Disclosure Project) assigned a disclosure score to a firm based on the number of points that the responding company was awarded for answering questions regarding the firm's carbon management and emissions (the numerator) as part of CDP's annual climate change questionnaire, divided by the maximum number that could have been awarded (the denominator). This fraction was then converted to a percentage by multiplying by 100 and was rounded to the nearest whole number. The higher the score, the more information a company provided to CDP about its carbon management and emissions.[a]	CDP	3–5
Carbon price	Coded as 1 or 0 otherwise if a firm has adopted an internal carbon price in a given year (available 2015–2020). Carbon price is based on responses to CC2.2c in the CDP annual climate change questionnaire ("Does your company use an internal price on carbon?"), which became part of the survey for the first time in 2015, and responses to C11.3 ("Does your organization use an internal price on carbon?") during 2018–2020.	CDP, corporate websites, annual reports	6, 8–10
CDP score	CDP assesses how well firms report on and reduce their environmental impact with a letter grade (A–D).	CDP	7, 9

CDP—transparency	Coded as 1 or 0 otherwise if a firm has received a letter grade in the range of D to D- from CDP; this designation means that the firm has responded to a majority of CDP's annual climate change questionnaire irrespective of the contents of the disclosure.	CDP	7, 9
CDP—awareness	Coded as 1 or 0 otherwise if a firm has received a letter grade in the range of C to C- from CDP; a firm has demonstrated an awareness about climate change issues through its evaluation of the impacts of business activities on the environment, how these activities affect people and ecosystems, and how the environment affects business activities.	CDP	7, 9
CDP—management	Coded as 1 or 0 otherwise if a firm has received a letter grade in the range of B to B- from CDP; a firm has demonstrated that management action has been taken to address issues that have been raised in its assessments of the company's impacts on the environment and the environment's impacts on business operations. Management action includes the implementation of an environmental management system and adoption of quantitative emissions targets.	CDP	7, 9
CDP—leadership	Coded as 1 or 0 otherwise if a firm has received a letter grade in the range of A to A- from CDP. To be designated a climate change A-list firm by CDP, companies must have disclosed climate actions that represent global best practice, such as third-party verification of at least 70 percent of total scope 1 and scope 2 emissions with no significant exclusions.	CDP	7, 9
CO_2 emissions (log)	Natural log of a firm's entity-wide scope 1 and scope 2 emissions in millions of metric tons	LSEG Data and Analytics	7, 9
CO_2 emissions per dollar (log)	Natural log of a firm's entity-wide scope 1 and scope 2 emissions divided by its corporate annual sales revenues	LSEG Data and Analytics	7, 9

(*continued*)

Table A2.1 (*continued*)

Variable	Description, construction, and operation	Source(s)	Chapter(s)
CO_2 emissions per full-time employees (log)	Natural log of a firm's entity-wide scope 1 and scope 2 emissions divided by entity-wide number of full-time employees	LSEG Data and Analytics	7, 9
Dedicated website	Coded as 1 and 0 otherwise if a company has a dedicated, separate website devoted to sustainability (available 2015)	Corporate websites, annual reports	3, 9
Environmental R&D	Coded as 1 and 0 otherwise if a company has invested in environmental research and development (R&D) (available 2015)	Corporate websites, annual reports	3, 9
Environmental innovation	This percentile rank score (0–100) measures the extent of a company's product innovation, R&D, and capital expenditures related to green technologies. It is one of the categories under the environmental pillar that comprises the environmental, social and governance (ESG) score.	LSEG Data and Analytics	6
ESG	Coded as 1 and 0 otherwise if there is an incorporation of ESG issues into decision-making processes and day-to-day operations	Corporate websites, annual reports	3, 9
ESG score	This percentile rank score (0–100) measures a company's relative ESG performance, commitment, and effectiveness, based on company-reported data, which include information covering ten categories across ESG pillars—namely, resource use, emissions, environmental product innovation, workforce, human rights, community, product responsibility, management, shareholders, and corporate social responsibility (CSR) strategy. Environmental and social factors are measures relative to a firm's sector. In order to calculate the governance categories, data based on a firm's country of incorporation are used as the benchmark.[b]	LSEG Data and Analytics	8–10

ESG score (adjusted)	This is an adjusted ESG score (0–100) that has been discounted for significant ESG controversies impacting firms. When firms are involved in ESG controversies, the ESG score (adjusted) is calculated as the weighted average of the ESG scores and ESG controversies score per fiscal period, with recent controversies reflected in the latest completed period. When companies are not involved in ESG controversies, the ESG score (adjusted) is equal to the ESG score.	LSEG Data and Analytics	10
ESG environment	A firm's environmental pillar score (0–100) is the relative sum of the category weights from emissions, innovation, and resource use categories, which vary per industry. The emissions category covers carbon emissions, waste, biodiversity, and environmental management systems. The innovation category consists of product innovation, environmental R&D and capital expenditures, and green revenues. Resource use includes water, energy, sustainability packaging, and environmental supply chain.	LSEG Data and Analytics	8–10
ESG social	A firm's social pillar score (0–100) is the relative sum of the category weights from community, human rights, product responsibility, and workforce categories, which vary per industry. Product responsibility covers responsible marketing, product quality, and data privacy. Workforce includes diversity and inclusion, career development and training, working conditions, and health and safety.	LSEG Data and Analytics	8–10
ESG governance	A firm's corporate governance pillar score (0–100) is the relative sum of the category weights from the CSR strategy, management, and shareholder categories, which is the same across all industries. CSR strategy covers CSR strategy and ESG reporting and transparency. Management comprises corporate structure (independence, diversity, committees) and compensation. Shareholders include shareholder rights and takeover defenses.		8–10

(*continued*)

Table A2.1 (*continued*)

Variable	Description, construction, and operation	Source(s)	Chapter(s)
ESG controversies	This percentile rank score (0–100) is calculated based on 23 ESG controversy topics across 10 ESG categories, which are aggregated into one ESG controversies score. During the year, if a scandal occurs, the company involved is penalized, and this affects their overall ESG (adjusted) score and grading. The impact of the event may still be seen the following year if there are new developments related to the negative event—for example, lawsuits, ongoing legislation disputes, or fines. All new media materials are captured as the controversy progresses.[c]	LSEG Data and Analytics	8–10
Employees (log)	Natural log of the number of entity-wide full-time employees	Fidelity, Bloomberg, LSEG Data and Analytics	3, 9
Global 100 rank	This score (1–100) represents a firm's rank on Corporate Knight's annual list of Global 100, or the world's most sustainable publicly listed firms with a gross revenue of at least $1 billion.[d] Ranking is based on publicly disclosed data (e.g., financial filings, sustainability reports, and company websites). Methodology is based on up to 25 key performance indicators covering resource management, employee management, financial management, sustainable revenue and sustainable investment, and supplier performance.	Corporate Knights	8, 9
Government-owned	Coded as 1 or 0 otherwise if the company is at least 50 percent government-owned (available 2015)	Fortune, corporate websites	3, 9

ISO 14001 certification	Coded as 1 or 0 otherwise if a company is certified with ISO 14001 (available 2015)	Corporate websites, annual reports	3, 9
Manager	Coded as 1 or 0 otherwise if a firm houses a senior- or executive-level manager responsible for climate change, environmental sustainability, or environmental policy. Manager is also coded 1 if a firm has a committee responsible for setting the vision and planning for climate risk management as part of its board of directors. Manager is based on the response to CC1.1 in the CDP annual climate change questionnaire ("Where is the highest level of direct responsibility for climate change within your organization?").[e]	CDP, corporate websites, annual reports	4–10
Mission statement	Coded as 1 or 0 otherwise if sustainability is stated to be core to the mission of the firm (available 2015)	Corporate websites, annual reports	3, 9
Paris Agreement	Coded as 1 in 2015 and thereafter or 0 otherwise to demarcate a regime shift in global climate change governance and policy	UN Framework Convention on Climate Change	7
Participation	Coded as 1 or 0 otherwise for participation in CDP's annual climate change questionnaire. A firm chooses on an annual basis whether to participate in voluntary carbon disclosure through CDP; it may decide to participate in CDP in one year but not the next year.	CDP	3–5, 7–10
Policy supporter—upper management	Coded as 1 or 0 otherwise if a firm has a designated director- or vice president–level officer for sustainability or if the firm has a designated chief sustainability officer (available 2015)	Corporate websites, annual reports	3, 9

(*continued*)

Table A2.1 (*continued*)

Variable	Description, construction, and operation	Source(s)	Chapter(s)
Policy supporter—analyst	Coded as 1 or 0 otherwise if a firm houses a designated analyst responsible for climate change or sustainability activities or has a sustainability-related committee as part of its board of directors; not the traditional "health, safety, and environment" positions or committee (available 2015)	Corporate websites, annual reports	3, 9
Policy supporter—vice president	Coded as 1 or 0 otherwise if a firm has a designated director- or vice president–level officer for sustainability (available 2015)	Corporate websites, annual reports	3, 9
Policy supporter—chief sustainability officer	Coded as 1 or 0 otherwise if a firm has a designated chief sustainability officer (available 2015)	Corporate websites, annual reports	3, 9
Target	Coded as 1 or 0 otherwise if a firm has adopted a quantitative emissions target, regardless whether it is an absolute or intensity target, in a given year. Target is based on responses to CC3.1 in the CDP annual climate change questionnaire ("Did you have an emission reduction target that was active (ongoing or reached completion) in the reporting year?") during 2011–2017 and responses to C4.1 ("Did you have an emissions target that was active in the reporting year?") during 2018–2020.[e]	CDP, corporate websites, annual reports	4–10
Target and Price	Coded as 1 or 0 otherwise if a firm has adopted both an emissions target and internal carbon price, in a given year (available 2015–2020)	CDP, corporate websites, annual reports	6, 8–10
UNGC member	Coded as 1 or 0 otherwise if a firm is a member of the UN Global Compact in a given year	UN Global Compact	4, 9, 10

Revenues (log)	Natural log of corporate annual sales revenues in millions of dollars; revenue figures include consolidated subsidiaries and reported revenues from discontinued operations but exclude excise taxes. For banks, revenue is the sum of gross interest income and gross noninterest income. For insurance companies, revenue includes premium and annuity income, investment income, realized capital gains or losses, and other income, but excludes deposits.	Fidelity, Bloomberg, LSEG Data and Analytics	3–9

[a] Information about how the CDP scores individual company responses is given in appendix 1.

[b] Information about LSEG Data and Analytics's suite of environmental, social, and governance scores, including calculation methodology and industry group and country benchmarks, can be found at https://www.lseg.com/en/data-analytics/sustainable-finance/esg-scores.

[c] According to LSEG Data and Analytics, firms' actions have been verified against corporate sustainability pledges and commitments. Moreover, market cap bias is addressed by applying severity weights, which adjust controversy scores based on a company's size. The assumption is that large firms are more scrutinized by media attention than smaller firms. See page 10 in https://www.lseg.com/content/dam/data-analytics/en_us/documents/methodology/lseg-esg-scores-methodology.pdf.

[d] Information about Toronto-based. Corporate Knights' Global 100 sustainability ratings, including methodology, can be found at https://www.corporateknights.com/resources/global-100/.

[e] Information about this book's treatment of missing data for *manager* and *target* is given in appendix 1.

Table A2.2

Market- or sector-level variables

Variable	Description, construction, and operation	Source(s)	Chapter(s)
Consumer-oriented	Coded as 1 or 0 otherwise if a firm operates in one of the following non-carbon-intensive sector categories, as defined by the Global Industrial Classification Standard: consumer discretionary, consumer staple, financial services, and health care	Global Industrial Classification Standard	7, 8
GHG-intensive	Coded as 1 or 0 otherwise if a firm operates in the materials and utilities sectors	Global Industrial Classification Standard	4, 7, 9
GHG-intensive (broad) or GHG (broad)	Coded as 1 or 0 otherwise if a firm operates in the energy, industrials, materials, and utilities sectors	Global Industrial Classification Standard	3, 6–9
Natural gas price (log)	Natural log of the annual average of the Dow Jones Commodity Index for Natural Gas (total returns). The Dow Jones index is a broad-market commodity index comprising equally weighted futures contracts of commodities in energy, agriculture and livestock, and metals.	S&P Global	4–6
Natural gas price (S&P GSCI) (log)	Natural log of the annual average of the S&P GSCI Natural Gas Index. The S&P GSCI Natural Gas Index is a production-weighted index that measures commodity market performance through futures contracts.	S&P Global	4–6
Technology	Coded as 1 or 0 otherwise if a firm operates in one of the following non-carbon-intensive sector categories, as defined by the Global Industrial Classification Standard: information technology and telecommunications	Global Industrial Classification Standard	7–10

Table A2.3
Country-level variables

Variable	Description, construction, and operation	Source(s)	Chapter(s)
Clean Power Plan (CPP)	Coded as 1 or 0 otherwise for the US EPA's introduction of the CPP in 2014 through 2016 In 2017 and thereafter, CPP in its original form was repealed by President Donald Trump's administration.	Environmental Protection Agency (EPA)	5, 7, 8
Climate change laws (log)	Natural log of the cumulative or year-to-date numbers of climate change–related laws (i.e., legislation and executive actions) that a country has passed	LSE Grantham Research Institute on Climate Change and the Environment	6
Civil liberties	Based on Freedom House's measure of civil liberties, which measures freedom of expression and belief, associational and organizational rights, rule of law, and personal autonomy and individual rights; the score is on a scale 0 to 7, with a lower score meaning more civil liberties and a higher score meaning fewer civil liberties. Countries with a rating of 1 or 2 enjoy a wide range of civil liberties, including freedoms of expression, assembly, association, education, and religion. At the other end, a rating of 6 indicates limits on the rights of expression and association, including highly restrictive private business activity. A rating of 7 means a country has virtually no civil liberties; in this book's empirical analyses, no company among the Fortune Global 500 originates from a country with a rating of 7.	Freedom House	4, 6, 9

(*continued*)

Table A2.3 (*continued*)

Variable	Description, construction, and operation	Source(s)	Chapter(s)
Environmental Performance Index (EPI)	The EPI measures the ambitiousness of a firm's country of origin's (or export country of largest sales) environmental policies, including climate policies. The EPI comprises 32 performance indicators across 11 issue categories: air quality, sanitation and drinking water, heavy metals, waste management, biodiversity and habitat, ecosystem services, fisheries, climate change, pollution emissions, agriculture, and water resources.[a]	Yale University Center for Environmental Law and Policy	4
EU member	Coded as 1 or 0 otherwise when a firm's country of origin (or export country of largest sales) is a member state of the EU	EU Directorate-General for Communication	4, 6, 9
Federalism	Coded as 1 or 0 otherwise if a firm's country of origin possesses a federalist system of government	Forum of Federations	4, 6, 9
GDP per capita (log)	Natural log of a country's gross domestic product	World Bank's World Development Indicators	4, 6, 9
ISO 14001 (log)	Natural log of the count of ISO 14001 certifications at the country level of a firm's country of origin or export country of largest sales	International Organization for Standardization	4, 6, 9
Political rights	Based on Freedom House's measure of political rights, which measures a firm's country of origin's (or export country of largest sales) electoral process, political pluralism and participation, and functioning of government; the score is on a scale of 0 to 7, with a lower score meaning more political rights and a higher score meaning fewer political rights to outright and extreme government oppression.	Freedom House	4, 6, 9

Regulatory stringency (log)	Natural log of the count of a firm's country of origin's (or export country of largest sales) ratification of international environmental treaties; this reflects what each country is willing to commit to with respect to the breadth and depth of environmental regulation.[b]	International Environmental Agreements (IEA) Database Project, Université Laval	4, 6, 9
USA	Coded as 1 or 0 otherwise when a firm's country of origin (or export country of largest sales) is the United States	LSEG Data and Analytics	4, 7, 9

[a] Information about the Environmental Performance Index (EPI) can be found at https://epi.yale.edu/about-epi.

[b] Information about country-level ratifications of international environmental treaties and how they are collected by the International Environmental Agreement (IEA) Database Project can be found at https://www.iea.ulaval.ca/en.

Appendix 3

Explanation of Data, Models, and Robustness Checks, Chapter 3

Data and Variables

Data on the Fortune Global 500 firms' participation in voluntary carbon disclosure and their level of disclosure come from CDP's 2015 climate change questionnaire. As explicated in appendix 1, the CDP's climate change questionnaire requests information from corporate executives about their company's management structure, risks, and opportunities related to climate change; corporate strategies for managing these risks and opportunities; and an inventory of their corporation's greenhouse gas (GHG) emissions.[1]

Based on questionnaire responses, CDP grades firms annually on the comprehensiveness of their information disclosure by assigning disclosure scores (with a maximum score of 100). CDP's disclosure scores serve as this chapter's proxy for the intensity of participation (i.e., the level of carbon disclosure by firms). A disclosure score is assigned to a company based on the number of points a company has been awarded for answering questions regarding their carbon management and emissions (the numerator) as part of CDP's climate change questionnaire, divided by the maximum number that could have been awarded (the denominator).[2] This fraction is then converted to a percentage by multiplying by 100 and is rounded to the nearest whole number.[3] The higher the score, the more information a company has provided to CDP about its carbon emissions and related management plans. Information about how CDP scores individual firm responses is given in appendix 1.

The *carbon disclosure score* for the eighty-eight firms that did not participate in CDP's 2015 climate change questionnaire—which make up less

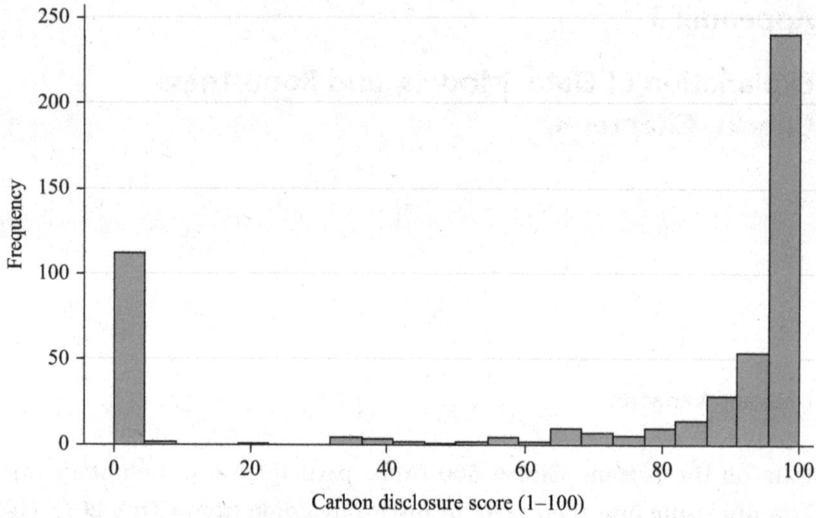

Figure A3.1
Distribution of carbon disclosure scores (2015).
Data source: CDP.

than 20 percent of the sample—has been coded as 0. This coding scheme is robust to an alternative modeling approach, namely the Heckman selection model, in which nonparticipation is coded as missing values.

In 2015, 5 percent (or twenty-four) of the Global 500 firms that disclosed to CDP requested to keep their disclosure scores private. In the analysis in chapter 3, *carbon disclosure score* has been coded 0 for these twenty-four companies.[4] Taken altogether, there are 388 companies (approximately 78 percent) that have a *carbon disclosure score* greater than 0 in the main analysis.

Figure A3.1 shows the distribution of the disclosure scores of the Global 500 companies that have participated in voluntary carbon disclosure. The thicker tail on the right side of the distribution suggests that while variation exists in carbon disclosure levels, there is a bias toward higher levels of carbon disclosure among companies that report their carbon emissions and related information to CDP. In fact, the disclosure scores take on a bimodal distribution with a concentration of zeros and a density of high scores. The double-hurdle model used in the empirical analysis is especially well suited for accounting for this problem of a corner solution (i.e., the phenomenon in which an actor or agent—a global firm in this book—is either unwilling or unable to make a tradeoff between choices).

Table A3.1

Collinearity diagnostics of independent variables in main models

	VIF	SQRT VIF[b]	Tolerance	R^2
Policy supporter—upper management	1.09	1.05	0.91	0.09
Mission statement	1.13	1.06	0.88	0.12
ESG principles[a]	1.03	1.02	0.97	0.03
Dedicated website	1.03	1.01	0.97	0.03
Environmental R&D	1.39	1.18	0.72	0.28
Revenues (log)	1.26	1.12	0.80	0.20
Government-owned	1.06	1.03	0.95	0.05
GHG-intensive (broad)	1.30	1.14	0.77	0.23
Mean VIF		1.16		

[a] Environmental, social, and governance (ESG) principles.

[b] Square root of the variance inflation factor (VIF), which is a measure of how much the variance of a regression coefficient is inflated due to multicollinearity between independent variables in the model.

The bimodal distribution with a density of high disclosure scores is not surprising: it has been shown in the literature that stakeholders are more likely to punish a firm for its "partial disclosure" than for being dangerous or dirty.[5] That is to say, firms have the incentive to disclose at higher levels or not to disclose at all. This upward bias in the distribution of disclosure scores notwithstanding, the existing variation in scores represents these firms' differential costs in voluntary carbon disclosure. The analysis in chapter 3 uncovers the characteristics of the leading Global 500 firms that choose not only to disclose to CDP but also engage in carbon disclosure at high levels.

One might be concerned that the firm-level independent variables (*mission statement, ESG, dedicated website, environmental R&D*, and *ISO 14001 certification*) in chapter 3's empirical analysis are highly correlated. For example, a firm's environmental research and development (R&D) may be correlated with its adoption of environmental, social, and governance (ESG) principles or with firm size. Table A3.1 reports the results of a standard collinearity diagnostic of the explanatory variables, which shows that chapter 3's analysis does not suffer from multicollinearity concerns. The variance inflation factor (VIF) is less than 10, indicating that the explanatory variables are orthogonal (i.e., uncorrelated).

Table A3.2
Summary statistics of internal firm determinants

	All Global 500 firms		
Variable	*N*	Mean	Standard deviation
Dependent variables			
Participation in CDP	500	0.776	0.417
Carbon disclosure score (0–100)	500	71.084	40.322
Independent variables			
Policy supporter—upper management	500	0.568	0.496
Policy supporter—analyst (only)	500	0.116	0.321
Policy supporter—vice president	500	0.500	0.501
Policy supporter—chief sustainability officer	500	0.068	0.252
Mission statement	500	0.164	0.371
ESG principles[a]	500	0.292	0.455
Dedicated website	500	0.100	0.300
Environmental R&D	500	0.378	0.485
ISO 14001 certification	500	0.626	0.484
Revenues (log)	500	9.993	1.167
Assets (log)	500	10.995	1.491
Employees (log)	489	10.709	1.266
Government-owned	500	0.060	0.238
GHG-intensive (broad)	500	0.288	0.453

[a] Environmental, social, and governance (ESG) principles.

Table A3.2 presents summary statistics of the dependent and independent variables, including alternative measures of the variables in chapter 3 in the robustness checks.

Double-Hurdle Model

Chapter 3 employs a double-hurdle model to model a Global 500 firm's decision to participate in voluntary carbon disclosure and the related, but separate and sequential, decision about the company's intensity of participation or level of carbon disclosure.[6] This estimation approach accounts for the fact that global firms may participate in voluntary carbon disclosure but choose to disclose different levels of information about their carbon management strategies and carbon emissions; this suggests that the incentives and conditions driving the (binary) decision to participate may be different from the decision about the level of effort.

Studies of corporate environmentalism and environmental voluntary programs have found that firms may advertise environmental leadership by the virtue of their participation in voluntary programs without actually fulfilling their pledges; that is, firms engage in greenwashing behavior.[7] Specifications that ignore the fact that the decision to disclose and the decision about the level of disclosure are influenced by different motivating factors could lead to biased and inconsistent estimates of carbon disclosure levels by firms.

The double-hurdle model is more general than the standard truncated regression model, or tobit model (which is a special case of Cragg's model), because it allows participation and effort decisions to be determined by separate processes through the incorporation of two stages or tiers of estimation. In doing so, it allows parameters and variables to differentially affect the two decisions. By contrast, the tobit model assumes that the same mechanism generates both the zeros and the positive values of disclosure levels.

Of note, the Heckman selection model is less appropriate of a model here because this is not a problem about sample selection. There are no missing data: we have complete information about whether the Global 500 firms choose to participate in CDP and their level of disclosure. Rather, this is a problem of corner solutions: some global businesses choose not to disclose their climate change information. The problem to be solved in this incidence is how to better model $D(y \mid x)$, where y or the decision about whether to disclose climate change information (and by how much) takes on a 0.

In the first (participation) stage of the double-hurdle model, the binary choice of whether to participate in carbon disclosure is modeled using a probit regression. In the second (effort) stage, a truncated normal regression is used to model a firm's level of carbon disclosure as proxied by its carbon disclosure score (d), conditional on engaging a positive level of carbon disclosure ($d>0$). Following Wooldridge (2002), the density of d is then given by

$$f(d|x_1, x_2) = [1 - \Phi(x_1\gamma)]^{1[d=0]}\{\Phi(x_1\gamma)[\Phi(x_2\beta/\sigma)]^{-1}[\phi(\{d - x_2\beta\}/\sigma)/\sigma]\}^{1[d>0]} \quad (1)$$

where x_1 and γ and x_2 and β are vectors of explanatory variables and parameters for the first and second stage, respectively, and Φ and φ are the standard normal cumulative distribution function and probability density function, respectively. The firm-level independent variables contained in x_1

and x_2, respectively, are the same variables in the first (participation) and second (effort) stages of the double-hurdle model.[8] Signs and significance levels of the estimated coefficients may vary between the two hurdles, because different types of decisions are made.

Equation (1) is estimated using maximum likelihood with robust standard errors and industry sector-level cluster correction using the "churdle" command in Stata, and the results are displayed in table 3.1 in chapter 3.

Estimating Average Marginal Effects

To estimate the average marginal effects of the chapter's independent variables of interest on the probability of participation in voluntary carbon disclosure and on the level of disclosure, the author first estimated the probability of participation for each individual firm *i* as

$$P(d_i > 0 \mid x_{1i}) = \Phi(x_{1i}\,\gamma)$$

The conditional expected disclosure effort can then be estimated as:

$$E(d_i \mid d_i > 0, x_{2i}) = x_{2i}\,\beta + \sigma \times \lambda(x_{2i}\,\beta/\sigma)$$

where $\lambda(x)$ is the inverse Mills ratio: $\lambda(x) = \varphi(x)/\Phi(x)$.

The first-stage average marginal effects, or AMEs, are based on the first-hurdle estimates, while the conditional average marginal effects (CAMEs) express the second-hurdle effect, conditional on the first hurdle being met—that is, conditional on participating in CDP; both sets of marginal effects of each independent variable are estimated following procedures outlined in Burke (2009). See chapter 3, table 3.2, for the estimated AMEs and CAMEs.

Robustness Checks

Several robustness checks have been conducted to assess the sensitivity of the main model specifications in chapter 3. These results are presented in table A3.3. First, *policy supporter—upper management* is replaced with similar but narrower measures of senior- or executive-level managers—namely, *policy supporter—vice president* and *policy supporter—chief sustainability officer* in both the first and second hurdles (i.e., tier 1 and tier 2). See the results for these alternative specifications in columns 1 and 2, respectively, in table A3.3. Another alternative specification, *policy supporter—analyst (only)*, represents firms that have only installed a lower-level policy analyst to be responsible for environmental sustainability.

Table A3.3

Internal firm determinants of participation and effort in voluntary carbon disclosure, double-hurdle model (alternative specifications)

	1	2	3	4	5	6
Tier 1 (Participation in voluntary carbon disclosure)						
Policy supporter—upper management				0.541***	0.653***	0.536***
Policy supporter—vice president	0.396**					
Policy supporter—chief sustainability officer		0.631*				
Policy supporter—analyst (only)			0.191			
Mission statement	0.13	0.184	0.179	0.088	0.101	0.142
ESG principles[a]	0.692***	0.820***	0.811***	0.618***	0.538***	0.667***
Dedicated website	0.053	0.113	0.141	0.028	0.011	0.003
Environmental R&D	-0.056	-0.062	-0.05		-0.036	-0.093
ISO 14001 certification				0.267		
Revenues (log)	0.313***	0.332***	0.344***	0.270***		
Assets (log)					0.202***	
Employees (log)						0.307***
Government-owned	–0.132	–0.130	–0.135	–0.089	–0.035	–0.390
GHG-intensive (broad)	–0.136	–0.143	–0.143	–0.226	–0.005	–0.016
Constant	3.961	3.788	3.712	4.049	4.704	3.747
Tier 2 (Level of voluntary carbon disclosure)						
Policy supporter—upper management				6.021***	6.733***	5.858***
Policy supporter—vice president	5.043***					
Policy supporter—chief sustainability officer		1.346				
Policy supporter—analyst (only)			1.611			

(*continued*)

Table A3.3 (*continued*)

	1	2	3	4	5	6
Mission statement	3.048**	3.281**	3.327**	3.112**	2.627*	2.681*
ESG principles[a]	5.209***	5.893***	5.835***	5.009***	4.815***	4.599***
Dedicated website	2.67	2.947	3.045	3.018	2.636	2.126
Environmental R&D	4.225***	4.069***	4.143***		4.618***	4.332***
ISO 14001 certification				3.714***		
Revenues (log)	1.635***	1.947***	1.946***	1.745***		
Assets (log)					0.358	
Employees (log)						1.337**
Government-owned	–0.321	0.543	0.637	-0.673	0.271	–4.894
GHG-intensive (broad)	–2.377*	–2.479*	–2.616*	–1.451	–1.859	–1.663
Constant	72.994***	71.966***	71.489***	68.598***	83.799***	74.437***
Lnsigma						
Constant	2.498***	2.515***	2.515***	2.492***	2.498***	2.472***
Chi-square	49.344	1,133.225	668.199	24.868	179.858	2.50E+09
N	500	500	500	500	500	489
Country fixed effects	Yes	Yes	Yes	Yes	Yes	Yes

Note: $^{*}p<0.1$, $^{**}p<0.05$, $^{***}p<0.01$.

[a] Environmental, social, and governance (ESG) principles.

Second, firms' certifications with the ISO 14001 environment management system, which has been used in the literature as a proxy for complementary assets,[9] serves as an alternative specification for *environmental R&D*. Third, *revenues* is replaced with other related measures—log forms of *assets* and *employees*—as alternative measures for firm size. Table A3.3 reports results for these alternative specifications in columns 4–6.

The chapter 3 double-hurdle results for the Global 500 firms (see table 3.2) are by and large robust to these different operationalizations of policy supporter, complementary assets, and firm size. Moreover, additional evidence is marshalled for this book's proposition about the critical role of policy supporters in upper management (see the lack of statistical significance for *policy supporter—analyst (only)* in alternative specification 3 in table A3.3).

When only lower-level policy supporters are responsible for climate mitigation, firms may not be compelled to participate in voluntary carbon disclosure or increase their level of participation, conditional on participation. This is because lower-level advocates of environmental sustainability inside a firm do not have the decision-making authority to alter business operations or make financial investments in carbon reduction activities. By contrast, the existence of a chief sustainability officer is correlated with firms' higher propensity to participate in CDP (although not correlated with a higher level of disclosure).

Appendix 4

Explanation of Data, Models, and Robustness Checks, Chapter 4

Data and Variables

Data for chapter 4's empirical analysis are drawn from the CDP annual climate change questionnaire from 2011 to 2015. This is the same data sample frame used in chapter 5's empirical analysis. As appendix 1 details, all disclosure scores are public by default, but companies can request privacy of their climate change information, including their disclosure scores. To avoid making assumptions about the missing disclosure scores of the "private" responses, the analysis sample consists of a panel of Fortune Global 500 companies in 2011–2015, excluding the 115 firm×year observations in which a company has requested privacy of its score.[1] The result is an unbalanced panel of 683 companies over 5 years, namely, 3,300 firm×year observations. The chapter's main analysis pertains to voluntary public disclosure by the Fortune Global 500.

Table A4.1 presents summary statistics for the dependent and independent variables, including alternative measures in the robustness checks.

Heckman Selection Model

Chapter 4 employs the Heckman selection (HS) model as the main model. An implication of the fact that not all global business invitees responded to CDP's information request is a truncation in the carbon disclosure data; that is, *carbon disclosure score* is not observed for those firms in the sample where the value of the *participation* variable is zero. In the HS model, companies that did not disclose to the CDP are coded as missing values for the

Table A4.1
Summary statistics

	Fortune Global 500 firms		
Variable	*N*	Mean	Standard deviation
Dependent variables			
Participation	3,300	0.728	0.445
Carbon disclosure score	2,404	80.191	19.152
Firm, market, and sector variables			
Manager	3,300	0.701	0.458
Target	3,300	0.585	0.493
UNGC member	3,300	0.329	0.470
Revenues (log)	3,258	9.731	1.215
Assets (log)	3,261	10.675	1.494
Natural gas price (Dow Jones)	3,300	0.697	0.377
Natural gas price (S&P GSCI)	3,300	4.174	0.377
GHG-intensive[a]	3,300	0.143	0.350
GHG-intensive (broad)[b]	3,300	0.341	0.474
Country-level variables			
Regulatory stringency (log)	3,300	4.695	0.887
Environmental performance index	3,175	81.910	7.271
Civil liberties	3,300	1.503	1.025
Political rights	3,300	1.523	1.289
GDP per capita (log)	3,300	10.337	0.945
Federal	3,300	0.621	0.485
ISO 14001 (log) (last year)	2,617	8.533	1.138
EU member	3,300	0.222	0.416

[a] Includes materials and utilities sectors.
[b] Includes chemicals, industrials, materials, and utilities sectors.

carbon disclosure score, unlike the alternative endogenous binary-variable (EBV) model (see below).

Firms' participation and intensity of participation are separate equations in the HS model. In the participation stage of the HS model, the likelihood of voluntary carbon disclosure is predicted using a probit model and the exclusion restriction;[2] an inverse Mills ratio, $\hat{\lambda}$, is also predicted for each observation. In the second stage, the level of carbon disclosure is estimated using the $\hat{\lambda}$ as a predictor in the model.[3] If the coefficient on $\hat{\lambda}$ is statistically equal to zero, there is no evidence of sample selection, and the ordinary least squares results are consistent and will be presented. By contrast, if the coefficient on $\hat{\lambda}$ is statistically significantly different from zero, the coefficients from the correlated model will be presented.

A Wald test of independent equations is rejected for model specifications representing corporate management and domestic regulation, and business corporate and global governance interactions, respectively, which suggests the appropriateness of the modeling approach.

Endogenous Binary-Variable Model

As an alternative model the EBV model requires an additional assumption to be made about firms' level of carbon disclosure: nonparticipating firms have not disclosed their carbon management strategies and practices and emissions to other institutions. Unlike the Heckman selection model, in which *carbon*

Table A4.2

Base model (no cross-level interactions) for multilevel determinants of participation and effort in voluntary carbon disclosure, Heckman selection model (Fortune Global 500 firms)

	Participation in voluntary carbon disclosure b/se[a]	Level of voluntary carbon disclosure b/se[a]
Firm, market, and sector variables		
Manager[b]	1.618*** (0.12)	
Target[b]		13.581*** (1.61)
UNGC member	0.823*** (0.17)	3.103*** (1.10)
Revenues[c] (log)	0.218*** (0.06)	1.368*** (0.50)
Natural gas price (log)	0.006 (0.09)	–10.280*** (0.75)
GHG-intensive	–0.441** (0.22)	4.667** (1.89)
Country-level variables		
Regulatory stringency (log)	0.121 (0.08)	–0.573 (1.70)
Civil liberties	–0.150** (0.07)	–8.080*** (1.59)

(continued)

Table A4.2 (*continued*)

	Participation in voluntary carbon disclosure b/se[a]	Level of voluntary carbon disclosure b/se[a]
GDP per capita (log)	0.210**	–3.183**
	(0.08)	(1.42)
Federalism	0.029	–0.533
	(0.21)	(1.54)
ISO 14001 (log)	0.004	–0.140
	(0.06)	(0.66)
EU member	0.154	–0.525
	(0.26)	(1.61)
Constant	–5.011***	115.103***
	(1.15)	(16.73)
Athrho Constant	–0.172**	
	(0.07)	
Lnsigma Constant	2.672***	
	(0.04)	
N	2,588	
Sector fixed effects	Yes	
Year fixed effects	Yes	

Note: $^{**}p<0.05$, $^{***}p<0.01$. Year indicator variables for 2011 and the technology sector, which includes information technology and telecommunications, serve as the base.

[a] Robust standard errors with firm-level cluster correction.

[b] *Manager* and *target* are lagged by one year to allow for the possibility of reverse causation. Moreover, the installation of a manager responsible for climate mitigation and the adoption of a quantitative emissions target may be jointly determined with the decision about participation in voluntary carbon disclosure or the level of disclosure. Companies that commit to voluntary carbon disclosure are more likely to devote resources to meet the program's goals, including integrating climate risks and/or hiring a manager dedicated to carbon management and climate risks. There could also be unobserved factors that influence participation in CDP that are also likely to influence current management choices.

[c] These contemporaneous time-varying variables are lagged by one year in the analysis to mitigate the possibility of reverse causation in the sense that larger, more deep-pocketed firms may be financially better positioned to cope with the costs of meeting CDP's requirements (including but not limited to disclosure requirements) and therefore more likely to self-select into CDP.

disclosure score is coded as a missing value, *carbon disclosure score* is coded 0 for nonparticipants during 2011–2015 in the endogenous binary-variable model. This assumption arguably has at least some support since no other institutions have built a more comprehensive international database of self-reported climate change information and have developed a reputation for impartiality.[4] Technical details about the EBV model are given in appendix 5.

Robustness Checks

As robustness checks to model 1 and model 2 (corporate×regulation and corporate×global, respectively), tables A4.3–A4.9 present the results of alternative specifications and an alternative model. A base model without the cross-level interactions is included in all the tables. First, *civil liberties* is replaced with *political rights* as an alternative measure of a country's level of civic engagement in table A4.3. Table A4.4 employs an alternative measure of *regulatory stringency*: the Environmental Performance Index (EPI) measures the ambitiousness of environmental policies, including climate policy, across countries. The third alternative specification replaces *revenues* (log) with *assets* (log) to control for firm size (see table A4.5).

In table A4.6, the Dow Jones Natural Gas Index has been replaced with the S&P GSCI Natural Gas Index as an alternative measure of natural gas prices. Moreover, GHG-intensive is defined more broadly to include the energy and industrial sectors in table A4.7. In table A4.8, a firm's country of origin has been replaced with its export country of largest sales. This means that the *corporate×regulation* interaction terms are made up of *manager* or *target* and *regulatory stringency*, respectively, for a firm's largest export market (i.e., the country where a firm earns its largest sales revenue) instead of a firm's domicile country. Finally, results based on the endogenous binary-variable model such that the omitted variable is an endogenous treatment variable rather than a selection variable, are presented in table A4.9.

On balance, chapter 4's main results are robust to these alternative specifications.[5] In three alternative specifications—political rights, EPI, and export country of largest sales—the estimated coefficient for *target×UNGC member*—is not statistically significant, contradicting the chapter's main results in table 4.3, although the estimated coefficient on *target×UNGC member* in table 4.3 is weakly significant (at the 10 percent level) to begin with. Despite this, the results of the alternative specifications are all in the same direction and of similar magnitude as the chapter's main results.

Table A4.3
Multilevel determinants of participation and effort in voluntary carbon disclosure, Heckman selection model (alternative specification: political rights)

	Base b/se[a]	Corporate × regulation b/se[a]	Corporate × global b/se[a]
Participation			
Revenue (log)	0.207*** (0.06)	0.189*** (0.06)	0.240*** (0.06)
Natural gas price (log)	0.008 (0.09)	0.005 (0.08)	0.006 (0.09)
GHG-intensive	–0.404* (0.22)	–0.366* (0.22)	–0.353 (0.22)
Regulatory stringency	0.064 (0.08)	–0.073 (0.08)	0.113 (0.08)
GDP per capita (log)	0.265*** (0.08)	0.257*** (0.07)	0.201*** (0.07)
Federalism	0.128 (0.20)	0.128 (0.19)	0.033 (0.18)
ISO 14001 (log)	0.033 (0.06)	0.032 (0.06)	0.021 (0.06)
EU member	0.270 (0.25)	0.250 (0.25)	0.287 (0.24)
Target	1.635*** (0.12)		1.545*** (0.12)
UNGC member	0.822*** (0.17)	0.835*** (0.16)	
Political rights[b]	–0.083 (0.05)	–0.089* (0.05)	–0.084* (0.05)
Manager × regulatory stringency		0.332*** (0.03)	
Manager × UNGC member			0.590*** (0.19)
Constant	–5.672*** (1.02)	–4.702*** (1.01)	–5.273*** (0.98)
Carbon disclosure score			
Revenue (log)	1.183** (0.51)	1.180** (0.51)	1.323** (0.52)
Natural gas price (log)	–10.422*** (0.73)	–10.403*** (0.74)	–10.465*** (0.74)
GHG-intensive	5.680*** (1.93)	5.717*** (1.95)	5.945*** (1.93)
Regulatory stringency	–2.697 (2.01)	–4.569** (1.94)	–2.522 (2.01)

	Base b/se[a]	Corporate × regulation b/se[a]	Corporate × global b/se[a]
GDP per capita (log)	−0.974 (1.36)	−1.027 (1.36)	−1.194 (1.37)
Federalism	1.858 (1.73)	1.858 (1.73)	1.493 (1.75)
ISO 14001 (log)	0.193 (0.75)	0.155 (0.75)	0.116 (0.76)
EU member	2.867* (1.67)	2.704 (1.65)	3.161* (1.69)
Target	13.342*** (1.64)		12.956*** (1.80)
UNGC member	2.862*** (1.10)	2.905*** (1.10)	
Political rights	−5.337*** (1.47)	−5.616*** (1.46)	−5.247*** (1.48)
Target × regulatory stringency		2.805*** (0.33)	
Target × UNGC member			1.641 (1.12)
Constant	95.300*** (18.13)	105.314*** (18.07)	97.070*** (18.28)
Athrho Constant	−0.182** (0.08)	−0.147** (0.07)	−0.205*** (0.08)
Lnsigma Constant	2.686*** (0.04)	2.683*** (0.04)	2.691*** (0.04)
N	2,588	2,588	2,588
Sector fixed effects	Yes	Yes	Yes
Year fixed effects	Yes	Yes	Yes

Note: *$p<0.1$, **$p<0.05$, ***$p<0.01$.

[a] Robust standard errors with firm-level cluster correction.

[b] Data for political rights come from Freedom House.

Table A4.4
Multilevel determinants of participation and effort in voluntary carbon disclosure, Heckman selection model (alternative specification: Environmental Performance Index)

	Base b/se[a]	Corporate × regulation b/se[a]	Corporate × global b/se[a]
Participation			
Revenue (log)	0.237*** (0.06)	0.233*** (0.06)	0.272*** (0.06)
Natural gas price (log)	0.057 (0.10)	0.059 (0.10)	0.056 (0.10)
GHG-intensive	–0.450** (0.22)	–0.467** (0.22)	–0.396* (0.22)
Civil liberties	–0.191** (0.08)	–0.200*** (0.08)	–0.194*** (0.07)
GDP per capita (log)	–0.011 (0.14)	–0.016 (0.14)	–0.077 (0.13)
Federalism	0.012 (0.20)	0.026 (0.20)	–0.057 (0.19)
ISO 14001 (log)	0.032 (0.07)	0.029 (0.07)	0.028 (0.07)
EU member	0.093 (0.28)	0.104 (0.28)	0.135 (0.27)
Manager	1.574*** (0.12)		1.474*** (0.13)
UNGC member	0.828*** (0.16)	0.829*** (0.16)	
EPI[b]	0.031* (0.02)	0.019 (0.02)	0.032** (0.02)
Manager × EPI		0.019*** (0.00)	
Manager × UNGC member			0.632*** (0.19)
Constant	–4.961*** (1.20)	–3.856*** (1.17)	–4.539*** (1.14)
Carbon disclosure score			
Revenue (log)	1.401*** (0.50)	1.407*** (0.50)	1.575*** (0.50)
Natural gas price (log)	–10.895*** (0.82)	–10.875*** (0.82)	–10.935*** (0.82)
GHG-intensive	4.286** (1.86)	4.263** (1.88)	4.645** (1.87)

	Base b/se[a]	Corporate × regulation b/se[a]	Corporate × global b/se[a]
Civil liberties	–8.029***	–8.099***	–7.925***
	(1.59)	(1.59)	(1.60)
GDP per capita (log)	–1.414	–1.33	–1.658
	(1.26)	(1.26)	(1.27)
Federalism	–0.056	–0.169	–0.444
	(1.60)	(1.60)	(1.62)
ISO 14001 (log)	–0.218	–0.257	–0.306
	(0.64)	(0.64)	(0.65)
EU member	0.605	0.493	1.082
	(1.72)	(1.72)	(1.74)
Target	13.786***		13.466***
	(1.62)		(1.77)
UNGC member	3.245***	3.289***	
	(1.09)	(1.10)	
EPI	–0.294*	–0.421***	–0.288*
	(0.16)	(0.16)	(0.16)
Target × EPI		0.165***	
		(0.02)	
Target × UNGC member			1.664
			(1.10)
Constant	117.936***	128.103***	120.079***
	(17.38)	(17.68)	(17.49)
Athrho	–0.176**	–0.166**	–0.195**
Constant	(0.08)	(0.07)	(0.08)
Lnsigma	2.656***	2.657***	2.661***
Constant	(0.04)	(0.04)	(0.04)
N	2,588	2,588	2,588
Sector fixed effects	Yes	Yes	Yes
Year fixed effects	Yes	Yes	Yes

Note: *$p<0.1$, **$p<0.05$, ***$p<0.01$.

[a] Robust standard errors with firm-level cluster correction.

[b] Data for EPI come from the Yale University Center for Environmental Law & Policy.

Table A4.5
Multilevel determinants of participation and effort in voluntary carbon disclosure, Heckman selection model (alternative specification: assets)

	Base b/se[a]	Corporate × regulation b/se[a]	Corporate × global b/se[a]
Participation			
Natural gas price (log)	0.010 (0.09)	0.007 (0.09)	0.006 (0.09)
GHG-intensive	–0.430* (0.22)	–0.396* (0.23)	–0.385* (0.22)
Regulatory stringency	0.140* (0.08)	0.000 (0.08)	0.192** (0.08)
Civil liberties	–0.144* (0.07)	–0.149** (0.07)	–0.144** (0.07)
GDP per capita (log)	0.216*** (0.08)	0.210*** (0.08)	0.149* (0.08)
Federalism	0.022 (0.21)	0.016 (0.21)	–0.071 (0.19)
ISO 14001 (log)	0.021 (0.07)	0.013 (0.06)	0.009 (0.06)
EU member	0.167 (0.26)	0.142 (0.26)	0.200 (0.25)
Target	1.658*** (0.12)		1.569*** (0.12)
UNGC member	0.851*** (0.17)	0.861*** (0.17)	
Assets (log)	0.159*** (0.06)	0.148*** (0.06)	0.193*** (0.05)
Manager × regulatory stringency		0.339*** (0.02)	
Manager × UNGC member			0.585*** (0.19)
Constant	–4.906*** (1.14)	–3.949*** (1.13)	–4.527*** (1.08)
Carbon disclosure score			
Natural gas price (log)	–10.177*** (0.75)	–10.168*** (0.76)	–10.231*** (0.76)
GHG-intensive	4.555** (1.92)	4.556** (1.94)	4.853** (1.92)
Regulatory stringency	–0.312 (1.70)	–2.126 (1.62)	–0.149 (1.69)

	Base b/se[a]	Corporate × regulation b/se[a]	Corporate × global b/se[a]
Civil liberties	−7.918*** (1.59)	−7.992*** (1.60)	−7.794*** (1.60)
GDP per capita (log)	−3.055** (1.41)	−3.044** (1.43)	−3.277** (1.43)
Federalism	−0.238 (1.55)	−0.234 (1.56)	−0.603 (1.58)
ISO 14001 (log)	0.057 (0.65)	0.031 (0.65)	−0.035 (0.66)
EU member	−0.44 (1.62)	−0.609 (1.62)	−0.09 (1.65)
Target	13.855*** (1.67)		13.318*** (1.81)
UNGC member	3.390*** (1.15)	3.411*** (1.15)	
Assets (log)	0.43 (0.50)	0.415 (0.50)	0.621 (0.49)
Target × regulatory stringency		2.870*** (0.33)	
Target × UNGC member			2.077* (1.13)
Constant	119.085*** (16.47)	128.187*** (16.38)	120.595*** (16.55)
Athrho Constant	−0.195** (0.08)	−0.177** (0.08)	−0.214** (0.08)
Lnsigma Constant	2.677*** (0.04)	2.676*** (0.04)	2.682*** (0.04)
N	2,588	2,588	2,588
Sector fixed effects	Yes	Yes	Yes
Year fixed effects	Yes	Yes	Yes

Note: *$p<0.1$, **$p<0.05$, ***$p<0.01$.

[a] Robust standard errors with firm-level cluster correction.

Table A4.6
Multilevel determinants of participation and effort in voluntary carbon disclosure, Heckman selection model (alternative specification: S&P GSCI Natural Gas Price Index)

	Base b/se[a]	Corporate × regulation b/se[a]	Corporate × global b/se[a]
Participation			
Natural gas price (S&P GSCI)[b] (log)	–0.002 (0.09)	–0.006 (0.09)	–0.008 (0.09)
Revenue (log)	0.193*** (0.06)	0.172*** (0.06)	0.228*** (0.06)
GHG-intensive	–0.412* (0.22)	–0.376* (0.22)	–0.358 (0.22)
Regulatory stringency	0.132* (0.08)	–0.004 (0.08)	0.183** (0.08)
Civil liberties	–0.146** (0.07)	–0.149** (0.07)	–0.145** (0.07)
GDP per capita (log)	0.213*** (0.08)	0.210*** (0.08)	0.150* (0.08)
Federalism	0.024 (0.21)	0.02 (0.21)	–0.072 (0.20)
ISO 14001 (log)	0.013 (0.06)	0.008 (0.06)	0.001 (0.06)
EU member	0.158 (0.26)	0.136 (0.26)	0.181 (0.25)
Manager	1.641*** (0.12)		1.551*** (0.12)
UNGC member	0.832*** (0.17)	0.845*** (0.17)	
Manager × regulatory stringency		0.334*** (0.03)	
Manager × UNGC member			0.587*** (0.19)
Constant	–4.963*** (1.19)	–3.974*** (1.17)	–4.569*** (1.13)
Carbon disclosure score			
S&P GSCI natural gas price (log)	–10.189*** (0.75)	–10.180*** (0.75)	–10.239*** (0.76)
Revenue (log)	1.273** (0.51)	1.259** (0.52)	1.428*** (0.51)
GHG-intensive	4.617** (1.90)	4.618** (1.91)	4.917*** (1.89)

	Base b/se[1]	Corporate × regulation b/se[1]	Corporate × global b/se[1]
Regulatory stringency	–0.531	–2.312	–0.379
	(1.70)	(1.63)	(1.69)
Civil liberties	–8.052***	–8.126***	–7.924***
	(1.59)	(1.60)	(1.59)
GDP per capita (log)	–3.224**	–3.214**	–3.420**
	(1.42)	(1.43)	(1.43)
Federalism	–0.511	–0.506	–0.868
	(1.54)	(1.54)	(1.56)
ISO 14001 (log)	–0.098	–0.126	–0.179
	(0.66)	(0.66)	(0.66)
EU member	–0.562	–0.733	–0.224
	(1.61)	(1.61)	(1.64)
Target	13.670***		13.190***
	(1.62)		(1.77)
UNGC member	3.176***	3.193***	
	(1.10)	(1.10)	
Target × regulatory stringency		2.829***	
		(0.32)	
Target × UNGC member			1.984*
			(1.10)
Constant	151.188***	160.118***	152.902***
	(16.55)	(16.44)	(16.60)
Athrho	–0.184**	–0.166**	–0.205***
Constant	(0.08)	(0.07)	(0.08)
Lnsigma	2.673***	2.673***	2.678***
Constant	(0.04)	(0.04)	(0.04)
N	2,588	2,588	2,588
Sector fixed effects	Yes	Yes	Yes
Year fixed effects	Yes	Yes	Yes

Note: $^{*}p<0.1$, $^{**}p<0.05$, $^{***}p<0.01$.

[a] Robust standard errors with firm-level cluster correction.

[b] Data for S&P GSCI Natural Gas Price Index come from S&P Global.

Table A4.7
Multilevel determinants of participation and effort in voluntary carbon disclosure, Heckman selection model (alternative specification: GHG-intensive [broad])

	Base b/se[a]	Corporate × regulation b/se[a]	Corporate × global b/se[a]
Participation			
GHG-intensive (broad)[b]	–0.412*	–0.376*	-0.358
	(0.22)	(0.22)	(0.22)
Natural gas price (log)	–0.002	–0.006	–0.008
	(0.09)	(0.09)	(0.09)
Revenue (log)	0.193***	0.172***	0.228***
	(0.06)	(0.06)	(0.06)
Regulatory stringency	0.132*	0.004	0.183**
	(0.08)	(0.08)	(0.08)
Civil liberties	–0.146**	–0.149**	–0.145**
	(0.07)	(0.07)	(0.07)
GDP per capita (log)	0.213***	0.210***	0.150*
	(0.08)	(0.08)	(0.08)
Federalism	0.024	0.020	–0.072
	(0.21)	(0.21)	(0.20)
ISO 14001 (log)	0.013	0.008	0.001
	(0.06)	(0.06)	(0.06)
EU member	0.158	0.136	0.181
	(0.26)	(0.26)	(0.25)
Manager	1.641***		1.551***
	(0.12)		(0.12)
UNGC member	0.832***	0.845***	
	(0.17)	(0.17)	
Manager × regulatory stringency		0.334***	
		(0.03)	
Manager × UNGC member			0.587***
			(0.19)
Constant	–4.971***	–3.995***	–4.596***
	(1.14)	(1.13)	(1.08)
Carbon disclosure score			
GHG-intensive (broad)[b]	4.617**	4.618**	4.917***
	(1.90)	(1.91)	(1.89)
Natural gas price (log)	–10.193***	–10.184***	–10.243***
	(0.75)	(0.75)	(0.76)
Revenue (log)	1.273**	1.259**	1.428***
	(0.51)	(0.52)	(0.51)

	Base b/se[a]	Corporate × regulation b/se[a]	Corporate × global b/se[a]
Regulatory stringency	–0.531	–2.312	–0.379
	(1.70)	(1.63)	(1.69)
Civil liberties	–8.052***	–8.126***	–7.924***
	(1.59)	(1.60)	(1.59)
GDP per capita (log)	–3.224**	–3.214**	–3.420**
	(1.42)	(1.43)	(1.43)
Federalism	–0.511	–0.506	–0.868
	(1.54)	(1.54)	(1.56)
ISO 14001 (log)	–0.098	–0.126	–0.179
	(0.66)	(0.66)	(0.66)
EU member	–0.562	–0.733	–0.224
	(1.61)	(1.61)	(1.64)
Target	13.670***		13.190***
	(1.62)		(1.77)
UNGC member	3.176***	3.193***	
	(1.10)	(1.10)	
Target × regulatory stringency		2.829***	
		(0.32)	
Target × UNGC member			1.984*
			(1.10)
Constant	115.761***	124.721***	117.302***
	(16.64)	(16.51)	(16.67)
Athrho	–0.184**	–0.166**	–0.205***
Constant	(0.08)	(0.07)	(0.08)
Lnsigma	2.673***	2.673***	2.678***
Constant	(0.04)	(0.04)	(0.04)
N	2,588	2,588	2,588
Sector fixed effects	Yes	Yes	Yes
Year fixed effects	Yes	Yes	Yes

Note: *$p<0.1$, **$p<0.05$, ***$p<0.01$.

[a] Robust standard errors with firm-level cluster correction.

[b] Includes chemicals, industries, materials, and utilities sectors.

Table A4.8
Multilevel determinants of participation and effort in voluntary carbon disclosure, Heckman selection model (alternative specification: export country of largest sales)

	Base b/se[a]	Corporate × regulation b/se[a]	Corporate × global b/se[a]
Participation			
Natural gas price (log)	0.080 (0.11)	0.070 (0.11)	0.054 (0.12)
Revenue (log)	0.258*** (0.08)	0.242*** (0.08)	0.286*** (0.08)
GHG-intensive	–0.369 (0.27)	–0.356 (0.27)	–0.318 (0.27)
Manager	1.691*** (0.15)		1.550*** (0.16)
UNGC member	1.043*** (0.20)	1.046*** (0.20)	
Manager × regulatory stringency[b]		0.357*** (0.03)	
Manager × UNGC member			0.883*** (0.23)
Constant	–2.053** (0.90)	–1.850** (0.89)	–2.189** (0.86)
Carbon disclosure score			
Natural gas price (log)	–10.869*** (0.94)	–10.826*** (0.94)	–10.965*** (0.94)
Revenue (log)	1.969*** (0.67)	1.976*** (0.67)	2.020*** (0.68)
GHG-intensive	5.439** (2.20)	5.518** (2.21)	5.707*** (2.19)
Target	13.940*** (1.96)		13.733*** (2.12)
UNGC member	1.920 (1.42)	1.992 (1.41)	
Target × regulatory stringency[b]		2.928*** (0.41)	
Target × UNGC member			1.005 (1.41)
Constant	64.475*** (7.79)	64.307*** (7.76)	64.360*** (7.92)
Athrho Constant	–0.248** (0.11)	–0.231** (0.10)	–0.270*** (0.10)

	Base b/se[a]	Corporate × regulation b/se[a]	Corporate × global b/se[a]
Lnsigma Constant	2.612*** (0.05)	2.611*** (0.05)	2.615*** (0.05)
N	1,649	1,649	1,649
Sector fixed effects	Yes	Yes	Yes
Year fixed effects	Yes	Yes	Yes
Country fixed effects[b]	Yes	Yes	Yes

Note: ** $p<0.05$, *** $p<0.01$.

[a] Robust standard errors with firm-level cluster correction.

[b] Country of origin is replaced with export country of largest sales in this model.

Table A4.9
Multilevel determinants of participation and effort in voluntary carbon disclosure, EBV model (alternative model)

	Base b/se[a]	Corporate × regulation b/se[a]	Corporate × global b/se[a]
Participation			
Natural gas price (log)	0.014 (0.09)	0.010 (0.09)	0.012 (0.09)
Revenue (log)	0.196*** (0.06)	0.175*** (0.06)	0.229*** (0.06)
GHG-intensive	–0.427** (0.22)	–0.390* (0.22)	–0.375* (0.22)
Regulatory stringency	0.130* (0.08)	–0.005 (0.08)	0.180** (0.08)
Civil liberties	–0.150** (0.07)	–0.152** (0.07)	–0.149** (0.07)
GDP per capita (log)	0.211** (0.08)	0.208** (0.08)	0.149* (0.08)
Federalism	0.025 (0.21)	0.021 (0.21)	–0.07 (0.20)
ISO 14001 (log)	0.011 (0.06)	0.006 (0.06)	–0.002 (0.06)
EU member	0.150 (0.26)	0.128 (0.26)	0.170 (0.25)

(continued)

Table A4.9 (*continued*)

	Base b/se[a]	Corporate × regulation b/se[a]	Corporate × global b/se[a]
Target	1.631*** (0.12)		1.543*** (0.12)
UNGC member	0.831*** (0.17)	0.842*** (0.16)	
Manager × regulatory stringency		0.333*** (0.03)	
Manager × UNGC member			0.591*** (0.19)
Constant	–4.947*** (1.16)	–3.978*** (1.15)	–4.558*** (1.10)
Carbon disclosure score[b]			
Natural gas price (log)	–7.763*** (0.60)	–7.729*** (0.60)	–7.755*** (0.60)
Revenue (log)	0.887** (0.38)	0.773** (0.38)	0.964** (0.39)
GHG-intensive	2.435 (1.52)	2.362 (1.53)	2.784* (1.51)
Regulatory stringency	–0.200 (0.66)	–0.799 (0.62)	–0.053 (0.66)
Civil liberties	–2.901*** (0.82)	–2.828*** (0.82)	–2.913*** (0.83)
GDP per capita (log)	–0.886 (0.84)	–0.900 (0.84)	–1.187 (0.83)
Federalism	0.965 (1.28)	1.107 (1.27)	0.633 (1.29)
ISO 14001 (log)	–0.041 (0.49)	–0.042 (0.48)	–0.112 (0.49)
EU member	1.447 (1.41)	1.076 (1.41)	1.364 (1.44)
Target	12.127*** (1.45)		11.261*** (1.55)
UNGC member	3.335*** (1.00)	3.254*** (1.00)	
Participation	72.760*** (2.07)	72.905*** (2.01)	73.737*** (2.10)
Target × regulatory stringency		2.575*** (0.29)	

	Base b/se[a]	Corporate × regulation b/se[a]	Corporate × global b/se[a]
Target × UNGC member			3.125*** (1.05)
Constant	11.266 (9.30)	14.983 (9.26)	13.787 (9.16)
Athrho Constant	–0.084 (0.07)	–0.074 (0.07)	–0.112 (0.07)
Lnsigma Constant	2.588*** (0.04)	2.585*** (0.04)	2.590*** (0.04)
N	2,588	2,588	2,588
Sector fixed effects	Yes	Yes	Yes
Year fixed effects	Yes	Yes	Yes

Note: *$p<0.1$, **$p<0.05$, ***$p<0.01$.

[a] Robust standard errors with firm-level cluster correction.

[b] *Carbon disclosure score* is coded 0 for nonparticipants in this model.

Appendix 5

Explanation of Models and Robustness Checks, Chapter 5

In addition to chapter 5's political economy argument for the Clean Power Plan's (CPP) validity as an exogenous policy shock, table A5.1 reports the results of a formal parallel trends test, where an indicator variable representing greenhouse gas (GHG)-intensive firms is interacted with year indicator variables as regressors in an ordinary least squares (OLS) regression of firms' participation in CDP (formerly the Carbon Disclosure Project). The treatment and control groups—namely, the GHG- and non-GHG-intensive firms, respectively, both of which experienced the threat of regulation differently after the introduction of the CPP—share a common support (i.e., they share the same distributions of observed and unobserved attributes), that they are in a common political and economic environment.

Difference-in-Differences and Difference-in-Difference-in-Differences Frameworks

Consider two groups of firms, US and non-US companies. Neither group of firms received the treatment in the first period, and only one group of firms received it in the second period. The idea is to calculate the change in the outcomes among the treated group, or US companies, between the two periods and then subtract the change in outcomes among the untreated group, or non-US firms.

The difference-in-differences (DD) estimator will produce a valid estimate of the average treatment effect under the assumption that in the absence of the treatment—which in chapter 5 is the US Environmental Protection Agency's (EPA) introduction of the CPP in 2014—the outcome in the US and non-US firms, respectively, would have changed identically in

Table A5.1
Formal test of common trends assumption

	1 b/se[a]	2 b/se[a]	3 b/se[a]
USA×2012	−2.180 (2.51)	1.669 (1.87)	1.669 (1.87)
USA×2013	2.516 (2.64)	0.140 (1.79)	0.140 (1.79)
USA×2014	6.120** (2.62)	2.404 (1.89)	2.404 (1.89)
USA×2015	12.536*** (2.79)	3.813* (2.13)	3.813* (2.13)
Constant	56.600*** (0.82)	68.717*** (3.98)	42.750*** (2.86)
Year fixed effects		Yes	Yes
Company fixed effects		Yes	
Sector fixed effects			Yes
R^2	0.008	0.897	0.897
N	3,251	3,251	3,251

Note: $^{*}p<0.1$, $^{**}p<0.05$, $^{***}p<0.01$.
[a] Robust standard errors.

the treatment and control firms between the two periods, that is, the pretreatment and posttreatment periods.[1]

This assumption is nontrivial and could be invalid in some settings, especially when behavioral responses are possible. In this setting, the introduction of the CPP by the EPA affecting chiefly the US-based companies was an exogenous event as part of a regulatory process (or sanctioned by law) rather than an initiative of individual firms in response to economic shocks. As such, the well-known "Ashenfelter's dip"[2] is probably unlikely: it is reasonable to assume that the estimated change between the treatment and control groups of firms (i.e., US versus non-US firms, respectively) is the "impact" that can be attributable to the CPP. Table A5.1 presents a formal test of the common trends assumption.

Endogenous Binary-Variable Model

The primary regression equation of interest is

$$Y_j = x_j\beta + \delta t_j + T\theta_j + \gamma_i + \epsilon_j, \quad (1)$$

where t_j is a binary participation variable that is assumed to stem from an unobserved latent variable,

$$t_j^* = w_j\gamma + u_j$$

In the outcome equation 1, x_j is a vector containing the nested DD or DDD estimator, as well as individual firm characteristics and controls explaining the level of voluntary carbon disclosure by firm j. The DD estimator is made up of the following explanatory variables, which are described in detail in the next section: *USA*, *USA × CPP*, *revenues*, as well as *natural gas price*, and *target*.[3] By contrast, the DDD estimator augments the DD estimator with additional variables and interactions: *manager*, *USA × manager*, *CPP × manager*, and *USA × CPP × manager*.

The endogenous binary-participation treatment variable in both the DD and DDD versions of the EBV model is a function of the same independent variables except for *target*, which is a proxy for whether a firm has integrated climate risks into its modus operandi. *Target* serves as an exclusion restriction; it is postulated to explain the level of carbon disclosure but not the decision about participation in voluntary carbon disclosure.

The adoption of a quantitative target affects the level of voluntary carbon disclosure but does not, on its own, cause firms to be more likely to participate in voluntary carbon disclosure, for several reasons. First, participating in CDP is relatively less costly than setting quantitative emissions targets, which requires relatively large operational if not infrastructural investments. Second, closing the gap between policy (climate mitigation) and practice (GHG reduction)—via quantitative targets, which furthers the objectives of policy implementation—is likely to lead to higher levels of carbon disclosure by companies because there is now presumably more climate change information to be disclosed. Third, a Hausman specification test for overidentification (i.e., no exclusion restriction versus overidentified version) indicates that the null—which is that the difference in coefficients is not systematic—can be rejected with a χ^2 value of 1,208.50 with probability $\geq \chi^2$ is 0.

T is a vector of time fixed effects that control for contemporaneous shocks in the world economy that affect all firms. γ_i represents a host of not readily observed factors in a firm's industry sector, where $i = 1, \ldots 6,8,9$ for the nine industry sectors, excluding the technology sector, which serves as the reference sector.

The decision to participate in voluntary carbon disclosure is made according to the rule

$$t_j = \begin{cases} 1, \textit{if } t_j^* > 0 \\ 0, \textit{otherwise} \end{cases}$$

where ϵ and u are bivariate normal with mean zero and covariate matrix

$$\begin{bmatrix} \sigma^2 & \rho\sigma \\ \rho\sigma & 1 \end{bmatrix}.$$

Interactions between x_j and the participation treatment t_j are also allowed in equation 1. The likelihood function for this model is given in Maddala (1983, 122). Greene (2000, 180) discusses the standard method of reducing a bivariate normal to a function of a univariate normal and correlation ρ. The following is the log likelihood for observation j,

$$\ln L_j = \begin{cases} \ln\Phi\left\{\dfrac{w_j\gamma + (y_j - X_j\beta - \delta)\rho/\sigma}{\sqrt{1-\rho^2}}\right\} - \dfrac{1}{2}\left(\dfrac{y_j - X_j\beta - \delta}{\sigma}\right)^2 - \ln(\sqrt{2\pi}\sigma) & t_j = 1 \\ \ln\Phi\left\{\dfrac{-w_j\gamma - (y_j - X_j\beta)\rho/\sigma}{\sqrt{1-\rho^2}}\right\} - \dfrac{1}{2}\left(\dfrac{y_j - X_j\beta}{\sigma}\right)^2 - \ln(\sqrt{2\pi}\sigma) & t_j = 0 \end{cases}$$

where $\Phi(\cdot)$ is the cumulative distribution function of the standard normal distribution. In the maximum likelihood estimation, σ and ρ are not directly estimated. Rather, $\ln\sigma$ and $a\ tan\ h\ \rho$ are directly estimated, where

$$a\ tan\ h\ \rho = \frac{1}{2}\ln\left(\frac{1+\rho}{1-\rho}\right).$$

The standard error of $\lambda = \rho\sigma$ is approximated through the delta method, which is given by

$$Var\,(\lambda) \approx D\ Var\{(a\ tan\ h\ \rho\ \ln\sigma)\}D',$$

where D is the Jacobian of λ with respect to $a\ tan\ h\ \rho$ and $\ln\sigma$.

The estimation is done in Stata using the "etregress" command, which fits the endogenous binary-variable model using the maximum likelihood estimator. Robust standard errors with firm-level cluster correction are included to correct for heterogeneity and serial correlation in the empirical analysis.

Table A5.2
Level of voluntary carbon disclosure by manager (pre- and post-CPP)

	Manager		Difference in means
	Yes	No	t-test
Pre-CPP	71.9	18.0	–41.531***
Post-CPP	81.3	11.1	–37.205***
Average	75.9	15.8	–55.593***

Note: ***$p<0.01$.

Trimmed Matching Sample

Table A5.3 and table A5.4 present summary statistics, as well as results for models 1–3 in chapter 5 based on a trimmed matching sample. The purpose is to formally establish balance on observables between treatment and control groups (i.e., US versus non-US firms) in order to confirm the comparability of the treatment and control groups. To assess overlap in covariate distributions, simple t-tests are conducted using the full sample to establish that the treatment and control groups are comparable on firm-level characteristics. Results show that US and non-US firms are not statistically different before or after the CPP for firm-level covariates, except for assets.

To create a subsample with more overlap, firm × year observations were discarded from the original dataset to align the treatment and control groups based on assets, while maintaining balance on the other covariates.[4]

Next, models 1–3 were replicated using the trimmed matching sample to show that chapter 5, table 5.2, results based on the full sample are robust to the matched sample. The results show that all estimated coefficients are qualitatively similar but differ to a small degree in magnitude. These results lend evidence to corroborate the plausibility of the chapter's quasi-experimental research design.

Further Robustness Checks

After establishing robustness to a trimmed matching sample, a series of robustness checks conducted on the sensitivity of models 1–3 to changes in specifications and modeling assumptions are presented in tables A5.5—A5.7.

Table A5.3
Summary statistics on the trimmed matching sample

Variable	Pre-CPP (2011–2013) Mean	Pre-CPP (2011–2013) Standard deviation	Post-CPP (2014–2015) Mean	Post-CPP (2014–2015) Standard deviation
Participation in the CDP (% share)	72.08	44.90	74.57	43.61
Carbon disclosure score (0–100)	51.86	36.76	63.30	39.89
Revenues (millions of dollars)	19,076.07	20,006.64	20,711.50	21,195.22
Assets (millions of dollars)	26,560.36	17,970.77	29,723.49	18,305.12
Manager (% share)	69.08	46.26	78.03	41.46
Target (% share)	49.12	50.04	57.51	49.50
Natural gas price (Dow Jones)	2.53	0.90	1.65	0.47
Natural gas price (S&P GSCI)	81.90	29.10	53.28	15.30
N	566		346	
Participation in the CDP (% share)	64.88	47.76	64.36	47.94
Carbon disclosure score (0–100)	47.38	37.99	57.20	44.29
Revenues (millions of dollars)	18,242.24	17,799.83	18,655.65	18,420.39
Assets (millions of dollars)	27,512.80	19,003.09	28,482.79	19,022.90
Manager (% share)	59.15	49.19	69.50	46.08
Target (% share)	50.44	50.03	60.20	49.00
Natural gas price (Dow Jones)	2.52	0.89	1.66	0.47
Natural gas price (S&P GSCI)	81.42	28.92	53.60	15.28
N	803		505	

Table A5.4

Quasi-experimental approach to participation and effort in voluntary carbon disclosure, DD and DDD estimations in OLS and nested in EBV models (trimmed matching sample)

	Model 1	Model 2		Model 3	
	DD Level of voluntary carbon disclosure b/se[a]	Participation in voluntary carbon disclosure b/se[a]	DD Level of voluntary carbon disclosure b/se[a]	Participation in voluntary carbon disclosure b/se[a]	DDD Level of voluntary carbon disclosure b/se[a]
USA	6.349*** (2.34)	0.261** (0.12)	0.869 (1.21)	0.074 (0.19)	0.032 (1.74)
Clean Power Plan (CPP)	N/A	N/A	N/A	N/A	N/A
USA×CPP	1.307 (1.92)	0.036 (0.08)	–0.343 (1.12)	0.388** (0.20)	0.97 (1.80)
Manager				1.909*** (0.17)	5.416* (2.12)
USA×manager				–0.024 (0.26)	0.244 (2.15)
CPP×manager				0.483*** (0.14)	10.008*** (1.33)
USA×CPP×manager				–0.424 (0.26)	–2.578 (2.26)
Revenues (log)	5.118*** (1.32)	0.418*** (0.07)	0.900* (0.50)	0.323*** (0.07)	0.184 (0.46)
Natural gas price (log)	–6.714*** (1.41)	0.010 (0.05)	–12.411*** (0.82)	0.730*** (0.09)	–5.767*** (0.86)

(*continued*)

Table A5.4 (*continued*)

	Model 1	Model 2		Model 3	
	DD Level of voluntary carbon disclosure b/se[a]	Participation in voluntary carbon disclosure b/se[a]	DD Level of voluntary carbon disclosure b/se[a]	Participation in voluntary carbon disclosure b/se[a]	DDD Level of voluntary carbon disclosure b/se[a]
Participation last year			62.028*** (2.42)		61.714*** (2.63)
Constant	–15.945 (12.34)	–3.276*** (0.65)	–3.280 (4.543)	–4.204*** (0.70)	–1.280 (4.48)
Athrho Constant		0.303*** (0.06)		0.163** (0.05)	
Lnsigma Constant		2.640*** (0.04)		2.601*** (0.04)	
Year fixed effects	Yes	Yes	Yes	Yes	Yes
Sector fixed effects	Yes	Yes	Yes	Yes	Yes
R^2	0.48				
F-stat	62.14***				
Chi-square			4,452.624***		13,188.452***
N	2,220		2,220		2,220

Note: $^{*}p<0.1$, $^{**}p<0.05$, $^{***}p<0.01$. Model 1 is the difference-in-differences estimation in the OLS model; model 2 is difference-in-differences estimation nested in the EBV model; model 3 is difference-in-difference-in-differences estimation nested in the EBV model. Clean Power Plan (CPP) is excluded from the model because it is collinear with the year fixed effects; N/A or "not applicable" denotes this fact.

[a] Robust standard errors with firm-level cluster correction.

Table A5.5
Quasi-experimental approach to participation and effort in voluntary carbon disclosure, DD estimation in OLS (alternative specifications for model 1)

	1 b/se[a]	2 b/se[a]	3 b/se[b]	4 b/se[c]
USA	3.217 (2.02)	2.865 (1.98)	2.718 (2.00)	2.718 (2.65)
Clean Power Plan (CPP)	N/A	N/A	N/A	N/A
USA × CPP	1.455 (1.50)	1.297 (1.49)	1.730 (1.56)	1.730 (1.56)
Assets (log)	4.808*** (1.06)			
Target	48.478*** (2.31)	48.569*** (2.26)	48.483*** (1.19)	48.483*** (3.28)
Natural gas price (log)	−6.670*** (1.16)	−10.813*** (2.22)	−7.054*** (1.85)	−7.054*** (2.16)
Revenues (log)		5.420*** (0.94)	5.420*** (1.17)	5.420*** (0.92)
Constant	−15.052 (10.66)	−14.911 (9.51)	−17.922 (11.75)	−17.922* (8.90)
Year fixed effects	Yes	Yes	Yes	Yes
Sector fixed effects	Yes	Yes	Yes	Yes
Sector × year effects	No	Yes	No	No
R^2	0.485	0.495	0.492	0.492
F-stat	77.308***	32.777***	N/A	N/A
N	3,212	3,209	3,209	3,209

Note: *$p<0.1$, ***$p<0.01$. Clean Power Plan (CPP) is excluded from the model because it is collinear with the year fixed effects; N/A or "not applicable" denotes this fact. F-stat is "not applicable" in the alternative specifications with sector- and country-level cluster error corrections because of a non-invertible variance-covariance matrix due to collinearity.

[a] Robust standard errors with firm-level cluster correction.

[b] Robust standard errors with sector-level cluster correction.

[c] Robust standard errors with country-level cluster correction.

Table A5.6
Quasi-experimental approach to participation and effort in voluntary carbon disclosure, DDD estimation nested in EBV model (alternative specifications for model 2)

	1 b/se[a]	2 b/se[a]	3 b/se[a]	4 b/se[a]	5 b/se[b]	6 b/se[c]
Participation in voluntary carbon disclosure						
USA	0.170 (0.11)	0.121 (0.11)	0.123 (0.11)	0.123 (0.11)	0.121 (0.12)	0.121 (0.17)
Clean Power Plan (CPP)	N/A	N/A	N/A	N/A	N/A	N/A
USA × CPP	0.051 (0.07)	0.058 (0.07)	0.057 (0.07)	0.061 (0.07)	0.058 (0.05)	0.058* (0.03)
Assets (log)	0.418*** (0.06)					
Revenues (log)		0.425*** (0.05)	0.427*** (0.05)	0.422*** (0.05)	0.425*** (0.08)	0.425*** (0.05)
Natural gas price (log)	0.030 (0.04)		–0.061 (0.10)	0.025 (0.04)	–0.002 (0.05)	–0.002 (0.04)
Natural gas price (GSCI Index) (log)		–0.002 (0.04)				
Constant	–3.541*** (0.57)	–3.342*** (0.54)	–3.332*** (0.51)	–3.345*** (0.49)	–3.349*** (0.78)	–3.349*** (0.47)
Level of voluntary carbon disclosure						
USA	0.012 (1.06)	–0.098 (1.05)	–0.019 (1.05)	–0.157 (1.35)	–0.098 (0.87)	–0.098 (0.93)
Clean Power Plan (CPP)	N/A	N/A	N/A	N/A	N/A	N/A
USA × CPP	–0.018 (0.90)	–0.024 (0.90)	–0.256 (0.89)	–1.063 (1.06)	–0.024 (1.14)	–0.024 (1.20)
Assets (log)	1.648*** (0.39)					

Revenues (log)		1.968*** (0.36)	1.967*** (0.36)	2.194*** (0.49)	1.968*** (0.31)	1.968*** (0.45)
Natural gas price (log)	–12.304*** (0.68)		–14.692*** (1.51)	–17.361*** (0.81)	–12.411*** (0.90)	–12.411*** (1.497)
Natural gas price (GSCI Index) (log)		–12.410*** (0.70)				
Target	15.299*** (1.50)	15.272*** (1.48)	15.312*** (1.48)	17.818*** (1.68)	15.272*** (1.56)	15.272*** (1.65)
Participation last year	62.453*** (1.83)	62.683*** (1.82)	62.670*** (1.81)		62.683*** (2.47)	62.683*** (1.92)
Constant	–3.866*** (3.97)	37.113*** (4.70)	–4.317 (3.61)	57.000*** (5.57)	–6.037** (3.00)	–6.037 (4.16)
Athrho Constant	0.306*** (0.03)	0.281*** (0.03)	0.280*** (0.03)	0.090*** (0.03)	0.281*** (0.03)	0.281*** (0.03)
Lnsigma Constant	2.646*** (0.03)	2.641*** (0.03)	2.638*** (0.03)	2.712*** (0.03)	2.641*** (0.03)	2.641*** (0.04)
Year fixed effects	Yes	Yes	Yes	Yes	Yes	Yes
Sector fixed effects	Yes	Yes	Yes	Yes	Yes	Yes
Chi-square	9270.960***	10239.147***	10896.191***	1233.313***	N/A	N/A
N	3,212	3,209	3,209	3,207	3,209	3,209

Note: *$p<0.1$, **$p<0.05$, ***$p<0.01$. *Clean Power Plan (CPP)* is excluded from the model because it is collinear with the year fixed effects; N/A or "not applicable" denotes this fact. F-stat is "not applicable" in the alternative specifications with sector- and country-level cluster error corrections because of a non-invertible variance-covariance matrix due to collinearity.

[a] Robust standard errors with firm-level cluster correction.

[b] Robust standard errors with sector-level cluster correction.

[c] Robust standard errors with country-level cluster correction.

Table A5.7

Quasi-experimental approach to participation and effort in voluntary carbon disclosure, DDD estimation nested in EBV model (alternative specifications for model 3)

	1 b/se[a]	2 b/se[a]	3 b/se[a]	4 b/se[a]	5 b/se[b]	6 b/se[c]	7 b/se[a]	8 b/se[a]	9 b/se[a]
Participation in voluntary carbon disclosure									
USA	0.062 (0.17)	0.057 (0.17)	0.058 (0.17)	0.032 (0.17)	0.057 (0.19)	0.057 (0.22)	0.053 (0.16)	0.181 (0.19)	0.127 (0.20)
Clean Power Plan (CPP)	N/A	N/A	N/A	N/A	N/A	N/A	N/A	N/A	N/A
USA×CPP	0.436*** (0.17)	0.456*** (0.17)	0.464*** (0.17)	0.469*** (0.17)	0.456*** (0.13)	0.456*** (0.08)	0.229** (0.11)	0.253** (0.13)	0.108 (0.15)
Manager	2.005*** (0.14)	2.037*** (0.14)	2.054*** (0.14)	2.053*** (0.14)	2.037*** (0.18)	2.037*** (0.13)			
Manager 2011							1.807*** (0.15)		
Manager 2012								1.994*** (0.16)	
Manager 2013									2.083*** (0.15)
USA× manager	–0.252 (0.22)	–0.291 (0.22)	–0.297 (0.22)	–0.256 (0.22)	–0.291 (0.19)	–0.291 (0.26)			
USA× manager 2011							–0.169 (0.24)		

USA × manager 2012								−0.470* (0.24)	
USA × manager 2013									−0.428* (0.25)
CPP × manager	0.546*** (0.13)	0.518*** (0.12)	0.530*** (0.12)	0.474*** (0.12)	0.518*** (0.12)	0.518*** (0.13)			
CPP × manager 2011							−0.091 (0.10)		
CPP × manager 2012								0.019 (0.11)	
CPP × manager 2013									0.093 (0.11)
USA × CPP × manager	−0.360* (0.22)	−0.384* (0.22)	−0.389* (0.22)	−0.397* (0.22)	−0.384*** (0.13)	−0.384** (0.15)			
USA × CPP × manager 2011							−0.177 (0.17)		
USA × CPP × manager 2012								−0.127 (0.17)	
USA × CPP × manager 2013									0.108 (0.19)
Assets (log)	0.288*** (0.06)								
Revenues (log)		0.304*** (0.05)	0.307*** (0.06)	0.298*** (0.05)	0.304*** (0.04)	0.304*** (0.05)	0.329*** (0.05)	0.321*** (0.06)	0.340*** (0.06)
Natural gas price (log)	0.820*** (0.08)		0.742*** (0.15)	0.782*** (0.08)	0.784*** (0.10)	0.784*** (0.11)	0.064 (0.06)	0.148** (0.07)	0.209** (0.08)

(*continued*)

Table A5.7 *(continued)*

	1 b/se[a]	2 b/se[a]	3 b/se[a]	4 b/se[a]	5 b/se[b]	6 b/se[c]	7 b/se[a]	8 b/se[a]	9 b/se[a]
Natural gas price (GSCI Index) (log)		0.784*** (0.08)							
Constant	–4.190*** (0.60)	–6.870*** (0.67)	–4.076*** (0.57)	4.110*** (0.56)	–4.143*** (0.54)	–4.143*** (0.52)	–3.263*** (0.54)	–3.575*** (0.57)	–4.033*** (0.56)
Level of voluntary carbon disclosure									
USA	–1.281 (1.64)	–0.932 (1.64)	–0.849 (1.65)	–5.037 (4.81)	–0.932 (0.84)	–0.932 (1.64)	–0.473 (1.71)	–1.256 (1.72)	0.276 (1.80)
Clean Power Plan (CPP)	N/A	N/A	N/A	N/A	N/A	N/A	N/A	N/A	N/A
USA × CPP	1.702 (1.70)	1.805 (1.73)	1.698 (1.74)	–0.865 (6.87)	1.805 (1.91)	1.805* (0.98)	2.332 (1.64)	1.456 (1.65)	1.123 (1.85)
Manager	5.035*** (1.71)	5.135*** (1.72)	5.158*** (1.74)	6.158** (2.69)	5.135*** (1.50)	5.135*** (1.48)			
Manager 2011							3.244** (1.53)		
Manager 2012								4.724*** (1.81)	
Manager 2013									6.122*** (2.04)
USA × manager	0.953 (1.95)	0.449 (1.95)	0.444 (1.95)	4.861 (4.86)	0.449 (1.08)	0.449 (2.62)			

USA× manager 2011							−0.112 (2.11)		
USA× manager 2012								0.591 (2.09)	
USA× manager 2013									−1.117 (2.15)
CPP× manager	9.157*** (1.09)	9.103*** (1.10)	9.144*** (1.09)	−0.464 (4.31)	9.103*** (0.92)	9.103*** (0.76)			
CPP× manager 2011							7.415*** (1.07)		
CPP× manager 2012								7.596*** (1.07)	
CPP× manager 2013									8.685*** (1.08)
USA×CPP× manager	−2.604 (2.04)	−2.743 (2.06)	−2.883 (2.07)	−0.181 (7.01)	−2.743*** (1.00)	−2.743 (1.95)			
USA×CPP× manager 2011							−3.867** (1.94)		
USA×CPP× manager 2012								−2.413 (1.94)	
USA×CPP× manager 2013									−1.845 (2.08)
Assets (log)	0.947*** (0.35)								

(continued)

Table A5.7 (*continued*)

	1 b/se[a]	2 b/se[a]	3 b/se[a]	4 b/se[a]	5 b/se[b]	6 b/se[c]	7 b/se[a]	8 b/se[a]	9 b/se[a]
Revenues (log)		1.343*** (0.35)	1.349*** (0.35)	1.905*** (0.50)	1.343*** (0.49)	1.343*** (0.26)	1.398*** (0.35)	1.352*** (0.36)	1.351*** (0.35)
Natural gas price (log)	–5.885*** (0.78)		–8.247*** (1.49)	–17.050*** (3.675)	–5.973*** (0.73)	–5.973*** (0.73)	–8.550*** (0.86)	–8.206*** (0.864)	–7.360*** (0.863)
Natural gas price (GSCI Index) (log)		–5.972*** (0.78)							
Target	13.898*** (1.48)	13.847*** (1.46)	13.881*** (1.46)	15.574*** (1.75)	13.847*** (1.77)	13.847*** (1.40)	14.349*** (1.43)	13.612*** (1.47)	13.410*** (1.46)
Participation last year	61.980*** (2.06)	61.748*** (2.06)	61.665*** (2.07)		61.748*** (2.14)	61.748*** (2.53)	63.559*** (1.93)	62.979*** (2.10)	62.442*** (2.20)
Constant	–7.337** (3.61)	10.416** (4.80)	–8.486** (3.43)	56.672*** (7.33)	–10.349*** (2.24)	–10.349** (4.35)	–7.918*** (3.52)	–8.307** (3.50)	–10.434*** (3.50)
Athrho Constant	0.187*** (0.03)	0.185*** (0.03)	0.187*** (0.03)	0.005 (0.03)	0.185*** (0.03)	0.185*** (0.04)	0.185*** (0.04)	0.183*** (0.04)	0.158*** (0.04)
Lnsigma Constant	2.616*** (0.03)	2.614*** (0.03)	2.611*** (0.03)	2.700*** (0.03)	2.614*** (0.04)	2.614*** (0.03)	2.603*** (0.03)	2.593*** (0.03)	2.601*** (0.03)
Year fixed effects	Yes	Yes	Yes	Yes	Yes	Yes	Yes	Yes	Yes
Sector fixed effects	Yes	Yes	Yes	Yes	Yes	Yes	Yes	Yes	Yes

Sector × year effects	No	No	Yes	No	No	No	No	No	No
Chi-square	18,905.340***	20,202.868***	22,333.381***	1,263.066***	N/A	N/A	1,6111.060***	17,927.878***	21,528.345***
N	3,212	3,209	3,209	3,207	3,209	3,209	3,163	3,147	3,150

Note: $^{*}p<0.1$, $^{**}p<0.05$, $^{***}p<0.01$. *Clean Power Plan (CPP)* is excluded from the model because it is collinear with the year fixed effects; N/A or "not applicable" denotes this fact. Chi-square is "not applicable" in the alternative specifications with sector- and country-level cluster error corrections because of a non-invertible variance-covariance matrix due to collinearity.

[a] Robust standard errors with firm-level cluster correction.

[b] Robust standard errors with sector-level cluster correction.

[c] Robust standard errors with country-level cluster correction.

First, an alternative specification that replaces *revenues* (log) with *assets* (log) is included. In the second alternative specification (in tables A5.6 and A5.7 only), the Dow Jones Natural Gas Index is replaced with the S&P GSCI Natural Gas Index as an alternative measure of natural gas prices. The next alternative specification includes *sector*×*year*, along with sector and year fixed effects. This specification controls for the time variant, the sector-specific market structure, and competitive pressures from rival firms in the same sector, such as variation in the intensity of carbon disclosure by rival firms from one year to another; these dynamics could be interpreted as learning and diffusion effects.

In another alternative specification in tables A5.6 and A5.7, the Heckman selection (HS) model is employed (see appendix 4 for HS model assumptions). The HS model includes the same covariates as model 2 and model 3 in table 5.2 (see chapter 5) except that it replaces carbon disclosure score with an alternative measure of the level of voluntary carbon disclosure that codes nonparticipants as missing values. This allows for the possibility that some of the nonparticipants may have disclosed their carbon management activities outside the CDP framework.

Furthermore, two alternative specifications are included in which standard errors are clustered at two separate, more aggregated levels—namely, sector level and country level. As Bertrand et al. (2004) have pointed out and Cameron and Miller (2015) have demonstrated, inference from DD models (and DDD models) will be misleading if standard errors are not clustered at the proper level.

A possible objection to the DDD analysis is a concern about the exogeneity of the existence of a manager responsible for climate mitigation from one year to the next. To mitigate this possibility, table A5.7 includes three additional alternative specifications that fix *manager* at 2011, 2012, and 2013 levels in model 3. Chapter 5's main results for the DDD estimator in the endogenous binary-variable model are robust to the alternative specifications with *manager* fixed at 2011 and 2012 levels but not at the 2013 levels, in the participation stage of the EBV model.

Finally, tables A5.8—A5.10 show that there is considerable sector heterogeneity with respect to the effects of regulatory pressure by way of the CPP for US firms. What is consistent across industry sectors, with the exception of the consumer discretionary sector, is the positive and statistically significant response to regulatory pressure by companies that have installed a manager

Table A5.8

Quasi-experimental approach to participation and effort in voluntary carbon disclosure, DD estimation in OLS (sector-specific regressions, model 1)

	Consumer discretionary b/se[a]	Consumer staples b/se[a]	Energy b/se[a]	Financials b/se[a]	Health care b/se[a]	Industrials b/se[a]	Technology[b] b/se[a]	Materials b/se[a]	Utilities b/se[a]
USA	2.446	1.258	0.641	4.567	–5.406	–2.675	9.929**	17.322**	–8.462
	(5.30)	(5.15)	(6.74)	(4.39)	(6.09)	(6.32)	(4.51)	(7.41)	(10.75)
Clean Power Plan (CPP)	N/A	N/A	N/A	N/A	N/A	N/A	N/A	N/A	N/A
USA×CPP	6.768	3.8	–2.536	3.669	–1.946	5.689	–0.150	–5.893	–9.117
	(4.34)	(4.59)	(5.11)	(3.18)	(4.80)	(4.80)	(3.50)	(4.90)	(7.35)
Assets (log)	10.815***	6.357**	–0.052	5.962**	5.797**	8.110	4.148**	1.364	7.380
	(2.42)	(2.53)	(2.86)	(2.31)	(2.76)	(4.93)	(1.76)	(3.09)	(5.40)
Target	45.879***	51.806***	46.106***	48.704***	49.339***	41.231***	52.567***	44.752***	45.350***
	(7.00)	(6.48)	(6.85)	(4.58)	(7.04)	(7.90)	(5.81)	(7.79)	(10.77)
Natural Gas Price (log)	–5.760*	–7.690**	–11.135**	–1.595	–7.908**	–11.350***	–10.787***	–12.560***	1.224
	(3.32)	(3.80)	(4.34)	(2.59)	(3.85)	(3.39)	(2.39)	(3.81)	(3.93)
Constant	–79.838***	–31.088	37.595	–25.877	–14.893	–36.516	–7.776	32.698	–44.443
	(20.35)	(24.00)	(28.73)	(21.33)	(24.88)	(50.03)	(16.98)	(30.02)	(49.99)
Year fixed effects	Yes	Yes	Yes	Yes	Yes	Yes	Yes	Yes	Yes
R^2	0.630***	0.586***	0.372***	0.503***	0.609***	0.408***	0.558***	0.437***	0.308***
F-stat	72.922	21.427	11.701	37.765	25.683	12.999	43.214	14.808	5.949
N	392	276	311	725	257	316	473	282	177

Note: $^*p<0.1$, $^{**}p<0.05$, $^{***}p<0.01$. *Clean Power Plan (CPP)* is excluded from the model because it is collinear with the year fixed effects; N/A or "not applicable" denotes this fact.

[a] Robust standard errors with firm-level cluster correction.

[b] Technology comprises information technology and telecommunications sectors.

Table A5.9

Quasi-experimental approach to participation and effort in voluntary carbon disclosure, DD estimation nested in EBV model (sector-specific regressions, model 2)

	Consumer discretionary b/se[a]	Consumer staples b/se[a]	Energy b/se[a]	Financials b/se[a]	Health care b/se[a]	Industrials b/se[a]	Technology[b] b/se[a]	Materials b/se[a]	Utilities b/se[a]
Participation in voluntary carbon disclosure									
USA	–0.053 (0.31)	0.029 (0.43)	–0.333 (0.31)	0.193 (0.23)	–0.543 (0.36)	0.038 (0.36)	0.522* (0.31)	6.708*** (0.29)	–0.125 (0.43)
Clean Power Plan (CPP)	N/A	N/A	N/A	N/A	N/A	N/A	N/A	N/A	N/A
USA × CPP	0.426** (0.21)	0.474 (0.41)	–0.031 (0.19)	0.048 (0.14)	0.049 (0.24)	0.062 (0.24)	–0.045 (0.18)	0.424* (0.23)	–0.250 (0.25)
Revenues (log)	0.896*** (0.17)	0.661*** (0.21)	0.075 (0.11)	0.510*** (0.10)	0.552*** (0.20)	0.412** (0.20)	0.322*** (0.12)	0.204 (0.14)	0.366* (0.20)
Natural gas price (log)	0.148 (0.15)	–0.133 (0.16)	0.01849 (0.15)	0.118 (0.10)	0.001 (0.21)	–0.140 (0.13)	–0.099 (0.09)	–0.194* (0.11)	0.240 (0.20)
Constant	–8.438*** (1.63)	–5.635*** (2.10)	–0.241 (1.12)	–4.332*** (0.98)	–4.116** (1.95)	–3.055 (1.91)	–2.456** (1.20)	–1.246 (1.32)	–3.260 (1.99)
Level of voluntary carbon disclosure									
USA	–2.012 (2.75)	–3.767 (2.87)	4.423 (2.72)	1.011 (2.35)	–1.532 (3.38)	–0.362 (4.11)	0.264 (2.48)	4.086 (3.83)	–3.316 (3.64)
Clean Power Plan (CPP)	N/A	N/A	N/A	N/A	N/A	N/A	N/A	N/A	N/A
USA × CPP	3.537 (2.40)	0.972 (2.34)	–5.830** (2.96)	2.969 (1.94)	–3.822 (3.57)	1.777 (2.91)	–1.052 (2.17)	–2.592 (3.52)	–2.498 (3.26)

Revenues (log)	3.645*** (1.41)	2.414* (1.31)	1.074 (1.05)	1.484* (0.88)	1.579 (1.24)	2.951 (1.87)	2.303*** (0.77)	2.234** (1.07)	0.841 (1.17)
Natural gas price (log)	–10.256*** (2.07)	–13.342*** (2.11)	–15.248*** (2.06)	–9.878*** (1.55)	–13.828*** (3.12)	–14.418*** (2.10)	–14.533*** (1.64)	–13.073*** (2.10)	–10.930*** (2.22)
Target	17.764*** (4.57)	13.317*** (4.31)	13.001*** (3.30)	17.104*** (3.22)	22.017*** (5.68)	16.717*** (5.50)	18.972*** (4.44)	6.944** (2.89)	3.563 (2.53)
Participation last year	58.652*** (5.97)	63.642*** (4.63)	59.601*** (4.88)	63.105*** (3.46)	50.721*** (8.67)	60.257*** (6.58)	58.463*** (5.69)	69.950*** (5.11)	85.417*** (3.61)
Constant	–25.762** (12.04)	–7.453 (11.22)	4.570 (10.41)	–4.157 (8.15)	5.439 (10.64)	–14.698 (18.18)	–6.658 (7.89)	–4.546 (9.86)	–0.833 (10.52)
Athrho Constant	0.206 (0.14)	0.369** (0.15)	0.398*** (0.11)	0.216*** (0.05)	0.465** (0.19)	0.267*** (0.09)	0.306** (0.13)	0.408* (0.23)	0.076 (0.09)
Lnsigma Constant	2.628*** (0.10)	2.444*** (0.07)	2.681*** (0.09)	2.654*** (0.08)	2.634*** (0.12)	2.761*** (0.09)	2.612*** (0.07)	2.531*** (0.10)	2.262*** (0.10)
Year fixed effects	Yes	Yes	Yes	Yes	Yes	Yes	Yes	Yes	Yes
Chi-square	1,865.676***	1,397.572***	499.063***	3,545.564***	710.850***	757.319***	859.657***	792.292***	4,303.473***
N	392	276	311	725	257	316	473	282	177

Note: $^{*}p<0.1$, $^{**}p<0.05$, $^{***}p<0.01$. *Clean Power Plan (CPP)* is excluded from the model because it is collinear with the year fixed effects; N/A or "not applicable" denotes this fact.

[a] Robust standard errors with firm-level cluster correction.

[b] Technology comprises information technology and telecommunications sectors.

Table A5.10

Quasi-experimental approach to participation and effort in voluntary carbon disclosure, DDD estimation nested in EBV model (sector-specific regressions, model 3)

	Consumer discretionary b/se[a]	Consumer staples b/se[a]	Energy b/se[a]	Financials b/se[a]	Health care b/se[a]	Industrials b/se[a]	Technology[b] b/se[a]	Materials b/se[a]	Utilities b/se[a]
Participation in voluntary carbon disclosure[c]									
USA	–0.093 (0.42)	0.125 (0.42)	–0.39 (0.31)	0.442 (0.31)	–1.177*** (0.44)	–0.331 (0.54)	0.739 (0.49)	6.426*** (0.33)	–0.094 (0.43)
Clean Power Plan (CPP)	N/A	N/A	N/A	N/A	N/A	N/A	N/A	N/A	N/A
USA × CPP	0.593 (0.52)	N/A	N/A	0.182 (0.31)	1.011* (0.52)	0.767 (0.49)	0.601 (0.41)	–0.643** (0.31)	N/A
Manager	1.511*** (0.42)	N/A	N/A	2.572*** (0.39)	N/A	2.080*** (0.48)	2.245*** (0.41)	N/A	N/A
USA × manager	–0.11 (0.61)	N/A	N/A	–1.030** (0.51)	0.943** (0.44)	–0.093 (0.72)	–0.446 (0.57)	N/A	N/A
CPP × manager	0.299 (0.39)	3.040*** (0.59)	2.575*** (0.45)	0.551 (0.36)	1.871*** (0.62)	0.25 (0.31)	0.681*** (0.23)	2.894*** (0.55)	2.128*** (0.47)
USA × CPP × manager	–0.23 (0.78)	0.078 (0.66)	–0.229 (0.38)	0.171 (0.45)	–1.796** (0.74)	–0.829 (0.51)	–0.908 (0.55)	N/A	–0.17 (0.57)
Revenues (log)	0.553*** (0.18)	0.657*** (0.21)	0.058 (0.10)	0.345*** (0.13)	0.457** (0.21)	0.302 (0.20)	0.232** (0.11)	0.205 (0.15)	0.414** (0.19)
Natural gas price (log)	0.097 (0.31)	–0.335 (0.33)	0.815*** (0.26)	0.615** (0.26)	0.577* (0.33)	0.545 (0.40)	0.263* (0.15)	0.035 (0.28)	0.433*** (0.16)
Constant	–5.681*** (1.64)	–5.353** (2.11)	–1.099 (0.99)	–4.299*** (1.31)	–3.988* (2.15)	–3.537* (2.06)	–3.059*** (1.09)	–1.554 (1.42)	–3.988** (1.94)

(continued)

Level of voluntary carbon disclosure[c]									
USA	–0.237 (4.29)	–2.909 (2.82)	4.207* (2.46)	–4.436 (2.98)	–5.536 (4.01)	–5.661 (6.92)	3.93 (4.88)	4.297 (3.98)	–3.16 (3.24)
Clean Power Plan (CPP)	3.846 (3.29)	–5.026 (4.15)	–4.82 (4.70)	–1.896 (2.55)	1.735 (5.75)	–1.311 (4.83)	–0.839 (2.61)	–7.537** (3.59)	5.778*** (2.06)
USA × CPP	N/A	N/A	N/A	N/A	N/A	N/A	N/A	N/A	N/A
Manager	–0.753 (6.27)	N/A	N/A	5.311 (3.57)	N/A	–1.886 (5.03)	11.523* (6.02)	N/A	N/A
USA × manager	–2.818 (5.56)	N/A	N/A	8.290** (3.85)	5.445 (4.20)	7.655 (8.29)	–6.002 (5.25)	N/A	N/A
CPP × manager	5.47 (4.28)	11.273*** (4.23)	18.570*** (3.53)	9.679*** (2.05)	12.930** (6.25)	11.752*** (4.48)	9.352*** (2.56)	13.244*** (3.43)	7.847*** (2.26)
USA × CPP × manager	0.669 (6.64)	–2.201 (2.46)	–7.446** (3.44)	–6.659 (4.49)	–3.767 (7.35)	–4.435 (6.62)	–4.193 (5.21)	N/A	–2.582 (3.87)
Revenues (log)	3.394*** (1.05)	1.927 (1.33)	0.817 (0.96)	0.866 (0.92)	0.483 (1.31)	2.053 (1.80)	1.929** (0.78)	2.133** (1.05)	0.898 (1.16)
Natural gas price (log)	–3.893* (2.24)	–10.144*** (2.11)	–7.121** (3.05)	–5.119*** (1.66)	–3.651 (3.25)	–7.886*** (2.47)	–8.220*** (1.61)	–10.513*** (2.62)	–0.639 (1.40)
Target	18.077*** (5.47)	12.866*** (4.39)	12.542*** (3.21)	15.350*** (3.44)	20.458*** (5.38)	15.049** (6.61)	16.042*** (3.41)	6.631** (2.90)	4.014 (2.75)
Participation last year	59.467*** (5.65)	64.947*** (4.99)	60.673*** (5.43)	57.980*** (4.03)	52.091*** (7.85)	62.486*** (6.43)	56.115*** (7.45)	69.504*** (4.61)	84.747*** (2.83)

(continued)

Table A5.10 (*continued*)

	Consumer discretionary b/se[a]	Consumer staples b/se[a]	Energy b/se[a]	Financials b/se[a]	Health care b/se[a]	Industrials b/se[a]	Technology[b] b/se[a]	Materials b/se[a]	Utilities b/se[a]
Constant	–32.143***	–7.853	–4.028	–3.147	1.992	–13.859	–15.209*	–6.545	–14.871
	(10.00)	(11.68)	(10.27)	(8.40)	(11.81)	(17.84)	(7.79)	(10.27)	(12.50)
Athrho Constant	0.195**	0.214	0.231	0.282***	0.358**	0.180*	0.146*	0.331*	0.003
	(0.10)	(0.13)	(0.16)	(0.05)	(0.17)	(0.10)	(0.08)	(0.20)	(0.06)
Lnsigma Constant	2.619***	2.418***	2.629***	2.634***	2.597***	2.739***	2.561***	2.508***	2.243***
	(0.10)	(0.07)	(0.08)	(0.09)	(0.11)	(0.09)	(0.07)	(0.10)	(0.10)
Year fixed effects	Yes	Yes	Yes	Yes	Yes	Yes	Yes	Yes	Yes
Chi-square	4,070.193***	2,480.427***	847.131***	5,253.527***	1,511.878***	1,947.857***	4,818.727***	2,692.558***	5,981.223***
N	392	276	311	725	257	316	473	282	177

Note: $^{*}p<0.1$, $^{**}p<0.05$, $^{***}p<0.01$. *Clean Power Plan (CPP)* is excluded from the model because it is collinear with the year fixed effects; N/A or "not applicable" denotes this fact.

[a] Robust standard errors with firm-level cluster correction.

[b] Technology comprises information technology and telecommunications sectors.

[c] Several variables have been dropped to ensure that the variance matrix is symmetric.

with respect to both their extensive and intensive margins of voluntary carbon disclosure. In fact, both US and non-US firms with dedicated managers operating in GHG-intensive sectors were about 20 to 50 percent more likely to participate in voluntary carbon disclosure and disclosed at higher levels (8–18 points) in the post-CPP period than firms in these sectors without managerial leadership capacity to address climate risks.[5] The responsiveness of multinational companies toward a US-promulgated rule may be because the policy action by the EPA and President Barack Obama's related proclamations and activities about increased US engagement on climate change globally signaled during 2014 and 2015 the significant role that the United States would play in the Paris Agreement.

Appendix 6
Explanation of Data and Robustness Checks, Chapter 6

Table A6.1 reports summary statistics for firm, market, sector, and country variables, including alternative measures used in the robustness checks, for Fortune Global 500 firms that are members and nonmembers of the United Nations Global Compact (UNGC).

Table A6.2 reports results for a reduced-form first-stage logistics panel data regression of global firms' participation in the UN Global Compact.

Robustness Checks

Aside from selection bias, which the reduced-form first-stage participation regression attempts to resolve, the nonexperimental nature of the data means that there are other potential threats of endogeneity that could undermine causal inference. Tables A6.3–A6.7 present results based on alternative specifications: *climate change laws* is an alternative measure of a country's regulatory stringency; it is the year-to-date numbers of climate change–specific legislation and executive actions that a country passed from 2011 to 2020. *Political rights* is an alternative measure to *civil liberties* of a country's level of civil rights and freedoms. *Assets* (log) replaces *revenues* (log) as an alternative measure of firm size. Moreover, the Dow Jones Commodity Index for Natural Gas is replaced with the S&P GSCI Natural Gas Index as a measure for natural gas price globally. An alternative specification employs *GHG broad*, which also includes energy and industrial sectors in its definition for carbon-intensive sectors.

In tables A6.8–A6.15, *manager* is replaced with alternative specifications that fix *manager* at 2011–2018 levels. This mollifies the concern that the installation of a senior- or executive-level manager dedicated to climate

Table A6.1
Summary statistics of non-UNGC members and UNGC members (Fortune Global 500 firms)

Variable	Non-UNGC members			UNGC members		
	N	Mean	Standard deviation	*N*	Mean	Standard deviation
Dependent variables						
Emissions target (0/1)	4,287	0.54	0.50	2,435	0.83	0.38
Internal carbon price (0/1)	2,505	0.22	0.42	1,550	0.46	0.50
Emissions target and internal carbon price (0/1)	2,526	0.19	0.40	1,553	0.45	0.50
Firm, market, and sector variables[a]						
Manager	4,265	0.56	0.50	2,427	0.81	0.39
UNGC member (0/1)	4,359	N/A	N/A	2,446	1.00	0.00
Revenues (log)	4,088	9.59	1.31	2,391	10.11	1.13
Assets (log)	4,119	10.62	1.46	2,404	11.20	1.64
Natural gas price (Dow Jones) (log)	4,359	4.69	0.73	2,446	4.59	0.74
Natural gas price (S&P GSCI) (log)	4,359	3.56	0.73	2,446	3.47	0.74
GHG-intensive (0/1)	4,359	0.12	0.33	2,446	0.18	0.38
GHG broad (0/1)	4,359	0.33	0.47	2,446	0.36	0.48
Country variables						
Regulatory stringency (IEA ratifications) (log)	4,359	4.58	1.03	2,446	4.97	0.43
Climate change laws (log)	4,108	2.43	0.38	2,437	2.57	0.43
Civil liberties	4,359	1.60	1.24	2,446	1.49	0.99
Political rights	4,359	1.86	1.58	2,446	1.44	1.04
GDP per capita (log)	4,359	10.43	0.90	2,446	10.24	0.94
Federal	4,359	0.68	0.47	2,446	0.50	0.50
EU member	4,359	0.05	0.22	2,446	0.34	0.47
ISO 14001 (country-level) (log)	4,359	8.41	1.08	2,446	8.59	0.98

[a] "GHG-intensive" includes materials and utilities sectors, and "GHG broad" includes chemicals, industrials, materials, and utilities sectors.

Table A6.2
Reduced-form logistics panel data model of participation in UNGC, 2011–2020 (Fortune Global 500 firms)

	UNGC membership b/se[a]
Manager	4.744*** (0.727)
Revenues (log)	1.425*** (0.124)
Constant	0.780 (0.132)
Chi-square	277.96
N	6,103
Sector fixed effects	Yes
Year fixed effects	Yes
Country fixed effects	Yes

Note: ***$p < 0.01$.
[a] Robust standard errors with firm-level cluster correction.

mitigation could be jointly determined with (rather than exogenous of) a firm's decision about the adoption of quantitative emission targets or an internal price on carbon—that is, reverse causation. The logic is that global firms that adopt costly carbon management tools could be more likely to devote resources to climate change, including hiring a dedicated manager who helps to integrate climate risks into business operations.

On the whole, chapter 6's main results for *target, carbon price,* and *target and price*, the dependent variables representing increasingly costlier voluntary climate action, are robust to the above-mentioned alternative specifications. Estimated coefficients are in the same direction and of similar magnitude as the main results.

Table A6.3

Adoption of quantitative emissions target, an internal carbon price, or both—stage 2 logistics panel data models (alternative specification: climate change laws)

	Emissions target		Internal carbon price		Emissions target and internal carbon price	
	Model 1	Model 2	Model 1	Model 2	Model 1	Model 2
	Base b/se[a]	Regulation × global b/se[a]	Base b/se[a]	Regulation × global b/se[a]	Base b/se[a]	Regulation × global b/se[a]
Manager	4.719*** (0.73)	4.736*** (0.74)	2.971*** (0.62)	2.931*** (0.62)	3.098*** (0.65)	3.078*** (0.65)
UNGC member	4.047*** (2.18)		3.619* (2.54)		3.682* (2.48)	
Revenues (log)	1.448*** (0.13)	1.449*** (0.13)	1.248** (0.11)	1.244** (0.11)	1.228** (0.11)	1.226** (0.11)
Natural gas price (log)	0.782 (0.14)	0.781 (0.14)	0.914 (0.09)	0.913 (0.09)	0.958 (0.10)	0.958 (0.10)
GHG-intensive	0.765 (0.25)	0.769 (0.25)	6.575*** (2.22)	6.525*** (2.21)	5.482*** (1.81)	5.456*** (1.80)
Climate change laws (log)	0.732 (0.22)	0.540* (0.19)	1.114 (0.40)	0.795 (0.38)	1.143 (0.40)	0.829 (0.38)
Civil liberties	0.780*** (0.07)	0.765*** (0.07)	0.628*** (0.08)	0.620*** (0.07)	0.658*** (0.08)	0.650*** (0.08)
GDP per capita (log)	1.234* (0.14)	1.221* (0.14)	0.791 (0.12)	0.791 (0.12)	0.773* (0.11)	0.770* (0.11)

Federal	0.711 (0.16)	0.680* (0.15)	0.687 (0.17)	0.668* (0.16)	0.683 (0.17)	0.659* (0.16)
ISO 14001 (country level) (log)	0.956 (0.09)	0.962 (0.09)	0.810* (0.10)	0.819 (0.11)	0.835 (0.10)	0.841 (0.10)
EU member	0.571* (0.19)	0.578* (0.19)	0.916 (0.29)	0.895 (0.29)	0.996 (0.31)	0.988 (0.31)
Post–Paris Agreement (2016–onward)	2.398** (1.05)	2.491** (1.09)				
Climate change laws × UNGC member		1.731*** (0.36)		1.653* (0.45)		1.637* (0.42)
Constant	0.030* (0.06)	0.071 (0.13)	1.587 (3.09)	3.733 (6.65)	1.323 (2.46)	3.213 (5.49)
Chi-square	477.73	474.493	226.669	228.047	227.385	229.156
N	5,853	5,853	3,489	3,489	3,492	3,492
Sector fixed effects	Yes	Yes	Yes	Yes	Yes	Yes
Year fixed effects	Yes	Yes	Yes	Yes	Yes	Yes

Note: *$p<0.1$, **$p<0.05$, ***$p<0.01$.

[a] Robust standard errors with firm-level cluster correction.

Table A6.4

Adoption of quantitative emissions target, an internal carbon price, or both—stage 2 logistics panel data models (alternative specification: political rights)

	Emissions target		Internal carbon price		Emissions target and carbon price	
	Model 1	Model 2	Model 1	Model 2	Model 1	Model 2
	Base b/se[a]	Regulation × global b/se[a]	Base b/se[a]	Regulation × global b/se[a]	Base b/se[a]	Regulation × global b/se[a]
Manager	5.093*** (0.68)	5.065*** (0.68)	3.198*** (0.57)	3.188*** (0.56)	3.270*** (0.58)	3.259*** (0.58)
UNGC member	2.722*** (0.50)		2.061*** (0.36)		2.146*** (0.37)	
Revenues (log)	1.475*** (0.12)	1.476*** (0.12)	1.286*** (0.10)	1.287*** (0.10)	1.272*** (0.10)	1.272*** (0.10)
Natural gas price (log)	0.808 (0.13)	0.809 (0.13)	0.913 (0.08)	0.914 (0.08)	0.953 (0.09)	0.954 (0.09)
GHG-intensive	0.855 (0.27)	0.856 (0.27)	7.643*** (2.46)	7.645*** (2.46)	6.373*** (2.02)	6.375*** (2.02)
Regulatory stringency (log)	1.203* (0.13)	1.187 (0.13)	1.096 (0.17)	1.078 (0.17)	1.036 (0.16)	1.018 (0.16)
Political rights	0.827*** (0.05)	0.829*** (0.05)	0.658*** (0.07)	0.662*** (0.07)	0.670*** (0.07)	0.674*** (0.07)
GDP per capita (log)	1.227** (0.10)	1.217** (0.10)	0.86 (0.09)	0.853 (0.09)	0.829** (0.08)	0.823** (0.08)

Federal	0.873 (0.16)	0.885 (0.16)	0.789 (0.15)	0.802 (0.15)	0.778 (0.14)	0.792 (0.14)
ISO 14001 (country level) (log)	0.967 (0.08)	0.967 (0.08)	0.91 (0.08)	0.912 (0.08)	0.945 (0.08)	0.947 (0.08)
EU member	0.834 (0.21)	0.796 (0.21)	1.011 (0.22)	0.986 (0.22)	1.131 (0.24)	1.103 (0.24)
Post–Paris Agreement (2016–onward)	2.595** (0.98)	2.586** (0.98)				
Regulatory stringency × UNGC member		1.232*** (0.05)		1.157*** (0.04)		1.166*** (0.04)
Constant	0.003*** (0.01)	0.004*** (0.01)	0.175 (0.27)	0.195 (0.30)	0.219 (0.33)	0.245 (0.37)
Chi-square	522.238	518.858	236.126	237.253	233.664	234.469
N	6,358	6,358	3,791	3,791	3,794	3,794
Sector fixed effects	Yes	Yes	Yes	Yes	Yes	Yes
Year fixed effects	Yes	Yes	Yes	Yes	Yes	Yes

Note: $*p<0.1$, $**p<0.05$, $***p<0.01$.

[a] Robust standard errors with firm-level cluster correction.

Table A6.5

Adoption of quantitative emissions target, an internal carbon price, or both—stage 2 logistics panel data models (alternative specification: assets)

	Emissions target		Internal carbon price		Emissions target and internal carbon price	
	Model 1	Model 2	Model 1	Model 2	Model 1	Model 2
	Base b/se[a]	Regulation × global b/se[a]	Base b/se[a]	Regulation × global b/se[a]	Base b/se[a]	Regulation × global b/se[a]
Manager	4.536*** (0.69)	4.611*** (0.70)	2.701*** (0.54)	2.708*** (0.55)	2.750*** (0.55)	2.772*** (0.56)
UNGC member	5.129*** (2.64)		3.738** (2.18)		4.221*** (2.35)	
Assets (log)	1.381*** (0.10)	1.384*** (0.10)	1.401*** (0.13)	1.398*** (0.13)	1.351*** (0.12)	1.350*** (0.12)
Natural gas price (log)	0.830 (0.14)	0.840 (0.14)	0.950 (0.09)	0.950 (0.09)	0.990 (0.10)	0.990 (0.10)
GHG-intensive	0.670 (0.21)	0.680 (0.22)	5.921*** (1.90)	5.949*** (1.91)	4.878*** (1.55)	4.912*** (1.56)
Regulatory stringency (log)	1.357** (0.17)	1.333** (0.17)	1.447* (0.28)	1.370 (0.27)	1.411* (0.28)	1.330 (0.27)
Civil liberties	0.850* (0.08)	0.855* (0.08)	0.668*** (0.08)	0.672*** (0.08)	0.695*** (0.08)	0.700*** (0.08)
GDP per capita (log)	0.910 (0.19)	0.920 (0.20)	0.760 (0.17)	0.790 (0.19)	0.770 (0.17)	0.800 (0.19)

Federal	1.232* (0.14)	1.200 (0.14)	0.766* (0.11)	0.760* (0.11)	0.760** (0.10)	0.751** (0.10)
ISO 14001 (country level) (log)	0.970 (0.08)	0.970 (0.08)	0.813** (0.08)	0.821** (0.08)	0.850* (0.08)	0.858* (0.08)
EU member	0.530** (0.17)	0.524** (0.17)	0.800 (0.24)	0.770 (0.24)	0.850 (0.24)	0.830 (0.25)
Post–Paris Agreement (2016–onward)	2.113* (0.82)	2.142** (0.82)				
Regulatory stringency × UNGC member		1.368*** (0.15)		1.305** (0.16)		1.330** (0.16)
Constant	0.002*** (0.00)	0.003*** (0.01)	0.100 (0.20)	0.130 (0.25)	0.090 (0.19)	0.130 (0.24)
Chi-square	530.75	525.32	223.21	225.03	221.30	223.18
N	6,082	6,082	3,628	3,628	3,631	3,631
Sector fixed effects	Yes	Yes	Yes	Yes	Yes	Yes
Year fixed effects	Yes	Yes	Yes	Yes	Yes	Yes

Note: *$p<0.1$, **$p<0.05$, ***$p<0.01$.

[a] Robust standard errors with firm-level cluster correction.

Table A6.6

Adoption of quantitative emissions target, an internal carbon price, or both—stage 2 logistics panel data models (alternative specification: S&P GSCI Natural Gas Index)

	Emissions target		Internal carbon price		Emissions target and internal carbon price	
	Model 1	Model 2	Model 1	Model 2	Model 1	Model 2
	Base b/se[a]	Regulation × global b/se[a]	Base b/se[a]	Regulation × global b/se[a]	Base b/se[a]	Regulation × global b/se[a]
Manager	4.744***	4.819***	2.792***	2.778***	2.839***	2.844***
	(0.73)	(0.74)	(0.56)	(0.56)	(0.56)	(0.57)
UNGC member	3.857***		4.255**		4.686***	
	(2.00)		(2.58)		(2.73)	
Revenue (log)	1.425***	1.432***	1.222**	1.220**	1.198**	1.199**
	(0.12)	(0.13)	(0.11)	(0.11)	(0.10)	(0.10)
Natural gas price (S&P GSCI) (log)	0.780	0.780	0.900	0.900	0.940	0.94
	(0.13)	(0.13)	(0.08)	(0.08)	(0.09)	(0.09)
GHG-intensive	0.780	0.790	6.485***	6.502***	5.305***	5.337***
	(0.25)	(0.26)	(2.16)	(2.17)	(1.74)	(1.75)
Regulatory stringency (log)	1.389**	1.371**	1.413*	1.330	1.390	1.300
	(0.18)	(0.18)	(0.28)	(0.26)	(0.28)	(0.26)
Civil liberties	0.843*	0.846*	0.660***	0.665***	0.687***	0.692***
	(0.07)	(0.08)	(0.08)	(0.08)	(0.08)	(0.08)
GDP per capita (log)	1.208*	1.180	0.800	0.800	0.790*	0.783*
	(0.14)	(0.14)	(0.12)	(0.12)	(0.11)	(0.11)

Federal	0.800 (0.17)	0.800 (0.17)	0.750 (0.18)	0.780 (0.20)	0.760 (0.18)	0.790 (0.20)
ISO 14001 (country level) (log)	0.940 (0.08)	0.930 (0.08)	0.839* (0.08)	0.848* (0.08)	0.870 (0.08)	0.880 (0.08)
EU member	0.586* (0.18)	0.584* (0.19)	0.800 (0.24)	0.760 (0.24)	0.860 (0.25)	0.820 (0.25)
Post–Paris Agreement (2016–onward)	2.010* (0.78)	2.035* (0.79)				
Regulatory stringency × UNGC member		1.291** (0.14)		1.351** (0.17)		1.367** (0.17)
Constant	0.004*** (0.01)	0.005*** (0.01)	0.250 (0.51)	0.320 (0.61)	0.220 (0.44)	0.290 (0.55)
Chi-square	524.95	520.37	218.69	220.28	217.31	218.95
N	6,091	6,091	3,631	3,631	3,634	3,634
Sector fixed effects	Yes	Yes	Yes	Yes	Yes	Yes
Year fixed effects	Yes	Yes	Yes	Yes	Yes	Yes

Note: $^{*}p<0.1$, $^{**}p<0.05$, $^{***}p<0.01$.

[a] Robust standard errors with firm-level cluster correction.

Table A6.7

Adoption of quantitative emissions target, an internal carbon price, or both—stage 2 logistics panel data models (alternative specification: GHG broad)

	Emissions target		Internal carbon price		Emissions target and internal carbon price	
	Model 1	Model 2	Model 1	Model 2	Model 1	Model 2
	Base b/se[a]	Regulation × global b/se[a]	Base b/se[a]	Regulation × global b/se[a]	Base b/se[a]	Regulation × global b/se[a]
Manager	4.772***	4.846***	2.512***	2.500***	2.596***	2.600***
	(0.73)	(0.74)	(0.49)	(0.49)	(0.50)	(0.51)
UNGC member	3.610**		7.401***		7.684***	
	(1.86)		(4.26)		(4.30)	
Revenue (log)	1.435***	1.442***	1.130	1.130	1.120	1.120
	(0.13)	(0.13)	(0.09)	(0.09)	(0.09)	(0.09)
Natural gas price (log)	0.780	0.780	0.900	0.890	0.930	0.930
	(0.13)	(0.13)	(0.08)	(0.08)	(0.09)	(0.09)
GHG broad	0.700	0.700	2.474***	2.447***	2.372***	2.347***
	(0.19)	(0.19)	(0.67)	(0.66)	(0.65)	(0.65)
Regulatory stringency (log)	1.390**	1.374**	1.330	1.220	1.330	1.210
	(0.18)	(0.18)	(0.26)	(0.23)	(0.27)	(0.23)
Civil liberties	0.838**	0.841**	0.674***	0.682***	0.699***	0.708***
	(0.07)	(0.07)	(0.08)	(0.08)	(0.08)	(0.08)
GDP per capita (log)	1.200	1.180	0.840	0.840	0.820	0.820
	(0.14)	(0.14)	(0.12)	(0.12)	(0.11)	(0.11)

Federal	0.780 (0.17)	0.790 (0.17)	0.860 (0.20)	0.920 (0.22)	0.860 (0.20)	0.910 (0.22)
ISO 14001 (country level) (log)	0.940 (0.08)	0.940 (0.08)	0.829** (0.08)	0.842* (0.08)	0.860 (0.08)	0.880 (0.08)
EU member	0.598* (0.19)	0.600 (0.19)	0.660 (0.19)	0.610 (0.19)	0.720 (0.20)	0.670 (0.20)
Post–Paris Agreement (2016–onward)	2.015* (0.79)	2.040* (0.79)				
Regulatory stringency × UNGC member		1.274** (0.14)		1.515*** (0.19)		1.516*** (0.18)
Constant	0.006*** (0.01)	0.007*** (0.01)	0.520 (1.00)	0.700 (1.30)	0.380 (0.73)	0.540 (0.98)
Chi-square	518.38	514.51	196.11	197.32	204.87	206.40
N	6,091	6,091	3,631	3,631	3,634	3,634
Sector fixed effects	Yes	Yes	Yes	Yes	Yes	Yes
Year fixed effects	Yes	Yes	Yes	Yes	Yes	Yes

Note: $^{*}p<0.1$, $^{**}p<0.05$, $^{***}p<0.01$.

[a] Robust standard errors with firm-level cluster correction.

Table A6.8

Adoption of quantitative emissions target, an internal carbon price, or both—stage 2 logistics panel data models (alternative specification: manager—fixed at 2011 level)

	Emissions target		Internal carbon price		Emissions target and internal carbon price	
	Model 1	Model 2	Model 1	Model 2	Model 1	Model 2
	Base b/se[a]	Regulation × global b/se[a]	Base b/se[a]	Regulation × global b/se[a]	Base b/se[a]	Regulation × global b/se[a]
Manager—fixed at 2011 level	2.969*** (0.53)	2.985*** (0.53)	1.912*** (0.35)	1.913*** (0.35)	1.862*** (0.34)	1.865*** (0.34)
UNGC member	13.213*** (6.68)		16.074*** (8.46)		17.174*** (8.75)	
Revenue (log)	1.376*** (0.12)	1.377*** (0.12)	1.10 (0.08)	1.100 (0.08)	1.090 (0.09)	1.090 (0.09)
Natural gas price (log)	0.601*** (0.09)	0.603*** (0.09)	0.793*** (0.06)	0.792*** (0.06)	0.825** (0.07)	0.824** (0.07)
GHG-intensive	0.680 (0.19)	0.670 (0.19)	2.431*** (0.68)	2.400*** (0.67)	2.326*** (0.65)	2.298*** (0.65)
Regulatory stringency (log)	1.304* (0.18)	1.254* (0.17)	1.340 (0.27)	1.190 (0.22)	1.340 (0.29)	1.18 (0.23)
Civil liberties	0.88 (0.08)	0.890 (0.08)	0.687*** (0.08)	0.699*** (0.09)	0.709*** (0.09)	0.722*** (0.09)
GDP per capita (log)	1.425*** (0.17)	1.397*** (0.16)	0.920 (0.12)	0.920 (0.12)	0.910 (0.12)	0.900 (0.12)

Federal	1.010 (0.24)	1.050 (0.24)	0.970 (0.22)	1.070 (0.26)	0.980 (0.22)	1.080 (0.26)
ISO 14001 (country-level) (log)	0.950 (0.09)	0.950 (0.09)	0.806** (0.08)	0.824* (0.08)	0.840* (0.09)	0.860 (0.09)
EU member	0.401*** (0.14)	0.371*** (0.13)	0.482** (0.14)	0.430*** (0.13)	0.519** (0.15)	0.467** (0.14)
Post-Paris Agreement (2016-onward)	1.210 (0.42)	1.210 (0.41)				
Regulatory stringency × UNGC member		1.686*** (0.18)		1.787*** (0.20)		1.801*** (0.20)
Constant	0.006*** (0.01)	0.008*** (0.02)	0.440 (0.88)	0.650 (1.22)	0.320 (0.64)	0.490 (0.91)
Chi-square	431.553	422.728	193.259	194.205	194.977	196.229
N	6,033	6,033	3,591	3,591	3,594	3,594
Sector fixed effects	Yes	Yes	Yes	Yes	Yes	Yes
Year fixed effects	Yes	Yes	Yes	Yes	Yes	Yes

Note: *$p<0.1$, **$p<0.05$, ***$p<0.01$.

[a] Robust standard errors with firm-level cluster correction.

Table A6.9

Adoption of quantitative emissions target, an internal carbon price, or both—stage 2 logistics panel data models (alternative specification: manager—fixed at 2012 level)

	Emissions target		Internal carbon price		Emissions target and internal carbon price	
	Model 1	Model 2	Model 1	Model 2	Model 1	Model 2
	Base b/se[a]	Regulation × global b/se[a]	Base b/se[a]	Regulation × global b/se[a]	Base b/se[a]	Regulation × global b/se[a]
Manager—fixed at 2012 level	3.438*** (0.63)	3.467*** (0.63)	1.979*** (0.41)	1.975*** (0.41)	1.930*** (0.40)	1.931*** (0.40)
UNGC member	9.332*** (4.99)		15.094*** (8.11)		15.952*** (8.33)	
Revenue (log)	1.417*** (0.14)	1.422*** (0.14)	1.110 (0.09)	1.110 (0.09)	1.090 (0.09)	1.090 (0.09)
Natural gas price (log)	0.584*** (0.09)	0.585*** (0.09)	0.794*** (0.06)	0.793*** (0.06)	0.827** (0.07)	0.826** (0.07)
GHG-intensive	0.690 (0.19)	0.680 (0.19)	2.485*** (0.69)	2.446*** (0.68)	2.371*** (0.67)	2.334*** (0.66)
Regulatory stringency (log)	1.301** (0.17)	1.264* (0.17)	1.320 (0.26)	1.180 (0.22)	1.310 (0.27)	1.160 (0.22)
Civil liberties	0.870 (0.08)	0.880 (0.08)	0.693*** (0.09)	0.707*** (0.09)	0.713** (0.10)	0.728** (0.10)
GDP per capita (log)	1.363*** (0.16)	1.333** (0.16)	0.900 (0.13)	0.900 (0.12)	0.890 (0.12)	0.880 (0.12)

Federal	0.910 (0.21)	0.930 (0.21)	0.940 (0.21)	1.030 (0.25)	0.950 (0.22)	1.040 (0.25)
ISO 14001 (country level) (log)	0.960 (0.09)	0.960 (0.09)	0.811** (0.08)	0.830* (0.08)	0.850 (0.09)	0.870 (0.09)
EU member	0.419*** (0.14)	0.401*** (0.14)	0.497** (0.14)	0.448*** (0.14)	0.542** (0.15)	0.493** (0.15)
Post–Paris Agreement (2016–onward)	1.210 (0.42)	1.210 (0.42)				
Regulatory stringency × UNGC member		1.555*** (0.17)		1.755*** (0.20)		1.764*** (0.20)
Constant	0.008*** (0.02)	0.011** (0.02)	0.500 (1.00)	0.710 (1.35)	0.360 (0.72)	0.530 (1.00)
Chi-square	420.195	411.722	185.873	187.071	185.856	187.640
N	5,971	5,971	3,543	3,543	3,546	3,546
Sector fixed effects	Yes	Yes	Yes	Yes	Yes	Yes
Year fixed effects	Yes	Yes	Yes	Yes	Yes	Yes

Note: $*p<0.1$, $**p<0.05$, $***p<0.01$.

[a] Robust standard errors with firm-level cluster correction.

Table A6.10

Adoption of quantitative emissions target, an internal carbon price, or both—stage 2 logistics panel data models (alternative specification: manager—fixed at 2013 level)

	Emissions target		Internal carbon price		Emissions target and internal carbon price	
	Model 1	Model 2	Model 1	Model 2	Model 1	Model 2
	Base b/se[a]	Regulation × global b/se[a]	Base b/se[a]	Regulation × global b/se[a]	Base b/se[a]	Regulation × global b/se[a]
Manager—fixed at 2013 level	4.651***	4.682***	2.197***	2.191***	2.090***	2.089***
	(0.89)	(0.89)	(0.51)	(0.51)	(0.47)	(0.47)
UNGC member	8.300***		13.154***		14.209***	
	(4.37)		(6.98)		(7.34)	
Revenue (log)	1.398***	1.403***	1.120	1.110	1.100	1.100
	(0.13)	(0.13)	(0.09)	(0.09)	(0.09)	(0.09)
Natural gas price (log)	0.645***	0.646***	0.793***	0.793***	0.826**	0.826**
	(0.10)	(0.10)	(0.06)	(0.06)	(0.07)	(0.07)
GHG-intensive	0.680	0.680	2.559***	2.519***	2.438***	2.401***
	(0.20)	(0.19)	(0.70)	(0.69)	(0.67)	(0.66)
Regulatory stringency (log)	1.384**	1.343**	1.330	1.190	1.330	1.180
	(0.18)	(0.18)	(0.27)	(0.22)	(0.29)	(0.23)
Civil liberties	0.900	0.910	0.701***	0.712***	0.720**	0.732**
	(0.09)	(0.09)	(0.09)	(0.09)	(0.09)	(0.10)
GDP per capita (log)	1.378***	1.349**	0.920	0.920	0.910	0.900
	(0.16)	(0.16)	(0.13)	(0.13)	(0.12)	(0.12)

Federal	0.940 (0.21)	0.960 (0.22)	0.970 (0.22)	1.070 (0.26)	0.980 (0.22)	1.080 (0.26)
ISO 14001 (country level) (log)	0.930 (0.09)	0.930 (0.09)	0.829* (0.08)	0.847* (0.09)	0.860 (0.09)	0.880 (0.09)
EU member	0.411*** (0.14)	0.392*** (0.13)	0.515** (0.15)	0.463*** (0.14)	0.556** (0.15)	0.504** (0.15)
Post–Paris Agreement (2016–onwards)	1.520 (0.53)	1.530 (0.53)				
Regulatory stringency × UNGC member		1.521*** (0.17)		1.715*** (0.19)		1.731*** (0.19)
Constant	0.004*** (0.01)	0.005*** (0.01)	0.270 (0.54)	0.380 (0.73)	0.200 (0.41)	0.300 (0.57)
Chi-square	418.392	411.027	180.194	181.460	179.468	181.331
N	5,975	5,975	3,546	3,546	3,549	3,549
Sector fixed effects	Yes	Yes	Yes	Yes	Yes	Yes
Year fixed effects	Yes	Yes	Yes	Yes	Yes	Yes

Note: $^{*}p<0.1$, $^{**}p<0.05$, $^{***}p<0.01$.

[a] Robust standard errors with firm-level cluster correction.

Table A6.11

Adoption of quantitative emissions target, an internal carbon price, or both—stage 2 logistics panel data models (alternative specification: manager—fixed at 2014 level)

	Emissions target		Internal carbon price		Emissions target and internal carbon price	
	Model 1	Model 2	Model 1	Model 2	Model 1	Model 2
	Base b/se[a]	Regulation × global b/se[a]	Base b/se[a]	Regulation × global b/se[a]	Base b/se[a]	Regulation × global b/se[a]
Manager—fixed at 2014 level	4.817*** (0.96)	4.854*** (0.96)	2.453*** (0.61)	2.443*** (0.61)	2.383*** (0.58)	2.382*** (0.58)
UNGC member	10.011*** (5.47)		13.701*** (7.37)		14.496*** (7.60)	
Revenue (log)	1.331*** (0.12)	1.338*** (0.13)	1.090 (0.08)	1.090 (0.08)	1.080 (0.08)	1.080 (0.09)
Natural gas price (log)	0.594*** (0.10)	0.596*** (0.10)	0.783*** (0.06)	0.782*** (0.06)	0.816** (0.07)	0.815** (0.07)
GHG-intensive	0.720 (0.21)	0.710 (0.20)	2.580*** (0.71)	2.542*** (0.70)	2.463*** (0.68)	2.427*** (0.67)
Regulatory stringency (log)	1.329** (0.18)	1.289* (0.17)	1.30 (0.26)	1.160 (0.21)	1.290 (0.27)	1.150 (0.22)
Civil liberties	0.900 (0.09)	0.910 (0.09)	0.687*** (0.09)	0.701*** (0.09)	0.710** (0.10)	0.726** (0.10)
GDP per capita (log)	1.385*** (0.16)	1.351*** (0.16)	0.910 (0.12)	0.900 (0.12)	0.890 (0.12)	0.890 (0.12)

Federal	0.940 (0.21)	0.960 (0.22)	0.930 (0.21)	1.020 (0.25)	0.950 (0.21)	1.040 (0.25)
ISO 14001 (country level) (log)	0.940 (0.09)	0.950 (0.09)	0.826* (0.08)	0.845* (0.09)	0.870 (0.09)	0.890 (0.09)
EU member	0.399*** (0.13)	0.384*** (0.13)	0.505** (0.14)	0.457*** (0.14)	0.550** (0.15)	0.502** (0.15)
Post–Paris Agreement (2016–onward)	1.300 (0.49)	1.310 (0.49)				
Regulatory stringency × UNGC member		1.572*** (0.18)		1.720*** (0.20)		1.730*** (0.19)
Constant	0.008*** (0.01)	0.010** (0.02)	0.450 (0.88)	0.620 (1.16)	0.310 (0.62)	0.450 (0.84)
Chi-square	409.315	404.172	178.55	180.181	177.531	180.1
N	5,952	5,952	3,529	3,529	3,532	3,532
Sector fixed effects	Yes	Yes	Yes	Yes	Yes	Yes
Year fixed effects	Yes	Yes	Yes	Yes	Yes	Yes

Note: *$p<0.1$, **$p<0.05$, ***$p<0.01$.

[a] Robust standard errors with firm-level cluster correction.

Table A6.12

Adoption of quantitative emissions target, an internal carbon price, or both—stage 2 logistics panel data models (alternative specification: manager—fixed at 2015 level)

	Emissions target		Internal carbon price		Emissions target and internal carbon price	
	Model 1	Model 2	Model 1	Model 2	Model 1	Model 2
	Base b/se[a]	Regulation × global b/se[a]	Base b/se[a]	Regulation × global b/se[a]	Base b/se[a]	Regulation × global b/se[a]
Manager—fixed at 2015 level	7.871*** (1.78)	7.952*** (1.80)	2.774*** (0.84)	2.775*** (0.85)	2.942*** (0.86)	2.959*** (0.88)
UNGC member	9.617*** (5.48)		14.896*** (8.54)		14.900*** (8.41)	
Revenue (log)	1.371*** (0.14)	1.379*** (0.14)	1.080 (0.08)	1.080 (0.08)	1.080 (0.09)	1.090 (0.09)
Natural gas price (log)	0.569*** (0.10)	0.572*** (0.10)	0.782*** (0.07)	0.782*** (0.07)	0.817** (0.08)	0.817** (0.08)
GHG-intensive	0.660 (0.20)	0.660 (0.20)	2.764*** (0.77)	2.715*** (0.76)	2.632*** (0.74)	2.587*** (0.73)
Regulatory stringency (log)	1.220 (0.17)	1.190 (0.17)	1.230 (0.23)	1.110 (0.20)	1.210 (0.24)	1.090 (0.20)
Civil liberties	0.850 (0.09)	0.860 (0.09)	0.640*** (0.09)	0.655*** (0.10)	0.663*** (0.10)	0.680*** (0.10)
GDP per capita (log)	1.419*** (0.18)	1.381** (0.18)	0.910 (0.13)	0.900 (0.13)	0.890 (0.12)	0.880 (0.12)

Federal	0.740 (0.18)	0.760 (0.19)	0.830 (0.20)	0.910 (0.23)	0.850 (0.20)	0.920 (0.23)
ISO 14001 (country level) (log)	0.920 (0.09)	0.920 (0.09)	0.830* (0.09)	0.850 (0.09)	0.870 (0.09)	0.890 (0.09)
EU member	0.344*** (0.13)	0.339*** (0.13)	0.443*** (0.13)	0.405*** (0.13)	0.490** (0.14)	0.453** (0.14)
Post–Paris Agreement (2016–onward)	1.250 (0.50)	1.260 (0.50)				
Regulatory stringency × UNGC member		1.551*** (0.19)		1.738*** (0.21)		1.728*** (0.21)
Constant	0.010** (0.02)	0.013** (0.03)	0.670 (1.35)	0.910 (1.77)	0.400 (0.83)	0.560 (1.10)
Chi-square	364.198	360.486	180.306	181.833	188.41	190.318
N	5,643	5,643	3,363	3,363	3,366	3,366
Sector fixed effects	Yes	Yes	Yes	Yes	Yes	Yes
Year fixed effects	Yes	Yes	Yes	Yes	Yes	Yes

Note: *$p<0.1$, **$p<0.05$, ***$p<0.01$.

[a] Robust standard errors with firm-level cluster correction.

Table A6.13

Adoption of quantitative emissions target, an internal carbon price, or both—stage 2 logistics panel data models (alternative specification: manager—fixed at 2016 level)

	Emissions target		Internal carbon price		Emissions target and internal carbon price	
	Model 1	Model 2	Model 1	Model 2	Model 1	Model 2
	Base b/se[a]	Regulation × global b/se[a]	Base b/se[a]	Regulation × global b/se[a]	Base b/se[a]	Regulation × global b/se[a]
Manager—fixed at 2016 level	8.993*** (1.70)	9.064*** (1.71)	4.113*** (0.91)	4.109*** (0.91)	3.903*** (0.86)	3.913*** (0.87)
UNGC member	4.073*** (2.10)		6.432*** (3.52)		7.193*** (3.82)	
Revenue (log)	1.379*** (0.13)	1.384*** (0.13)	1.110 (0.09)	1.100 (0.09)	1.090 (0.09)	1.090 (0.09)
Natural gas price (log)	0.574*** (0.10)	0.575*** (0.10)	0.785*** (0.07)	0.784*** (0.07)	0.818** (0.07)	0.818** (0.07)
GHG-intensive	0.700 (0.21)	0.700 (0.21)	2.709*** (0.77)	2.677*** (0.77)	2.572*** (0.74)	2.542*** (0.74)
Regulatory stringency (log)	1.261* (0.17)	1.240 (0.17)	1.290 (0.26)	1.190 (0.23)	1.280 (0.27)	1.180 (0.23)
Civil liberties	0.890 (0.08)	0.890 (0.08)	0.702*** (0.08)	0.709*** (0.08)	0.730*** (0.08)	0.739*** (0.08)
GDP per capita (log)	1.331** (0.16)	1.306** (0.16)	0.850 (0.12)	0.850 (0.12)	0.840 (0.11)	0.840 (0.11)

Federal	1.010 (0.25)	1.010 (0.25)	0.910 (0.21)	0.980 (0.24)	0.920 (0.21)	0.990 (0.24)
ISO 14001 (country level) (log)	0.950 (0.10)	0.950 (0.10)	0.820** (0.08)	0.833** (0.08)	0.856* (0.08)	0.870 (0.08)
EU member	0.630 (0.22)	0.620 (0.22)	0.690 (0.20)	0.640 (0.19)	0.730 (0.20)	0.680 (0.20)
Post–Paris Agreement (2016–onward)	1.630 (0.63)	1.630 (0.63)				
Regulatory stringency × UNGC member		1.312** (0.14)		1.475*** (0.17)		1.500*** (0.17)
Constant	0.013** (0.02)	0.016** (0.03)	0.850 (1.67)	1.110 (2.09)	0.580 (1.15)	0.800 (1.50)
Chi-square	437.699	433.689	193.397	194.109	194.895	196.066
N	6,086	6,086	3,630	3,630	3,633	3,633
Sector fixed effects	Yes	Yes	Yes	Yes	Yes	Yes
Year fixed effects	Yes	Yes	Yes	Yes	Yes	Yes

Note: $^{*}p<0.1$, $^{**}p<0.05$, $^{***}p<0.01$.

[a] Robust standard errors with firm-level cluster correction.

Table A6.14

Adoption of quantitative emissions target, an internal carbon price, or both—stage 2 logistics panel data models (alternative specification: manager—fixed at 2017 level)

	Emissions target		Internal carbon price		Emissions target and internal carbon price	
	Model 1	Model 2	Model 1	Model 2	Model 1	Model 2
	Base b/se[a]	Regulation × global b/se[a]	Base b/se[a]	Regulation × global b/se[a]	Base b/se[a]	Regulation × global b/se[a]
Manager—fixed at 2017 level	11.025*** (2.10)	11.093*** (2.11)	3.600*** (0.83)	3.594*** (0.83)	3.665*** (0.83)	3.671*** (0.84)
UNGC member	4.908*** (2.71)		7.753*** (4.17)		8.355*** (4.36)	
Revenue (log)	1.342*** (0.13)	1.350*** (0.13)	1.100 (0.09)	1.100 (0.09)	1.090 (0.09)	1.090 (0.09)
Natural gas price (log)	0.565*** (0.10)	0.566*** (0.10)	0.788*** (0.07)	0.788*** (0.07)	0.821** (0.07)	0.821** (0.07)
GHG-intensive	0.586* (0.17)	0.586* (0.18)	2.462*** (0.69)	2.433*** (0.68)	2.356*** (0.66)	2.328*** (0.66)
Regulatory stringency (log)	1.220 (0.18)	1.200 (0.18)	1.290 (0.26)	1.170 (0.23)	1.280 (0.27)	1.160 (0.23)
Civil liberties	0.910 (0.09)	0.920 (0.09)	0.722*** (0.08)	0.730*** (0.08)	0.748** (0.09)	0.757** (0.09)
GDP per capita (log)	1.373** (0.17)	1.339** (0.17)	0.880 (0.12)	0.880 (0.12)	0.870 (0.11)	0.860 (0.11)

Federal	1.170 (0.28)	1.180 (0.28)	1.000 (0.23)	1.070 (0.26)	1.000 (0.23)	1.070 (0.26)
ISO 14001 (country level) (log)	0.970 (0.09)	0.960 (0.09)	0.835* (0.08)	0.849* (0.08)	0.870 (0.08)	0.880 (0.09)
EU member	0.590 (0.19)	0.590 (0.20)	0.650 (0.19)	0.594* (0.18)	0.700 (0.20)	0.650 (0.19)
Post–Paris Agreement (2016–onward)	1.720 (0.69)	1.730 (0.69)				
Regulatory stringency × UNGC member		1.352*** (0.16)		1.533*** (0.18)		1.547*** (0.17)
Constant	0.009** (0.02)	0.013** (0.03)	0.450 (0.91)	0.610 (1.18)	0.340 (0.67)	0.480 (0.90)
Chi-square	440.184	437.111	187.277	187.877	194.159	195.327
N	6,075	6,075	3,627	3,627	3,630	3,630
Sector fixed effects	Yes	Yes	Yes	Yes	Yes	Yes
Year fixed effects	Yes	Yes	Yes	Yes	Yes	Yes

Note: *$p<0.1$, **$p<0.05$, ***$p<0.01$.

[a] Robust standard errors with firm-level cluster correction.

Table A6.15

Adoption of quantitative emissions target, an internal carbon price, or both—stage 2 logistics panel data models (alternative specification: manager—fixed at 2018 level)

	Emissions target		Internal carbon price		Emissions target and internal carbon price	
	Model 1	Model 2	Model 1	Model 2	Model 1	Model 2
	Base b/se[a]	Regulation × global b/se[a]	Base b/se[a]	Regulation × global b/se[a]	Base b/se[a]	Regulation × global b/se[a]
Manager—fixed at 2018 level	8.371*** (1.62)	8.406*** (1.63)	2.163*** (0.44)	2.158*** (0.44)	2.363*** (0.49)	2.365*** (0.49)
UNGC member	9.111*** (5.02)		12.166*** (6.52)		12.193*** (6.45)	
Revenue (log)	1.265*** (0.10)	1.268*** (0.10)	1.090 (0.08)	1.080 (0.08)	1.070 (0.08)	1.070 (0.08)
Natural gas price (log)	0.591*** (0.10)	0.593*** (0.10)	0.790*** (0.06)	0.789*** (0.06)	0.821** (0.07)	0.820** (0.07)
GHG-intensive	0.545** (0.16)	0.542** (0.16)	2.388*** (0.66)	2.355*** (0.66)	2.293*** (0.65)	2.261*** (0.64)
Regulatory stringency (log)	1.210 (0.19)	1.170 (0.18)	1.290 (0.26)	1.160 (0.21)	1.280 (0.27)	1.150 (0.22)
Civil liberties	0.920 (0.09)	0.930 (0.09)	0.678*** (0.08)	0.688*** (0.08)	0.705*** (0.08)	0.716*** (0.08)
GDP per capita (log)	1.400*** (0.17)	1.373** (0.17)	0.910 (0.13)	0.900 (0.13)	0.880 (0.12)	0.880 (0.12)

Federal	0.940 (0.22)	0.970 (0.23)	0.950 (0.22)	1.040 (0.25)	0.950 (0.22)	1.030 (0.25)
ISO 14001 (country level) (log)	1.020 (0.10)	1.030 (0.10)	0.845* (0.08)	0.860 (0.08)	0.880 (0.09)	0.900 (0.09)
EU member	0.462** (0.16)	0.438** (0.15)	0.556** (0.16)	0.503** (0.15)	0.611* (0.17)	0.559* (0.17)
Post–Paris Agreement (2016–onward)	1.630 (0.64)	1.630 (0.63)				
Regulatory stringency × UNGC member		1.558*** (0.18)		1.684*** (0.19)		1.674*** (0.19)
Constant	0.007** (0.01)	0.010** (0.02)	0.490 (0.98)	0.700 (1.33)	0.380 (0.75)	0.560 (1.05)
Chi-square	437.951	434.006	184.569	186.177	188.66	190.864
N	6,075	6,075	3,627	3,627	3,630	3,630
Sector fixed effects	Yes	Yes	Yes	Yes	Yes	Yes
Year fixed effects	Yes	Yes	Yes	Yes	Yes	Yes

Note: *$p<0.1$, **$p<0.05$, ***$p<0.01$.

[a] Robust standard errors with firm-level cluster correction.

Appendix 7

Explanation of Models and Robustness Checks, Chapter 7

Parallel Trends Test for Difference-in-Difference-in-Differences Model

The divergence in parallel trends in the post–Clean Power Plan (CPP) period is confirmed with a formal parallel trends test, where an indicator variable representing greenhouse gas (GHG)–intensive firms is interacted with year indicator variables as regressors in an ordinary least squares (OLS) regression of firms' participation in CDP. In table A7.1, results show that the coefficients associated with pre-CPP year indicator variables are statistically insignificant for models 2 and 3. This can be interpreted to mean that the outcome trends between the GHG-intensive firms (treatment group) and the non-GHG-intensive firms (control group) are the same, which suggests that the chapter's regressions are not significantly different between the GHG-intensive and non-GHG-intensive companies in the pretreatment period or pre-CPP period.

In what follows, table A7.2 contains a full set of results (including control variables) for stage 1 (voluntary carbon disclosure) and stage 2 (entity-wide carbon emissions) of the difference-in-difference-in-differences (DDD) estimations in endogenous binary-variable (EBV) models for models 1–3 in chapter 7. A full set of stage 1 and stage 2 results are reported in table A7.3 for the S&P 500 firms and table A7.4 for firms in the GHG-intensive sector.

Model 1 is the main model, which contains the DDD estimator on a full sample of the S&P 500 firms. Model 2 represents a split sample of the S&P 500 firms in the broad GHG-intensive sectors (i.e., energy, industrials, materials, and utilities), whereas model 3 is a split sample comprising firms in non-GHG-intensive or consumer-oriented sectors (i.e., consumer discretionary, consumer staples, financial services, and health care).

Table A7.1
Formal test of parallel trends assumption

	1	2	3
	b/se[a]	b/se[a]	b/se[a]
GHG-intensive × 2012	0.052 (0.06)	–0.026 (0.09)	–0.029 (0.08)
GHG-intensive × 2013	0.023 (0.06)	–0.076 (0.09)	–0.079 (0.08)
GHG-intensive × 2014	0.008 (0.06)	–0.114 (0.09)	–0.118 (0.08)
GHG-intensive × 2015	–0.022 (0.06)	–0.156* (0.09)	–0.159* (0.08)
GHG-intensive × 2016	–0.067 (0.06)	–0.193** (0.09)	–0.196** (0.08)
constant	0.634*** (0.01)	0.686*** (0.03)	0.647*** (0.06)
Year fixed effects	No	Yes	Yes
Sector fixed effects	No	Yes	Yes
State fixed effects	No	No	Yes
R^2	0.001	0.063	0.142
N	3,432	3,432	3,432

Note: *$p<0.1$, **$p<0.05$, ***$p<0.01$.
[a] Robust standard errors.

Of note, *manager* is included in the endogenous binary-participation treatment equation (first stage) but not in the outcome equation (second stage). *Manager* serves as an exclusion restriction; it is postulated to explain participation in voluntary carbon disclosure but is not directly linked to a firm's decision to reduce (or not) entity-wide carbon emissions. The presence of a manager responsible for carbon management and climate risks affects participation in voluntary carbon disclosure but does not, on its own, cause firms to be more likely to reduce carbon emissions, for a couple of reasons. First, participating in CDP is a relatively inexpensive activity compared to reducing entity-wide carbon emissions, which requires relatively large investments in operational if not infrastructural changes. Second, the author's interviews with senior- and executive-level managers indicate that during much of the 2011–2020 decade, the chief focus of these nascent offices of corporate

Table A7.2

Participation in voluntary carbon disclosure and entity-wide carbon emissions, a full set of results for stage 1 and stage 2 DDD estimation in EBV models

	Model 1		Model 2		Model 3	
	All S&P 500		GHG-intensive (broad)[a]		Consumer-oriented[b]	
	Voluntary carbon disclosure b/se[c]	Entity-wide carbon emissions b/se[c]	Voluntary carbon disclosure b/se[c]	Entity-wide carbon emissions b/se[c]	Voluntary carbon disclosure b/se[c]	Entity-wide carbon emissions b/se[c]
CDP—transparency		–0.203** (0.10)		–0.665*** (0.20)		–0.071 (0.13)
CDP—awareness		0.012 (0.11)		–0.241 (0.21)		0.081 (0.13)
CDP—management		0.229** (0.12)		–0.096 (0.22)		0.350** (0.14)
CDP—leadership		0.181 (0.15)		–0.219 (0.28)		0.537*** (0.18)
GHG-intensive	–0.698* (0.41)	4.476*** (0.34)				
Clean Power Plan (CPP)	N/A	N/A				
CPP × GHG-intensive	–0.645 (0.45)	–0.024 (0.33)				
CPP × manager	0.282 (0.25)	0.179 (0.22)	0.273 (0.43)	0.564** (0.24)	0.633* (0.34)	0.334 (0.28)
GHG-intensive × manager	0.059 (0.33)	–0.237 (0.27)				

(continued)

Table A7.2 (*continued*)

	Model 1		Model 2		Model 3	
	All S&P 500		GHG-intensive (broad)[a]		Consumer-oriented[b]	
	Voluntary carbon disclosure b/se[c]	Entity-wide carbon emissions b/se[c]	Voluntary carbon disclosure b/se[c]	Entity-wide carbon emissions b/se[c]	Voluntary carbon disclosure b/se[c]	Entity-wide carbon emissions b/se[c]
CPP × GHG-intensive × manager	0.341 (0.50)	–0.031 (0.36)				
Revenues (log)	0.263*** (0.07)	0.827*** (0.05)	0.284*** (0.11)	0.933*** (0.09)	0.374** (0.16)	0.700*** (0.07)
Natural gas price (log)	0.329*** (0.05)	0.194*** (0.04)	0.329*** (0.05)	0.125** (0.06)	0.323*** (0.09)	0.326*** (0.05)
Manager	1.190*** (0.16)		1.391*** (0.24)		1.049*** (0.24)	
Participation last year		0.181 (0.23)		0.381 (0.44)		–0.229 (0.30)
Constant	–4.474*** (0.87)	3.629*** (0.49)	–5.605*** (1.07)	7.525*** (0.73)	0.310 (2.87)	4.538*** (0.63)
Athrho Constant	–0.051 (0.09)		–0.026 (0.19)		0.078 (0.10)	
Lnsigma Constant	0.122*** (0.04)		0.109* (0.06)		0.013 (0.06)	
Sector fixed effects	Yes	Yes	Yes	Yes	Yes	Yes

State fixed effects	Yes	Yes	Yes	Yes	Yes	Yes
Year fixed effects	Yes	Yes	Yes	Yes	Yes	Yes
N	3,209		1,184		1,504	

Note: *$p<0.1$, **$p<0.05$, ***$p<0.01$. *Clean Power Plan (CPP)* is excluded from the model because it is collinear with the year fixed effects; N/A or "not applicable" denotes this fact.

[a] Energy, industrials, materials, and utilities.

[b] Consumer discretionary, consumer staples, financial services, and health care.

[c] Robust standard errors with firm-level cluster correction.

Table A7.3

Participation in voluntary carbon disclosure and carbon emissions intensity, a full set of results for stage 1 and stage 2 DDD estimation in EBV models (S&P 500 index firms)

	Voluntary carbon disclosure b/se[a]	CO_2 emissions per dollar b/se[a]	Voluntary carbon disclosure b/se[a]	CO_2 emissions per full-time employees b/se[a]
CDP—transparency		–0.190* (0.10)		–0.360*** (0.12)
CDP—awareness		0.020 (0.11)		–0.168 (0.13)
CDP—management		0.243** (0.12)		0.076 (0.14)
CDP—leadership		0.199 (0.15)		0.064 (0.19)
GHG-intensive	–0.711* (0.41)	4.486*** (0.34)	–0.677 (0.42)	5.594*** (0.38)
Clean Power Plan (CPP)	N/A	N/A	N/A	N/A
CPP × GHG-intensive	–0.612 (0.44)	–0.039 (0.33)	–0.730 (0.45)	–0.279 (0.35)
CPP × manager	0.310 (0.25)	0.162 (0.22)	0.186 (0.26)	0.107 (0.23)
GHG-intensive × manager	0.064 (0.33)	–0.224 (0.28)	–0.056 (0.33)	–0.362 (0.32)
CPP × GHG-intensive × manager	0.292 (0.50)	–0.029 (0.36)	0.469 (0.51)	0.248 (0.38)

Revenues (log)	0.258*** (0.07)	–0.172*** (0.05)	0.258*** (0.08)	–0.075 (0.06)
Natural gas price (log)	0.331*** (0.05)	0.181*** (0.04)	0.322*** (0.07)	0.128*** (0.04)
Manager	1.199*** (0.16)		1.283*** (0.17)	
Participation last year		0.175 (0.24)		0.195 (0.28)
Constant	–4.449*** (0.87)	3.684*** (0.50)	–4.738*** (0.95)	1.827*** (0.61)
Athrho Constant	–0.048 (0.09)		–0.116 (0.08)	
Lnsigma Constant	0.133*** (0.04)		0.290*** (0.05)	
Sector fixed effects	Yes	Yes	Yes	Yes
State fixed effects	Yes	Yes	Yes	Yes
Year fixed effects	Yes	Yes	Yes	Yes
N	3,203		2,881	

Note: $^{*}p<0.1$, $^{**}p<0.05$, $^{***}p<0.01$. *Clean Power Plan (CPP)* is excluded from the model because it is collinear with the year fixed effects; N/A or "not applicable" denotes this fact.

[a] Robust standard errors with firm-level cluster correction.

Table A7.4

Participation in voluntary carbon disclosure and carbon emissions intensity, a full set of results for stage 1 and stage 2 DDD estimation in EBV models (GHG-intensive firms)

	Voluntary carbon disclosure b/se[a]	CO_2 emissions per dollar b/se[a]	Voluntary carbon disclosure b/se[a]	CO_2 emissions per full-time employees b/se[a]
CDP—transparency		–0.669*** (0.20)		0.982*** (0.24)
CDP—awareness		–0.260 (0.21)		–0.645*** (0.25)
CDP—management		–0.117 (0.23)		–0.537* (0.27)
CDP—leadership		–0.238 (0.28)		–0.595* (0.31)
Clean Power Plan (CPP)	N/A	N/A	N/A	N/A
CPP × manager	0.327 (0.42)	0.536** (0.24)	0.213 (0.44)	0.680** (0.27)
Revenues (log)	0.269** (0.10)	–0.043 (0.08)	0.299*** (0.11)	0.153 (0.11)
Natural gas price (log)	0.318*** (0.09)	0.094* (0.06)	0.354*** (0.11)	0.003 (0.07)
Manager	1.438*** (0.24)		1.441*** (0.24)	
Participation last year		0.369 (0.46)		0.677 (0.47)

Constant	–5.575***	7.492***	–6.395***	6.326***
	(1.08)	(0.74)	(1.31)	(1.05)
Athrho	–0.004		–0.11	
Constant	(0.20)		(0.15)	
Lnsigma	0.112*		0.282***	
Constant	(0.06)		(0.06)	
Sector fixed effects	Yes	Yes	Yes	Yes
State fixed effects	Yes	Yes	Yes	Yes
Year fixed effects	Yes	Yes	Yes	Yes
N	1,180		1,072	

Note: *$p<0.1$, **$p<0.05$, ***$p<0.01$. *Clean Power Plan (CPP)* is excluded from the model because it is collinear with the year fixed effects; N/A or "not applicable" denotes this fact.

[a] Robust standard errors with firm-level cluster correction.

sustainability was on outputs, such as membership in private or public voluntary programs and/or the design and reporting of emission targets rather than on environmental outcomes or performance.[1] Moreover, a Hausman specification test for overidentification (i.e., no exclusion restriction versus the overidentified version) indicates that the null—which is that the difference in coefficients is not systematic—can be rejected with a statistically significant chi-square value of 10.9.

Robustness Checks

A series of robustness tests assess the chapter 7 models (models 1–3) for sensitivity to changes in modeling assumptions, specifications, and error structures (see tables A7.5–A7.7). By and large, chapter 7's empirical results in all three models are robust to alternative specifications with respect to signs and magnitudes.

For the purpose of comparison, the first alternative specification is an endogenous binary-variable (EBV) model that contains only a firm's participation in CDP (from the previous year) on the right-hand side of the regression (outcome) equation. The measures on firms' intensity of participation—namely, *CDP—transparency*, *CDP—awareness*, *CDP—measurement*, and *CDP—leadership*—have been dropped from the models. Across all three models, the *participation* covariate on its own in the stage 2 equation is not statistically significant; this result lends further evidence to chapter 7's argument that firms' intensity of participation—namely, firms' disclosures about the substantive contents of their climate mitigation activity—is linked to their carbon emissions and carbon emissions intensity.

Revenues (log) is replaced with *assets* (log) (see the third column in tables A7.5–A7.7). Moreover, the standard errors are clustered at the sector level because difference-in-differences (as well as difference-in-difference-in-differences) models could be misleading if standard errors are not clustered at the proper level, as reported in the fourth column.[2]

In another specification, *sector×year* is included, along with sector and year fixed effects. This specification controls for time-variant, sector-specific market structures and competitive pressures from rival firms in the same sector, such as variation in rival firms' level of carbon disclosure from one year to the next; these dynamics could be interpreted as learning, diffusion, and peer effects. The next alternative specification differentiates between A and A-disclosers because, unlike the other performance-grade categories, the existence of an A-subcategory is potentially nonnegligible because close to 50 percent of firms in the A-range received an A-rather than an A grade. For other grades, no more than 1 percent of firms received a grade of B–, C–, or D–. Table A7.7 also includes an alternative specification that includes information technology and telecommunications as part of the split sample of consumer-oriented sectors in model 3.

An alternative specification includes *environmental innovation* as a measure of the extent of a company's product innovation, research and development, and capital expenditures related to green technologies, normalized to percentages ranging from 0 to 100. In another regression, an indicator variable for *Paris Agreement* is turned on in 2014 and thereafter to demarcate a regime shift in global climate change governance and policy. Moreover, a possible objection to the difference-in-difference-in-differences analysis is a concern about the exogeneity of the existence of a climate change manager from one year to the next. To mitigate this possibility, tables A7.5–A7.7 include several additional alternative specifications that fix *manager* at different time periods (years); see the last five columns of the tables.

Table A7.5
Entity-wide carbon emissions, stage 2 DDD estimation nested in EBV models (alternative specifications for model 1, S&P 500 index firms)

	Participation only b/se[a]	Assets b/se[a]	Sector SE b/se[a]	State SE b/se[a]	Sector × year b/se[a]	Grade A vs A– b/se[a]
CDP—transparency		–0.081 (0.10)	–0.203 (0.15)	–0.203** (0.10)	–0.214** (0.10)	–0.203** (0.10)
CDP—awareness		0.070 (0.11)	0.012 (0.12)	0.012 (0.13)	0.017 (0.11)	0.013 (0.11)
CDP—management		0.277** (0.12)	0.229** (0.12)	0.229 (0.15)	0.232** (0.12)	0.230** (0.12)
CDP—leadership		0.175 (0.15)	0.181 (0.18)	0.181 (0.16)	0.189 (0.15)	
CDP—leadership (A)						0.070 (0.17)
CDP—leadership (A–)						0.269* (0.16)
Participation in CDP	0.266 (0.24)					
Controls	Yes	Yes	Yes	Yes	Yes	Yes
Sector fixed effects	Yes	Yes	Yes	Yes	Yes	Yes
State fixed effects	Yes	Yes	Yes	Yes	Yes	Yes
Year fixed effects	Yes	Yes	Yes	Yes	Yes	Yes
Sector × year fixed effects	No	No	No	No	Yes	No
N	3,209	3,209	3,209	3,209	3,209	3,209

Note: $^{*}p<0.1$, $^{**}p<0.05$, $^{***}p<0.01$. This table contains stage 2 results on the main independent variables based on alternative specifications to model 1 (all S&P 500 firms), which is a difference-in-difference-in-differences estimation nested in an endogenous binary-variable (EBV) model. Alternative specifications include a regression with only a firm's participation in CDP from the previous year, an alternative measure of firm size (assets), inclusion of standard errors clustered at the sector and state levels, inclusion of sector × year fixed effects, differentiation between A

Environmental innovation b/se[a]	Paris Agreement b/se[a]	Manager 2011 b/se[a]	Manager 2012 b/se[a]	Manager 2013 b/se[a]	Manager 2014 b/se[a]	Manager 2015 b/se[a]
–0.206**	–0.203**	–0.186*	–0.199*	–0.202**	–0.211**	–0.210**
(0.10)	(0.10)	(0.10)	(0.10)	(0.10)	(0.10)	(0.10)
0.012	0.012	0.034	0.019	0.006	–0.004	–0.011
(0.11)	(0.11)	(0.11)	(0.11)	(0.11)	(0.11)	(0.11)
0.223*	0.229**	0.247**	0.230**	0.214*	0.205*	0.201*
(0.11)	(0.12)	(0.11)	(0.11)	(0.12)	(0.12)	(0.12)
0.168	0.181	0.200	0.180	0.150	0.136	0.138
(0.15)	(0.15)	(0.15)	(0.15)	(0.15)	(0.15)	(0.15)
Yes	Yes	Yes	Yes	Yes	Yes	Yes
Yes	Yes	Yes	Yes	Yes	Yes	Yes
Yes	Yes	Yes	Yes	Yes	Yes	Yes
Yes	Yes	Yes	Yes	Yes	Yes	Yes
No	No	No	No	No	No	No
3,209	3,209	3,209	3,209	3,209	3,209	3,209

and A– grades, inclusion of a measure of the extent of a company's product innovation, research and development, and capital expenditures related to green technologies, an indicator that signifies the 2015 Paris Agreement as a governance regime change, and the existence of a senior- or executive-level manager (i.e., *manager*) fixed at different years.

[a] Robust standard errors with firm-level cluster correction.

Table A7.6
Entity-wide carbon emissions, stage 2 DDD estimation nested in EBV models (alternative specifications for model 2, GHG-intensive firms)

	Participation only b/se[a]	Assets b/se[a]	State SE b/se[a]	Sector × year b/se[a]	Grade A vs. A– b/se[a]
CDP—transparency		–0.625*** (0.19)	–0.665*** (0.18)	–0.641*** (0.19)	–0.664*** (0.20)
CDP—awareness		–0.323* (0.19)	–0.241 (0.24)	–0.213 (0.20)	–0.242 (0.21)
CDP—management		–0.239 (0.20)	–0.096 (0.21)	–0.053 (0.22)	–0.097 (0.22)
CDP—leadership		–0.353 (0.24)	–0.219 (0.33)	–0.157 (0.28)	
CDP—leadership (A)					–0.035 (0.34)
CDP—leadership (A–)					–0.320 (0.27)
Participation in CDP	0.374 (0.38)				
Controls	Yes	Yes	Yes	Yes	Yes
Sector fixed effects	Yes	Yes	Yes	Yes	Yes
State fixed effects	Yes	Yes	Yes	Yes	Yes
Year fixed effects	Yes	Yes	Yes	Yes	Yes
Sector × Year fixed effects	No	No	No	Yes	No
N	1,184	1,184	1,184	1,184	1,184

Note: *$p<0.1$, ***$p<0.01$. This table contains stage 2 results on the main independent variables based on alternative specifications to model 2 (GHG-intensive firms), which is a difference-in-difference-in-differences estimation nested in an endogenous binary-variable (EBV) model. Alternative specifications include a regression with only a firm's participation in CDP from the previous year, an alternative measure of firm size (assets), inclusion of standard errors clustered at the sector and state

Environmental innovation b/se[a]	Paris Agreement b/se[a]	Manager 2011 b/se[a]	Manager 2012 b/se[a]	Manager 2013 b/se[a]	Manager 2014 b/se[a]	Manager 2015 b/se[a]
–0.633***	–0.665***	–0.621***	–0.660***	–0.676***	–0.693***	–0.705***
(0.18)	(0.20)	(0.19)	(0.19)	(0.20)	(0.19)	(0.19)
–0.231	–0.241	–0.187	–0.236	–0.265	–0.256	–0.290
(0.21)	(0.21)	(0.21)	(0.21)	(0.21)	(0.21)	(0.21)
–0.014	–0.096	–0.031	–0.088	–0.123	–0.146	–0.161
(0.21)	(0.22)	(0.22)	(0.22)	(0.23)	(0.23)	(0.23)
–0.150	–0.219	–0.163	–0.203	–0.244	–0.272	–0.284
(0.27)	(0.28)	(0.27)	(0.28)	(0.28)	(0.28)	(0.28)
Yes	Yes	Yes	Yes	Yes	Yes	Yes
Yes	Yes	Yes	Yes	Yes	Yes	Yes
Yes	Yes	Yes	Yes	Yes	Yes	Yes
Yes	Yes	Yes	Yes	Yes	Yes	Yes
No	No	No	No	No	No	No
1,184	1,184	1,184	1,184	1,184	1,184	1,184

levels, inclusion of sector × year fixed effects, differentiation between A and A– grades, inclusion of a measure of the extent of a company's product innovation, research and development, and capital expenditures related to green technologies, an indicator that signifies the 2015 Paris Agreement as a governance regime change, and the existence of a senior- or executive-level manager (i.e., *manager*) fixed at different years.

[a] Robust standard errors with firm-level cluster correction.

Table A7.7

Entity-wide carbon emissions, stage 2 DDD estimation nested in EBV models (alternative specifications for model 3, consumer-oriented firms)

	Participation only b/se[a]	Assets b/se[a]	State SE b/se[a]	Sector × year b/se[a]	Grade A vs. A– b/se[a]	Technology b/se[a]
CDP—transparency		0.052 (0.13)	–0.071 (0.10)	–0.099 (0.13)	–0.072 (0.13)	0.165 (0.13)
CDP—awareness		0.129 (0.14)	0.081 (0.12)	0.052 (0.14)	0.082 (0.14)	0.135 (0.17)
CDP—management		0.430*** (0.14)	0.350** (0.15)	0.331** (0.14)	0.349** (0.14)	0.220 (0.19)
CDP—leadership		0.606*** (0.19)	0.537*** (0.16)	0.512*** (0.18)		0.031 (0.28)
CDP—leadership (A)					0.441** (0.21)	
CDP—leadership (A–)					0.603*** (0.19)	
Participation in CDP	0.136 (0.32)					
Controls	Yes	Yes	Yes	Yes	Yes	Yes
Sector fixed effects	Yes	Yes	Yes	Yes	Yes	Yes
State fixed effects	Yes	Yes	Yes	Yes	Yes	Yes
Year fixed effects	Yes	Yes	Yes	Yes	Yes	Yes
Sector × year fixed effects	No	No	No	Yes	No	No
N	1,504	1,504	1,504	1,504	1,504	1,504

Note: ** $p < 0.05$, *** $p < 0.01$. This table contains stage 2 results on the main independent variables based on alternative specifications to model 3 (consumer-oriented firms), which is a difference-in-difference-in-differences estimation nested in an endogenous binary-variable (EBV) model. Alternative specifications include a regression with only a firm's participation in CDP from the previous year, an alternative measure of firm size (assets), inclusion of standard errors clustered at the sector and state levels, inclusion of sector × year fixed effects, differentiation between A and A– grades, inclusion of technology (i.e., information technology and telecommunications)

Environmental innovation b/se[a]	Paris Agreement b/se[a]	Manager 2011 b/se[a]	Manager 2012 b/se[a]	Manager 2013 b/se[a]	Manager 2014 b/se[a]	Manager 2015 b/se[a]
–0.069	–0.071	–0.055	–0.058	–0.056	–0.064	–0.071
(0.12)	(0.13)	(0.13)	(0.13)	(0.13)	(0.13)	(0.13)
0.068	0.081	0.094	0.095	0.082	0.068	0.041
(0.13)	(0.13)	(0.13)	(0.14)	(0.14)	(0.14)	(0.13)
0.322**	0.350**	0.365***	0.364***	0.349**	0.330**	0.307**
(0.14)	(0.14)	(0.14)	(0.14)	(0.14)	(0.14)	(0.14)
0.430**	0.537***	0.544***	0.541***	0.505***	0.485***	0.464**
(0.18)	(0.18)	(0.18)	(0.18)	(0.18)	(0.18)	(0.18)
Yes	Yes	Yes	Yes	Yes	Yes	Yes
Yes	Yes	Yes	Yes	Yes	Yes	Yes
Yes	Yes	Yes	Yes	Yes	Yes	Yes
Yes	Yes	Yes	Yes	Yes	Yes	Yes
No	No	No	No	No	No	No
1,504	1,504	1,504	1,504	1,504	1,504	1,504

firms as part of the consumer-oriented sectors, inclusion of a measure of the extent of a company's product innovation, research and development, and capital expenditures related to green technologies, an indicator that signifies the 2015 Paris Agreement as a governance regime change, and the existence of a senior- or executive-level manager (i.e., *manager*) fixed at different years.

[a] Robust standard errors with firm-level cluster correction.

Appendix 8

Explanation of Data and Robustness Checks, Chapters 8 and 9

Data and Variables

Data for empirical analyses in chapters 8 and 9 come from a plethora of sources: the CDP climate change questionnaire from 2011 to 2020, LSEG Data & Analytics, the *Financial Times*'s Europe's Climate Leaders lists 2021–2023, and Corporate Knights' Global 100 rankings 2011–2020. Construction and coding of firm-, market-, sector-, and country-level variables for the discrete-continuous econometric analyses in chapters 8 and 9 can be found in appendix 2.

Table A8.1 reports the summary statistics for internal firm management and organizational structures for all Fortune Global firms versus European Union–based Fortune Global 500 firms.

Robustness Checks

Table A8.2 presents the results of robustness checks on the double-hurdle model of the EU-based global firms' participation and effort in voluntary carbon disclosure (see table 9.4 in chapter 9). In models 1 and 2, *policy supporter—vice president* and *policy supporter—chief sustainability officer* replace *policy supporter—upper management* as similar but narrower measures of managerial agency. Another alternative specification, *policy supporter—analyst (only)*, represents firms that have only installed a lower-level policy analyst to be responsible for environmental sustainability (see model 3).

ISO 14001 certification by global firms serves as an alternative specification for *environmental R&D*. *Revenues* is replaced with other related measures—log forms of *assets* and *employees*—as the alternative specification for firm size.

Table A8.1

Internal firm management and organizational structures (all versus EU-based Fortune Global 500 firms, 2015)

Variable	All Global 500 firms			EU-based Global 500 firms		
	N	Mean	Standard deviation	*N*	Mean	Standard deviation
Participation in voluntary carbon disclosure	500	78%	42%	114	89%	32%
Carbon disclosure score (0–100)	500	71.1	40.3	114	85.3	31.3
Policy supporter—upper management	500	57%	50%	114	72%	45%
Policy supporter—analyst	500	12%	32%	114	9%	28%
Policy supporter—vice president	500	50%	50%	114	65%	48%
Policy supporter—chief sustainability officer	500	7%	25%	114	7%	26%
Mission statement	500	16%	37%	114	21%	41%
ESG principles[a]	500	29%	46%	114	45%	50%
Dedicated website	500	10%	30%	114	7%	26%
Environmental R&D	500	38%	49%	114	52%	50%
ISO 14001 certification	500	63%	48%	114	82%	39%
Revenues (log)	500	10.0	1.2	114	10.3	1.1
Assets (log)	500	11.0	1.5	114	11.4	1.7
Employees (log)	489	10.7	1.3	110	11.1	1.0
Government-owned	500	6%	24%	114	0%	0%
GHG-intensive (broad)	500	29%	45%	114	27%	45%

[a] Environmental, social, and governance (ESG) principles

Table A8.2

Internal firm determinants of participation and effort in voluntary carbon disclosure, double-hurdle model (alternative specifications for EU-based Fortune Global 500 firms)

	1	2	3	4	5	6	7
Tier 1 (Participation in voluntary carbon disclosure)							
Policy supporter—upper management				0.422	0.385	0.765*	0.527
Policy supporter—vice president	0.203						
Policy supporter—chief sustainability officer		4.254***					
Policy supporter—analyst (only)			–0.349				
Mission statement	0.119	0.116	0.159	0.241	–0.035	–0.086	0.198
ESG principles[a]	0.154	0.157	0.172	0.170	–0.088	–0.242	0.196
Dedicated website	0.055	0.099	0.106	–0.017	–0.164	0.338	–0.019
Environmental R&D	0.146	0.263	0.166		0.091	–0.151	0.208
ISO 14001 certification				–0.888			
Revenues (log)	0.365***	0.352***	0.393***	0.430***			0.339***
Assets (log)					0.252***		
Employees (log)						0.756***	
Government-owned	N/A	N/A	N/A	N/A	N/A	N/A	–1.217
GHG-intensive (broad)	0.686	0.658	0.628*	0.803*	1.152***	1.423***	0.662
Constant	–1.978***	–1.749***	–2.115**	–2.112***	–1.059**	–6.707***	–1.973***
Tier 2 (Level of voluntary carbon disclosure)							
Policy supporter—upper management				1.626	1.761	1.459	1.800
Policy supporter—vice president	0.744						
Policy supporter—chief sustainability officer		1.750					
Policy supporter—analyst (only)			–1.231				

(continued)

Table A8.2 (*continued*)

	1	2	3	4	5	6	7
Mission statement	4.154**	4.008**	4.072**	4.259**	4.033*	4.383**	2.33
ESG principles[1]	2.524*	2.416*	2.594*	2.604**	2.046	2.621*	2.979**
Dedicated website	–0.916	–0.718	–0.693	–0.886	–0.716	–1.275	–0.612
Environmental R&D	1.993**	1.940**	1.989**		2.305**	2.319**	1.389*
ISO 14001 certification				2.171			
Revenues (log)	1.287**	1.313**	1.433**	1.461***			1.424**
Assets (log)					0.483		
Employees (log)						0.254	
Government-owned	N/A	N/A	N/A	N/A	N/A	N/A	7.229**
GHG-intensive (broad)	–3.511**	–3.410**	–3.576**	–3.008	–2.423	–2.996*	–2.776
Constant	81.717***	81.988***	80.872***	78.272***	88.221***	91.371***	79.600***
Lnsigma							
Constant	1.681***	1.679***	1.681***	1.674***	1.687***	1.689***	1.758***
Chi-square	26.668	20.945	45.495	29.863	226.241	224.167	73.964
N	114	114	114	114	114	110	137
Country fixed effects	Yes	Yes	Yes	Yes	Yes	Yes	Yes

Note: *$p<0.1$, **$p<0.05$, ***$p<0.01$; N/A or "not applicable" denotes that *Government-owned* has been dropped from the model due to collinearity.

[a] Environmental, social, and governance (ESG) principles.

Table A8.3

Full set of results for multilevel determinants of participation and effort in voluntary carbon disclosure, Heckman selection model (developed countries–based Fortune Global 500 firms)

	Base model		Model 1		Model 2	
	No cross-level interactions		Corporate × regulation		Corporate × global	
	Participation in voluntary carbon disclosure b/se[a]	Level of voluntary carbon disclosure b/se[a]	Participation in voluntary carbon disclosure b/se[a]	Level of voluntary carbon disclosure b/se[a]	Participation in voluntary carbon disclosure b/se[a]	Level of voluntary carbon disclosure b/se[a]
Firm, market, and sector variables						
Manager	1.668*** (0.13)				1.558*** (0.14)	
Target		13.488*** (1.71)				13.183*** (1.84)
UNGC member	1.197*** (0.22)	3.078*** (1.10)	1.201*** (0.22)	3.104*** (1.10)		
Revenues (log)	0.206*** (0.06)	1.944*** (0.52)	0.183*** (0.06)	1.915*** (0.53)	0.241*** (0.06)	2.085*** (0.53)
Natural gas price (log)	0.022 (0.10)	–9.840*** (0.82)	0.017 (0.09)	–9.851*** (0.82)	0.02 (0.10)	–9.875*** (0.82)
GHG-intensive	–0.687*** (0.25)	5.331*** (1.99)	–0.609** (0.26)	5.380*** (2.01)	–0.645** (0.26)	5.667*** (1.99)

(continued)

Table A8.3 (*continued*)

	Base model		Model 1		Model 2	
	No cross-level interactions		Corporate × regulation		Corporate × global	
	Participation in voluntary carbon disclosure b/se[a]	Level of voluntary carbon disclosure b/se[a]	Participation in voluntary carbon disclosure b/se[a]	Level of voluntary carbon disclosure b/se[a]	Participation in voluntary carbon disclosure b/se[a]	Level of voluntary carbon disclosure b/se[a]
Country-level variables						
Regulatory stringency	0.029 (0.11)	–0.191 (1.67)	–0.109 (0.12)	–1.931 (1.66)	0.128 (0.11)	–0.036 (1.68)
Civil liberties	–0.424*** (0.16)	–6.450 (4.05)	–0.405*** (0.16)	–6.490 (4.10)	–0.352** (0.14)	–6.330 (4.09)
GDP per capita (log)	0.430* (0.24)	–3.464 (3.15)	0.452* (0.25)	–3.200 (3.16)	0.280 (0.24)	–3.680 (3.20)
Federalism	–0.296 (0.28)	–0.552 (1.57)	–0.277 (0.27)	–0.541 (1.58)	–0.381 (0.26)	–0.870 (1.61)
ISO 14001 (log)	0.021 (0.09)	–0.499 (0.66)	0.016 (0.09)	–0.483 (0.66)	–0.001 (0.09)	–0.586 (0.67)
EU member	–0.076 (0.31)	–0.597 (2.11)	–0.079 (0.30)	–0.707 (2.13)	–0.052 (0.28)	–0.207 (2.12)
Cross-level interactions						
Manager × regulatory stringency			0.331*** (0.03)			

Target × regulatory stringency				2.760*** (0.34)		
Manager × UNGC member					0.984*** (0.25)	
Target × UNGC member						1.749 (1.13)
Constant	–6.392** (2.81)	110.693*** (37.39)	–5.678** (2.80)	116.575*** (37.11)	–5.314* (2.75)	112.416*** (37.70)
Athrho Constant	–0.107 (0.07)		–0.095 (0.06)		–0.128* (0.07)	
Lnsigma Constant	2.651*** (0.05)		2.651*** (0.05)		2.655*** (0.05)	
N	2,228		2,228		2,228	
Sector fixed effects	Yes		Yes		Yes	
Year fixed effects	Yes		Yes		Yes	

Note: $^{*}p<0.1$, $^{**}p<0.05$, $^{***}p<0.01$.

[a] Robust standard errors with firm-level cluster correction.

Table A8.4

Full set of results for multilevel determinants of participation and effort in voluntary carbon disclosure, Heckman selection model (developing countries–based Fortune Global 500 firms)

	Base model		Model 1		Model 2	
	No cross-level interactions		Corporate × regulation		Corporate × global	
	Participation in voluntary carbon disclosure b/se[a]	Level of voluntary carbon disclosure b/se[a]	Participation in voluntary carbon disclosure b/se[a]	Level of voluntary carbon disclosure b/se[a]	Participation in voluntary carbon disclosure b/se[a]	Level of voluntary carbon disclosure b/se[a]
Firm, market, and sector variables						
Manager	1.861*** (0.23)				1.886*** (0.32)	
Target		14.750*** (3.70)				16.961*** (3.80)
UNGC member	0.366 (0.31)	–1.916 (3.86)	0.370 (0.31)	–1.80 (3.86)		
Revenues (log)	0.231 (0.15)	–3.027 (1.89)	0.227 (0.15)	–2.950 (1.88)	0.260* (0.14)	–3.033* (1.79)
Natural gas price (log)	0.082 (0.27)	–17.543*** (3.90)	0.083 (0.27)	–17.611*** (3.88)	0.060 (0.27)	–17.593*** (3.76)
GHG-intensive	0.255 (0.46)	–4.962 (5.39)	0.239 (0.45)	–5.030 (5.39)	0.310 (0.47)	–4.740 (5.46)
Country-level variables						
Regulatory stringency	1.376 (0.89)	–20.093** (9.54)	1.126 (0.89)	–22.722** (9.39)	1.335 (0.90)	–21.458** (9.49)

Civil liberties	0.070 (0.17)	–11.818*** (3.05)	0.062 (0.17)	–11.866*** (3.03)	0.010 (0.17)	–11.850*** (2.88)
GDP per capita (log)	–0.046 (0.25)	–0.359 (4.70)	–0.041 (0.25)	–0.330 (4.71)	–0.041 (0.25)	–0.583 (4.71)
Federalism	0.343 (0.42)	–1.748 (6.52)	0.342 (0.42)	–1.749 (6.51)	0.236 (0.41)	–0.986 (6.08)
ISO 14001 (log)	–0.188 (0.19)	2.043 (2.83)	–0.184 (0.18)	1.954 (2.84)	–0.165 (0.18)	2.097 (2.82)
Cross-level interactions						
Manager × regulatory stringency			0.420*** (0.05)			
Target × regulatory stringency				3.277*** (0.82)		
Manager × UNGC member					0.002 (0.40)	
Target × UNGC member						–3.914 (2.78)
Constant	–8.459** (3.77)	232.898*** (63.22)	–7.365** (3.75)	244.564*** (62.15)	–7.365** (3.75)	238.849*** (62.22)
Athrho Constant	–0.339 (0.22)		–0.319 (0.21)		–0.319 (0.21)	

(continued)

Table A8.4 (*continued*)

	Base model		Model 1		Model 2	
	No cross-level interactions		Corporate × regulation		Corporate × global	
	Participation in voluntary carbon disclosure b/se[a]	Level of voluntary carbon disclosure b/se[a]	Participation in voluntary carbon disclosure b/se[a]	Level of voluntary carbon disclosure b/se[a]	Participation in voluntary carbon disclosure b/se[a]	Level of voluntary carbon disclosure b/se[a]
Lnsigma	2.613***		2.611***		2.611***	
Constant	(0.10)		(0.10)		(0.10)	
N	360		360		360	
Sector fixed effects	Yes		Yes		Yes	
Year fixed effects	Yes		Yes		Yes	

Note: *$p<0.1$, **$p<0.05$, ***$p<0.01$.

[a] Robust standard errors with firm-level cluster correction.

See models 5 and 6 for these results. The last alternative specification, or model 7, in table A8.2 employs an expanded definition of "European" to include countries that are part of the continent of Europe but are not part of the EU—namely Iceland, Liechtenstein, Norway, and Switzerland.

Finally, tables A8.3 and A8.4 report the full set of results for models 1 and 2 in table 9.9, panels A and B, respectively.

Appendix 9
Field Research and Interviews

To identify the firm, regulatory, and global governance factors and their interactions that have influenced the supply and demand for corporate self-regulation on climate change, this book draws primarily on secondary data for the quasi-experiments, econometric modeling, and panel data analyses. To supplement and complement the large-*N* quantitative analyses, original qualitative data were collected from 2020 to 2023 to inform theory building in chapter 2 and substantiate illustrative cases in chapters 6, 8, and 9. In-person field research was conducted by the author in February 2020, just before the commencement of the global outbreak of the COVID-19 pandemic. Over the next couple of years, further field research and interviews were conducted by Zoom videoconferencing software on in person post-pandemic. Altogether, fifty semistructured interviews were conducted with senior- or executive-level corporate leaders, regulators, global governance leaders, and practitioners in corporate sustainability.[1]

Interviewees represent diverse stakeholders in corporate sustainability and related fields and issue areas, including corporate climate disclosures, carbon management and accounting, voluntary carbon markets, carbon capture technology, and natural climate solutions. These stakeholders include, but are not limited to, Fortune Global 500 firms, US and other government agencies, international organizations, industry associations, private consultancies, research institutes, and higher education institutions.

There was a synergetic relationship between this book's large-*N* quantitative analyses and the qualitative research. The author employed the results of large-*N* quantitative analyses to frame this book's field research and to help structure the interview protocol. A chief objective of the qualitative research was to contextualize the firm, regulatory, and global governance factors that characterize corporate (global firm) leaders in proactive climate action, which informed the illustrative case studies. The field research and interviews also helped the author to further refine this book's multilevel governance framework on climate change with global firms and managers inside them as the central nodes of decision-making.

Field Research

The author's original qualitative data collection began with field research at the GreenBiz 20 conference, the twentieth annual gathering of sustainability leaders from business, nongovernmental organizations, and academia on February 4–6, 2020. GreenBiz Group (renamed Trellis Group in 2024) is a media and event company that, according to its website, "accelerates the just transition to a clean economy."[2] The fifteen hundred conference attendees that gathered in Scottsdale, Arizona, consisted of chief executive officers, chief sustainability officers, policy experts, nongovernmental organization representatives, practitioners, and students. Before the official start of GreenBiz 20, the United Nations Global Compact (UNGC) hosted a Sustainable Development Goal (SDG) Summit to celebrate the twentieth anniversary of the founding of the UN Global Compact, launch the SDG Action Manager, a tool developed by the UNGC and B Lab for tracking corporate commitments related to the SDGs, and to promote SDGs in supply chains and in climate finance.[3] At the invitation of Arizona State University's Thunderbird School of Global Management, which was a sponsor of the GreenBiz 20 and a university partner to Global Compact Network USA (i.e., the US chapter of the UNGC), the author attended the SDG Summit and GreenBiz 20 as an observer.

In addition, the author attended the UN Global Compact's weeklong SDG Innovation Accelerator Workshop,[4] which was held at the ASU Thunderbird School of Global Management during the same week as GreenBiz 20. Young professionals from US or Canadian UNGC member firms were paired with senior- and executive-level managers to design and develop carbon management or climate solution products that could be scaled and executed inside the organization. The author observed multiple interactive sessions with young professionals, managers, and experts focused on corporate sustainability program design, impact, and execution, as well as team presentations. The author also observed a public-private partnership dialogue and exchange between the UNGC Young Innovators and US State Department officials.

Although the author did not conduct ethnographic research, these visits helped the author understand the dynamic relationship between corporate and global governance and the ways in which public policy and regulatory governance facilitated and impeded corporate climate action.

Between 2020 and 2023, the author also attended multiple webinars and online live sessions hosted by Global Compact Network USA or the UN Global Compact Academy. These meetings and e-learning courses offered corporate members introductions to topics such as setting science-based targets and carbon pricing and step-by-step guides for advancing corporate action across industry, function, geography, or jurisdiction. The author gained insights into the ways in which global governance institutions like the UNGC incentivized and supported the development and implementation of innovative solutions, new business models, and global best practices within the national and subnational regulatory contexts. These stakeholder meetings enabled the author to collect key information about the role of global governance in corporate sustainability and the kind of exchanges that frequently take place.

Semistructured Interviews

At GreenBiz 20, the SDG Summit, and the SDG Innovation Accelerator Workshop, the author met and spoke with potential interviewees working in business, government, and global governance and in diverse issues areas related to corporate sustainability. To arrange these and other interviews, the author followed up with potential interviewees who had been identified through public and private forums on corporate sustainability and on corporate websites and annual reports, as well as through a snowball sampling strategy. An effort was made to maximize representation across industry sectors, government, global governance, and nonprofit organizations. In some cases, initial introductions were facilitated by academic and private sector colleagues. Once voluntary participation was secured via email, the author set up a thirty-minute to one-hour Zoom or in-person interview.

The semistructured interviews were conducted by the author using an interview protocol created for firms, regulators, and civil society. Interviews with firm representatives were by and large conducted with companies' senior- or executive-level leaders and officers responsible for corporate sustainability or corporate social responsibility. In these interviews, the objective was to uncover the internal firm and external political economy drivers that a company attributes to its beyond compliance climate mitigation. Interview questions were constructed to elicit insights on what corporate management practices and structures facilitate a company's sustainability and climate leadership among its peers; what factors characterize a company's engagement with stakeholders worldwide, from consumers to regulators; as well as whether and to what extent a company participates in subnational (local and state), national, and global voluntary programs and initiatives on climate change. Furthermore, the interview questions elicit corporate executives' insights on a company's most significant accomplishments and challenges related to climate risks and opportunities.

Interviews with policymakers in government and leaders in global governance were based on similar questions but elicited unique perspectives about their views and insights on the supply of and demand for corporate climate action. The author also asked interviewees about the ways in which global firms navigated different levels of governance and their interactions with regulators and global governance leaders and personnel vis-à-vis sustainability and climate-specific policies or programs. Interviewees were asked about their perspectives on the major opportunities and challenges that global firms across sectors have faced and are facing in climate solutions and decarbonization efforts.

During 2022–2023, the author was a visiting scholar at Stanford University during the inaugural year of the Stanford Doerr School of Sustainability. At Stanford and in the San Francisco Bay Area, the author interacted with and interviewed stakeholders in academia, the private sector, and nonprofit organizations, all of which informed the theorizing and testing of this book's multilevel governance framework on climate change as well as the author's evidence-based proposal for a portfolio approach to climate change—namely, a polycentric governance structure with checks and balances from diverse stakeholders, with both bottom-up and top-down pressures and incentives.

To maintain anonymity and confidentiality, all interviews were codified for references. In this book, direct attribution of quotes by interviewees was made with permission. Table A9.1 lists the date, location, and description of interviewees without disclosing their affiliations.

Table A9.1
List of interviews

No.	Code	Interviewee	Date (mm/dd/yyyy)	Location	Format
1	O8	Account manager in corporate climate disclosure, a nonprofit consultancy	11/17/2015	London, UK	Phone
2	HE1	Consultant on energy projects to multinational companies, a consultancy specialized in the oil and gas sector	11/5/2019	Boston, MA, USA	Email
3	GF1	Director of social performance, a Global 500 company in the materials sector	1/17/2020	Phoenix, AZ, USA	In person
4	HE2	Executive director of global development and global citizenship, a higher education institution	1/21/2020	Phoenix, AZ, USA	In person
5	GG1	Executive director of a United Nations–initiated global governance institution	2/3/2020	New York, NY, USA	In person
6	GF2	Sustainability manager, a Global 500 company in the health care sector	2/5/2020	New York, NY, USA	In person
7	GF3	Business analyst in sustainability, a Global 500 company in the technology sector	2/5/2020	Raleigh, NC, USA	In person
8	GF4	Communications manager, a Global 500 company in the technology sector	2/5/2020	Raleigh, NC, USA	In person
9	GF5	Global communications manager, a Global 500 company in the technology sector	2/5/2020	New York, NY, USA	In person
10	GF6	Sustainability solutions and engagement specialist, a Global 500 company in the technology sector	2/5/2020	New York, NY, USA	In person
11	GF7	Sustainability solutions principal, a Global 500 company in the technology sector	2/5/2020	Amsterdam, Netherlands	In person

(*continued*)

Table A9.1 (*continued*)

No.	Code	Interviewee	Date (mm/dd/yyyy)	Location	Format
12	GF10	Energy consultant, a Global 500 company in the energy sector	2/7/2020	Austin, TX, USA	In person
13	GF8	Global marketing and innovation brand manager, a Global 500 company in the consumer staples sector	2/7/2020	New York, NY, USA	In person
14	GF9	Compliance manager, a Global 500 company in the energy sector	2/7/2020	Philadelphia, PA, USA	In person
15	HE4	Area expert instructor on corporate sustainability, a higher education institution, and United Nations–initiated global governance institution	2/24/2020	Phoenix, AZ, USA	In person
16	GF11	Executive vice president and head of corporate responsibility, a Global 500 company in financial services	5/1/2020	Newport Beach, CA, USA	Zoom
17	GF12	Executive vice president and head of environmental, social, and governance (ESG) business strategy, a Global 500 company in financial services	5/13/2020	Newport Beach, CA, USA	Zoom
18	O9	Account manager in corporate climate disclosure, a nonprofit consultancy	8/6/2020	London, UK	Zoom
19	GF13	Director of corporate responsibility, a Global 500 company in information technology and telecommunications	10/2/2020	Phoenix, AZ, USA	Zoom
20	GF14	Global director of community engagement and social performance, a Global 500 company in the energy sector	10/8/2020	Toronto, Canada	Zoom
21	GF15	Director of supply chain development, a Global 500 company in the consumer discretionary sector	12/14/2020	Portland, OR, USA	Zoom
22	GF16	Head of operations, environmental, social, and governance, and managing director, a Global 500 company in financial services	1/20/2021	London, UK	Zoom

23	GF17	Senior director of health and safety, environment and energy, a Global 500 company in the consumer discretionary sector	2/2/2021	Herzoge-naurach, Germany	Zoom
24	GF18	Head of sustainability, a Global 500 company in the consumer discretionary sector	10/21/2021	Medellin, Colombia	Zoom
25	HE5	Area expert in geography land use changes, a higher education institution	2/3/2022	Stanford, CA, USA	In person
26	HE6	Area expert in climate science, a higher education institution	5/11/2022	Stanford, CA, USA	In person
27	O1	Founder of luxury apparel collection focused on sustainable and American-made fashion and associate director at nonprofit research institute focused on business policy and innovation	8/19/2022	Washington, DC, USA	Zoom
28	O2	Senior manager of membership program for sustainability professionals, a consultancy that brings together sustainability brands and sustainability and design innovation professionals for networking and peer-to-peer learning groups	9/21/2022	Palo Alto, CA, USA	In person
29	O3	Area expert in ESG in climate and startup ecosystem, a law and consulting firm specializing in sustainability start-ups	9/27/2022	Menlo Park, CA, USA	In person
30	G1	Assistant chief counsel and senior adviser on environmental quality, California state and US federal government agencies	12/1/2022	Sacramento, CA, USA	In person
31	G2	Chair of climate-related market risk committee, an independent US federal government agency	12/2/2022	Palo Alto, CA, USA	In person
32	O4	Environmental and energy lawyer with expertise in climate change litigation and emerging laws in India, a higher education institution	1/13/2023	Stanford, CA, USA	In person

(*continued*)

Table A9.1 (*continued*)

No.	Code	Interviewee	Date (mm/dd/yyyy)	Location	Format
33	HE12	Expert on harmonizing global carbon accounting, a higher education institution	4/12/2023	Stanford, CA, USA	In person
34	O5	Consultant in energy systems, a Global 500 company in the oil and gas sector	5/19/2023	Pleasanton, CA, USA	In person
35	HE13	Expert in climate science and lead author of an IPCC report, a higher education institution	5/23/2023	Zurich, Switzerland	In person
36	HE15	Expert in climate engineering, a higher education institution	6/16/2023	Ithaca, NY, USA	In person
37	O6	Director of interdisciplinary collaborations, a global sustainability nonprofit	6/20/2023	Palo Alto, CA, USA	In person
38	GF20	Head of public relations and branding, a Global 500 company in the technology sector	6/21/2023	Hinchu, Taiwan	Email
39	O7	Co-organizer of student activist organization and campaign, a higher education institution	8/28/2023	Stanford, CA, USA	In person

Notes

Chapter 1

1. Intel, "Letter from Intel CEO Pat Gelsinger about the Company's CSR Progress in 2022–23," May 11, 2023, https://www.intc.com/news-events/press-releases/detail/1618/opinion-intel-ceo-letter-2022-23-corporate-responsibility.

2. ASML Holdings NV, a Netherlands-based company, landed on Corporate Knight's top 100 list six times, whereas South Korea's Samsung Electronics has been ranked in the top 100 five times. The Taiwan Semiconductor Manufacturing Company, or TSMC, has been ranked in the top 100 three separate years during 2011–2020. Nvidia Corporation was ranked among the Top 100 companies in 2018 for the first time.

3. Suzanne Fallender (former global director of corporate responsibility at Intel Corporation) in discussion with the author, October 2, 2020 (interview GF13).

4. John Harland, "Designing for the Environment Turns Intel Green," GreenBiz, November 30, 2005, https://www.greenbiz.com/article/designing-environment-turns-intel-green.

5. Bill Baue, "Footprints and Handprints: Stephen Harper on Intel's New Science-Based Climate Policy," Sustainable Brands, May 16, 2014, https://sustainablebrands.com/read/new-metrics/footprints-and-handprints-stephen-harper-on-intel-s-new-science-based-climate-policy-part.

6. Suzanne Fallender in discussion with the author, October 2, 2020 (interview GF13).

7. "National Top 100," EPA Green Power Partnership, accessed August 9, 2023, https://www.epa.gov/system/files/documents/2023-10/top100_july2023.pdf.

8. "Our Vision," Intel's contribution to Europe, Intel Corporation, accessed April 23, 2024, https://www.intel.com/content/www/us/en/corporate/eu-chipmaking/vision.html.

9. The terms "global business," "multinational corporation," "global firm," "firm," and "company" are used interchangeably to refer to publicly traded companies that operate globally and are listed on international stock exchanges.

10. Griffin 2017. The term "carbon emission" is used interchangeably with "GHG emission" to refer to the release of carbon dioxide and other greenhouse gases into the atmosphere, primarily human activities such as burning fossil fuels for energy, transportation, and industrial processes. These emissions are a major contributor to global climate change and have significant implications for the health and well-being of humans and other living beings. This book refers to climate change as a human-caused phenomenon, which encompasses global warming (i.e., Earth's rising surface temperature) and the "side effects" of warming (i.e., melting glaciers, heavier rainstorms, and more frequent drought). That being said, throughout the book "climate change" is used interchangeably with "global warming" to refer to the larger phenomenon of human-caused climate change.

11. "Voluntary climate action" is also referred to as "corporate self-regulation" in the climate change area, which involves a decentralized approach for firms' adoption and implementation of environmentally friendly measures that are not required by law or the "private provision of public goods" by firms. The literature on corporate self-regulation is expansive across economics, political science, and management (see, e.g., Buchanan 1965; Arora and Gangopadhyay 1995; Besley and Ghatak 2001, 2007; Prakash 2001; McWilliams and Siegel 2001; Lyon and Maxwell 2004, 2008; Graff and Small 2005; Bénabou and Tirole 2006, 2010; Baron 2010; Kotchen 2006, 2013; van't Veld and Kotchen 2011; Potoski and Prakash 2013; Banzhaf et al. 2013; Hsueh 2020).

12. Chapter 2 introduces the multilevel governance framework on climate change and the book's hypotheses in the form of propositions. Figure 2.2 illustrates the causal mechanism that links multilevel governance interactions and voluntary climate action by global firms. The rest of the book substantiates the book's arguments.

13. There is rich literature in state and local or subnational climate policy and governance, which is beyond the scope of this book. That being said, chapter 10 (conclusion) discusses the role of subnational actors and the regulatory process to underscore the fact that regulatory pressures and drivers for corporate self-regulation on climate change can also come from subnational levels and sources, notably in countries with federalist systems where the state/provincial-level and city/local-level have substantial implementation and enforcement roles.

14. Seneviratne et al. 2012, Kennedy and Lindsey 2015; Hoegh-Guldberg et al. 2018.

15. As greenhouse gas emissions from human and industrial activities increase, they build up in the atmosphere and warm the climate, leading to many other changes in and destruction of the global commons.

16. Interviews HE5, HE6, and HE13. Oreskes 2004; Geist and Lambin 2004; Seneviratne et al. 2012; Pachauri et al. 2014; Diffenbaugh et al. 2021.

17. Kolstad et al. 2014; Kunreuther et al. 2014.

18. By contrast, the Paris Agreement is a bottom-up approach. In the accord's pledge and review negotiation structure, countries themselves determine how much emissions to cut nationally (Harstad 2023a).

19. See, e.g., Victor 2011; Hoffmann 2011; Hale et al. 2013; Nordhaus 2013.

20. In other words, an externality is an indirect cost or benefit to an uninvolved party that arises as an effect of another party's activity. There are negative and positive externalities. An example of a positive externality is the pollination of surrounding crops by bees kept for honey. By contrast, fracking, which pollutes drinking water sources, is a negative externality. In the context of climate change, GHG emissions that build up in the atmosphere and warm the climate are another prominent example of a negative externality.

21. Mas-Colell et al. (1995) provide a textbook proof of the Coase theorem showing the additional assumptions are needed: no income effects, perfect information, rationality, and no endowment effects. A more nuanced interpretation of the Coase theorem indicates that decentralized approaches involving private actors can happen once information provision helps to resolve transaction costs (Tietenberg 1998). Coasean bargaining alone is likely to efficiently resolve externality problems in a limited set of circumstances where the number of parties involved is small (Deryugina et al. 2021; Costello and Kotchen 2022). Nevertheless, Elinor Ostrom, a political scientist and the 2009 recipient of the Nobel Prize in Economics, documented dozens of well-functioning private arrangements in irrigation, fisheries, and forest use in a wide range of countries. These local communities are able to self-organize in ways that punish those who free ride on the common resource. Ostrom asserted that this was because of rules in place that clearly define who gets what, what the conflict resolution methods are, how to set up monitoring and punitive actions for nonadherence that involve users and/or a third party accountable to the users, and how to set and modify rules that involve common resource users themselves (Ostrom 1990, 2007b, 2009, 2010).

22. Tirole 2017, 209.

23. Harstad 2023b. In a companion paper, Harstad (2023a) shows that under different bargaining procedures, when free riding is accounted for and participation is voluntary, the Paris Agreement's pledge and review could in fact lead to a large sum of contributions in emission cuts, investments, and social welfare relative to the Kyoto Protocol.

24. Avant et al. 2010.

25. Cutler et al. 1999; Vogel 2005; Vandenbergh 2013; Vandenbergh and Gilligan 2017.

26. Avant et al. 2010, 2.

27. Kotchen 2013.

28. See Alberini and Segerson 2002; Prakash and Potoski 2006; Khanna et al. 2007, 2009; Morgenstern and Pizer 2007; Borck and Coglianese 2009; Hsueh and Prakash 2012; Hsueh 2020.

29. Arora and Gangopadhyay 1995; Bénabou and Tirole 2003, 2006; Besley and Ghatak 2005; Graff and Small 2005.

30. Buchanan 1965.

31. Grossman and Hart 1986; Bergstrom et al. 1986; Hart and Moore 1990; Besley and Ghatak 2001; Andreoni and Kanbur 2007; Schmitz 2015.

32. Besley and Ghatak 2007; Kitzmueller and Shimshack 2012.

33. Lyon and Maxwell (2004, xi) define corporate environmentalism as "environmental-friendly measures that are not required by law." As such, corporate environmentalism is akin to industry self-regulation in the environmental area.

34. Henriques and Sadorsky 1996; Maxwell et al. 2000; Feddersen and Gilligan 2001; Khanna and Anton 2002; Decker 2003; Lyon and Maxwell 2004, 2008; Innes 2006; Baron and Diermeier 2007; Shimshack and Ward 2008; Reid and Toffel 2009; Baron 2010; Kitzmueller and Shimshack 2012; Egorov and Harstad 2017.

35. Arora and Gangopadhyay 1995; Bénabou and Tirole 2003, 2006; Besley and Ghatak 2005; Graff and Small 2005.

36. Decker 2003; Doonan et al. 2005; Bandyopadhyay and Horowitz 2006; Delmas and Toffel 2008; Shimshack and Ward 2008; Lyon and Shimshack 2015; McDonnell and Werner 2016; Demirel et al. 2018. Other microlevel theories include a consumer market explanation, which argues that firms attempt to attract a clientele of "green consumers" willing to pay more for goods produced in an environmentally friendly way (see Arora and Gangopadhyay 1995). A producer market argument suggests firms may engage in self-regulation in order to spur tighter environmental standards that "raise rivals' costs" (see Innes and Bial 2002).

37. Baron 2001, 2009; Feddersen and Gilligan 2001; Lyon and Maxwell 2004, 2008, 2011; Innes 2006; Baron and Diermeier 2007; Kitzmueller and Shimshack 2012; Gupta and Innes 2014.

38. Decker 2003.

39. Meckling 2015.

40. Malhotra et al. 2019.

41. Kotchen and Segerson 2019; Malhotra et al. 2019.

42. Toffel and Short 2011.

43. Kolk and Pinkse 2007; Reid and Toffel 2009; Freedman and Jaggi 2011; Cotter and Najah 2012; Jira and Toffel 2013; Stanny 2013; Peters and Romi 2014; Ben-Amar and McIlkenny 2015; Liao et al. 2015; D'Amico et al. 2016; Delgado-Márquez et al. 2017; Ott et al. 2017; Ott et al. 2017; Li et al. 2018; Luo et al. 2018.

44. Stanny and Ely 2008; Kim and Lyon 2011; Matisoff 2012; Lee et al. 2015; Doda et al. 2016; Ben-Amar and Chelli 2018; Hassan and Romilly 2018; Jung et al. 2018; Lemma et al. 2019.

45. Aragòn-Correa et al. 2020.

46. Green 2010, 2013; Newell and Paterson 2010; Clapp and Dauvergne 2011; Hoffmann 2011; Bulkeley et al. 2014; Paterson et al. 2014; Hadden 2015; O'Neill 2017, 2019; Roger et al. 2017.

47. Ronit and Schneider 1999; Knill and Lehmkuhl 2002; Levy and Newell 2005; Avant et al. 2010; Weiss and Wilkinson 2014; Bartley 2018b.

48. Blok et al. 2012.

49. Cutler et al. 1999; Ronit and Schneider 1999; Cashore 2002; Eisner 2004; Newman and Bach 2004; Pattberg 2005; Bernstein and Cashore 2007; Auld et al. 2008; Vogel 2008; ; Buthe and Mattli 2011; Tsutsui and Lim 2015; Chan et al. 2018.

50. Vogel 1995, 2008, 2010; Garcia-Johnson 2000; Prakash and Potoski 2006; Bartley 2010; Dauvergne and Lister 2010; Perkins and Neumayer 2010.

51. Inter alia, Conconi and Perroni 2002; Barrett 2003, 2006, 2007; Eyckmans and Tulkens 2003; Finus et al. 2006; Stern 2007; Wiener 2007; Ostrom 2009; Stavins 2011; Bernauer 2013; Nordhaus 2015; Keohane and Victor 2016.

52. Aklin and Mildenberger 2020.

53. Colgan et al. 2021.

54. Hysing 2009; Bartley 2014, 2018a; Berliner and Prakash 2014a; Andonova et al. 2017; Roger et al. 2017.

55. Kollman and Prakash 2001; Koppell 2010; Buthe and Mattli 2011; Prakash and Potoski 2014; Andonova et al. 2017.

56. Green 2017.

57. Andonova et al. 2017.

58. Orts and Deketelaere 2001; Tosun et al. 2016.

59. Hsueh 2017.

60. Ostrom 2007b.

61. March 1962; Cyert and March 1992.

62. Appendices 1 and 2 provide details about the scope, data, and variables of the Global Sustainable Business and Climate Action Database. In this book, corporate environmental performance is measured by firms' entity-wide direct and indirect operational carbon emissions (i.e., scope 1 and scope 2 emissions) because of the lack of consistent and comparable indirect supply chain emissions (scope 3) data for entities that use or emit fossil fuels. Chapter 10 underscores the need for a universal protocol for measuring scope 3 emissions in emerging mandatory carbon disclosure rules around the globe.

63. CDP has been called "the most powerful green NGO you've never heard of" by the Harvard Business Review (Winston 2010).

64. "The A List 2023," CDP, accessed August 29, 2023, https://www.cdp.net/en/companies/companies-scores.

65. Elliott et al. 2023.

66. Outside the scope of this book, CDP also encourages voluntary disclosure of water usage and management and biodiversity impacts and deforestation risks by companies, cities, and governments worldwide. "Who We Are," CDP, accessed August 29, 2023, https://www.cdp.net/en/info/about-us.

67. Appendix 1 provides an explanation of the climate disclosure data from the CDP and the methods by which missing information has been separately collected for companies that did not voluntarily reported to the CDP.

68. Somini Sengupta, "An American Climate Failure," *New York Times*, July 15, 2022.

69. While outside the scope of this book, the US Inflation Reduction Act of 2022 is a landmark US federal law to curb inflation through reductions in the federal government budget deficit, lowering prescription drug prices, and investing in domestic energy production while promoting clean energy. Inflation Reduction Act of 2022, Pub. L. No. 117–169, 117 (2022). Stat. 1818.

70. In the absence of federal action, a majority of climate-related actions in the first two decades of the millennium occurred at the state and local levels in US states like California, and the Regional Greenhouse Gas Initiative states (namely, Connecticut, Delaware, Maine, Maryland, Massachusetts, New Hampshire, New Jersey, New York, Pennsylvania, Rhode Island, and Vermont) enacted ambitious GHG emission reduction regimes. According to Fowlie et al. (2014), cross-state coordination is key to cost-effective CO_2 reductions under the CPP. Chapter 7's analysis, which spotlights US-based global firms, includes state-fixed effects to control for heterogeneity across states with respect to climate-related polices.

71. Hsueh 2019c.

72. Ruggie 2017, 2018.

Chapter 2

1. "Green" behavior refers to reduced entity-wide carbon emissions and carbon emissions intensity in this book.

2. "Act globally. Engage locally." United Nations Global Compact, accessed June 25, 2023, https://unglobalcompact.org/engage-locally/about-local-networks.

3. "Fast-track your sustainability strategy and skills," United Nations Global Compact, accessed May 29, 2023, https://unglobalcompact.org/academy.

4. Examples of public and private cooperative initiatives include RE100, Climate Ambition Alliance, Business Ambition for 1.5° C, and We Mean Business Coalition.

5. "The world's largest corporate sustainability initiative," United Nations Global Compact, accessed May 12, 2022, https://www.unglobalcompact.org/what-is-gc.

6. Milton Friedman, "A Friedman Doctrine: The Social Responsibility of Business Is to Increase Its Profits," *New York Times*, September 13, 1970, https://www.nytimes.com/1970/09/13/archives/a-friedman-doctrine-the-social-responsibility-of-business-is-to.html.

7. According to Schwab (2021), "stakeholder capitalism is a form of capitalism in which companies seek long-term value creation by taking into account the needs of all their stakeholders, and society at large."

8. Fama 2021, 193, 194.

9. A 2019 statement by the Business Roundtable, a prominent US lobby made up of CEOs of leading US companies from Apple to Walmart, appeared to counter this view. One hundred eighty-one CEOs, representing nearly 30 percent of total US market capitalization, declared, "Each of our stakeholders is essential. We commit to deliver value to all of them, for the future success of our companies, our communities and our country." Corporations are, according to the statement, accountable to five constituencies, of which shareholders are only one (customers, employees, suppliers, and communities are the others). Business Roundtable, "Business Roundtable Redefines the Purpose of a Corporation to Promote 'An Economy That Serves All Americans,'" August 19, 2021, https://www.businessroundtable.org/business-roundtable-redefines-the-purpose-of-a-corporation-to-promote-an-economy-that-serves-all-americans.

10. Seneviratne et al. 2012; Hoegh-Guldberg et al. 2018; Dubash et al. 2022.

11. Elster 1989, 2009.

12. This definition reflects both the political science and sociology usage of norms. Political scientists have traditionally defined norms as "collective expectations for the proper behavior of actors with a given identity" (Katzenstein 1996, 5). By contrast, sociologists refer to norms as institutions and define them as a "relatively stable collection of practices and rules defining appropriate behavior for specific groups of actors in specific situations" (March and Olsen 1998, 948).

13. Finnemore and Sikkink 1998, 891.

14. This is in line with but a slight modification of Elster's (1989, 99) formulation, which states that norms range from a simple form of the type "Do X." or "Don't do X." to more complex forms, such as "If you do Y, then do X." or "Do X if it would be good if everyone did X."

15. Simon 1957.

16. Simon 1979, 1991; Bendor et al. 2009; Bendor 2010.

17. Prakash 2001.

18. Eccles and Taylor's (2023) interviews with chief sustainability officers (CSOs) and investors across diverse industries and countries find that CSOs are increasingly involved in investor meetings, notably in controversial carbon-intensive sectors that are viewed to have mismanaged their negative external impacts. According to the authors, managers have shifted from leading internal firm voluntary programs such as recycling and waste reduction to helping to articulate a company's strategy, capital allocation, or business model.

19. Nevertheless, what constitute best practices in management could vary across and within sectors and countries (e.g., see Bloom and Van Reenen 2007, 2010; Bloom et al. 2016; Scur et al. 2021).

20. A 2022 survey of fifty global sustainability leaders by a consulting company shows that businesses are 50 percent more likely to achieve organizational environmental, social, and governance (ESG) targets when their sustainability leader reports directly to a CEO than organizations with other reporting structures. "CSOs Have More Impact When They're Aligned to the CEO," Harvard Law School Forum on Corporate Governance, accessed September 13, 2022, https://corpgov.law.harvard.edu/2022/08/12/csos-have-more-impact-when-aligned-to-the-ceo/.

21. Van den Steen 2005, 2010.

22. Gartenberg et al. (2019) show empirically that firms with employees with strong beliefs in the purpose of their organization and clarity in the path toward that purpose experience higher future accounting and stock market performance, all else being equal. This may be because, as Henderson and Van den Steen (2015) contend, firms that adopt a corporate purpose—namely, the aggregate sense of meaning and impact felt by employees of a corporation—employ workers who accept lower wages when they derive identity and reputation benefits from working for the firm. In fact, Krueger et al. (2022) find that in Sweden, private sector workers earn close to 10 percent lower wages in firms that operate in more sustainable sectors. A "sustainable wage gap" arises because workers, especially those with higher skills and from younger cohorts, value environmental sustainability and accept lower wages to work in more environmentally sustainable firms and sectors.

23. Barnett 2017b.

24. Fligstein and McAdam 2012.

25. Sutton (2010) differentiates good and bad "bosses" and writes that the hallmark of a "great" boss is one that "stays in tune" with how their followers (and superiors, peers, and customers) react to what they say and do. The "best" bosses are aware that their success depends on having the self-awareness to control their moods and actions, to accurately interpret their impact on others, and to continuously adjust to incentivize effort, dignity, and pride among subordinates. By contrast, "bad" bosses possess poor social skills: notably, their ability to take the perspective of the "other" is wanting.

26. Goffman 1974; Barnett 2017a.

27. Rotemberg and Saloner 2000; Truelove et al. 2014.

28. Goffman 1974.

29. Public politics can be broader, rather than a narrowly defined piece of legislation or regulation: it can be about better policies that address the origin of the opposition, better policy design, and/or more incentives.

30. Meckling et al. 2015; Meckling 2015; Aklin and Mildenberger 2020; Colgan et al. 2021; Green et al. 2021.

31. Chapter 10 circles back to political lobbying by firms and discusses corporate political responsibility as an area of study for both academics and practitioners.

32. Fearon 1995, 1998a, 1998b.

33. In international relations theory, firm A would be replaced with country A and the government would be replaced with country B. The warring nations decide whether to bargain or not for a peaceful resolution, with the alternative being war.

34. Climate policies that are deemed the most cost-effective may in fact exhibit low political feasibility. This is because they impose high visible costs on powerful polluters to change emitting behavior in ways that minimize the total cost to the society as whole, but tend to concentrate on high emitters, while spreading the benefits of climate mitigation diffusely across society, leaving few supporters (Meckling and Karplus 2023).

35. Costello and Kotchen (2022) theorize that the government's policy instrument choice determines whether corporate self-regulation along with the centralized policy (which the authors call "Coasean provision," or Coasean bargaining, that occurs in the presence or shadow of centralized policy) produce a "first-best level of pollution" (i.e., the level of minimum pollution for a given level of economic development). Given uncertainty about the marginal benefits or costs of pollution, carbon taxes (as opposed to a cap on carbon emissions) provide an implicit subsidy to voluntary climate action, which helps to offset welfare losses from getting the policy "wrong" ex post facto.

Costello and Kotchen's theory shares a similar implication as the MGFCC, which is that self-regulation by firms is a complement to rather than a substitute for public politics.

36. Fearon 1995, 1998a, 1998b; Buthe and Mattli 2011; Mach et al. 2019; Malhotra et al. 2019.

37. That being said, in the aggregate a signal of commitment by firm A requires that other firms also signal their commitment to self-regulate, resulting in an aggregate commitment to self-regulation; otherwise, there is an incentive for firm A to engage in free riding and underperform. In this way, corporate self-regulation could be characterized as a global commons problem just like climate change.

38. Maxwell and Lyon (2011, 9) define greenwashing as the "selective disclosure of positive information about a company's environmental or social performance, without full disclosure of negative information on these dimensions, so as to create an overly positive corporate image."

39. Westphal and Zajac 1998; Ramus and Montiel 2005.

40. Meyer and Rowan 1977; Bromley and Powell 2012.

41. Delmas and Burano 2011; Lyon and Montgomery 2015.

42. One indicator that environmental issues and climate risks in particular have been accounted for and mainstreamed into business operations is the adoption of a science-based emissions target, which in turn serves as a driver of a firm's intensity of participation in the face of regulatory stringency. Global firms have increasingly adopted science-based, quantitative emissions targets, from 50 percent during the first half of the decade to greater than 75 percent of the Fortune Global 500 firms by the latter half of the decade (2015–2020).

43. Navarro 1988; Arora and Gangopadhyay 1995; Dasgupta et al. 2000; Graff and Small 2005.

44. Abbott and Snidal 2009; Alter and Meunier 2009; Abbott and Snidal 2010; Koppell 2010; Keohane and Victor 2011; Bulkeley et al. 2014; Eberlein et al. 2014; Hale and Roger 2014.

45. Green 2013, 2.

46. Finnemore 1993; Finnemore and Sikkink 1998; Avant et al. 2010; Overdevest and Zeitlin 2014; Abbott et al. 2016.

47. Thrall 2021.

48. Bendor 2010, 10.

49. May 1992.

50. Arrow 1962; Rosenberg and Nathan 1982; Fudenberg and Tirole 1983; Malerba 1992; Fagerberg 1995; Foster and Rosenzweig 1995; Matsuo and Schmidt 2019.

51. Cyert and March 1963; Fudenberg and Tirole 1983.

52. Sabatier 1988; Haas 1992; Gough and Shackley 2001; Dunlop 2009; Cross 2013; Jenkins-Smith et al. 2018.

53. Stone 2012.

54. Cyert and March 1992.

55. Levinthal and March 1993, 96.

56. Deutsch 1966; Bardach 1977; Elmore 1979; Bobrow and Dryzek 1987; Goggin et al. 1990; deLeon and deLeon 2002.

57. Dunlop 2010.

58. Global businesses also respond to regulatory pressures from countries where firms carry out their main activities or generate their largest sales. To address the ambiguity embedded in the term "originating," in the empirical analysis, regulatory stringency of a firm's country of origin is replaced with that of a firm's largest country export market. Anecdotal evidence from the *New York Times* indicated that multinational corporations based in China have responded to tougher trade restrictions placed on China by Western countries by relocating their headquarters and factories to the United States and Europe, where they generate large sales (see, for example, https://www.nytimes.com/2023/06/15/business/economy/china-business-tiktok-shein.html?searchResultPosition=2).

59. Baccaro and Mele 2011.

60. "Frequently Asked Questions," United Nations Global Compact, accessed November 14, 2023, https://unglobalcompact.org/about/faq.

Chapter 3

1. Parts of this chapter are based on the author's previously published article: Lily Hsueh (November 2019), "Opening Up the Firm: What Explains Participation and Effort in Voluntary Carbon Disclosure by Businesses? An Analysis of Internal Firm Factors and Dynamics," *Business Strategy and the Environment* 28 (7): 1302–1322, https://doi.org/10.1002/bse.2317.

2. Voluntary climate action is defined here as it is in Hsueh 2017, namely, a Fortune Global 500 firm's participation in at least one Global Climate Action–listed initiative. Global Climate Action (formerly NAZCA) is an online portal hosted by the United Nations Framework of Climate Change Conference (UNFCCC) to track firms' pledges of climate action.

3. Teece 1986.

4. Information about CDP's annual climate change questionnaire and the data sample frames used in this book are in appendix 1.

5. Winston 2010.

6. Maxwell et al. 2000; Lyon and Maxwell 2011; Bowen and Aragon-Correa 2014; Lyon and Montgomery 2015.

7. Esty and Lubin 2010.

8. A sizable empirical literature that spans voluntary environmental programs, corporate social performance and accounting, corporate finance, and organizational behavior and management strategy underscores corporate management's role (including the corporate board of directors) in increasing firms' participation in voluntary environmental programs and market-driven environmental performance ratings, such as the Dow Jones Sustainability Indices. See Rivera and De Leon 2005; Berthelot and Robert 2011; Strand 2013; Borghesi et al. 2014; Peters and Romi 2014; Ben-Amar and Mclkenny 2015; Liao et al. 2015.

9. Teece (1986, 285) was the first to introduce complementary assets' vital role in firms' innovative capability.

10. Christmann 2000.

11. Hart 1995; Sharma and Vredenburg 1998; Graff and Small 2005; Kotchen 2006; Eiadat et al. 2008; Chang 2011; Amores-Salvadó et al. 2014.

12. Darnall et al. 2008; Arimura et al. 2011.

13. McWilliams and Siegel 2001.

14. Matten and Moon 2005, 2008; Videaver-Cohen and Bronn 2013.

15. Porter and Kramer 2006.

16. Matten and Moon 2005; Moon and Knudsen 2018.

17. Matten and Moon 2005, 2008.

18. Waddock 2008; Scherer and Palazzo 2008; Eccles et al. 2014.

19. Peiró-Signes and Segarra-Oña 2013.

20. "Our Mission," United Nations Principles for Responsible Investment, accessed September 13, 2021, http://www.unpri.org/.

21. Interview O3. A data provider that has developed a market niche is MSCI. "About Us," MSCI, accessed September 13, 2022, https://www.msci.com/our-story.

22. Fisher-Vanden and Thorburn 2011; Gans and Hintermann 2013; Fatemi et al. 2015; Barbier and Burgess 2018; Borghesi et al. 2019; Vestrelli et al. 2024.

23. See appendix 3 for technical details about the double-hurdle model.

24. See Maxwell et al. 2000; Lyon and Maxwell 2011; Bowen and Aragon-Correa 2014; Lyon and Montgomery 2015.

25. After 2016, CDP restructured its carbon disclosure scoring system to rank firms based on letter grades rather than numerical scores. Chapter 7 uses CDP's letter grade system to link global firms' substantive level of voluntary carbon disclosure to their entity-wide carbon emissions and carbon emissions intensity.

26. Given the cross-sectional nature of the empirical analysis, data for all independent variables are from 2012, 2013, or 2014, all of which precede the dependent variables. The collection of the lagged data and the sequencing of the dependent and independent variables (e.g., a firm's participation in voluntary carbon disclosure occurred after the installation of sustainability officers) are intentional, the purpose of which is to mitigate potential concerns about the direction of impact between the dependent and independent variables.

27. In subsequent chapters, "policy supporter—upper management" is referred to as "manager" since the rest of the book is focused on the role of senior- and executive-level managers and their interactions with regulatory and global governance, respectively.

28. Data on this chapter's various measures of policy supporters have been collected and coded for the entire set of Fortune Global 500 firms, which include firms that did not respond to the CDP's climate change information request. Independent sources are corporate websites and sustainability or CSR reports. To the best of the author's knowledge, CDP does not differentiate among these different levels of environmental champions inside the firm.

29. Global firms that emphasize sustainable economic growth rather than a sustainable environment are excluded from this measure.

30. Borghesi et al. 2014; Gillan et al. 2021.

31. Arora and Cason 1996; Henriques and Sadorsky 1996; DeCanio and Watkins 1998; Videras and Alberini 2000; Khanna et al. 2007; Stanny and Ely 2008.

32. Aerts et al. 2008 ; Luo et al. 2012; Guenther et al. 2015.

33. Darnall and Edwards 2006.

34. Arora and Cason 1996.

35. Cho and Patten 2007; Kolk and Pinkse 2008; Haigh and Griffiths 2012; Hsueh and Prakash 2012; Kotchen and Moon 2012; Luo et al. 2012.

36. Additional evidence is marshalled for the important role of policy supporters in upper management for corporate self-regulation on climate change by the fact that when there are only lower-level policy supporters in the firm [see (3) in table A3.3 in appendix 3], companies are not compelled to participate in voluntary carbon disclosure or increase their effort if they do participate.

37. See appendix 1 for information about the CDP administrative fee that companies pay in order to disclose through CDP.

38. Lyon and Maxwell 2011.

39. Avant et al. 2010.

40. Hassan and Romilly 2018.

Chapter 4

1. This chapter draws from and extends the author's published article: Lily Hsueh, 2019. "Corporations at a Crossroads: How Multilevel Governance Interactions Shape Participation and Effort in Private Governance Regimes," *Governance* 32 (4): 715–760.

2. The models employed in this chapter represent an alternative modeling approach from the previous and subsequent chapters in order to, together, demonstrate the robustness of the book's empirical evidence for the book's multilevel governance framework on climate change.

3. Henriques and Sadorsky 1996; Maxwell et al. 2000; Baron 2001; Feddersen and Gilligan 2001; Khanna and Anton 2002; Decker 2003; Lyon and Maxwell 2004, 2008; Innes 2006; Baron and Diermeier 2007; Shimshack and Ward 2008; Kitzmueller and Shimshack 2012.

4. Berliner and Prakash 2012, 2014b, 2015.

5. Chapter 6 delves into a mechanism of learning and norming by global firms to explicate the complementary interplay between domestic and global governance in advancing voluntary climate action. By contrast, this chapter examines the interaction between managerial agency and global governance as a driver of firms' decision to self-regulate with respect to climate mitigation.

6. See table A2.1 in appendix 2 for the CDP climate change questionnaire questions that the *manager* and *target* variables are based on.

7. Lerner and Osgood (2023) argue and show that corporate board of directors' active engagement on climate issues, including climate innovations, could be influenced by other companies through shared board members in common. The learning, socialization, and competitive dynamics vis-à-vis company boards that the authors describe is captured in the *manager* variable but not separately identified in this book's empirical analyses.

8. Zielinski n.d.

9. See, for example, Andonova et al. (2017) and Prakash and Potoski (2014).

10. Mitchell 2018.

11. "About the EPI," Yale University, accessed March 28, 2023, https://epi.yale.edu/about-epi.

12. Yale University 2018.

13. ISO 14001, published by the International Organization for Standards, obligates firms to establish environmental management systems and to be certified by third-party certification bodies for meeting standard requirements.

14. Betsill and Bulkeley 2004; Selin and VanDeveer 2009; Dolšak and Prakash 2016.

15. Harrison and Sundstrom 2010; Folke 2014; Finnegan 2023; Guy et al. 2023; Meckling and Karplus 2023.

16. Berliner and Prakash 2014a; Andonova et al. 2017; Dolšak and Prakash 2016; Moon and Kundsen 2018.

17. Prakash and Potoski 2007b.

18. Hetig 2018.

19. Andonova et al. 2017; Dolšak and Prakash 2016.

20. *Target* and *manager* have been dropped from both the participation and intensity of participation equations of the Heckman selection model due to multicollinearity. Collinearity diagnostics based on the inclusion of these variables, along with the interaction terms, show that the variance inflation factor scores were above generally accepted boundaries.

21. *UNGC member* has also been dropped from the participation and intensity of participation equations due to multicollinearity.

22. This is a predicted probability of voluntary carbon disclosure with estimated covariates entering into the fitted models at their mean values.

23. Pretty and Ward 2001; Andonova et al. 2017; Green 2017; Roger et al. 2017.

24. To acknowledge that the regulations (and other characteristics) of the country in which a firm is most active with respect to business operations could be just as or more salient than a firm's country of origin, this chapter includes an alternative specification in which a firm's country of origin is replaced with its export country of largest sales (see table A4.8 in appendix 4). The chapter's main results are robust to this alternative specification.

Chapter 5

1. This chapter draws from and extends the author's published article: Lily Hsueh, "Voluntary Climate Action and Credible Regulatory Threat: Evidence from the Carbon Disclosure Project," *Journal of Regulatory Economics* 56, no. 2–3 (2019): 188–225.

2. The study period is 2011–2015, which was before President Donald Trump's first term and subsequent policy reversal.

3. The global commons, also known as common resources, are nonexcludable and rival in consumption: it is very costly and nearly impossible to exclude potential users. Since individuals or groups cannot be excluded from enjoying or consuming these goods, each has an incentive to overuse the commons. Ultimately, global commons face problems of congestion, overuse, or degradation because more consumption by one person or group means less is available for everyone else.

4. "What Is the Kyoto Protocol?" United Nations Climate Change, accessed November 27, 2023, https://unfccc.int/kyoto_protocol.

5. See Cohen and Viscusi 2012; Bransteller and Pizer 2013; Meckling and Nahm 2018; Stokes and Breetz 2020.

6. Lyon and Maxwell 2004; Morgenstern and Pizer 2007; Cohen and Viscusi 2012; Hsueh 2020.

7. Rabe 2007, 2010.

8. Meng 2017.

9. In the absence of federal action, the majority of climate-related actions occurred at the state and local levels in US states like California, and the Regional Greenhouse Gas Initiative states (namely, Connecticut, Delaware, Maine, Maryland, Massachusetts, New Hampshire, New Jersey, New York, Pennsylvania, Rhode Island, and Vermont) enacted ambitious GHG emissions reduction regimes. According to Fowlie et al. (2014), cross-state coordination is key to cost-effective CO_2 reductions under the CPP. Chapter 7's analysis, which focuses exclusively on US-based global firms, includes state fixed effects to control for heterogeneity across states with respect to climate-related polices.

10. Meng 2017.

11. Meckling and Nahm 2018.

12. Massachusetts v. EPA, 549 U.S. 497 (2007).

13. US EPA 2009.

14. Kotchen and Mansur 2014.

15. Potential caveats, however, are questions about the CPP's stringency and efficacy. According to Kotchen and Mansur's (2014) analysis, more than 90 percent of the constructed natural gas CCGT, or combined-cycle gas turbine, units during that period already complied with the proposed emission standard for new power plants.

16. Legal challenges and a new Trump administration kept the CPP from ever taking effect. See Adler 2016; US EPA 2018; and Greshko et al. 2018. Nevertheless, there was little reason to expect a different regulatory world than the one that was emerging in the early to mid-2010s.

17. United Nations Framework Convention on Climate Change, "U.S, China Climate Moves Boost Paris Prospects," November 12, 2014, https://unfccc.int/news/us-china-climate-moves-boost-paris-prospects.

18. See table A5.1 in appendix 5 for a parallel trends test for the CPP's validity as a plausible exogenous policy shock.

19. Maddala 1983.

20. A Fisher-type panel unit root test (Choi 2001) has been conducted on the carbon disclosure score for US firms and non-US firms to confirm that the OLS DD estimator and the nested DD and DDD estimators in the EBV models do not lead to spurious results in the regression analysis.

21. The UNFCC's Global Climate Action database partners with CDP as its primary source of carbon management data.

22. All calculations of the marginal impacts of participation follow the standard approach in the empirical literature. The indicator variables (*CPP* and *USA* in this case) are set to 1, and all other variables are held at their mean, and the standard normal distribution is utilized.

23. From model 3 (level of voluntary carbon disclosure), estimated coefficients for *manager* and *CPP×manager* have been summed (5.135+9.103) to obtain 14.238.

24. This is based on the author's calculations from sales data from Mint Global.

25. Appendix 1 describes the administrative fees that global firms paid to participate in the CDP program during 2011–2020. Firms' substantive climate mitigation can be, albeit not always, reflected in their higher carbon disclosure scores. To earn higher scores, firms need to disclose not only information about their carbon management but also their climate risks, global scope 1 and 2 emissions, third-party verification of GHG emissions, and sources of uncertainty in data gathering and calculations (CDP 2017).

Chapter 6

1. Fudenberg and Tirole 1983; Malerba 1992; Lamoreaux et al. 1999.

2. "Schumpeterian" here refers to a fundamental change that is an outcome of a process of "creative destruction," as popularized by the Austrian economist Joseph Schumpeter.

3. Kingdon 1995; Birkland 1997, 1998.

4. While the majority of firms are unlikely to be involved in a Schumpeterian-style generation of new ideas in their interactions with global governance institutions, international organizations' "creative learning" (Allan and Meckling 2021) process could

very well involve firms. For example, the UN Global Compact's Think Labs "convene leading businesses, academia, civil society, and the United Nations to develop solutions to critical corporate sustainability challenges. They help to define our thinking, curate best practices and develop knowledge, guidance and tools that empower business sector on urgent topics." That being said, less than 1 percent of more than 9,000 corporate members of the UNGC are invited to "shape future thinking . . . [and] deliver thought leadership content including new frameworks . . . [and] innovate around new themes and topics." "Think Labs," United Nations Global Compact, accessed November 17, 2023, https://www.unglobalcompact.org/take-action/think-labs.

5. May 1992.

6. Morrison et al. 2008.

7. Arrow 1962; Rosenberg and Nathan 1982; Fudenberg and Tirole 1983; Malerba 1992; Fagerberg 1995; Foster and Rosenzweig 1995; Matsuo and Schmidt 2019.

8. Sabatier 1988; Haas 1992; Gough and Shackley 2001; Dunlop 2009; Cross 2013; Jenkins-Smith et al. 2018.

9. Stone 2012.

10. Levinthal and March 1993.

11. Deutsch 1966; Bardach 1977; Elmore 1979; Bobrow and Dryzek 1987; Goggin et al. 1990; May 1992; deLeon and deLeon 2002.

12. Dunlop 2010.

13. Ruggie 2017.

14. "We Are Driving Change Across All Aspects of Corporate Sustainability," United Nations Global Compact, accessed November 20, 2023, https://www.unglobalcompact.org/what-is-gc/our-work/.

15. UNGC n.d.b, 8.

16. UNGC 2018, 6.

17. "Fast Track Your Sustainability Strategy and Skills," United Nations Global Compact, accessed November 20, 2023, https://www.unglobalcompact.org/academy.

18. "A Local Lens for Global Change," United Nations Global Compact, accessed November 20, 2023, https://www.unglobalcompact.org/engage-locally.

19. For example, Network USA permits subsidiary participation for companies with headquarters outside the US but have significant staff and/or operations within the US or companies that are 100 percent owned by another participating company. "Participation for Subsidiary Companies," Global Compact Network USA, accessed November 20, 2023, https://www.globalcompactusa.org/join/subsidiary-companies.

20. "Act globally. Engage locally," United Nations Global Compact, accessed November 20, 2023, https://unglobalcompact.org/engage-locally/about-local-networks.

21. Interviews HE2 and HE4. The UN Compact Young SDG Innovators are young professionals selected through a competitive process to participate in an "accelerator programme" and to "collaborate and accelerate innovation toward the Sustainable Development Goals (SDGs) . . . and to develop and drive innovative solutions through new technologies, initiatives, and business models and deliver on their company's sustainability objectives." The Young SDG Innovators Programme operates out of and by the Local Networks. There are Young SDG Innovators based in Brazil, China, Kenya, Mexico, South Africa, Ukraine, the United Kingdom, and the United States. "SDG Innovation Accelerator for Young Professionals," UN Global Compact, accessed November 20, 2023, https://unglobalcompact.org/sdgs/young-sdg-innovators.

22. Interview GG1. The author was an observer at this lunch learning forum, which took place on February 5, 2020, during Network USA's Young SDG Innovators' Third Workshop at Arizona State University's Thunderbird School of Management. ASU Thunderbird has been an academic partner for Global Compact Network USA since 2019.

23. "Events," Global Compact Network USA, accessed November 20, 2023, https://www.globalcompactusa.org/events.

24. "SEC Climate Disclosure: How Investors Can Get Involved," accessed September 27, 2020, https://globalcompactusa.org/events-and-webinars/sec-climate-disclosure-how-investors-can-get-involved.

25. UNGC 2018, 25.

26. UNGC n.d.a.

27. "UN Global Compact Academy: Hear from Our Learners," United Nations Global Compact, accessed November 22, 2023, https://www.youtube.com/watch?v=_yu3P6ymqaM.

28. Interview O2.

29. "The Ambition Loop," accessed May 4, 2020, https://www.unglobalcompact.org/take-action/events/1688-the-ambition-loop.

30. This chapter does not differentiate between the three standard forms of internal carbon prices: an internal carbon fee, a shadow price, or an implicit price. A carbon fee is a monetary value on each ton of carbon emission. A shadow price is a theoretical price that primarily supports long-term business planning and investment strategies. An implicit price is how much a company spends to reduce existing emissions or the cost of complying with government regulation. "Internal Carbon Pricing," Center for Climate and Energy Solutions, accessed December 6, 2023, https://www.c2es.org/content/internal-carbon-pricing/.

31. Hsueh 2017, 2019a, 2019b; Prakash 2000, 2001.

32. *UNGC member* on its own has been dropped from model 2 because of multicollinearity. Collinearity diagnostics based on the inclusion of *UNGC member*, along with the interaction terms, show that the variance inflation factor scores were above generally accepted boundaries.

33. An odds ratio allows the comparison of the group of interest—which in this chapter would be firms that participate in the UNGC—with that of firms that do not participate in the global governance institution. If the outcome is the same in both groups, the ratio will be 1, which implies there is no difference between participants and nonparticipants.

34. See Aklin and Mildenberger 2020 and Hale 2020.

35. Purdon 2015, 2.

Chapter 7

1. Kim and Lyon 2011b.

2. Matisoff 2012, 2013.

3. By contrast, Delmas et al. (2010) assess the impact of mandatory carbon disclosure on major investor-owned electric utility firms' percentage of power generation attributable to clean fuels. The authors found that state-mandated information disclosure programs had a statistically and economically significant negative impact on the proportion of fossil fuels, whereas the proportion of clean fuels increased in response to mandatory disclosure programs. A recent study of the UK's 2013 disclosure mandate for UK-listed firms found that companies reduced their operational emissions by about 8 percent relative to a control group, with no significant changes to their profitability (Downar et al. 2021).

4. In the accounting literature a cross-sectional study by Luo and Tang (2014) answers a reverse question: the authors ask whether low-carbon-intensity-emissions firms (i.e., higher performers) disclose more to the CDP. The authors' findings show a significant positive association between carbon disclosure and performance. In other words, good performers are more forthright in their carbon disclosures. This chapter's findings do not contradict Luo and Tan's study, because high performers have the incentive to signal their high performance to distinguish themselves for investors and other stakeholders. What this chapter shows, however, is that by and large, when selection bias and other sources of endogeneity, such as reverse causation (i.e., higher performers disclose at higher levels) are accounted for, on average, firms that have received a B grade from CDP did not reduce entity-wide carbon emissions during 2011–2020.

5. Klassen and McLaughlin 1996; Khanna and Damon 1999; Fisher-Vanden and Thorburn 2011; Kim and Lyon 2011a; Oberndorfer et al. 2013; Lyon and Shimshack 2015; Wang et al. 2019.

6. Kim and Lyon 2011a; Lyon and Shimshack 2015.

7. Wang et al. 2019.

8. Lyon and Maxwell 2008, 2011; Tell 2013; Lyon and Montgomery 2015; Dahm et al. 2018.

9. Henriques and Sadorsky 1996; Maxwell et al. 2000; Khanna and Anton 2002; Lyon and Maxwell 2004.

10. Prakash 2001; Henderson and Van den Steen 2015; Hsueh 2019a.

11. Notably, Malhotra et al. (2019) found in their field experiments with voters, activists, and government officials that their demand for draconian environmental regulations lessened when firms participated in voluntary environmental programs.

12. Van den Steen 2005; Henderson and Van den Steen 2015; Barnett 2017; Henderson 2020; Henderson and Serafeim 2020.

13. Power plants are the largest source of global warming pollutants in the United States, accounting for more than a quarter of all domestic greenhouse gas emissions in 2022. See "GHGRP Power Plants," United States Environmental Protection Agency, accessed October 10, 2023, https://www.epa.gov/ghgreporting/ghgrp-power-plants.

14. CDP 2016a, 2017.

15. For example, there were seven companies that disclosed their carbon emissions to the CDP in 2014 but not in 2015.

16. Kotchen and Moon 2012; Haigh and Griffiths 2012; Kolk and Pinkse 2012; Kolk and Pinske 2008.

17. Guy et al. 2023.

18. Lyon and Maxwell 2011.

19. Aldy and Pizer 2015.

20. "Ambitious Corporate Climate Action," Science Based Targets, accessed November 9, 2023, https://sciencebasedtargets.org/; "ISO 14001: 2015 Environmental Management Systems," ISO, accessed November 9, 2023, https://www.iso.org/standard/60857.html.

21. CDP 2016c.

22. In this chapter and book, the term "transparency" is used to represent firms' carbon transparency irrespective of the substantive contents of their disclosures. This is different from CDP's official designation of "disclosure" as the lowest disclosure level in its grading system.

23. CDP 2016b, 8.

24. CDP 2016b, 9.

25. CDP 2016b, 9.

26. CDP 2016b.

27. "The A List 2023," CDP, accessed October 11, 2023, https://www.cdp.net/en/companies/companies-scores.

28. There are 7 B- as opposed to 556 B company×year observations, 5 C- as opposed to 492 C company×year observations, and 7 D- as opposed to 345 D company×year observations. Only in the A category was the A- subcategory potentially nonnegligible; there are 136 A- as opposed to 162 company×year observations. As such, in the empirical analysis there is a trade-off between a little less precision in favor of greater statistical power. Nevertheless, an alternative specification differentiates between A and A- disclosers, which does not change the chapter's empirical results (see appendix 7).

29. Keyes et al. 2019.

30. For example, an alternative specification of the EBV model controls for time variant, sector-specific market structure, and competitive pressures from rival firms in the same sector; these dynamics could be interpreted as learning, diffusion, and peer effects, respectively.

31. CDP 2016b, 2019.

32. The qualitative results and their statistical significance do not change when the technology sector (i.e., information technology and telecommunications) is included as part of the consumer-oriented sectors. See appendix 7.

33. "CDP Scores," CDP, accessed March 4, 2021, https://www.cdp.net/en/scores.

34. Elfenbein et al. 2019; Farrell and Rabin 1996.

35. Sweeney 2016.

36. "Climate Change and President Barack Obama's Action Plan," The White House, https://obamawhitehouse.archives.gov/president-obama-climate-action-plan.

37. Hsueh 2019b.

38. Climate scientists have warned that while reduced carbon emissions intensities are laudable and necessary, what is just as important is reduction in aggregate carbon emissions. See Sonia Seneviratne, "Climate Extremes in a Warming Climate: Why Every Year Matters," Stanford University, May 16, 2023, https://events.stanford.edu/event/environmental_forum_climate_extremes_in_a_warming_climate_why_every_year_matters.

39. "Pepco Advances Climate Action in DC: New Initiative Provides Model for Action by Local Electricity Distribution Companies," National Resources Defense Council, accessed November 9, 2023, https://www.nrdc.org/bio/ben-longstreth/pepco-advances-climate-action-dc.

40. Natasha Bernal, "Google, Microsoft and the Strange World of Corporate Greenwashing," *Wired UK*, January 31, 2020, https://www.wired.co.uk/article/corporate-greenwashing.

41. Sergio Chapa, "Schlumberger, Chevron, and Microsoft Launch Artificial Intelligence Platform for Oil Field," *Houston Chronicle*, September 17, 2019, https://www.chron.com/business/energy/article/Schlumberger-Chevron-and-Microsoft-launch-14445539.php.

42. "The Higg Index Tools," Sustainable Apparel Coalition, accessed November 9, 2023, https://apparelcoalition.org/the-higg-index/.

43. Hiroko Tabuchi, "How Fashion Giants Recast Plastic as Good for the Planet," *New York Times*, June 12, 2022, https://www.nytimes.com/2022/06/12/climate/vegan-leather-synthetics-fashion-industry.html.

44. "Eco-Friendly and Green Marketing Claims," Federal Trade Commission, accessed November 9, 2023, https://consumer.ftc.gov/articles/eco-friendly-green-marketing-claims; Lesley Fair, "$5.5 Million Total FTC Settlements with Kohl's and Walmart Challenge "Bamboo" and Eco Claims, Shed Light on Penalty Offense Enforcement," Business Blog, Federal Trade Commission, April 8, 2022, https://www.ftc.gov/business-guidance/blog/2022/04/55-million-total-ftc-settlements-kohls-and-walmart-challenge-bamboo-and-eco-claims-shed-light.

45. Daniel Graeber, "Big Oil's Generosity and the Cloak of Social Responsibility," Oilprice.com, February 22, 2012, https://oilprice.com/Energy/Energy-General/Big-Oils-Generosity-and-the-Cloak-of-Social-Responsibility.html; Javier E. David, "Shell Tries to Spin Oil into a Green (as in the Environment) Future," CNBC, September 7, 2014, https://www.cnbc.com/2014/09/05/shell-tries-to-spin-oil-into-a-green-as-in-the-environment-future.html; Paul Barret and Ben Elgin, "Inside Shell's Extreme Plan to Drill for Oil in the Arctic," *Bloomberg*, August 5, 2015, https://www.bloomberg.com/news/features/2015-08-05/inside-shell-s-extreme-plan-to-drill-for-oil-in-the-arctic.

46. Cohen and Viscusi 2012.

47. Potoski and Prakash 2005; Lyon and Maxwell 2011; Bowen and Aragon-Correa 2014; Kim and Lyon 2014.

48. Nives Dolsak and Aseem Prakash, "Amazon Pledges $2 Billion Climate Fund, As Its Carbon Emissions Grow," *Forbes*, June 24, 2020, https://www.forbes.com/sites/prakashdolsak/2020/06/24/amazons-2019-sustainability-report-some-progress-but-critical-challenges-remain/#18b07d796254; Nives Dolsak and Aseem Prakash,

"Unilever's Climate Plan: Emissions from Supply Chain and Consumers Are the Real Challenge," *Forbes*, June 18, 2020, https://www.forbes.com/sites/prakashdolsak/2020/06/18/unilevers-climate-plan-emissions-from-supply-chain-and-consumers-are-the-real-challenge/?sh=4145e0101fba.

49. Interviews G2, GF11, and GF12. Disclosure rules about third-party audits in an adjacent policy area, such as hedge fund oversight, has been shown to minimize misreporting and lead organizations to alter their internal governance, thus strengthening the quality of reporting (Honigsberg 2019).

50. Huang 2024.

51. Vogel 2005; Lyon et al. 2018.

Chapter 8

1. Mecking 2015; Colgan et al. 2021.

2. Arora and Cason 1996.

3. Cho and Patten 2007; Kolk and Pinkse 2008; Kotchen and Moon 2012.

4. Lenox and Chatterji 2018; Lenox and Duff 2021.

5. Global firms refer to either the world's largest firms by revenue that were part of the Fortune Global 500 or those listed in the S&P 500 index at least once from 2011 to 2015.

6. Consumer-oriented firms include consumer discretionary, consumer staples, financial services, and health care sectors. Technology firms comprise information technology and telecommunications sectors.

7. Appendix 9 provides a rationale for this book's illustrative company case selection and information about semistructured interviews with senior and executive leaders in corporate sustainability. The names of several interviewees quoted in this book are withheld by request and mutual agreement.

8. Interviews GF2, GF3, GF4, GF10, GF11, GF12, GF14, GF16, and GF20.

9. "Actor Tracking," Global Climate Action Portal, accessed July 31, 2023, https://climateaction.unfccc.int/Actors.

10. Renckens 2020a.

11. Falkner 2016; Harstad 2023a.

12. David G. Victor and Parker Bolstad, "Good News about Global Warming: The Public's Paying Attention," Brookings Institution, February 10, 2023, https://www.brookings.edu/articles/good-news-about-global-warming-the-publics-paying-attention/.

13. Technical details on the quasi-experiments and the endogenous binary-variable model are given in appendix 5.

14. "Higg Index Tools," Sustainable Apparel Coalition, accessed July 28, 2023, https://apparelcoalition.org/the-higg-index/.

15. Interview O1. Hiroko Tabuchi, "How Fashion Giants Recast Plastic as Good for the Planet," *New York Times*, accessed June 12, 2022, https://www.nytimes.com/2022/06/12/climate/vegan-leather-synthetics-fashion-industry.html?searchResultPosition=1.

16. Lesley Fair, "5.5 Million Total FTC Settlements with Kohl's and Walmart Challenge 'Bamboo' and Eco Claims, Shed Light on Penalty Offense enforcement," Business Blog, US Federal Trade Commission, April 8, 2022, https://www.ftc.gov/business-guidance/blog/2022/04/55-million-total-ftc-settlements-kohls-and-walmart-challenge-bamboo-and-eco-claims-shed-light.

17. "Rayon Manufacturing Process," accessed July 28, 2023, https://idoc.pub/documents/rayon-manufacturing-processpdf-19n0r6ozpknv.

18. "Federal Trade Commission Act," US Federal Trade Commission, accessed December 22, 2023, https://www.ftc.gov/legal-library/browse/statutes/federal-trade-commission-act; "The Textile Products Identification Act," US Federal Trade Commission, accessed December 22, 2023, https://www.ftc.gov/legal-library/browse/rules/textile-products-identification-act-text.

19. Johannes Wassenberg (former head of operations, ESG, and managing director in Moody's London office) in discussion with the author, January 20, 2021 (interview GF16).

20. Johannes Wassenberg (interview GF16).

21. Moody's, "Moody's Acquires Majority Stake in Vigeo Eiris, a Global Leader in ESG Assessments," April 15, 2019, https://ir.moodys.com/press-releases/news-details/2019/Moodys-Acquires-Majority-Stake-in-Vigeo-Eiris-a-Global-Leader-in-ESG-Assessments/default.aspx; Moody's, "Moody's Acquires Majority Stake in Four Twenty Seven, Inc., a Leader in Climate Data and Risk Analysis," July 24, 2019, https://www.businesswire.com/news/home/20190724005169/en/Moody%E2%80%99s-Acquires-Majority-Stake-in-Four-Twenty-Seven-Inc.-a-Leader-in-Climate-Data-and-Risk-Analysis.

22. Johannes Wassenberg (interview GF16). By year-end 2024, Moody's has ceased its in-house ESG activities and entered into a strategic partnership agreement with MSCI, to obtain their ESG input from MSCI (save for Moody's Ratings, which continues its ESG work insofar as it is relevant for credit ratings). According to Moody's CEO Rob Fauber, this is a business imperative and a "real win-win, as Moody's customers gain access to MSCI's renowned ESG content and MSCI customers will gain access to

Moody's world-class risk assessment expertise, data and insights." See https://ir.moodys.com/press-releases/news-details/2024/Moodys-and-MSCI-Announce-a-Strategic-Partnership-to-Enhance-Transparency-and-Deliver-Data-Driven-Risk-Solutions/default.aspx.

23. Moody's Investors Service, "Rating Action: Moody's Downgrades Alpha Natural Resources' CFR to B1 from Ba2, Outlook Stable," June 27, 2012, https://www.moodys.com/research/Moodys-downgrades-Alpha-Natural-Resources-CFR-to-B1-from-Ba2-Rating-Action—PR_249284 (registration required).

24. Johannes Wassenberg (interview GF16).

25. Johannes Wassenberg (interview GF16).

26. Johannes Wassenberg (interview GF16).

27. Interviews GF15 and GF17; S&P Global, "Environmental, Social, And Governance Evaluation: Adidas AG," November 4, 2021, https://www.spglobal.com/esg/scores/documents/170654890.pdf.

28. For example, RobecoSAM, a global investment group focused on sustainable investing, awarded Adidas as industry best in "environmental policy and management systems" and "eco-efficiency."

29. Adidas ranked first for its ESG score out of 110 global businesses from 22 countries in the textile and apparel industry group. See "LSEG Peer Analysis," LSEG Data & Analytics, accessed June 15, 2023, https://www.lseg.com/en/data-analytics/financial-data/analytics/lseg-analytics.

30. Interview with a senior-level director at Adidas' Green Company, February 2, 2021 (interview GF17).

31. Interview GF17.

32. Interview GF17.

33. Adidas Group, "Sustainability Reports," https://www.adidas-group.com/en/sustainability/transparency/reporting/sustainability-reports?tag=2015; Adidas Group, "Annual Report 2020," March 10, 2021, https://report.adidas-group.com/2020/en/.

34. Adidas Group, "Adidas Group Joins UN Climate Neutral Now Initiative," September 22, 2015, https://www.adidas-group.com/en/media/press-releases/adidas-group-joins-un-climate-neutral-now-initiative.

35. Adidas Group, "Green Company Reports," https://www.adidas-group.com/en/sustainability/transparency/reporting/green-company-reports?tag=2019.

36. Interview GF17.

37. "LSEG ESG Peer Analysis," LSEG Data & Analytics, accessed June 15, 2023, https://www.lseg.com/en/data-analytics/financial-data/analytics/lseg-analytics.

38. "Actor Tracking: Adidas AG," Global Climate Action Portal, accessed December 17, 2024, https://climateaction.unfccc.int/Actors/Companies/GCAP3126.

39. "Our Mission," Adidas AG, accessed December 17, 2024, https://www.adidas.com/us/go/campaign/impact/planet.

40. Interview GF17.

41. Interview GF17.

42. Natalie Schwertheim, "Colombia Launches National Plastics Pact Targeting 50% Recycling Rate," Packaging Insights, February 27, 2023, https://www.packaginginsights.com/news/colombia-launches-national-plastics-pact-targeting-50-recycling-rate.html.

43. Interview GF17.

44. Hsueh 2015.

45. Hsueh 2017.

46. Dating back to 2002, the ESG performance scores cover 85 percent of the global market cap, across more than 630 different ESG metrics covering 10 main categories, including emissions, environmental product innovation, human rights, and shareholders. See https://www.lseg.com/en/data-analytics/sustainable-finance/esg-scores.

47. Race to Zero is an UN-based global campaign rallying non-state actors across the global economy to take rigorous and immediate action to halve global emissions by 2030. See https://climatechampions.unfccc.int.

48. Led by the governments of the United Kingdom and Chile, with support from the United Nations, the Climate Ambition Alliance brings together countries, businesses, investors, cities, and regions "to enhance collaboration in the achievement of net-zero CO_2 emissions by 2050." See https://climateaction.unfccc.int/Initiatives?id=Climate_Ambition_Alliance.

49. Business Ambition for 1.5°C is an international cooperative climate initiative of the "world's largest and fastest-growing group of companies taking urgent action." See https://climateaction.unfccc.int/Initiatives?id=Business_Ambition_for_1.5%C2%B0C.

50. Elizabeth Willmott, "How Microsoft Is Using an Internal Carbon Fee to Reach Its Carbon Negative Goal," *Microsoft Sustainability Blog*, March 24, 2022, https://www.microsoft.com/en-us/industry/blog/sustainability/2022/03/24/how-microsoft-is-using-an-internal-carbon-fee-to-reach-its-carbon-negative-goal/.

51. Natasha Bernal, "Google, Microsoft and the Strange World of Corporate Greenwashing," *Wired UK*, January 31, 2020, https://www.wired.co.uk/article/corporate-greenwashing.

52. Sergio Chapa, "Schlumberger, Chevron and Microsoft Launch Artificial Intelligence Platform for Oil Field," Houston Chronicle, September 17, 2019, https://www.chron.com/business/energy/article/Schlumberger-Chevron-and-Microsoft-launch-14445539.php.

53. "About Green Power Partnership," US Environmental Protection Agency, accessed August 9, 2023, https://www.epa.gov/greenpower/about-green-power-partnership.

54. "Actor Tracking: Microsoft Corporation," Global Climate Action Portal, accessed August 1, 2023, https://climateaction.unfccc.int/Actors/Companies/GCAP1778.

55. Stanford Precourt Institute for Energy, "Global Energy Dialogues: Corporate Sustainability: Going Far Beyond Advocacy," YouTube, October 28, 2020, https://www.youtube.com/watch?v=nb-0KT_8-5k.

56. "Emissions Impact Dashboard," Microsoft, accessed August 2, 2023, https://www.microsoft.com/en-us/sustainability/emissions-impact-dashboard.

57. Along with Microsoft, TONZ's founding firms include Danone, GSK, HSBC, Maersk, Mercedes-Benz, Natura & Co., Nike, Inc., Ørsted, Starbucks, Unilever, and Wipro. The Environmental Defense Fund is a founding nongovernmental organization member. Business for Social Responsibility, which is a non-profit organization, acts as TONZ's Secretariat, managing the administrative and operational aspects of the initiative. See https://www.bsr.org/en/collaboration/groups/transform-to-net-zero.

58. Each year Corporate Knights announces the top 100 firms at the World Economic Forum in Davos, Switzerland. All publicly listed firms with $1 billion revenue are screened for a financially based Piotroski F-score to ensure financial stability and fines, penalties, or settlements paid out by the company for sustainability-related violations. Firms involved in certain products or services and behaviors, such as the use of thermal coal and corporate lobbying against climate policy and deforestation, are disqualified from consideration. Global firms are scored on up to 25 key performance indicators, including percent sustainable revenue, percent sustainable investment, percent taxes paid, carbon productivity, and racial and gender diversity. See https://www.corporateknights.com/resources/global-100/.

59. Intel, "Letter from Intel CEO Pat Gelsinger about the Company's CSR Progress in 2022–23," May 11, 2023, https://www.intc.com/news-events/press-releases/detail/1618/opinion-intel-ceo-letter-2022-23-corporate-responsibility.

60. Intel, "Letter from Intel CEO."

61. Intel, "Letter from Intel CEO."

62. "Green Power Partnership National Top 100," US Environmental Protection Agency, accessed August 9, 2023, https://www.epa.gov/system/files/documents/2023-10/top100_july2023.pdf.

63. Suzanne Fallender (former global director of corporate responsibility at Intel Corporation) in discussion with the author, October 2, 2020 (interview GF13).

64. John Harland, "Designing for the Environment Turns Intel Green," GreenBiz, November 30, 2005, https://www.greenbiz.com/article/designing-environment-turns-intel-green.

65. Interview GF13.

66. Intel has won numerous awards on water stewardship, including water restoration. For example, Intel is a winner of the 2019 *Portland Business Journal* Innovation in Philanthropy Award for the firm's numerous water restoration projects in the United States (notably, the Willamette River Basin in Oregon), India, Costa Rica, Ireland, Malaysia, and Mexico.

67. In a white paper, Kevin Geoghegan, a sustainability manager at Intel Ireland, writes, "Sustainability has moved from voluntary, to peer pressure, to a community, employee, and shareholder expectation. Now, sustainability is moving towards being a requirement in our buildings, workplaces and homes to protect our planet and economies."

68. Stephanie Mehta, "Why Intel's CEO Attends a Monthly Diversity Committee Meeting," Fast Company, October 6, 2020, https://www.fastcompany.com/90558460/why-intels-ceo-attends-a-monthly-diversity-committee-meeting.

69. Bill Baue, "Footprints and Handprints: Stephen Harper on Intel's New Science-Based Climate Policy," Sustainable Brands, May 16, 2014, https://sustainablebrands.com/read/new-metrics/footprints-and-handprints-stephen-harper-on-intel-s-new-science-based-climate-policy-part.

70. Interview GF13.

71. Intel pioneered the "Copy EXACTLY!" system whereby production could ramp up quickly without sacrificing consistency in form, fit, function, and appearance in the semiconductor manufacturing process. See https://www.vse.com/blog/2019/07/25/finding-a-copy-exact-manufacturing-partner-for-your-pcb-assembly/. See also Joel Hruska, "Deliberate Excellence: Why Intel Leads the World in Semiconductor Manufacturing," May 1, 2012, https://www.extremetech.com/computing/127987-deliberate-excellence-why-intel-leads-the-world-in-semiconductor-manufacturing.

72. The world's largest publicly traded and investor-owned oil and gas firms are commonly referred to by the international news media as the "big oil" or "supermajors." See "Inside the Big Oil Game" *Time*, May 7, 1979, https://time.com/archive/6854296/inside-the-big-oil-game/. See also Simon Mundy and Patrick Temple-West, "How Big Oil's COP 28 Strategy Backfired," December 4, 2023, https://www.ft.com/content/4725c8ed-7d74-4e7c-bdbd-13b1bc4b50ab.

73. Emily Godsen, "Oil Chiefs Try to Boost Green Credentials with New Investment Fund," *The Telegraph*, November 2, 2016, https://www.telegraph.co.uk/business/2016/11/02/oil-chiefs-try-to-boost-green-credentials-with-new-investment-fu/.

74. This calculation of year over year change in 2011–2020 entity-wide (scope 1 and scope 2) emissions does not include Shell, China National Petroleum Corporation, and Saudi Aramco due to unavailable emissions data for these companies.

75. See https://www.corporateknights.com/rankings/global-100-rankings/.

76. See Neville Hawcock, "Europe's Climate Leaders 2023: Interactive Listing," April 19, 2023, https://www.ft.com/climate-leaders-europe-2023.

77. Sandra Laville, "'Greenwashing': Fossil Fuel Execs to Hold Invite-Only Forum at UN Climate Summit," *The Guardian*, September 18, 2019, https://www.theguardian.com/environment/2019/sep/18/fossil-fuel-invite-only-forum-un-climate-summit.

78. Laville, "'Greenwashing.'"

79. By 2021 and 2022, both Chevron and ExxonMobil had set quantitative emissions targets, catching up with their industry peers. See "Exxon pledges net-zero carbon emissions from operations by 2050," CNBC, January 18, 2022, https://www.cnbc.com/2022/01/18/exxon-pledges-net-zero-carbon-emissions-from-operations-by-2050.html.

Chapter 9

1. This book defines developed versus developing countries based on the World Bank's designations for high-income economies (developed countries) and upper-middle-income, low-income, and lower-middle-income economies (developing countries), respectively. See https://datahelpdesk.worldbank.org/knowledgebase/articles/906519-world-bank-country-and-lending-groups. Developed countries represented by the Fortune Global 500 firms in this book are the following: Australia, Belgium, Canada, Czech Republic, Denmark, Finland, Germany, Hong Kong, Ireland, Israel, Italy, Japan, Luxembourg, Netherlands, Norway, Poland, Singapore, South Korea, Spain, Sweden, Switzerland, Taiwan, United States, and United Kingdom. Developing countries are Brazil, Chile, China, Colombia, India, Indonesia, Malaysia, Mexico, Peru, Russia, South Africa, Thailand, and Turkey.

2. The twenty-seven countries that make up the European Union are Austria, Belgium, Bulgaria, Croatia, Cyprus, Czech Republic, Denmark, Estonia, Finland, France, Germany, Greece, Hungary, Ireland, Italy, Latvia, Lithuania, Luxembourg, Malta, Netherlands, Poland, Portugal, Romania, Slovakia, Slovenia, Spain, and Sweden. This book's corporate climate action database contains 107 firms listed at least once in the Fortune Global 500 from 2011 to 2015 that are domiciled in Belgium, Czech Republic, Denmark, Finland, France, Germany, Italy, Luxembourg, Netherlands, Poland, Spain, and Sweden.

3. Ye Qi, "China's Perspective on the US Withdrawal from the Paris Agreement," Brookings Institution, June 29, 2017, https://www.brookings.edu/articles/chinas-perspective-on-the-us-withdrawal-from-the-paris-agreement/.

4. Interview O4.

5. Neville Hawcock, "Europe's Climate Leaders 2021: Interactive Listing," *Financial Times*, May 26, 2021, https://www.ft.com/climate-leaders-europe-2021. The *Financial Times* defines GHG emissions intensity as tons of emissions of CO_2-equivalent per 1 million euros of revenue. GHG emissions intensity is the compound annual reduction rate (CARR) based on the sum of scope 1 and scope 2 emissions and adjusted by revenue growth during a five-year period (e.g., 2015–2020). Scope 3, or indirect emissions—which account for the bulk of a firm's emissions, but are not always disclosed or measured in a consistent manner—are not factored into the intensity calculation.

6. "Actor Tracking," Global Climate Action Portal, accessed January 19, 2024, https://climateaction.unfccc.int/Actors.

7. "The Europe A List 2020," CDP, accessed January 19, 2924, https://www.cdp.net/en/companies/companies-scores/a-list-europe-2020.

8. Bradford 2019.

9. Boasson and Wettestad 2016. In a review of research findings on the impacts of the European Union Emissions Trading System (ETS), Martin et al. (2016) found that the EU ETS had a robust negative effect on carbon emissions and had a small positive impact on innovation in clean technologies, without strong detrimental effect on firms' economic performance.

10. Renckens 2020a, 2021; Elliott et al. 2023.

11. See Habisch et al. 2005; Matten and Moon 2005, 2008; and Porter and Kramer 2006.

12. Mirroring table 3.2 in chapter 3, table 9.4 reports results of internal firm managerial and organizational determinants of participation and effort in voluntary carbon disclosure, based on the double-hurdle model. The tier 1 results cover firms' first-hurdle decision of participation, and tier 2 results cover firms' second-hurdle decision about their effort or intensity of participation, conditional on positive participation in the CDP. Appendix 3 contains technical details of the double-hurdle model.

13. Deakin and Walsh 1996; Moon 2002.

14. Table 3.2 reports positive and statistically significant results for the existence of senior- or executive-level managers and explicit CSR activities, such as firms' adoption of ESG principles, for all Global 500 firms.

15. Eberhard-Harribey 2006; Matten and Moon 2008; Carson et al. 2015.

16. Djelic 2001.

17. Strand 2012.

18. "Action Plan: Financing Sustainable Growth," European Commission, March 8, 2018, https://eur-lex.europa.eu/legal-content/EN/TXT/?uri=CELEX:52018DC0097.

19. "Action Plan."

20. "Implementing and Delegated Acts—SFDR," European Commission, accessed January 17, 2024, https://finance.ec.europa.eu/regulation-and-supervision/financial-services-legislation/implementing-and-delegated-acts/sustainable-finance-disclosures-regulation_en.

21. See https://transparency-register.europa.eu/index_en. "Communication from the Commission: Guidelines on Non-Financial Reporting," European Union, July 5, 2017, https://eur-lex.europa.eu/legal-content/EN/TXT/?uri=CELEX%3A52017XC0705%2801%29.

22. Renckens 2020b; Elliott et al. 2023.

23. Lily Hsueh, "SEC's Climate Disclosure Plan Could Be in Trouble after a Recent Supreme Court Ruling, but a Bigger Question Looms: Does Disclosure Work?" *The Conversation*, July 7, 2022, https://theconversation.com/secs-climate-disclosure-plan-could-be-in-trouble-after-a-recent-supreme-court-ruling-but-a-bigger-question-looms-does-disclosure-work-185371.

24. West Virginia v. Environmental Protection Agency, 597 U.S (2022); Avery Ellfedt, "Up Next: West Virginia AG Targets SEC Climate Proposal," *E&E News*, July 1, 2022, https://www.eenews.net/articles/up-next-west-virginia-ag-targets-sec-climate-proposal/.

25. "Fact Sheet: Enhancement and Standardization of Climate-Related Disclosures," US Securities and Exchange Commission, assessed January 19, 2024, https://www.sec.gov/files/33-11042-fact-sheet.pdf.

26. Elizabeth Small, "3 Vital Things to Know about the SEC's New Proposed Climate Disclosure Rule—and Where CDP Fits In," CDP, March 25, 2022, https://www.cdp.net/en/articles/climate/3-vital-things-to-know-about-the-secs-new-proposed-climate-disclosure-rule-and-where-cdp-fits-in.

27. "China Sustainability Leaders Council: About the Council," The Conference Board, accessed February 2, 2024, https://www.conference-board.org/councils/china-sustainability-leaders.

28. Zhu and Sarkis 2007.

29. Blackman et al. 2010.

30. Rivera 2002, 2004.

31. Buthe and Mattli 2005, 2011; Blackman 2008; Prakash and Potoski 2014.

32. These are predicted probabilities of voluntary carbon disclosure based on the empirical models for the developed country split sample (i.e., model 1 in table 9.9, panel A) and developing country split sample (i.e., model 1 in table 9.9, panel B), with estimated covariates entering into the fitted models at their mean values.

33. These average marginal effects are based on the author's calculations for the participation stage of the Heckman selection model. By contrast, the reported estimated coefficients in table 9.9 are estimates that maximize the likelihood function rather than estimated average marginal effects.

34. Vogel 2008, 2010; R. Hsueh 2011, 2012, 2016, 2022; Bartley 2014, 2018a.

35. Berliner et al. 2015; Mayer and Phillips 2017; Seabrooke and Wigan 2017.

36. Chan et al. 2018. See also Global Climate Action's (formerly NAZCA) Actor Tracking portal by country (https://climateaction.unfccc.int/Actors).

37. Bartley 2018b.

38. In 2021, JinkoSolar was awarded the Sustainability Awards 2022 Outstanding Enterprise by Ernst & Young. At the end of 2021, JinkoSolar joined the Science-Based Carbon Targeting Initiative (SBTi) and committed to the ten principles of the UN Global Compact as a corporate member. See https://www.jinkosolar.com/en/site/newsdetail/1787.

39. Ana Swanson, "As Ties to China Turn Toxic, Even Chinese Companies Are Breaking Them," *New York Times*, June 15, 2023, https://www.nytimes.com/2023/06/15/business/economy/china-business-tiktok-shein.html?searchResultPosition=1.

Chapter 10

1. See https://www.ipcc.ch/site/assets/uploads/2021/08/IPCC_WGI-AR6-Press-Release_en.pdf. See also IPCC Sixth Assessment Reports Working Group 1 Report, https://www.ipcc.ch/report/ar6/wg1/.

2. In this calculation electricity use has been allocated to the industrial end-use sector.

3. Lily Hsueh, "Exxon, Apple and other Corporate Giants Will Have to Disclose all Their Emissions under California's New Climate Laws—That Will Have a Global Impact," *The Conversation*, October 10, 2023, https://theconversation.com/exxon-apple-and-other-corporate-giants-will-have-to-disclose-all-their-emissions-under-californias-new-climate-laws-that-will-have-a-global-impact-214630.

4. About 40 percent of the firms listed in the S&P 500 index are also part of the Fortune Global 500.

5. "Our Work," United Nations Global Compact, accessed November 14, 2023, https://www.unglobalcompact.org/what-is-gc/our-work/.

6. Hsueh 2015.

7. Dating back to 2002, ESG performance scores cover 85 percent of the global market cap, across more than 630 different ESG metrics covering 10 main categories, including emissions, environmental product innovation, human rights, and shareholders. See https://www.lseg.com/en/data-analytics/sustainable-finance/esg-scores.

8. "A UN-based global campaign rallying non-state actors across the global economy to take rigorous and immediate action to halve global emissions by 2030." See https://climatechampions.unfccc.int.

9. Led by the governments of the UK and Chile, with support from the United Nations, the Climate Ambition Alliance brings together countries, businesses, investors, cities, and regions "to enhance collaboration in the achievement of net-zero CO_2 emissions by 2050." See https://climateaction.unfccc.int/Initiatives?id=Climate_Ambition_Alliance.

10. Business Ambition for 1.5°C is an international initiative of the "world's largest and fastest-growing group of companies taking urgent action." See https://sciencebasedtargets.org/companies-taking-action.

11. Chapa, "Schlumberger, Chevron and Microsoft."

12. The OGCI's stated mission is to reduce unabated carbon emissions through carbon capture, utilization and storage, and methane emissions reduction, among other initiatives, as discussed in chapter 8.

13. This calculation of year-over-year change in 2011–2020 entity-wide (scope 1 and 2) emissions does not include Shell, China National Petroleum Corporation, and Saudi Aramco due to unavailable emissions data for these companies.

14. "Global 100," Corporate Knights, accessed February 21, 2024, https://www.corporateknights.com/rankings/global-100-rankings/.

15. "Europe's Climate Leaders 2023: Interactive Listing," *Financial Times*, https://www.ft.com/climate-leaders-europe-2023.

16. Sandra Laville, "'Greenwashing': Fossil Fuel Execs to Hold Invite-Only Forum at UN Climate Summit," *The Guardian*, September 18, 2019, https://www.theguardian.com/environment/2019/sep/18/fossil-fuel-invite-only-forum-un-climate-summit.

17. Laville, "'Greenwashing.'"

18. Renckens 2020a, 2021; Elliott et al. 2023.

19. See, for example, Porter and Kramer 2006.

20. "Action Plan: Financing Sustainable Growth," European Commission, March 8, 2018, https://eur-lex.europa.eu/legal-content/EN/TXT/?uri=CELEX:52018DC0097.

21. "Transparency Register," European Union, https://transparency-register.europa.eu/index_en.

22. These average marginal effects are based on the author's calculations for the participation stage of the Heckman selection model. By contrast, the reported estimated coefficients in table 9.9 are estimates that maximize the likelihood function rather than estimated average marginal effects.

23. In 2021, Jinko Solar was awarded the "Sustainability Awards 2022 Outstanding Enterprise" by Ernst & Young. At the end of 2021, Jinko Solar joined the Science-Based Carbon Targeting Initiative (SBTi) and committed to the ten principles of the UN Global Compact as a corporate member. See "JinkoSolar Recognised as the "Sustainability Awards 2022 Outstanding Company of the Year" by Ernst & Young," JinkoSolar, https://www.jinkosolar.com/en/site/newsdetail/1787.

24. Ana Swanson, "As Ties to China Turn Toxic, Even Chinese Companies Are Breaking Them," *New York Times*, June 15, 2023, https://www.nytimes.com/2023/06/15/business/economy/china-business-tiktok-shein.html?searchResultPosition=1.

25. CDP, "The A List," https://www.cdp.net/en/companies/companies-scores.

26. Natasha Bernal, "Google, Microsoft and the Strange World of Corporate Greenwashing," *Wired UK*, January 31, 2020, https://www.wired.co.uk/article/corporate-greenwashing.

27. Sergio Chapa, "Schlumberger, Chevron and Microsoft Launch Artificial Intelligence Platform for Oil Field," *Houston Chronicle*, September 17, 2019, https://www.chron.com/business/energy/article/Schlumberger-Chevron-and-Microsoft-launch-14445539.php.

28. See https://apparelcoalition.org/why-become-a-member/sac-for/brands-retailers/.

29. Hitoko Tabuchi, "How Fashion Giants Recast Plastic as Good for the Planet," *New York Times*, June 12, 2022, https://www.nytimes.com/2022/06/12/climate/vegan-leather-synthetics-fashion-industry.html.

30. See https://apparelcoalition.org/the-higg-index/.

31. Eco-Friendly and Green Marketing Claims, "Federal Trade Commission," accessed November 9, 2023, https://consumer.ftc.gov/articles/eco-friendly-green-marketing-claims.

32. Downar et al. 2021.

33. Tinglong Dai, Christopher S. Tang, and Hau L. Lee, "Lego's ESG Dilemma: Why an Abandoned Plan to Use Recycled Plastic Bottles Is a Wake-Up Call for Supply

Chain Sustainability," *The Conversation,* October 5, 2023, https://theconversation.com/legos-esg-dilemma-why-an-abandoned-plan-to-use-recycled-plastic-bottles-is-a-wake-up-call-for-supply-chain-sustainability-214573.

34. Cingano and Pinotti 2013; Zingales 2014; Bessen 2016; Decker et al. 2016.

35. Giddens 2011; Werner 2012; Mildenberger 2020; Stokes 2020; Perlman 2023.

36. Interview HE1. Supran et al. 2023; Neela Banerjee et al., "The Road Not Taken," *Inside Climate News,* accessed February 17, 2024, https://insideclimatenews.org/project/exxon-the-road-not-taken/.

37. Peter Frumhoff and Naomi Oreske, "Fossil Fuel Firms Are Still Bankrolling Climate Denial Lobby Groups," *The Guardian,* March 25, 2015, https://www.theguardian.com/environment/2015/mar/25/fossil-fuel-firms-are-still-bankrolling-climate-denial-lobby-groups; Suzanne Goldenberg, "Conservative Groups Spend up to $1BN a Year to Fight Action on Climate Change," *The Guardian,* December 20, 2013, https://www.theguardian.com/environment/2013/dec/20/conservative-groups-1bn-against-climate-change.

38. Interviews O5 and HE15. Alastair Marsh, "Oil Majors' Carbon Capture Plans Dubbed a 'Dangerous Delusion,'" *Bloomberg,* November 16, 2023, https://www.bloomberg.com/news/articles/2023-11-16/oil-majors-carbon-capture-plans-dubbed-a-dangerous-delusion?embedded-checkout=true.

39. Welton and Eisen 2019; Welton 2020; Scott-Buechler et al. 2024.

40. See, for example, Lyon et al. 2018, Skaife and Werner 2020, and Lyon 2023. Broek (2021) shows evidence that EU-based signatory firms of the UN Global Compact are more likely to lobby for stricter regulation in the EU than nonsignatory firms and industry associations. It is unclear whether these firms are engaged in subtle strategies to erect barriers to entry that lessen competition and boost the profits of businesses protected by the regulatory barriers or that their political positions are more aligned with nonbusiness stakeholders' interests. In fact, Kennard (2020) shows that in the presence of market competition and open borders, firms facing a lower cost of adjustment to climate regulation and export competition may lobby for stringent regulation, particularly when regulation raises the costs of domestically produced intermediate goods.

41. Krueger et al. 2020.

42. Yadin 2023b, 2023a. Naming and shaming of climate laggards can and have occurred at the country level. Falkner (2016b) posits that shaming is the main tool countries use to "exhort [country] laggards to raise their game" in the Paris Agreement. Tingley and Tomz (2022) show through survey experiments that shaming by foreign countries shifted domestic US public opinion in favor of compliance—notably for partial compliers compared to countries that took no action—increasing the political incentives to honor the Paris Agreement.

43. Shawn Mccarthy, "The Global 100 List: How the World's Most Sustainable Corporations are Driving the Green Transition," Corporate Knights, January 17, 2024, https://www.corporateknights.com/rankings/global-100-rankings/2024-global-100-rankings/the-20th-annual-global-100/. The Global 100 rates firms in thirty-eight industry groups, including banking, utilities, mining, oil and gas, and manufacturing, based on twenty-five metrics. It applies different weighting to certain metrics given the nature of the sector. Sustainable revenue and sustainable investment are key measures; others include gender and racial diversity, chief executive officer (CEO) pay versus employee average, CEO bonuses based on sustainability performance, taxes paid, and contributions to employee pensions.

44. MSCI ACWI Investable Market Index is a widely quoted global equity index, known formally as the Morgan Stanley Capital International All Country World Investable Market Index. Between February 1, 2005, and December 15, 2023, the Global 100 saw a return of 287 percent on a US dollar basis, while the MSCI ACWI had a return of 272 percent. The Dow Jones Sustainability World Index posted a return of 254 percent over that period.

45. In the policy process literature, the act of finding a decision setting that maximizes one's policy goals is called venue shopping, the theory of which was first laid out by Baumgartner and Jones (1993) and extended by Pralle (2003, 2006a, 2006b), among others.

46. Interview O6. Nielsen et al. 2021.

47. Interview O7. Dissociation is a newer movement than divestment. While dissociation may often include divestment, it is a broader term to mean a refrain from any relationships, such as research funding, gifts, or grants, that involve a financial component from a company that does not align with the value of a particular higher education institution. See "Fossil Fuel Dissociation FAQ," Princeton University, https://fossilfueldissociation.princeton.edu/faq.

48. David Gelles, "Stanford Gets $1.1 Billion for New Climate School from John Doerr," *New York Times*, May 4, 2022, https://www.nytimes.com/2022/05/04/climate/john-doerr-stanford-climate.html.

49. Felicia Yan, "Fossil Fuels Fund Doerr School of Sustainability Research, Data Shows," *Stanford Daily*, January 29, 2024, https://stanforddaily.com/2024/01/29/doerr-funding/.

50. David Palumbo-Liu, "What Would a True School of Sustainability Look Like? Rejecting Oil Money, for a Start," September 28, 2023, *Speaking Out of Place* podcast, 33:09, https://speakingoutofplace.com/2023/09/28/what-would-a-true-school-of-sustainability-look-like-rejecting-oil-money-for-a-start/.

51. "Office of the Dean: Statement on the Foundation for a Smoke-Free World," Harvard TH Chan School of Public Health, January 25, 2018, https://www.hsph.harvard.edu/deans-office/2018/01/26/smoke-free-world-letter/.

52. "WHO Statement on Philip Morris Funded Foundation for a Smoke-Free World," World Health Organization, September 28, 2017, https://www.who.int/en/news-room/detail/28-09-2017-who-statement-on-philip-morris-funded-foundation-for-a-smoke-free-world.

53. Evan Castillo, "These Colleges Have Divested from Fossil Fuels," Best Colleges, September 19, 2023, https://www.bestcolleges.com/news/list-of-colleges-divested-from-fossil-fuels/.

54. https://divestmentdatabase.org/.

55. "About," Fossil Free Research, accessed February 22, 2024, https://mauve-copper-lnj4.squarespace.com/mission.

56. X, October 4, 2023, https://twitter.com/weareyellowdot/status/1709607101646180592.

57. Jack Johnson and Noah Herfort, "Mapping the Global Youth Climate Movement," Green Economy Coalition, March 3, 2023, https://www.greeneconomycoalition.org/news-and-resources/mapping-the-global-youth-climate-movement. The climate youth movement's emphasis on "collective futures" is in line with research showing that individuals who internalize the welfare of others in society beside themselves—that is, possess other-regarding preferences—are more likely to express serious concern and take action about global warming (Kennard 2020).

58. Palumbo-Liu, "What Would a True School."

59. "June Choi et al., "Letter to the Editor," *Stanford Daily*, October 5, 2023, https://stanforddaily.com/2023/10/05/letter-to-the-editor-across-diverse-backgrounds-we-are-more-aligned-on-how-to-approach-stanfords-fossil-fuel-engagement-than-you-might-think/. Other Coalition-affiliated recommendations include specific criteria for dissociation when fossil fuel companies do not provide a credible transition plan that is based on quantifiable, Paris Agreement–aligned criteria or provide transparent data; the establishment of a third-party enforcement board that oversees dissociation; and future re-association processes, among other recommendations.

60. "Climate Action 100+ Net Zero Company Benchmark v1.1," Climate Action 100+, https://www.climateaction100.org/wp-content/uploads/2021/10/Climate-Action-100-v1.1-Benchmark-Indicators-Oct21.pdf.

61. https://influencemap.org.

62. https://sciencebasedtargets.org/.

63. Palumbo-Liu, "What Would a True School."

64. Stephanie M. Lee, "Big Oil Helped Shape Stanford's Latest Climate-Research Focus," *Chronicle of Higher Education*, May 4, 2023, https://www.chronicle.com/article/big-oil-helped-shape-stanfords-latest-climate-research-focus.

65. Palumbo-Liu, "What Would a True School."

66. Amy Adams, "Members Named to Committee Reviewing Fossil Fuel Funding of Research," Stanford Report, February 23, 2024, https://news.stanford.edu/report/2023/02/24/members-named-committee-reviewing-fossil-fuel-funding-research/.

67. Andrew Myers, "New Committee Will Evaluate Stanford Doerr School of Sustainability Affiliate Programs," Stanford Doerr School of Sustainability, February 8, 2024, https://sustainability.stanford.edu/news/new-committee-will-evaluate-stanford-doerr-school-sustainability-affiliate-programs.

68. "Industrial Affiliates Programs," Stanford Doerr School of Sustainability, https://sustainability.stanford.edu/school/industrial-affiliate-programs.

69. Beyond the scope of this book, subnational actors, institutions, policymaking, and dynamics in the environmental area, including climate change, are active research agendas in political science and public administration and policy. For US-centric studies, see Potoski 2001; Potoski and Woods 2002; Rabe et al. 2005; Rabe 2007, 2010; Carley 2009, 2011; Krause 2011, 2012; Egan and Mullin 2012; Hsueh and Prakash 2012c; Li and Yi 2014; Yi and Feiock 2014; Kim and Verweij 2016; Krause et al. 2016; and Konisky 2007, 2024. For non-US-focused studies, see Bulkeley and Betsill 2005, 2012; Bulkeley and Kern 2009; Bulkeley et al. 2014; Yi and Liu 2015; Anderson et al. 2019; and Shen 2022.

70. Vogel 2018.

71. "California Senate Bill 253," LigiScan, https://legiscan.com/CA/text/SB253/id/2841248. For US federal rules, see "Greenhouse Gas Reporting Program (GHGRP)," US EPA, https://www.epa.gov/ghgreporting. For US state rules, see "Mandatory Greenhouse Gas Emissions Reporting," California Air Resources Board, https://ww2.arb.ca.gov/our-work/programs/mandatory-greenhouse-gas-emissions-reporting.

72. "The Enhancement and Standardization of Climate-Related Disclosures for Investors," US Securities and Exchange Commission, accessed February 23, 2024, https://www.sec.gov/files/rules/proposed/2022/33-11042.pdf; "Federal Supplier Climate Risks and Resilience Proposed Rule," Office of the Federal Chief Sustainability Officer, Council on Environmental Quality, accessed February 23, 2024, https://www.sustainability.gov/federalsustainabilityplan/fed-supplier-rule.html.

73. Interviews G1, HE12, and G2.

74. Bartley 2018a; Distelhorst and Locke 2018; Grab 2020; Cory et al. 2021; Amengual and Bartley 2022; Luer et al. 2022; Schleifer et al. 2022.

75. See "Sustainable Finance Disclosure Regulation," Morgan Stanley, https://www.morganstanley.com/im/en-be/intermediary-investor/about-us/newsroom/press-release/sustainable-finance-disclosure-regulation.html.

76. See "Implementing and delegated acts—SFDR," European Commission, https://finance.ec.europa.eu/regulation-and-supervision/financial-services-legislation/implementing-and-delegated-acts/sustainable-finance-disclosures-regulation_en.

77. Madeleine Ngo, "Republican Attacks on Biden's Climate Law Raise Concerns Ahead of Election," *New York Times*, February 19, 2024, https://www.nytimes.com/2024/02/19/us/politics/inflation-reduction-act-republican-attacks.html.

78. Inflation Reduction Act of 2022, Pub. L. No. 117–169, 117 Stat. 1818 (2022).

79. "Global: Record Number of Fossil Fuel Lobbyists at COP Undermines Critical Climate Talks," Amnesty International, December 5, 2023, https://www.amnesty.org/en/latest/news/2023/12/global-record-number-of-fossil-fuel-lobbyists-at-cop-undermines-critical-climate-talks/.

80. US Environmental Protection Agency, "Biden-Harris Administration Finalizes Standards to Slash Methane Pollution, Combat Climate Change, Protect Health, and Bolster American Innovation," December 2, 2023, https://www.epa.gov/newsreleases/biden-harris-administration-finalizes-standards-slash-methane-pollution-combat-climate; European Commission, "Commission Welcomes Deal on First-Ever EU Law to Curb Methane Emission in the EU and Globally," November 15, 2023, https://ec.europa.eu/commission/presscorner/detail/en/IP_23_5776.

81. Eric Niiler, "COP28 Climate Summit Takes Aim at Powerful Methane Emissions," *Wall Street Journal*, December 2, 2023, https://www.wsj.com/us-news/climate-environment/environmental-protection-agency-methane-rules-oil-gas-industry-ff05fa1b.

82. Gernot Wagner, "How to Assess the Outcome of COP28," Project Syndicate, December 13, 2023, https://www.project-syndicate.org/commentary/cop28-pledges-methane-still-matters-even-if-oil-gas-industry-focusing-on-own-interests-by-gernot-wagner-2023-12.

83. Goulder et al. 2016; Goulder and Hafstead 2017; and Goulder et al. 2019.

Appendix 1

1. During this book's study period (2011–2020), firms dropped out of the sample due to merger or acquisition; this explains the slight variation in the number of firms across the empirical analyses.

2. CDP 2015b.

3. The Task Force for Climate-Related Financial Disclosure was established by the Financial Stability Board to set global standards on the type of information that firms should disclose to support investors, lenders, and insurance underwriters in order to assess and price risks related to climate change. See https://www.fsb-tcfd.org/.

4. Interview with account manager at the CDP on August 6, 2020 (interview O9). See also CDP 2016a, 2017.

5. "Admin Fee FAQ," CDP, accessed December 5, 2023, https://www.cdp.net/en/info/admin-fee-faq.

6. CDP 2015a.

7. See "Our Collaborations," CDP, https://www.cdp.net/en/info/collaborations.

8. More information about CDP's scoring methodology before 2016 can be found in this CDP video: https://vimeo.com/121236413.

9. Email exchange between the author and former corporate partnership executive of CDP's London office on November 17, 2015 (interview O8).

10. CDP 2016b.

11. van den Heuvel 2012; Busch et al. 2018.

12. Building on a twenty-year partnership between the World Resources Institute and the World Business Council for Sustainable Development, GHG Protocol works with governments, industry associations, nongovernmental organizations, businesses, and other organizations.

13. LSEG Data & Analytics, Environmental, Social, and Governance Scores from LSEG, December 2023, https://www.lseg.com/content/dam/data-analytics/en_us/documents/methodology/lseg-esg-scores-methodology.pdf.

Appendix 3

1. A firm's disclosures on scope 1, scope 2, and scope 3 GHG emissions must be reported at the "entity level" so as to prevent the firm from reporting only on the outcomes of successful projects (CDP 2017, 2016).

2. In general, the number of points allocated to each question depends on the amount of data requested. Questions that have more than one point attached to a single piece of information are deemed of particularly high importance by the CDP (e.g., gross scope 1 and scope 2 emissions) (CDP 2015a).

3. CDP 2015a.

4. This chapter's analysis is robust to an alternative specification that drops these 24 cases from the analysis. Results are available by request from the author.

5. Lyon and Maxwell 2011.

6. Cragg 1971; Cameron and Trivedi 2005; Burke 2009.

7. See Lyon and Maxwell 2011; Bowen and Aragon-Correa 2014; Lyon and Montgomery 2015; Prakash and Potoski 2007a, 2012.

8. If there are obvious exclusion restrictions (which there are not for voluntary carbon disclosure), this can be relaxed (Cameron and Trivedi 2005).

9. See Arimura et al. 2011; Darnall et al. 2008.

Appendix 4

1. A separate robustness check that includes the 115 firm × year observations shows that the chapter's empirical results are robust to the exclusion of these observations.

2. The exclusion restriction separately identifies the participation and intensity of participation equations: *manager* and *target* are distinct to the participation and the intensity of participation equations, respectively. See appendix 7 for rationale for *manager* as an exclusion restriction.

3. Woodridge 2010.

4. Winston 2010.

5. In table A4.8, the lack of model sensitivity to whether one is controlling for a firms' country of origin or export country of largest sales may be in part because a majority (over 60 percent) of the Fortune Global 500 firms are domiciles of or export to the United States, Japan, the UK, Canada, and France.

Appendix 5

1. Greenstone and Gayer 2009; Deschenes and Meng 2018.

2. Ashenfelter and Card 1985.

3. The standard approach in the empirical literature is followed for specifying DD models with multiple time periods, which is to exclude *Clean Power Plan (CPP)*, the indicator variable that represents the posttreatment or post-CPP period, so as to thwart collinearity with year effects.

4. Imbens 2015.

5. The marginal impacts of participation for firms with dedicated managers to climate mitigation operating in GHG-intensive sectors in the post-CPP period have been computed by setting *CPP* = 1 and *manager* = 1 and holding other variables at their mean and using the standard normal distribution.

Appendix 7

1. Interviews GF5, GF6, GF7, GF8, GF9, GF10, GF11, and GF12.

2. Bertrand et al. 2004; Cameron and Miller 2015.

Appendix 9

1. To conduct these interviews and field research, the author underwent an institutional review board human subjects review process at Arizona State University, and the study was approved as an exempt study pursuant to federal regulations 45CFR46 (2) Tests, surveys, interviews, or observation and (4) Data, documents, or specimens.

2. See https://www.greenbiz.com/about-us.

3. B Lab is a global nonprofit network known for certifying B corporations, which are firms that meet high standards of social and environmental performance, accountability, and transparency. See https://www.bcorporation.net/en-us/movement/about-b-lab/.

4. The SDG Innovation Accelerator Training Workshop was part of a series of local training workshops, live case studies, and interactive sessions as part of UNGC's SDG Innovation Accelerator for Young Professionals. The accelerator is a nine-month program to "empower the young talent within [participating companies of the UN Global Compact] to collaborate and drive business innovation that aligns with the Sustainable Development Goals." See https://unglobalcompact.org/take-action/sdg-innovation-accelerator.

Bibliography

Abbott, Kenneth W., Jessica F. Green, and Robert O. Keohane. 2016. "Organizational Ecology and Institutional Change in Global Governance." *International Organization* 70 (02): 247–77. https://doi.org/10.1017/S0020818315000338.

Abbott, Kenneth W., and Duncan Snidal. 2009. "Strengthening International Regulation through Transmittal New Governance: Overcoming the Orchestration Deficit." *Vanderbilt Journal of Transnational Law* 42: 501–578.

Abbott, Kenneth W., and Duncan Snidal. 2010. "International Regulation without International Government: Improving IO Performance through Orchestration." *Review of International Organizations* 5 (3): 315–344. https://doi.org/10.1007/s11558-010-9092-3.

Adler, Jonathan H. 2016. "Opinion: Supreme Court Puts the Brakes on the EPA's Clean Power Plan." *Washington Post*, February 9, 2016, https://www.washingtonpost.com/news/volokh-conspiracy/wp/2016/02/09/supreme-court-puts-the-brakes-on-the-epas-clean-power-plan/.

Aerts, Walter, Denis Cormier, and Michel Magnan. 2008. "Corporate Environmental Disclosure, Financial Markets and the Media: An International Perspective." *Ecological Economics* 64 (3): 643–659. https://doi.org/10.1016/j.ecolecon.2007.04.012.

Aklin, Michaël, and Matto Mildenberger. 2020. "Prisoners of the Wrong Dilemma: Why Distributive Conflict, Not Collective Action, Characterizes the Politics of Climate Change." *Global Environmental Politics* 20 (4): 4–27. https://doi.org/10.1162/glep_a_00578.

Alberini, Anna, and Kathleen Segerson. 2002. "Assessing Voluntary Programs to Improve Environmental Quality." *Environmental and Resource Economics* 22 (1–2): 157–84. https://doi.org/10.1023/A:1015519116167.

Allan, Bentley B., and Jonas O. Meckling. 2021. "Creative Learning and Policy Ideas: The Global Rise of Green Growth." *Perspectives on Politics*, April 1–19. https://doi.org/10.1017/S1537592721000037.

Alter, Karen J., and Sophie Meunier. 2009. "The Politics of International Regime Complexity." *Perspectives on Politics* 7 (1): 13–24. https://doi.org/10.1017/S1537592709090033.

Amengual, Matthew, and Tim Bartley. 2022. "Global Markets, Corporate Assurances, and the Legitimacy of State Intervention: Perceptions of Distant Labor and Environmental Problems." *American Sociological Review* 87 (3): 383–414. https://doi.org/10.1177/00031224221092340.

Amores-Salvadó, Javier, Gregorio Martín-de Castro, and José E. Navas-López. 2014. "Green Corporate Image: Moderating the Connection between Environmental Product Innovation and Firm Performance." *Journal of Cleaner Production* 83 (November): 356–365. https://doi.org/10.1016/j.jclepro.2014.07.059.

Amran, Azlan, Vinod Periasamy, and Abdul Hadi Zulkafli. 2014. "Determinants of Climate Change Disclosure by Developed and Emerging Countries in Asia Pacific." *Sustainable Development* 22 (3): 188–204. https://doi.org/10.1002/sd.539.

Anderson, Sarah E., Mark T. Buntaine, Mengdi Liu, and Bing Zhang. 2019. "Non-Governmental Monitoring of Local Governments Increases Compliance with Central Mandates: A National-Scale Field Experiment in China." *American Journal of Political Science* 63 (3): 626–643. https://doi.org/10.1111/ajps.12428.

Andonova, Liliana B., Thomas N. Hale, and Charles B. Roger. 2017. "National Policy and Transnational Governance of Climate Change: Substitutes or Complements?" *International Studies Quarterly* 61 (2): 253–268. https://doi.org/10.1093/isq/sqx014.

Andreoni, James, and Ravi Kanbur. 2007. "Special Issue: Celebrating the 20th Anniversary of Bergstrom, Blume, and Varian's 'On the Private Provision of Public Goods': Guest Editor's Introduction: Twenty Surprising Years of BBV." *Journal of Public Economics* 91 (9): 1643–1644. https://doi.org/10.1016/j.jpubeco.2007.08.002.

Aragòn-Correa, J. Alberto, Alfred A. Marcus, and David Vogel. 2020. "The Effects of Mandatory and Voluntary Regulatory Pressures on Firms' Environmental Strategies: A Review and Recommendations for Future Research." *Academy of Management Annals* 14 (1): 339–365. https://doi.org/10.5465/annals.2018.0014.

Arimura, Toshi H., Nicole Darnall, and Hajime Katayama. 2011. "Is ISO 14001 a Gateway to More Advanced Voluntary Action? The Case of Green Supply Chain Management." *Journal of Environmental Economics and Management* 61 (2): 170–182.

Arora, Seema, and Timothy N. Cason. 1996. "Why Do Firms Volunteer to Exceed Environmental Regulations? Understanding Participation in EPA's 33/50 Program." *Land Economics* 72 (4): 413–32. https://doi.org/10.2307/3146906.

Arora, Seema, and Shubhashis Gangopadhyay. 1995. "Toward a Theoretical Model of Voluntary Overcompliance." *Journal of Economic Behavior & Organization* 28 (3): 289–309. https://doi.org/10.1016/0167-2681(95)00037-2.

Arrow, K. 1962. "The Economic Implications of Learning by Doing." *Review of Economic Studies* 29 (3): 155–173.

Ashenfelter, Orley, and David Card. 1985. "Using the Longitudinal Structure of Earnings to Estimate the Effect of Training Programs." *Review of Economics and Statistics* 67 (4): 648–660. https://doi.org/10.2307/1924810.

Auld, Graeme, Lars H. Gulbrandsen, and Constance L. McDermott. 2008. "Certification Schemes and the Impacts on Forests and Forestry." *Annual Review of Environment and Resources* 33 (1): 187–211. https://doi.org/10.1146/annurev.environ.33.013007.103754.

Avant, Deborah D., Martha Finnemore, and Susan K. Sell. 2010. *Who Governs the Globe?* Cambridge University Press.

Baccaro, Lucio, and Valentina Mele. 2011. "For Lack of Anything Better? International Organizations and Global Corporate Codes." *Public Administration* 89 (2): 451–470. https://doi.org/10.1111/j.1467-9299.2011.01918.x.

Bandyopadhyay, Sushenjit, and John Horowitz. 2006. "Do Plants Overcomply with Water Pollution Regulations? The Role of Discharge Variability." *Topics in Economic Analysis & Policy* 6 (1): 1–32. https://doi.org/10.2202/1538-0653.1486.

Banzhaf, H. Spencer, Timothy Fitzgerald, and Kurt Schnier. 2013. "Nonregulatory Approaches to the Environment: Coasean and Pigouvian Perspectives." *Review of Environmental Economics and Policy* 7 (2): 238–258. https://doi.org/10.1093/reep/ret013.

Bardach, Eugene. 1977. *The Implementation Game: What Happens After a Bill Becomes a Law*. MIT Press.

Barnett, William P. 2017a. "Framing Work in Metacompetition." In *Emerging Trends in the Social and Behavioral Sciences*, edited by Robert A. Scott and Marlis C. Buchmann, 1–8. John Wiley & Sons. https://doi.org/10.1002/9781118900772.etrds0422.

Barnett, William P. 2017b. "Metacompetition: Competing over the Game to Be Played." *Strategy Science* 2 (4): 212–219. https://doi.org/10.1287/stsc.2017.0049.

Baron, David P. 2001. "Private Politics, Corporate Social Responsibility, and Integrated Strategy." *Journal of Economics & Management Strategy* 10 (1): 7–45.

Baron, David P. 2009. "A Positive Theory of Moral Management, Social Pressure, and Corporate Social Performance." *Journal of Economics & Management Strategy* 18 (1): 7–43. https://doi.org/10.1111/j.1530-9134.2009.00206.x.

Baron, David P. 2010. "Morally Motivated Self-Regulation." *American Economic Review* 100 (4): 1299–1329. https://doi.org/10.1257/aer.100.4.1299.

Baron, David P., and Daniel Diermeier. 2007. "Strategic Activism and Nonmarket Strategy." *Journal of Economics & Management Strategy* 16 (3): 599–634.

Barrett, Scott. 2003. *Environment and Statecraft: The Strategy of Environmental Treaty-Making: The Strategy of Environmental Treaty-Making*. Oxford University Press.

Barrett, Scott. 2006. "Climate Treaties and 'Breakthrough' Technologies." *American Economic Review* 96 (2): 22–25.

Barrett, Scott. 2007. *Why Cooperate?: The Incentive to Supply Global Public Goods*. OUP Oxford.

Bartley, Tim. 2010. "Transnational Private Regulation in Practice: The Limits of Forest and Labor Standards Certification in Indonesia." *Business & Politics* 12 (3): 1–34. https://doi.org/10.2202/1469-3569.1321.

Bartley, Tim. 2014. "Transnational Governance and the Re-Centered State: Sustainability or Legality?" *Regulation & Governance* 8 (1): 93–109. https://doi.org/10.1111/rego.12051.

Bartley, Tim. 2018a. *Rules without Rights: Land, Labor, and Private Authority in the Global Economy*. Oxford University Press.

Bartley, Tim. 2018b. "Transnational Corporations and Global Governance." *Annual Review of Sociology* 44: 145–165. https://doi.org/10.1146/annurev-soc-060116-053540.

Barbier, Edward. 2022. *Economics for a Fragile Planet: Rethinking Markets, Institutions and Governance*. Cambridge University Press.

Barbier, Edward B., and Joanne C. Burgess. 2018. "Innovative Corporate Initiatives to Reduce Climate Risk: Lessons from East Asia." *Sustainability* 10 (1): 13. https://doi.org/10.3390/su10010013.

Baumgartner, Frank R., and Bryan D. Jones. 1993. *Agendas and Instability in American Politics*. 1st ed. University of Chicago Press.

Bénabou, Roland, and Jean Tirole. 2003. "Intrinsic and Extrinsic Motivation." *Review of Economic Studies* 70 (3): 489–520. https://doi.org/10.1111/1467-937X.00253.

Bénabou, Roland, and Jean Tirole. 2006. "Incentives and Prosocial Behavior." *American Economic Review* 96 (5): 1652–1678. https://doi.org/10.1257/aer.96.5.1652.

Bénabou, Roland, and Jean Tirole. 2010. "Individual and Corporate Social Responsibility." *Economica* 77 (305): 1–19. https://doi.org/10.1111/j.1468-0335.2009.00843.x.

Ben-Amar, Walid, and Mohamed Chelli. 2018. "What Drives Voluntary Corporate Water Disclosures? The Effect of Country-Level Institutions." *Business Strategy and the Environment* 27 (8): 1609–1622. https://doi.org/10.1002/bse.2227.

Ben-Amar, Walid, and Philip McIlkenny. 2015. "Board Effectiveness and the Voluntary Disclosure of Climate Change Information." *Business Strategy and the Environment* 24 (8): 704–719. https://doi.org/10.1002/bse.1840.

Bendor, Jonathan B. 2010. *Bounded Rationality and Politics*. University of California Press.

Bendor, Jonathan, Bernardo A. Huberman, and Fang Wu. 2009. "Management Fads, Pedagogies, and Other Soft Technologies." *Journal of Economic Behavior & Organization* 72 (1): 290–304. https://doi.org/10.1016/j.jebo.2009.07.002.

Bergstrom, Theodore, Lawrence Blume, and Hal Varian. 1986. "On the Private Provision of Public Goods." *Journal of Public Economics* 29 (1): 25–49. https://doi.org/10.1016/0047-2727(86)90024-1.

Berliner, Daniel, Anne Regan Greenleaf, Milli Lake, Margaret Levi, and Jennifer Noveck. 2015. *Labor Standards in International Supply Chains: Aligning Rights and Incentives*. Edward Elgar Publishing.

Berliner, Daniel, and Aseem Prakash. 2012. "From Norms to Programs: The United Nations Global Compact and Global Governance." *Regulation & Governance* 6 (2): 149–166.

Berliner, Daniel, and Aseem Prakash. 2014a. "Public Authority and Private Rules: How Domestic Regulatory Institutions Shape the Adoption of Global Private Regimes." *International Studies Quarterly* 58 (4): 793–803. https://doi.org/10.1111/isqu.12166.

Berliner, Daniel, and Aseem Prakash. 2014b. "The United Nations Global Compact: An Institutionalist Perspective." *Journal of Business Ethics* 122 (2): 217–223. https://doi.org/10.1007/s10551-014-2217-5.

Berliner, Daniel, and Aseem Prakash. 2015. "'Bluewashing' the Firm? Voluntary Regulations, Program Design, and Member Compliance with the United Nations Global Compact." *Policy Studies Journal* 43 (1): 115–138. https://doi.org/10.1111/psj.12085.

Bernauer, Thomas. 2013. "Climate Change Politics." *Annual Review of Political Science* 16: 421–448. https://doi.org/10.1146/annurev-polisci-062011-154926.

Bernstein, Steven, and Benjamin Cashore. 2007. "Can Non-State Global Governance Be Legitimate? An Analytical Framework." *Regulation & Governance* 1 (4): 347–371. https://doi.org/10.1111/j.1748-5991.2007.00021.x.

Berthelot, Sylvie, and Anne-Marie Robert. 2011. "Climate Change Disclosures: An Examination of Canadian Oil and Gas Firms." *Issues in Social and Environmental Accounting* 5 (1–2): 106–123.

Bertrand, Marianne, Esther Duflo, and Sendhil Mullainathan. 2004. "How Much Should We Trust Differences-In-Differences Estimates?" *Quarterly Journal of Economics* 119 (1): 249–275. https://doi.org/10.1162/003355304772839588.

Besley, Timothy, and Maitreesh Ghatak. 2001. "Government Versus Private Ownership of Public Goods." *Quarterly Journal of Economics* 116 (4): 1343–1372. https://doi.org/10.1162/003355301753265598.

Besley, Timothy, and Maitreesh Ghatak. 2005. "Competition and Incentives with Motivated Agents." *American Economic Review* 95 (3): 616–636. https://doi.org/10.1257/0002828054201413.

Besley, Timothy, and Maitreesh Ghatak. 2007. "Retailing Public Goods: The Economics of Corporate Social Responsibility." *Journal of Public Economics* 91 (9): 1645–1663.

Bessen, James E. 2016. "Accounting for Rising Corporate Profits: Intangibles or Regulatory Rents?" Boston University School of Law, Law and Economics research paper no. 16–18. https://doi.org/10.2139/ssrn.2778641.

Betsill, Michele M., and Harriet Bulkeley. 2004. "Transnational Networks and Global Environmental Governance: The Cities for Climate Protection Program." *International Studies Quarterly* 48 (2): 471–493. https://doi.org/10.1111/j.0020-8833.2004.00310.x.

Birkland, Thomas A. 1997. *After Disaster: Agenda Setting, Public Policy, and Focusing Events*. Georgetown University Press.

Birkland, Thomas A. 1998. "Focusing Events, Mobilization, and Agenda Setting." *Journal of Public Policy* 18 (1): 53–74.

Blackman, Allen. 2008. "Can Voluntary Environmental Regulation Work in Developing Countries? Lessons from Case Studies." *Policy Studies Journal* 36 (1): 119–141. https://doi.org/10.1111/j.1541-0072.2007.00256.x.

Blackman, Allen, Bidisha Lahiri, William Pizer, Marisol Rivera Planter, and Carlos Muñoz Piña. 2010. "Voluntary Environmental Regulation in Developing Countries: Mexico's Clean Industry Program." *Journal of Environmental Economics and Management* 60 (3): 182–192. https://doi.org/10.1016/j.jeem.2010.05.006.

Blok, Kornelis, Niklas Höhne, Kees van der Leun, and Nicholas Harrison. 2012. "Bridging the Greenhouse-Gas Emissions Gap." *Nature Climate Change* 2 (7): 471–174. https://doi.org/10.1038/nclimate1602.

Bloom, Nicholas, Raffaella Sadun, and John Van Reenen. 2016. "Management as a Technology?" Working Paper. Working Paper Series. National Bureau of Economic Research. https://doi.org/10.3386/w22327.

Bloom, Nicholas, and John Van Reenen. 2007. "Measuring and Explaining Management Practices Across Firms and Countries." *Quarterly Journal of Economics* 122 (4): 1351–1408. https://doi.org/10.1162/qjec.2007.122.4.1351.

Bloom, Nicholas, and John Van Reenen. 2010. "Why Do Management Practices Differ across Firms and Countries?" *Journal of Economic Perspectives* 24 (1): 203–224. https://doi.org/10.1257/jep.24.1.203.

Boasson, Elin Lerum, and Jørgen Wettestad. 2016. *EU Climate Policy: Industry, Policy Interaction and External Environment*. Routledge. https://doi.org/10.4324/9781315580623.

Bobrow, Davis B., and John S. Dryzek. 1987. *Policy Analysis by Design*. University of Pittsburgh Press.

Boiral, Olivier, Jean-François Henri, and David Talbot. 2012. "Modeling the Impacts of Corporate Commitment on Climate Change." *Business Strategy and the Environment* 21 (8): 495–516.

Borck, Jonathan, and Cary Coglianese. 2009. "Voluntary Environmental Programs: Assessing Their Effectiveness." *Annual Review of Environment & Resources* 34: 305.

Borghesi, Richard, Kiyoung Chang, and Ying Li. 2019. "Firm Value in Commonly Uncertain Times: The Divergent Effects of Corporate Governance and CSR." *Applied Economics* 51 (43): 4726–4741. https://doi.org/10.1080/00036846.2019.1597255.

Borghesi, Richard, Joel F. Houston, and Andy Naranjo. 2014. "Corporate Socially Responsible Investments: CEO Altruism, Reputation, and Shareholder Interests." *Journal of Corporate Finance* 26 (June):164–181. https://doi.org/10.1016/j.jcorpfin.2014.03.008.

Bouten, Lies, Patricia Everaert, and Robin W. Roberts. 2012. "How a Two-Step Approach Discloses Different Determinants of Voluntary Social and Environmental Reporting." *Journal of Business Finance & Accounting* 39 (5–6): 567–605. https://doi.org/10.1111/j.1468-5957.2012.02290.x.

Bowen, Frances, and J. Alberto Aragon-Correa. 2014. "Greenwashing in Corporate Environmentalism Research and Practice: The Importance of What We Say and Do." *Organization & Environment* 27 (2): 107–112. https://doi.org/10.1177/1086026614537078.

Bradford, Anu. 2019. *The Brussels Effect: How the European Union Rules the World*. Oxford University Press. https://doi.org/10.1093/oso/9780190088583.001.0001.

Branstetter, Lee, and William Pizer. 2013. *Facing the Climate Change Challenge in a Global Economy*. NBER Book Chapter Series, no. c12587. National Bureau of Economic Research.

Broek, Onna van den. 2021. "Soft Law Engagements and Hard Law Preferences: Comparing EU Lobbying Positions between UN Global Compact Signatory Firms and Other Interest Group Types." *Business and Politics* 23 (3): 383–405. https://doi.org/10.1017/bap.2021.2.

Bromley, Patricia, and Walter W. Powell. 2012. "From Smoke and Mirrors to Walking the Talk: Decoupling in the Contemporary World." *Academy of Management Annals* 6 (1): 483–530. https://doi.org/10.1080/19416520.2012.684462.

Buchanan, James M. 1965. "An Economic Theory of Clubs." *Economica*, New Series, 32 (125): 1–14.

Bulkeley, Harriet. 2012. *Cities and Climate Change*. Routledge. https://doi.org/10.4324/9780203077207.

Bulkeley, Harriet, Liliana Andonova, Michele M. Betsill, et al. 2014. *Transnational Climate Change Governance*. Cambridge University Press.

Bulkeley, Harriet, and Michele M. Betsill. 2005. "Rethinking Sustainable Cities: Multilevel Governance and the 'Urban' Politics of Climate Change." *Environmental Politics* 14 (1): 42–63. https://doi.org/10.1080/0964401042000310178.

Burke, William. 2009. "Fitting and Interpretting Cragg's Tobit Alternative Using Stata." *Stata Journal* 9 (4): 584–592.

Busch, Timo, M. Johnson, T. Pioch, and M. Kopp. 2018. "Consistency of Corporate Carbon Emission Data." University of Hamburg/WWF Deutschland.

Buthe, Tim, and Walter Mattli. 2005. "Accountability in Accounting? The Politics of Private Rule-Making in the Public Interest." *Governance* 18 (3): 399–429.

Buthe, Tim, and Walter Mattli. 2011. *New Global Rulers: The Privatization of Regulation in the World Economy*. Princeton University Press.

Cameron, A. Colin, and Douglas L. Miller. 2015. "A Practitioner's Guide to Cluster-Robust Inference." *Journal of Human Resources* 50 (2): 317–372. https://doi.org/10.3368/jhr.50.2.317.

Cameron, Adrian Colin, and P. K Trivedi. 2005. *Microeconometrics: Methods and Applications*. Cambridge University Press.

Carley, Sanya. 2009. "State Renewable Energy Electricity Policies: An Empirical Evaluation of Effectiveness." *Energy Policy* 37 (8): 3071–3081. https://doi.org/10.1016/j.enpol.2009.03.062.

Carley, Sanya. 2011. "The Era of State Energy Policy Innovation: A Review of Policy Instruments." *Review of Policy Research* 28 (3): 265–294. https://doi.org/10.1111/j.1541-1338.2011.00495.x.

Carson, Siri Granum, Øivind Hagen, and S. Prakash Sethi. 2015. "From Implicit to Explicit CSR in a Scandinavian Context: The Cases of HÅG and Hydro." *Journal of Business Ethics* 127 (1): 17–31. https://doi.org/10.1007/s10551-013-1791-2.

Cashore, Benjamin. 2002. "Legitimacy and the Privatization of Environmental Governance: How Non–State Market–Driven (NSMD) Governance Systems Gain Rule–Making Authority." *Governance* 15 (4): 503–529. https://doi.org/10.1111/1468-0491.00199.

CDP. 2015a. "CDP 2015 Climate Change Scoring Methodology." CDP.

CDP. 2015b. "CDP's 2015 Climate Change Information Request." CDP.

CDP. 2016a. "Accounting of Scope 2 Emissions: Technical Notes for Reporting to CDP Climate Change and Supply Chain in 2016." CDP. https://www.cdp.net/en/research/global-reports/tracking-climate-progress-2016

CDP. 2016b. "Out of the Starting Blocks: Tracking Progress on Corporate Climate Action." Climate Change Report. London, UK: CDP.

CDP. 2017. "Guidance for Companies Reporting on Climate Change on Behalf of Investors & Supply Chain Members 2017." Climate Change Report. https://b8f65cb373b1b7b15feb-c70d8ead6ced550b4d987d7c03fcdd1d.ssl.cf3.rackcdn.com/cms/guidance_docs/pdfs/000/000/224/original/CDP-Climate-Change-Reporting-Guidance.pdf?1478542692.https://b8f65cb373b1b7b15feb-c70d8ead6ced550b4d987d7c03fcdd1d.ssl.cf3.rackcdn.com/cms/guidance_docs/pdfs/000/000/224/original/CDP-Climate-Change-Reporting-Guidance.pdf?1478542692

Chan, Sander, Robert Falkner, Matthew Goldberg, and Harro van Asselt. 2018. "Effective and Geographically Balanced? An Output-Based Assessment of Non-State Climate Actions." *Climate Policy* 18 (1): 24–35. https://doi.org/10.1080/14693062.2016.1248343.

Chang, Ching-Hsun. 2011. "The Influence of Corporate Environmental Ethics on Competitive Advantage: The Mediation Role of Green Innovation." *Journal of Business Ethics* 104 (3): 361–370. https://doi.org/10.1007/s10551-011-0914-x.

Cho, Charles H., and Dennis M. Patten. 2007. "The Role of Environmental Disclosures as Tools of Legitimacy: A Research Note." *Accounting, Organizations and Society* 32 (7–8): 639–647. https://doi.org/10.1016/j.aos.2006.09.009.

Choi, In. 2001. "Unit Root Tests for Panel Data." *Journal of International Money and Finance* 20 (2): 249–272. https://doi.org/10.1016/S0261-5606(00)00048-6.

Christmann, Petra. 2000. "Effects of 'Best Practices' of Environmental Management on Cost Advantage: The Role of Complementary Assets." *Academy of Management Journal* 43 (4): 663–680. https://www.researchgate.net/publication/237686471_Effects_of_Best_Practices_of_Environmental_Management_on_Cost_Advantage_The_Role_of_Complementary_Assets.

Cingano, Federico, and Paolo Pinotti. 2013. "Politicians at Work: The Private Returns and Social Costs of Political Connections." *Journal of the European Economic Association* 11 (2): 433–465. https://doi.org/10.1111/jeea.12001.

Clapp, Jennifer, and Peter Dauvergne. 2011. *Paths to a Green World: The Political Economy of the Global Environment*, 2nd ed. MIT Press.

Cohen, Mark A., and W. Kip Viscusi. 2012. "The Role of Information Disclosure in Climate Mitigation Policy." *Climate Change Economics* 03 (04): 1250020. https://doi.org/10.1142/S2010007812500200.

Colgan, Jeff D., Jessica F. Green, and Thomas N. Hale. 2021. "Asset Revaluation and the Existential Politics of Climate Change." *International Organization* 75 (2): 586–610. https://doi.org/10.1017/S0020818320000296.

Conconi, Paola, and Carlo Perroni. 2002. "Issue Linkage and Issue Tie-in in Multilateral Negotiations." *Journal of International Economics* 57 (2): 423–447. https://doi.org/10.1016/S0022-1996(01)00157-X.

Cory, Jared, Michael Lerner, and Iain Osgood. 2021. "Supply Chain Linkages and the Extended Carbon Coalition." *American Journal of Political Science* 65 (1): 69–87. https://doi.org/10.1111/ajps.12525.

Costello, Christopher, and Matthew Kotchen. 2022. "Policy Instrument Choice with Coasean Provision of Public Goods." *Journal of the Association of Environmental and Resource Economists* 9 (5): 947–980. https://doi.org/10.1086/717345.

Cotter, Julie, and Muftah M. Najah. 2012. "Institutional Investor Influence on Global Climate Change Disclosure Practices." *Australian Journal of Management*, 37 (2), 169–187. https://doi.org/10.1177/0312896211423945.

Cragg, John G. 1971. "Some Statistical Models for Limited Dependent Variables with Application to the Demand for Durable Goods." *Econometrica* 39 (5): 829–844. https://doi.org/10.2307/1909582.

Cross, Mai'a K. Davis. 2013. "Rethinking Epistemic Communities Twenty Years Later." *Review of International Studies* 39 (1): 137–160. https://doi.org/10.1017/S0260210512000034.

Cutler, A. Claire, Virginia Haufler, and Tony Porter. 1999. *Private Authority and International Affairs*. SUNY Press.

Cyert, Richard, and James G. March. 1963. *A Behavioral Theory of the Firm*. Blackwell.

Cyert, Richard Michael, and James G. March. 1992. *A Behavioral Theory of the Firm*. 2nd ed. Blackwell Business.

D'Amico, Eugenio, Daniela Coluccia, Stefano Fontana, and Silvia Solimene. 2016. "Factors Influencing Corporate Environmental Disclosure." *Business Strategy and the Environment* 25 (3): 178–192. https://doi.org/10.1002/bse.1865.

Darnall, Nicole, and Daniel Edwards. 2006. "Predicting the Cost of Environmental Management System Adoption: The Role of Capabilities, Resources and Ownership Structure." *Strategic Management Journal* 27 (4): 301–320. https://doi.org/10.1002/smj.518.

Darnall, Nicole, G. Jason Jolley, and Robert Handfield. 2008. "Environmental Management Systems and Green Supply Chain Management: Complements for Sustainability?" *Business Strategy and the Environment* 17 (1): 30–45. https://doi.org/10.1002/bse.557.

Dasgupta, Susmita, Hemamala Hettige, and David Wheeler. 2000. "What Improves Environmental Compliance? Evidence from Mexican Industry." *Journal of Environmental Economics and Management* 39 (1): 39–66.

Dauvergne, Peter, and Jane Lister. 2010. "The Power of Big Box Retail in Global Environmental Governance: Bringing Commodity Chains Back into IR." *Millennium—Journal of International Studies* 39 (1): 145–160. https://doi.org/10.1177/0305829810371018.

Deakin, Nicholas, and Kieron Walsh. 1996. "The Enabling State: The Role of Markets and Contracts." *Public Administration* 74 (1): 33–47. https://doi.org/10.1111/j.1467-9299.1996.tb00856.x.

DeCanio, Stephen J., and William E. Watkins. 1998. "Investment in Energy Efficiency: Do the Characteristics of Firms Matter?" *Review of Economics and Statistics* 80 (1): 95–107. https://doi.org/10.1162/003465398557366.

Decker, Christopher S. 2003. "Corporate Environmentalism and Environmental Statutory Permitting." *Journal of Law & Economics* 46 (1): 103–129. https://doi.org/10.1086/345586.

Decker, Ryan A., John Haltiwanger, Ron S. Jarmin, and Javier Miranda. 2016. "Declining Business Dynamism: What We Know and the Way Forward." *American Economic Review* 106 (5): 203–207. https://doi.org/10.1257/aer.p20161050.

deLeon, Peter, and Linda deLeon. 2002. "What Ever Happened to Policy Implementation? An Alternative Approach." *Journal of Public Administration Research and Theory* 12 (4): 467–492. https://doi.org/10.1093/oxfordjournals.jpart.a003544.

Delgado-Márquez, Blanca L., Luis E. Pedauga, and Eulogio Cordón-Pozo. 2017. "Industries Regulation and Firm Environmental Disclosure: A Stakeholders' Perspective on the Importance of Legitimation and International Activities." *Organization & Environment*, 30 (2): 103–121.https://doi.org/10.1177/1086026615622028.

Delmas, Magali A., and Vanessa Cuerel Burbano. 2011. "The Drivers of Greenwashing." *California Management Review* 54 (1): 64–87. https://doi.org/10.1525/cmr.2011.54.1.64.

Delmas, Magali A., and Michael W. Toffel 2008. "Organizational Responses to Environmental Demands: Opening the Black Box." *Strategic Management Journal* 29 (10): 1027–1055. https://doi.org/10.1002/smj.701.

Demirel, Pelin, Konstantinos Iatridis, and Effie Kesidou. 2018. "The Impact of Regulatory Complexity upon Self-Regulation: Evidence from the Adoption and Certification of Environmental Management Systems." *Journal of Environmental Management* 207 (February): 80–91. https://doi.org/10.1016/j.jenvman.2017.11.019.

Deryugina, Tatyana, Frances Moore, and Richard S. J. Tol. 2021. "Environmental Applications of the Coase Theorem." *Environmental Science & Policy* 120 (June): 81–88. https://doi.org/10.1016/j.envsci.2021.03.001.

Deschenes, Olivier, and Kyle C Meng. 2018. "Quasi-Experimental Methods in Environmental Economics: Opportunities and Challenges." Working Paper 24903. National Bureau of Economic Research. https://doi.org/10.3386/w24903.

Deutsch, KW. 1966. *The Nerves of Government*. Free Press.

Diffenbaugh, Noah S., Alexandra G. Konings, and Christopher B. Field. 2021. "Atmospheric Variability Contributes to Increasing Wildfire Weather but Not as Much as Global Warming." *Proceedings of the National Academy of Sciences* 118 (46): e2117876118. https://doi.org/10.1073/pnas.2117876118.

Distelhorst, Greg, and Richard M. Locke. 2018. "Does Compliance Pay? Social Standards and Firm-Level Trade." *American Journal of Political Science* 62 (3): 695–711. https://doi.org/10.1111/ajps.12372.

Djelic, Marie-Laure. 2001. *Exporting the American Model: The Post-War Transformation of European Business*. Oxford University Press.

Doda, Baran, Caterina Gennaioli, Andy Gouldson, David Grover, and Rory Sullivan. 2016. "Are Corporate Carbon Management Practices Reducing Corporate Carbon Emissions?" *Corporate Social Responsibility and Environmental Management* 23 (5): 257–270. https://doi.org/10.1002/csr.1369.

Dolsak, Nives, and Aseem Prakash. 2016. "Join the Club: How the Domestic NGO Sector Induces Participation in the Covenant of Mayors Program." *International Interactions* 43 (1): 26–47. https://doi.org/10.1080/03050629.2017.1226668.

Doonan, Julie, Paul Lanoie, and Benoit Laplante. 2005. "Determinants of Environmental Performance in the Canadian Pulp and Paper Industry: An Assessment from inside the Industry." *Ecological Economics* 55 (1): 73–84. https://doi.org/10.1016/j.ecolecon.2004.10.017.

Downar, Benedikt, Jurgen Ernstberger, Stefan Reichelstein, Sebastian Schwenen, and Aleksandar Zaklan. 2021. "The Impact of Carbon Disclosure Mandates on Emissions and Financial Operating Performance." *Review of Accounting Studies* 26 (3):1137–1175.

Dubash, N. K., C. Mitchell, E. L. Boasson, et al. 2022. "National and Sub-National Policies and Institutions. In IPCC, 2022: Climate Change 2022: Mitigation of Climate Change. Contribution of Working Group III to the Sixth Assessment Report of the Intergovernmental Panel on Climate Change." Intergovernmental Panel on Climate Change. https://www.ipcc.ch/report/ar6/wg3/downloads/report/IPCC_AR6_WGIII_Chapter13.pdf.

Dunlop, Claire A. 2009. "Policy Transfer as Learning: Capturing Variation in What Decision-Makers Learn from Epistemic Communities." *Policy Studies* 30 (3): 289–311. https://doi.org/10.1080/01442870902863869.

Dunlop, Claire A. 2010. "The Temporal Dimension of Knowledge and the Limits of Policy Appraisal: Biofuels Policy in the UK." *Policy Sciences* 43 (4): 343–363. https://doi.org/10.1007/s11077-009-9101-7.

Eberhard-Harribey, Laurence. 2006. "Corporate Social Responsibility as a New Paradigm in the European Policy: How CSR Comes to Legitimate the European Regulation Process." *Corporate Governance* 6 (4): 358–368. https://doi.org/10.1108/14720700610689487.

Eberlein, Burkard, Kenneth W. Abbott, Julia Black, E. E Meidinger, and Stepan Wood. 2014. "Transnational Business Governance Interactions: Conceptualization and Framework for Analysis." *Regulation & Governance* 8 (1): 1–21.

Eccles, Robert G., Ioannis Ioannou, and George Serafeim. 2014. "The Impact of Corporate Sustainability on Organizational Processes and Performance." *Management Science* 60 (11): 2835–2857. https://doi.org/10.1287/mnsc.2014.1984.

Eccles, Robert G., and Alison Taylor. 2023. "The Evolving Role of Chief Sustainability Officers." *Harvard Business Review*, 2023. https://hbr.org/2023/07/the-evolving-role-of-chief-sustainability-officers.

Egan, Patrick J., and Megan Mullin. 2012. "Turning Personal Experience into Political Attitudes: The Effect of Local Weather on Americans' Perceptions about Global Warming." *Journal of Politics* 74 (3): 796–809. https://doi.org/10.1017/S0022381612000448.

Egorov, Georgy, and Bård Harstad. 2017. "Private Politics and Public Regulation." *Review of Economic Studies* 84 (4): 1652–1682. https://doi.org/10.1093/restud/rdx009.

Eiadat, Yousef, Aidan Kelly, Frank Roche, and Hussein Eyadat. 2008. "Green and Competitive? An Empirical Test of the Mediating Role of Environmental Innovation Strategy." *Journal of World Business* 43 (2): 131–145. https://doi.org/10.1016/j.jwb.2007.11.012.

Eisner, Marc Allen. 2004. "Corporate Environmentalism, Regulatory Reform, and Industry Self-Regulation: Toward Genuine Regulatory Reinvention in the United States." *Governance* 17 (2): 145–167. https://doi.org/10.1111/j.1468-0491.2004.00241.x.

Elliott, Christian, Amy Janzwood, Steven Bernstein, and Matthew Hoffmann. 2023a. "Rethinking Complementarity: The Co-Evolution of Public and Private Governance in Corporate Climate Disclosure." *Regulation & Governance* 18 (3): 802–819. https://doi.org/10.1111/rego.12550.

Elmore, Richard F. 1979. "Backward Mapping: Implementation Research and Policy Decisions." *Political Science Quarterly* 94 (4): 601–616. https://doi.org/10.2307/2149628.

Elster, Jon. 1989. "Social Norms and Economic Theory." *Journal of Economic Perspectives* 3 (4): 99–117. https://doi.org/10.1257/jep.3.4.99.

Elster, Jon. 2009. *Reason and Rationality*. Princeton University Press.

Lubin, David A., and Daniel C. Esty. 2010. "The Sustainability Imperative." *Harvard Business Review*. 2010. https://hbr.org/2010/05/the-sustainability-imperative.

Eyckmans, Johan, and Henry Tulkens. 2003. "Simulating Coalitionally Stable Burden Sharing Agreements for the Climate Change Problem." *Resource and Energy Economics* 25 (4): 299–327. https://doi.org/10.1016/S0928-7655(03)00041-1.

Fagerberg, J. 1995. "User–Producer Interaction, Learning and Comparative Advantage." *Cambridge Journal of Economics* 19 (1): 243–256. https://doi.org/10.1093/oxfordjournals.cje.a035306.

Falkner, R. 2016a. "A Minilateral Solution for Global Climate Change? On Bargaining Efficiency, Club Benefits, and International Legitimacy." *Perspectives on Politics* 14 (1): 87–101. https://doi.org/10.1017/S1537592715003242.

Falkner, Robert. 2016b. "The Paris Agreement and the New Logic of International Climate Politics." *International Affairs* 92 (5): 1107–1125. https://doi.org/10.1111/1468-2346.12708.

Fama, Eugene F. 2021. "Contract Costs, Stakeholder Capitalism, and ESG." *European Financial Management* 27 (2): 189–195. https://doi.org/10.1111/eufm.12297.

Fatemi, Ali, Iraj Fooladi, and Hassan Tehranian. 2015. "Valuation Effects of Corporate Social Responsibility." *Journal of Banking & Finance* 59 (October):182–192. https://doi.org/10.1016/j.jbankfin.2015.04.028.

Fearon, James D. 1995. "Rationalist Explanations for War." *International Organization* 49 (3): 379–414. https://doi.org/10.1017/S0020818300033324.

Fearon, James D. 1998a. "Bargaining, Enforcement, and International Cooperation." *International Organization* 52 (2): 269–305. https://doi.org/10.1162/002081898753162820.

Fearon, James D. 1998b. "Domestic Politics, Foreign Policy, and Theories of International Relations." *Annual Review of Political Science* 1: 289. https://doi.org/10.1146/annurev.polisci.1.1.289.

Fearon, James D. 1999. "What Is Identity? (As We Now Use the Word)?" Stanford University. http://www.web.stanford.edu/group/fearon-research/cgi-bin/wordpress/wp-content/uploads/2013/10/What-is-Identity-as-we-now-use-the-word-.pdf.

Feddersen, Timothy J., and Thomas W. Gilligan. 2001. "Saints and Markets: Activists and the Supply of Credence Goods." *Journal of Economics & Management Strategy* 10 (1): 149–171. https://doi.org/10.1111/j.1430-9134.2001.00149.x.

Finnegan, Jared J. 2023. "Changing Prices in a Changing Climate: Electoral Competition and Fossil Fuel Taxation." *Comparative Political Studies* 56 (8): 1257–1290. https://doi.org/10.1177/00104140221141853.

Finnemore, Martha. 1993. "International Organizations as Teachers of Norms: The United Nations Educational, Scientific, and Cultural Organization and Science Policy." *International Organization* 47 (4): 565–597. https://doi.org/10.1017/S0020818300028101.

Finnemore, Martha, and Kathryn Sikkink. 1998. "International Norm Dynamics and Political Change." *International Organization* 52 (4): 887–917. https://doi.org/10.1162/002081898550789.

Finus, Michael, Ekko van Ierland, and Rob Dellink. 2006. "Stability of Climate Coalitions in a Cartel Formation Game." *Economics of Governance* 7 (3): 271–291. https://doi.org/10.1007/s10101-005-0009-1.

Fisher-Vanden, Karen, and Karin S. Thorburn. 2011. "Voluntary Corporate Environmental Initiatives and Shareholder Wealth." *Journal of Environmental Economics and Management* 62 (3): 430–445. https://doi.org/10.1016/j.jeem.2011.04.003.

Fligstein, Neil, and Doug McAdam. 2012. *A Theory of Fields*. Oxford University Press.

Folke, Olle. 2014. "Shades of Brown and Green: Party Effects in Proportional Election Systems." *Journal of the European Economic Association* 12 (5): 1361–1395. https://doi.org/10.1111/jeea.12103.

Foster, Andrew D., and Mark R. Rosenzweig. 1995. "Learning by Doing and Learning from Others: Human Capital and Technical Change in Agriculture." *Journal of Political Economy* 103 (6): 1176–1209. https://doi.org/10.1086/601447.

Fowlie, Meredith, Lawrence Goulder, Matthew Kotchen, et al. 2014. "An Economic Perspective on the EPA's Clean Power Plan." *Science* 346 (6211): 815–816. https://doi.org/10.1126/science.1261349.

Freedman, Martin, and Bikki Jaggi. 2005. "Global Warming, Commitment to the Kyoto Protocol, and Accounting Disclosures by the Largest Global Public Firms from Polluting Industries." *International Journal of Accounting* 40 (3): 215–232. https://doi.org/10.1016/j.intacc.2005.06.004.

Freedman, Martin, and Bikki Jaggi. 2011. "Global Warming Disclosures: Impact of Kyoto Protocol Across Countries." *Journal of International Financial Management & Accounting* 22 (1): 46–90. https://doi.org/10.1111/j.1467-646X.2010.01045.x.

Fudenberg, Drew, and Jean Tirole. 1983. "Learning-by-Doing and Market Performance." *Bell Journal of Economics* 14 (2): 522–530. https://doi.org/10.2307/3003653.

Gans, Will, and Beat Hintermann. 2013. "Market Effects of Voluntary Climate Action by Firms: Evidence from the Chicago Climate Exchange." *Environmental and Resource Economics* 55 (2): 291–308. https://doi.org/10.1007/s10640-012-9626-7.

Garcia-Johnson, Ronie. 2000. *Exporting Environmentalism: U.S. Multinational Chemical Corporations in Brazil and Mexico*. MIT Press.

Gartenberg, Claudine, Andrea Prat, and George Serafeim. 2019. "Corporate Purpose and Financial Performance." *Organization Science* 30 (1): 1–18. https://doi.org/10.1287/orsc.2018.1230.

Geist, Helmut J., and Eric F. Lambin. 2004. "Dynamic Causal Patterns of Desertification." *BioScience* 54 (9): 817–829. https://doi.org/10.1641/0006-3568(2004)054[0817:DCPOD]2.0.CO;2.

Giddens, Anthony. 2011. *The Politics of Climate Change*. 2nd ed. Polity.

Goffman, Erving. 1974. *Frame Analysis: An Essay on the Organization of Experience*. Harvard University Press.

Goggin, Malcolm L., Anne O. Bowman, James P. Lester, and Laurence J. O'Toole. 1990. *Implementation Theory and Practice: Toward a Third Generation*. Scott, Foresman/Little, Brown Higher Education.

Gough, Clair, and Simon Shackley. 2001. "The Respectable Politics of Climate Change: The Epistemic Communities and NGOs." *International Affairs* 77 (2): 329–346. https://doi.org/10.1111/1468-2346.00195.

Grabs, Janina. 2020. *Selling Sustainability Short? The Private Governance of Labor and the Environment in the Coffee Sector*. Cambridge University Press.

Goulder, Lawrence H., Marc A. C. Hafstead, GyuRim Kim, and Xianling Long. 2019. "Impacts of a Carbon Tax across US Household Income Groups: What Are the Equity-Efficiency Trade-Offs?" *Journal of Public Economics* 175 (July):44–64. https://doi.org/10.1016/j.jpubeco.2019.04.002.

Goulder, Lawrence H., Marc A. C. Hafstead, and Roberton C. Williams III. 2016. "General Equilibrium Impacts of a Federal Clean Energy Standard." *American Economic Journal: Economic Policy* 8 (2): 186–218. https://doi.org/10.1257/pol.20140011.

Goulder, Lawrence, and Marc Hafstead. 2017. *Confronting the Climate Challenge: U.S. Policy Options*. Columbia University Press.

Graff, Zivin Joshua, and Arthur Small. 2005. "A Modigliani-Miller Theory of Altruistic Corporate Social Responsibility." *B.E. Journal of Economic Analysis & Policy* 5 (1): 1–19. https://doi.org/10.1515/1538-0653.1369.

Green, Jessica F. 2010. "Private Standards in the Climate Regime: The Greenhouse Gas Protocol." *Business & Politics* 12 (3): 1–37. https://doi.org/10.2202/1469-3569.1318.

Green, Jessica F. 2013. "Order out of Chaos: Public and Private Rules for Managing Carbon." *Global Environmental Politics* 13 (2): 1–25. https://doi.org/10.1162/GLEP_a_00164.

Green, Jessica F. 2017. "Blurred Lines: Public-Private Interactions in Carbon Regulations." *International Interactions* 43 (1): 103–128. https://doi.org/10.1080/03050629.2016.1210943.

Green, Jessica, Jennifer Hadden, Thomas Hale, and Paasha Mahdavi. 2021. "Transition, Hedge, or Resist? Understanding Political and Economic Behavior toward

Decarbonization in the Oil and Gas Industry." *Review of International Political Economy* 9 (6): 2036–2063. https://doi.org/10.1080/09692290.2021.1946708.

Greene, W. H. 2000. *Econometric Analysis*. 4th ed. Prentice Hall.

Greenstone, Michael, and Ted Gayer. 2009. "Quasi-Experimental and Experimental Approaches to Environmental Economics." *Journal of Environmental Economics and Management* 57 (1): 21–44. https://doi.org/10.1016/j.jeem.2008.02.004.

Greshko, Michael, Laura Parker, and Brian Clark Howard. 2018. "A Running List of How Trump Is Changing the Environment." *National Geographic News*.

Griffin, Paul. 2017. "CDP Carbon Majors Report 2017." CDP. https://cdn.cdp.net/cdp-production/cms/reports/documents/000/002/327/original/Carbon-Majors-Report-2017.pdf.

Grossman, Sanford J., and Oliver D. Hart. 1986. "The Costs and Benefits of Ownership: A Theory of Vertical and Lateral Integration." *Journal of Political Economy* 94 (4): 691–719.

Guenther, Edeltraud, Thomas Guenther, Frank Schiemann, and Gabriel Weber. 2015. "Stakeholder Relevance for Reporting Explanatory Factors of Carbon Disclosure." *Business & Society*. https://doi.org/10.1177/0007650315575119.

Gupta, Sonam, and Robert Innes. 2014. "Private Politics and Environmental Management." *Journal of Environmental Economics and Management* 68 (2): 319–339. https://doi.org/10.1016/j.jeem.2014.05.002.

Guy, Johnathan, Esther Shears, and Jonas Meckling. 2023. "National Models of Climate Governance among Major Emitters." *Nature Climate Change* 13 (2): 189–195. https://doi.org/10.1038/s41558-022-01589-x.

Haas, Peter M. 1992. "Introduction: Epistemic Communities and International Policy Coordination." *International Organization* 46 (1): 1–35.

Habisch, André, Jan Jonker, Martina Wegner, and René Schmidpeter, eds. 2005. *Corporate Social Responsibility Across Europe*. Springer-Verlag. https://www.springer.com/us/book/9783540232513.

Hadden, Jennifer. 2015. *Networks in Contention*. Cambridge University Press.

Haigh, Nardia, and Andrew Griffiths. 2012. "Surprise as a Catalyst for Including Climatic Change in the Strategic Environment." *Business & Society* 51 (1): 89–120. https://doi.org/10.1177/0007650311427425.

Hale, Thomas. 2020. "Catalytic Cooperation." *Global Environmental Politics* 20 (4): 73–98. https://doi.org/10.1162/glep_a_00561.

Hale, Thomas, David Held, and Kevin Young. 2013. *Gridlock: Why Global Cooperation Is Failing When We Need It Most*. Polity.

Hale, Thomas, and Charles Roger. 2014. "Orchestration and Transnational Climate Governance." *Review of International Organizations* 9 (1): 59–82. https://doi.org/10.1007/s11558-013-9174-0.

Harrison, Kathryn, and Lisa McIntosh Sundstrom. 2010. *Global Commons, Domestic Decisions: The Comparative Politics of Climate Change*. MIT Press.

Harstad, Bård. 2023a. "Pledge-and-Review Bargaining: From Kyoto to Paris." *Economic Journal* 133 (651): 1181–1216. https://doi.org/10.1093/ej/ueac076.

Harstad, Bård. 2023b. "Pledge-and-Review Bargining." *Journal of Economic Theory* 207: 105574. https://doi.org/10.1016/j.jet.2022.105574.

Hart, Oliver, and John Moore. 1990. "Property Rights and the Nature of the Firm." *Journal of Political Economy* 98 (6): 1119–1158.

Hart, Stuart L. 1995. "A Natural-Resource-Based View of the Firm." *Academy of Management Review* 20 (4): 986–1014. https://doi.org/10.5465/amr.1995.9512280033.

Hassan, Omaima A. G., and Peter Romilly. 2018. "Relations between Corporate Economic Performance, Environmental Disclosure and Greenhouse Gas Emissions: New Insights." *Business Strategy and the Environment* 27 (7): 893–909. https://doi.org/10.1002/bse.2040.

Helfaya, Akrum, and Mark Whittington. 2019. "Does Designing Environmental Sustainability Disclosure Quality Measures Make a Difference?" *Business Strategy and the Environment* 28 (4): 525–541. https://doi.org/10.1002/bse.2262.

Henderson, Rebecca. 2020. *Reimagining Capitalism in a World on Fire*. Public Affairs.

Henderson, Rebecca, and George Serafeim. 2020. "Tackling Climate Change Requires Organizational Purpose." *AEA Papers and Proceedings*. https://www.hbs.edu/faculty/Pages/item.aspx?num=57586.

Henderson, Rebecca, and Eric Van den Steen. 2015. "Why Do Firms Have 'Purpose'? The Firm's Role as a Carrier of Identity and Reputation." *American Economic Review* 105 (5): 326–330. https://doi.org/10.1257/aer.p20151072.

Henriques, Irene, and Perry Sadorsky. 1996. "The Determinants of an Environmentally Responsive Firm: An Empirical Approach." *Journal of Environmental Economics and Management* 30 (3): 381–395. https://doi.org/10.1006/jeem.1996.0026.

Hertig, Gerard. 2018. "Governance by Institutional Investors in a Stakeholder World." In *The Oxford Handbook of Corporate Law and Governance*, edited by Jeffrey Gordon and Wolf-Georg Ringe. Oxford University Press. http://www.oxfordhandbooks.com/view/10.1093/oxfordhb/9780198743682.001.0001/oxfordhb-9780198743682-e-35.

Heuvel, Remco van den. 2012. "How Robust Are CSR Benchmarks? Comparing ASSET4 with Sustainalytics." Tilburg University. http://arno.uvt.nl/show.cgi?fid=127705.

Hoegh-Guldberg, O., D. Jacob, M. Bindi, et al. 2018. "Impacts of 1.5°C Global Warming on Natural and Human Systems," In Global Warming of 1.5°C. An IPCC Special Report on Impacts of Global Warming of 1.5°C above Pre-Industrial Levels and Related Global Greenhouse Gas Emission Pathways, in the Context of Strengthening the Global Response to the Threat of Climate Change, Sustainable Development, and Efforts to Eradicate Poverty, edited by V. Masson-Delmotte, P. Zhai, H.O. Pörtner, et al., 175–311.

Hoffmann, Matthew J. 2011a. *Climate Governance at the Crossroads: Experimenting with a Global Response after Kyoto*. Oxford University Press.

Honigsberg, Colleen. 2019. "Hedge Fund Regulation and Fund Governance: Evidence on the Effects of Mandatory Disclosure Rules." *Journal of Accounting Research* 57 (4): 845–888. https://doi.org/10.1111/1475-679X.12270.

Hsueh, Lily. 2015. "Why IT Companies Lead on Proactive Climate Action?" *TechTank* (blog). December 5. https://www.brookings.edu/articles/why-it-companies-lead-on-proactive-climate-action/.

Hsueh, Lily. 2017. "Transnational Climate Governance and the Global 500: Examining Private Actor Participation by Firm-Level Factors and Dynamics." *International Interactions* 43 (1): 48–75. https://doi.org/10.1080/03050629.2016.1223929.

Hsueh, Lily. 2019a. "Corporations at a Crossroads: How Multilevel Governance Interactions Shape Participation and Effort in Private Governance Regimes." *Governance* 32 (4): 715–760. https://doi.org/10.1111/gove.12406.

Hsueh, Lily. 2019b. "Opening Up the Firm: What Explains Participation and Effort in Voluntary Carbon Disclosure by Global Businesses? An Analysis of Internal Firm Factors and Dynamics." *Business Strategy and the Environment* 28 (7): 1302–1322. https://doi.org/10.1002/bse.2317.

Hsueh, Lily. 2019c. "Voluntary Climate Action and Credible Regulatory Threat: Evidence from the Carbon Disclosure Project." *Journal of Regulatory Economics* 56 (2–3): 188–225. https://doi.org/10.1007/s11149-019-09390-z.

Hsueh, Lily. 2020. "Calling All Volunteers: Industry Self-Regulation on the Environment." In *Handbook of U.S. Environmental Policy*, edited by David Konisky, 243–256. Edward Elgar Publishing Limited.

Hsueh, Lily, and Aseem Prakash. 2012. "Incentivizing Self-Regulation: Federal vs. State-Level Voluntary Programs in US Climate Change Policies." *Regulation & Governance* 6 (4): 445–473. https://doi.org/10.1111/j.1748-5991.2012.01140.x.

Hsueh, Lily, and Aseem Prakash. 2012c. "Private Voluntary Programs on Climate Change: U.S. Federal Government as the Sponsoring Actor." In *Business and Climate Policy: The Potentials and Pitfalls of Private Voluntary Programs*, edited by Karsten Ronit, 77–110. United Nations University Press.

Hsueh, Roselyn. 2011. *China's Regulatory State: A New Strategy for Globalization*. Cornell University Press.

Hsueh, Roselyn. 2012. "China and India in the Age of Globalization: Sectoral Variation in Postliberalization Reregulation." *Comparative Political Studies* 45 (1): 32–61. https://doi.org/10.1177/0010414011421305.

Hsueh, Roselyn. 2016. "State Capitalism, Chinese-Style: Strategic Value of Sectors, Sectoral Characteristics, and Globalization." *Governance* 29 (1): 85–102. https://doi.org/10.1111/gove.12139.

Hsueh, Roselyn. 2022. *Micro-Institutional Foundations of Capitalism*. Cambridge University Press.

Huang, Janna Z. 2024. "Greenhoused Organizations: Climate Information and the Transformation of Corporate Sustainability." *Academy of Management Annual Meeting Proceedings*. https://journals.aom.org/doi/abs/10.5465/AMPROC.2024.12263abstract.

Hysing, Erik. 2009. "From Government to Governance? A Comparison of Environmental Governing in Swedish Forestry and Transport." *Governance* 22 (4): 647–672. https://doi.org/10.1111/j.1468-0491.2009.01457.x.

Imbens, Guido W. 2015. "Matching Methods in Practice: Three Examples." *Journal of Human Resources* 50 (2): 373–419. https://doi.org/10.3368/jhr.50.2.373.

Innes, R., and J. J. Bial. 2002. "Inducing Innovation in the Environmental Technology of Oligopolistic Firms." *Journal of Industrial Economics* 50 (3): 265–287. https://doi.org/10.1111/1467-6451.00177.

Innes, Robert. 2006. "A Theory of Consumer Boycotts under Symmetric Information and Imperfect Competition." *Economic Journal* 116 (511): 355–381. https://doi.org/10.1111/j.1468-0297.2006.01084.x.

Jenkins-Smith, H. C., D. Nohrstedt, C. M. Weible, and K. Ingold. 2018. "The Advocacy Coalition Framework: An Overview of the Research Program." In *Theories of the Policy Process*, edited by C. M. Weible and P. A. Sabatier, 4th ed., 135–171. Westview Press.

Jira, Chonnikarn (Fern), and Michael W. Toffel. 2013. "Engaging Supply Chains in Climate Change." *Manufacturing & Service Operations Management* 15 (4): 559–577. https://doi.org/10.1287/msom.1120.0420.

Jung, Juhyun, Kathleen Herbohn, and Peter Clarkson. 2018. "Carbon Risk, Carbon Risk Awareness and the Cost of Debt Financing." *Journal of Business Ethics* 150 (4): 1151–1171. https://doi.org/10.1007/s10551-016-3207-6.

Katzenstein, Peter J. 1996. "Introduction: Alternative Perspective on International Security." In *The Culture of National Security: Norms and Identity in World Politics*, edited by Peter J. Katzenstein, 1–32. Columbia University Press.

Kennard, Amanda. 2020. "The Enemy of My Enemy: When Firms Support Climate Change Regulation." *International Organization* 74 (2): 187–221. https://doi.org/10.1017/S0020818320000107.

Kennedy, Caitlyn, and Rebecca Lindsey. 2015. "What's the Difference between Global Warming and Climate Change?" NOAA Climate Q&A, June 17. https://www.climate.gov/news-features/climate-qa/whats-difference-between-global-warming-and-climate-change.

Keohane, Robert O., and David G. Victor. 2011. "The Regime Complex for Climate Change." *Perspectives on Politics* 9 (01): 7–23. https://doi.org/10.1017/S1537592710004068.

Keohane, Robert O., and David G. Victor. 2016. "Cooperation and Discord in Global Climate Policy." *Nature Climate Change* 6 (6): 570–575. https://doi.org/10.1038/nclimate2937.

Kern, Kristine, and Harriet Bulkeley. 2009. "Cities, Europeanization and Multi-Level Governance: Governing Climate Change through Transnational Municipal Networks." *JCMS: Journal of Common Market Studies* 47 (2): 309–332. https://doi.org/10.1111/j.1468-5965.2009.00806.x.

Khanna, Madhu, George Deltas, and Donna Harrington. 2009. "Adoption of Pollution Prevention Techniques: The Role of Management Systems and Regulatory Pressures." *Environmental and Resource Economics* 44 (1): 85–106. https://doi.org/10.1007/s10640-009-9263-y.

Khanna, Madhu, Patricia Koss, Cody Jones, and David Ervin. 2007. "Motivations for Voluntary Environmental Management." *Policy Studies Journal* 35 (4): 751–772. https://doi.org/10.1111/j.1541-0072.2007.00246.x.

Khanna, Madhu, and William Rose Q. Anton. 2002b. "Corporate Environmental Management: Regulatory and Market-Based Incentives." *Land Economics* 78 (4): 539–558. https://doi.org/10.2307/3146852.

Kim, Eun-Hee, and Thomas Lyon. 2011. "When Does Institutional Investor Activism Increase Shareholder Value? The Carbon Disclosure Project." *B.E. Journal of Economic Analysis & Policy* 11 (1): 1–27. https://doi.org/10.2202/1935-1682.2676.

Kim, Yushim, and Stefan Verweij. 2016. "Two Effective Causal Paths That Explain the Adoption of US State Environmental Justice Policy." *Policy Sciences* 49 (4): 505–523. https://doi.org/10.1007/s11077-016-9249-x.

Kingdon, John. 1995. *Agendas, Alternatives, and Public Policies*. 2nd ed. Longman.

Kitzmueller, Markus, and Jay Shimshack. 2012. "Economic Perspectives on Corporate Social Responsibility." *Journal of Economic Literature* 50 (1): 51–84.

Knill, Christoph, and Dirk Lehmkuhl. 2002. "Private Actors and the State: Internationalization and Changing Patterns of Governance." *Governance* 15 (1): 41–63. https://doi.org/10.1111/1468-0491.00179.

Kolk, Ans, and Jonatan Pinkse. 2007. "Towards Strategic Stakeholder Management? Integrating Perspectives on Sustainability Challenges Such as Corporate Responses to Climate Change." *Corporate Governance* 7 (4): 370.

Kolk, Ans, and Jonatan Pinkse. 2008. "A Perspective on Multinational Enterprises and Climate Change: Learning from 'an inconvenient truth'?" *Journal of International Business Studies* 39 (8): 1359–1378. https://doi.org/10.1057/jibs.2008.61.

Kollman, Kelly, and Aseem Prakash. 2001. "Green by Choice? Cross-National Variations in Firms' Responses to EMS-Based Environmental Regimes." *World Politics* 53 (03): 399–430. https://doi.org/10.1353/wp.2001.0010.

Kolstad, Charles, Kevin Urama, John Broome, et al. 2014. "Social, Economic, and Ethical Concepts and Methods." In *Climate Change 2014: Mitigation of Climate Change. Contribution of Working Group III to the Fifth Assessment Report of the Intergovernmental Panel on Climate Change*, edited by P. K. Pachauri and L. A. Meyer, 207–282. Cambridge University Press. https://openresearch-repository.anu.edu.au/handle/1885/55464.

Konisky, David M. 2007. "Regulatory Competition and Environmental Enforcement: Is There a Race to the Bottom?" *American Journal of Political Science* 51 (4): 853–872. https://doi.org/10.1111/j.1540-5907.2007.00285.x.

Konisky, David M. 2024. "The Politics of Climate Policy Instruments." *PS: Political Science & Politics* 57 (1): 21–24. https://doi.org/10.1017/S1049096523000434.

Koppell, Jonathan G. S. 2010. *World Rule: Accountability, Legitimacy, and the Design of Global Governance*. University of Chicago Press.

Kotchen, M., and J. J. Moon. 2012. "Corporate Social Responsibility for Irresponsibility." *B.E. Journal of Economic Analysis & Policy* 12 (1): 1–21. http://www.degruyter.com/view/j/bejeap.2012.12.issue-1/1935-1682.3308/1935-1682.3308.xml.

Kotchen, Matthew J. 2006. "Green Markets and Private Provision of Public Goods." *Journal of Political Economy* 114 (4): 816–834.

Kotchen, Matthew J. 2013. "Voluntary- and Information-Based Approaches to Environmental Management: A Public Economics Perspective." *Review of Environmental Economics and Policy* 7 (2): 276–295. https://doi.org/10.1093/reep/ret012.

Kotchen, Matthew J., and Erin T. Mansur. 2014. "How Stringent Are the US EPA's Proposed Carbon Pollution Standards for New Power Plants?" *Review of Environmental Economics and Policy* 8 (2): 290–306. https://doi.org/10.1093/reep/reu003.

Kotchen, Matthew J., and Kathleen Segerson. 2019. "On the Use of Group Performance and Rights for Environmental Protection and Resource Management."

Proceedings of the National Academy of Sciences 116 (12): 5285–5292. https://doi.org/10.1073/pnas.1802881115.

Krause, Rachel M. 2011. "Policy Innovation, Intergovernmental Relations, and the Adoption of Climate Protection Initiatives by U.S. Cities." *Journal of Urban Affairs* 33 (1): 45–60. https://doi.org/10.1111/j.1467-9906.2010.00510.x.

Krause, Rachel M. 2012. "An Assessment of the Impact That Participation in Local Climate Networks Has on Cities' Implementation of Climate, Energy, and Transportation Policies." *Review of Policy Research* 29 (5): 585–604. https://doi.org/10.1111/j.1541-1338.2012.00582.x.

Krause, Rachel M., Richard C. Feiock, and Christopher V. Hawkins. 2016. "The Administrative Organization of Sustainability within Local Government." *Journal of Public Administration Research and Theory* 26 (1): 113–127. https://doi.org/10.1093/jopart/muu032.

Krueger, Philipp, Daniel Metzger, and Jiaxin Wu. 2022. "The Sustainability Wage Gap." *SSRN Electronic Journal*, April. https://doi.org/10.2139/ssrn.3672492.

Krueger, Philipp, Zacharias Sautner, and Laura T. Starks. 2020. "The Importance of Climate Risks for Institutional Investors." *Review of Financial Studies* 33 (3): 1067–1111.

Kunreuther, H., S. Gupta, R. Bosetti, et al. 2014. "2014: Integrated Risk and Uncertainty Assessment of Climate Change Response Policies." In *Climate Change 2014: Mitigation of Climate Change: Working Group III Contribution to the Fifth Assessment Report of the Intergovernmental Panel on Climate Change*, edited by Ottmar Edenhofer, Ramón Pichs-Madruga, Youba Sokona, et al., 151–205. Cambridge University Press. https://doi.org/10.1017/CBO9781107415416.

Lambin, Eric F., and Paul R. Furumo. 2023. "Deforestation-Free Commodity Supply Chains: Myth or Reality?" *Annual Review of Environment and Resources* 48: 237–261. https://doi.org/10.1146/annurev-environ-112321-121436.

Lamoreaux, Naomi R., Daniel M. G. Raff, and Peter Temin. 1999. *Learning by Doing in Markets, Firms, and Countries*. University of Chicago Press.

Lee, Su-Yol, Yun-Seon Park, and Robert D. Klassen. 2015. "Market Responses to Firms' Voluntary Climate Change Information Disclosure and Carbon Communication." *Corporate Social Responsibility and Environmental Management* 22 (1): 1–12. https://doi.org/10.1002/csr.1321.

Lemma, Tesfaye T., Martin Feedman, Mthokozisi Mlilo, and Jin Dong Park. 2019. "Corporate Carbon Risk, Voluntary Disclosure, and Cost of Capital: South African Evidence." *Business Strategy and the Environment* 28 (1): 111–126. https://doi.org/10.1002/bse.2242.

Lenox, Michael, and Aaron Chatterji. 2018. *Can Business Save the Earth? Innovating Our Way to Sustainability*. Stanford University Press.

Lenox, Michael, and Rebecca Duff. 2021. *The Decarbonization Imperative: Transforming the Global Economy by 2050*. Stanford University Press.

Lerner, Michael, and Iain Osgood. 2023. "Across the Boards: Explaining Firm Support for Climate Policy." *British Journal of Political Science* 53 (3): 934–957. https://doi.org/10.1017/S0007123422000497.

Levinthal, Daniel A., and James G. March. 1993. "The Myopia of Learning." *Strategic Management Journal* 14 (S2): 95–112. https://doi.org/10.1002/smj.4250141009.

Levy, David L., and Peter John Newell. 2005. *The Business of Global Environmental Governance*. MIT Press.

Li, Dayuan, Min Huang, Shenggang Ren, Xiaohong Chen, and Lutao Ning. 2018. "Environmental Legitimacy, Green Innovation, and Corporate Carbon Disclosure: Evidence from CDP China 100." *Journal of Business Ethics* 150 (4): 1089–1104. https://doi.org/10.1007/s10551-016-3187-6.

Li, Hui, and Hongtao Yi. 2014. "Multilevel Governance and Deployment of Solar PV Panels in U.S. Cities." *Energy Policy* 69 (June): 19–27. https://doi.org/10.1016/j.enpol.2014.03.006.

Liao, Lin, Le Luo, and Qingliang Tang. 2015. "Gender Diversity, Board Independence, Environmental Committee and Greenhouse Gas Disclosure." *British Accounting Review* 47 (4): 409–424. https://doi.org/10.1016/j.bar.2014.01.002.

Luers, Amy, Leehi Yona, Christopher B. Field, et al. 2022. "Make Greenhouse-Gas Accounting Reliable—Build Interoperable Systems." *Nature* 607 (7920): 653–656. https://doi.org/10.1038/d41586-022-02033-y.

Luo, Le, Yi-Chen Lan, and Qingliang Tang. 2012. "Corporate Incentives to Disclose Carbon Information: Evidence from the CDP Global 500 Report." *Journal of International Financial Management & Accounting* 23 (2): 93–120. https://doi.org/10.1111/j.1467-646X.2012.01055.x.

Luo, Le, Qingliang Tang, and Juan Peng. 2018. "The Direct and Moderating Effects of Power Distance on Carbon Transparency: An International Investigation of Cultural Value and Corporate Social Responsibility." *Business Strategy and the Environment* 27 (8): 1546–1557. https://doi.org/10.1002/bse.2213.

Lyon, Thomas P. 2023. *Corporate Political Responsibility*. Cambridge University Press.

Lyon, Thomas P., Magali A. Delmas, John W. Maxwell, et al. 2018. "CSR Needs CPR: Corporate Sustainability and Politics." *California Management Review* 60 (4): 5–24. https://doi.org/10.1177/0008125618778854.

Lyon, Thomas P., and John W. Maxwell. 2004a. *Corporate Environmentalism and Public Policy*. Cambridge University Press.

Lyon, Thomas P., and John W. Maxwell. 2008. "Corporate Social Responsibility and the Environment: A Theoretical Perspective." *Review of Environmental Economics and Policy* 2 (2): 240–260. https://doi.org/10.1093/reep/ren004.

Lyon, Thomas P., and John W. Maxwell. 2011. "Greenwash: Corporate Environmental Disclosure under Threat of Audit." *Journal of Economics & Management Strategy* 20 (1): 3–41.

Lyon, Thomas P., and A. Wren Montgomery. 2015. "The Means and End of Greenwash." *Organization & Environment* 28 (2): 223–249. https://doi.org/10.1177/1086026615575332.

Lyon, Thomas P., and Jay P. Shimshack. 2015. "Environmental Disclosure Evidence from Newsweek's Green Companies Rankings." *Business & Society* 54 (5): 632–675. https://doi.org/10.1177/0007650312439701.

Mach, Katharine J., Caroline M. Kraan, W. Neil Adger, et al. 2019. "Climate as a Risk Factor for Armed Conflict." *Nature* 571 (7764): 193–197. https://doi.org/10.1038/s41586-019-1300-6.

Maddala, G. S. 1983. *Limited-Dependent and Qualitative Variables in Econometrics*. Cambridge University Press.

Malerba, Franco. 1992. "Learning by Firms and Incremental Technical Change." *Economic Journal* 102 (413): 845–859. https://doi.org/10.2307/2234581.

Malhotra, Neil, Benoît Monin, and Michael Tomz. 2019. "Does Private Regulation Preempt Public Regulation?" *American Political Science Review* 113 (1): 19–37. https://doi.org/10.1017/S0003055418000679.

March, James G. 1962. "The Business Firm as a Political Coalition." *Journal of Politics* 24 (4): 662–678. https://doi.org/10.1017/S0022381600016169.

March, James G., and Johan P. Olsen. 1998. "The Institutional Dynamics of International Political Orders." *International Organization* 52 (4): 943–969. https://doi.org/10.1162/002081898550699.

Martin, Ralf, Mirabelle Muûls, and Ulrich J. Wagner. 2016. "The Impact of the European Union Emissions Trading Scheme on Regulated Firms: What Is the Evidence after Ten Years?" *Review of Environmental Economics and Policy* 10 (1): 129–148. https://doi.org/10.1093/reep/rev016.

Mas-Colell, Andreu, Michael D. Whinston, and Jerry R. Green. 1995. *Microeconomic Theory*. Oxford University Press.

Matisoff, Daniel C. 2012. "Privatizing Climate Change Policy: Is There a Public Benefit?" *Environmental and Resource Economics* 53 (3): 409–433. https://doi.org/10.1007/s10640-012-9568-0.

Matsuo, Tyeler, and Tobias S. Schmidt. 2019. "Managing Tradeoffs in Green Industrial Policies: The Role of Renewable Energy Policy Design." *World Development* 122 (October): 11–26. https://doi.org/10.1016/j.worlddev.2019.05.005.

Matten, Dirk, and Jeremy Moon. 2005. "A Conceptual Framework for Understanding CSR." In *Corporate Social Responsibility Across Europe*, edited by André Habisch, Jan Jonker, Martina Wegner, and René Schmidpeter, 335–356. Springer Nature.

Matten, Dirk, and Jeremy Moon. 2008. "'Implicit' and 'Explicit' CSR: A Conceptual Framework for a Comparative Understanding of Corporate Social Responsibility." *Academy of Management Review* 33 (2): 404–424. https://doi.org/10.5465/amr.2008.31193458.

Maxwell, John W., Thomas P. Lyon, and Steven C. Hackett. 2000. "Self-Regulation and Social Welfare: The Political Economy of Corporate Environmentalism." *Journal of Law & Economics* 43 (2): 583–618.

May, Peter J. 1992. "Policy Learning and Failure." *Journal of Public Policy* 12 (4): 331–354. https://doi.org/10.1017/S0143814X00005602.

Mayer, F. W., and N. Phillips. 2017. "Outsourcing Governance: States and the Politics of a 'global Value Chain World.'" *New Political Economy* 22 (2): 13–52.

McDonnell, Mary-Hunter, and Timothy Werner. 2016. "Blacklisted Businesses: Social Activists' Challenges and the Disruption of Corporate Political Activity." *Administrative Science Quarterly* 61 (4): 584–620. https://doi.org/10.1177/0001839216648953.

McWilliams, Abagail, and Donald Siegel. 2001. "Corporate Social Responsibility: A Theory of the Firm Perspective." *Academy of Management Review* 26 (1): 117–127. https://doi.org/10.5465/amr.2001.4011987.

Meckling, Jonas. 2015. "Oppose, Support, or Hedge? Distributional Effects, Regulatory Pressure, and Business Strategy in Environmental Politics." *Global Environmental Politics* 15 (2): 19–37. https://doi.org/10.1162/GLEP_a_00296.

Meckling, Jonas, and Valerie J. Karplus. 2023. "Political Strategies for Climate and Environmental Solutions." *Nature Sustainability*, May, 1–10. https://doi.org/10.1038/s41893-023-01109-5.

Meckling, Jonas, Nina Kelsey, Eric Biber, and John Zysman. 2015. "Winning Coalitions for Climate Policy." *Science* 349 (6253): 1170–1171. https://doi.org/10.1126/science.aab1336.

Meckling, Jonas, and Jonas Nahm. 2018. "The Power of Process: State Capacity and Climate Policy." *Governance*, 1–27. https://doi.org/10.1111/gove.12338.

Meng, Kyle C. 2017. "Using a Free Permit Rule to Forecast the Marginal Abatement Cost of Proposed Climate Policy." *American Economic Review* 107 (3): 748–784. https://doi.org/10.1257/aer.20150781.

Meyer, John W., and Brian Rowan. 1977. "Institutionalized Organizations: Formal Structure as Myth and Ceremony." *American Journal of Sociology* 83 (2): 340–363. https://doi.org/10.1086/226550.

Mildenberger, Matto. 2020. *Carbon Captured: How Business and Labor Control Climate Politics*. MIT Press.

Mitchell, Ronald B. 2018. "Data from Ronald B. Mitchell." International Environmental Agreements Database Project (Version 2018.1), Université Laval. http://iea.uoregon.edu/.

Moon, Jeremy. 2002. "The Social Responsibility of Business and New Governance 1." *Government and Opposition* 37 (3): 385–408. https://doi.org/10.1111/1477-7053.00106.

Moon, Jeremy, and Jette Steen Knudsen. 2018. "Corporate Social Responsibility and Government." *Academy of Management Proceedings* 2018 (1): 12777. https://doi.org/10.5465/AMBPP.2018.12777abstract.

Morgenstern, Richard D., and William Aaron Pizer. 2007. *Reality Check: The Nature and Performance of Voluntary Environmental Programs in the United States, Europe, and Japan*. Resources for the Future.

Morrison, Andrea, Carlo Pietrobelli, and Roberta Rabellotti. 2008. "Global Value Chains and Technological Capabilities: A Framework to Study Learning and Innovation in Developing Countries." *Oxford Development Studies* 36 (1): 39–58. https://doi.org/10.1080/13600810701848144.

Navarro, Peter. 1988. "Why Do Corporations Give to Charity?" *Journal of Business* 61 (1): 65.

Nelson, Richard R., and Sidney G. Winter. 2002. "Evolutionary Theorizing in Economics." *Journal of Economic Perspectives* 16 (2): 23–46. https://doi.org/10.1257/0895330027247.

Newell, Peter, and Matthew Paterson. 2010. *Climate Capitalism: Global Warming and the Transformation of the Global Economy*. Cambridge University Press.

Newman, Abraham L., and David Bach. 2004. "Self-Regulatory Trajectories in the Shadow of Public Power: Resolving Digital Dilemmas in Europe and the United States." *Governance* 17 (3): 387–413. https://doi.org/10.1111/j.0952-1895.2004.00251.x.

Nielsen, Kristian S., Kimberly A. Nicholas, Felix Creutzig, Thomas Dietz, and Paul C. Stern. 2021. "The Role of High-Socioeconomic-Status People in Locking in or Rapidly Reducing Energy-Driven Greenhouse Gas Emissions." *Nature Energy* 6 (11): 1011–1016. https://doi.org/10.1038/s41560-021-00900-y.

Nordhaus, William. 2015. "Climate Clubs: Overcoming Free-Riding in International Climate Policy." *American Economic Review* 105 (4): 1339–1370. https://doi.org/10.1257/aer.15000001.

Nordhaus, William D. 2013. *The Climate Casino: Risk, Uncertainty, and Economics for a Warming World*. Yale University Press.

O'Neill, Kate. 2017. *The Environment and International Relations*. Cambridge University Press.

O'Neill, Kate. 2019. "Linking Wastes and Climate Change: Bandwagoning, Contention, and Global Governance." *Wiley Interdisciplinary Reviews: Climate Change* 10 (2): e568. https://doi.org/10.1002/wcc.568.

Oreskes, Naomi. 2004. "The Scientific Consensus on Climate Change." *Science* 306 (5702): 1686–1686. https://doi.org/10.1126/science.1103618.

Orts, Eric W., and Kurt Deketelaere. 2001. *Environmental Contracts: Comparative Approaches to Regulatory Innovation in the United States and Europe*. Kluwer Law International B.V.

Ostrom, Elinor. 1990. *Governing the Commons: The Evolution of Institutions for Collective Action*. Cambridge University Press.

Ostrom, Elinor. 2007a. "A Diagnostic Approach for Going beyond Panaceas." *Proceedings of the National Academy of Sciences of the United States of America* 104 (39): 15181–15187. https://doi.org/10.1073/pnas.0702288104.

Ostrom, Elinor. 2007b. "Institutional Rational Choice: An Assessment of the Institutional Analysis and Development Framework." In *Theories of the Policy Process*, edited by Paul Sabatier, 21–64. Westview Press.

Ostrom, Elinor. 2009. "A General Framework for Analyzing Sustainability of Social-Ecological Systems." *Science* 325 (5939): 419–422. https://doi.org/10.1126/science.1172133.

Ostrom, Elinor. 2010. "Beyond Markets and States: Polycentric Governance of Complex Economic Systems." *American Economic Review* 100 (3): 641–672. https://doi.org/10.1257/aer.100.3.641.

Ott, Christian, Frank Schiemann, and Thomas Günther. 2017. "Disentangling the Determinants of the Response and the Publication Decisions: The Case of the Carbon Disclosure Project." *Journal of Accounting and Public Policy* 36 (1): 14–33. https://doi.org/10.1016/j.jaccpubpol.2016.11.003.

Overdevest, Christine, and Jonathan Zeitlin. 2014. "Assembling an Experimentalist Regime: Transnational Governance Interactions in the Forest Sector." *Regulation & Governance* 8 (1): 22–48.

Pachauri, R. K., M. R. Allen, V. R. Barros, et al. 2014. *Climate Change 2014: Synthesis Report. Contribution of Working Groups I, II and III to the Fifth Assessment Report of the Intergovernmental Panel on Climate Change*. IPCC. https://epic.awi.de/id/eprint/37530/.

Paterson, Matthew, Matthew Hoffmann, Michele Betsill, and Steven Bernstein. 2014. "The Micro Foundations of Policy Diffusion Toward Complex Global Governance: An Analysis of the Transnational Carbon Emission Trading Network." *Comparative Political Studies* 47 (3): 420–449. https://doi.org/10.1177/0010414013509575.

Pattberg, Philipp. 2005. "The Institutionalization of Private Governance: How Business and Nonprofit Organizations Agree on Transnational Rules." *Governance* 18 (4): 589–610. https://doi.org/10.1111/j.1468-0491.2005.00293.x.

Peiró-Signes, Angel, and María-del-Val Segarra-Oña. 2013. "Trends in ESG Practices: Differences and Similarities Across Major Developed Markets." In *Sustainability Appraisal: Quantitative Methods and Mathematical Techniques for Environmental Performance Evaluation*, edited by Marina G. Erechtchoukova, Peter A. Khaiter, and Paulina Golinska, 125–140. Springer. https://doi.org/10.1007/978-3-642-32081-1_6.

Perkins, Richard, and Eric Neumayer. 2010. "Geographic Variations in the Early Diffusion of Corporate Voluntary Standards: Comparing ISO 14001 and the Global Compact." *Environment and Planning A* 42 (2): 347–365.

Perlman, Rebecca L. 2023. *Regulating Risk: How Private Information Shapes Global Safety Standards*. Cambridge University Press. https://doi.org/10.1017/9781009291880.

Peters, Gary F., and Andrea M. Romi. 2014. "Does the Voluntary Adoption of Corporate Governance Mechanisms Improve Environmental Risk Disclosures? Evidence from Greenhouse Gas Emission Accounting." *Journal of Business Ethics* 125 (4): 637–666. https://doi.org/10.1007/s10551-013-1886-9.

Porter, Michael E., and Mark R. Kramer. 2006. "Strategy and Society: The Link Between Competitive Advantage and Corporate Social Responsibility." *Harvard Business Review*, December. https://hbr.org/2006/12/strategy-and-society-the-link-between-competitive-advantage-and-corporate-social-responsibility.

Potoski, Matthew. 2001. "Clean Air Federalism: Do States Race to the Bottom?" *Public Administration Review* 61 (3): 335–343. https://doi.org/10.1111/0033-3352.00034.

Potoski, Matthew, and Aseem Prakash. 2013. "Green Clubs: Collective Action and Voluntary Environmental Programs." *Annual Review of Political Science* 16: 399–419. https://doi.org/10.1146/annurev-polisci-032211-211224.

Potoski, Matthew, and Neal D. Woods. 2002. "Dimensions of State Environmental Policies." *Policy Studies Journal* 30 (2): 208–226. https://doi.org/10.1111/j.1541-0072.2002.tb02142.x.

Prakash, Aseem. 2000. *Greening the Firm: The Politics of Corporate Environmentalism*. Cambridge University Press.

Prakash, Aseem. 2001. "Why Do Firms Adopt 'Beyond-Compliance' Environmental Policies?" *Business Strategy and the Environment* 10 (5): 286–299. https://doi.org/10.1002/bse.305.

Prakash, Aseem, and Matthew Potoski. 2006. *The Voluntary Environmentalists: Green Clubs, ISO 14001, and Voluntary Regulations*. Cambridge University Press.

Prakash, Aseem, and Matthew Potoski. 2007a. "Collective Action through Voluntary Environmental Programs: A Club Theory Perspective." *Policy Studies Journal* 35 (4): 773–792. https://doi.org/10.1111/j.1541-0072.2007.00247.x.

Prakash, Aseem, and Matthew Potoski. 2007b. "Investing Up: FDI and the Cross-Country Diffusion of ISO 14001 Management Systems." *International Studies Quarterly* 51 (3): 723–744. https://doi.org/10.1111/j.1468-2478.2007.00471.x.

Prakash, Aseem, and Matthew Potoski. 2012. "Voluntary Environmental Programs: A Comparative Perspective." *Journal of Policy Analysis and Management* 31 (1): 123–138.

Prakash, Aseem, and Matthew Potoski. 2014. "Global Private Regimes, Domestic Public Law ISO 14001 and Pollution Reduction." *Comparative Political Studies* 47 (3): 369–394. https://doi.org/10.1177/0010414013509573.

Pralle, Sarah. 2006a. *Branching Out, Digging In: Environmental Advocacy and Agenda Setting*. Georgetown University Press.

Pralle, Sarah. 2006b. "Timing and Sequence in Agenda-Setting and Policy Change: A Comparative Study of Lawn Care Pesticide Politics in Canada and the US." *Journal of European Public Policy* 13 (7): 987–1005.

Pralle, Sarah B. 2003. "Venue Shopping, Political Strategy, and Policy Change: The Internationalization of Canadian Forest Advocacy." *Journal of Public Policy* 23 (3): 233–260.

Pretty, Jules, and Hugh Ward. 2001. "Social Capital and the Environment." *World Development* 29 (2): 209–227. https://doi.org/10.1016/S0305-750X(00)00098-X.

Purdon, Mark. 2015. "Advancing Comparative Climate Change Politics: Theory and Method." *Global Environmental Politics* 15 (3): 1–26. https://doi.org/10.1162/GLEP_e_00309.

Rabe, Barry. 2007. "Beyond Kyoto: Climate Change Policy in Multilevel Governance Systems." *Governance* 20 (3): 423–444. https://doi.org/10.1111/j.1468-0491.2007.00365.x.

Rabe, Barry G. 2010. "The Aversion to Direct Cost Imposition: Selecting Climate Policy Tools in the United States." *Governance* 23 (4): 583–608. https://doi.org/10.1111/j.1468-0491.2010.01499.x.

Rabe, Barry G., Mikael Roman, and Arthur N. Dobelis. 2005. "State Competition as a Source Driving Climate Change Mitigation." *New York University Environmental Law Journal* 14 (1): 1–53.

Ramus, Catherine A., and Ivan Montiel. 2005. "When Are Corporate Environmental Policies a Form of Greenwashing?" *Business and Society; Chicago* 44 (4): 377–414.

Reid, Erin M., and Michael W. Toffel. 2009. "Responding to Public and Private Politics: Corporate Disclosure of Climate Change Strategies." *Strategic Management Journal* 30 (11): 1157–1178. https://doi.org/10.1002/smj.796.

Renckens, Stefan. 2020a. *Private Governance and Public Authority: Regulating Sustainability in a Global Economy*. Cambridge University Press.

Renckens, Stefan. 2020b. "The Instrumental Power of Transnational Private Governance: Interest Representation and Lobbying by Private Rule-Makers." *Governance* 33 (3): 657–674. https://doi.org/10.1111/gove.12451.

Renckens, Stefan. 2021. "Disaggregating Public-Private Governance Interactions: European Union Interventions in Transnational Private Sustainability Governance." *Regulation & Governance* 15 (4): 1230–1247. https://doi.org/10.1111/rego.12332.

Rivera, Jorge. 2002. "Assessing a Voluntary Environmental Initiative in the Developing World: The Costa Rican Certification for Sustainable Tourism." *Policy Sciences* 35 (4): 333–60. https://doi.org/10.1023/A:1021371011105.

Rivera, Jorge. 2004. "Institutional Pressures and Voluntary Environmental Behavior in Developing Countries: Evidence from the Costa Rican Hotel Industry." *Society & Natural Resources* 17 (9): 779–797.

Rivera, Jorge, and Peter De Leon. 2005. "Chief Executive Officers and Voluntary Environmental Performance: Costa Rica's Certification for Sustainable Tourism." *Policy Sciences* 38 (2–3): 107–127. https://doi.org/10.1007/s11077-005-6590-x.

Roger, Charles, Thomas Hale, and Liliana Andonova. 2017. "The Comparative Politics of Transnational Climate Governance." *International Interactions* 43 (1): 1–25. https://doi.org/10.1080/03050629.2017.1252248.

Ronit, Karsten, and Volker Schneider. 1999. "Global Governance through Private Organizations." *Governance* 12 (3): 243–266. https://doi.org/10.1111/0952-1895.00102.

Rosenberg, Nathan, and Rosenberg Nathan. 1982. *Inside the Black Box: Technology and Economics*. Cambridge University Press.

Rotemberg, Julio J., and Garth Saloner. 2000. "Visionaries, Managers, and Strategic Direction." *RAND Journal of Economics* 31 (4): 693–716. https://www.jstor.org/stable/2696355.

Ruggie, John Gerard. 2017. "The Theory and Practice of Learning Networks: Corporate Social Responsibility and the Global Compact." In *Learning to Talk: Corporate Citizenship and the Development of the UN Global Compact*, edited by Malcolm McIntosh, Sandra Waddock, and Georg Kell, 27–35. Taylor & Francis. https://www.taylorfrancis.com/books/e/9781351281157/chapters/10.4324%2F9781351281164-12.

Ruggie, John Gerard. 2018. "Multinationals as Global Institution: Power, Authority and Relative Autonomy." *Regulation & Governance* 12 (3): 317–333. https://doi.org/10.1111/rego.12154.

Sabatier, Paul A. 1988. "An Advocacy Coalition Framework of Policy Change and the Role of Policy-Oriented Learning Therein." *Policy Sciences* 21 (2–3): 129–168.

Scherer, Andreas Georg, and Guido Palazzo. 2008. *Handbook of Research on Global Corporate Citizenship*. Edward Elgar Publishing.

Schleifer, Philip. 2023. *Global Shifts: Business, Politics, and Deforestation in a Changing World Economy*. MIT Press.

Schleifer, Philip, Clara Brandi, Rupal Verma, Katharina Bissinger, and Matteo Fiorini. 2022. "Voluntary Standards and the SDGs: Mapping Public-Private Complementarities for Sustainable Development." *Earth System Governance* 14 (December): 100153. https://doi.org/10.1016/j.esg.2022.100153.

Schmitz, Patrick W. 2015. "Government versus Private Ownership of Public Goods: The Role of Bargaining Frictions." *Journal of Public Economics* 132 (December): 23–31. https://doi.org/10.1016/j.jpubeco.2015.09.009.

Schwab, Klaus. 2021. *Stakeholder Capitalism: A Global Economy That Works for Progress, People and Planet*. John Wiley & Sons.

Scott-Buechler, Celina, Bruce Cain, Khalid Osman, et al. 2024. "Communities Conditionally Support Deployment of Direct Air Capture for Carbon Dioxide Removal in the United States." *Communications Earth & Environment* 5 (1): 1–13. https://doi.org/10.1038/s43247-024-01334-6.

Scur, Daniela, Raffaella Sadun, John Van Reenen, Renata Lemos, and Nicholas Bloom. 2021. "The World Management Survey at 18: Lessons and the Way Forward." *Oxford Review of Economic Policy* 37 (2): 231–258. https://doi.org/10.1093/oxrep/grab009.

Seabrooke, Leonard, and Duncan Wigan. 2017. "The Governance of Global Wealth Chains." *Review of International Political Economy* 24 (1): 1–29. https://www.tandfonline.com/doi/abs/10.1080/09692290.2016.1268189.

Selin, Henrik, and Stacy D. VanDeveer. 2009. *Changing Climates in North American Politics: Institutions, Policymaking, and Multilevel Governance*. MIT Press.

Seneviratne, Sonia, Neville Nicholls, David Easterling, et al. 2012. "Changes in Climate Extremes and Their Impacts on the Natural Physical Environment," 109–230. https://doi.org/10.7916/d8-6nbt-s431.

Sharma, Sanjay, and Harrie Vredenburg. 1998. "Proactive Corporate Environmental Strategy and the Development of Competitively Valuable Organizational Capabilities." *Strategic Management Journal* 19 (8): 729–753. https://doi.org/10.1002/(SICI)1097-0266(199808)19:8<729::AID-SMJ967>3.0.CO;2-4.

Shen, Shiran Victoria. 2022. *The Political Regulation Wave: A Case of How Local Incentives Systematically Shape Air Quality in China*. Cambridge University Press.

Shimshack, Jay P., and Michael B. Ward. 2008. "Enforcement and Over-Compliance." *Journal of Environmental Economics and Management* 55 (1): 90–105. https://doi.org/10.1016/j.jeem.2007.05.003.

Simon, Herbert A. 1957. *Models of Man: Social and Rational; Mathematical Essays on Rational Human Behavior in Society Setting*. Wiley.

Simon, Herbert A. 1979. "Rational Decision Making in Business Organizations." *American Economic Review* 69 (4): 493–513.

Simon, Herbert A. 1991. "Bounded Rationality and Organizational Learning." *Organization Science* 2 (1): 125–134. https://doi.org/10.1287/orsc.2.1.125.

Skaife, Hollis A., and Timothy Werner. 2020. "Changes in Firms' Political Investment Opportunities, Managerial Accountability, and Reputational Risk." *Journal of Business Ethics* 163 (2): 239–263. https://doi.org/10.1007/s10551-019-04224-6.

Stanny, Elizabeth. 2013. "Voluntary Disclosures of Emissions by US Firms." *Business Strategy and the Environment* 22 (3): 145–158. https://doi.org/10.1002/bse.1732.

Stanny, Elizabeth, and Kirsten Ely. 2008a. "Corporate Environmental Disclosures about the Effects of Climate Change." *Corporate Social Responsibility and Environmental Management* 15 (6): 338–348. https://doi.org/10.1002/csr.175.

Stavins, Robert N. 2011. "The Problem of the Commons: Still Unsettled after 100 Years." *American Economic Review* 101 (1): 81–108. https://doi.org/10.1257/aer.101.1.81.

Stern, Nicholas Herbert. 2007. *The Economics of Climate Change: The Stern Review*. Cambridge University Press.

Stokes, Leah C., and Hanna L. Breetz. 2020. "States of Crisis: Subnational Inaction on Climate Change in the United States." In *Handbook of U.S. Environmental Policy*, edited by David M. Konisky, 289–301. Edward Elgar Publishing.

Stokes, Leah Cardamore. 2020. *Short Circuiting Policy: Interest Groups and the Battle Over Clean Energy and Climate Policy in the American States*. Studies in Postwar American Political Development. Oxford University Press.

Stone, Diane. 2012. "Transfer and Translation of Policy." *Policy Studies* 33 (6): 483–499. https://doi.org/10.1080/01442872.2012.695933.

Strand, Robert. 2012. "The Chief Officer of Corporate Social Responsibility: A Study of Its Presence in Top Management Teams." *Journal of Business Ethics* 112 (4): 721–734. https://doi.org/10.1007/s10551-012-1568-z.

Strand, Robert. 2013. "The Chief Officer of Corporate Social Responsibility: A Study of Its Presence in Top Management Teams." *Journal of Business Ethics* 112 (4): 721–734.

Strange, Susan. 1996. *The Retreat of the State: The Diffusion of Power in the World Economy*. Cambridge University Press.

Supran, G., S. Rahmstorf, and N. Oreskes. 2023. "Assessing ExxonMobil's Global Warming Projections." *Science* 379 (6628): eabk0063. https://doi.org/10.1126/science.abk0063.

Sutton, Robert I. 2010. *Good Boss, Bad Boss: How to Be the Best . . . and Learn from the Worst*. Grand Central Publishing.

Sweeney, James L. 2016. *Energy Efficiency: Building a Clean, Secure Economy*. Hoover Press.

Teece, David J. 1986. "Profiting from Technological Innovation: Implications for Integration, Collaboration, Licensing and Public Policy." *Research Policy* 15 (6): 285–305. https://doi.org/10.1016/0048-7333(86)90027-2.

Thrall, Calvin. 2021. "Public-Private Governance Initiatives and Corporate Responses to Stakeholder Complaints." *International Organization* 75 (3): 803–836. https://doi.org/10.1017/S0020818321000199.

Tietenberg, Tom. 1998. "Disclosure Strategies for Pollution Control." *Environmental and Resource Economics* 11 (3–4): 587–602. https://doi.org/10.1023/A:1008291411492.

Tingley, Dustin, and Michael Tomz. 2022. "The Effects of Naming and Shaming on Public Support for Compliance with International Agreements: An Experimental Analysis of the Paris Agreement." *International Organization* 76 (2): 445–468. https://doi.org/10.1017/S0020818321000394.

Tirole, Jean. 2017. *Economics for the Common Good*. Princeton University Press.

Toffel, Michael W., and Jodi L. Short. 2011. "Coming Clean and Cleaning up: Does Voluntary Self-Reporting Indicate Effective Self-Policing." *Journal of Law & Economics* 54 (3): 609–650.

Tosun, Jale, Sebastian Koos, and Jennifer Shore. 2016. "Co-Governing Common Goods: Interaction Patterns of Private and Public Actors." *Policy and Society* 35 (1): 1–12. https://doi.org/10.1016/j.polsoc.2016.01.002.

Truelove, Heather Barnes, Amanda R. Carrico, Elke U. Weber, Kaitlin Toner Raimi, and Michael P. Vandenbergh. 2014. "Positive and Negative Spillover of Pro-Environmental Behavior: An Integrative Review and Theoretical Framework." *Global Environmental Change* 29 (November): 127–138. https://doi.org/10.1016/j.gloenvcha.2014.09.004.

Tsutsui, Kiyoteru, and Alwyn Lim. 2015. *Corporate Social Responsibility in a Globalizing World*. Cambridge University Press.

UNGC. 2018. "Global Compact Local Networks: Accelerating National SGD Implementation." United Nations Global Compact. https://www.unglobalcompact.org/docs/publications/GCLNs-Accelerating_National-SDG-Implementation.pdf.

UNGC. n.d.a. "UN Global Compact Academy Q&A." Accessed August 2, 2019. https://www.unglobalcompact.org/docs/about_the_gc/UN%20Global%20Compact%20Academy%20FAQs.pdf.

UNGC. n.d.b. "United Nations Global Compact: A Call to Action for Sustainable Business." United Nations Global Compact. https://www.unglobalcompact.org/docs/publications/UNGC-Value-Proposition.pdf.

US EPA, OA. 2009. "Endangerment and Cause or Contribute Findings for Greenhouse Gases under the Section 202(a) of the Clean Air Act." Reports and Assessments. US EPA. December. https://19january2017snapshot.epa.gov/climatechange/endangerment-and-cause-or-contribute-findings-greenhouse-gases-under-section-202a_.html.

US EPA, OA. 2018. "EPA Proposes Affordable Clean Energy (ACE) Rule." Speeches, Testimony and Transcripts. US EPA. August 21, 2018. https://www.epa.gov/stationary-sources-air-pollution/proposal-affordable-clean-energy-ace-rule.

Vandenbergh, Michael P. 2013. "Private Environmental Governance." *Cornell Law Review* 99 (1): 129–199.

Vandenbergh, Michael P., and Jonathan M. Gilligan. 2017. *Beyond Politics*. Cambridge University Press.

Van den Steen, Eric. 2005. "Organizational Beliefs and Managerial Vision." *Journal of Law, Economics, and Organization* 21 (1): 256–283. https://doi.org/10.1093/jleo/ewi011.

Van den Steen, Eric. 2010. "Culture Clash: The Costs and Benefits of Homogeneity." *Management Science* 56 (10): 1718–1738.

van't Veld, Klaas, and Matthew J. Kotchen. 2011. "Green Clubs." *Journal of Environmental Economics and Management* 62 (3): 309–322. https://doi.org/10.1016/j.jeem.2011.03.009.

Ven, Hamish van der, Yixian Sun, and Benjamin Cashore. 2021. "Sustainable Commodity Governance and the Global South." *Ecological Economics* 186 (August): 107062. https://doi.org/10.1016/j.ecolecon.2021.107062.

Vestrelli, Roberto, Andrea Fronzetti Colladon, and Anna Laura Pisello. 2024. "When Attention to Climate Change Matters: The Impact of Climate Risk Disclosure on Firm Market Value." *Energy Policy* 185 (February): 113938. https://doi.org/10.1016/j.enpol.2023.113938.

Victor, David G. 2011. *Global Warming Gridlock: Creating More Effective Strategies for Protecting the Planet.* Cambridge University Press.

Vidaver-Cohen, Deborah, and Peggy Simcic Brønn. 2013. "Reputation, Responsibility, and Stakeholder Support in Scandinavian Firms: A Comparative Analysis." *Journal of Business Ethics* 127 (1): 49–64. https://doi.org/10.1007/s10551-013-1673-7.

Videras, Julio, and Anna Alberini. 2000. "The Appeal of Voluntary Environmental Programs: Which Firms Participate and Why?" *Contemporary Economic Policy* 18 (4): 449–461. https://doi.org/10.1111/%28ISSN%291465-7287.

Vogel, David. 1995. *Trading Up: Consumer and Environmental Regulation in a Global Economy*. Harvard University Press.

Vogel, David. 2005. *The Market for Virtue: The Potential and Limits of Corporate Social Responsibility*. Brookings Institution Press.

Vogel, David. 2008. "Private Global Business Regulation." *Annual Review of Political Science* 11: 261–282.

Vogel, David. 2010. "The Private Regulation of Global Corporate Conduct: Achievements and Limitations." *Business and Society* 49 (1): 68–87.

Vogel, David. 2018. *California Greenin': How the Golden State Became an Environmental Leader*. Princeton University Press. https://doi.org/10.23943/9781400889594.

Waddock, Sandra. 2008. "The Development of Corporate Responsibility/Corporate Citizenship." *Organization Management Journal* 5 (1): 29–39. https://doi.org/10.1057/omj.2008.5.

Weiss, Thomas G., and Rorden Wilkinson. 2014. "Rethinking Global Governance? Complexity, Authority, Power, Change." *International Studies Quarterly* 58 (1): 207–215. https://doi.org/10.1111/isqu.12082.

Welton, Shelley. 2020. "Decarbonization in Democracy." *UCLA Law Review* 67 (1): 56–120.

Welton, Shelley, and Joel Eisen. 2019. "Clean Energy Justice: Charting an Emerging Agenda." *Harvard Environmental Law Review* 43 (2): 307–372.

Werner, Timothy. 2012. *Public Forces and Private Politics in American Big Business*. Business and Public Policy. Cambridge University Press. https://doi.org/10.1017/CBO9781139149150.

Westphal, James D., and Edward J. Zajac. 1998. "The Symbolic Management of Stockholders: Corporate Governance Reforms and Shareholder Reactions." *Administrative Science Quarterly* 43 (1): 127–153. https://doi.org/10.2307/2393593.

Wiener, Jonathan B. 2007. "Think Globally, Act Globally: The Limits of Local Climate Policies." *University of Pennsylvania Law Review* 155 (6): 1961–179.

Winston, Andrew. 2010. "The Most Powerful Green NGO You've Never Heard Of." *Harvard Business Review*, 2010. https://hbr.org/2010/10/the-most-powerful-green-ngo.

Wooldridge, Jeffrey M. 2002. *Econometric Analysis of Cross Section and Panel Data*. MIT Press.

Wooldridge, Jeffrey M. 2010. *Econometric Analysis of Cross Section and Panel Data*. MIT Press.

Yadin, Sharon. 2023a. *Fighting Climate Change through Shaming*. Organizational Responses to Climate Change: Business, Governments. Cambridge University Press. https://www.cambridge.org/core/elements/fighting-climate-change-through-shaming/FE9DA69D7DE60C8FDA2FBD2521FD540A.

Yadin, Sharon. 2023b. "Regulatory Shaming and the Problem of Corporate Climate Obstruction." *Harvard Journal on Legislation* 60 (2): 337–382.

Yale University. 2018. "About the EPI. 2018." Environmental Performance Index. https://epi.envirocenter.yale.edu/about-epi.

Yi, Hongtao, and Richard C. Feiock. 2014. "Renewable Energy Politics: Policy Typologies, Policy Tools, and State Deployment of Renewables." *Policy Studies Journal* 42 (3): 391–415. https://doi.org/10.1111/psj.12066.

Yi, Hongtao, and Yuan Liu. 2015. "Green Economy in China: Regional Variations and Policy Drivers." *Global Environmental Change* 31 (March): 11–19. https://doi.org/10.1016/j.gloenvcha.2014.12.001.

Zhu, Qinghua, and Joseph Sarkis. 2007. "The Moderating Effects of Institutional Pressures on Emergent Green Supply Chain Practices and Performance." *International Journal of Production Research* 45 (18–19): 4333–4355. https://doi.org/10.1080/00207540701440345.

Zielinski, Sarah. n.d. "Natural Gas Really Is Better Than Coal." *Smithsonian*. Accessed December 15, 2016. http://www.smithsonianmag.com/science-nature/natural-gas-really-better-coal-180949739/.

Zingales, Luigi. 2014. *A Capitalism for the People: Recapturing the Lost Genius of American Prosperity*. Basic Books.

Index

Note: Photos, figures, and tables are indicated by italicized page numbers.

Publisher contact:
The MIT Press
Massachusetts Institute of Technology
77 Massachusetts Avenue, Cambridge, MA 02139
mitpress.mit.edu

EU Authorised Representative:
Easy Access System Europe, Mustamäe tee 50,
10621 Tallinn, Estonia
gpsr.requests@easproject.com

Printed by Integrated Books International,
United States of America